Computers and Information Systems

Computers and Information Systems

Robert A. Szymanski

Donald P. Szymanski

Donna M. Pulschen

Prentice Hall

Englewood Cliffs, New Jersey 07632

Library of Congress Cataloging-in-Publication Data

Szymanski, Robert A.
    Computers and information systems / Robert A. Szymanski, Donald P.
Szymanski, Donna M. Pulschen.
        p.   cm.
    Includes index
    ISBN 0-02-418767-4
    1. Computers. 2. Computer software.   I.   Szymanski, Donald P.
II.   Pulschen, Donna M.
QA76.5.S98 1994
004—dc20   94-16833
                                                                              CIP

Cover art: Marjory Dressler
Editor: P. J. Boardman
Production Editor: Christine M. Harrington
Photo Editor: Chris Migdol
Text/Cover Designer: Julia Zonneveld Van Hook
Production Buyer: Pamela D. Bennett

 © 1995 by Prentice-Hall, Inc.
A Simon & Schuster Company
Englewood Cliffs, New Jersey 07632

Printed in the United States of America

10 9 8 7 6 5 4 3 2 1

ISBN: 0-02-418767-4

Prentice-Hall International (UK) Limited, *London*
Prentice-Hall of Australia Pty. Limited, *Sydney*
Prentice-Hall of Canada, Inc., *Toronto*
Prentice-Hall Hispanoamericana, S.A., *Mexico*
Prentice-Hall of India Private Limited, *New Delhi*
Prentice-Hall of Japan, Inc., *Tokyo*
Simon & Schuster Asia Pte. Ltd., *Singapore*
Editora Prentice-Hall do Brasil, Ltda., *Rio de Janeiro*

Part opening artwork courtesy of: Alias Research Inc., pp. 258, 524; Michael Miller, Head Spin Studio, p. 2; Lasergraphics LFR, p. 400; Reginald Wickham, pp. 3, 259, 401, 525.

Chapter opening artwork courtesy of: Alias Research Inc., pp. 48 (top); 494 (top, bottom); David E. Breen, p. 208 (bottom); Luz Bueno, p. 434 (bottom); Digital Equipment Corporation, pp. 123, 298 (top); Marjory Dressler, pp. 4 (middle), 48 (middle), 80 (middle), 122 (middle), 164 (middle), 208 (middle), 260 (middle), 298 (middle), 328 (middle), 370 (middle), 402 (middle), 434 (middle), 460 (middle), 494 (middle), 526 (middle); David S. Ebert, p. 208 (top); Michael Miller, Head Spin Studio, pp. 5, 49, 80 (top), 165, 209, 261, 299, 329, 371, 403, 435, 461, 495, 527; Lasergraphics LFR, pp. 4 (top), 80 (bottom), 164 (top), 260 (top), 328 (top, bottom), 370 (top, bottom), 402 (bottom), 434 (top), 526 (top, bottom); Marsha McDevitt, p. 122 (top); PIXAR, pp. 81, 260 (bottom), 460 (bottom); S.K. Robinson, K.C. Hu, P.R. Spalart, NASA Ames Research Center, p. 402 (top); Bob Sabiston, p. 122 (bottom); Time Arts, p. 48 (bottom); Reginald Wickham, p. 4 (bottom); John S. Willette/Emerald City, p. 164 (bottom).

Profile artwork courtesy of: Marjory Dressler.

Miscellaneous photos courtesy of: Albertson's, Inc., p. 141; Brooks Shoe, Inc., and Michigan State University, p. 359; Burlington Industries Inc., p. 93 (top, right); The Babcock and Wilcox Co., p. 362; Cobalt Productions/Merrill, pp. 29, 93 (bottom, right); Daimler-Benz and Evans & Sutherland, p. 8; Honda America, Marysville, Ohio, p. 361; Honeywell, Inc., p. 363; International Business Machines Corp., p. 447 (bottom); Mattel Toys, p. 98; Gene Moore/Phototake/NYC, and Inset: Joseph Klemp and Richard Rotunno/National Center for Atmospheric Research, p. 34; National Semiconductor Co., p. 86 (bottom); Preston Lyon/Index Stock, Inc., p. 365 (top, left); Time Arts, p. 499 (bottom); TRW, Inc., p. 134.

For Laura and Eric, your love has brought true happiness and joy into my life

R. A. S.

For the truly meaningful part of my life, my wife Sue and children Paul, Stacy, and Michael

D. P. S.

For the Chip in my main memory and my dear Mother "bored"

D. M. P.

Preface

This textbook presents a thorough and nontechnical guide for the practical use of computers and information systems to acquire, manage, and use information that will be vital to your personal and professional lives. We'll look at how technology works and describe how that technology is applied. Current examples are found throughout this text to illustrate these applications. Because there is no consensus in the way that various instructors prefer to present this material, the book has been designed with a unique organization through the use of Infomodules (subchapters). This makes it possible to cover all the current, important topics, but allows the instructor to choose and order them.

Note to the Student

How does this book prepare you for the future? Using computers and information systems to achieve your information needs will be an important part of your professional and personal lives. Some experts think that if you do not know how to use a computer, you will be just as handicapped in performing your job as the person who cannot read.

It is important to be both information- and computer-literate. You must understand what information you need and how to use it effectively once you have acquired it. To remain competitive in today's computerized world, you also need to know how and where computers and information systems can be used to help you acquire the needed information. *Computers and Information Systems* is an interesting and informative guide on your journey to understanding the world of computers and information systems. If you intend to become a computer professional, this book gives you the broad-based background you need to pursue more advanced course work.

After you have completed this course, your book will remain a handy reference. When you select and purchase your own personal computer system, you can use the consumer information and checklists in the Infomodule "Buying and Caring for a Microcomputer System." The chapters on popular application packages will provide additional information when you are ready to evaluate and select your own software. The Infomodules that describe document and spreadsheet design as well as the creation of business graphs and charts will be valuable references as you use these applications in your education and career. The primers on MS-DOS 6.0, Microsoft Windows 3.1 and SQL offer a solid foundation, allowing you to begin experimenting with and using these applications.

Although computers played an important role in the preparation of this text, so did a talented group of publishing professionals. Computers and people working together made this book possible.

Key Features of the Text

To present thorough coverage of concepts, hardware, software, computer systems, information systems, and related topics that educators have indicated are important, we have included these key features:

> **Unique organization** through the use of subchapters called Info-modules, which allow for flexibility and expandability in structuring a course.
>
> **Readability** at the appropriate level, and a conversational writing style to hold the student's interest.
>
> **Sound and effective pedagogy** designed to facilitate student understanding and interest in the subject matter.
>
> **Current examples** of computer applications that relate concepts to actual situations.
>
> **Comprehensive coverage** which, beyond the usual core coverage, includes discussions of contemporary issues such as:
>
> Information and its value
>
> Ethics and legal issues
>
> Artificial intelligence, neural networks, and virtual reality
>
> Expert systems
>
> Trends in technology, such as optoelectronics, parallel processing, and communication
>
> Object-oriented programming language, object-oriented databases, and computer-assisted systems engineering (CASE)
>
> Popular types of application software
>
> Tips on document design, spreadsheet design, and business graph and chart design
>
> Increasing use of communication technology
>
> Thorough coverage of local-area networks
>
> Increasing use of networks, commercial information services, and database services by professionals, organizations, businesses, and home users
>
> Increasing home use of computers and helpful microcomputer and software buyers' tips
>
> Career information about computer professions and about noncomputer professions that use computers

DOS 6.0, Windows 3.1, and SQL primers

International issues focusing on the current global nature of businesses and information systems

Written for everyone—not only introductory-level students who may be interested in continuing their study of computers and information systems as a career, but also for those who plan to pursue other career opportunities

Pedagogy

The following pedagogical devices were chosen with both student and instructor in mind:

Chapter objectives alert students and instructor to the major points or concepts to be gleaned from the chapter.

Chapter outlines preview chapter topics and organization so students can see the relationships among the topics covered.

Profiles acquaint students with people who have made major contributions to the Information Age.

Highlight boxes focus on current computer uses and issues.

Sidebars, placed in the margin near relevant text, reiterate key points and serve as memory joggers.

Summaries review major concepts in the chapter.

Vocabulary self-tests spotlight words that are important to understanding the material. These key words are boldfaced and defined in the text at their first usage and listed alphabetically at the end of the chapter or Infomodule with text page numbers for reference and review. They are also listed in the glossary.

Review questions check the student's understanding of the main topics in the chapter. They appear at the end of each chapter as a self-test comprised of about 30 questions.

Issues for thought encourage discussion and instill group participation in problem solving.

Infomodules provide significant coverage of special-interest topics. These subchapters (one per chapter) offer flexibility in structuring course content. Most include key terms in boldface as well as review questions.

Glossary, a handy reference at the end of the book, defines all of the key terms.

Index, a detailed guide to text and Infomodule topics.

Finally, full-color functional illustrations and more than 220 photographs clarify concepts, depict applications, and show equipment.

Expandability/Flexibility

The unique feature of this text is the series of subchapters called Infomodules. These enable instructors to modify courses by expanding or deleting topics according to time constraints and individual preference. The Infomodules present succinct but significant coverage of additional topics, such as ethics, crime and privacy, buying and caring for a microcomputer system, document design, spreadsheet design, hypertext and multimedia, creating business graphs and charts, among others. Infomodules include key terms and review questions so the material can be treated as separate chapters. If preferred, the material can be assigned as outside reading.

Organization

The text is divided into four parts:

- Part One (Chapters 1 through 6) is an overview of computing and computers.
- Part Two (Chapters 7 through 10) describes information system concepts.
- Part Three (Chapter 11 through 14) describes popular application software.
- Part Four (Chapter 15) examines international computing, trends in technology, and history of computers.

Here is a quick look at the topics discussed in each chapter and Infomodule.

Chapter 1, "Computers in Your World," introduces students to the concept of information, how it is created, managed, and used. It also introduces them to the powerful tools of computers and information systems used in the creation and management of information. The chapter provides examples of where computers are used and briefly explains how they work, what they can and cannot do, and the need to become computer and information literate. The **Infomodule, "Computer Ethics, Crime, and Privacy,"** defines ethics and looks at it in the context of corporate, individual, and government responsibility; it discusses crimes, legislation, and privacy issues.

Chapter 2, "The Processing Unit," overviews the internal design and operation of the processing unit. The chapter also explains data representation. The **Infomodule, "Number Systems,"** describes various number systems used to represent data, including the binary system used by computers.

Chapter 3, "Input," explains input concepts and describes devices, including those used for physically challenged users. The **Infomodule, "MS-DOS 6.0 Primer,"** provides an overview of the concepts and commands required to work with MS-DOS 6.0.

Chapter 4, "Output," explains output concepts and describes both hard and soft copy output devices; ports and device drivers are also covered. The **Infomodule, "Microsoft Windows 3.1 Primer,"** provides an overview of the concepts and commands required to work with Microsoft Windows 3.1.

Chapter 5, Secondary Storage," describes various secondary storage media and ways to organize and access data on these media; it addresses common secondary storage problems and solutions. The **Infomodule, "Buying and Caring for a Microcomputer System,"** offers suggestions for selecting and purchasing hardware and software for a microcomputer system and gives helpful tips on maintaining and protecting systems and data.

Chapter 6, **"Computer Software,"** describes systems and application software, emphasizing operating systems and their importance. The **Infomodule, "Developing Computer Programs,"** looks at different levels of computer programming languages; introduces the latest programming techniques, including object-oriented programming; and lists criteria for choosing a programming language.

Chapter 7, **"Data Communication,"** explains what data communication is and how data are transferred from one computer to another. The chapter introduces computer networks and distributed data processing and covers some of the challenges presented by the use of data communications. The **Infomodule, "Putting Data Communication to Work for You,"** describes applications of data communications, including bulletin boards, electronic mail, facsimile, voice messaging, teleconferencing, commercial online services, and gateway services.

Chapter 8, **"Local-Area Networks,"** provides detailed coverage of a technology gaining widespread use in business and describes the components and benefits of using LANs. The **Infomodule, "Microcomputer Communications,"** describes the uses and features of typical communications software.

Chapter 9, **Information Systems and the System Development Life Cycle,"** defines information systems and describes the different levels of management—their information needs and the basic types of information systems used, the systems development life cycle, prototyping, and the use of computer-aided systems engineering (CASE) software. The **Infomodule, "Applications of Information Systems,"** examines the application of information systems in various functional areas of business and selected industries.

Chapter 10, **"Files and Databases,"** describes the use of files and databases. It covers file management systems, database management systems, database models, and concerns about developing and managing a database. The **Infomodule, "A Structured Query Language (SQL) Primer,"** presents the basic SQL concepts and commands to build a foundation for further study for those individuals who will be required to access information from a database.

Chapter 11, **"Document Preparation: Word Processing and Desktop Publishing Software,"** describes the uses and features of a typical word processor and examines the features and benefits of using desktop publishing. The **Infomodule, "Document Design,"** describes the elements to consider when designing a document for the effective communication of ideas.

Chapter 12, **"Managing Data: Database Management Systems,"** describes the uses and features of a typical database management system. The **Infomodule, "Hypertext and Multimedia,"** looks at software that allow text, graphs, pictures, sound, and video to be combined into one application.

Chapter 13, **"Manipulating Numeric Data: The Spreadsheet,"** describes the uses and features of a typical electronic spreadsheet. The

Infomodule, "Spreadsheet Design," prescribes some basic rules for designing effective spreadsheets.

Chapter 14, "Data Presentation and Graphics Software," features applications of typical graphics software. The **Infomodule, "Creating Business Graphs and Charts,"** describes factors to consider when creating graphs and the appropriate type of graphs and methods to convey particular information.

Chapter 15, "International Computing and Trends in Technology," looks at the increasing global use of computers and information systems in business and government, and examines some technological trends—chip technologies, neural networks, virtual reality, parallel processing, and optoelectronics. The **Infomodule, "A History of Computers,"** provides a summary of events, significant people, and their contributions throughout the history of computers and computing.

The Instructional Package

Instructor's Resource Manual contains chapter-by-chapter lecture outlines, answers to questions in the text, suggestions for using alternative instructional material, and a list of sources for additional reading.

Computerized Test Bank includes true/false, short answer, multiple choice, and fill-in questions. All questions are coded with the chapter or Infomodule number and organized by objective. This versatile test bank program allows the instructor to generate tests, edit existing questions, and add new questions.

Printed Test Bank is a hard-copy version of all questions in the computerized test bank.

Transparency Package consists of overhead transparencies that illustrate concepts presented in the text.

Electronic Transparency Package utilizing Powerpoint allows instructors to present transparencies in the classroom using their personal computer.

Data Diskettes are files that save keyboarding time for instructors and eliminate the possibility of introducing incorrect data during rekeyboarding.

Videotapes can be purchased by adopters of *Computers and Information Systems* directly from American Micro Media at a discounted rate:

"Electronic Words"—Word processing and microcomputers

"Keeping Track"—Database management and microcomputers

"Computer Calc"—Electronic spreadsheets and microcomputers

"Computer Talk"—Microcomputer communications

"Computer Images"—Computer graphics

ABC News/Prentice Hall Video Library, which consists of interviews, critical analyses, and network news reports drawn from the ABC news library, is available to instructors who adopt this book for their classes and have their bookstore order it from the publisher. The videos, chosen for their widespread applicability to business and their usefulness and appeal to students, draw on such ABC News programs as *Nightline, World News Tonight,* and *This Week With David Brinkley.*

The *New York Times* **"Themes of the Times."** Computers and information systems are constant themes in the news, both because of developments in the computer industry itself and because of the ways businesses use them on a day-to-day basis. To enhance access to important news items, the *New York Times* and Prentice Hall are sponsoring "Themes of the Times." Twice a year, Prentice Hall will deliver complimentary copies of a "mini newspaper" containing reprints of selected *Times* articles to instructors who use this book for their classes. "Themes of the Times" is an excellent way of keeping students abreast of the ever-changing world of computers and information systems.

Multimedia Toolkit. The CD-ROM package that accompanies *Computers and Information Systems* is designed to support the text through visuals, sound, and motion. More information is available from your PH sales representative.

Reviewers

We wish to thank the following people who reviewed the manuscript and provided thoughtful and helpful suggestions for this edition of *Computers and Information Systems:* Professor Bennett, Nashville State Technical Institute; Diane Delisio, Miami University; Richard Ender, University of Alaska; James Gatza, Insurance Institute of America; Robert Harris, Holmes Junior College; Richard Hatch, San Diego State University; Judy Ann Hill, Purdue University, Calumet; Sharon Hill, Prince George Community College; Carl Hommer, Purdue University; Sandy Juergens, Great Falls Vocational Technical Center; C. Kiklas, Anoka Ramsey Community College; Diane Larsan, Purdue University, Calumet; Chang-Yang Lin, Eastern Kentucky University; Mack Lundy, Trident Technical College; Ron Mummaw, Antelope Valley College; Jon Persavich, Kennebec Valley Vocational Technical College; Jerry Ralya; Al Schroeder, Richland College; Dorothy Smalley, Arizona Western College; Wanda Staggers, Anderson College; Ralph Szweda, Monroe Community College; Pat Tormey, University of Wisconsin, Madison; Marianne P. Vakalis, Western Michigan University; Lister Wayne, Pensicola Junior College; and Paul Wolotikin, State University of New York at Farmingdale.

Acknowledgments

Once again, we have had the pleasure of working with a very professional and friendly group of individuals throughout this endeavor. So many people were involved in the development, production, and creative aspects of this project that the list of names would go on and on. Special acknowledgment, however, goes to the professionals at Prentice Hall who provided support, enthusiasm, and helpful suggestions: P. J. Boardman, administrative editor; Christine Harrington, production editor; and Julia Zonneveld Van Hook, designer. Thanks also to Sheryl Rose for her fine copyediting.

Brief Contents

Contents

PART 3

Computers and
Information Systems

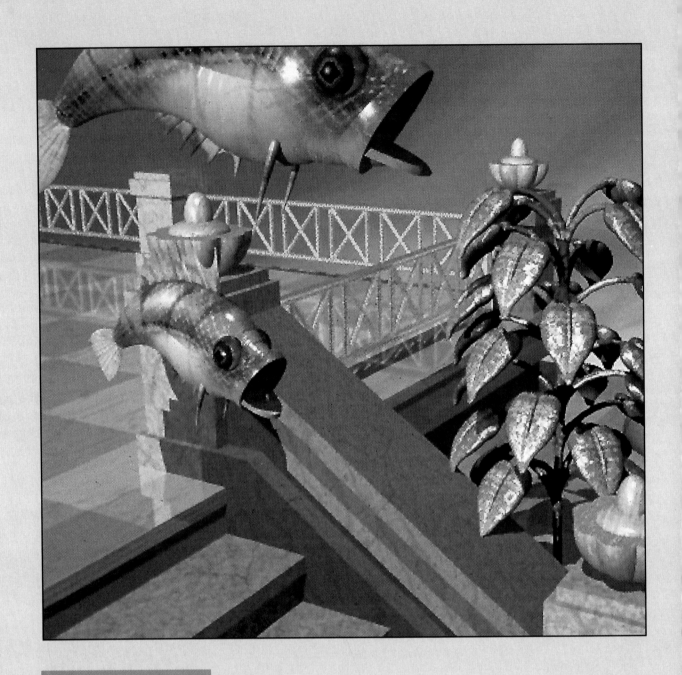

Part 1

Information Age: An Overview of Computing and Computers

The revolution manifest in this new age—this age of intelligent machines—is in its earliest stages. The impact of these new machines that augment our mental resources will be greater than the radical technological and social changes that have come before. It cannot be stopped. Today's challenges are to be found in our need to understand it, to learn to live creatively and harmoniously with it, and to harness it to constructive uses.

Raymond Kurzweil, researcher in artificial intelligence and chairman of Kurzweil Applied Intelligence, Inc.

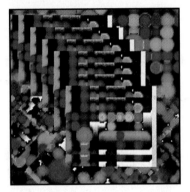

OUTLINE

OBJECTIVES

1.1 Describe several ways in which computer technology has changed the way you conduct your personal and professional business.

1.2 Differentiate between data and information, identify the attributes of information, identify the sources of information, and discuss the concerns with information sources.

1.3 Explain what is meant by the value of information and describe several ways in which information is used in decision making.

1.4 Define the terms computer and information system.

1.5 Recognize the importance of possessing a basic level of knowledge, understanding, and skill in using computers and information systems.

1.6 Describe some of the effects that computers and information systems have had on the generation and management of information.

1.7 State the purpose of a computer, describe the three basic functions that computers perform, and explain the advantage of using a computer to accomplish them.

1.8 Identify the components that make up a computer.

1.9 Understand the purpose of software and describe the two main types.

1.10 Describe the steps involved in transforming data into information.

1.11 Identify four basic ways in which computers are used.

1.12 Understand the limitations of computers.

1.13 Specify the criteria used to categorize computers and describe the major computer categories.

Chapter 1

Computers in Your World

Profile

John V. Atanasoff

Computers! Could it all really have begun with something as elementary as ABC? Yes, the Atanasoff-Berry Computer (ABC).

At Iowa State University, Dr. John Vincent Atanasoff was a professor of mathematics and physics. In 1937, he was interested in discovering a way to solve complex math problems known as simultaneous differential equations. Atanasoff was a driven scientist, often working in his lab until the early morning hours. Taking long automobile drives helped him to perceive solutions. After one 200-mile expedition, his mind began to focus on the potential of building a machine with regenerative memory. The concept of the logic circuit was born.

Neither Atanasoff nor his graduate assistant, Clifford Berry, was disheartened by the fact that the college offered them a grant of only $650. By 1939, they succeeded in building the prototype of the first electronic, digital computer. The ABC contained vacuum tubes whose on and off electrical states were controlled by implementing the binary system of 1s and 0s. Both IBM and Remington Rand were interested in producing a commercial version, but the companies wanted Atanasoff to sign away his rights to the invention. He refused.

The officials at Iowa State and a patent lawyer were supposed to handle the technicalities of filing for Atanasoff's patent rights. But in 1942 he left the university to work for the Naval Ordinance Laboratory in Washington, D.C. and the patent application was never finalized. Unfortunately, other inventors were aware of the ABC, and they used the ideas to build the Electronic Numerical Integrator and Computer (ENIAC). The ENIAC was christened, arguably, as the first large-scale programmable electronic computer. The argument was finally settled in 1973 when a U.S. District Court held that the patents that had been granted under an Army contract during 1943–46 to build the ENIAC were invalid. The court found that the concepts of the ABC should take precedence.

At last the recognition was where it belonged. Now, John Vincent Atanasoff could be acknowledged as the father of the modern computer. And to think that it all started with ABC.

It is nearly impossible to escape the effects of computers and information systems today. Organizations and individuals like you, from artists to zoologists, are discovering the potential of computers and information systems to meet their information needs and reach their desired goals.

On a personal level, you may find them beneficial for tasks such as managing investments and finances, calculating taxes, preparing resumes, catching up at home on your school or office work, educating your children, and entertaining yourself and your family. Businesses large and small have long seen advantages in using computers and information systems. The pace of technological innovations and the pressures of competition keep businesses constantly searching for new and better ways to use computers and information systems.

No matter what your career path, you will likely be responsible for identifying and solving problems and for making decisions. Some decisions will be inconsequential; others may have monumental impact on you and your organization. To ensure that the decisions you make are in the best interests of all concerned, you should understand how to recognize and acquire the appropriate information. You need to be aware of and understand how to use the powerful tools of computers and information systems to gather and manage the information you need. This text lays the foundation for you to function in a world that makes extensive use of computers and information systems.

So let's discover what information, computers, and information systems are; what they can do for you; and how to go about using them in ways that will be beneficial to your personal and career goals. We'll start by seeing the changes in your world.

Objective 1.1   Describe several ways in which computer technology has changed the way you conduct your personal and professional business.

How Is Computer Technology Changing Your World?

Even when you don't see them, computers and information systems are working behind the scenes—at home, at school, and where you shop, work, or transact business. Some computers aid in your leisure enjoyment and entertainment; others are found in government operations and most professions.

Computers and information systems are used in business for many information processing tasks. These tasks include word processing, filing, and assembling numbers and facts associated with general office functions, such as accounting, payroll processing, personnel record keeping, and compliance with federal regulations.

The ability to simulate hazardous conditions without risk to humans has brought progress in space flight and earth-bound vehicle safety testing (Figure 1.1). NASA astronauts train by studying computer simulations of problems they could encounter during launch, in space, or upon return to Earth. In addition, computers are instrumental in the design of aircraft models; they can simulate the effects of wind and other environmental forces on those designs.

Hospitals use computers extensively, recording information on each patient's admission, prescribed medications, doctor visits, other hospital services, and of course the itemized bill. Computers and information

FIGURE 1.1
This body model is designed to simulate the mass and other characteristics of an actual human body to test a proposed seat belt design. Computer simulation aids engineers in identifying the most effective seat belt design to eliminate shoulder belt slack on impact.

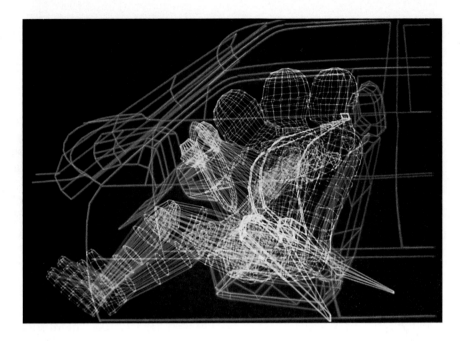

systems are valuable as tools to diagnose and treat medical conditions. Diagnostic equipment such as computer-aided tomography (CAT) and magnetic resonance imaging (MRI) relies on computers. Pharmaceutical companies and medical research facilities use information systems to help discover, design, and test new medicines and treatments. Some of today's medical students are learning anatomy and physiology by means of *The Electric Cadaver*. This "electronic book" displays text and images on the computer screen—even depictions of muscles and tendons at work—and gives students the ability to study the body's internal organs and skeletal structure.

Most schools in the United States have computers located in laboratories, classrooms, and registration offices. Many educators find computers to be valuable aids for instruction and tutoring. Computer tutors are tireless and nonjudgmental when drilling students on mathematical facts or offering specialized lessons on particular subjects. Because many science laboratory experiments can be simulated by computer, young students become interested and excited by the interaction, the vivid color graphics, and the feeling of accomplishment gained from giving the right answers. The Boston Computer Society and Lotus Development Corp. sponsor a competition in search of our future programmers. Four-year-olds are not too young to learn about the computer mouse and preteens develop computer games and create computer art work.

The federal government is the largest user of computers and information systems and one of the largest funders of computer research. By one estimate, the federal government holds over 4 billion personal files on U.S. citizens. The U.S. Patent and Trademark Office receives over 20,000 documents every day, and the Securities and Exchange Commission receives more than 6 million pages of documents and reports a year. These agencies could not function efficiently without modern information systems.

Highlight 1.1

What's Up, Doc?

Computers and neurosurgery? Why not? At Stanford University Medical Center, Dr. John Adler uses the Neurosurgical Operating Arm System (NOAS) attached to a workstation to look inside the brain of his patients. CAT scan and X-ray data are fed into the computer to give the surgeon a three-dimensional view of the brain. In this way a tumor or diseased portion of the brain is pinpointed with the precision necessary for this delicate procedure. The operating arm contains a probe end which is placed on the patient's head. Appropriate images can be displayed on the screen of the workstation. Other images can be examined by accessing specific menus. Because the surgeon's hands are necessarily occupied, a foot pedal located on the floor gives the physician the freedom of motion required.

Hard copies of X-rays and scans have been available for the surgeon for some time, but they were positioned on a frame that was attached to the skull of the patient. This device was ungainly and got in the way of the surgeon. It was not capable of providing the specific data required to locate the appropriate position in the brain.

The NOAS, which costs approximately $150,000, is comparatively inexpensive for a highly qualified brain surgery assistant.

In most professional sports, computers compile statistics, track ticket sales, create training programs and diets for athletes, and suggest strategies based on the past performance of competitors. The graphic art displays flashed on scoreboards also are generated by computers. Even if you're a sports fan watching in an armchair, computers affect you. Television networks use computers in the control room to bring you play-by-play action. With the help of a computer, a technician calls up replays of the action and inserts the commercial breaks on schedule.

A musical instrument digital interface (MIDI) exists to link musical instruments to a personal computer, thereby enabling the computer to control a wide variety of instrument sounds (Figure 1.2). The background music in many movies, television shows, and commercials is electronically generated. In addition, when you buy concert tickets, the ticket agency is probably part of a computerized network that registers the number of seats sold.

Computers have long since gone Hollywood. Computer-generated art lets designers create sets, special effects, and even imaginary characters in movies, videos, and commercials. Creatures, spaceships, and entire galaxies are created and manipulated by computers and then photographed by computer-driven cameras. Computer-controlled lighting systems on sound stages or in theaters produce a dramatic range of atmospheres.

Want to get away from it all? Computers help prepare your ticket, confirm your hotel room and rental car reservations, monitor the route of your train, or guide your plane to a safe landing. Tulsa, Oklahoma, is the hub for American Airlines' reservation system, SABRE, the world's largest network of computers not used for military purposes. The system processes data at the rate of 1,400 messages per second. With the aid of over 700,000

miles of wires and circuits connecting five large computers, SABRE confirms your reservations while you wait.

In more and more home offices, people use computers to continue their daytime work, organize personal information needs, or conduct business for themselves. Microwaves, sewing machines, and coffee makers are among the standard computerized appliances in most households. In addition, home automation systems with prices ranging from $1,500 to many thousands of dollars create so-called "smart" homes that maximize computer use. Lighting, heating, cooling, and security systems are among the computer-controlled functions. Sensors warn owners of fire or vandalism. Lawns are sprinkled automatically, hot tub temperatures are regulated, and motion sensors turn lights and heat on or off when a person enters or leaves a room.

But wait, the latest gadget coming to your home will be a combination of technologies and services. The blend depends on digital information being carried via fiber-optic cable directly into your television, computer, printer, and probably devices that have not been invented yet. Promoters say that you will be able to replay your favorite television shows and access books and periodicals, classic movies, and contemporary films. You will be able to make bank transactions and travel arrangements, and perhaps shop in "virtual reality" stores. This coming technology has been dubbed the "information highway." Can you imagine speed limits on this kind of highway?

SFX

Computers are invaluable in the million-dollar business of special effects (SFX). You've seen these SFX in movies such as *Tron, The Abyss, Willow,* and all of the *Terminator* series. The graphic technique known as visualization creates images from numerical data. To create the T-1000 cyborg, photos and images were scanned, digitized, distorted, and manipulated with computers.

The 1993 smash hit movie *Jurassic Park* brought high-tech to prehistoric subjects in the form of dinosaurs of various sizes and species. Stan Winston Studios and George Lucas's Industrial Light and Magic (ILM) in San Rafael, California, collaborated for months to create these digital dinosaurs. Rough drawings were created on monitors, rendered digitally, and then inserted into the film. Because many of the movements are manipulated by individual pixels, or points, on the screen, the animals look and move more realistically. The combination of human actors with these computer creations blends many technologies. For example, one scene takes place in the kitchen where a meat-eating dinosaur traps the children. Filming begins with a close-up of the animated raptor's head, but then a person in a rubber suit chases the children around. The total effect, however, is one that looks terrifyingly real.

The "Gallimi" animals were digital creations. Their galloping motion was accomplished by means of a computer program, Softimage. The animator sculpted the skin, bones, and movement of the creatures. ILM has created custom software that gives the digitally created muscle realism, so if the muscle is supposed to twitch or move during an action, it will.

The software that allowed the villain to ooze from the floor tiles in *Terminator 2* has applications for morphing, or changing. For example, it can be important to update the appearance of children who have been missing for a long time since their photographs were first made available, for enhancing the mug shots of criminals who may alter their "look" through hair style or other appearance changes, and for giving us the option of "trying out" new makeup or hair styles before we commit to a purchase.

Without doubt, computers are a part of your world. Surveys of recent graduates indicate that the need is critical for more computer education and hands-on application training so you'll be prepared for real-world experiences. Developing the knowledge and skills to put computers to work for you is essential to a well-rounded education in the information age in which you live.

Turning to that education, let's discover the roles of data and information.

Objective 1.2   Differentiate between data and information, identify the attributes of information, identify the sources of information, and discuss the concerns with information sources.

What Are Data and Information?

How can I track personal finances? How can I make an inventory of personal belongings and easily update it for insurance purposes? I have an idea for a novel, but the thought of using a typewriter and having to make corrections and revisions prevents me from starting. What can I do?

How can my business keep track of and reduce the cost of inventory? We need a way to analyze our sales data so we can make more cost-effective advertising decisions. All of my employees have computers on their desks, but nobody seems to be working with the same information. How can I remedy this?

You may have these and many other questions in your personal or professional lives. To make appropriate decisions and solve problems, you need to gather data and turn them into information to help answer those questions.

Data are raw facts (numbers, letters, special characters, or combinations thereof) that convey little meaning by themselves. **Information** is processed data that appears in context and conveys meaning to people. Strange as it may seem, one person's data may be another's information. For example, your first test grade of, say, 93 is information to you but is probably regarded only as data by your teacher.

Data are readily available to an organization. Every transaction that occurs supplies data. A **transaction** is a business activity or event. The receipt of an order or the sale of a product constitutes a transaction. Typically there is much more data available than needs to be collected for the decision making, problem solving, and control activities of most managers. With computers and improved data communications, the problem for most managers is not the lack of data or the subsequent information that its processing can generate, but the fact that they receive more information than they can possibly absorb. This condition is referred to as "information overload"; too much of the decision maker's time is spent trying to determine what is relevant and what is not. The greatest difficulty is not in gathering data but in deciding what data need to be gathered to provide the necessary information and making sure the information gets distributed to the right people at the right time.

Information can be of two general types: qualitative or quantitative. Quantitative information tells how much or how many. For example, there are 12 roses in the vase. Quantitative information is used heavily throughout businesses. How many units were sold, or how many dollars are being spent on employee salaries? Quantitative information appears in one of two forms: numerical or graphical. Information represented by numbers is called numerical information. A business' balance sheet or income statement contains numerical information. Information represented pictorially is called graphical information. Common graphical representations of quantitative business information include pie charts and bar and line graphs. Qualitative information describes something using nonquantitative characteristics. For example, the roses in the vase are red. Qualitative characteristics can be used to describe job categories or positions, such as marketing manager, graphics designer, or programmer.

Data

■ Raw facts conveying little meaning

Information

■ Processed data seen in context and conveying meaning

Attributes of Information

Information can be expressed in terms of its attributes, or characteristics. These give the user a framework by which to judge the meaningfulness and usefulness of information. We will look at seven basic attributes of information: accuracy, relevance, completeness, timeliness, cost-effectiveness, auditability, and reliability.

Accuracy refers to whether information is accurate (true) or inaccurate (false). Information is accurate if it represents a fact or situation as it really is. Inaccurate information can result from errors in the collecting, processing, or reporting activities involved in producing and transmitting it. You might think that inaccurate information is not really information. However, if users are unaware that it is inaccurate and they use it in decision making, then it is information to them. This is one of the problems with the generation and distribution of information within organizations. In most cases the user of the information is not the same person(s) who collected, processed, and distributed it. Users assume that what they have received is accurate information. It is therefore the responsibility of the provider to ensure its accuracy.

Relevance refers to whether information is needed and useful in a particular situation. If it is needed, then the information is relevant. However, relevance is not a static attribute. What is relevant for a chief executive officer (CEO) may not be relevant for a purchasing clerk, and vice versa. In addition, what is relevant today may not be relevant tomorrow in making the same decision.

Completeness refers to how thorough or inclusive a set of information is. It tells everything you need to know about a situation. Because of the complexity of most business decision-making situations, it is virtually impossible to attain a complete set of information. The aim is to acquire the most complete set possible.

Timeliness refers to two conditions: Is the information available when it is needed, and is it outdated when it is received or when it is to be used? If the information is not available when needed or if it is outdated by the time it is used, then it has little or no value in decision making, problem solving, or control activities. Outdated information may also be counterproductive or worse than no information at all.

Cost-effectiveness refers to the relationship between the benefit to be derived from using information and the cost of producing it. If the cost is more than the benefit, the information is not cost-effective and is usually not produced.

Auditability, also known as verifiability, refers to the ability to check the accuracy and completeness of information. Without auditability it is not possible to determine accuracy, thus bringing into question the information's usefulness. The term audit trail is used to indicate that summarized information can be traced back to its original source(s) to verify its accuracy.

Reliability summarizes how closely information fits the other six attributes. Information is not always perfect. It may not be totally accurate, or it may not be 100 percent verifiable. Reliability takes into consideration the expected averages of the other six attributes. If they are near what was expected, then the information is considered reliable. If they deviate significantly from what was expected, then it is considered unreliable.

Sources of Information

It is important to become aware of the many potential sources of information available. Decision-making efforts can be hampered if you do not know where to get the information you need or if you fail to realize that it exists. Information can be acquired from two basic sources—internal and external.

Internal sources of information are found within an organization. Three common sources are internally generated documents, observations, and surveys. Internal documents—such as balance sheet, income statement, employee files, scheduled and unscheduled reports, and other files and reports—supply a great deal of information about how a business operates and what its financial condition is.

Observation is a method of obtaining information about a situation or event by observing it and thus gaining firsthand knowledge. It is important for an observer to be complete and accurate in recording information so that it will not be misinterpreted later on. It is also important to realize that the process of observation itself may alter the situation or event being observed. Internal surveys in the form of questionnaires, telephone interviews, or personal interviews are another popular means of obtaining information about an organization from individuals within that organization.

External sources of information are produced outside an organization. Common sources include external surveys, annual reports from other organizations, statistics from government agencies, trade publications, and research reports. External surveys are similar to internal surveys except that the individuals surveyed are outside the organization that is conducting the survey.

Government agencies provide an external source by compiling large amounts of information about a wide variety of topics, including items such as the gross national product (GNP) and population estimates, which can be very important to some businesses. Most of the information collected by government agencies is available upon request.

Publications of a commercial, trade, government, or professional business nature are available through subscriptions, libraries, or special purchase. They provide valuable information on topics including industry trends, new technologies, and government regulations.

Information can also be purchased from outside sources such as research houses, like A. C. Nielsen Company, and public opinion polls, like Gallup Poll. An organization can buy information or commission specific research and polls to gather needed information.

Concerns with Information Sources

You need to ensure that the decision-making information is of the highest quality. There are several concerns for the user about information sources. The information supplied by a source should not contain bias but should be valid, reliable, consistent, and timely (i.e., have minimal time delay between its request and its receipt).

Bias refers to the impartiality of the information source. Unbiased information is impartial and does not attempt to distort reality.

Valid information is meaningful and relevant to the purpose for which it is used. For example, you might notice that sales of a product went down after its price was increased. You might conclude that the increase in price caused the sales to go down. But in fact, a decrease in quality or availability of the product might account for the diminished sales. An information user should examine all possible factors before determining the validity of any specific information.

Reliable information gives a true picture of a given event or situation. For example, a report that 90 percent of those surveyed used a particular brand of product might suggest that that brand was the most popular. However, it is important to know other things, such as what percentage of the total market was surveyed. If the total market consists of 100,000 product users and the survey reflects the views of only 10, then the reliability of the result is questionable. If the survey randomly sampled 10,000 users, the results reflect a more significant portion of the market and would be more reliable.

Information obtained from a source should be based on consistent factors so they can be compared each time to ensure that the information will be meaningful. For example, you might want to compare first quarter sales to second quarter sales. If total sales in the first quarter are based on four products, then the second quarter total sales should be based on the same four products. If the total number of products in the second quarter report increases or decreases or the products are not the same, the comparison will not be meaningful.

The time delay in receiving information from a source is also important in assessing the value of the information. Many of the concerns in the design of information systems center around decreasing the delay between a user's request for and receipt of information.

Objective 1.3   Explain what is meant by the value of information and describe several ways in which information is used in decision making.

How Can I Identify the Value of Information and Use It to Make Decisions?

How do you determine the value of information? This question faces managers daily. Computers do not have the ability to "understand" what the data they process represents. Determining the value is up to you. Generally, people judge the **value of information**, i.e., its meaningfulness and usefulness based on the attributes of information discussed above. It is important to look closely at the information to determine if it is correct and in a form that meets your needs. You can't assume it is merely because it was generated by a computer.

Value must be determined by the user on a case-by-case basis. Valuable information for one user in one situation may have no value for another user or another situation.

The value of information should be viewed in terms of its incremental value. The important factor is not how much information an item contains but how much additional knowledge it adds to what was previously known and stored.

Costs and benefits must also be examined. Costs are relatively easy to identify because they are quantifiable. They include things such as the costs of personnel, equipment, and supplies for collecting, processing, and transmitting information. Benefits are harder to pin down. They can range from the quantifiable (e.g., faster order processing) to the intangible (e.g., better decision making). The likelihood of actually obtaining the expected benefit also needs to be weighed.

You must use the information wisely and ethically. **Computer ethics** refers to a standard of behavior that conforms to societal and professional principles for the use of computers and the information they generate. The Infomodule at the end of this chapter takes a closer look at this important topic.

How you use information to make decisions depends on the circumstances. Some decisions can be made easily based on the generated information. For example, as a salesperson you could verify that a specific quantity of a particular item is in stock by checking the company's computerized inventory system. You would know if it was available.

Other situations require that the decision maker be more knowledgeable. Knowledge refers to the range of information or understanding accumulated. You then combine your knowledge with the information generated to make the decision. For example, your customer might want to know if an order can be shipped and reach its destination by a particular date. Simply determining if the requested items are in stock would not be enough. You would have to apply your knowledge about things such as the average shipping time to the desired destination, how long it would take to obtain any items that were not in stock, availability of transportation (e.g., is a strike in process?), and so on.

Critical decisions often require that decision makers not only use the generated information and their knowledge but also apply their instincts. For example, introducing a new product is a critical process for most businesses. The time and money committed to this task can be enormous. Computer-generated numbers and statistics can be misleading. You must combine this information with your knowledge about how it was generated, who the competitors are, what your company's financial position is, and so on, along with your instincts. Those instincts can be based on your confidence in the information and what you believe the market will want in the future. Since a computer has no understanding of how or why it processes data—it simply follows instructions—you must apply your instincts and good judgment in combination with the knowledge acquired from the computer-generated information when making critical decisions. Computers are a tremendous help in preparing the information, but it is people like you who ultimately bear the responsibility of decision making.

Objective 1.4   Define the terms computer and information system.

What Are Computers and Information Systems?

Two tools that are used to convert data into information and communicate it to the people who need it are computers and information systems. A **computer** is an electronic device that can accept input, process it in a prescribed manner, output the results, and store the results for later use. A computer is a tool used to process data into information. There is no single type of computer, but a wide assortment with varying capabilities, as we will examine later in this chapter. Figure 1.3 shows a computer that you might recognize, a microcomputer.

A *system* is any set of components that work together to perform a task. An **information system** is a set of components that work together to manage the acquisition, storage, manipulation, and distribution of information. The components of an information system are hardware, software, people, data, and procedures. **Hardware** includes all the physical equipment that make up a computer. **Software** is the instructions that cause the hardware to do the work. People, like you, make products, deliver services, solve problems, and make decisions. A person who uses computer hardware and software to perform a task is often referred to as an **end user** or simply **user**. As an end user of an information system, you will need to understand what it can do for you and how to use it effectively to accomplish your information needs. Data also play an important role in an information system; as you saw above, data provide the basis for information. The final component in an information system is **procedures**, the instructions that tell a user how to operate and use an information system.

> ### Information System Components
>
> - Hardware
> - Software
> - People
> - Data
> - Procedures

FIGURE 1.3
Most of you have seen or used a microcomputer, such as the ones pictured here.

TABLE 1.1
Functions of an Information System in Determining Customer Credit

Input	Process	Output
Data	*Data to Information*	*Information*
Customer specifics Lending policy Interest rate	Algorithms to convert data into desired information (e.g., customer credit worthiness, recommendation of whether to grant loan or not)	Transformed into a form usable by loan officer (e.g., screen display, paper copy)

Functions of an Information System

- Accept data (Input)
- Convert data to information (Process)
- Produce and communicate information (Output)

Information systems designed to be used by many users are called **multiuser information systems**. These are found in most businesses and organizations, and are vital to their successful operation. Information systems that are designed for use by an individual user are called **personal information systems**. You might set up a personal information system on your home computer to manage your financial portfolio.

An information system has three basic functions: (1) to accept data (*input*), (2) to convert data to information (*process*), and (3) to produce and communicate information in a timely fashion to users for decision making (*output*). For example, many banks and other financial institutions use information systems to help determine whether a customer applying for a loan is a good risk (Table 1.1). Data about the customer, lending policies, and interest rates are input into the information system. The data is then processed using previously defined procedures for determining credit worthiness. Finally, information is communicated to the loan officer (the user in this case) in the form of a recommendation to grant or deny the loan. It is important to note, however, that no matter what the output indicates, the user of an information system makes the actual decision.

Many of today's products could not be produced without the effective use of information systems on the factory floor. Aerospace, automotive, and industrial manufacturers use information systems to automate production and streamline engineering, speed development time, reduce costs, and keep up with the competition. These industries need a strong commitment to and investment in information systems to compete successfully in cost, quality, and delivery.

Objective 1.5   Recognize the importance of possessing a basic level of knowledge, understanding, and skill in using computers and information systems.

Why Learn About Computers and Information Systems?

We are in the midst of a revolution where the possession and dissemination of information has replaced industrialization as the driving force. Computers and information systems are the tools that allow you to transform data efficiently and effectively into information and distribute it to where it is needed. If used properly they can also improve your productivity. Productivity refers to the amount of time and resources required to gain a desired result. Ideally, you'd like to use less time and fewer resources to get the same or better results. In recent years, the growing use of microcomputers has brought the benefits of these tools to almost anyone who wants to take advantage of them.

As you examine potential career choices, you will find that many require—or soon will require—knowledge and understanding of computers and information systems as well as the ability to use them. Possessing knowledge and understanding of computers and information systems in combination with the ability to use them effectively is called **computer literacy**. Judging the value of information and using the information generated wisely is called **information literacy**. You will need both to compete for many jobs. This doesn't mean, however, that you'll have to be a technical wizard, because there are many levels of ability. These range from users who only need to know how to turn the computer on and off and use the software required by their job to generate or gain access to needed information; to those who must decide what data should be gathered and how that data should be processed; to those who repair, install, or design computers and information systems.

If you have ever used a computer, then you have had an introduction to this remarkable tool. You already realize its impact on your efficiency and productivity. However, if you have never used a computer, just ask a friend who uses a word processor about the differences in preparing a term paper. Ask your friend to go back to typing rough and final drafts on a typewriter. The answer will definitely be a resounding "No way!"

Objective 1.6   Describe some of the effects that computers and information systems have had on the generation and management of information.

How Do Computers and Information Systems Affect the Creation and Management of Information?

Over the last several decades the management of information and, thus, of computers and information systems has become increasingly more important to the attainment of an organization's goals. Information is the life blood of an organization. Most activities performed by managers in an organization—such as problem identification and solution, control, and decision making—are based on information. Managers need to receive accurate and timely information to accomplish these activities effectively. Computers and information systems permit information to be acquired, processed, and distributed efficiently. They enable businesses to gain a competitive edge because accurate, timely, and more complete information allows better decisions to be made.

Most organizations change as a result of both internal and external influences. Computers and information systems provide the means to gather and manage the appropriate information to keep pace with change. For example, a merger between two organizations may result in new goals and objectives. The managers must quickly acquire the information to meet the requirements of the new business and the philosophy of new top management. Changes in the marketplace, availability of resources, economic factors, and a host of other considerations force managers to reevaluate their goals and objectives. Computers and information systems help them gather and manage the information required to do this quickly and easily.

Communicating with an increasing number of other departments, managers, and staff; dealing with new technologies; and maintaining an edge over a growing number of competitors are all factors that increase the complexity of a manager's job. An information system helps to control this increasing complexity by ensuring that appropriate information is communicated in an accurate and timely manner.

When designed, developed, and used correctly, computers and information systems are powerful tools that increase the efficiency and effectiveness with which an organization acquires, processes, communicates, and uses information. Effective information systems can enable organizations to make better decisions and reach their goals.

Objective 1.7   State the purpose of a computer, describe the three basic functions that computers perform, and explain the advantage of using a computer to accomplish them.

Why Use a Computer?

Because of the move to an economy based on information, your ability to perform on a job may depend on how well you acquire and use it. Imagine that the Marketing Department manager plops down a two-inch thick pile of statistics and asks you to summarize it and prepare a report to the marketing director by 8 A.M. tomorrow! If you know how to use it, the computer can help. It processes data into information through three basic functions: (1) performing arithmetic operations on numeric data, (2) testing relationships between data items by logically comparing values, and (3) storing and retrieving data. These functions allow the computer to calculate numeric data, create documents, and manage data.

If you can perform these functions already, why use a computer? Computers can work faster, more accurately, and more reliably than people. Consider the formidable task the IRS faces each year processing millions of tax returns. It would be possible to process them manually; however, this would be extremely difficult, time consuming, and prone to human error. None of us would be too happy to wait years for a refund check or to have payment amounts miscalculated.

Advantages of Computers Over Humans

- Faster
- More accurate
- More reliable

Objective 1.8   Identify the components that make up a computer.

What Hardware Makes Up a Computer?

Computer hardware includes the system unit, input devices, output devices, and secondary storage devices (Figure 1.4). The **system unit**, or housing, contains the major components and controls of the computer. Hardware that is externally attached to the system unit is sometimes referred to as a **peripheral device**. An **input device** allows instructions and data to be entered into the computer for processing, e.g., keyboard and mouse. An **output device** receives information from the computer, e.g., monitor and printer. A **secondary storage device** provides permanent or relatively permanent storage of data and instructions. Instructions and data can be reentered without retyping them. Common secondary storage devices are hard disk drives and floppy disk drives.

Objective 1.9   Understand the purpose of software and describe the two main types.

FIGURE 1.4
The components of a computer are identified on this microcomputer.

What Is Software?

Computer hardware is no more than an extremely expensive paperweight or doorstop without a key to unlock the computer's enormous potential. The key is software. Software, or **computer programs**, are the instructions that cause the hardware to do the work. A computer program consists of numerous instructions, often tens of thousands. There are two main types of software: system software and application software.

System software directly controls and monitors the operation of the computer hardware. The computer is a general-purpose tool designed to perform a wide variety of tasks. **Application software** allows you to perform a specific task or set of tasks. Tasks include preparing documents, managing data, performing numeric calculations, creating graphic images, and transferring data between computers electronically. The types of application software that perform these tasks are word processors, database management systems, electronic spreadsheets, graphics programs, and communication programs. Application software also includes specialized tasks related to such fields as business, engineering, science, education, and entertainment. Business-oriented applications include accounting programs

FIGURE 1.5
The relationship among system
software, application software,
hardware, and the user.

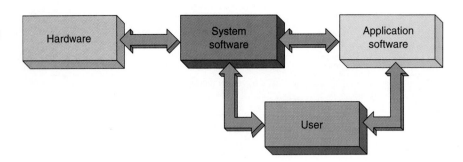

Types of Hardware and Examples

- **System unit**
    **Contains major
    components and
    controls**
- **Input devices**
    Keyboard
    Mouse
- **Output devices**
    Monitors
    Printers
- **Storage devices**
    Disk drives
    Tape drives

such as payroll, accounts receivable, accounts payable, general ledger, budgeting, and financial planning, which are used in almost every kind of business. Engineering and scientific applications include programs for computer-aided design (CAD), which automates mechanical drawings; chemical engineering; scientific calculations; and structural analysis. Educational applications include computer-assisted instruction (CAI) that guides a student through a course of study, typing tutors, and grade book programs to assist instructors in the process of recording student scores. Entertainment applications include games, flight simulators, and music programs. You interact with the application software by entering commands and data. The application software interacts with the system software requesting specific computer hardware resources. You can also interact directly with system software to control the computer hardware (Figure 1.5). You do not need to create computer programs for the computer to be useful. In fact, most people purchase the software they need rather than create it themselves.

Objective 1.10   Describe the steps involved in transforming data into information.

How Do Computers Transform Data into Information?

Information Processing Steps

- **Input**
- **Processing**
- **Output**
- **Storage**

Information processing, or more traditionally **data processing**, refers to all the steps associated with converting data into information. These steps include input, processing, output, and storage (Figure 1.6).

   Input refers to the data and instructions entered into a computer for processing and also describes the act of entering data and instructions. It is important that correct data be input because the information generated is based on the manipulation of that data. If the input is incorrect the output will also be incorrect, creating a situation referred to as **garbage in, garbage out (GIGO)**.

   Processing involves manipulating data into the desired form. Be sure that the programs you design or buy will process the data in the manner required.

   Output refers to the results of processing and also describes the act of generating results. Once the computer generates the information, it must be output so you can use it. Output can take numerous forms including informal drafts, formal reports, and graphics. One advantage in using a computer is that a single set of data entered can be manipulated in a variety of ways to produce many different outputs. For example, a company's corporate sales data could be manipulated to produce reports on sales of

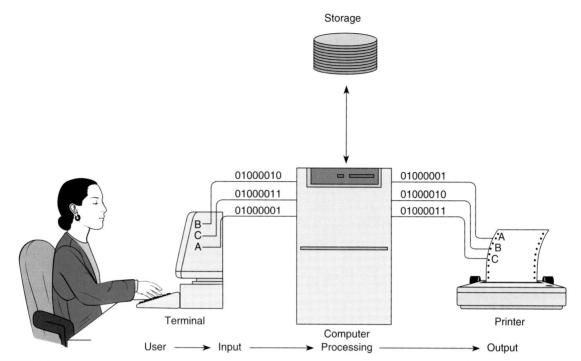

FIGURE 1.6
The basic flow of data through a computer system involves three steps: (1) input, (2) processing, and (3) output. A user enters data at an input device, and the computer converts the data to machine-readable form. In this example, the computer's instructions specify that the data should be alphabetized. After the computer completes that procedure, the output, in human-readable form, prints out on the output device. Data can be stored during this flow.

each product by region, total sales of each product, performance of each individual salesperson, and charts that graphically display these results.

Storage refers to the computer's ability to maintain data or information for use at a later time. A computer has two primary means of storage: internal storage called **main memory**, or **primary storage**, and external storage called **secondary storage**. The instructions in a computer program and the data they work on must be stored in main memory to be executed. Secondary storage preserves programs and data permanently or relatively permanently.

Let's see how this process works. Imagine you work for a newspaper and you've just received three thousand completed surveys on what readers want in a national health-care program. Your editor wants a breakdown of the data by age, income, and political affiliation. She wants the results displayed in both tabular and graphic forms for the paper's editorial page.

The first step is to carefully input the data from each survey into the computer. You could use a keyboard to enter the data into an application program called a database management system. This program easily manipulates data to meet your information needs. You enter each individual's age, income, political affiliation, and preferences into the computer.

Next comes processing of the data into the information you need. By selecting the appropriate data manipulation and graphics features of the program you can extract the information you require and arrange it in both tabular and graphic form.

Once you've generated the information and selected the presentation format, you output the results. They can be displayed on the computer's monitor, sent to a printer, or transferred electronically to another computer, or you could store the information for later use. For example, the editor may want to review and approve a printed copy. Later you could retrieve it for modification, if required, and then send it electronically to the computer that controls the typesetting process.

Objective 1.11   Identify four basic ways in which computers are used.

What Are the Basic Ways Computers Are Used?

Ways Computers Are Commonly Used

- General information processing
- Design and development
- Monitor and control
- Data communication

Typically, computers are used for general information-processing tasks where output is required in forms that can be read, understood, and used by people (end users), e.g., reports or graphs.

Design and development of products is another way the power of the computer can be used. Products are designed and tested on the computer before resources are spent on actual manufacturing. This saves time and money and is important for expensive products or products that are dangerous for people to test such as airplane designs or pharmaceuticals.

Computers can also be used to monitor and control other computers, equipment, or processes, e.g., your home environment (heating, cooling, lights, security), robots on assembly lines, or the flight of an airplane.

Another way in which computers are used is to send data electronically from one point to another—a process called **data communication**. A **computer network** links one computer to another, thus making it possible for data to be shared and updated at different locations (Figure 1.7).

Objective 1.12   Understand the limitations of computers.

What Are the Limitations of Computer Use?

Criteria for Classifying Computers

- Architecture
- Processing speed
- Amount of main memory
- Capacity of external storage devices
- Speed of output devices
- Number of users
- Cost

Computers are merely tools, useless without humans. A computer cannot identify a problem to be solved, decide the output needed to solve a problem, identify and collect the data needed to produce output, design the software necessary to transform data into a desired output, or interpret and use the accumulated information to solve a problem. These tasks must be completed by people like you. If a computer system is conceived and designed properly, then it becomes a valuable tool allowing you to accomplish your task faster, more accurately, and more reliably.

In some cases, it may seem that a computer is doing its work without the benefit of human involvement, for example, when a computer automatically generates software instructions or initiates a process. However, the software that automatically generates other instructions was conceived and designed by humans and the decision criteria that led to a particular process initiated by a computer were defined and programmed by humans. You play an important part in ensuring the successful use of a computer. In the end the information generated by a computer is only as good as the data that you decided to enter into it for processing, the quality of the software designed to process the data, and your ability to wisely use the information produced to make decisions and solve problems.

FIGURE 1.7
A travel agent uses a computer network to access information stored on a remote computer. She can quickly identify availability and the price that suits a client's needs when booking airline flights, hotel rooms, and car rentals. She can also immediately update the information on the remote computer so that once a reservation is made it is no longer available to other agents.

Objective 1.13 | Specify the criteria used to categorize computers and describe the major computer categories.

How Are Computers Categorized?

Categories of Computers

- **Microcomputers**
    - **Desktop**
    - **Portable**
        - **Laptop**
        - **Notebook**
        - **Palmtop**
        - **Pen-based**
- **Workstations**
- **Minicomputers**
- **Mainframes**
- **Supercomputers**

The criteria used to sort computers into classifications include architecture (design), processing speed, amount of main memory, capacity of external storage devices, speed of output devices, number of users, and cost.

The architecture of a computer refers to the design of the internal circuitry. It includes the number and type of the components that perform the actual computing tasks.

Processing speed is measured by the number of instructions that a computer can process per second, usually in millions of instructions per second (MIPS). Generally, the larger the classification, the faster a computer can process data.

Main memory includes the internal storage that a computer can access and use. Larger computers have more main memory than do smaller computers. Generally, the larger the classification of computer, the larger the number of secondary storage devices that a computer is capable of supporting.

The speed of an output device is how fast it can print or otherwise produce output. Usually, the larger the computer, the faster the output devices. Output from a small computer is typically measured in characters per second (cps); output from larger computers is usually measured in lines or pages per minute.

Typically, small computers are single-user computers that can be accessed by only one user at one time. Large computers can easily support hundreds of users at one time and are called multiuser systems.

The price of a computer is usually a reflection of the power of the system. Therefore, the larger the classification, the higher the price. The price of a computer also depends on the options purchased. Thus, a complete computer system classified in a lower category may actually cost more than one in a higher category. Small computers range from hundreds to thousands of dollars, and the largest computers cost millions of dollars.

According to these criteria, computers are grouped into five size classifications: (1) microcomputers, (2) workstations, (3) minicomputers, (4) mainframes, and (5) supercomputers. You should understand what is meant by each.

Distinctions in computing power are becoming blurred because of technological innovations that increase processing speed and store greater amounts of data in smaller areas. Therefore, many of the small newer machines have characteristics and capabilities of the large older ones of a few years ago. Figure 1.8 illustrates how the various computer systems overlap in computing power.

Microcomputers

The computer that you will likely come in contact with is the microcomputer. A **microcomputer** is a computer that is built around a single-chip processor called the microprocessor. These computers are relatively small in

FIGURE 1.8
Because technological advances have increased computing power and decreased prices, categorical distinctions among computer systems are becoming increasingly blurred.

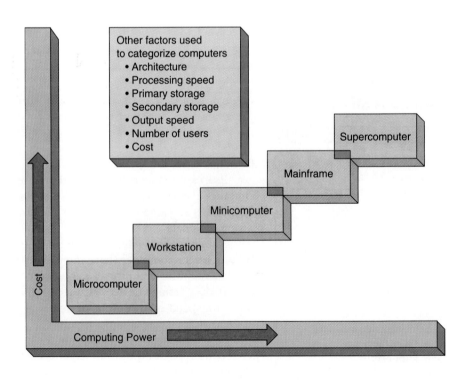

Other factors used to categorize computers
• Architecture
• Processing speed
• Primary storage
• Secondary storage
• Output speed
• Number of users
• Cost

Supercomputer

Mainframe

Minicomputer

Workstation

Microcomputer

Cost

Computing Power

size but some of today's models pack as much processing power and speed as larger systems of only a few years ago and at significantly lower cost. Microcomputers are designed to be used primarily by a single individual, which explains why they are called **personal computers** or PCs for short. However, most microcomputers can share resources if the appropriate software is used and hardware connections are made. Microcomputers are the least expensive computers, ranging from a few hundred dollars to several thousands of dollars. PCs are categorized as desktop or portable. A **desktop computer** can fit conveniently on a standard business desk (Figure 1.9). Portables are divided into laptop, notebook, palmtop, and pen-based computers. Weight, readability of the screen, layout and ease of use of the keyboard, and durability are some of the most important features to look for in a portable. The advent of truly portable microcomputers has allowed users to take computers where they are needed (Figure 1.10).

Portable computers also have evolved in the past few years. The first portables were called transportables, required AC power, and weighed around 30 pounds. Next came the **laptop computer**, which ran on both AC and batteries and weighed around 10 to 15 pounds (Figure 1.11). Further shrinking in size but increasing power and flexibility resulted in a **notebook computer** (Figure 1.12). About the size of an 8½ × 11 inch notebook, it is very popular and has both AC and battery power options. Notebook computers weigh around 6 to 8 pounds, have display screens from 7 to 10 inches, and keyboards that are smaller than those of desktop microcomputers. However, many challenge desktop models in power and speed. Some notebooks can be inserted into a docking station to take full advantage of the desktop's peripheral devices, including the full-sized

FIGURE 1.9
A typical desktop microcomputer.

(a)

(c)

(b)

FIGURE 1.10
Portable computers have allowed individuals to use computers in a wide variety
of circumstances: (a) in the library, (b) in the field at a construction site, and (c)
on the go.

keyboard and large monitor (Figure 1.13). The docking station uses the notebook's microprocessor and storage units and eliminates the need to transfer data from the notebook to a separate desktop computer in order to use the desktop's features. A **palmtop computer** weighs less than one pound and is as easy to carry around as your wallet or checkbook (Figure 1.14). It fits easily into your pocket and can provide you with quick access to the data wherever you need it. Palmtops can be connected to your PC to transfer and share information between them. Most operate for up to 60 hours on standard alkaline AA or AAA batteries, which can be easily replaced. Palmtop computers can be used with peripherals such as printers, fax/modems, and integrated circuit cards, which can supply additional

FIGURE 1.11
These two men in hardhats are using a laptop computer at a construction site.

memory and software applications. Drawbacks with palmtops include their small keyboard and display screen. A **pen-based computer** uses a penlike device to input data rather than a keyboard or a mouse (Figure 1.15). It is ideal for mobile workers and those who regularly fill out forms such as law enforcement personnel, insurance claim adjusters, delivery personnel, and doctors.

Workstations

A term you will often hear is "workstation." A **workstation** is a category of powerful stand-alone computer whose base price includes a 32-bit processor, very large main memory, considerable calculating and graphics capability, and all of the hardware and software needed to connect it to a network (see Chapters 7 and 8). Workstations can range in cost from $10,000 to $100,000. Typical users of workstations are engineers and architects. The

FIGURE 1.12
A notebook computer fits easily into a standard briefcase for convenient transport to where you need it.

FIGURE 1.13
A docking station allows notebook computer users to take full advantage of desktop microcomputer features without transferring data between computers.

FIGURE 1.14
A palmtop computer is about the size of a checkbook and can be carried just as easily.

workstation can provide the power needed for sophisticated design programs without the expense of larger computers.

Minicomputers

Minicomputers are the next step up in processing power, speed, and cost (Figure 1.16). Minis are designed to accept input from and produce output to a large number of users, supporting from 10 to 100 terminals. Typically the minicomputers perform complex computations such as those involved in the use of computer-aided design (CAD) programs that create engineering and architectural drawings, transaction-processing applications such as order-entry systems, and as interfaces between mainframe computers linked into a computer network. The top of the line minicomputers are designated superminis. Minicomputers range in price from tens of thousands of dollars to several hundred thousand dollars.

Mainframes

Mainframes provide an increase in processing power, speed, and cost over minicomputers (Figure 1.17). They typically handle greater volumes of input, output, and storage activities and can support hundreds of users. The mainframe is for more intensive computational tasks than minicomputers and is associated with the manipulation of large volumes of data by businesses and the government. Because mainframe computers are sensitive to temperature and humidity changes and dust they are usually found in environmentally controlled computer rooms. Mainframes are priced from several hundred thousand dollars to several million dollars.

FIGURE 1.15
An insurance claims adjuster uses a pen-based computer to complete a claim form electronically. The information can later be transferred to a computer in the main office and the claim processed.

FIGURE 1.16
Minicomputers generally have less power than do mainframes. They are used in many small and medium-sized organizations.

FIGURE 1.17
An IBM ES/9000 mainframe is shown here. Mainframes are most often used for business processing in medium-sized to large organizations.

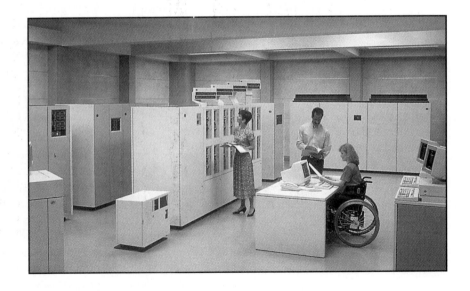

(a)

(b)

FIGURE 1.18
(a) The Cray YMP supercomputer. (b) Terminals and other hardware needed to support the Cray YMP.

FIGURE 1.19
A Cray supercomputer produced this three-dimensional schematic simulation of a thunderstorm. The position of the arrows indicates that the low-level rotation is intensifying. This type of simulation helps meteorologists to predict the paths and intensities of severe storms.

Supercomputers

Supercomputers are the most powerful, fastest, and most expensive computers, supporting hundreds of users (Figure 1.18). A supercomputer is used for complex or sophisticated applications such as weather forecasting (Figure 1.19), genetic decoding, aerodynamics, and processing of geological data. Supercomputers can process up to several billions of instructions per second (bips), but they require environmentally controlled computer rooms and can cost millions of dollars.

Summary

Data are raw facts that convey little meaning by themselves. Information is processed data that is seen in context and conveys meaning to people. Information can be of two general types: Quantitative information tells how much or how many and can be presented in two forms, as numerical or graphical information. Qualitative information describes something in non-quantitative terms. A transaction is a business activity or event. The attributes of information include accuracy, relevance, completeness, timeliness, cost-effectiveness, auditability, and reliability. The two basic sources of information are internal, those gathered within an organization, and external, those gathered outside the organization. Information received from any source should not contain bias and should be valid, reliable, consistent, and timely.

The value of information (its meaningfulness and usefulness) is determined by how much additional knowledge the information adds to what was already known. The costs and benefits of obtaining information are also important in determining its value. Computer ethics refers to a standard of behavior that conforms to societal and professional standards for the use of computers and the information they generate. The information can then be put to use in decision making by itself or in combination with your knowledge and instincts, depending on the type of decision to be made.

A computer is an electronic device that can accept input, process it in a prescribed way, present the results as output, and store the results for use in later processing.

A system is any set of components that work together to perform a task. An information system is a set of hardware, software, people, data, and procedures that work together to manage the acquisition, storage, manipulation, and distribution of information. The physical equipment that makes up a computer is called hardware. Software is the instructions that cause the hardware to do the work that you desire. A person who uses computers and software to perform tasks is called an end user or user. Data provide the basis for the information generated by an information system. Each information system has a set of procedures, which are the instructions that tell you how to operate and use it.

A multiuser information system is designed to be used by many users. A personal information system is designed to be used by an individual user.

Information systems are designed to perform three basic functions: (1) to accept data (input), (2) to convert data to information (process), and (3) to produce and communicate information in a timely fashion to users for decision making (output).

The shift to a society that emphasizes the possession and dissemination of information has brought about an increasing use and reliance on computers and information systems in many professions. To compete in the marketplace you should possess a basic level of knowledge and understanding of computers and have the ability to effectively use them and the information they generate.

The purpose of a computer is to transform data into information. Computers perform three basic functions. They can perform arithmetic functions on numeric data, they can test relationships between data items by logically comparing values, and they can store and retrieve data. The advantage of using computers for these functions is that they can perform them faster, more accurately, and with more reliability than humans.

Computer hardware includes the system unit, input devices, output devices, and secondary storage devices. Peripheral devices are hardware that are externally attached to the system unit.

Software, or computer programs, are the instructions that cause the hardware to do the work that you desire. There are two main types of software: system software and application software.

Data are transformed into information through a series of steps referred to as information processing, or data processing. These steps include input, processing, output, and storage.

Computers are used in several basic ways. They are used for general information processing tasks, to design, develop, and test products, to monitor and control other computers, equipment, and processes, and to send data from point to point electronically.

Computers cannot operate alone. They require humans to identify a problem, decide how to solve it, identify and collect the data to solve it, design the software to solve it, and interpret the information that is obtained.

Computers are classified by architecture, processing speed, main memory, external storage capacity, speed of output devices, number of users that can access a system at one time, and cost. Small computers are classified as microcomputers and workstations. Large computers are categorized as supercomputers, mainframe computers, and minicomputers.

Microcomputers are often called personal computers since they are primarily designed to be used by a single individual. Microcomputers are divided into desktop computers and portable computers. Portables are divided into laptop, notebook, palmtop, and pen-based computers. Some notebook computers can be inserted into a docking station to take advantage of the full range of desktop computer features.

Minicomputers are more powerful than microcomputers. The next step in power is the mainframe computer, followed by the most powerful computer, the supercomputer.

Computers and information systems have affected most people's personal and professional lives. They have provided better customer service and greater convenience. On the other hand, the increased ability they provide to acquire, store, manipulate, and distribute information can lead to the potential misuse of that information.

VOCABULARY SELF-TEST

Can you define the following terms?

application software (p. 21)
computer (p. 17)
computer ethics (p. 16)
computer literacy (p. 19)
computer network (p. 23)
computer programs (p. 21)
data (p. 12)
data communication (p. 23)
data processing (p. 22)
desktop computer (p. 27)
end user (p. 17)
garbage in, garbage out (GIGO) (p. 22)
hardware (p. 17)
information (p. 12)
information literacy (p. 19)
information processing (p. 22)
information system (p. 17)
input (p. 22)
input device (p. 20)
laptop computer (p. 27)
mainframes (p. 31)
main memory (p. 23)
microcomputer (p. 26)
minicomputers (p. 31)

multiuser information systems (p. 18)
notebook computer (p. 27)
output (p. 22)
output device (p. 20)
palmtop computer (p. 28)
pen-based computer (p. 29)
peripheral devices (p. 20)
personal computers (PCs) (p. 27)
personal information systems (p. 18)
primary storage (p. 23)
procedures (p. 17)
processing (p. 22)
secondary storage (p. 23)
secondary storage device (p. 20)
software (p. 17)
storage (p. 23)
supercomputers (p. 23)
system software (p. 21)
system unit (p. 20)
transaction (p. 12)
user (p. 17)
value of information (p. 15)
workstation (p. 29)

REVIEW QUESTIONS

Multiple Choice

1. Which of the following is true about data?
   a. convey little or no meaning to people
   b. are seen in context and convey meaning to people

     c. are the primary product of processing

     d. are not necessary for processing

2. Which of the following is not a function of an information system?

     a. accepts input

     b. produces output

     c. communicates output in a timely fashion

     d. makes decisions for users

3. Computer literacy means _____.

     a. being knowledgeable in advanced mathematics and electronics

     b. having a complete understanding of how computers work internally

     c. being able to use the most advanced and complex features of a computer

     d. having a general knowledge and understanding of computers

4. Which of the following is not an advantage of computers over humans?

     a. faster

     b. more reliable

     c. more accurate

     d. smarter

5. Which of the following is not a function of a computer?

     a. stores and retrieves data

     b. interprets output

     c. tests relationships logically

     d. performs arithmetic operations

6. A(n) _____ allows information to be retrieved from the computer.

     a. output device

     b. input device

     c. storage device

     d. system unit

7. _____ refers to computer programs that help users perform specific tasks.

     a. System software

     b. User software

     c. Application software

     d. Hardware

8. _____ involves the manipulation of data to produce information.

     a. Storage

     b. Processing

     c. Input

     d. Output

9. Which of the following is false?

     a. computers process data into information

     b. computers are more accurate than people

     c. computers can interpret and use information to solve a problem

     d. computers are faster than people

10. Which of the following is the fastest and most powerful category of computers?

a. personal computer
b. minicomputer
c. mainframe computer
d. supercomputer

Fill-In

1. _____ are raw facts that convey little meaning by themselves.
2. Data that have been processed into a form that can be seen in context and convey meaning to people are called _____.
3. A(n) _____ is an electronic device that can accept input, process it in a prescribed way, present the results as output, and store the results for use in later processing.
4. A(n) _____ is a set of hardware, software, people, data, and procedures that work together to manage the acquisition, storage, manipulation, and distribution of information.
5. _____ refers to being able to judge the value of information and use the generated information wisely.
6. _____ is the components, or physical equipment, that make up a computer.
7. The instructions that cause the hardware to do work are called _____.
8. _____ refers to the input, processing, output, and storage stages involved in converting data into information.
9. _____ refers to the data entered into a computer for processing.
10. A(n) _____ is a computer small enough and light enough to carry around with you.

Short Answer

1. Differentiate between data and information and give several examples of each.
2. In order to use computers effectively it is necessary to have detailed knowledge of electronics and mathematics. Defend or refute this statement.
3. Describe the three basic tasks that a computer can perform.
4. Describe the advantages that computers have over humans in processing data into information.
5. Describe the components that make up a computer.
6. Describe the steps involved in transforming data into information and give an example.
7. Describe what is meant by the value of information and define computer ethics.
8. Describe four ways in which computers are commonly used.
9. Discuss some of the limitations of computer use.
10. Discuss several ways in which computers and information systems have affected either your personal, educational, or professional life.

Issues for Thought

1. Some airplanes are controlled by computers that do not let the pilot override the computer's control. Do you think this is a good idea? Why or why not?

2. When you make a transaction, many companies use computers and information systems to gather data about you such as your name, address, telephone number, buying habits, and credit history. They then sell this information to other companies without your permission and without giving you the chance to verify the information. What potential problems can you see in this? Explain your answer.

Infomodule

Computer Ethics, Crime, and Privacy

WHAT IS COMPUTER ETHICS?

Webster's New World Dictionary defines "ethics" as "the study of standards of conduct and moral judgment; the system of morals of a particular person, religion, group, etc." **Computer ethics,** then, refers to a set of rules that govern the standards or conduct of computer users; and to principles used with computers and the information they produce. The terms "property" and "stealing" are difficult to define as they relate to hardware, information, access, and privacy. Although there may be disagreement on what is right and what is wrong in given instances, there are areas of agreement. Those common areas serve as a beginning, and controversies can be handled on a case-by-case basis. Additionally, standards and codes of computer ethics must change and adapt as new dimensions are added; e.g., virtual reality, a different concept of computer use, has brought a whole series of problems along with its applications.

WHAT DOES PROFESSIONAL ETHICS EMBODY?

The concept of ethical standards is not new. For thousands of years people have recognized the need for regulations or codes of ethics. In Babylon from 1792 to 1750 B.C. one of the greatest kings developed the famous Code of Hamurabi, the credo of which was that "the strong shall not injure the weak." Probably one of the most recognizable standards is the Hippocratic Oath, the code of ethics to which physicians subscribe. Its foundation dates back to 2000 B.C. Most professional organizations acknowledge the need for principles; a code of ethics offers a framework for accountability. In 1992 the Association for Computing Machinery (ACM) adopted a revised

Code of Ethics, as have other professional organizations. The ACM Code asks members to abide by the following eight principles:

> Make a contribution to society.
>
> Avoid injury to others; consider long-range impacts.
>
> Be honest.
>
> Be tolerant of others.
>
> Do not condone copyright or patent infringement.
>
> Respect intellectual property.
>
> Maintain privacy.
>
> Revere confidentiality.

You will notice that computers are not actually mentioned. In fact, this general code could be adapted for other professions. However, a study described in the *Computer Professionals for Social Responsibility Newsletter* indicates that fewer than half of the businesses surveyed had a written code of ethics.

WHAT DOES INDIVIDUAL ETHICS EMBODY?

Ethical behavior on the part of an individual is basically the choice of the individual. Although there are laws that govern us all, some people will inevitably seek to circumvent those laws. Unfortunately it is the same with computer use standards. It is up to each of us to behave ethically and to persuade other users to behave in ethical ways. Some ethical behaviors for individuals include:

> Refusing to borrow or share illegally obtained programs.

Protecting your password and not using another person's password.

Encouraging others to behave ethically.

WHAT DOES GOVERNMENT ETHICS EMBODY?

Although there is no specific code of ethics for all government entities, the U.S. Constitution does set certain standards. For example, the First Amendment of the Constitution grants us freedom of association, of speech, and of the press. And the Fourth Amendment guarantees that "the right of the people to be secure in their persons, houses, papers, and effects, against unreasonable searches and seizures, shall not be violated and no warrants shall issue but upon probable cause . . . ." Of course, wiretapping and eavesdropping are limited by state and federal statutes, but what's to prevent another individual from doing it? It's an individual's personal code of ethics that dominates in those situations.

In 1991 the Computer Crime Unit (CCU) was organized by the Department of Justice. It is charged with prosecuting computer criminals and supports stiffer punishments and expanding the area covered by federal computer crime statutes. In 1993 a proposal that network services expose their equipment to wiretaps by the FBI was introduced. The proposal wants the FBI to be given the power to tap into data or voice transmissions without having to deal with an encryption device; to be able to tap into the transmission at the time it is happening; and to achieve the tap from another location. Most users, however, want to keep their networks secure.

WHAT IS NETWORK ETHICS?

In 1986 the Federal Electronic Communications Privacy Act offered protection for a person's electronic mail sent over public networks, but the act does not apply to a person's electronic mail if it is sent via corporate networks. Electronic eavesdropping, however, is not prevented. Two of the largest on-line services, Prodigy (an IBM and Sears joint venture) and CompuServe (an H&R Block subsidiary), have different philosophies about their services. CompuServe lets users publish their own subject matter without approval from them. Prodigy, on the other hand, stirred up great controversy in its attempt to control the contents of its on-line bulletin boards, giving rise to many questions about censorship.

Censorship vs. Free Speech

In 1993 a USENET user implemented a program that prevented what he considered irrelevant or abusive messages from being posted on a public network. Preventing someone from posting notices is unacceptable, but should networks post everything? The ethical dilemma that this creates is similar to debates about sexually explicit material in art, movies, and magazines. There is no pat answer, but networks may choose to limit their liability by warning users that on-line material may be inappropriate for children.

WHAT IMPACT DOES ETHICS HAVE ON INFORMATION USE?

Personal information about each of us is readily available through the technology of computers. It is not difficult for that information to find its way into unauthorized hands. There is a definite need for ethical conduct as it relates to personal information in computer files. The Freedom of Information Act of 1970 allows individuals to secure the records that federal agencies have collected about them. See Table 1 for a synopsis of legislation dealing with information and computer privacy matters.

Misuse of Information

Is it a misuse of information when your name and buying habits find their way into a database available to other merchants? Merely buying something from a mail order catalog can cause that information to appear in a database that is sold to others. For example, if you buy a set of gourmet cooking utensils from an all-purpose catalog, that company can put your name on a list to be sold to other chef supply dealers. The chef supply catalog will soon be in your mailbox and after you order a recipe book from them your name will be on yet another mailing list,

TABLE 1
Computer and Privacy
Legislation

Freedom of Information Act of 1970
Permits individuals to get copies of the data that federal agencies have gathered.

Fair Credit Reporting Act of 1970
Gives the right to people to review their credit records.

Crime Control Act of 1973
Ensures the security and privacy of data in state criminal records that were produced using federal funds.

Privacy Act of 1974
Prevents abuse of a person's privacy; prohibits data collected for one reason to be used for another without prior consent; grants right to see the government information collected; provides copies of that information; allows correction of wrong data; requires the information be current and correct; and keeps them from misuse, to name a few.

Tax Reform Act of 1976
Limits IRS access to personal data and restricts sharing of that data with other federal agencies.

Copyright Act of 1976
Prohibits books and other written works, including computer programs, from being illegally copied.

Privacy Protection Act of 1980
Prevents unwarranted searches of offices and files by government agents.

Debt Collection Act of 1982
Specifies prerequisites for releasing bad debt information.

Cable Communications Policy Act of 1984
Provides that subscribers are advised if personal information is being accumulated or broadcast.

Semiconductor Chip Protection Act of 1984
Gives the chip developer an exclusive 10-year period for rights and prevents others from reproducing chip patterns.

Electronic Communications Privacy Act of 1986
Makes interception of computer communications illegal.

Computer Fraud and Abuse Act of 1986
Grants jurisdiction to the federal government in matters of computer crimes. Pertains to federal government and federally insured financial institution computers.

to be sold perhaps to a bookstore. In the meantime, a profile of your buying habits is being accumulated and added to with each purchase. Many people feel this is an invasion of their privacy.

Liability for Incorrect Information

Some computer errors are comical. For example, if you received a computer-generated letter announcing that you, "Ms. Philadelphia, PA" are a million-dollar sweepstakes winner, you would quickly realize that your city and state were inserted where your name should have been. Other errors, however, can be devastating if lives are lost through faulty data. What if a patient's medical records are confused with another's because of a data entry error? Who is liable for such incorrect information? The question is ambiguous at best, since placing blame is usually quite an involved process, and generally disputes are settled in court. Two methods that software providers are using to protect themselves are verifying and testing their data to make sure their product or service is reputable, and entering into contracts in advance with disclaimers that limit their liability.

Software Workability

What happens and who pays when software doesn't do what it's supposed to? Sellers expect the consumers to beware. Consumers, on the other hand, expect the sellers to deliver a software package that works. Software usually carries no guarantee by the seller. In fact, when there are accidents or losses, blame can be placed on the hardware, software, database, or the user. Any combination of them could be at fault. Regulations and laws concerning software workability are not yet well defined. This brings us to a series of ethical issues.

WHY ARE ETHICAL ISSUES DIFFICULT TO RESOLVE?

There are no hard and fast rules and methods that apply in *all* instances. As new technology appears, values also are still emerging. In "virtual reality," where the computer simulates imagery and the user enters into the picture, a whole new series of problems is created along with its applications. Physicians envision using virtual reality to develop a body suit that could enable quadriplegic patients to experience movement that is unavailable to them in their real world. What if the patients chose to spend time in the computer-generated world instead of living with the challenges of daily life? This is only one aspect of technology that professionals must anticipate may have negative effects on its users. A myriad of problems needs to be taken into consideration in preparing that code of ethics.

You can see from the list below that computer users are wrestling with issues such as:

Is it a threat to employees' privacy to use a computer to monitor their work?

Is the employer obligated to compensate an employee displaced by a computer?

Should all data that is input be considered confidential by the individual at the keyboard?

Is it ethical to read someone's electronic mail? View their files? Share their password? Use their employer's computer for personal tasks?

Is it ethical for a student to use the facilities in the campus computer lab to play games while other students wait for a computer to complete assignments or do research?

Is it ethical for someone to censor messages on computer bulletin boards? Post pornographic messages?

The issues are not easily resolved. You will no doubt think of many other issues that should be considered by companies and individuals in formulating codes of ethics.

HOW DOES COMPUTER CRIME AFFECT SOCIETY?

A **computer crime** may be described as one in which computers and software are used with illegal intentions. Computers allow crimes like embezzlement, theft, sabotage, and vandalism to be carried out faster and with a lower chance of discovery. Computer crimes are costly—just how costly is the question, but even conservative estimates start in the billions of dollars.

Piracy and Copyright Infringement

Software piracy is the unauthorized duplication of copyrighted computer programs. **Copyright infringement** occurs when the appropriate royalty payment is not made for use of the protected work. Software developers incur the often costly expenses of research and development to produce their programs; thus, each time a "pirated" (i.e., no fee is paid and no royalty is collected by the owner of the work) version is shared, but not paid for, they lose the profit. Federal copyright laws cover most computer software, prohibiting unauthorized distribution. Some experts estimate that piracy costs range from $20 billion to $60 billion each year. This is obviously a serious concern for software developers. Some of the methods that developers use to deter piracy are:

■ Licensing, or allowing manufacturers to produce the programs upon payment of appropriate royalties to the developer.
■ Sealing the packages and stating on the outside of the package that only the buyer may use the software.
■ "Locking" the programs to keep the buyer from making unauthorized copies.
■ Providing the instructions about using the programs in extensive documentation. Anyone who copies the program will also have to copy the explanations. This can be a real deterrent when the documentation is hundreds of pages in length.
■ Educating users. Software Publishers Association in Washington, D.C. has an interesting approach. It produced a rap video called "Don't Copy That Floppy," aimed at educating preteens about the illegality of copying software. Articles alerting young people about computer crimes are even found in magazines such as *Boys' Life*.

Pirating software, a felony, can bring up to five years in prison and as much as $250,000 in fines.

Types of Computer Crime

Computers can be used to commit crimes, such as theft or fraud; but they can also be the object of a crime (someone may want to steal the hardware),

and can be used in the commission of crimes intrinsic to computers, i.e., spreading viruses, worms, bombs, Trojan horses, manipulating data, and stealing data. Employees are being taught how to spot the fraud and forgeries that computer criminals try to pass. Undercover officers have conducted sting operations in which as many as 30 people were arrested for stealing computer chips that were then sold at three times their value.

Virus, Worms, Bombs, and Trojan Horses. A computer **virus** is a program that can get into a computer to destroy or alter data and spread itself to other computers. It can be spread through sharing software, downloading files from a bulletin board, or logging on to a computer network. John von Neumann (see Chapter 5 Profile) proposed a theory that programs could be made to multiply automatically, not a problem in itself. But during the 1970s, when criminal users created programs that were destructive and could multiply quickly, the concept became a real threat. During the 1980s viruses "caught on" and became even worse. They are often set to attack at a specific time or date, e.g., the Michelangelo virus that wreaks havoc when the computer system is turned on on March 6th, the birthday of the famous artist. Now there are hundreds of viruses worldwide.

A computer **worm** is a surreptitious program that issues false or misleading commands. It occupies computer memory and spreads quickly, as does a virus—they both stop normal computer operation. Because they are designed not to be readily apparent it is hard to detect viruses and worms until they have done their damage. In 1988 a graduate student introduced a worm into Internet, the network used by universities and government agencies.

A **time bomb** is created when a program is put into a computer that is set to destroy itself either at a certain time or after a specified number of times the program is run. Time bombs have been used by employees who feel they have an ax to grind with their employer. However, the concept has also been used by developers to prevent nonpayment for services. After the bill for software development has been paid, the developer tells the purchaser how the bomb can be defused. If payment is not received, the program destroys itself. The program labeled a **Trojan horse** disguises itself as a legitimate program, but once it is installed the rogue program does its damage—garbling data, destroying indexes, or erasing all the data in the computer. Even mail bombs can be "delivered" via electronic mail services.

Data Manipulation and Data Stealing. **Data manipulation** (sometimes called "data diddling") occurs when a user alters data in the computer. This kind of manipulation ranges from changing a grade, to accessing and changing medical records or credit records. When a user steals information that has been gathered for a legitimate purpose, it is called **data stealing**. For example, if an address list that had been legally obtained was then sold to someone else for another use, it would be considered data stealing.

There are many reasons for the proliferation of computer crimes. Some of them are:

> There are more computers in use.
>
> More people are familiar with computers and what they can do.
>
> More computers are linked together and communicating with each other.
>
> More databases can be accessed by microcomputer users.

Computers are used in the apprehension of criminals, too. Automated fingerprint identification systems are set up around the country. Fingerprint records that have been obtained by pressing the inked finger onto a card can be scanned by computers. The information about the patterns and distinguishing features is stored in computer files where they can be retrieved and matched to prints found at the scene of a crime. This system was instrumental in convicting the infamous "Night Stalker" in California. So beware, if you commit crimes using a computer, you might be convicted by the computer as well.

The Criminal

Most of the computer crime headlines are given over to the knowledgeable computer user who enjoys the challenge of breaking into large computer systems, usually for the fun of it, without criminal intent; but this is still considered a crime. The greatest number of computer crimes however, are committed by insiders—employees of a company. It's very hard to guard against them.

Detection

Because computer crime is often committed by an employee in the employer's place of business, detection is often difficult. The crime may be so complex that it is not discovered for months or years, adding to the problem. Even after the crime is disclosed, finding the perpetrator may be next to impossible. The savvy criminal does not leave fingerprints or a paper trail. Investigators may not have the expertise or money to pursue the criminals. Although there may be plenty of co-workers around, no one can be sure just who is doing legitimate work and who may be committing a crime. The statistics on computer crime are inexact since many victims never report a violation of their computer system. It could be perceived as a sign of weakness to a bank, credit company, or investment company's customers. Often company managers and law enforcement personnel have little expertise in dealing with computer criminals. Many police divisions in larger cities find that having a computer crime unit is helpful. As more law schools offer specializations in computer law, the criminal will be up against his/her peers. But juries may still have difficulty handling the complexities and terminology of computer crime.

Prevention

Many techniques can be used in prevention and protection against computer crimes. The most important first step is to be sure that you have backup copies of all your data. Another important safeguard is to write-protect the disk that contains the software programs; this prevents anyone from adding other data to that disk. Do not copy software from a questionable origin. Don't let other people use your program disks or your computer. Remember that bulletin boards can contain contaminated software. Many antivirus software programs are available to specifically combat viruses. The three services that this software renders are prevention, diagnosis, and recovery. By running monitoring routines these programs can prevent a virus from taking effect. But if you already have a virus, the program can recognize the identifying codes and then help eliminate the virus by erasing the infected files. Unfortunately, piracy and infringement cannot be cured by antivirus software.

Disaster Recovery

Even with the best prevention strategies in place, the unthinkable can occur. What if something happens to your computers or your data? There are experts called **disaster recovery teams** whose job it is to help recover data that may have been destroyed by fire, flood, or virus attack. Large businesses that are particularly dependent on their computer system are at risk, but even small businesses can suffer when their normal functions are interrupted. The experts suggest the following:

- Institute a backup power supply in case of power failure.
- Create backup copies of programs and data and store them at another location.
- Share resources with a similar business.
- Accumulate backup spare parts for your computers to minimize "down" time.

Legislation

It would seem that with the laws found in Table 1 and the constitutional protections afforded us, there would be plenty of legislation to guard our rights. Some constitutional scholars feel that the document as it is written covers all possible areas of computer applications; others, however, argue that a new amendment should be added granting rights and privileges regardless of the technology involved. Legislators are faced with decisions about what actions constitute computer crimes. Our laws may be inadequate to deal with the burgeoning problems; therefore, lawmakers need to become more knowledgeable about computers and their operation to continue to assure freedoms for all.

HOW CAN PRIVACY ISSUES AFFECT YOU?

The U.S. government is the largest user of computers and one of the largest funders of computer research. The federal government holds more than 4 billion personal files on its citizens. The IRS alone processes over 100 million tax returns a year. Even though federal agencies are prohibited by legislation from using their information for other than its intended purpose, they employ a system known as "matching" whereby they can compare data on a particular individual. Welfare rolls can be compared with Social Security records and income tax records, too. The giant database that uses this matching process robs the citizen of any privacy.

A hot topic under discussion is the privacy that someone can expect from E-mail, that is, electronic mail delivered to a computer "mailbox." Can an individual expect that messages delivered in this way are protected from prying eyes as are the letters received in sealed envelopes? The Federal Electronic Communications Privacy Act does not protect mail sent over private networks. Unless the company has a written policy, the recipient should expect that the employer is accessing those messages, even if just to monitor and maintain its network. Perhaps if everyone acted in an ethical manner, there would be fewer instances of computer crimes and invasions of privacy.

VOCABULARY SELF-TEST

Can you define the following terms?

computer crime (p. 43)

computer ethics (p. 40)

copyright infringement (p. 44)

data manipulation (p.45)

data stealing (p. 45)

disaster recovery team (p. 46)

software piracy (p. 44)

time bomb (p. 44)

Trojan horse (p. 45)

virus (p. 44)

worm (p. 44)

REVIEW QUESTIONS

Multiple Choice

1. Codes of ethics have been traced to _____.
   a. 2000 B.C.
   b. 200 B.C.
   c. 200 A.D.
   d. the Magna Carta
2. _____ occurs when someone copies a software program illegally.
   a. Program infringement
   b. Software piracy
   c. Data manipulation
   d. Data stealing
3. A computer program that is made to destroy other programs is known as a _____.
   a. computer infection
   b. worm
   c. data manipulation
   d. virus
4. Most computer crimes are committed by _____.
   a. computer professionals
   b. teenagers
   c. employees
   d. persons with a previous criminal record
5. Antivirus software cannot protect your computer from _____ and _____.
   a. copyright infringement and piracy
   b. time bombs and worms
   c. Trojan horses and viruses
   d. worms and viruses

Fill-In

1. If your computer or data suffer damage in a flood or fire, you would contact a(n) _____.
2. The _____ is the legislation enacted that allows an individual to have access to his/her file accumulated by the federal government.
3. When someone changes data in an existing file, it is called _____.
4. _____ is a process used by federal agencies to compare data on individuals.
5. The program that disguises itself as a legitimate program is known as a(n) _____.

Short Answer

1. Illustrate how someone's personal privacy could be invaded by computers.
2. Give several reasons why a company would *not* report a computer crime.
3. Should networks be subject to limits on pornography?
4. Recount ways that a computer could be involved in a crime.
5. Describe three ways that developers can protect themselves from piracy.

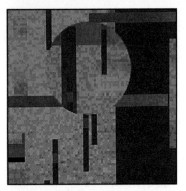

OUTLINE

OBJECTIVES

2.1 Understand why it is important to learn about computer terminology.

2.2 Explain how data are represented in a computer.

2.3 Comprehend the functions of the central processing unit.

2.4 Explain what makes up a microprocessor.

2.5 Describe the internal storage of a computer.

2.6 Contrast the roles of RAM and ROM.

2.7 Define memory in terms of conventional, extended, and expanded.

2.8 Differentiate the types of buses and their role in compatibility.

2.9 Describe the instruction cycle.

2.10 Identify items that affect processing power and speed.

2.11 Describe factors to consider when deciding which CPU you want in a personal computer.

Chapter 2

The Processing Unit

M. E. (Ted) Hoff

It's hard to imagine the world today if it weren't for people with vision like Ted Hoff. Even he probably didn't realize what would become of the work he started on that fateful day in 1969.

After working at Stanford University as a research assistant, Ted Hoff joined Intel Corporation in 1969. At Intel, Hoff led a team that helped a Japanese firm, Busicom, design a custom circuit for its calculator. The Busicom design called for 12 integrated circuit chips, each with 3,000–5,000 transistors. The chips that made up the processor were matched to the specific tasks of the calculator. After reviewing the design, however, Hoff decided it was too complex and would be too expensive to produce. Consequently, he used a totally different approach. He decided to design the calculator around a general-purpose processor, relying more on software than on electronics. Although more memory space was needed to store the software, this approach enabled Hoff to put the entire processor on a single integrated-circuit chip, called a microprocessor.

What a chip it was! The Intel 4004 could handle four bits of information at a time, and its computational powers came close to those of the ENIAC, one of the early electronic digital computers that required an entire room to house it. This single microprocessor performed as well as some of the early (1960s) IBM machines that cost around $30,000 and had processing units the size of a large desk. Hoff's microprocessor was about one-sixth by one-eighth inch and cost about $200. The reductions in size and cost made it possible to design small, relatively inexpensive computers. This discovery heralded the beginning of the microcomputer revolution. Thanks to Ted Hoff's creativeness, microprocessors are everywhere—in our computers, homes, cars, factories, and yes, still in our calculators.

"Sue just upgraded her office with 33 megahertz, 486 machines."

"Yeah, with all the new larger, more powerful software we run, she made sure they came with 8 megabytes of RAM."

"With the built-in coprocessor and the cache memory we can be more productive."

If you overheard the above conversation, would you understand what they were talking about? Or would you ask, "Why would I need to know that technical stuff?"

In the conversation above, people were describing what goes on in the computer. All of those parameters concern internal operations, but they are essential for selecting the right computer for the right application. The terms refer to how much and how fast a computer can process data. In this chapter you will find an overview of those concepts, descriptions of the central processing unit, and learn how data are represented in the computer. You will enhance your general knowledge of computers and learn how to apply that knowledge.

Objective 2.1   Understand why it is important to learn about computer terminology.

Why Do You Need to Know About What's Inside a Computer?

Specialized terminology is associated with any new subject (Figure 2.1). The value of understanding these terms can be seen in everyday applications. For example:

■ You load your software and try to run an application but . . . OUT OF MEMORY. You have only 640 *kilobytes* of RAM and the software requires at least 1 *megabyte* of RAM.

FIGURE 2.1
Learning the language is a part of computer education.

- As manager you need to select and purchase the computers used in your department. Do you rely entirely on the salesperson, or can you interpret the information in the computer ad yourself?
- You bought the latest release of the drafting software Autocad. You try to install and run it on your computer, but it doesn't work. By reading the instruction manual, you find that it requires a *coprocessor.*

You can solve the above problems, if you understand the technical terminology. Your career path and the ways in which it will incorporate computers are unknown, so it is important to prepare for those future challenges. Understanding the terminology associated with computers is one part of that preparation. First, let's talk a bit about the byte.

Objective 2.2   Explain how data are represented in a computer.

How Does the Computer Understand What You Input?

One way humans communicate is by depicting ideas through characters. This representation can be in the form of alphabetic (letters), numeric (digits), and other special characters, collectively called alphanumerics.

But, because computers are made of electronic circuits, they can only recognize two distinct electrical states—ON or OFF. The on and off states are commonly represented with the numbers 1 and 0, respectively. The **binary system** is the number system using only 1s and 0s. Various combinations of 1s and 0s can be entered and stored in a computer to represent all of the numbers, letters, and symbols. Although you see numbers, letters, and symbols assembled to form English words and phrases, the computer "sees" things differently. For example, the uppercase letter *D* is represented by the binary sequence 1000100.

Because the language of the computer, machine language, is based on the binary system, data and instructions must be interpreted into binary code before they can be used by the computer. There are computer programs that take care of this conversion.

Bits and Bytes

Each individual 1 or 0 is called a bit, a *b*inary dig*it*. A **bit** is the smallest piece of data that a computer can process. To represent an alphanumeric character requires multiple bits. A grouping of eight bits is a **byte**. The byte is the basic unit for measuring the size of memory. However, with today's memory sizes, it is more common to hear the term *kilobyte* (K or KB), *megabyte* (MB), or *gigabyte* (GB) (Figure 2.2).

There is some confusion over the prefixes *kilo-* and *mega-*. In strict scientific notation, *kilo-* means 1,000 and *mega-* means 1,000,000. However, in the language of computers, *kilo-* actually is 1,024 and *mega-* is 1,048,576. The disparity occurs because computers, as binary machines, are based on the powers of 2. If 2 is raised to the 10th power (2^{10}), the decimal number is 1,024. Since this is very near 1,000 (10^3), the prefix *kilo-* was adopted for computer use. The same rationale explains the prefixes *mega-* (1 million) and *giga-* (1 billion).

FIGURE 2.2
Comparison of sizes of bits and
bytes.

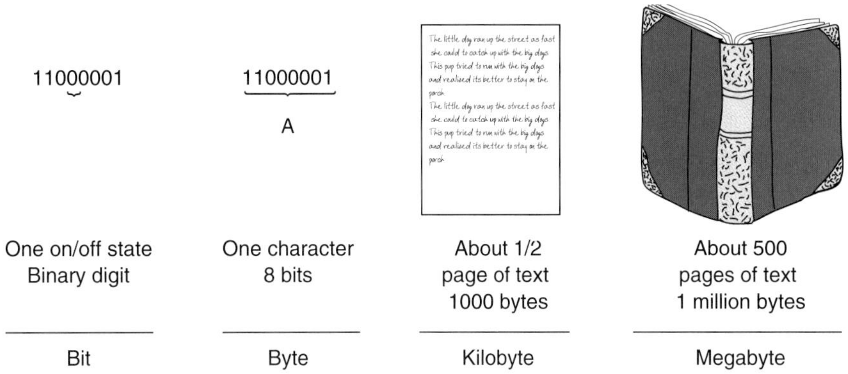

11000001	11000001		
	A		
One on/off state Binary digit	One character 8 bits	About 1/2 page of text 1000 bytes	About 500 pages of text 1 million bytes
Bit	Byte	Kilobyte	Megabyte

Computer Words

Although individual pieces of data are represented by a byte, the computer handles them in units of words. A computer **word** is the number of adjacent bits that can be manipulated as a unit. Just as English vocabulary words are of varying lengths, so are computer words; e.g., 16-, 32- and 64-bit words are common. A computer with a 16-bit word manipulates a number up to 2^{16}, or 65,536, as a unit. A computer with a 32-bit word manipulates a number as large as 2^{32}, or 4,294,967,296, as a unit. Numbers larger than these in a calculation require the computer to break down the operation into smaller steps.

You might compare word size and its relationship to computer power and speed as you would the size of a truck to move your belongings. For example, you have a 16-foot truck, but enough furniture to fill a 32-foot truck. After filling the truck, you drive to the new location, empty the truck, and drive back to load the remainder of the furniture. But if you had a 32-foot truck in the first place, everything could have been loaded at once and you would have made only one trip.

Encoding Systems

Data Representation

- Bit
- Byte
- Word
- Encoding systems
  - ASCII
  - EBCDIC

With all the bits and bytes, how does the computer know how to represent each individual character? An **encoding system** is used that permits alphanumeric characters to be coded in terms of bits using 1s and 0s. The two most widely used encoding systems are ASCII (*A*merican *S*tandard *C*ode for *I*nformation *I*nterchange), developed by several computer manufacturers, and EBCDIC (*E*xtended *B*inary *C*oded *D*ecimal *I*nterchange *C*ode), developed by IBM.

The standard ASCII character set consists of 128 distinct 7-bit binary codes (numbered 0 to 127) that are used by almost every microcomputer. This permits data or programs to be exchanged by different programs and computers. For example, when the Macintosh or an IBM sees the bit pattern 1010001, they both understand this to be a capital letter Q. The first 32 codes are communication and printer control codes, such as tab, backspace, and carriage return. The remaining 96 are used for letters, numbers and other special characters.

TABLE 2.1
ASCII and EBCDIC alphanumeric chart

Character	8-Bit ASCII	8-Bit EBDCIC	Character	8-Bit ASCII	8-Bit EBCDIC
0	1011 0000	1111 0000	K	1100 1011	1101 0010
1	1011 0001	1111 0001	L	1100 1100	1101 0011
2	1011 0010	1111 0010	M	1100 1101	1101 0100
3	1011 0011	1111 0011	N	1100 1110	1101 0101
4	1011 0100	1111 0100	O	1100 1111	1101 0110
5	1011 0101	1111 0101	P	1101 0000	1101 0111
6	1011 0110	1111 0110	Q	1101 0001	1101 1000
7	1011 0111	1111 0111	R	1101 0010	1101 1001
8	1011 1000	1111 1000	S	1101 0011	1110 0010
9	1011 1001	1111 1001	T	1101 0100	1110 0011
A	1100 0001	1100 0001	U	1101 0101	1110 0100
B	1100 0010	1100 0010	V	1101 0110	1110 0101
C	1100 0011	1100 0011	W	1101 0111	1110 0110
D	1100 0100	1100 0100	X	1101 1000	1110 0111
E	1100 0101	1100 0101	Y	1101 1001	1110 1000
F	1100 0110	1100 0110	Z	1101 1010	1110 1001
G	1100 0111	1100 0111	+	1010 1011	0100 1110
H	1100 1000	1100 1000	$	1010 0100	0101 1011
I	1100 1001	1100 1001	.	1010 1110	0100 1011
J	1100 1010	1101 0001	<	1011 1000	0100 1100

There is also an extended ASCII character set composed of 128 additional 8-bit codes (numbered 128 through 255). This set includes graphic characters, Greek letters, and scientific characters; however, this character set is not standard among computers.

EBCDIC is an 8-bit code of 256 distinct binary possibilities that are mainly used on IBM's minicomputers and mainframes. Table 2.1 lists some alphanumeric characters, their ASCII codes, and their EBCDIC codes.

Objective 2.3   Comprehend the functions of the central processing unit.

What Is the Central Processing Unit?

The **central processing unit (CPU)** is that part of the computer that decodes and executes instructions. The CPU is comprised of the arithmetic-logic unit (ALU) and the control unit (Figure 2.3).

All CPUs carry out the processing of data and instructions for a computer. Large system computers often contain more than one CPU because of the additional processing requirements. Multiple CPUs allow parallel processing. **Parallel processing** divides a task among the various processors. This allows more complex tasks, such as simulations, to be performed. A microcomputer is a single CPU computer and does **serial processing**, that is, it must finish one instruction before starting the next.

The **arithmetic-logic unit (ALU)** is the part of a CPU where all arithmetic and logical functions are performed. Some arithmetic functions are addition, subtraction, multiplication, and division. A logic function is one that compares numbers or conditions. Some logic functions are greater

---

Main Components of a CPU

- Arithmetic-logic unit (ALU)
- Control unit

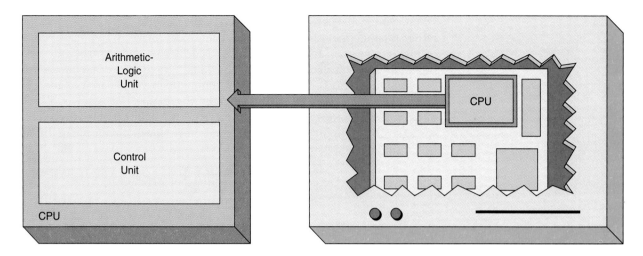

FIGURE 2.3
The central processing unit (CPU) consists of the control unit and the
arithmetic-logic unit. In a microcomputer the CPU is combined on a single chip
called a microprocessor.

than, less than, equal to, not equal to, greater than or equal to, and less than or equal to.

The **control unit** directs the sequence of events necessary to execute each instruction. It is basically the "traffic cop" of the system. For example, data can flow both in and out of the central processing unit, but the control unit keeps this from happening simultaneously to prevent garbled information. The synchronization of tasks is accomplished through electrical timing signals delivered by control circuitry called the **system clock**.

Objective 2.4   Explain what makes up a microprocessor.

What Is a Microprocessor?

Microcomputers as we know them would not be possible without technological developments such as semiconductor technology. Semiconductors use transistors to form electronic circuits that can serve as conductors (allowing the transmission of electricity) or as insulators (inhibiting the transmission of electricity). This capability is ideal, because computer data are represented by combinations of high-voltage states (binary 1) and low-voltage states (binary 0).

Through a process called etching, circuits are engraved onto a silicon wafer. A complete electronic semiconductor circuit contained on a piece of silicon is called an **integrated circuit (IC)**. An integrated circuit, also called a **microchip** or just **chip**, is used for logic and memory circuitry. For example, an IC can be designed to function as part of the ALU or as a memory chip.

Until the developmental work by Ted Hoff (described in the Profile), the parts of the central processing unit were on separate chips. Hoff combined them onto a single chip called a **microprocessor**, the CPU of a microcomputer. Microprocessors made the rapid development of microcomputers possible. In the opening conversation the reference to a "486 machine" described the microprocessor being used, i.e., an Intel 80486.

Often, you will hear a microcomputer described by its microprocessor rather than its brand name. For microcomputers there are two main series of microprocessors: Intel (Figure 2.4), used by IBM and compatibles; and the Motorola equivalent (i.e., 68030 and 68040), used by the Macintosh line of computers. This is one reason why computers by Apple are not entirely compatible with those by IBM. Generally the higher the number of the microprocessor series, the faster and more powerful it is. The microprocessor and other support chips are mounted on the main circuit board, often called the motherboard or system board (Figure 2.5).

Objective 2.5   Describe the internal storage of a computer.

FIGURE 2.4
An Intel microprocessor.

FIGURE 2.5
The motherboard, or main circuit board, of a computer.

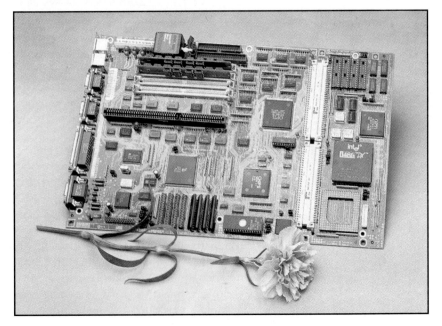

How many times have you bought a bag of apples, taken one out, bit into it, and had it go squish instead of crunch? Well, researchers from Michigan State University and the U.S. Department of Agriculture are using computers to find out where in their transit to market the apples pick up their bruises. Each computer is in the form of a bright blue apple that contains a device for measuring pressure, a microprocessor, a memory chip, and a battery. Yum-yum!

These computer "apples" are placed with the edible ones as they travel to their destination. Researchers compare the condition of the real apples to the data contained in the computer apples. Because apples sustain the most damage during bagging, the researchers are working on new methods of bagging. Damaged fruit amounts to millions of dollars of losses annually, so the little blue apples may be just what the doctor ordered.

What Is Main Memory?

For the CPU to function efficiently it needs a place to store data and instructions. **Main memory** is the internal storage component of a computer. The amount is important in determining the software that can be used because each program requires a specific amount of memory to be functional. The two types of main memory are random-access memory and read-only memory (Figure 2.6).

Random-access memory (RAM) is the part of main memory where data and program instructions are held temporarily while being manipulated or executed. This type of memory allows you to enter data into memory (write) and then to retrieve it (read).

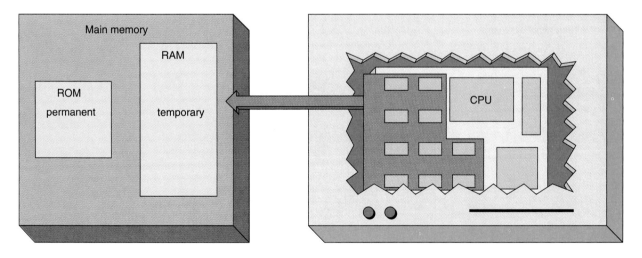

FIGURE 2.6
The computer's internal main memory contains both RAM and ROM.

Most of main memory consists of RAM. The two most common types are dynamic RAM and static RAM. The first, dynamic RAM (DRAM), is used in almost all personal computers. DRAM has the advantages of more memory per chip (high density) and low cost, but to maintain the contents of its memory, it must have periodic pulses of electricity, which is referred to as "refreshing its memory."

The second type of RAM is called static RAM (SRAM). SRAM has faster access times and does not need to be refreshed, but its main disadvantage over DRAM is cost.

In either case, when the power to a computer is shut off, everything stored in RAM is lost. In other words, RAM is **volatile**.

Part of the main memory may contain permanently stored instructions that tell a computer what to do when it is turned on, such as checking that everything is working properly and seeing what peripheral equipment is attached. As the name implies, the contents of **read-only memory (ROM)** can only be read. The actual contents of ROM are usually set by the computer manufacturer; they are unchangeable and permanent. The contents of ROM are often referred to as **firmware**. ROM is nonvolatile because the contents cannot be altered and they are not lost when the electric current is turned off.

Some read-only memory can be programmed according to a user's specifications. Programmable read-only memory (PROM) allows a chip to be programmed by a user once; then it cannot be altered further. Another ROM in which the contents can be changed is called erasable programmable read-only memory (EPROM) (Figure 2.7). An EPROM chip has a transparent quartz window covering the internal circuitry. By removing the chip from the circuit and exposing the window to ultraviolet light, the contents can be erased. Then the chip can be programmed for another application.

Another type of ROM chip is electrically erasable programmable read-only memory (EEPROM). This chip can be erased and reprogrammed

FIGURE 2.7
By removing the chip and exposing the transparent quartz window to ultraviolet light, this EPROM can be erased and later reprogrammed.

electrically, so there is no need to remove it from the circuit as with an EPROM. One use for this chip is in point-of-sale applications such as grocery store computers, where price changes occur frequently.

The CPU also uses some special-named memories to improve the overall performance of a computer. These memories, vital to moving data in and out of the CPU, are called registers, buffers, and cache.

A **register** holds an instruction or data to be worked on immediately and can hold only one piece of data at a time. Registers are part of the CPU, so transfer of data into and out of them is very fast. In fact, the size and number of registers help determine the overall speed of a computer. Registers are used to store the result of the last processing step of the ALU, hold the location of the next piece of data, and hold the location of the next instruction to be executed.

A **buffer**, another temporary holding space for data, may be part of main memory or it may be built into devices used to input or output data, e.g., printers. Unlike a register, a buffer can hold more than one piece of data at a time. The buffer acts as an intermediary between the CPU and the input or output device that operates at much slower rates than does the CPU. A temporary holding place avoids too much idle CPU time.

A special type of buffer memory used in microcomputers is **cache memory**, which is high-speed SRAM logically located between the CPU and the main memory. The purpose is to increase the speed at which data are accessed by storing only the most frequently used data in the cache. The CPU looks to the cache first. If it finds the data it is looking for, it is a "hit," if not, a "miss." A miss means main memory must be searched—this additional step adds time to the data search. Cache efficiency is a measure of the numbers of hits made. Hit rates can be as much as 90–95%, so you can see that this can increase the speed at which a task is completed. Cache memory has been a staple for over 20 years in mainframe computers, but microcomputers have reached speeds that make cache memory necessary to take full advantage of the capabilities of their microprocessors. However, software is required to access and manage a cache memory.

Objective 2.6   Contrast the roles of RAM and ROM.

How Is Memory Used?

Let's represent your microcomputer's main memory as the cube in Figure 2.8a. The cube is composed of two parts, RAM and ROM. ROM is shown as the thin portion along the top of the cube. When the computer is first turned on, ROM firmware performs predetermined operations, such as checking the system for errors. Notice that nothing is contained in RAM at this point.

Before a computer can be used, it must have operating instructions; that software is called the operating system. Instructions in ROM initially load the operating system. The typical microcomputer operating system is said to "reside" on a disk and must be transferred, or loaded, into RAM. Figure 2.8b shows the part of RAM that is occupied by the operating system.

If you want to write a letter, the computer needs more instructions in the form of an application software program to function as a word

FIGURE 2.8
An example of RAM and ROM
use in a microcomputer.

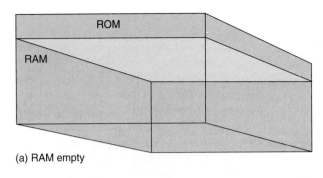

(a) RAM empty

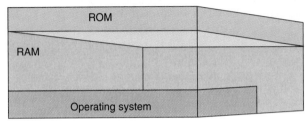

(b) Operating system loaded into RAM

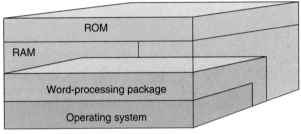

(c) Word-processing package
    loaded into RAM

processor. This word-processing software also has to be loaded into RAM. Once it has been loaded, it is ready to use (Figure 2.8c). Remember, though, that RAM is volatile. If you turn the computer off, main memory will contain only ROM and again will look like Figure 2.8a.

Objective 2.7   Define memory in terms of conventional, extended, and expanded.

How Much Main Memory Can You Have?

The amount of main memory in a computer is important in determining its capabilities. Many applications require a specific amount of memory or the software may not work or may run slowly. Most computers have provisions for adding individual RAM chips, installing a *Single Inline Memory Module* (SIMM) to the main circuit board, or adding RAM cards (Figure 2.9). RAM chips are available in different memory sizes and are inserted directly into the motherboard. A RAM card is a group of integrated circuits already assembled on a printed circuit board which can be plugged into the expansion slots found on the main circuit board of a computer.

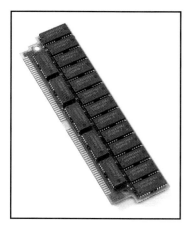

FIGURE 2.9

Plug-in memory boards are one option for increasing the amount of main memory in your computer.

You will encounter the terms conventional, extended, and expanded memory, with computers using Intel microprocessors (IBMs and compatibles). Early microprocessors were designed to access (address) only 1,024 kilobytes (1 megabyte, or 1 million bytes) of memory. The upper 384 KB of this memory was reserved for accessories such as the ROM-BIOS (Basic Input-Output System), video devices, and disk controllers. The remaining 640 KB kilobytes, called **conventional memory**, is all that's left for applications.

Many programs require more than 640 KB, especially memory-intensive applications like graphics. This barrier was overcome beginning with the 80286 microprocessor. With the appropriate software, applications could access memory above the 640 KB. This memory is referred to as **extended memory** (Figure 2.10). The 384 KB reserved area can be used as extended memory by giving it new addresses from 1,024 KB to 1,408 KB. The 80286 can address 16 megabytes (16 million bytes) of extended memory, while the 80386 and 80486 can address up to 4 gigabytes (4 billion bytes).

FIGURE 2.10

A pictorial representation of conventional, extended, and expanded memory.

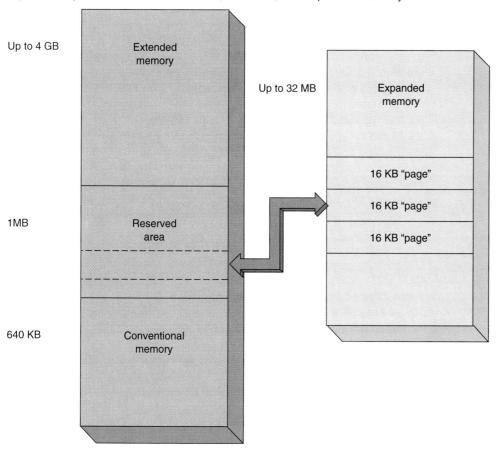

Certain application programs, such as Lotus 1-2-3 (a spreadsheet program), make use of an additional type of memory. To bypass the limitations of the 640 KB of conventional memory, Lotus, Intel, and Microsoft (LIM) developed expanded memory. **Expanded memory** is accessed through paging. Requiring special software, paging is a way to bring a block (page) of memory into the reserved memory area. Up to four 16 KB pages can be swapped in and out of the reserved memory area between 640 KB and 1 MB. The software "fools" the computer into treating this as conventional memory. This creates the illusion of more conventional memory. Expanded memory can support up to 2,000 pages, the equivalent of 32 MB.

Objective 2.8   Differentiate the types of buses and their role in compatibility.

What Are the Communication Pathways?

Communication Pathways

- Control bus
- Address bus
- Data bus

The arithmetic and logic unit, the control unit, and the main memory unit must communicate to function. The links among and within the various units are called buses. A **bus** is an electrical path for signals to flow from point to point in a circuit. A bus is classified according to its function. For example, a **control bus** is a unidirectional pathway for all timing and controlling functions. Signals sent by the control unit regulate what happens on the other two buses. An **address bus** is a unidirectional pathway used to locate the storage position in memory of the next instruction to be executed or the next piece of data. A **data bus** is a bidirectional pathway where actual data transfer takes place. The bus width is the number of bits that the bus can transfer at a time, e.g., 16 bits and 32 bits.

Major characteristics of **bus architecture** include the speed at which a bus can transfer data, the amount of data that the bus can transfer, and the number of extra circuit boards that can be used. Internal sockets where additional computer boards can be plugged in are called **expansion slots**. Why would you care about the internal bus structure of a computer? Well, not all microcomputers use the same bus architecture. For example, an expansion board using a 32-bit bus architecture will not work in the expansion slot of a computer using a 16-bit bus. Whether you are choosing a complete system or selecting an accessory card, compatibility is a key issue.

More than one bus architecture is used. IBM PS/2 models use Micro Channel Architecture (MCA). Others embrace the Extended Industry Standard Architecture (EISA), which was developed by nine computer manufacturers. The XT bus is used for the 8-bit IBM and compatibles, the AT bus for the 16-bit IBM and compatibles, and NuBus for the Apple Macintosh. Some architectures are only partially compatible while others, like MCA and EISA, are not compatible at all.

Graphical images require large amounts of memory and therefore take longer to access. But they are playing a larger role in computing, so data transfer speed is becoming more crucial. Although your monitor may be connected to a 16- or 32-bit expansion slot, these input/output slots transfer data at rates much slower than the CPU can operate. To speed this process, many are opting for a local bus. A **local bus** allows video to be connected to the CPU's bus, bypassing the slower input/output bus of the expansion slot, and thereby operating at the CPU's speed.

Objective 2.9   Describe the instruction cycle.

How Does the CPU Process an Instruction?

Thanks in part to the control unit, the elements of a computer act with and react to one another with amazing precision. Depending on the instruction, certain computer components may or may not be used. In one instance, the instruction may involve computations by the ALU; another may simply look for and display the contents of a memory location.

Regardless of the actual instruction, a computer always proceeds through the same instruction cycle. The **instruction cycle** is composed of two steps: (1) **instruction time** and (2) **execution time**. The instruction time is the time required to fetch an instruction from memory and place it in a temporary location in the CPU called the register. This is equivalent to opening a drawer and pulling out a cookbook. Execution time involves the decoding and execution of that instruction. During decoding, the instruction is translated and sent to the ALU along with any necessary data for processing. Compare this to reading the recipe instructions and gathering all the ingredients for the recipe.

During the execution phase, the instruction is executed by the ALU, and the result is stored in memory until needed (Figure 2.11). To complete the analogy, this would be baking the recipe and placing the dish aside to cool until it's time to eat. The CPU is then ready to fetch the next instruction and the instruction-execution sequence of operations is repeated until the program ends.

Instruction Cycle

- **Instruction time**
  Fetch
- **Execution time**
  Decode
  Execute
  Store

FIGURE 2.11
The CPU and main memory during the instruction cycle.

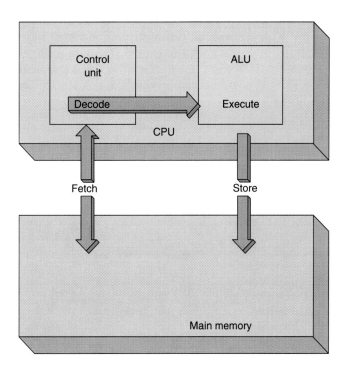

How Do CPU Properties Affect Processing Power and Speed?

Computer Power and Speed Determinants

- Microprocessor
- Clock speed
- Word size
- Data bus width
- Instruction set
- Memory type
- Support chips

The CPU may be thought of as the engine of the computer. Just as a race car engine has more power and performance than the family sedan, CPUs are not equal either. Generally each new generation of CPUs is more powerful and faster than the last. Many factors determine the power and speed at which a computer processes data. These include the microprocessor and its clock speed, word size and data bus width, the instruction set, memory type, and other support chips.

The Microprocessor and Its Clock Speed

The number of pulses, or cycles per second that the system clock sends out is a main element in determining the speed of a microprocessor. Clock speed is measured in megahertz (MHz). Hertz is the basic unit of frequency and is a measure of the number of cycles per second in a periodic, or repeating, signal. A megahertz is equal to 1 million hertz. All other things being equal, a 66-MHz microprocessor will execute instructions twice as fast as a 33-MHz microprocessor.

Microprocessor design improvements are increasing their speeds at a tremendous rate. Clock speeds for some 32-bit computers are 33 and 66 MHz as compared to 4.77 MHz for microcomputers of the mid-1980s. Many of the microcomputer advertisements tout a particular computer as being "a 33-MHz computer." Use the clock speed as a general guide for comparison, but because there are many other considerations, switching from a 33-MHz to a 66-MHz computer does not necessarily mean a twofold increase in computing speed.

More and more components are being placed on a single chip to increase speed. Consider that the 4004 microprocessor contained 2,300 transistors, but the P5 (Pentium or 80586) has 3.1 million transistors (see Table 2.2 for a comparison of microprocessor chips). Many people predict that microprocessors will contain 15–20 million transistors and will reach

TABLE 2.2
Comparison of Intel microprocessor features

Chip	Clock Speed	Data Bus Width	MIPS	Memory	Number of Transistors
8086	4.77–10MHz	16 Bit	.33–.75	1MB	29,000
8088	4.77–10MHz	16 Bit	.33–.66	1MB	29,000
80286	8–12MHz	16 Bit	1.2–2.66	16MB	130,000
80386SX	16–33MHz	16 Bit	2.5–4.2	16MB	275,000
80386DX	16–33MHz	32 Bit	6–11.4	4GB	275,000
80486SX	16–33MHz	32 Bit	13–20	4GB	1.2 Million
80486DX	25–66MHz	32 Bit	20–40.7	4GB	1.2 Million
Pentium (586) (P5)	66MHz	64 Bit	≈100	4GB	3.1 Million

speeds of 250 MHz and 2,000 millions of instructions per second by the year 2000. Microprocessors are starting to encroach into what was once supercomputer territory.

Word Size and Data Bus Width

A computer that can handle a longer computer word can process the data faster. Word size is dependent on the size of the registers of the processor. A 16-bit register would require two operations to handle a 32-bit word, while a 32-bit register could handle it all at once.

The width of the data bus, or how many bits it can handle at a time, is a major factor in how fast a computer can process data. Let's say Computer One has a 32-bit data bus and Computer Two has a 16-bit data bus. Computer One would require half the time to transfer a 32-bit instruction as would Computer Two. So even if the word size in both computers was the same, Computer Two would require twice the time to transfer the word.

Instruction Set

The **instruction set** is the group of commands available to a CPU. It determines which basic computer operations (arithmetic, logic, storage, and retrieval functions) can be performed. A CPU is designed with an instruction set to direct and coordinate the operations of the computer.

Two major software designs are used to implement the instruction set. Reduced-instruction-set computers (RISC) use microprocessors that contain only the simpler and most used instructions. By reducing the number of clock cycles needed to execute one of those instructions, the processor is faster. Complex-instruction-set computers (CISC) contain most of the instructions on the processor, so the processor must access memory fewer times.

Computer speed is also measured by the number of instructions completed per second, or **millions of instructions per second (MIPS)**. This designation compares the processing power of computer systems.

Computer speeds are continually increasing. New chips can put the power of a mainframe on your desk. High-powered microprocessors may find new uses for microcomputers in areas such as banking, where high-precision calculations are needed to avoid rounding errors.

A typical microcomputer can execute an instruction, such as adding two numbers, in a few milliseconds. Mainframes and supercomputers can execute this instruction in microsecond and nanosecond ranges. The difference between a millisecond and a microsecond may seem insignificant; however, it is roughly the same as the difference between 1 minute and 1 day, or 1 hour and 1 month. Just think how much more you can accomplish in a month than you can in an hour! Table 2.3 compares computer speeds to 1 second of time. The speed differences become evident when running programs that process larger volumes of data.

TABLE 2.3
Computer speeds compared to 1 second of time

1 millisecond	=	.001 second
1 microsecond	=	.000001 second
1 nanosecond	=	.000000001 second
1 picosecond	=	.000000000001 second
1 second	=	1 thousand milliseconds
1 second	=	1 million microseconds
1 second	=	1 billion nanoseconds
1 second	=	1 trillion picoseconds

Memory Type

Memory also plays a part in processing speed. The wait state while DRAM chips are being refreshed temporarily idles the CPU. The more expensive SRAM chips have a zero wait state.

Access times given for memory chips are listed in billions of seconds, or nanoseconds, indicating how long it takes to access and retrieve data. The lower the number, the faster the chip. In order for the microprocessor to operate at a given speed, the memory chips must be able to keep up with it. So it is important when adding memory that you consult the manufacturer's manual for the speed range of any additional chips you may install. The trade-off for faster memory chips is an increase in the cost of the chips.

Some operations that involve large arrays of data, such as those involved in saving a video image, can be sped up by using direct memory access (DMA). DMA allows data to go directly to memory without passing through the CPU. In operations where data or instructions are transferred from memory to the CPU, a memory cache can increase the speed.

Support Chips

A microprocessor usually does not carry all of the burden of a computer system. Many other chips control other functions, such as sound, video, and peripheral devices. Some of these chips are contained on circuit boards that can be plugged into the expansion slots on the motherboard.

Many computers also contain a coprocessor, which is a chip used along with the main microprocessor dedicated to speed large number-crunching activities. This adds more speed and power to the computer system. Some software programs require that your computer be equipped with a coprocessor. Autocad, a popular computer-aided design program, cannot function without a coprocessor. Be careful how you read a computer ad. Most say they *support* a coprocessor. This means a socket in the computer is available for one but that the chip itself is a separate option. Chips such as the 80486DX have the coprocessor already built into the microprocessor.

Hallmark Cards is known for its slogan. Now, the very best is something that you can create. Hallmark has installed more than 1,200 in-store kiosks containing Macintosh Centris 610 computers. Each computer runs on the Motorola 68040 microprocessor chip. Since each computer has 12 MB of RAM and a 230 MB hard drive and CD-ROM, more than 800 card designs are available. The memory also allows for automatic recordkeeping. Each kiosk can report which card design is the best seller so those designs will be presented to users first. The unit will keep track of sales and its own maintenance data and someday contain repair diagnostic programs. The kiosks take up about as much space as a video arcade game and Hallmark plans to install them at grocery stores and pharmacies as well. There is 24-hour on-line technical support available and service calls are guaranteed within four hours with service restored within eight hours.

The Macintosh reputation as a user-friendly system made it the first choice. An image of a salesperson guides you through the various menus as you design your card. Selections are made on a touch screen. You can personalize your message and have it printed on the front, back, or inside of the card. Card selections will coincide with the change of seasons and holidays. The completed work of art is printed on an ink-jet color printer. Although the cards are comparatively expensive, approximately $3.50 each, Hallmark expects that the novelty will appeal to many people.

Maybe soon you'll be able to fax it directly to your sweetheart!

Objective 2.11   Describe factors to consider when deciding which CPU you want in a personal computer.

Which CPU Should Your Personal Computer Contain?

A complete computer system includes peripherals such as the monitor, disk drives, and printers, and most important, the CPU that the system uses. The microprocessor that contains the CPU determines to a great extent what you can do and how fast you can do it. The microprocessor is on the motherboard along with other chips inside the main "box." Personal computers are sold with a particular microprocessor, for example, 386 SX 16 MHz or 486 DX 66 MHz.

When it comes time to select a personal computer, what factors should you consider when deciding which CPU it should have? While there are many reasons, the most important fall into four categories: cost, applications, compatibility, and expandability.

Cost is usually one of the most important determinations. Generally, the more powerful and faster the CPU, the more it will cost. You may have many options such as buying a slower CPU but getting more memory for the same price.

The applications you intend to use will help you decide how powerful a CPU is necessary. A self-employed plumber or a small business on a limited budget might be satisfied with an older, less powerful CPU that is adequate, yet relatively inexpensive. Applications such as text-based word processing

Selecting a CPU

- Cost
- Applications
- Compatibility
- Expandability

can be used with this CPU. If you expect to manipulate large spreadsheets and databases or if you are interested in applications that involve intensive graphics such as desktop publishing and designing programs, then a more powerful CPU is preferable.

Compatibility is another reason for buying a computer with a specific CPU. If most of your clients use Macintosh computers that contain Motorola microprocessors, it may not make sense to buy an IBM or compatible that contains Intel or compatible microprocessors. If you already have an IBM or compatible and have built up an extensive library of software, it may be impractical to purchase a Macintosh. Processor cards are available so that an IBM or compatible can run Macintosh software and vice versa, however.

The Power PC chip introduced by Motorola promises to be the solution to compatibility issues, allowing Macintosh and IBM computers to run each other's software. Apple's Power PC hit the market in March 1994 and IBM's entries appeared later.

When determining which CPU your personal computer should have, also consider future expandability. At a minimum, you will want to be able to add additional memory or insert other expansion boards, such as modems or video cards. To predict too far into the future is difficult, at best. No one knows for sure what to expect over the next ten to twenty years. See Chapter 15 for insight about what might be in store.

Summary

Data are represented as binary system numbers. The smallest piece of data that a computer understands is a bit. A grouping of 8 bits is a byte. A kilobyte is 1,024 bytes. A computer word is the number of adjacent bits that a register can hold. ASCII and EBCDIC are two of the encoding schemes used to represent all alphanumeric characters and control codes.

A central processing unit (CPU) is comprised of the arithmetic-logic unit (ALU) and control unit. The ALU handles mathematical and comparison operations. The control unit regulates the timing and sequence of all processing within a computer. Large system computers may contain many CPUs while a microcomputer usually has only one. Large-system computers with more than one CPU have the ability to accomplish parallel processing, while microcomputers execute one instruction after another, called serial processing. In a microcomputer the parts of the CPU are on one chip called a microprocessor.

The computer's main memory is the internal storage unit of a computer where programs and data are stored. Program instructions or data can be stored internally in random-access memory (RAM) or read-only memory (ROM). RAM is used primarily for temporary storage and is volatile. ROM is used for permanent storage and is nonvolatile; that is, it does not rely on a continuous source of power.

Special-purpose memories are registers and buffers. A register is a temporary holding place for instructions or data that are to be worked on immediately. A buffer holds data going into and out of the central processing unit. A special high-speed buffer memory is cache memory.

The amount of main memory is important in determining the capabilities of a computer. Most computers have provisions for adding individual

RAM chips, installing a single inline memory module (SIMM) to the main circuit board, or adding RAM cards to increase the amount of main memory.

Main memory terms you will encounter include conventional, extended, and expanded memory. The first 640 kilobytes of addressable memory is called conventional memory. Many programs require more than this amount. With the appropriate software, memory could be accessed above 1 MB. This memory is referred to as extended memory and is memory that has a physical address above 1 MB. Certain application programs use expanded memory, which is memory that is accessed through paging, not through addressing.

The instruction cycle is composed of two steps, instruction time and execution time. The instruction time is the time required to fetch an instruction from memory and place it in a temporary location in the CPU. Execution time involves the decoding and execution of that instruction. During decoding, the instruction is translated and sent to the ALU along with any necessary data for processing. During the execution phase, the instruction is executed by the ALU, and the result is stored in memory until needed.

The links among and within the various units are called buses. A bus is an electrical path for signals to flow from point to point in a circuit. A bus is classified according to its function. For example, a control bus is a unidirectional pathway for all timing and controlling functions. An address bus is a unidirectional pathway used to locate the storage position in memory for the next instruction to be executed or the next piece of data. A data bus is a bidirectional pathway in which actual data transfer takes place.

Many factors determine the power and speed at which a computer processes data. These include the microprocessor and its clock speed, word size and data bus width, the instruction set, memory type, and other support chips.

Factors you should consider when buying a CPU include how much it costs, your applications, compatibility, and expandability.

VOCABULARY SELF-TEST

Can you define the following terms?

address bus (p. 62)	control bus (p. 62)
arithmetic-logic unit (ALU) (p. 54)	control unit (p. 55)
binary system (p. 52)	conventional memory (p. 61)
bit (p. 52)	data bus (p. 62)
buffer (p. 59)	encoding system (p. 53)
bus (p. 62)	execution time (p. 63)
bus architecture (p. 62)	expanded memory (p. 62)
byte (p. 52)	expansion slots (p. 62)
cache memory (p. 59)	extended memory (p. 61)
central processing unit (CPU) (p. 54)	firmware (p. 58)
chip (p. 55)	

instruction cycle (p. 63)

instruction set (p. 65)

instruction time (p. 63)

integrated circuit (IC) (p. 55)

local bus (p. 62)

main memory (p. 57)

microchip (p. 55)

microprocessor (p. 55)

millions of instructions per second (MIPS) (p. 65)

parallel processing (p. 54)

random-access memory (RAM) (p. 57)

read-only memory (ROM) (p. 58)

register (p. 59)

serial processing (p. 54)

system clock (p. 55)

volatile (p. 58)

word (p. 53)

REVIEW QUESTIONS

Multiple Choice

1. The number of adjacent bits that can be stored and manipulated as a unit is called a _____.
   a. byte
   b. nibble
   c. word
   d. MIP

2. Which one of the following is a binary representation of a character?
   a. 1101100
   b. +
   c. 10,100
   d. A

3. The central processing unit is the part of the computer that _____.
   a. includes all peripheral devices
   b. is used to determine the size of the computer
   c. decodes and executes instructions
   d. stores application programs

4. A microprocessor contains both the _____.
   a. ALU and main memory
   b. control unit and RAM
   c. RAM and ROM
   d. ALU and control unit

5. Which of the following is a logic function?
   a. addition
   b. greater than
   c. division
   d. logarithmic

6. Main memory refers to _____.
   a. permanent ROM storage only
   b. internal storage for programs or data
   c. disk storage of data
   d. external permanent storage only

7. When application software, such as a word processor, is loaded into a computer, it resides in _____.
   a. RAM
   b. the operating system
   c. ROM
   d. the instruction set
8. A(n) _____ allows more than one piece of data to be stored temporarily, thus freeing the CPU for other tasks.
   a. buffer
   b. accumulator
   c. register
   d. controller
9. A(n) _____ is used to electronically link the parts of a computer.
   a. microchip
   b. battery
   c. operating system
   d. bus
10. During instruction time, the instruction is _____.
   a. loaded into RAM
   b. decoded
   c. executed
   d. fetched from memory

Fill-In

1. The processing unit responsible for mathematical computations is the _____.
2. _____ is a type of internal memory that can only be read from and not written to.
3. Software programs stored in ROM are called _____.
4. ASCII and EBCDIC are two types of _____ systems.
5. A circuit that contains both the ALU and the control unit on a single microchip is call a(n) _____.
6. A(n) _____ bus allows peripherals, such as a monitor, to be connected to the CPU's bus, thus bypassing the slower input/output bus of the expansion slot.
7. The _____ number system is used to represent the electrical conditions of on or off in computers.
8. The smallest unit of data that a computer recognizes is called a(n) _____.
9. _____ memory is memory that is accessed through paging.
10. The _____ is the group of commands available to a CPU that determines which basic computer operations can be performed.

Short Answer

1. What two major units comprise the CPU? Briefly describe the function of each unit.
2. Give four examples of a logic function.

3. How are large system CPUs different from microcomputer CPUs?
4. What does the term *volatile* mean as it pertains to computer memory?
5. Describe the roles that RAM and ROM play within a computer, the main purpose of each, and the factors that distinguish the two types of memory.
6. What is the function of a register? A buffer? Cache?
7. List and briefly describe the steps of the instruction cycle.
8. Discuss some of the factors involved in determining the overall processing speed of a computer.
9. Describe the form that data must take for the computer to identify and use it.
10. Discuss how the specifications might differ when looking for a microcomputer that was to be used for a small business versus one that would be used for running spreadsheets in a large accounting office.

Issues for Thought

1. Having products that do not work with each other can be very frustrating. In computer systems, software and hardware often are not compatible. Should standards be set to cover all aspects of computing, or should the free market rule and the best product win?
2. As a class project, bring in various computer advertisements and discuss the information contained in them. Are you able to decipher them yourself? Can you determine the speed, amount of memory, peripheral equipment? Discuss how you would choose one for a specific task.

Infomodule

Number Systems

Most of you are comfortable counting and manipulating numbers with the decimal system and can picture in your minds the quantities that each number represents, but what if you were asked to picture the quantity 6A7C? At first, you might say this doesn't represent a quantity because it contains letters. But in the hexadecimal number system 6A7C is a number. If you were to use the various number systems presented in this text as often as you use the decimal system, they would become easier to use over time.

WHAT IS THE DECIMAL SYSTEM?

Because the decimal system is the most familiar number system, our discussion begins there. The **decimal system** is a base-10 system, which means that there are ten distinct digits—0 through 9—to represent any quantity. Any number greater than 9 can be represented by a combination of these digits. The value that the digits represent depends on the weight, or position, they hold. The weights are based on powers of 10, as shown in Figure 1.

Figure 2 shows how to determine the value of a group of digits in the base-10 system using the digits 1, 0, 2, and 4. Many combinations of these four digits can be made. The exact position in which they are placed determines the final value. In Figure 2, 4 is in the first position, 2 in the second position, 0 in the

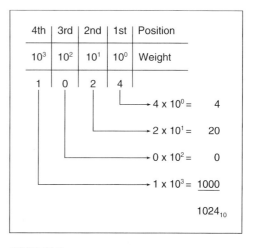

FIGURE 2
Representation of a decimal value.

third position, and 1 in the fourth position. The final value can be figured by multiplying each digit by the weight and then adding all of the intermediate results to achieve the final value. This same technique can be applied to the other number systems.

To distinguish one number system from the next, a subscript can be used to indicate the base. For example, 1024_{10} is a base-10, or decimal, number, while 1001_2 is a base-2 number. Many times in common use, however, the subscript is not shown.

WHAT IS THE BINARY SYSTEM?

As you read earlier in this chapter, computer circuitry represents data as a pattern of on or off electrical states. Because there are only two states, they are represented by a 1 for on and a 0 for off. This two-digit representation is called the **binary system**.

4th	3rd	2nd	1st	Position
$10^3 = 1000$	$10^2 = 100$	$10^1 = 10$	$10^0 = 1$	Weight

FIGURE 1
Position weights in base 10.

8th	7th	6th	5th	4th	3rd	2nd	1st	Position
$2^7 = 128$	$2^6 = 64$	$2^5 = 32$	$2^4 = 16$	$2^3 = 8$	$2^2 = 4$	$2^1 = 2$	$2^0 = 1$	Weight

FIGURE 3
Position weights in base 2.

The binary system is a base-2 system, meaning the position weights are based on the powers of 2 (Figure 3). Again, evaluate a group of digits using the procedure applied to the decimal system. Use the binary number 10000000000_2. Remember that you are in base 2, so this number is not 10 billion. Notice that commas are not used in base-2 numbers. Figure 4 evaluates the number 10000000000_2. From the calculations, $1024_{10} = 10000000000_2$. Now, look at one more. Figure 5 converts the binary number 1011011_2 to its decimal equivalent.

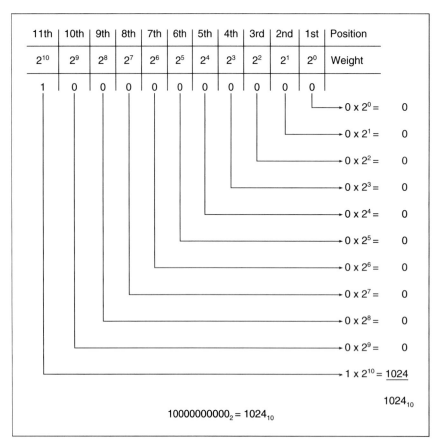

FIGURE 4
Evaluation of a base 2 number.

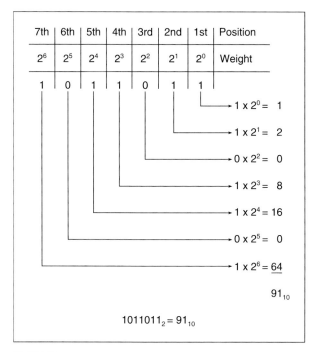

FIGURE 5
Conversion of 1011011_2 to its decimal equivalent.

WHAT IS THE OCTAL SYSTEM?

Octal and hexadecimal systems are used to provide shorthand ways to deal with the long strings of 1's and 0's created in binary. As the name suggests, the **octal system** is a base-8 system. It uses the digits 0 through 7. For evaluating purposes, again use a weighted system to convert from base 8 to base 10 (decimal). Figure 6 shows the conversion of 3137_8 to its decimal equivalent.

Converting Octal Numbers to Binary Numbers

As shown in Figure 7, an octal number can easily be converted to a binary number by replacing each octal digit with the corresponding three binary digits. Groups of three are used because any octal number $(0-7)$ can be represented by three binary digits. For example, 7_8 is 111_2 in binary.

WHAT IS THE HEXADECIMAL SYSTEM?

The **hexadecimal system** is a base-16 system. It contains the digits 0 through 9 and the letters *A* through *F*. The letters *A* through *F* are used because 16 placeholders are needed, and there are only 10 distinct digits in the decimal system. The letters *A* through *F* represent the decimal numbers 10 through

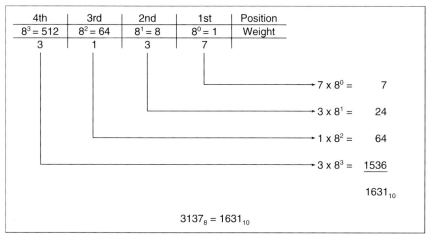

FIGURE 6
Conversion of 3137_8 to its decimal equivalent.

$$
\begin{array}{ccc}
1 & 3 & 4 \\
\underbrace{001} & \underbrace{011} & \underbrace{100}
\end{array}
\qquad \text{therefore } 134_8 = 001011100_2
$$

$$
\begin{array}{cccc}
7 & 4 & 3 & 2 \\
\underbrace{111} & \underbrace{100} & \underbrace{011} & \underbrace{010}
\end{array}
\qquad \text{therefore } 7432_8 = 111100011010_2
$$

FIGURE 7
Conversion of an octal number to a binary number.

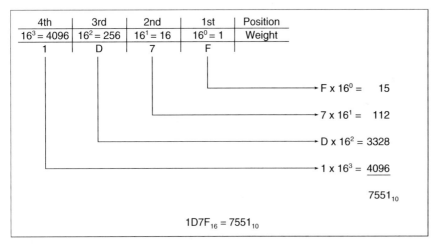

$1D7F_{16} = 7551_{10}$

4th	3rd	2nd	1st	Position
$16^3 = 4096$	$16^2 = 256$	$16^1 = 16$	$16^0 = 1$	Weight
1	D	7	F	

$F \times 16^0 = 15$

$7 \times 16^1 = 112$

$D \times 16^2 = 3328$

$1 \times 16^3 = \underline{4096}$

7551_{10}

FIGURE 8
Conversion of a hexadecimal number to a decimal number.

15, respectively. This system is often used in programming as a shortcut to the binary number system. Figure 8 shows some position weights in the hexadecimal system and a conversion of $1D7F_{16}$ to its decimal equivalent. Table 1 shows a comparison of decimal, binary, octal, and hexadecimal numbers.

Converting Hexadecimal Numbers to Binary Numbers

Hexadecimal numbers can be transposed to binary numbers in the same way octal numbers are con

---

Number Systems

- Decimal—base 10
- Binary—base 2
- Octal—base 8
- Hexadecimal—base 16

TABLE 1
Decimal, binary, octal, and hexadecimal number chart

Decimal	Binary	Octal	Hexadecimal	Decimal	Binary	Octal	Hexadecimal
0	0	0	00	50	110010	62	32
1	1	1	01	51	110011	63	33
2	10	2	02	52	110100	64	34
3	11	3	03	53	110101	65	35
4	100	4	04	54	110110	66	36
5	101	5	05	55	110111	67	37
6	110	6	06	56	111000	70	38
7	111	7	07	57	111001	71	39
8	1000	10	08	58	111010	72	3A
9	1001	11	09	59	111011	73	3B
10	1010	12	0A	60	111100	74	3C
11	1011	13	0B	61	111101	75	3D
12	1100	14	0C	62	111110	76	3E
13	1101	15	0D	63	111111	77	3F
14	1110	16	0E	64	1000000	100	40
15	1111	17	0F	65	1000001	101	41
16	10000	20	10	66	1000010	102	42
17	10001	21	11	67	1000011	103	43
18	10010	22	12	68	1000100	104	44
19	10011	23	13	69	1000101	105	45
20	10100	24	14	70	1000110	106	46
21	10101	25	15	71	1000111	107	47
22	10110	26	16	72	1001000	110	48
23	10111	27	17	73	1001001	111	49
24	11000	30	18	74	1001010	112	4A
25	11001	31	19	75	1001011	113	4B
26	11010	32	1A	76	1001100	114	4C
27	11011	33	1B	77	1001101	115	4D
28	11100	34	1C	78	1001110	116	4E
29	11101	35	1D	79	1001111	117	4F
30	11110	36	1E	80	1010000	120	50
31	11111	37	1F	81	1010001	121	51
32	100000	40	20	82	1010010	122	52
33	100001	41	21	83	1010011	123	53
34	100010	42	22	84	1010100	124	54
35	100011	43	23	85	1010101	125	55
36	100100	44	24	86	1010110	126	56
37	100101	45	25	87	1010111	127	57
38	100110	46	26	88	1011000	130	58
39	100111	47	27	89	1011001	131	59
40	101000	50	28	90	1011010	132	5A

TABLE 1
Continued

Decimal	Binary	Octal	Hexadecimal	Decimal	Binary	Octal	Hexadecimal
41	101001	51	29	91	1011011	133	5B
42	101010	52	2A	92	1011100	134	5C
43	101011	53	2B	93	1011101	135	5D
44	101100	54	2C	94	1011110	136	5E
45	101101	55	2D	95	1011111	137	5F
46	101110	56	2E	96	1100000	140	60
47	101111	57	2F	97	1100001	141	61
48	110000	60	30	98	1100010	142	62
49	110001	61	31	99	1100011	143	63

verted to binary. This time, though, the binary digits are organized into groups of four because four digits are needed to represent 15 (1111_2), the largest hexadecimal digit. Examples are shown in Figure 9.

Converting Binary Numbers to Hexadecimal Numbers

To reverse the operation, break a binary number into groups of four and replace the groups with the hexadecimal equivalent. Two examples are shown in Figure 10.

```
  6     B     2
 ‿     ‿     ‿
0110  1011  0010        therefore 6B2₁₆ = 011010110010₂


  9     3     F     A
 ‿     ‿     ‿     ‿
1001  0011  1111  1010      therefore 93FA₁₆ = 1001001111111010₂
```

FIGURE 9
Conversion of hexadecimal numbers to binary numbers.

```
1101  1001  1111  1000
 ‿     ‿     ‿     ‿
  D     9     F     8       therefore 1101100111111000₂ = D9F8₁₆


1010  0001  0111
 ‿     ‿     ‿
  A     1     7         therefore 101000010111₂ = A17₁₆
```

FIGURE 10
Conversion of binary numbers to hexadecimal numbers.

VOCABULARY SELF-TEST

Can you define the following terms?

binary system (p. 73)

decimal system (p. 73)

hexadecimal system (p. 75)

octal system (p. 75)

REVIEW QUESTIONS

Multiple Choice

1. The equivalent decimal number of the binary number 101 is _____.
   a. 4
   b. 5
   c. 7
   d. 2
2. In the octal system the decimal number 8 is written as _____.
   a. 7
   b. 8
   c. 10
   d. 1000
3. The hexadecimal and octal systems are used _____.
   a. exclusively in ASCII
   b. to encode numbers
   c. because binary is outdated
   d. as a shorthand way of representing binary numbers
4. Which of the following number systems uses letters as placeholders?
   a. decimal
   b. binary
   c. octal
   d. hexadecimal
5. Which one of the following statements is true?
   a. The decimal system is a base-16 system.
   b. The octal system uses the digits 1 through 8.
   c. The binary system uses letters to represent numbers.
   d. The hexadecimal system is a base-16 system using the digits 0 through 9 and the letters *A* through *F.*

Fill-In

1. The base-10 system is called the _____ system.
2. The base of a system indicates the number of _____ used.
3. The value a digit represents depends on the _____ it holds.
4. The subscript 2 in 1001_2 is called the _____.
5. The hexadecimal system is a base-_____ system.

Short Answer

1. Why is the binary number system used for computers?
2. Convert the binary numbers 10101010_2 and 1111001_2 into their decimal equivalents.
3. What is the purpose of using the hexadecimal and the octal numbering systems?
4. Convert your age to binary, octal, and hexadecimal numbers.
5. Using what you have learned about number systems, write the numbers from 0 to 10 using the base-3 number system.

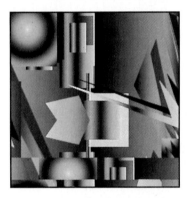

OUTLINE

OBJECTIVES

3.1 Understand the term "input" and the purpose of an input device.

3.2 Describe several ways to control the data entry process and increase the accuracy of the data input.

3.3 Know the purpose of a keyboard and describe its main features.

3.4 Define pointing devices, touch screens, and speech recognition input devices and identify applications for which they are used.

3.5 Identify and describe three special-purpose input devices.

3.6 Define optical recognition and describe three methods and devices used to accomplish it.

Chapter 3

Input

Profile

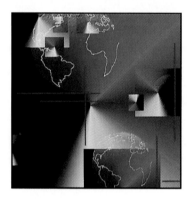

Douglas Engelbart

People who were there say that it was more like a rock concert than a scientific demonstration. But up on the platform, Douglas Engelbart was giving his audience a preview of their future as well as that of the computer. When computers were still in their infancy and viewed primarily as machines to manipulate numbers rapidly, Engelbart had the notion that computers could be used as extensions of the human mind. At this major computer conference in San Francisco in 1968, he was given the opportunity to demonstrate some of his ideas.

Engelbart was working for the Stanford Research Institute (SRI) in Menlo Park, California. Having been a radar technician during World War II and subsequently a graduate student in electrical engineering at the University of California at Berkeley, he had joined SRI in 1957. After only a few months, Engelbart convinced the administration of SRI to let him set up a unit within the famed think tank to devote itself to "human augmentation technology." This unit was the start of the Augmentation Research Center (ARC) at the institute.

As the head of the ARC, Engelbart began experiments to find a way to harness computers to a monitor instead of a teletype. At a time when some offices were still using only typewriters, Engelbart theorized about using computers as word processing units. He also experimented with computer-generated graphics. Engelbart's use of a monitor screen presented the problem of how best to move a cursor around the screen to activate the various processes. He tried light pens and joysticks and even knee-activated controls to shift the cursor, but none of these proved satisfactory. In 1964 Engelbart developed a hand-held device that could roll across a flat surface on wheels and cause a corresponding movement on the screen. It was hooked to the screen by an electric cord that looked something like a tail. Engelbart named this device a mouse.

But it wasn't only the mouse that he demonstrated at the 1968 conference. Using a giant screen that was connected by microwave transmission to his ARC computer 40 miles away, Engelbart showed the audience how graphics could be generated and text manipulated using the mouse as a right-hand control and a five-key chord keyset for left-hand inputting. It was a stunning display of human and computer interaction, and it earned the scientist, who had often worked in isolation, a standing ovation from the audience. From that day on, Engelbart's peers firmly believed in the computer potentials that Engelbart had so long visualized.

I n Chapter 2, you learned that the CPU is the engine used to turn raw data into usable information quickly and efficiently. But how do you, as the user, get data into the computer for processing? In this chapter you'll learn the meaning of input, the purpose of input devices, be introduced to some important data entry concepts, and examine some of the more common input devices and their purposes.

Objective 3.1   Understand the term "input" and the purpose of an input device.

What Is Input and What Is an Input Device?

You'll see the term **input** commonly used in two ways. As a noun or adjective it refers to the data and instructions entered into a computer for processing. For example, "What input was used to produce this information?" As a verb it describes the act of entering data and instructions into a computer. This process is often referred to as **data entry.** For example, "Input these journal entries by two o'clock."

An **input device** is the hardware that transfers data and instructions into the computer for processing. The input is converted into a digital form the computer can use. There is a wide variety of input devices, many with specialized uses. You will be introduced to a number of them in this chapter.

Objective 3.2   Describe several ways to help control the data entry process and increase the accuracy of the data input.

How Can the Data Entry Process Be Controlled and Kept Accurate?

One of the biggest challenges for a business is to ensure that the data entered are correct. This is crucial because the data you input into the computer are the basis for the information produced. If incorrect data are entered and processed, the result will be incorrect output. This is referred to as "garbage in, garbage out." The data should be entered into the computer in a timely manner and at a reasonable cost.

Several steps can be taken to control the data entry process and improve the accuracy of data. These include the use of appropriate procedures, well-designed user interfaces and input forms, the type of data collection methods used, the type of data entry mode used, the use of internal program checks, and well-designed work environments and machines.

Procedures

One factor that influences the input process is the data entry procedures used. In a business environment these are dictated by management. The procedures, found in training manuals, indicate such things as what data are needed, where they should be obtained, who should obtain them, who should input them, when they should be input, the type of input device to use, the method of processing, and what to do if an error is detected in the data. Well-developed procedures and consistent use of the procedures help avoid problems in the data-entry process.

User Interfaces

The software being used has some control over the data-entry process. The software's **user interface** is that portion of a program with which a user interacts. It allows entry of commands and data required by a program, directs where to enter them, and informs about certain types of errors in the data entered. To make the input process easier and more efficient, user interface features should be consistent from one application to another and the on-screen layout of fields (designated areas for entering specific data) and the cursor movement among those fields should be logical. A **cursor** is an on-screen indicator, such as a blinking underline or rectangle, that shows where the next keystroke will appear when typed.

Input Forms

Imagine that your boss gave you a stack of papers in no particular order. The papers have names and numbers, but no headings indicating the meaning of those values. You were asked to input the data into the payroll program. Without any headings or formalized structure to the documents it would be difficult to input them. You couldn't be certain which numbers indicated regular hours, overtime hours, and so on.

To give the input precise meaning, simplify the input process, and decrease errors, input forms are used. An **input form** is a structured document in which spaces are reserved for specific information. The original document, in this case the employee timecard, on which data are recorded is called a **source document**. When the accuracy of data entered into a computer is in question the source document is used to verify it.

Even when well-conceived input forms are used human error can occur when transcribing the data to the computer. A **transcription error** occurs when the wrong characters are entered, for example, if the product number "8751" was mistakenly entered as "8750." Transcription errors are often detected and corrected manually by the person entering the data by matching the data entered with the source document. A **transposition error** is a type of transcription error that occurs when two characters are reversed, for example, if the product number "8751" is entered as "8571."

Data Collection Methods

Two basic ways to collect data are through transcriptive data entry and source data entry. In **transcriptive data entry,** data are collected at the source, or place of origin, by entering them on input forms (for example, handwritten or typed sales invoices). The data from the input form must be keyed into the computer later or be transcribed to another medium that can be input for processing at a later time.

In **source data entry,** the data (called source data) are collected and prepared at the source in a *machine-readable* form that can be used by a computer without a separate, intermediate data-transcription step. This method is commonly found at many retail checkouts. You may have seen a clerk use a scanning device to read information about your purchase directly from merchandise tags (Figure 3.1a). Scanners also interpret bar codes that are found on many products (Figure 3.1b).

Source data entry reduces the number of errors made during input because it eliminates the transcription process. Human error and carelessness can occur when people transcribe data onto a new document or directly into the computer. Studies have shown that approximately 85 percent of all the errors detected in data are due to transcription errors and only 15 percent actually occur in the source data.

Data Entry Modes

There are two basic modes of data entry; each is closely associated with a mode of processing data. The first is batch input and batch processing. The second is on-line input and interactive processing. Before these are discussed some terms will be defined.

Data can be entered using either an on-line or an off-line input device. A device is **on-line** if it is ready for use and can communicate with or be controlled by a computer. A device is **off-line** if it cannot communicate with or be controlled by a computer.

Batch input involves the collection of data for a specified period of time. The source documents are grouped into "batches," entered all at one time into the computer, and stored until they are to be processed.

A common example of batch input is the payroll timecard. The hours worked and possibly the projects worked on are entered on a timecard, the source document, for a specified period of time. Then the timecards are assembled in a batch and the data are entered into the computer and stored for later processing. **Batch processing** involves processing this group, or "batch," of data without user intervention.

On-line input involves the immediate capture and entry of data into the computer for processing. The input device used for data entry must be on-line. On-line input is associated with interactive processing. **Interactive processing** involves the user in a command and response mode with the computer in more or less continuous participation. A type of interactive processing often associated with business uses is called on-line real-time processing or transaction processing. A **transaction** is a discrete activity such as the entering of a customer order or the updating of an inventory file on a computer system. **On-line real-time processing** involves the immediate processing of data upon input to the computer. Order-entry systems and airline reservation systems typically use on-line input and on-line real-time processing. A computer system that uses on-line input does not have to process the data immediately. Some systems store the data and process them at scheduled intervals, for example every two hours or at the end of the day.

Programming Controls

Programs can be designed to perform **validity checking** to determine if the data are consistent and complete. A **consistency check** verifies if the data entered conform to certain formats, boundaries, and other parameters.

(a)

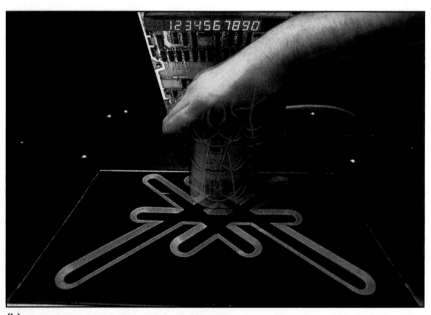

(b)
FIGURE 3.1
(a) A clerk uses a scanning device to read information about your purchase directly from merchandise tags. (b) Bar code scanners interpret bar codes that are found on many products.

For example, a program might check a value entered into a numeric field; if it contained any alphabetic characters, the program could inform you and allow you to reenter the data. A payroll program might check to see that data are within acceptable boundaries. For example, it might flag an entry of 800 hours worked during a two-week pay period or prevent the generation of a $1,000,000 payroll check. A **completeness check** determines if all the data are present. For example, if a program required the entry of a five-digit product code and four digits are entered, or if no entry is made, the program detects the error and allows the data to be reentered. Some programs require that critical data be keyed twice. If the entries match, they are assumed to be correct; if they don't, the error is brought to the user's attention.

Environmental Controls

One possible cause of errors is fatigue. Some companies have created a work environment that promotes comfort, efficiency, and safety through ergonomics. **Ergonomics** is the study of people in their work environments. It involves examining the physical characteristics of people and the way they function in relationship to the furnishings and machines at work. The results of such studies are used in **human engineering**, the design of furnishings and machines to meet the needs of people.

Objective 3.3   Know the purpose of a keyboard and describe its main features.

What Is a Keyboard?

Parts of Typical Keyboard

- Main keyboard
- Numeric keypad/cursor movement and editing keys
- Function keys

There are numerous devices used for input. The most common type of input device today is the keyboard.

The **keyboard** is an input device that resembles a typewriter keyboard. You press individual keys or combinations of keys to send data to the computer for processing. The data you type are usually viewed on the screen of a televisionlike device called a monitor. The keyboard will probably be your primary input device with either larger computers or microcomputers. Developing good keyboard skills is helpful to efficient computing. This discussion will address the commonly used IBM enhanced keyboard (Figure 3.2) and the Apple extended keyboard (Figure 3.3). The features discussed can usually be easily translated to most other keyboards. A typical keyboard is made up of several parts: the main keyboard, the numeric keypad/cursor movement and editing keys, and the function keys.

The Main Keyboard

The central portion of the main keyboard resembles a typewriter keyboard and contains the standard set of printable characters in what is called a QWERTY arrangement, named for the first six characters in the top row of letters. In addition to the printable characters Table 3.1 lists some other keys found here and their functions.

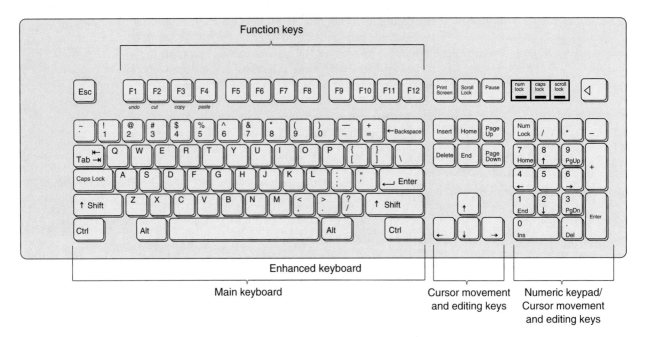

FIGURE 3.2
The IBM enhanced keyboard.

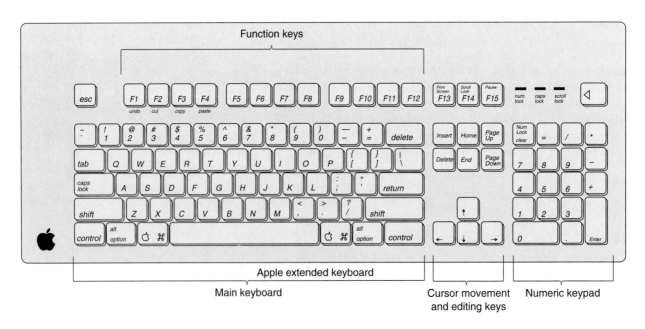

FIGURE 3.3
The Apple extended keyboard.

TABLE 3.1
Key Definitions

Keys found on both the IBM Enhanced Keyboard and the Apple Extended Keyboard:	
Shift keys	Used in combination with other keys to select commands and perform actions, notably to produce uppercase letters, but if the Shift key is used in combination with an alphabetic key when Caps Lock is on a lowercase letter will be typed.
Caps Lock	Shifts the alphabetic characters to uppercase. They remain uppercase until the Caps Lock key is pressed again. Does not affect numbers, punctuation marks, or other symbols.
Tab	Has a number of functions depending on the program. In programs such as word processors, it functions similarly to a typewriter's Tab key, indenting text. In other programs it might move the cursor from place to place, such as from field to field in a database management system.
Enter/Return	Found in the main portion of each keyboard. Called the Enter key on the IBM enhanced keyboard and the Return key on the Apple extended keyboard. Tells the operating system that a string of input is complete. Application programs use this key in a variety of ways. For example, a word processor program might use it to end a paragraph and a database management system program might use it to end a record and add that record to a database.
Enter	Found on the numeric keypad. Depending on the program this Enter key may function similarly or differently from the Enter/Return key on the main portion of the keyboard.
Esc	Its function depends on the program being run. On IBM enhanced keyboards it is typically used for functions such as going back one level in a menu structure, exiting a program, or canceling a function. Its primary purpose on the Apple extended keyboard is for compatibility when using a Macintosh to connect to a larger computer, or when the appropriate hardware or software is installed that allows a Macintosh to run programs designed for IBM and compatible computers.
Print Scrn	Sends a copy of the current screen contents to the printer on the IBM enhanced keyboard. On the Apple extended keyboard it is used primarily for compatibility when using a Macintosh to connect to a larger computer, or when the appropriate hardware or software is installed that allows a Macintosh to run programs designed for IBM and compatible computers.
Scroll Lock	Affects the use of the cursor movement keys, and depends on the application being used. Its name is a bit misleading. It suggests that pressing this key will stop text from scrolling, or moving, off the screen. This is true for some applications, but it is not always the case and depends on the program.
Pause	Temporarily stops the operation of a command or program.
Keys found only on the IBM Enhanced Keyboard:	
Alt (Alternate)	Used in combination with other keys to select commands and perform actions.
Ctrl	Used in combination with other keys to select commands and perform actions.
Backspace	Erases the character preceding the cursor.
Keys found only on the Apple Extended Keyboard:	
Command (Apple key)	Used in combination with other keys to select commands and perform actions.
Option (Alt key)	Used in combination with other keys to select commands and perform actions.
Control	Used in combination with other keys to select commands and perform actions.
Clear	Functions similarly to the Esc key on the IBM enhanced keyboard, typically clearing the current menu selection or deleting the current selection.

Numeric Keypad/Cursor Movement and Editing Keys

Many keyboards also contain a calculatorlike numeric keypad at one side to assist in data entry. The numbers on the keypad are arranged in the same type of pattern as on an adding machine or calculator, to allow individuals skilled in using these devices to enter numeric data quickly and efficiently.

On IBM enhanced keyboards some of the keys on the numeric keypad also perform cursor movement and editing functions. A toggle key called the Num Lock key is found at the upper left corner of the numeric keypad. This key switches between the numeric and the cursor movement/editing functions.

The cursor movement keys include left and right arrow keys that move the cursor one space left or right respectively, and up and down arrow keys that move the cursor one line up or down respectively. Also included are the Home, End, Page Up, and Page Down keys, which move the cursor to a position defined by the application software.

The editing keys include the Insert or Ins and the Delete or Del keys. The Insert key performs different functions depending on the application program. One of its most common uses is in text-editing applications to toggle between an insert mode where text is inserted and an overstrike mode where text is written over and thereby deleted. The Delete key also performs different functions depending on the application program. On the IBM enhanced keyboard the Delete key is commonly used to erase the character at the cursor. On the Apple extended keyboard the Delete key functions as a backspace key erasing the character preceding the onscreen cursor. The Delete key is also commonly used to erase highlighted text or graphics on both the IBM and Apple keyboards. On the IBM enhanced keyboard, the cursor movement and editing keys can also be found between the main part of the keyboard and the numeric keypad. On the Apple extended keyboard, that is the only place they are found.

Function Keys

Each keyboard contains a group of keys (numbered F1 through F12 on the IBM enhanced keyboard and F1 through F15 on the Apple extended keyboard) that are programmable keys. These are usually found along the top of the keyboard, but in older keyboards they are grouped at the left. Typically, the uses of the function keys are defined by an operating system or an application program. A common example is to call up the application program's help function. However, some programs allow the user to define a particular function.

Objective 3.4   Define pointing devices, touch screens, and speech recognition input devices and identify applications for which they are used.

What Are Some Other Devices for Input?

In addition to keyboards, many other devices are used for input. The most popular of these fall into a category called pointing devices. Others include touch screen and speech recognition.

Types of Pointing
Devices

- **Mouse**
- **Trackball**
- **Light pen**
- **Joystick**
- **Stylus (or pen)**
- **Puck**
- **Head position tracker**
- **Eye tracker**

Pointing Devices

A **pointing device** controls an on-screen cursor or creates drawings or graphical shapes. A pointing device is often used for actions such as choosing menu items, "pressing" on-screen "buttons" in dialog boxes, and selecting text or other values. Pointing devices include the mouse, trackball, light pen, joystick, stylus or pen, puck, and head position and eye trackers.

Mouse. A **mouse**, the most commonly used pointing device (Figure 3.4), is an excellent complement to the keyboard and is inexpensive and easy to use. The mouse was made popular by its inclusion as standard equipment with the Apple Macintosh. The current trend in the DOS, OS/2, and Unix operating systems toward graphical user interfaces has increased the popularity of the mouse. A graphical user interface is an operating environment that allows you to point to on-screen pictures and buttons rather than type commands. A mouse is a must for a graphical user interface.

A mouse is designed to be easily gripped in your hand and contains one or more buttons on the top which are used to select items and choose commands. Most are connected to the computer by a cable; however, a cordless mouse that uses infrared or radio-wave technologies is also available. On the underside of a mouse is a device that detects the direction and speed of its movement across a flat surface. This device is usually a ball that is rolled along the surface. When the mouse is moved, the rotation of the ball is translated into a digital signal that controls the movement of the cursor. This is called a **mechanical mouse**. The other basic type of mouse is an **optical mouse** that detects light reflected off a pad containing a precise set of grid lines to track the mouse's movements. An optical mouse is more precise in tracking a cursor across a screen and since there are no moving parts, it is more reliable. However, they are more expensive and most users don't require the precision they offer.

Trackball. A **trackball** is a pointing device that uses a sphere located on top that is rotated by hand to control cursor movement (Figure 3.5). In essence a trackball can be thought of as an upside-down mouse. Whereas the entire mouse is moved, a trackball is stationary and the ball is rotated by hand. A trackball may also contain one or more buttons to initiate other actions. Trackballs are suited for more precise movements than the mouse because of the user's fingertip control over the sphere. The growing use of laptop and notebook computers has spurred the development of minitrackballs that either attach easily to the side of these computers or are built into the keyboard. They allow control of the cursor as a mouse does.

Light Pen. The **light pen** is a pointing device that resembles a wand attached to the computer by a cable. It selects items or chooses commands (Figure 3.6). A light pen does not emit light. Rather, it contains sensors that send a signal back to the computer whenever they detect light. The entire screen is not lit at one time, even though it seems to be. The electron gun of a monitor scans the screen, lighting one screen position at a time. This happens so fast that to our eyes it appears that the screen is completely lit all the time. When light is detected, the computer determines the position of the electron beam at that time and ascertains the light pen's location on the screen. A light pen allows you to select precise points on the screen, but your arm may become tired from holding it up for long periods of time.

FIGURE 3.4
A mouse is a pointing device that is typically used to control an on-screen cursor.

FIGURE 3.5
Trackball.

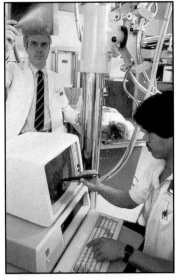

FIGURE 3.6
The light pen is a pointing device that uses a wand attached to the computer by a cable to select items or choose commands. An X-ray technician uses a light pen to enter data into a computer.

Joystick. A **joystick** is a pointing device that uses a lever to control the position of the cursor (Figure 3.7). It internally translates the position and speed of the lever into digital signals that are sent to the computer to control the cursor or other on-screen object. Joysticks usually have one or more buttons located on the base or stem that are used to control various software features. Most people are familiar with the joystick as a device used to play video games. They are also used by individuals who are physically unable to use other input devices.

Graphics Tablet/Stylus/Puck. A **graphics tablet** (also called a digitizing tablet) consists of a flat plastic rectangle that contains electronic circuitry below its surface to detect when an object makes contact with the tablet. The graphics tablet is used in conjunction with pointing devices such as the stylus and the puck. When a pointing device is moved across the graphics tablet its position is detected and converted to a digital signal to control the cursor's movement.

The **stylus** (also called a pen) is a pointing device that can be used with a graphics tablet. It is pressed against the graphics tablet to draw or point. Some graphics tablets have special areas where the stylus can be touched to select commands or items. A stylus also typically has a button it uses for selecting commands or items. The stylus is usually connected to the graphics tablet by a cord although cordless models exist. Using a stylus offers a great deal of manual control and closely resembles freehand drawing. For this reason it is often preferred by artists for illustrations.

A **puck** is a pointing device that is often used with a graphics tablet (Figure 3.8). It has a mouselike shape with buttons for selecting items or choosing commands. In addition, there is a clear plastic piece with crosshairs printed on it that extends out from the body. The place where these crosshairs intersect points to a specific location on the tablet. That location is mapped to a specific location on the screen. Because the cross hairs lie on a clear plastic piece drawings can be placed on the tablet and traced to enter them into the computer easily. Pucks are popular with engineers and architects.

Stylus/Pen-Based Computers. A pen-based computer uses a stylus as the primary input device (Figure 3.9). These computers do not use keyboards as standard equipment. When the pen is pressed against the computer screen a small electric current is generated. Special software interprets the pen strokes. Pen-based systems are designed to read handwriting and make the input process easier and more intuitive to the user. Currently they are being used by people such as inspectors, inventory takers, poll takers, police officers, and rail workers. Former noncomputer users easily use a stylus to check boxes or fill in blanks on computer-displayed forms that are nearly identical to the paper forms they traditionally used. The data can be stored and later transferred to other computers for processing.

Head Position and Eye Trackers. Although not common devices to the average user, head position and eye trackers can open up the world of computers to those who cannot use other input devices because of physical limitations.

Head position trackers use a headset that emulates a mouse. A control unit that sits on top of the computer measures the change in the

FIGURE 3.8
This engineer is using a puck to help design a new textile plant.

FIGURE 3.7
A joystick is a pointing device that uses a lever to control the position of the cursor.

FIGURE 3.9
A pen-based computer uses a stylus as the primary input device.

headset's angular position and translates this change into cursor movements. The headset also contains an attached mouth tube into which the user can lightly puff to select an item, such as a letter to be entered into a word processing document from a keyboard that is displayed on the screen.

Eye trackers use video cameras to track the position of the eye's pupils. These data are then translated into screen coordinates. Thus, the eye can focus and select items on the screen.

Touch Screens

A **touch screen** recognizes the location of a contact on the screen (Figure 3.10) through a built-in grid of sensing lines or a grid of infrared beams and sensors.

Many applications, such as automatic teller machines (ATMs) and information kiosks, make use of touch screens because they offer an easy and intuitive way for users to interact with the computer. They also are very durable and stand up well to use by numerous individuals since there are no moving parts involved.

Touch screens have not been popular with personal computer users. Their low resolution prevents users from pinpointing a specific place on the screen, thus limiting their uses. A user's hand can also become tired after being held in midair pointing at the screen.

Speech Recognition

Probably the easiest way for you to input commands and data into a computer would be to speak them. The ability of a computer to accept input by understanding the speech of a user is called **speech recognition**

FIGURE 3.10
Touch screens allow users to make selections by simply touching the screen.

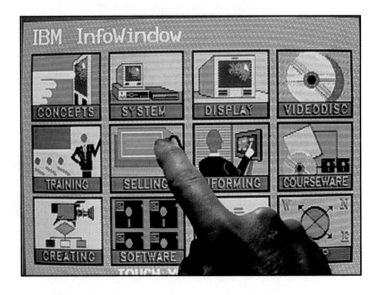

FIGURE 3.11
The IBM Voicetype voice recognition system allows commands and text to be entered by speaking.

or **voice recognition**. Many people who do a great deal of writing have dreamed of the day when the computer can easily and accurately convert speech to text.

Currently, systems exist that can recognize limited vocabularies spoken by specific individuals. However, developing a system that can recognize the variety of speech patterns and accents that exist and the numerous ways in which particular statements or requests can be made still poses some significant problems for designers. Applications that require intensive use of the hands or eyes for which a computer might be used are benefiting from speech recognition. For example, physicians performing surgery could receive information from the computer by simply asking for it. Speech recognition input is also valuable for individuals who have lost some or all of their eyesight or functional use of their hands (Figure 3.11).

Objective 3.5   Identify and describe three special-purpose input devices.

What Are Special-Purpose Input Devices?

Many input devices are designed to be general-purpose input devices, allowing for their use in a wide variety of applications. Some have been designed to accomplish specific tasks.

Special-Purpose Input Devices

- **Magnetic-ink character reader**
- **Magnetic strip reader**
- **Hand-tracking device**

Magnetic-Ink Character Recognition

Magnetic-ink character recognition (MICR) is the method by which a computer recognizes characters written in a special magnetic ink. The computer first determines the shape of the character by sensing the magnetic charge in the ink. The shapes, which can also be read by humans, are then matched to a stored set of character shapes and converted into computer text. You may have noticed a line of numbers and some

INPUT   **95**

Remember the Revolutionary War shot heard 'round the world? Today a process that translates speech from one language into two other languages is the technology that will literally be "heard" 'round the world. In 1993 in a demonstration an American confirmed his registration for a conference in Munich. That may not be particularly remarkable, but the stateside researcher spoke in English to his computer at Carnegie Mellon in Pittsburgh and thus directly to the researcher in Germany who received the message translated into German.

ATR Interpreting Telephone Laboratories in Kyoto, Japan; Siemens AG and Karlsruhe University in Germany; and Carnegie Mellon University in Pittsburgh have combined forces in the development of a speech-to-speech computerized translation system. The system must recognize the voice of someone inputting data, then translate the message into two other languages (for now they are German and Japanese), and finally synthesize the voice back into understandable speech in the receiving country.

The 2½ second sentence in the example above took approximately 20 seconds before it was received, including translation and time to transmit it overseas. With computer speeds measured in nanoseconds this delay is considered practically an eternity.

The system has a limited vocabulary of approximately 500 words, but terminology can be added relatively easily. However, teaching a computer the nuances of language is another challenge. Alex Waibel of Carnegie Mellon gives this example. If you ask the computer to "Give me a new display," that message is acoustically comparable to "Give me a nudist play."

Although we can't hear the bugs in the system, it seems there could be some misinterpretation.

odd-shaped characters on the bottom of your personal checks. These magnetic-ink characters are bank-processing symbols that represent the check number, customer account number, and bank identification number (Figure 3.12). When the bank receives the check, it also prints the amount of the check in magnetic ink. An input device called an MICR reader interprets the magnetic characters and sends the information to a computer to update the appropriate accounts. In some cases, the checks are sorted afterwards. Magnetic ink is used on documents such as bank checks and credit card slips because the MICR reader can read the magnetic characters no matter how much a user might have written over them.

Magnetic Strips

Magnetic strips are thin bands of magnetically encoded data found on the backs of many credit cards and automated teller cards. The data stored on a card vary from one application to another, but they often include account numbers or special access codes. For example, magnetic strip cards are used to limit access to high-security areas. To enter a secured area, a person

FIGURE 3.12
These magnetic-ink characters are bank-processing symbols. They represent the check number, customer account number, and bank identification number. Banks use magnetic-ink characters on checks to ensure fast and efficient processing.

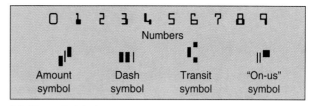

(a) Magnetic-ink character set

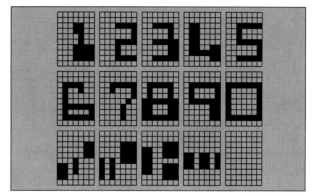

(b) Matrix patterns for magnetic-ink characters

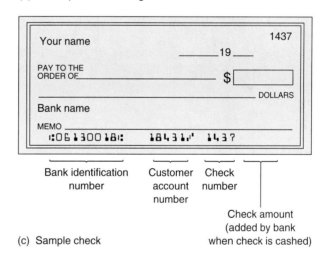

(c) Sample check

inserts the card into a computerized read device. If the card contains the right code, the door automatically opens. Because no one can see or interpret the data by simply looking at the card, the data can be highly sensitive or personal.

Hand-Tracking Devices

A **hand-tracking device** is a special-purpose input device that converts the movements of a hand into digital signals. These signals are sent to the computer and can be used to control various functions such as the

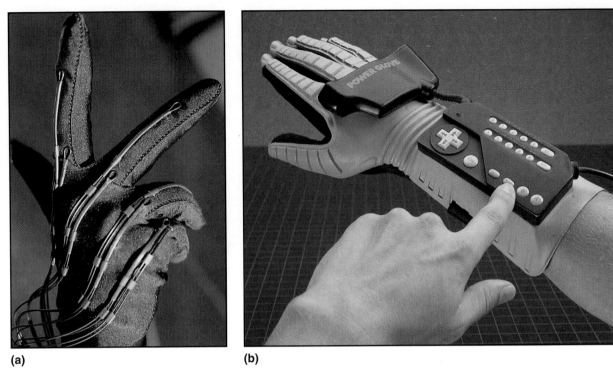

FIGURE 3.13
(a) Original DataGlove showing fiber-optic sensors. (b) Mattel Power Glove, a hand-tracker with programmable keyboard used with Nintendo game.

movement of a graphically produced hand displayed on the screen. A computer program can interpret these hand movements, which can be used, for example, to throw a graphically produced ball on the screen with the same arc, distance, and speed that a real ball would have been thrown. One of the better known hand trackers is the DataGlove developed by VPL Research in California. Applications for this technology are still being studied. Some video game manufacturers such as Mattel have adapted the hand tracker for use with their products (Figure 3.13). Developments such as this may lead to the use of computers in yet undreamed-of applications.

Objective 3.6   Define optical recognition and describe three methods and devices used to accomplish it.

What Is Optical Recognition?

Optical recognition is the process of using light-sensing equipment to scan paper or other sources and translate the pattern of light and dark, or in some cases color, into a digital signal that can be used by the computer. Optical recognition does not rely on the magnetic quality of the image, as MICR does. The three types of optical recognition described here are (1) optical-mark recognition, (2) optical-bar recognition, and (3) optical scanners.

Optical-Mark Recognition

Optical-mark recognition (OMR) employs mark sensing, one of the simplest forms of optical recognition, to scan and translate the locations of a series of pen or pencil marks into computer-readable form. A common use of OMR is to score test results. For example, answers to multiple-choice questions can be marked in pencil on a form. An input device called an optical-mark reader scans the form and identifies the *positions of the marks,* rather than the shapes, to score the test.

Optical-Bar Recognition

Optical-bar recognition (OBR) involves the scanning and translating of a bar code into digital signals to be used by a computer. A **bar code** is composed of a set of vertical lines of varying widths and may also include numbers and letters (Figure 3.14). OBR is designed to be a fast, error-free method of input. An input device called an optical-bar reader scans and interprets the pattern of lines printed on products.

The use of bar codes on products has given businesses faster and more accurate checkout procedures and better inventory control. The most common bar coding scheme is the Universal Product Code (UPC). Department and grocery stores have long used optical-bar recognition. However, the bar code on a product does not contain the price of the item; the price is actually stored in the computer, where the dollar amount can be easily reprogrammed to reflect sales prices or special offers. When a bar code reader passes over the bar code, the price and product are matched by the computer. Other stores, factories, and manufacturing operations use bar codes to provide more efficient, cost-effective control of inventory. The Defense Department and the automotive industry now use bar codes on materials and parts so that they can track these items automatically as they move through the manufacturing and distribution cycle. The U.S. Postal Service encourages businesses to encode their mail with a bar code that

FIGURE 3.14
A bar code is a special code composed of a set of vertical lines of varying widths and may also include numbers and letters.

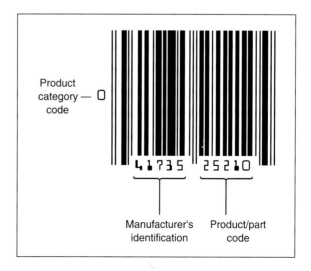

Product category — 0 code

Manufacturer's identification

Product/part code

FIGURE 3.15
Flatbed scanners resemble a photocopier.

identifies the nine-digit zip code. Discounts are offered on bulk mailings that are so encoded. The bar codes allow the mail to be automatically sorted.

Optical Scanners

An **optical scanner**, often simply called a scanner, is an input device that uses light to sense the patterns of black and white (or color) on paper or other medium and convert them into a digital signal that can be manipulated by graphical software or optical character recognition (OCR) software. Color scanners are available, although they are more expensive and require more computer memory to store the image and all the color information that goes with it.

The scanning process begins by shining a light on the material to be scanned. White areas reflect the light and black areas absorb it. The amount of light that the page absorbs or reflects helps determine what is on the page. The scanner contains a device called a charged couple device (CCD) that converts the light into digital signals.

The quality of a scanned image is determined by the number of dots per inch that the scanner can perceive. This is referred to as the resolution. The higher the dots per inch (dpi), the better the quality of the image. Scanners typically range between 50 and 300 dpi.

The scanner produces an image that can be stored on disk. Graphical software allows the display and manipulation of the image (light and dark, or color patterns) sensed by the optical scanner. These graphical images can be saved, manipulated, and incorporated into other programs.

Suppose you wanted to edit the text you just scanned. You can't because what you've scanned is an image of the text and not real text. In order to convert the image to actual text characters you need to use optical-character recognition software (OCR). The optical scanner determines the character's shape. **Optical-character recognition (OCR) software** translates these images into text files that can be used by programs capable of manipulating text.

Scanners are available in two basic types: **flatbed scanners** and **handheld scanners**. Flatbed scanners resemble photocopy machines (Figure 3.15) and are the best choice if you need to scan full-page

FIGURE 3.16
Handheld scanners are very popular. They are held in the user's hand and passed over the document.

Highlight

3.2

The Phoenix: Preserving the Past for the Future

A fire in Los Angeles destroyed over $5.5 millon worth of rare, original documents leaving them in ashes, according to Professor Robert D. Howell. Efforts are being made to protect existing documents, such as Benjamin Franklin's first issue of *Poor Richard's Almanac* and Mozart's original scores, so they don't suffer the same fate and become lost forever. Howell is director of the Department of Art and Design Multimedia Research Project at California Polytechnic University and the leader of the Phoenix Project. The Phoenix Project preserves documents by scanning them and storing the images on compact disks. Having these documents on compact disk means scholars and researchers can study them as much as they want without risking damage to the documents.

The first works scanned included images and text on astronomy that are part of the Huntington Library's permanent collection. Original manuscripts, sketches, and drawings by such noted scientists and astronomers as Copernicus, Galileo, Newton, Descartes, Halley, Hubble, and Einstein were among those scanned. Phoenix preserves a record of these documents and provides students with hands-on experience in the field of image digitizing and categorization. The project team works to discover the best methods of scanning and organizing many different types of information including CAD/CAE drawings, musical scores, literary manuscripts, and artistic masterpieces.

Currently Phoenix is funded and supported by industry, but in the future, the project plans to seek grant funding as well. However, the goal of the project continues to be the preservation of all irreplaceable documents since they, unlike the mythical phoenix bird, cannot be resurrected from the ashes.

documents. Many have sheet feeders that allow you to scan multiple pages automatically. Flatbed scanners take up more desk space and are more expensive than handheld scanners. Handheld scanners are best suited for scanning smaller images such as photos (Figure 3.16). One disadvantage of a handheld scanner is that it relies on the user's arm movements, thus moving the scanner too fast or in a crooked manner across an image results in distortion of the scanned image. Some handheld scanners have a speed indicator light and many also supply scanning guides to get a straight scan.

Summary

Input refers to the data and instructions entered into a computer for processing or to the act of entering data, which is often called data entry. Input devices transfer data and instructions to the computer.

It is important that data being input into the computer be accurate because they are the basis for producing the output generated.

The data entry process benefits from well-developed and consistently used procedures. Consistent and logical user interface design can help ensure efficient and accurate data entry. Structured documents called input forms are used to make data meaningful for input. The original document on which data are stored is called a source document. A source document is a valuable tool for identifying transcription errors that occur when the wrong characters are entered. A transposition error is a type of transcription error that occurs when two characters are reversed.

Data are collected through either a transcriptive data entry process or a source data entry process. Source data entry reduces the number of errors by eliminating the human error factor and carelessness often associated with the transcriptive process.

On-line refers to a device that is ready for use and is capable of communicating with and being controlled by a computer. Off-line refers to a device that cannot communicate with or be controlled by a computer. The two basic modes of data entry and their associated processing modes are batch input and batch processing, and on-line input and interactive processing. Batch input involves the collection of data on input forms for a specified period of time, grouping the documents into batches, and entering them at one time into the computer for storage until they are to be processed. Batch processing involves processing this batch of data without user intervention. On-line input involves the immediate capture and entry of data into the computer for processing. Interactive processing involves the more or less continuous participation of the user with the computer in a command and response mode. On-line real-time processing involves the immediate processing of data upon input to the computer.

Data accuracy can be improved by programs that perform validity checking to ensure the data are consistent and complete. A consistency check determines if the data entered conform to certain formats, boundaries, and other parameters. A completeness check is used to determine if all the data required are present.

Another way to reduce errors is to provide work environments that are comfortable, efficient, and safe through the use of ergonomics and human engineering.

The most commonly used input device for modern-day computers is the keyboard. It is important to develop good keyboard skills for efficient use of the computer. Most keyboards are divided into several parts; the main keyboard, the numeric keypad/cursor movement and editing keys, and the function keys.

Pointing input devices control an on-screen cursor or create drawings and graphical images. Pointing devices include the mouse, trackball, light pen, joystick, stylus and puck used with a graphics tablet, stylus used with pen-based computers, and head position and eye trackers.

A touch screen is an input device that can detect where a computer screen is touched and use this information to initiate an action.

Speech recognition, or voice recognition, is the ability of a computer to accept input by understanding the speech of a user. It is beneficial for any application that requires intensive use of the hands or eyes for which a computer might be used and is also valuable for individuals who have lost their eyesight or functional use of their hands.

Some input devices are designed for special purposes. These include the MICR reader used for magnetic ink character recognition, magnetic strips used to encode data on cards, and hand tracking devices used to digitize the movements of a hand to control computer operations.

Optical recognition is the process of using light-sensing equipment to scan paper and other media, and translate the patterns of light and dark (or color) into a digital signal for the computer. Optical recognition devices include the optical-mark reader for optical-mark recognition (OMR), the optical-bar reader for optical-bar recognition (OBR), and optical scanners used in combination with graphical software or optical-character recognition (OCR) software. Optical scanners are either flatbed scanners or handheld scanners.

VOCABULARY SELF-TEST

Can you define the following terms?

bar code (p. 99)

batch input (p. 85)

batch processing (p. 85)

completeness check (p. 87)

consistency check (p. 85)

cursor (p. 84)

data entry (p. 83)

ergonomics (p. 87)

eye trackers (p. 94)

flatbed scanner (p. 100)

graphics tablet (p. 92)

handheld scanner (p. 100)

hand-tracking device (p. 97)

head position trackers (p. 92)

human engineering (p. 87)

input (p. 83)

input device (p. 83)

input form (p. 84)

interactive processing (p. 85)

joystick (p. 92)

keyboard (p. 87)

light pen (p. 91)

magnetic-ink character recognition (MICR) (p. 95)

magnetic strips (p. 96)

mechanical mouse (p. 91)

mouse (p. 91)

off-line (p. 85)

on-line (p. 85)

on-line input (p. 85)

on-line real-time processing (p. 85)

optical-bar recognition (OBR) (p. 99)

optical-character recognition (OCR) software (p. 100)

optical-mark recognition (OMR) (p. 99)

optical mouse (p. 91)

optical recognition (p. 98)

optical scanner (p. 100)

pointing device (p. 91)

puck (p. 92)

source data entry (p. 84)

source document (p. 84)

speech recognition (p. 94)

stylus (p. 92)

touch screen (p. 94)

trackball (p. 91)

transaction (p. 85)

transcription error (p. 84)

transcriptive data entry (p. 84)

transposition error (p. 84)

user interface (p. 84)

validity checking (p. 85)

voice recognition (p. 95)

Multiple Choice

1. A(n) _____ is used to structure data for input to give them precise meaning.
   a. input device
   b. pointing device
   c. input form
   d. user interface

2. _____ is a data collection method that involves manually writing data on input forms that must later be keyed into the computer or converted to a machine-readable form to be input into the computer.
   a. Real-time data entry
   b. On-line data entry
   c. Source data entry
   d. Transcriptive data entry

3. A device that is ready for use and can communicate with and be controlled by a computer is _____.
   a. on-line
   b. an input device
   c. a real-time device
   d. off-line

4. _____ involves accumulating and storing data for processing at a later time without user intervention.
   a. Batch input
   b. Batch processing
   c. On-line input
   d. On-line real-time processing

5. Which of the following input devices is the most common device used for input?
   a. keyboard
   b. joystick
   c. trackball
   d. mouse

6. The special symbol or character that indicates a user's position on the screen is the _____.
   a. mouse
   b. digitizer
   c. cursor
   d. monitor

7. A(n) _____ is a type of input device used to control an on-screen cursor or to create drawings or graphical shapes.
   a. touch screen
   b. keyboard
   c. pointing device
   d. cursor

8. A(n) _____ is a pointing device that fits in your hand and is rolled along a flat surface to control an on-screen cursor.
   a. trackball
   b. joystick

    c. stylus

    d. mouse

9. One of the most complex input techniques, in which a user speaks into a microphone, is called _____.

    a. speech recognition

    b. voice output

    c. voice coding

    d. voice synthesis

10. An input device called a(n) _____ can be used to translate printed text into computer text.

    a. optical-bar reader

    b. optical-mark reader

    c. MICR reader

    d. optical scanner

Fill-In

1. A(n) _____ transfers data and instructions to the computer for processing.

2. A(n) _____ occurs when the wrong characters are mistakenly entered during the input process.

3. In _____, data are prepared at the source in a machine-readable form that can be used by a computer without a separate, intermediate data-transcription step.

4. _____ is a type of interactive processing in which transactions are input using an on-line input device and executed immediately after being received by the computer.

5. A(n) _____ is a pointing device that uses a sphere located on top that is rotated by hand to control cursor movement.

6. A(n) _____ is a pointing device that uses a lever to control the position of the cursor.

7. _____ and _____ are pointing devices that enable individuals with motor disabilities to use a computer.

8. A(n) _____ is an input device that can recognize the location of a touch on the screen.

9. _____ is the process of using light-sensing equipment to scan paper or other sources and translate the pattern of light and dark, or in some cases color, into a digital signal that can be used by the computer.

10. After an optical scanner recognizes the shape of characters, _____ is needed to translate these images into text files that can be used by programs capable of manipulating text.

Short Answer

1. Distinguish the meanings of the term "input" and describe the purpose of an input device.

2. Why is it important that the data entered into a computer be accurate?

3. Why is validity checking important? Describe the difference between a consistency check and a completeness check.

4. Differentiate between batch data entry and on-line data entry and their associated processing modes.
5. Describe ergonomics and human engineering and discuss how you think they can increase the accuracy of the data entered into a computer.
6. What are the main features of a keyboard?
7. Define pointing device and describe several devices that fit this category.
8. Give examples of situations in which speech recognition would be a valuable input method.
9. List and describe three special-purpose input devices.
10. What is meant by optical recognition? Describe three types of optical recognition.

Issues for Thought

1. Credit bureaus gather and enter a wealth of data about individuals and assign a credit rating based on these data. Do you feel it is important for you to be able to access and verify this data? Should you be informed when an organization receives and uses it to make a decision regarding your credit worthiness? Why or why not?
2. Optical scanners have made it relatively easy for individuals to digitize and incorporate text and graphics from nearly any source into their documents. From an ethical standpoint, what limits do you think should be placed on scanning and using preexisting text and graphics in your own materials without permission? Explain your position.

MS-DOS 6.0 Primer

Infomodule

WHAT IS MS-DOS?

Every computer requires an operating system to start and manage its operations. An operating system can be thought of as a "behind the scenes" manager. When the computer is first turned on, the operating system must be loaded into the computer's memory. Once it has been loaded, it takes care of all the details of performing requested tasks such as managing the attached peripheral devices (printers, keyboards, disk drives, monitors, modems) and running other system and application programs. **Microsoft Disk Operating System (MS-DOS)** is the most commonly used operating system for IBM and compatible microcomputers.

MS-DOS has gone through a number of versions to keep up with changing technology and to correct bugs, or errors, that occurred. Major changes are indicated by a change in version number, from 3.0 to 4.0 or 5.0. Minor changes or bug fixes are indicated by changes after the decimal point, for example, 3.01, 3.3, and 4.1. New versions have been designed to be upwardly compatible, which means that commands that work with older versions will also work with the new ones. Of course, newer versions usually contain new commands not previously available and some old commands may have enhanced features. We've used MS-DOS version 6 in developing this Infomodule.

HOW DO INTERNAL AND EXTERNAL COMMANDS DIFFER?

MS-DOS commands are actually small programs that instruct the computer to perform certain operations. There are two types of commands: internal and external. Each time MS-DOS is started, the file COMMAND.COM is stored in main memory. **Internal**

commands are part of the COMMAND.COM file. Because internal commands are stored in main memory they execute immediately after you type them and press Enter. **External commands** are in separate files stored on a hard disk or diskette. When you enter an external command the operating system must first access the disk containing the file and load it into main memory.

WHAT IS THE MS-DOS COMMAND PROMPT?

The **MS-DOS command prompt** indicates the current drive and consists of the current drive letter and the symbol >. The **current drive** is the drive on which DOS will put any files or search for any filenames or commands you type unless it is instructed to look elsewhere. For example, the MS-DOS command prompt C> means the current, or default, drive is drive C.

If at any MS-DOS command prompt you want to change the current drive, simply type the new drive name (letter of the new drive followed by a colon) and press Enter. For example, to change the current drive from C to A make sure drive A contains a diskette and at the prompt C>, type A: and press Enter. The new default drive is now drive A, and the MS-DOS command prompt is now A>.

HOW DO I START DOS?

The process of starting the computer and loading the operating system into main memory is called *booting* the system. We will assume the hard disk has been prepared and contains the system files necessary to boot MS-DOS.

After you turn on the computer it first performs some internal tests, and after a few moments checks drive A to see if it contains a diskette. If drive A contains a diskette when the computer is started, the system searches for the operating system on drive A. If the diskette in drive A contains MS-DOS, it will be loaded; but, if it does not, the following message will be displayed:

```
Non-System disk or disk error
Replace and strike any key when
ready
```

If there is no diskette in drive A the computer reads from the hard disk (usually drive C). When the MS-DOS command prompt C> appears on the screen, the system is booted and ready to execute a program or receive an MS-DOS command at the prompt.

WHAT ARE FILENAMES AND FILENAME EXTENSIONS?

Data, text, and programs used by MS-DOS are stored in files on either a floppy diskette or a hard disk. Each file must be identified by a unique name, which may consist of two parts: a filename and a filename extension.

A **filename** is a name given to a file to indicate the contents and to distinguish it from other files. It can be from one to eight characters long and may consist of numbers, letters, and the special characters underscore (_), caret (^), dollar sign ($), tilde (˜), exclamation point (!), number sign (#), percent sign (%), ampersand (&), hyphen (-), braces ({}), at sign (@), single quotation mark ('), apostrophe ('), and parentheses ( ). Examples of valid filenames are June, CHAPTER1, and TAXES_Q1. You can type a filename in either uppercase or lowercase, but spaces cannot be used between characters.

A **filename extension** identifies a file's type. It is optional and can be from one to three characters long. Characters that are valid for a filename are also valid for a filename extension. An extension may be typed in uppercase or lowercase. It is separated from the filename by a period (.).

MS-DOS gives special meaning to a few filename extensions. These include: EXE, COM, BAT, SYS, and

BAK. The EXE and COM extensions indicate files that can be executed by typing in their name and pressing Enter. The BAT extension indicates a batch file. Batch files are discussed later. The SYS extension indicates a system file that can only be used by MS-DOS. The BAK extension indicates a backup file, which is a copy of an original file. Do not choose these extensions when naming your files.

Wildcards may also be used in filenames and filename extensions. A **wildcard** is an MS-DOS character that can represent a character or characters. The wildcard ? represents one character in its position in the filename. The wildcard * stands for one or more characters in the filename. Wildcards may be used with most MS-DOS commands where filenames or extensions are entered.

WHAT ARE DIRECTORIES AND PATHS?

A **directory** holds files and lets you organize them into convenient groups so they can be easily located on disk. The main directory, or "root" directory, is created when you format a hard disk or diskette. Additional directories (subdirectories to the root directory) can also be created. A **subdirectory** is a directory within another directory. Subdirectories can also have subdirectories.

A multilevel directory structure can be viewed as an upside-down family tree. Figure 1 shows an example of a multilevel directory structure. The root directory is at the top. Under the root are two directories (subdirectories to the root): WORD, for a subdirectory containing a word processor, and SS, for a subdirectory containing a spreadsheet. Under the WORD directory are two directories (subdirectories to the WORD directory): LETTERS and REPORTS to organize files created with the word processor. Under the SS directory is the directory EXPENSES (a subdirectory to the SS directory) for spreadsheet files detailing expenses.

Each directory holds numerous files and subdirectories. The same rules apply for naming directories as for naming files. The directory that you are in at any time is called the current directory, or working directory. Any operations or commands you give to MS-

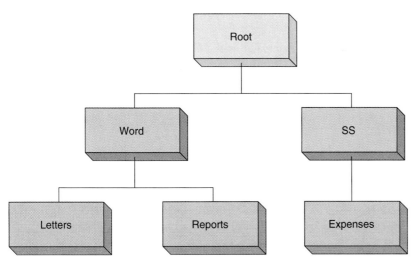

FIGURE 1
A multilevel directory structure.

DOS affect only the current directory unless you specify otherwise. When the root directory is the only directory, any operations or commands that you give affect the entire diskette or hard disk.

In a multilevel directory structure, you can move from the root directory downward along any branch of the structure, or move downward from the directory you are in to a directory below it on the same branch. However, to move to a directory that is in another branch of the directory structure, you must first move up to the root, and then move downward.

If you do not specify a particular directory when you want MS-DOS to find a file, only the current directory will be searched. However, MS-DOS can find files in other directories if you designate a **path** that tells MS-DOS where you want it to look for a file. A path can consist of a drive name, directory names, and the name of the file you want to find. If a sequence of directory names is needed, each is separated by a backslash character (\). For example, look at Figure 1. Suppose you are currently in the REPORTS directory and you want to load your word processor called WP.EXE contained in the WORD directory. At the system prompt you could enter the

path \WORD followed by another backslash and the name of the file you wish to execute, as follows:

```
C>\WORD\WP
```

When a path begins with a backslash character (\), as in this example, MS-DOS begins the search at the root directory; otherwise, it begins at the current directory and searches downward. When a path begins with a drive name MS-DOS looks for the file or command on the specified drive. For example,

```
A>COPY C:\EXPENSES\HOUSE\MORTGAGE.REP
```

will copy the file MORTGAGE.REP, located two levels below the root directory on drive C, to drive A. (The COPY command is described in detail later.)

WHAT IS THE AUTOEXEC.BAT FILE?

What is a batch file? You may need to perform the same sequence of commands numerous times. To do this quickly and easily you can create and use a batch file. A **batch file** contains a series of MS-DOS commands that when executed automatically performs all those commands as if each were typed and executed individually.

Batch files can contain any valid command and be of any length. A batch filename follows the same rules as any other filename; however, the filename extension must be BAT. Batch files can be created using a text editor such as the MS-DOS editor or a word processor and then saving the file in text (ASCII) format.

To execute a batch file, simply type its filename. You do not have to type the .BAT extension. The batch file must be in the default directory unless a path is designated. You can interrupt the execution by pressing Ctrl-Break.

An AUTOEXEC.BAT file is a batch file that is automatically executed when you boot your computer. MS-DOS looks for this file first and executes it if it exists. You create this file like any other batch file except that you name it AUTOEXEC.BAT.

We'll look at four commands, PATH, PROMPT, DATE, and TIME, that are often included in an AUTOEXEC.BAT file.

The PATH Command

The PATH command is used to search a specified directory or list of directories for executable files that were not found by a search of the current directory. You can specify a drive, directory, and any subdirectories to search, but the current directory is always searched first. The maximum length of the PATH command is 127 characters. Look at Figure 1. Suppose your word processor is located in the WP directory and you are currently in the EXPENSES directory. If you typed the command that executes the word processor, MS-DOS would return the message:

```
File not found
```

If you had designated the following PATH command,

```
PATH C:\WP
```

MS-DOS would find the word processor and load it.

To specify multiple directories in a PATH command, separate entries with a semicolon (;), for example:

```
PATH C:\WP;C:\SS
```

If the PATH command is executed without any parameters it displays the current search path. If a semicolon is the only parameter then it clears all search-path settings and specifies that only the current directory is to be searched.

A PATH command is really useful if it is put into an AUTOEXEC.BAT file where it is automatically executed each time you boot your computer. You can then execute any executable file whose path is in the PATH command from any directory by simply typing the command used to load it. If the program is not in the current directory MS-DOS searches the directories listed in the PATH command to find and load it.

The PROMPT Command

The PROMPT command lets you change the MS-DOS prompt text to anything you wish. For example, entering

```
PROMPT Get to work
```

causes the words "Get to work" to appear as the prompt. MS-DOS also provides some character combinations for use with the PROMPT command. Below are brief descriptions of the text or information that they add to your command prompt.

```
$Q    = (equal sign)
$$    $ (dollar sign)
$T    Current time
$D    Current date
$P    Current drive and path
$V    MS-DOS version number
$N    Current drive
$G    > (greater-than sign)
$L    < (less-than sign)
$B    : (pipe)
$_    ENTER-LINEFEED
$E    ASCII escape code (code 27)
$H    Backspace (to delete a character
      that has been written to the
      prompt command line)
```

You can reset the prompt to the system default (the current drive letter followed by a greater-than sign) by entering the PROMPT command without any parameters.

A common use for the PROMPT command is to show the current drive and path followed by the greater-than sign (>). This is very helpful when you have multiple directories and must keep track of where you are in the system. To change the prompt to reflect the current drive and path type PROMPT pg at the system prompt and press Enter. The $p represents the current drive and path and $g represents the symbol >. After the command is executed the prompt for the root directory of the diskette in drive A will be displayed as A:\>, the prompt for the root directory of drive C will be displayed as C:\>, and the prompt for the directory COLOR (a subdirectory of the root directory) on drive C would appear as C:\COLOR>. The PROMPT pg command must be typed each time the system is turned on if you want to display the current drive and path. To automatically execute the PROMPT pg command (or any other version of this command) you can add it to your AUTOEXEC.BAT file. Then every time you boot your computer the PROMPT command will be automatically executed.

The DATE and TIME Commands

To change the system date or time, use the DATE and TIME commands. Type DATE at the system prompt and press Enter. The following message is displayed:

```
Current date is Day xx-xx-xxxx
Enter new date (mm-dd-yy):
```

Enter a new date using the format of mm-dd-yy (for example, 01–23–94) or mm-dd-yyyy (01–23–1994) and press Enter. Or, press Enter to accept the default entry if the date is already correct. A **default entry** is a value that the computer uses if you don't supply another value. In this case, the default entry is displayed on the screen following the message "Current date is."

To enter the time type TIME and press Enter. The following message appears:

```
Current time is xx:xx:xx.xx
Enter new time:
```

Enter a new time using the 24-hour format (you only need to enter hours; however, entering minutes is

recommended for precision) and press Enter. Or, press Enter to accept the default entry if the time is already correct.

To update the date and time each time you turn on your computer, place these commands in your AUTOEXEC.BAT file.

WHAT IS THE CONFIG.SYS FILE FOR?

The CONFIG.SYS file is a text file (that is, a file containing only the letters, numerals, and special characters contained in the ASCII code). These commands configure your computer's hardware so that they can be used by MS-DOS and application programs. MS-DOS executes the commands in the CONFIG.SYS file every time you start your computer. Three commands commonly used in the CONFIG.SYS file are BUFFERS, FILES, and DEVICE.

The BUFFERS Command

The BUFFERS command allocates memory for a specified number of disk buffers (from 1 to 99) when your system starts. The buffers hold data during read and write operations. Application programs require a certain number of buffers to work efficiently. Most applications update this command when they are being installed, or you can update it if more buffers are needed. If an application program requires 30 buffers, add the following line to your CONFIG.SYS file:

```
BUFFERS=30
```

The FILES Command

Application programs require that MS-DOS be able to access a certain number of files at one time. The FILES command specifies the number of files (ranging from 8 through 255) that MS-DOS can access at one time. The default setting is 8. Many programs require a larger value such as 30. In order to allow access of up to 30 files at one time you would add the following line to your CONFIG.SYS file:

```
FILES=30
```

The DEVICE Command

The DEVICE command loads a device driver into memory. For example, when you purchase a mouse or a scanner the manufacturer usually includes device driver software. To use that hardware the appropriate device driver must be installed by specifying its location and name on a DEVICE command line in the CONFIG.SYS file. For example, to load the device driver for your scanner, SCAN.SYS, from the directory SCANNER, you would enter the following command in your CONFIG.SYS file:

```
DEVICE=C:\SCANNER\SCAN.SYS
```

HOW DO I GET ON-LINE HELP?

There are two ways to get on-line help using MS-DOS 6. First is the command FASTHELP, which gives a brief explanation of each of the MS-DOS 6 commands.

You can access FASTHELP two ways. For example, if you wanted help on the FORMAT command you could enter either of the following two lines:

```
FASTHELP FORMAT
```

or

```
FORMAT /?
```

Using the /? switch is slightly faster.

The second way to get on-line help is to use the HELP command. This command provides more detailed help. For help on the COPY command, you would type:

```
HELP COPY
```

Typing HELP without any parameter will display the help table of contents. Then the topic you want can be selected from the table of contents.

WHAT DOES THE CLS COMMAND DO?

The CLS command clears the screen. Typing CLS and pressing Enter clears the screen, except for the command prompt and the cursor.

HOW DO I MANAGE DIRECTORIES?

Let's examine the four commands that help you work with and manage your directories: the directory (DIR) command, the make directory (MKDIR) command, the change directory (CHDIR) command, and the remove directory (RMDIR) command.

The Directory (DIR) Command

The DIR (directory) command lists all the files and subdirectories contained in the current directory of a disk. A directory listing shows the filenames, extensions, file sizes in bytes, the dates and times the files were last updated in the current directory, and any subdirectories contained in the directory. The contents of the current directory can be viewed by entering the DIR command at the system prompt as follows:

```
C>DIR
```

You can also add some optional parameters after the DIR command. If a directory contains more files than will fit on the display screen, the list scrolls off the screen. To list one display screen at a time, the command DIR/P stops the scrolling when the display screen is full. Press any key to continue the scrolling through the rest of the files.

The command DIR/W displays files in a column format across the screen. More files can be seen in the same amount of screen space because only the filename and extension are listed.

To view the files on another drive, enter the drive name after the DIR command. To get a listing of files on drive A from the prompt C>, type DIR A:. To view files in a specific directory, simply add that directory to the parameter, for example, DIR C:\WP\LETTER. Wildcards can also be used with the DIR command. For example, to list all the files in the current directory with the extension .DOC, type DIR *.DOC.

The root directory is automatically opened when a hard disk or diskette is formatted. All files will be stored in the root directory if no other directories are created. But you may want to organize the files more efficiently as the number of files increases or as the topics become diverse. To do this you can create, move between, and delete directories.

The Make Directory (MKDIR) Command

To organize and locate files stored on a disk or diskette, you can create a new directory with the command MKDIR (make directory), or MD. All directories are subdirectories of the root directory and each can also have subdirectories. The directory structure resembles an upside-down tree with the trunk (root directory) at the top and branches extending downward into subdirectories.

Let's say a root directory contains many files, three of which are related. These files are called RED.TXT, BLUE.TXT, and GREEN.TXT. A directory called COLOR could be made by entering the command MD COLOR at the system prompt. Then the files RED.TXT, BLUE.TXT, and GREEN.TXT can be moved from the root directory into the new directory using the MOVE command. The MOVE command is discussed below. This places the three related files into a directory with a descriptive name, making them easier to locate.

The Change Directory (CHDIR) Command

To change, or move, from one directory to another, use the command CHDIR (change directory), or CD. To change from the root directory (labeled as \) to the subdirectory called WP, enter the command CD WP at the system prompt. If you are not currently in the root directory and want to change to a directory on the same level or above, you must always start with the root directory symbol (\). For example, if you are currently in the directory called WP and want to change to the directory SS, which is on the same level as WP, you would enter the command CD\SS. A shorthand way to change to the directory one level above the current directory, that is, to the parent directory, is to type CD.. and then press Enter.

The CHDIR command can also tell you what directory you are currently in by entering the CHDIR command without any parameters.

The Remove Directory (RMDIR) Command

Before you can remove a directory, all files in that directory must be removed or erased. This is MS-DOS's way of preventing accidental erasure of files stored in a directory. To erase a directory that contains no files, use the command RMDIR (remove directory), or RD. Entering the command RD DATA at

the system prompt will remove the subdirectory DATA from the root directory—if it contains no files. However, if the directory contains files, the following message appears:

```
Invalid path, not directory,
or directory not empty
```

If this message appears, it usually means that all the files have not been deleted from the directory or the directory name has been incorrectly typed.

HOW DO I MANAGE FILES?

In this section we will describe some commands that are used to work with files. These include the RENAME, COPY, MOVE, DELETE, ERASE, UNDELETE, TYPE, MORE, and PRINT commands.

The RENAME Command

If you want to change the filename, filename extension, or both, use the command RENAME or REN. RENAME does not allow you to specify a new drive or path. For example, if after reorganizing a manuscript you had a file named CHAPTER3.DOC that you now wanted to name CHAPTER4.DOC, type:

```
RENAME CHAPTER3.DOC CHAPTER4.DOC
```

Be careful when renaming files because some application programs require specific filename extensions for the file to be recognized and used.

The COPY Command

The COPY command duplicates an existing file. The duplicate file can be stored on a different disk, in a different directory, or in the same directory under another name. For safekeeping, a backup of the original should be copied to another disk. If the backup is on the same medium as the original and something happens, both the original and duplicate could be lost or destroyed.

The disk from which you copy is the *source disk* and the disk onto which the copy is placed is the *target disk*. The target disk must be formatted before you use the COPY command.

Make sure there is not an existing file on the target disk with the same filename as the one to be copied. If the file has the same name, the file on the target disk will be replaced by the file from the source disk. For example, if you enter at the C> prompt

```
COPY MUSIC.TXT A:
```

the text file MUSIC located on the source disk in drive C is copied to the target disk in drive A using the same filename. But if a file already exists on drive A with the name MUSIC.TXT, it will be written over.

If you enter at the C> prompt

```
COPY MUSIC.TXT A:CD.TXT
```

the text file MUSIC.TXT will be copied from source drive C to target drive A and stored under the filename CD.TXT.

Wildcards are often used with the COPY command. To illustrate, entering
    COPY *.* C:
at the A> prompt copies all files from drive A to drive C, regardless of the individual filename and filename extension. Entering

```
COPY *.TXT C:
```

at the A> prompt copies all files from drive A to drive C that have the file extension .TXT, regardless of the individual filename. For example, if a drive contains the text files A.TXT, TEST1.TXT, B.TXT, TEST2.TXT, and CD.TXT, they would all be copied to drive A by this command.

However, if the COPY command had been entered as

```
COPY ?.TXT C:
```

only A.TXT and B.TXT from the above files would be copied.

The MOVE Command

The MOVE command has two functions: It moves one or more files to a specified location and it renames directories.

If you are moving only one file, you can rename the file when you move it. Using the MOVE command overwrites the existing file without prompting you. To move more than one file, the destination must be a directory name. If you move more than one file, and specify one filename, you will see the following message:

```
Cannot move multiple files to a
single file
```

Suppose LETTERS is a directory on the C drive. To move the files LAURA.TXT and ERIC.TXT from the A drive to the LETTERS directory, at the command prompt type:

```
MOVE LAURA.TXT,ERIC.TXT C:\LETTERS
```

To move the Q1TAXES.TXT file from the current directory to the FINANCES directory on drive C and rename it Q2TAXES.TXT, type the following at the command prompt:

```
MOVE Q1TAXES.TXT C:\FINANCES\
Q2TAXES.TXT
```

You can rename a directory using the MOVE command by specifying the old directory name as the file you want to move, and the new directory name as the destination. For example, on drive C, to rename a directory called NEW to OLD, type the following command:

```
MOVE C:\NEW C:\OLD
```

You can change the directory name, but the MOVE command does not allow you to move a directory to another location in the tree. The following command is invalid because the new directory name is not in the same location as the old directory name:

```
MOVE C:\NEW C:\DOS\NEW
```

The DELETE and ERASE Commands

To erase a file or files, DEL (delete) or ERASE can be used. The commands are interchangeable. To erase the text file TAPES.TXT from a diskette in drive A, at the C> prompt, type

```
DEL A:TAPES.TXT
```

or

```
ERASE A:TAPES.TXT
```

To delete all the files in a directory type the DEL command followed by the drive and path. Wildcards allow you to delete more than one file at a time. Use wildcards cautiously, though, to avoid deleting files unintentionally. Suppose you type the following command:

```
DEL *.*
```

DEL displays the following prompt:

```
All files in directory will be
deleted! Are you sure (Y/N)?
```

If you press Y and then ENTER all files in the current directory will be deleted; if you press N and then ENTER the deletion is canceled.

Before you use wildcards with the DEL command to delete a group of files, you can use the same wildcards with the DIR command to see a list of the names of all the files included in the group.

Be careful when deleting files because you may not be able to retrieve a file that's been deleted. Although the UNDELETE command can retrieve some deleted files, that occurs with certainty only if no other files have been created or changed on the disk. If you accidentally delete a file that you want to keep, stop what you are doing and immediately use the UNDELETE command to retrieve the file. We will look at the UNDELETE command next.

The UNDELETE Command

The UNDELETE command restores files that were previously deleted by the DEL or ERASE commands. To recover the file CHAPTER1.DOC in the current directory:

```
UNDELETE CHAPTER1.DOC
```

UNDELETE cannot restore a directory that has been removed, and it cannot retrieve a file from a removed directory.

The TYPE and MORE Commands

To view the contents of a text file (that is one with the filename extension .TXT) on the display screen, without making a hard copy, use the command TYPE.

The contents of the text file README.TXT in the current directory will be displayed on the screen if, at the prompt, you type:

```
TYPE README.TXT
```

If there are many lines, the display will scroll off the screen. Press Ctrl-S or Ctrl-Num Lock to pause the scrolling. Press any key to continue the scrolling.

The MORE command displays the file one screen at a time. Assuming the MORE command file is stored on drive C in the DOS directory, you could enter:

```
TYPE README.TXT ¦ C:\DOS\MORE
```

The first full screen of text is displayed. Press any key to display the next screen.

The PRINT Command

A text file can be sent, or "printed," using the command PRINT. For example, many programs contain a text file usually called README.TXT, or something similar, that informs you of changes or corrections to the printed manuals. You may find it easier to print this material rather than reading it from the screen.

Suppose the PRINT file is in the DOS directory on drive C, the program disk containing the README.TXT file is in drive A, and the system prompt is C:\>. To print the contents of that text file, make sure the printer is on and ready; then at the C:\> prompt enter:

```
C:\DOS\PRINT A:README.TXT
```

A hard copy of the data stored in that text file is provided.

HOW DO I MANAGE DISKS?

In this section we'll look at four commands used to manage your disks. They are the FORMAT command, the UNFORMAT command, the CHKDSK command, and the DISKCOPY command.

The FORMAT Command

Before you can use either the hard disk or a floppy diskette, it must be formatted or made ready for use.

The command FORMAT prepares a hard disk or floppy diskette to store files. It checks for defects on the disk and indicates if the disk is usable. It also divides a disk into tracks and sectors and creates a File Allocation Table (FAT). MS-DOS uses the FAT to keep track of where data are stored on a disk.

CAUTION: *Formatting or reformatting a disk destroys all files currently on the disk.*

Take care not to format a hard disk, which may contain 40 or more megabytes of valuable programs and data. In classroom situations, you may be required to format a floppy diskette. You will not receive a warning message, so make sure you are formatting a new diskette—not one that contains active files. Examine the contents of a previously formatted diskette before formatting using the DIR command.

There are two ways to format a floppy diskette: (a) as a nonbootable data diskette or (b) as a bootable diskette. A nonbootable data diskette does not contain system files and cannot be used to start the computer and load MS-DOS. A bootable diskette contains the system files and starts the computer and loads MS-DOS.

Here's how to format a diskette in drive A on a hard disk system. Make sure the MS-DOS file FORMAT.COM is on your hard disk and is in the current directory, or enter the appropriate path name. To format a diskette as either bootable or nonbootable, follow the steps listed below.

1. Insert a blank diskette into drive A.

2. Format it as either a nonbootable or a bootable diskette:

   a. *Nonbootable:* At the C> prompt, type FORMAT A: and press Enter. The prompt "Insert new diskette for drive A: and press ENTER when ready" is displayed. Press Enter. In a minute or two, the diskette in drive A will be formatted with no MS-DOS system files transferred to the diskette. This leaves more space for data storage. To use this nonbootable disk, MS-DOS must already be booted.

   b. *Bootable:* At the C> prompt, type FORMAT A:/S and press Enter. The prompt "Insert new

diskette for drive A: and press ENTER when ready" is displayed. Press Enter. In a minute or two, the diskette in drive A will be formatted. This process puts two hidden system files and the file COMMAND.COM onto the diskette; therefore, less space is left for data.

3. When the diskette is formatted the following message appears:

   ```
   Format complete.
   Volume label (11 characters, ENTER
   for none)?
   ```

   You can type up to 11 characters for the volume label, for example, DONNADISK, to identify the contents or owner of a disk. If you do not want a volume label, press ENTER.

4. After you press ENTER information about the total bytes of disk space, total bytes available on disk, number of bytes in each allocation unit, and number of allocation units available on disk is displayed and the following message appears:

   ```
   Format another (Y/N)?
   ```

   To format another diskette type Y and press Enter. The prompt tells you to "Insert new diskette for drive A: and press ENTER when ready." When formatting is complete, MS-DOS displays messages showing the total disk space, any space marked as defective, the total space used by the operating system (if you formatted a bootable diskette), and the space available for your files. If you do not wish to format another diskette, type N and press Enter. The system prompt is displayed and you can enter other MS-DOS commands.

The UNFORMAT Command

If you formatted a diskette that already contained needed files the UNFORMAT command can restore the disk. For example, if you accidentally formatted the diskette in drive A you can recover the files by entering the following at the command prompt:

```
UNFORMAT A:
```

The CHKDSK Command

You can check the status of your disk and system with the command CHKDSK (check disk). Assume CHKDSK is stored on drive C in a directory called DOS and the current drive is A. To check the disk in drive A, enter C:\DOS\CHKDSK A: at the system prompt A>.

Once executed, CHKDSK does not give an opportunity to switch disks. It immediately checks the disk in the specified drive, or if no drive was specified, it checks the disk in the current drive. In either case a status report is displayed:

```
XXXXXX   bytes total disk space
XXXXXX   bytes in x hidden files
XXXXXX   bytes in xx directories
XXXXXX   bytes in xxx user files
XXXXXX   bytes in bad sectors
XXXXXX   bytes available on disk
XXXXXX   bytes in each allocation
         unit
XXXXXX   total allocation units on
         disk
XXXXXX   available allocation units
         on disk
XXXXXX   total bytes memory
XXXXXX   bytes free
```

The information supplied is measured in bytes. "Total disk space" is the amount available when the disk was formatted. Space used by any hidden files, directories, and all user files is listed. The number of bytes of bad sectors, or unusable disk space, is given if any exists. Space remaining in which to store files is given next. An allocation unit is the smallest part of a disk that can be allocated to a file. The next three lines report the number of bytes in each allocation unit, the total allocation units on the disk, and the number of allocation units currently available. The next line displays total system memory, followed by the amount of space in memory that is available for use.

CHKDSK finds and reports any errors in the file directory or file allocation table. It automatically corrects any errors it detects if the command is followed by a /F switch. For example, CHKDSK A:/F.

The DISKCOPY Command

When an entire diskette (called the source) is to be copied onto another diskette (called the target), the command DISKCOPY can be used. However, this command cannot be used to copy to or from a hard disk. This command automatically formats the target diskette if necessary.

The entire contents of the source diskette in drive A can be copied to the target diskette in drive B by entering the command

```
DISKCOPY A: B:
```

To use DISKCOPY with a single floppy-diskette drive enter

```
DISKCOPY A: A:
```

The system prompts you to swap between the target and source diskettes in drive A to complete the disk copy.

WHAT OTHER MS-DOS TOOLS ARE AVAILABLE?

We'll give a brief overview of some other tools available with MS-DOS 6. The HELP command or your MS-DOS User's Guide offer detailed information on how to use these tools.

The DoubleSpace (DBLSPACE) Command

If you are running out of disk space on either your hard disk or a floppy diskette, the DBLSPACE command gives you more space. DoubleSpace increases disk capacity by 50 to 100 percent by compressing the data on your disk.

The Defragment (DEFRAG) Command

Over time, normal use of your hard disk will eventually lead to some of the files becoming fragmented. This happens when files are stored in noncontiguous areas on the disk. While this condition will not harm your files, it slows down access to them because the hard disk's read/write head requires more movement as it searches for each piece of a file. The DEFRAG command reorganizes, or defragments, the noncontiguous files so that they occupy a single contiguous chunk of disk space. Using the defragment command optimizes disk performance.

The Microsoft Antivirus (MSAV) Command

Computer viruses can simply be a nuisance or they can devastate all the data stored on your hard disk. To protect your computer against viruses the MSAV command scans for and removes viruses from your system. In addition, a memory-resident program, VSAFE, can be loaded that continuously monitors your computer for viruses. When a virus is found a warning is displayed.

The Microsoft Backup (MSBACKUP) Command

Hard disks fail and human error causes us to accidentally overwrite or delete files that we need. The MS-BACKUP command prevents such disasters. It allows you to back up all files on a disk or those files that have changed since your last backup. You can schedule backups so they are done automatically on a regular basis and restore files that you have backed up. Performing scheduled backups protects your data and your investment of time and effort.

The MEM and MEMMAKER Commands

The MEM command displays the amount of used and free memory in your system. The MEMMAKER command automatically optimizes your computer's memory. It moves device drivers and memory-resident programs to upper memory to give your programs more memory to operate in. To use MEM-MAKER, your computer must have an 80386 or 80486 processor and extended memory.

The Microsoft Diagnostic (MSD) Command

Some programs require specific hardware in order to run, such as a specific level of microprocessor (i.e., 80386 or 80486), a coprocessor, or a particular type of video adapter. If your system has problems and you call for technical assistance, they will want information about your system. How do you find this information? The MSD program provides detailed technical information about your computer's model and processor, memory, video adapter, version of MS-DOS, mouse, other adapters, disk drives, LPT ports, COM ports, terminate-and-stay-resident (TSR) programs, and device drivers.

The Dosshell (DOSSHELL) Command

When MS-DOS 6 is first started it has a command line interface. You see the command prompt where you enter desired commands. Some users want a menu-oriented interface with a more visually oriented approach. Typing DOSSHELL at the command prompt starts the Dosshell, which looks similar to Figure 2. A menu bar at the top of the screen contains pull-down menus of MS-DOS commands. The available drives, directories, files, and applications are also displayed.

The MS-DOS Editor (EDIT) Command

The MS-DOS Editor uses a menu-oriented interface for choosing commands and provides extensive on-line help about techniques and commands. Entering the command EDIT at the MS-DOS command prompt starts the editor. You can create, edit, save, and print ASCII text files such as AUTOEXEC.BAT and CONFIG.SYS.

VOCABULARY SELF-TEST

Can you define the following terms?

batch file (p. 109)
current drive (p. 107)
default entry (p. 111)
directory (p. 108)
external commands (p. 107)
filename (p. 108)
filename extension (p. 108)
internal commands (p. 107)
Microsoft Disk Operating System (MS-DOS) (p. 107)
MS-DOS command prompt (p. 107)
path (p. 109)
subdirectory (p. 108)
wildcard (p. 108)

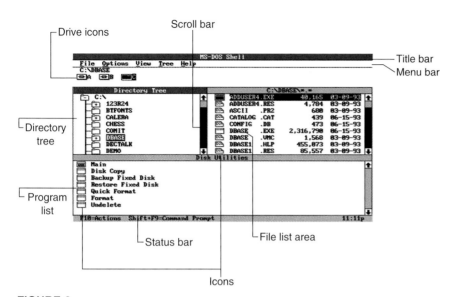

Drive icons

Scroll bar

Title bar

Menu bar

Directory tree

Program list

Status bar

Icons

File list area

FIGURE 2
The Dosshell screen.

REVIEW QUESTIONS

Multiple Choice

1. The command DIR CH??.* would not retrieve which of the following files?
   a. CH.TXT
   b. CHTWO.DOC
   c. CH1.DOC
   d. CH22

2. Which of the following commands is not used with the CONFIG.SYS file?
   a. buffers
   b. path
   c. device
   d. files

3. Which command creates a directory?
   a. DIR
   b. RMDIR
   c. CHDIR
   d. MKDIR

4. Which command renames a directory?
   a. COPY
   b. MOVE

   c. RENAME
   d. DELETE

5. The _____ command compresses data on a disk to increase the available storage space.
   a. DOSSHELL
   b. DEFRAG
   c. MSD
   d. DBLSPACE

Fill-In

1. _____ are DOS commands that are contained in separate files stored on disk.

2. The _____ consists of the current drive letter and the symbol > and indicates the current drive.

3. The drive on which DOS will put any files or search for any filenames or commands you type, unless it is instructed to look elsewhere, is called the _____.

4. A(n) _____ is an MS-DOS character that is entered to represent a character or characters.

5. A(n) _____ holds files and organizes them into convenient groups so they can be easily located on disk.

Short Answer

1. Define the terms filename, filename extension, directory, and path.
2. Describe the functions of the AUTOEXEC.BAT file and the CONFIG.SYS file and identify several commands commonly used in each.
3. State the purpose of the following directory management commands: DIR, MKDIR, CHDIR, and RMDIR.
4. Describe the function of the following file management commands: RENAME, COPY, MOVE, DELETE, ERASE, UNDELETE, TYPE, MORE, and PRINT.
5. Briefly describe the function of each of the following commands: the DoubleSpace (DBLSPACE) command, the Defragment (DEFRAG) command, the Microsoft Antivirus (MSAV) command, the Microsoft Backup (MSBACKUP) command, the MEM command, the MEMMAKER command, the Microsoft Diagnostic (MSD) command, the Dosshell (DOSSHELL) command, and the MS-DOS Editor (EDIT) command

OUTLINE

OBJECTIVES

4.1 Describe the concept of output and explain the purpose of an output device.

4.2 Contrast hard copy and soft copy output.

4.3 Identify ways in which output is made meaningful.

4.4 Briefly describe various hard copy output devices.

4.5 Briefly describe various soft copy output devices.

4.6 Define input/output devices and identify several input/output devices.

4.7 Understand the purpose of a port and describe several types.

4.8 Understand the purpose of a device driver and identify several devices that require one.

Chapter 4

Output

Profile

Raymond Kurzweil

Raymond Kurzweil is an inventor, scientist, businessman and author of the book *The Age of Intelligent Machines,* which examines human intelligence and suggests that machines can be built to imitate those abilities. Kurzweil was born in Queens, New York, in 1948. As a youngster he was a talented magician. But as soon as he was introduced to computers at the age of 12, the true magic began. Kurzweil was interested in recognizing patterns, especially those involving music. He created a program that could compose new works just by matching the sounds of a particular composer. Later he would develop the Kurzweil 250, a keyboard synthesizer that can be programmed to sound like any instrument in its memory—even a concert grand piano. By the time Kurzweil was 15 he had written a program and sold it to IBM for distribution to its customers. Not your "average" teenager.

Kurzweil's abilities with patterns are particularly important to the challenges of artificial intelligence (AI), where speech-pattern recognition is fundamental. AI was defined in 1956 by Marvin Minsky (one of Kurzweil's professors at MIT) as "the art of creating machines that perform functions that require intelligence when performed by people."

In 1976 Kurzweil came up with what would be called by some a machine as important to the blind as the development of Braille. The device could "read" and "speak" aloud in a robotlike voice. He went on the "Today Show" with the 350-pound Personal Reader. The apparatus caught the attention of Stevie Wonder, the blind singer, who wanted one. The $50,000 price tag did not deter Wonder, who took the unwieldy machine home and "read" all night. By 1991 the Personal Reader had become a briefcase-sized machine with a palm-size scanning device and a collection of nine "voices" that could even identify exclamation marks in the written word and read those passages with excitement.

Although machine intelligence is advancing rapidly and human intelligence is at a comparative standstill, human intelligence covers a broad expanse while today's computer intelligence works in rather narrow areas of expertise. For example, Kurzweil's VoiceRAD machine is used by radiologists. The device can be programmed to recognize individual voices and as a user utters specific words or terminology, the machine produces predetermined phrases and sentences that ultimately are compiled into written radiological reports. Using this machine saves doctors from the tedium of taking notes, dictating, and proofreading each report.

The future, according to Kurzweil, will likely include telephones that translate conversations into other languages; devices that could give "voice" to persons with speech problems, by recognizing voice patterns and printing the words; and robotic devices that paraplegics could fit on their legs to permit them to walk. The future will tell us whether computers will ever "speak" for themselves. But, whatever the future holds, it isn't hard to imagine more tricks up Kurzweil's sleeve.

Now that you have some insight into how data are entered into a computer for processing, let's examine how the results of that processing are communicated back to you. The results are used to make decisions and solve problems. In this chapter you'll learn the meaning of output, the purpose of output devices, and examine some of the more common output devices.

Objective 4.1   Describe the concept of output and explain the purpose of an output device.

What Is Output and What Is an Output Device?

Output is the process of translating data that are in machine-readable form into a form understandable to humans or readable by other machines. Information that is the result of processing is also often referred to as output. An **output device** is hardware that enables a computer to communicate information to humans or other machines so that it may be used. Output can be divided into two general categories: (1) output that is read and used by people, and (2) data that are sent to secondary-storage devices to be used later as input for further processing by a computer or for use by another machine.

Objective 4.2   Contrast hard copy and soft copy output.

What Is the Difference Between Hard Copy and Soft Copy Output?

In today's information society, clear, legible output is a necessity—a major consideration when purchasing output devices. Output that is readable by users is categorized as either hard copy or soft copy. **Hard copy** is output that can be read immediately or stored and read later, such as paper. It is a relatively stable and permanent form of output. **Soft copy** is a transient form of output, for example, text on a screen display. It is lost when the computer is turned off. However, if the data used to create that soft copy remain in the computer's memory or have been saved on disk or tapes, the soft copy can be reproduced repeatedly.

Objective 4.3   Identify ways in which output is made meaningful.

How Can Output Be Made Meaningful?

Types of output

- **Human-readable output**
  Hard copy
      relatively stable
      and permanent
  Soft copy
      transient
- **Stored in machine-readable form**

Output must be presented in a form that can be used by others. A computer will not automatically produce output in the form you want. The computer must be programmed to arrange the data that were input into some meaningful form.

Output is made more meaningful by ensuring the input is correct, by organizing it into reports, and by appropriately presenting it to the intended audience. Meaningful output must start with meaningful input. You can't expect to produce useful output if the data entered were in error, unorganized, or otherwise bad. Although the burden of entering good data is on the user, some programs provide methods of data entry that can catch many errors.

Output takes on meaning by incorporating it into reports. A **report** is an organized presentation of information in the form of text, charts, graphics, or combinations of all three.

The intended audience for the output in part determines how the output will look. A text representation of the data might be sufficient in an interoffice memo, while a color graph might be more appropriate to achieve visual impact for a formal presentation.

Soft copy output devices allow you to preview and make changes before creating hard copy output. In the next sections you will examine various hard and soft copy output devices.

Objective 4.4   Briefly describe various hard copy output devices.

What Are Hard Copy Output Devices?

Hard Copy Output Devices

- Printers
- Plotters
- Computer output microform (COM) machines

Hard copy output devices produce graphics and text on paper, or other media, that can be read by people. Printers and plotters are the most common hard copy output devices. Microfilm and microfiche, known as computer output microform, are often used when hard copy needs to be retained for extended periods of time. These devices are examined in the following sections.

Printers

Most output is produced by printers. A **printer** is an output device that produces output, on paper or other media, in the form of text or graphics. Printers are used with all types of computers, therefore there are a wide variety of printers with differing capabilities and features.

In general printers can be categorized by how they produce characters on a page. A printer uses one of two basic types of printing mechanisms: impact or nonimpact. An **impact printer** produces characters when a hammer or pin strikes an ink ribbon, which in turn presses against a sheet of paper and leaves an impression of the character on the paper. This is how an ordinary typewriter works. The two impact printers most often used with microcomputers are the dot-matrix printer and the daisy-wheel printer. A **nonimpact printer** does not use a striking device to produce characters on paper. Rather, it uses a variety of other technologies. Because nonimpact printers do not hammer against paper, they are much quieter. Nonimpact printers include ink-jet and laser printers.

Printers are either character, line, or page printers. **Character printers** print one character at a time. Most microcomputer printers are character-at-a-time printers with speeds up to several hundred characters-per-second (cps). Some printers have built-in memory to store succeeding lines of text. This memory makes possible bidirectional printing, that is, printing in which the print head prints from left to right and then from right to left. This capability significantly increases print speed. A **line printer,** or line-at-a-time printer, uses a special mechanism that prints a whole line at once. It can typically print in the range of a few hundred to a few thousand lines per minute. These are mainly used with large system computers. **Page printers** produce an entire page at one time. The largest of these are very fast and can achieve speeds of several thousand pages per minute.

Paper can move through a printer either as continuous connected sheets or as single sheets. Some printers allow both types of form feeds.

Continuous form paper is used on printers equipped with tractor feed mechanisms. Rotating pins engage holes in the paper and pull it through the printer. Friction feed printers use pressure to pinch the paper between rollers that hold the paper in place. As the rollers turn, the paper is moved through the printer.

The carriage is the area of the printer that holds the print head mechanism and the place where the paper passes through. Most printers have a carriage width that accepts 8½-inch wide paper on which 80 characters of normal size can be printed on each line. Wide carriages allow wider paper to be used. A typical wide carriage uses paper 14 inches wide and 132 characters of normal size are printed on a line.

Print Quality

Print quality is a major consideration in choosing a printer for a particular job. The quality of type that a printer produces is determined mainly by its printing mechanism. The quality of print varies widely among printers. At the top of the line in quality is **typeset-quality print**. This is the quality provided by commercial typesetters and is the type seen in most magazines and books. Letters and characters are fully formed, using solid lines.

Letter-quality print is the equivalent of good typewriter print. This print, too, is made using fully formed (solid line) characters, as opposed to characters made up of a series of lines or dots (Figure 4.1). Letter-quality print is used traditionally in business letters and formal correspondence.

Printers that produce characters composed of a series of dots or short lines, rather than continuous solid lines, print high-quality documents using a **near-letter-quality (NLQ) print** mode. This is achieved on some printers when the print head makes multiple passes over each letter, filling in the spaces between the dots or lines.

Standard-quality print, sometimes called draft-quality print, is produced when characters composed of dots or lines are formed by a single pass of the print head. Generally, standard-quality print is suitable for most informal applications and rough drafts.

At the low end of the quality scale is **compressed print,** which is sometimes used for listing or printing the code in computer programs. Characters in compressed print are very close together (compressed) to

FIGURE 4.1

A comparison of fully formed characters to those composed of dots or lines.

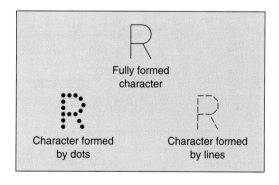

FIGURE 4.2
A comparison of the different
qualities of print.

This is an example of typeset-quality print.

This is an example of near-typeset quality print.

This is an example of letter-quality print.

This is an example of near-letter quality print.

This is an example of standard-quality print.

This is an example of draft-quality (compressed) print.

conserve space. The characters are formed with a minimum number of dots or lines and are smaller than the standard-quality characters. Figure 4.2 compares print qualities.

Common Printing Devices for Microcomputers

A variety of printing needs has led to the development of numerous types of printers. Several common types are dot-matrix, daisy wheel, ink-jet, and laser printers.

Dot-Matrix Printers. The **dot-matrix printer** uses print heads containing 9 or 24 pins. These pins produce patterns of dots to form the individual characters. The 24-pin dot-matrix printer produces more dots than a 9-pin dot-matrix printer, resulting in much crisper, clearer characters (Figure 4.3). Dot-matrix printers with 9-pin print heads typically produce compressed print, standard quality, and near-letter-quality print. Most 24-pin models have letter quality, compressed, standard, and NLQ modes. Dot-matrix printers have improved their print quality in general but marked improve-

This is an example of 24-pin dot-matrix print.

This is an example of 9-pin dot-matrix print.

FIGURE 4.3
A comparison of print quality between 9-pin and 24-pin dot-matrix printers.

ment can be seen when a film ribbon (as opposed to a cloth ribbon) is used. With the film ribbon some dot-matrix printers can reach 90–95 percent of laser quality. However, in some printers the higher print quality modes require the print head to make multiple passes over the same line, which drastically reduces the printing speed. Dot-matrix printers have print speeds ranging from 100 to 600 cps. They are known to be very loud; however, many newer models have been designed to substantially reduce the noise.

Dot-matrix printers are popular with home computer users because they are relatively inexpensive to purchase (approximately $100 and up) and have low operating costs of about .8 cent per page.

Daisy-Wheel Printers. A **daisy-wheel printer** produces letter-quality type, i.e., the type found on modern typewriters. This impact printer contains a print mechanism that looks like a daisy. At the end of each "petal" is a fully formed character. When a hammer strikes a petal against the ribbon, the character image prints on the paper. Daisy-wheels produce solid-line print (Figure 4.4) and wheels can be exchanged to choose different type fonts.

Ink-Jet Printers. An **ink-jet printer** is a nonimpact printer that forms characters on paper by spraying ink from tiny nozzles in the print head. The ink is absorbed into the paper and when dried is permanently bonded to the paper. Ink-jet printers produce high-quality output comparable to that of laser printers.

Laser Printers. When typeset quality is required, a laser printer is the solution. The **laser printer** is a nonimpact printer that produces images on paper by directing a laser beam at a mirror that bounces the beam onto a drum (Figure 4.5). The laser leaves a negative charge on the drum, to which positively charged black toner powder sticks. As paper rolls by the drum,

FIGURE 4.4
A daisy wheel.

FIGURE 4.5
A desktop laser printer

the toner is transferred to the paper. A hot roller then bonds the toner to the paper.

A laser printer's internal memory stores a page at a time. When the entire page is loaded, it is printed. Desktop laser printers typically print a few pages (4–12) per minute. Laser printers are quiet and provide high-quality text and images. The average cost per page is about 3 cents.

Portable Printers.   With the advent of portable microcomputers came the need for portable printers. A **portable printer** is generally smaller, lighter, and more rugged than desktop printers. Most are battery powered so you can take them anywhere. The quality of output from today's portable printers compares favorably with their larger desktop versions.

Common Printing Devices for Large System Computers

Mainframes or other large computer systems print enormous amounts of material and the character-at-a-time printers are too slow. They require line-at-a-time printers like the drum, chain, and band printers or laser printers that print an entire page at a time.

A **drum printer** has a complete character set engraved around the circumference of each print position of the drum. The number of print positions across the drum equals the number of characters in a line available on a page.

A **chain printer** uses a chain of print characters wrapped around two pulleys. Like the drum printer, a chain printer has one hammer for each print position. The chain rotates until all of the required print positions on the line have been filled. Then the page moves up to print the next line.

A **band printer** operates in a similar way. However, it uses a steel band instead of a chain and has fewer hammers. The steel bands can be interchanged to utilize different fonts.

Laser printers for large system computers use the same basic technology to produce printed copy as those used with desktop microcomputers. However, they are much larger and print up to several thousand pages per minute so they are often controlled by their own computer.

Common Color Printing Devices

We'll examine six types of printers commonly used to produce output in color: color dot-matrix printers, color ink-jet printers, color wax thermal printers, phase change printers, dye sublimation printers, and color laser printers. Choosing a color printer depends on how you will use it; what kind of prints you will make; who will see them; what kind of impression you need to make; and the price you are willing to pay.

Color Dot-Matrix Printers.   The least expensive entry into color printing is the color dot-matrix printer. A **color dot-matrix printer** works basically like the black-and-white counterpart, but instead of a black ribbon it has a four-color ribbon. For each line of print the head makes four passes, one for each color. A color ribbon costs around $20 and can produce about one million printed characters. The cost per page for color dot-matrix printed pages ranges from about 2 to 6 cents. These printers provide affordable color to all personal computer users with prices starting at around $200. They print at speeds ranging from 160 to 400 cps. Although resolution isn't as good as other color printer technologies, this printer does offer an inexpensive alternative to enhance documents with color. You can't expect color printouts simply by buying a color dot-matrix printer, because the software must provide a print driver capable of producing color.

Color dot-matrix printers are being used for rough drafts and review proofs by artists and graphic designers, by business people to highlight information in printed spreadsheets and reports, and by doctors and other professionals to highlight items such as past due amounts on invoices.

Color Ink-Jet Printers.   The **color ink-jet printer** is the least expensive entry in *true* color printing. It costs less than $1,000 and offers the lowest cost per page at about 15 cents. However, this cost varies depending on the amount of color on the page. With more than 50 percent of color coverage, the price can easily be $1 per page. Color ink-jet printers print at resolutions of 300 to 400 dots-per-inch (dpi) and can produce more than 16.7 million colors using a combination of cyan (light blue), magenta, yellow, and black inks.

Color ink-jet printers produce color graphs, charts and text of adequate quality for routine business letters, but the output might not be good enough for formal business presentations. They were not designed for more advanced graphics applications such as reproducing photographs or detailed drawings.

Color Wax Thermal Printers.   A **color wax thermal printer** is a step above color ink-jet printers in quality. While most print at 300 dpi the image is better than those produced by the color ink-jet printer, but costs range up to $4,000.

They operate by melting colored wax onto paper to produce images. The wax is carried on a polyester ribbon. The ribbon contains cyan, magenta, and yellow panels of wax. Each panel is the size of a sheet of paper. A glass-coated printing head presses the wax ribbon against the sheet of paper. As the page moves through the printer tiny heating elements in the print head turn on and off. Where they are turned on wax melts and adheres to the paper. An entire page of one color is printed. The page is then backed up and the ribbon advances to the next color. This is repeated for each color used. Special paper with a smooth, coated surface is required for the wax to adhere to. Because they use such large ribbons and need special paper, costs per page average about 50 cents.

Phase Change Printers. A **phase change printer** is more expensive, costing up to $7,000. It prints at 300 dpi and produces images of the same quality as color wax thermal printers. Their advantage is that no special paper is needed and thus they are cheaper to operate with costs averaging about 25 cents per page.

Phase change printers use colored wax pellets which are loaded into the print head. The print head melts the wax as it moves back and forth and sprays it on the paper as it moves through the printer. The solid wax is melted but cools to a solid again when it hits the paper. The printer gets its name from this change from solid to liquid to solid phases.

Dye Sublimation Printers. A **dye sublimation printer** offers ultra-high-resolution color images resembling photographs for around $10,000. Dye sublimation uses colored ribbons like wax thermal printers; however, the ribbons are opaque and saturated with a special dye. The print head presses the ribbon against the paper as it passes through the printer. The dye gets so hot that it actually penetrates the surface of the paper. The ink dots expand to fill the gaps between them and this allows the intensity of the colors to be varied by increasing or lowering the temperature of the heating elements in the print head. These benefits result in a continuous tone image with no apparent dots. The intense heat requires special paper made out of polyester material. Because of the unique ribbons and paper needed, operating costs for dye sublimation printers range from $2 to $3 per page. This printer is popular with graphic artists and others who combine photographs with text to produce desktop-publishing documents.

Color Laser Printers. A **color laser printer** produces the highest quality of color image but can cost from $20,000 to $40,000. It uses dry ink electrophotographic technology similar to photocopy machines or black-and-white laser printers. One pass over the page is made for each color of toner (cyan, magenta, yellow, and black). The image is printed on plain paper, which reduces the per-page operating costs.

Plotters

The growth of computer-aided design and drafting technology created a demand for devices that produce high-quality graphics in multiple colors on hard copy. A **plotter** is an output device that reproduces graphic images on paper using a pen that is attached to a movable arm (Figure 4.6). The pen is directed across the surface of a stationary piece of paper. Many plotters, however, combine a movable pen arm with a mechanism that rolls the

(a)

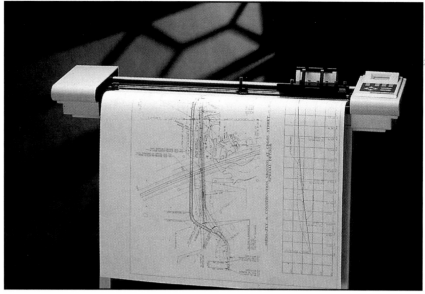
(b)

FIGURE 4.6
(a) Desktop plotters are used in offices to generate graphics that enhance business presentations. (b) Large plotters allow images such as this circuit diagram to be drawn to a size that users can view in detail.

paper back and forth to make the drawing. This two-way movement allows the plotter to draw any configuration.

Plotter applications are not limited to computer-aided design and drafting. High-quality bar graphs and pie charts created with a plotter can enhance business presentations, too.

Computer Output Microform

Hard copy of photographic images recorded on a microform such as microfilm or microfiche cards is called **computer output microform (COM)**. In some cases, a computer can output directly to a COM machine. In other cases, data are first recorded on magnetic tape, and the tape is used as input to a COM machine. Microfilm and microfiche readers are necessary to read the data.

COM provides low-cost storage for large amounts of data requiring infrequent access. It is ideal for businesses such as hospitals, which must keep patients' medical, financial, and insurance claim records. In the past, microforms were used primarily for archival purposes. Today, however, this technology is integrated into a **computer-assisted retrieval system (CARS)** to allow fast retrieval of data stored on the microforms. Microforms are useful to a business or organization because they reduce information storage and distribution costs and improve accessibility to information.

Objective 4.5   Briefly describe various soft copy output devices.

What Are Soft Copy Output Devices?

Ordinarily, users prefer to see output before making a permanent copy of it. Viewing work before printing permits users to make corrections or to rearrange material. Although most soft copy output appears on a visual display device or screen, a voice output device lets users hear it as well.

Monitors

The most popular soft copy output device is the monitor (Figure 4.7). A **monitor** is a television-like apparatus that displays data or information. It's what you'll be looking at every time you work with your computer. The earliest computers didn't have monitors. Users printed output on a teletype machine, a type of remote printer, in order to view it.

Monitor quality is often discussed in terms of **resolution,** a measure of the number of picture elements, or pixels for short, that the display screen of a monitor contains. A **pixel** is the smallest increment of a display screen that can be controlled individually. The more pixels, the clearer and sharper the onscreen image. You may see advertisements for monitors

FIGURE 4.7
Shown here are several monitors used to view output. Note the difference between the color display of the monitor on the left and the monochrome (single color) display of the monitor on the bottom right.

The U.S. Customs Service needs more than two eyes to watch the over 2 million people who come into the United States weekly. Most arrive legally, but others are bringing undeclared possessions. They bring contraband such as drugs, precious gems, guns, pirated software, and counterfeit merchandise.

An imaging system adds a far-ranging visual dimension and simplifies the customs inspectors' job. Over 40,000 digitized images of terrorists, criminals and those who have been caught previously bringing illegal goods into the country are now available for customs inspectors across the country.

In less than a minute a photo is digitized and entered into the U.S. Customs Service's northern Virginia mainframe. The system also records the different techniques that people use to bring the illegal goods into the country. This information can then be sent to any airport, seaport, or land crossing where an illegal entry might be under way. The digitized photos can be viewed on a monitor at any port of entry. An agent who has a likeness of a suspected drug smuggler, for example, avoids arresting an innocent person who could have the same name and date of birth as the suspected smuggler, or human "mule."

Customs agents usually watch arriving international passengers from booths in the center of the luggage carousels. Two-way mirrors keep them out of sight of their prey. Suspected smugglers may be getting their pictures taken without their knowledge.

Some time ago a woman smuggling heroin into New York in her beehive hairstyle was discovered by drug-sniffing dogs. When she was arrested, her photo was digitized and entered into the system. Later, when the same woman's name was listed as an arriving passenger in Boston, customs agents were watching for her. The distinctive hair piled high on her head was immediately recognized, and, as suspected, she was apprehended trying to smuggle more heroin.

The long arm of the law now has an eagle eye as well.

referring to the number of dots per inch (dpi). The higher the dpi, the greater the quality of the images will be. A 640 × 480 pixel screen contains 640 horizontal pixels and 480 vertical pixels, for a total of 307,200 individual pixels on the screen. An 800 × 600 pixel screen contains 800 horizontal pixels and 600 vertical pixels, for a total of 480,000 individual pixels on the screen.

Another measurement that is often referred to is the dot pitch. **Dot pitch** describes the size of the dots that make up the images. Dot pitch is measured in millimeters from a point (usually the center) on one dot to the corresponding point on an adjacent dot. The smaller the dot pitch, the sharper the image will be. Common dot pitch for high-resolution monitors is from .28 to .31mm.

The **refresh rate** is the number of times a screen is scanned to maintain an image. It is measured in Hertz, which indicates the number of times the screen is redrawn in one second. The refresh rate is important because it produces flicker. **Flicker** is a shimmering illusion created by the pixels going on and off. The flicker can cause eyestrain and fatigue during prolonged sessions at the computer. The slower the refresh rate, the greater the flicker and the more eyestrain you're likely to suffer. You will also see the terms interlaced and noninterlaced screens. An **interlaced screen** scans all the even lines first and then returns to scan all the odd lines. This approach makes the cost of the monitor lower but it also increases flicker. A **noninterlaced screen** scans every line from top to bottom sequentially and thus produces less flicker.

A **multisync** or multiscanning **monitor** supports refresh rates for VGA and higher resolutions (see the discussion on graphics adapter cards later). This is an advantage when upgrading to a higher resolution since it means that you only have to buy a new adapter card and not both a card and monitor.

You should consider several human factors when selecting monitors. First, be aware that people who work at monitors for long periods of time can suffer from eyestrain and fatigue that result from the glare and flicker of some monitors. Therefore, monitors should be positioned so that they are easy to read and antiglare screens should be used where needed. Screen resolution should be sufficient for text to be crisp and comfortable to read. In addition, users should take frequent breaks away from the monitor. Health concerns involving the emission of electromagnetic radiation by monitors are still unresolved. However, because of potential dangers, users should take reasonable precautions. Let's look at two kinds of viewing screens for monitors: cathode-ray tube and flat-panel display.

Cathode-Ray Tube. To produce an image on a **cathode-ray tube (CRT)**, an electron beam moves across a phosphor-coated screen. Intensifying the strength of the beam, the phosphor coating glows in certain places, forming the characters. The most common type of CRT has a display screen of 24 lines of 80 characters each. The standard CRT monitor size for desktop computers has been 14″. However, with increasing resolutions larger monitors such as 17″, 19″, 20″, and 21″ are required so that text can be large enough to be easily read while allowing for an adequate work area on the screen. This is especially true for applications that run under graphical user interfaces such as desktop publishing and computer-aided design applications. Other CRT monitor sizes are available, including those used in desktop publishing applications that display two full 8½ × 11-inch pages at their normal size. CRT monitors are large and bulky because of the size of the picture tube.

Flat-Panel Display. Monitors for portable computers need to be lighter weight and more energy efficient. A CRT is too large and cumbersome to use on today's small, portable computers because it is so thick and heavy, and demands a lot of power. A **flat-panel display** does not have a picture tube and can be manufactured small enough to fit on a battery-powered portable computer. Some desktop microcomputers also use flat-panel displays. Besides size and energy efficiency, another advantage of flat-panel screens over CRTs is that they do not use an electron gun and therefore do not flicker.

A common type of flat-panel display is the **liquid-crystal display (LCD),** which produces images by aligning molecular crystals. A backlight shines light through a polarized filter and into the liquid crystal substance. Backlight is a generic name for a light that shines through a flat-panel screen. The light is going in one direction. Electrical charges near the crystals cause them to twist the light into another angle. The light then comes to another polarized pane. If the light waves are moving in the direction of the filter they come through; if they are moving in the opposite direction they don't come through and you see black. This forms the characters on the screen. The greater the angle that the crystals can turn or "twist" the light, the sharper the contrast the screen will have. Newer LCDs with supertwist or double supertwist give greater screen contrast.

Two types of LCDs are passive matrix and active matrix. A **passive-matrix display** uses one set of transistors for each row and column on the screen. As soon as an LCD element is turned on it begins to fade. An **active-matrix display** uses one set of transistors for each LCD element. This provides steadier illumination, improves color selection, and reduces response time. Quicker response times eliminate the loss of cursor and shadowing common with passive matrix displays. Color saturation is also better with active matrix. Active matrix displays require more power and are more expensive.

Another type of flat-panel display is the **gas-plasma display,** which contains an ionized gas (plasma) between two glass plates. One glass plate contains a set of horizontal wires, and the other has a set of vertical wires. The intersection of each horizontal and vertical wire identifies a pixel. A pixel is turned on when electric current is sent through the appropriate vertical and horizontal wires. The plasma at the pixel emits light as the current is applied. Characters are formed by lighting the appropriate pixels. Gas-plasma displays are typically orange and black. Gas-plasma screens also provide a nonflickering bright picture. Figure 4.8 compares gas-plasma and LCD screens.

Graphics Adapter Cards

In order for your computer to communicate with the monitor it needs a graphics adapter card. A **graphics adapter card** is a circuit board inside the computer that converts the electronic signals sent by your computer into a form usable by the monitor. In some computers this circuitry is built-in, in others a separate card must be installed. We will use the term graphics adapter card to refer to both cases. The graphics adapter card determines the monitor display type.

There are several common types of graphics adapter cards found in IBM and compatible computers: MDA, Hercules Graphics Card, CGA, EGA, VGA, and SuperVGA.

Monochrome monitors display text and graphics in only one color. They are well suited to those who don't need to work in color. Two

(a)

(b)

FIGURE 4.8
(a) Gas-plasma display screen. (b) LCD display screen.

common graphics adapter cards for monochrome monitors for IBM-compatible computers are the Monochrome Display Adapter (MDA) and the Hercules Graphics Card (HGC). The MDA is designed to work with monochrome monitors for text-only display. The text is displayed in either green, amber, or black and white. The resolution is fairly high, 720 × 348 dpi, and is adequate if you work with text. The HGC also has a resolution of 720 × 348 dpi and displays only in green, amber, or black and white. However, unlike the MDA, the HGC displays graphics. Adapter cards for many monochrome monitors are proprietary and are sold with the monitors. These can have resolutions of up to 1,600 × 1,280 dpi. Many of them display in 256 shades of gray, which can produce photographic-quality images.

A color monitor is often preferred for output containing graphics. The Color Graphics Adapter (CGA), was the first color display that was available. Its resolution of 320 × 200 dpi displays 16 colors, but only four colors at one time. The next step up in resolution is the Enhanced Graphics Adapter (EGA) with a resolution of 640 × 350 dpi that displays 16 colors at one time. The Video Graphics Array (VGA) offers a resolution of 640 × 480 dpi. VGA is a widely accepted standard developed by IBM. The color VGA card displays 256 colors at one time while the gray-scale version allows 256 different shades of gray. The latest standard is the SuperVGA card, which has a resolution of 800 × 600 dpi. The next step up is high-resolution displays such as the IBM 8514/A, which is an interlaced monitor that has a resolution of 1024 × 768 dpi, or IBM's noninterlaced version of 1024 × 768 dpi, called XGA. These are much more expensive and are usually used by those individuals who need precise detail in their graphics such as engineers and architects.

A graphics adapter card needs to support the resolution and refresh rate of the monitor. It also determines the number of colors you will get. Although many of the current monitors display as many colors as the human eye can detect, it is the graphics adapter card that determines the color palette and the number of colors that can be displayed simultaneously. You'll see the terms 4-bit color, 8-bit color, 16-bit color, and 24-bit color. These terms refer to how many colors a card is capable of producing, not its throughput, as might be thought after reading about buses in Chapter 2. The numbers are just a shorthand way, using the binary number system, to indicate the number of colors. For example, 4-bit color produces two to the fourth power or 16 colors; 8-bit color produces 256 colors; 16-bit color produces 65,536 colors; and 24-bit color produces 16,777,216 colors. If you want to generate the maximum number of colors you need to have the appropriate amount of memory on your graphics adapter card. The more colors you want to produce, the more memory you will need per pixel. Color depth is the amount of memory required in bits per pixel to produce a certain number of colors.

Voice Output

Another type of soft copy output is **voice output,** the technology in which a computer uses a voice. Voice output systems are used where a display screen would not work or be appropriate, for example, in automobile warning systems, systems designed for the blind and visually impaired, and in toys and games.

    Speech coding, one type of voice output, is the storage of a bank of human sounds. The sounds are coded to be selected in building the words and phrases to be spoken. You may have heard the supermarket checkout computer give the total of your purchases. On the other hand, **voice synthesis** is the process of electronically reproducing the human voice in recognizable patterns. Producing these patterns is not easy. The English language and its rules of syntax are enough to confuse many humans. Imagine the difficulty in programming a computer to decipher how to say "I can record a record." Advances are being made and you can expect voice output, as well as voice input, to play significant roles in future computer design.

Objective 4.6   Define input/output devices and identify several input/output devices.

What Is an Input/Output Device?

An **input/output (I/O) device** is used both to transfer data and instructions to the computer and to receive information from the computer. Terminals and disk drives are examples of input/output devices.

Terminals

A **terminal**, also called a video display terminal (VDT), is an input/output device that consists of a keyboard and a monitor. Terminals are almost exclusively used with multiuser systems. They attach to a computer via a cable and communication software. Numerous terminals can be attached to

A computer system can be a declaration of independence. Ask Norman Coombs, a blind history professor at Rochester Institute of Technology. In 1961 there weren't many options for people with impaired vision. Coombs was dependent on friends, relatives, and others who read his books and assignments to him for most of his life. The readers helped Coombs obtain his doctorate in history from the University of Wisconsin. But at age 60 Coombs found his independence through a computer equipped with a speech synthesizer and scanning device. The scanning device inputs printed material into the computer and the speech synthesizer outputs it by "reading" it aloud.

Dr. Coombs regularly "reads" *The New York Times* and *USA Today*. It's not the Braille edition, either, since those translations often don't come out until as much as a week later. Many newspapers are available on computer networks so that whenever Dr. Coombs has the time he can have the news directly in his home, not delivered in the conventional manner, but rather via a modem in the computer system. Additionally, since the card catalog in his campus library appears on-line, Dr. Coombs is able to do his own research by modem too.

But the story only begins here! A deaf student in one of Dr. Coombs's computerized history classes found that by using these devices, she was able to participate in discussions with classmates and the instructor for the first time. In a world of computer communication, work is judged on its merit without notice of disabilities or bias of prejudice. No one knows your impairment, your gender, your race, or your image. Indeed, a declaration of independence for everyone!

minicomputers, mainframes, and supercomputers allowing many individuals to input data and receive output. Two major categories of terminals are dumb terminals and intelligent terminals.

A **dumb terminal** does not contain a microprocessor and, therefore, cannot do any of its own processing. This basic device is attached to a computer system and used for data entry and output display. If such a terminal is disconnected from the computer system, it cannot function on its own. An **intelligent terminal** contains a microprocessor that enables it to process data independently of the computer system to which it is connected. They typically perform a variety of error-checking functions and can often store data.

Terminals can be designed as either general-purpose devices capable of being used for a variety of tasks or special-purpose devices dedicated to a specific task or set of tasks. Often, microcomputers are used as general purpose terminals. A **point-of-sale (POS) terminal** is a special-purpose terminal that reads data at the source of a transaction and immediately turns them into usable information (Figure 4.9). Such terminals record data found on bar codes or magnetic-ink character recognition (MICR) price tags on

FIGURE 4.9
This point-of-sale terminal enables the salesclerk to enter data about a product by simply passing the item's UPC bar code over a bar code scanner connected to the POS terminal.

each product. Special scanning devices calculate cost, verify credit, provide the consumer with detailed receipts of transactions, and maintain sales records. Some directly update inventory files.

Disk and Tape Drives

Disk and tape drives input data and programs stored on magnetic media into the computer. They function as input/output devices, as well as secondary storage devices. They provide a means to store and retrieve data and instructions so that they can be input again at a later time without having to be rekeyed. Output can be stored and retrieved later for viewing or modification. These devices will be examined more closely in Chapter 5.

Objective 4.7   Understand the purpose of a port and describe several types.

What Are Ports?

You will see a number of pluglike connectors at the back of your computer. These are called **expansion ports**, or **input/output (I/O) ports**. Their purpose is to allow your computer to physically connect to and communicate with peripheral devices such as printers and mice. Communication can

Types of Expansion Ports

■ Parallel
■ Serial
■ Mouse
■ Game
■ SCSI
■ Video
■ Modular phone jack
■ Audio

take place from the computer to the peripheral device, from the peripheral device to the computer, or both ways. The cable that connects a peripheral device to the computer is called an **interface cable**. You'll notice that there are a number of different ports. Let's look at two main types of ports: parallel ports and serial ports.

A **parallel port** transmits information over eight wires eight bits at a time. Parallel ports are often called printer ports because they connect many types of printers to the computer. You can identify a parallel port by the 25-pin female connector. A female port has a number of holes; a male port is identified by little pins sticking out of the connector. Most parallel ports are capable of only one-way communication—from the computer to the peripheral device—and are used primarily with printers. Some parallel ports have two-way communication.

A **serial port** transmits information over one wire one bit at a time. It is capable of two-way communication and is used by a variety of peripheral devices. Common devices include laser printers, serial printers, and scanners. Serial ports have male connectors and are often referred to as COM ports or RS-232 ports. The two main types of serial connectors that you will find on IBM and compatible computers are the DB-25 and the DB-9, which have 25 and 9 pins, respectively. Adapters are available to convert from one to the other.

Parallel ports are faster than serial ports because they move more data at one time; however, serial ports are more versatile and can be used by a wider number of peripherals.

Other ports found on your computer include mouse ports, game ports, small computer system interface ports, video connectors, phone jacks, and audio output jacks.

A **mouse port** is a round serial port especially for connecting the mouse. A mouse that connects directly into a mouse port is called a bus mouse. A serial mouse can be connected to a standard serial port, but that renders the port unavailable for other devices.

A **game port**, or **analog-to-digital port**, connects joysticks or paddles. These devices move the cursor around on-screen and are often used with games, hence the name game port. A DB-15 female connecter is commonly used.

A **small computer system interface (SCSI) port** (pronounced "scuzzy") is a fast, versatile parallel port that is capable of transferring up to 32 bits of information at a time. This type of port is seeing greater use as more and more peripheral devices are becoming available. Many laser printers and scanners use SCSI ports. Because of its speed, a SCSI port allows you to connect up to seven peripheral devices together and hook them up to one port. This is called daisy chaining.

Your computer also has a **video port** into which the monitor is plugged. Common video ports on IBM and compatible computers include a 9-pin female connector or a 15-pin female connector. The 9-pin connector is used by monochrome monitors and color CGA and EGA monitors. The 15-pin connector is used by VGA and other high-resolution monitors.

There are some other special connectors on your computer such as modular phone jacks on the back of a modem card or minijacks to connect headphones for audio output.

What Are Device Drivers?

A **device driver** is software that allows peripheral devices to communicate with your computer and other peripheral devices. Common examples of peripherals that require device drivers include printers, mice, and monitors.

DOS and the Macintosh operating systems use device drivers differently. Device drivers are part of the Macintosh operating system and require little or no setup by the user. For example, every Macintosh program can automatically use a mouse because the driver is part of the operating system. On the other hand, for many programs DOS requires that you install one or more software files that make up a device driver. Some programs install these files automatically.

Device drivers for printers and a mouse are the ones you will most likely have to deal with when working with DOS. Every DOS application requires a printer driver. A **printer driver** tells the computer what kind of printer it will be working with and what type of printing capabilities the printer has (such as font availability and page layout). When ready to print, the driver converts text and graphics into a series of codes the printer understands. Laser printers and others that print a variety of fonts use a set of codes known as the **page description language (PDL).** The PDL dictates character size, font style, line spacing, and other features. The two most common PDLs are Adobe System's PostScript and Hewlett-Packard's PCL (Printer Control Language).

A **mouse driver** enables programs to use a mouse. The driver comes with the mouse itself instead of with an application program. The mouse driver is installed on a hard disk and must be loaded into memory each time the computer is started.

Summary

The process of translating machine-readable data into a form that can be understood by humans or a form that can be read by other machines is called output. The information that is the result of processing is also referred to as output. An output device is the hardware that enables a computer to communicate information to humans or other machines.

Output that people can read is categorized as either hard copy or soft copy. Hard copy is a relatively stable and permanent form of output, such as paper, that can be read immediately or stored and read later. Soft copy, for example, screen-displayed output or voice output, is a transient form of output.

Output is made more meaningful by ensuring the input is correct, by organizing it into reports, and by appropriately presenting it to the intended audience.

Hard copy output devices include printers, plotters, and computer output microform devices. Printers are categorized as either impact or nonimpact printers, based on how the mechanism prints the characters. They can also be categorized by whether they print a character, line, or page at a time. Printers also differ in the type of form feed and carriage width.

A major characteristic of printers is the quality of the print produced. This includes typeset-quality print, letter-quality print, near-letter-quality print, standard quality print, and compressed print.

Dot-matrix, daisy-wheel, ink-jet, and laser printers are commonly used with microcomputers. Large computer systems generally use much faster printers, such as chain, drum, band, and commercial laser printers.

Six types of printers are commonly used to produce output in color: color dot-matrix printers, color ink-jet printers, color wax thermal printers, phase change printers, dye sublimation printers, and color laser printers.

A plotter is an output device that uses a pen attached to a movable arm to draw graphic images on paper.

Computer output microform (COM) involves producing hard copy in the form of photographic images recorded on microfilm or microfiche cards. A computer-assisted retrieval system (CARS) allows fast retrieval of data stored on microforms.

Soft copy output devices include monitors and voice-output systems.

A monitor is a televisionlike device that displays data or information. A monitor's quality is measured in terms of resolution, a measure of the number of pixels that the display screen of a monitor contains. A pixel is the smallest increment of a display screen that can be controlled individually. Dot pitch describes the size of the dots that make up the images. The smaller the dot pitch, the sharper the image will be. The refresh rate is the number of times a screen is scanned to maintain an image. It is important because it produces flicker. Flicker is a shimmering illusion created by the pixels going on and off. The slower the refresh rate, the greater the flicker and the more eyestrain. An interlaced screen scans all the even lines first and then returns to scan all the odd lines. This makes the cost of the monitor lower but it increases flicker. A noninterlaced screen scans every line from top to bottom sequentially and produces less flicker. A multisync or multiscanning monitor supports refresh rates for VGA and higher resolutions. This is an advantage when upgrading to a higher resolution since you only have to buy a new adapter card and not both a card and monitor.

Two popular types of monitor screen display are the cathode-ray tube (CRT) and the flat-panel display. Common types of flat-panel displays include liquid-crystal display (LCD) and gas-plasma display. Two types of LCDs are passive matrix and active matrix.

A graphics adapter card is a circuit board inside the computer that converts the electronic signals sent by your computer into a form usable by the monitor. In IBM and compatible computers there are several common types of graphics adapter cards: MDA, Hercules Graphics Card, CGA, EGA, VGA, and SuperVGA. Color depth is the amount of memory required in bits per pixel to produce a certain number of colors.

The use of a voice by the computer for output is called voice output. It is used where a display screen would not work or be appropriate, for example in automobile warning systems, systems designed for the blind and visually impaired, and in toys and games. Speech coding and voice synthesis are two different approaches to voice output.

Some devices are capable of both sending data and instructions to the computer and receiving information from the computer. They are called input/output devices. A terminal, also called a video display terminal (VDT), is an input/output device that consists of a keyboard and a monitor.

Terminals can be designed as dumb terminals that have no processing capabilities or intelligent terminals that have a microprocessor and can perform some processing. Terminals can be designed for special purposes such as a point-of-sale (POS) terminal. Disk and tape drives also function as input/output devices allowing data and instructions to be output to them, stored, and then input back into the computer.

Expansion ports, or input/output I/O ports, allow your computer to communicate with peripheral devices such as printers and mice.

An interface cable connects a peripheral device to the computer. A parallel port transmits information over eight wires eight bits at a time. A serial port transmits information over one wire one bit at a time. A mouse port is a round serial port made especially for connecting a bus mouse. A serial mouse can be connected to a standard serial port. A game port, or analog-to-digital port, connects joysticks or paddles. A small computer system interface (SCSI) port (pronounced "scuzzy") is a fast, versatile parallel port that is capable of transferring up to 32 bits of information at a time. Your monitor is plugged into a video port.

Some computers have ports for modular phone jacks and minijacks to connect headphones for audio output.

A device driver is software that allows peripheral devices to communicate with your computer and other peripheral devices. A printer driver tells the computer what kind of printer it will be working with and what printing capabilities that printer has. A page description language (PDL) is a series of codes into which text and graphics are translated so that the printer can understand them. This conversion is performed by the print driver.

A mouse driver lets programs use a mouse.

VOCABULARY SELF-TEST

Can you define the following terms?

active-matrix display (p. 137)

analog-to-digital port (p. 142)

band printer (p. 130)

cathode-ray tube (CRT) (p. 136)

chain printer (p. 130)

character printer (p. 126)

color dot-matrix printer (p. 131)

color ink-jet printer (p. 131)

color laser printer (p. 132)

color wax thermal printer (p. 131)

compressed print (p. 127)

computer-assisted retrieval system (CARS) (p. 133)

computer output microform (COM) (p. 133)

daisy-wheel printer (p. 129)

device driver (p. 143)

dot-matrix printer (p. 128)

dot pitch (p. 135)

drum printer (p. 130)

dumb terminal (p. 140)

dye sublimation printer (p. 132)

expansion port (p. 141)

flat-panel display (p. 136)

flicker (p. 136)

game port (p. 142)

gas-plasma display (p. 137)

graphics adapter card (p. 137)

hard copy (p. 125)

impact printer (p. 126)

ink-jet printer (p. 129)

input/output (I/O) device (p. 139)

input/output (I/O) port (p. 141)

intelligent terminal (p. 140)

interface cable (p. 142)

interlaced screen (p. 136)

laser printer (p. 129)

letter-quality print (p. 127)

line printer (p. 126)

liquid-crystal display (LCD) (p. 137)

monitor (p. 134)

mouse driver (p. 143)

mouse port (p. 142)

multisync monitor (p. 136)

near-letter-quality (NLQ) print
   (p. 127)

nonimpact printer (p. 126)

noninterlaced screen (p. 136)

output (p. 125)

output device (p. 125)

page description language (PDL)
   (p. 143)

page printer (p. 126)

parallel port (p. 142)

passive-matrix display (p. 137)

phase change printer (p. 132)

pixel (p. 134)

plotter (p. 132)

point-of-sale (POS) terminal
   (p. 140)

portable printer (p. 130)

printer (p. 126)

printer driver (p. 143)

refresh rate (p. 136)

report (p. 125)

resolution (p. 134)

serial port (p. 142)

small computer system interface
   (SCSI) port (p. 142)

soft copy (p. 125)

speech coding (p. 139)

standard-quality print (p. 127)

terminal (p. 139)

typeset-quality print (p. 127)

video port (p. 142)

voice output (p. 139)

voice synthesis (p. 139)

REVIEW QUESTIONS

Multiple Choice

1. A(n) _____ allows a computer to communicate information to humans or another machine by accepting data from the computer and translating them into a usable form.
    a. output device
    b. program
    c. input device
    d. print driver

2. _____ is a relatively stable and permanent form of output.
    a. A screen display
    b. Hard copy
    c. Voice output
    d. Soft copy

3. Which of the following is the highest quality print type?
    a. compressed
    b. letter-quality

    c. standard-quality

    d. near-letter quality

4. Printers produce characters on a page using two basic types of printing mechanisms; they are _____.

    a. electrical and mechanical

    b. impact and nonimpact

    c. hard and soft

    d. dot-matrix and daisy-wheel

5. A(n) _____ printer uses a print head composed of 9 to 24 pins to produce patterns of dots on paper.

    a. laser

    b. daisy-wheel

    c. nonimpact

    d. dot-matrix

6. _____ is a measure of monitor screen quality.

    a. Flicker

    b. Resolution

    c. Refresh rate

    d. Dot pitch

7. The smallest increment on a display screen that can be individually controlled is called a(n) _____.

    a. dot

    b. cursor

    c. electron

    d. pixel

8. A(n) _____ produces images by aligning molecular crystals.

    a. backlight

    b. LCD

    c. gas-plasma display

    d. CRT

9. The process of electronically reproducing human sounds is called _____.

    a. voice synthesis

    b. voice input

    c. voice recognition

    d. speech coding

10. A(n) _____ allows the computer to physically connect to and communicate with peripheral devices.

    a. intelligent terminal

    b. device driver

    c. terminal

    d. expansion port

Fill-In

1. A screen display is an example of _____ copy output.

2. The _____ is an impact printer that produces letter-quality print.

3. A drum printer is an example of a(n) _____ printer.

4. A(n) _____ is an output device that uses a pen attached to a movable arm to draw graphic images on paper.
5. Hard copy in the form of photographic images recorded on microforms is called _____.
6. The _____ is the number of times a screen is scanned to maintain an image.
7. The shimmering illusion created by the pixels going on and off is called _____.
8. A(n) _____ is a circuit board inside the computer that converts the electronic signals sent by your computer into a form usable by the monitor.
9. A terminal is an example of a(n) _____, which is used to transfer data and instructions to the computer, as well as to receive information from the computer.
10. A(n) _____ is software that allows peripheral devices to communicate with your computer and other peripheral devices.

Short Answer

1. Relate several ways in which output can be made meaningful.
2. List and describe the differences between four common printing devices for microcomputers.
3. Give a summary of the six types of printers that can produce color output.
4. Why aren't CRT displays practical for portable computers? Compare the displays used in portable computers.
5. What is a pixel and how does it relate to a monitor's resolution?
6. What is the purpose of a graphics adapter card?
7. Describe the difference between speech coding and voice synthesis.
8. What is an input/output device? Give several examples.
9. Define expansion port and describe several different ports found on a typical microcomputer.
10. What is the purpose of a device driver?

Issues for Thought

1. The day may come when all computers are capable of interacting with the user through voice output. How might it affect the workplace? What are the advantages or disadvantages of voice output?
2. Some printers are capable of output that very closely mimics the look of paper money. In fact, the U.S. government is redesigning how some bills are made. What other ethical questions might arise from the use of high-quality output devices?

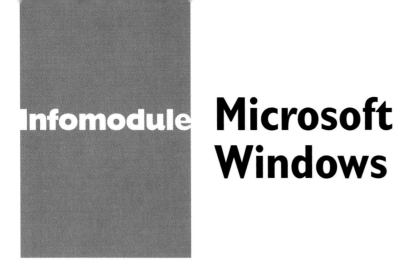

Microsoft Windows 3.1 Primer

Infomodule

Microsoft Windows (Windows) is a graphical environment for the DOS operating system that provides a graphical interface consistent from one application to the next. Learning new applications is easier because once you've learned the essentials for one application you've learned them for all other applications, too. This Infomodule introduces you to Microsoft Windows 3.1.

HOW DO I USE A MOUSE?

It is recommended and more efficient to use a mouse with Windows, but you can also use a keyboard. Four basic mouse techniques are pointing, clicking, double-clicking, and dragging. *Pointing* involves moving the mouse to maneuver a corresponding pointer on the screen. This pointer appears as an arrow, blinking underline, box, or other shape depending on the application. The pointer moves in the same direction and at the same speed as the mouse.

Once the pointer is placed where you want it, click the left mouse button to select an item, open an item, or move the cursor. *Clicking* is accomplished by pressing and then quickly releasing the mouse button. You might have heard or read the phrase "point and shoot" used when describing the use of a mouse. This refers to pointing and clicking.

Double-clicking involves quickly pressing the left mouse button twice before releasing it. Double-clicking is often the technique used to open or close an item. Another technique, *dragging,* is accomplished by holding down the left mouse button and moving the mouse so that the pointer moves (or drags) an object across the screen, resizes a portion of the screen, or selects text or objects.

HOW DO I START WINDOWS?

Starting Windows is easy: Type win at the DOS prompt and press ENTER. You may find it convenient to have Windows automatically started each time you turn on your computer. To do this, add the line win to the end of your AUTOEXEC.BAT file.

WHAT IS THE PROGRAM MANAGER?

When you start Windows, the Program Manager application starts. Figure 1 shows the Program Manager window. It lets you start applications, quit applications, and organize applications into groups so that they can be easily accessed. It runs the entire time that you are working in Windows.

When you run an application it appears in a rectangular area called a **window**. Windows appear on the background screen area called the **desktop**. Figure 1 shows the Program Manager application window on the desktop. The small graphical symbols inside a window are called **icons.** Icons represent groups or applications that you can run. Icons in the Program Manager window represent groups. A **group** is a collection of applications that can be run with Windows. Each window has a **title bar,** which identifies the group or application in the window. You will also see the **mouse pointer,** which selects and moves objects around the screen. By double-clicking on a group icon you open that group. A new window is opened and the icons representing the applications in that group are displayed. Figure 2 shows the applications in the Main Group. The Main Group window contains the applications included with Windows that help you work with it. Notice that the Main Group window is contained within the Program Manager

FIGURE 1
The Program Manager window.

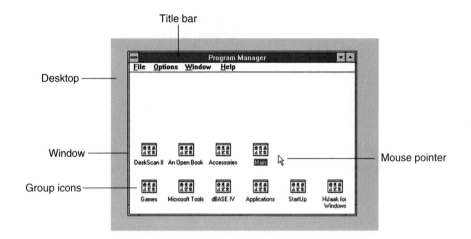

Title bar

Desktop

Window

Group icons

Mouse pointer

FIGURE 2
The Main Group window.

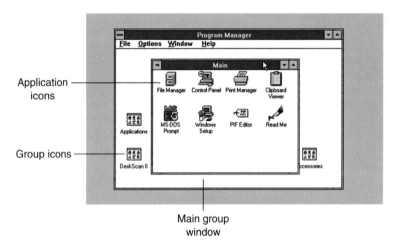

Application icons

Group icons

Main group window

window. Group windows always display within the Program Manager window.

Now let's start the Write application (a word processor), which is contained in the Accessories Group. First locate the Accessories Group icon and open it by placing the mouse pointer on it and double-clicking (Figure 3). Once the Accessories window is open, find the icon for Write and double-click on it. The Write word processor appears in an application window on the desktop ready for you to type in your text (Figure 4).

Once an application is running it may be easier to enlarge its window to use the full screen. Notice the button with the up arrow at the upper right corner of the Write window in Figure 4. This is the Maximize button. Clicking once on the Maximize button enlarges the window to the full screen (Figure 5). This is called maximizing the application window. When you maximize a window any other applications that are running continue to run but are hidden behind the maximized window. After maximizing a window the Maximize button is replaced with a Restore

FIGURE 3
The Accessories Group window.

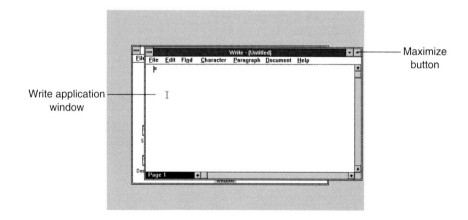

Write application icon

Accessories group window

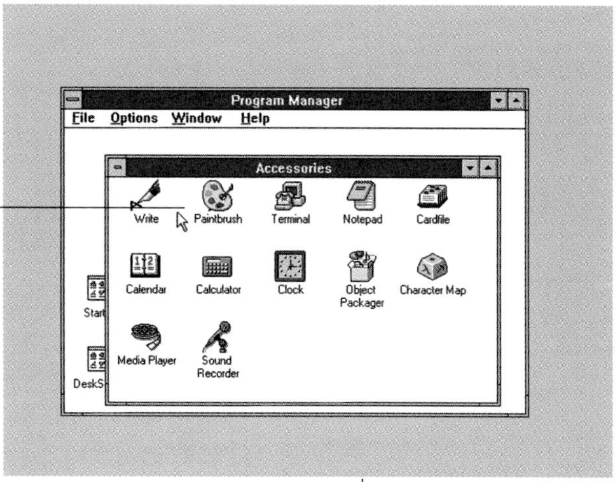

FIGURE 4
The Write application is displayed in its own window when running.

Maximize button

Write application window

button that contains both up and down arrows. Clicking once on the Restore button will return a maximized window to its previous size.

You may have a number of applications running on the desktop at one time. This leaves the desktop looking cluttered and makes it hard to work. To clear some space but still allow all the applications there to keep running, you can minimize some of the applica-

tions. Minimizing a window reduces it to an icon at the bottom of the screen. The application keeps running. The Minimize button in the upper right corner of a window contains a downward pointing arrow (Figure 5). To minimize an application, click once on the Minimize button. Figure 6 shows the Write window minimized. Any applications that are running, including the Program Manager, can be minimized. To

FIGURE 5
Clicking on the Maximize button enlarges a window to the full screen.

Minimize button

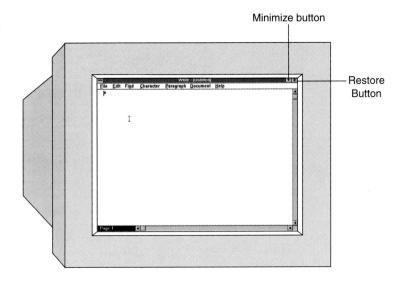

Restore Button

FIGURE 6
The Write application is minimized to an icon.

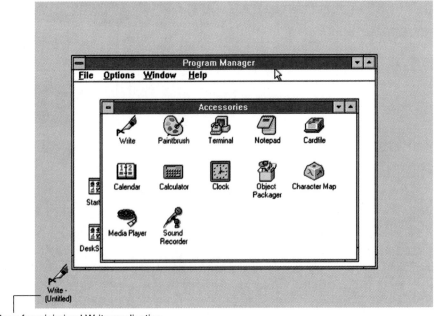

Icon for minimized Write application

restore a minimized application to its previous size, double-click on the icon at the bottom of the screen.

Another way to get organized is to move windows around on the desktop. Place the pointer on the title bar and drag the window to the desired location.

You can change the window's width, height, or both at the same time. To change the height, move the pointer slowly over the top or bottom border of a window until it changes to a double arrow pointer (Figure 7). Then drag the border until the window is the height you want. To change the width, follow the same steps using the left or right window borders. You change both the height and width at the same time by slowly moving the pointer to a corner of a window until you see a double-arrow pointer (Figure 8). Then drag the corner until the window is the desired height and width. When the size of a window is changed, it may cover other windows. These covered applications are still running. It is sometimes helpful to size the windows so you can see all the applications that are running at once.

When you have more than one application running at a time, the window that you are currently working in is called the **active window**. All other windows are inactive. The title bar in the active window changes color to differentiate it from inactive windows. To work with an application it must be the active window. Click anywhere on the window you wish to activate. The active window always appears in the foreground.

When windows overlap on the screen it can be difficult finding the application you need. If you resize the applications so they all fit on the screen, they may be too small to work with effectively. There are two choices that allow you to quickly and easily switch between applications. One is the Alt-Tab key sequence and the other is the Task List. You can quickly switch between applications if you press and

FIGURE 7
When you see the double-arrow pointer on the top or bottom border of a window you can drag the border to change the height of the window. A double-arrow pointer on the left or right side of a window can drag the border to change the width of a window.

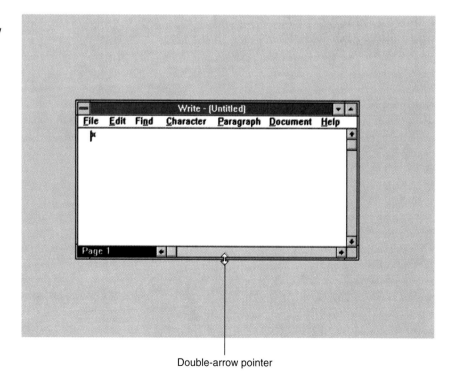

Double-arrow pointer

FIGURE 8
A double-arrow pointer on the
corner of a window can be used
to drag the corner and change
the height and width of a
window at the same time.

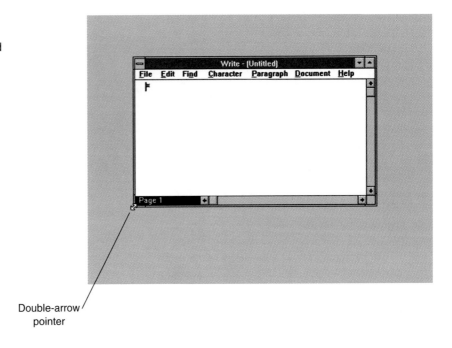

Double-arrow
pointer

hold the Alt key and then press the Tab key. This key combination can be used in two ways. Initially you should check the Desktop dialog box, which can be found in the Control Panel window by double-clicking on the Desktop icon. If the Fast "Alt+Tab" Switching check box is marked, each time you press the Tab key while holding down the Alt key, the title of an application that is currently running appears in the center of the screen. When the application you want to run appears, releasing the Alt-Tab keys brings that application to the foreground. However, if the Fast "Alt+Tab" Switching check box is *not* checked, the active window cycles among the currently running applications, but the name of the application will not be displayed on the screen.

The other option is the Task Switcher, which allows you to display a list of all the applications you are currently running, switch quickly to any running application, rearrange windows and icons on the desktop, and close an application. The Task List window is displayed either by double-clicking anywhere on the desktop, by pressing Ctrl-Esc, or by selecting the Switch To command from any application's

Control-Menu box. (The Control-Menu box is located in the upper left corner of a window and is particularly useful for keyboard users who work with Windows (Figure 9).) The Task List contains buttons that perform the following functions: Switch To switches to the selected application, End Task quits the selected application, Cascade layers windows on the screen so that you see the title of each, Tile resizes windows and arranges them side by side, Arrange Icons rearranges icons along the bottom of the display, and Cancel closes the Task List (Esc also closes the Task List).

Most windows have a **menu bar** at the top directly below the title bar (Figure 9), which contains a list of all the currently available menus for the application. Each menu contains a list of commands used for that application. To open a menu and view the list of commands, move the pointer to the desired menu and click. Figure 10 shows the list of commands found in the File menu. Choose a command by placing the pointer on the command and clicking. If you've opened a menu but do not choose a command, clicking anywhere outside the menu closes it.

FIGURE 9
A menu bar.

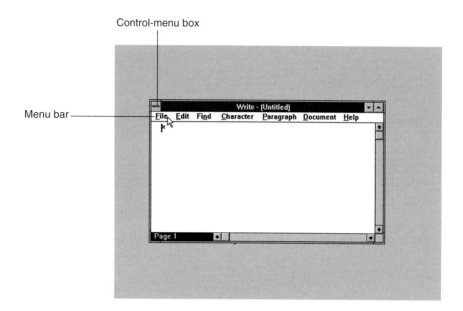

Control-menu box

Menu bar

FIGURE 10
Commands in a menu that are followed by three dots display a dialog box when they are selected.

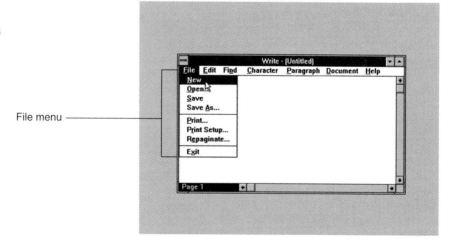

File menu

Figure 10 shows some commands in a menu. Commands not followed by three dots are executed immediately after they are selected. However, commands that do have three dots cause a dialog box to appear after being selected. A **dialog box** is displayed when a command needs more information before it can be executed. Figure 11 shows the dialog box for the Open command; it asks for the name of the file to open. Two ways in which dialog boxes ask for information are Text Boxes and List Boxes. Text Boxes allow you to enter text or data needed by a command. List Boxes give choices from which you select. You can enter a file name in one of two ways. Either type the name in the File Name Text Box with the flashing cursor or click on the file name in the List Box below the Text Box. It is highlighted and the name appears in the File Name Text Box. Or you can double-click on

FIGURE 11
The Open command dialog box.

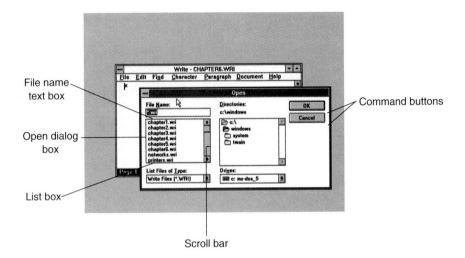

File name text box

Open dialog box

List box

Command buttons

Scroll bar

a file name in the List Box to immediately open the file. If more filenames are in the list than can appear in the List Box at one time you can use the scroll bars to look through the list to bring the additional information into view. They are found along the right side or bottom of a window whenever there is more information than can fit in the window. Clicking on the arrows in a vertical scroll bar displays information contained above or below the information currently in the window. The horizontal scroll bar located at the bottom of a window displays information to the right or left of what is currently in the window. Scrolling will be useful in most applications.

Dialog boxes also have command buttons for selecting actions. Two command buttons found in the Open dialog box are OK and Cancel (Figure 11). Once a filename is entered in the File Name Text Box clicking the OK button opens the file. Clicking the Cancel button exits the dialog box without opening a file. Help is another common command button that brings help for the current dialog box.

Dialog boxes also provide information through drop-down list boxes, option buttons, and check boxes. A drop-down list box appears initially as a rectangular box with the current selection marked by the cursor. When you click on the arrow at the right side of the rectangle a list of available choices appears (Figure 12a and b). Drop-down list boxes are often used in small or crowded dialog boxes. Option but-

tons are used when there are mutually exclusive options. Only one button can be selected at a time (Figure 13). Clicking on an option button selects the option and places a black dot in the button. All other options are dimmed. When one or more options can be selected at the same time check boxes are used (Figure 14). Clicking on a check box selects that option and places an X in the check box. Deselect an option by clicking on the check box to remove the X.

There are several methods you can use to close a window and quit an application. The quickest and easiest method is to double-click on the Control-Menu box. Or click once on the Control-Menu box and then select the Close command from the menu, or you could press Alt-F4. However, if you have any unsaved work you are first prompted to save the work before quitting the application (Figure 15).

You can perform other tasks with the Program Manager. These include adding or deleting applications to or from a group, creating or deleting groups, and adding applications to the startup group so that they start when Windows starts. Your Windows manual and the on-screen Help facilities give more details on the Program Manager.

WHAT IS THE FILE MANAGER?

The File Manager is the part of Windows that allows you to organize and maintain your files. We will look at a few basic file-related tasks: viewing the contents

FIGURE 12

(a) A drop-down list box as it appears before clicking on the down arrow box. (b) The same drop-down list box after clicking on the down arrow box to reveal the list of choices.

Drop-down list box (initial appearance)

Drop-down list box (opened)

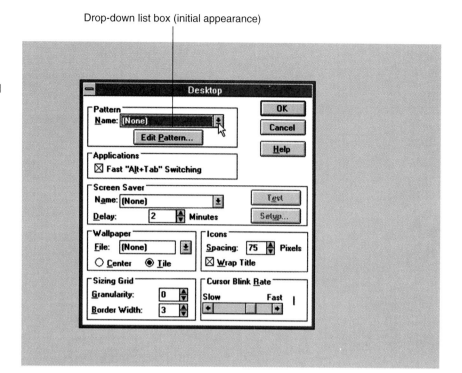

FIGURE 13
Option buttons represent
mutually exclusive options.

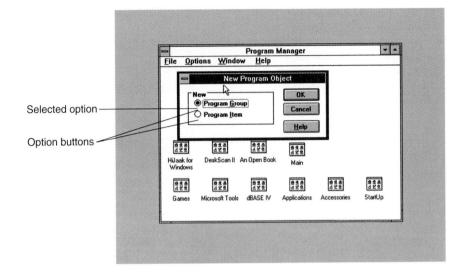

Selected option

Option buttons

FIGURE 14
Check boxes represent
nonexclusive options.

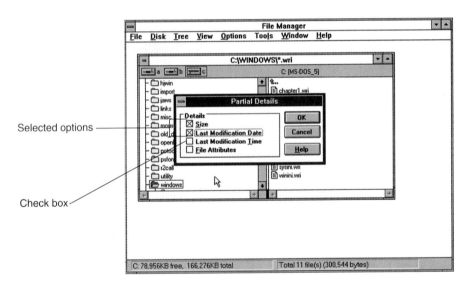

Selected options

Check box

of your directories; moving, copying and deleting files and directories; and changing to other disk drives.

The File Manager is started by finding the File Manager icon in the Main group window and double-clicking on the icon (Figure 16). The directory icons appear as file folders; the file icons take different forms depending on the nature of the file. The status bar at the bottom of the screen shows total disk space, the amount of space the open directory is

using, and the remaining space available. A directory window appears in the main File Manager window and shows the relationship of the files and directories stored on a disk. The directory tree is displayed on the left side of the window and the contents of the current directory are displayed on the right side.

The File Manager allows you to view the contents of any directory easily. Open the directory by clicking

FIGURE 15

If you have unsaved work when exiting an application, Windows prompts you to save the work before quitting.

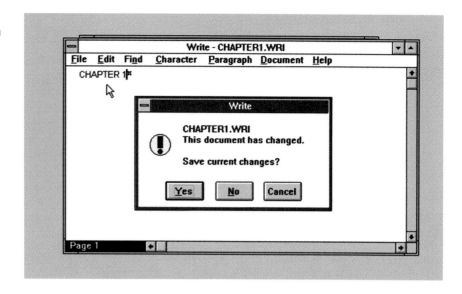

FIGURE 16

The File Manager window.

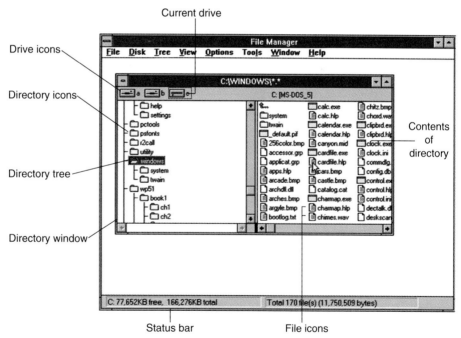

on its name or icon located on the left side of the window. Figure 16 shows the Windows directory opened with its contents displayed in the right side of the window. Once a directory is opened, to display the contents of another directory simply click on the

icon or name of the desired directory. The contents of the new directory replace the contents of the previous directory in the right-hand side of the window. If there is more text or graphics than can be displayed in a window at one time, use the scroll bar.

Files can be moved or copied quickly using the "drag and drop" feature of the File Manager. To move a file from your hard disk to a disk in drive A simply position the mouse pointer on the file icon, drag it to the icon for drive A, and release the mouse button. The same procedure is used to move from one directory to another. To copy a file, hold down the Ctrl key while dragging the icon to its destination.

Directly below the window title, the File Manager displays icons for all the drives on your system. The outlined icon represents the current drive. The directory window displays the directories and files on the current drive. To switch between drives, click on the drive icons. The directory window displays the contents of the chosen drive. For an additional directory window, double-click on the drive icon.

You can perform a number of other tasks with the File Manager including formatting and maintaining disks, printing documents, starting applications, changing the kind and amount of information displayed about each file, and connecting to network drives. Your Windows manuals and the on-line help facilities give more information about these options.

WHAT IS THE CONTROL PANEL?

From the Windows Control Panel you adjust system settings, for example, changing the look of the desktop and configuring certain hardware. The Control Panel is started by double-clicking its icon, found in the Main group window (Figure 17). Each icon in the Control Panel window represents a group of system settings that can be changed. Among those available are changing screen colors and desktop options, adding and removing fonts, and setting printer options. We'll look at the Desktop option used to change the look of your desktop. Double-click on the desktop icon to bring up the desktop dialog box. Locate the Wallpaper drop-down list box and click on the down arrow. Scroll through the list of files and click on marble.bmp. If you click on the OK command button at the top right of the dialog box, your desktop resembles the look of marble. Try other available options until you find a combination that is pleasing to you.

WHAT IS THE PRINT MANAGER?

Printing for all Windows applications is controlled by the Print Manager. The Print Manager window displays the status of your printer(s), the print jobs that are currently printing, and those waiting to be printed.

FIGURE 17
The Control Panel window.

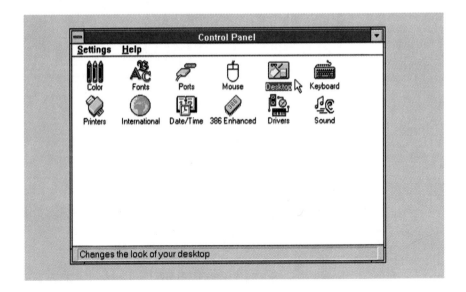

The Print Manager icon is found in the Main Group window and can be started by double-clicking on it. Some of the tasks it performs are checking the status of a print job, pausing and restarting a print job, and canceling a print job. To pause, restart, or cancel a print job you first need to select (highlight) an item and then click the appropriate button to carry out the desired action. The Print Manager also sets up a printer, changes priorities of a print job, displays printing messages, and connects to and disconnects from network printers.

HOW CAN I GET HELP?

Two manuals that are provided with the software, *Getting Started with Microsoft Windows* and the Microsoft Windows *User's Guide,* offer help. These manuals contain information on setting up and learning to use Microsoft Windows. In addition to the manuals, on-line help is also available. You can press the F1 key in any application to display a list of help topics for that application. Figure 18 shows the Help topics available for the Desktop option in the Control Panel group. Scroll through the list to find the topic you desire, place the mouse pointer on that topic, and click for a display on the desired topic. Many dialog boxes include a Help button. Clicking the mouse pointer on the Help button or pressing F1 when the dialog box is displayed brings up help for that particular dialog box. A third way to receive on-line help is to choose the Help menu from any application (Figure 19).

After you select a Help option a Help window is displayed (Figure 20) with a series of buttons along the top to guide you to the information you need. These include the Contents, Search, Back, History, and Glossary buttons. The Contents button displays a list of topics for an application. The Search button displays a dialog box for you to specify the searched for topic. Clicking on the Back button displays the previously viewed topic. To see a chronological list of all help topics viewed since the start of your current Windows session, click on the History box. Windows terms and definitions are displayed by clicking on the Glossary button. To get help to use Help, press the F1 key while a Help window is open or select How To Use Help from an applications Help menu.

FIGURE 18
The Desktop Help window.

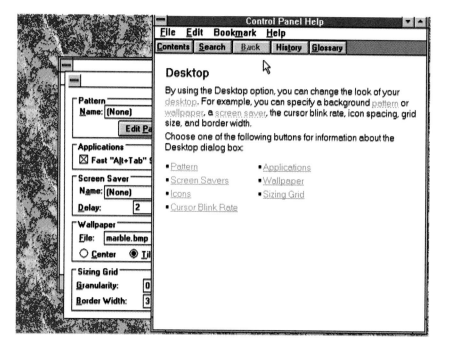

FIGURE 19
A Help menu.

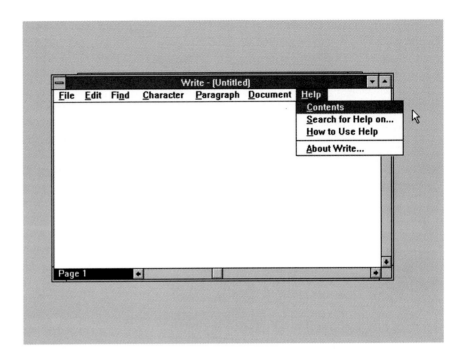

FIGURE 20
A Help window.

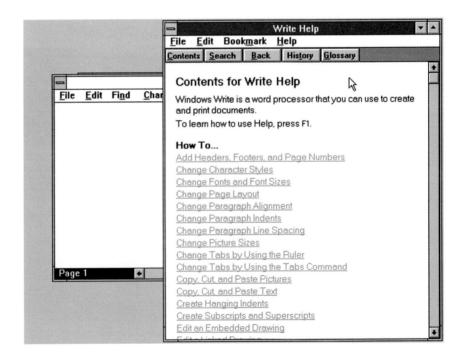

HOW DO I QUIT WINDOWS?

The quickest way to quit Windows is by double-clicking the Control-Menu box in the Program Manager. You can also select Exit from the Program Manager File Menu. The Exit Windows dialog box appears and advises that choosing this command ends your current Windows session. The dialog box has two command buttons, OK and Cancel. Clicking on Cancel resumes the current Windows session; clicking on OK ends the current Windows session and returns you to the DOS prompt.

VOCABULARY SELF-TEST

Can you define the following terms?

active window (p. 153)

desktop (p. 149)

dialog box (p. 155)

group (p. 149)

icons (p. 149)

menu bar (p. 154)

Microsoft Windows (p. 149)

mouse pointer (p. 149)

title bar (p. 149)

window (p. 149)

REVIEW QUESTIONS

Multiple Choice

1. Which of the following mouse moves relocates items around the screen and resizes portions of the screen?
   a. double-clicking
   b. pointing
   c. dragging
   d. clicking
2. How are group windows and applications opened?
   a. clicking on the icon
   b. dragging the icon outside of its window
   c. highlighting the icon and clicking on the File menu
   d. double-clicking on the icon

3. Which is not true of a minimized application?
   a. remains running
   b. no longer in the active window
   c. operations are temporarily suspended
   d. reduced to an icon at the bottom of the screen
4. What window is used to view a listing of the directories on your disk?
   a. File Manager
   b. Control Panel
   c. Program Manager
   d. Print Manager
5. What icon in the Main Group window is selected to view the icons for adjusting the settings on your system, such as screen color and the desktop appearance?
   a. File Manager
   b. Accessories
   c. Windows Setup
   d. Control Panel

Fill-In

1. The background screen area on which windows are displayed is called the _____.
2. The rectangular areas on the screen that enclose applications are called _____.
3. A(n) _____ is a collection of applications that can be run with Windows.
4. The _____ is used to select and move objects around the screen.
5. A(n) _____ is displayed when a command needs more information before it can be executed.

Short Answer

1. What are the effects of maximizing and minimizing windows?
2. Describe how to move and resize a window.
3. Differentiate the two methods that allow you to switch between running applications.
4. Summarize three ways that dialog boxes provide information needed by a command.
5. Identify the basic functions of the File Manager, Control Panel, and Print Manager.

OUTLINE

OBJECTIVES

5.1 State the purpose of secondary storage.

5.2 Describe the basic hierarchy of data organization.

5.3 Contrast three methods of storing and accessing a file.

5.4 Identify main types of magnetic secondary storage.

5.5 Identify several different forms of optical secondary storage.

5.6 Describe the general characteristics of secondary storage.

5.7 Recognize common secondary storage problems and possible solutions.

Chapter 5

Secondary Storage

165

Profile

John von Neumann

"You know he's a Martian disguised as a human being." That's what the neighbors said.

Who was this alleged alien whose findings would have a resounding impact on the future of computers? Well, in a 1945 scientific draft paper that has served as the basis for the logic structure of subsequent computers, he explained how the computer processed information. This man was John von Neumann—one of the pioneers of the "stored-program concept." Von Neumann proposed a way to encode instructions so they could reside inside the computer. He based his theory on the idea that an internally stored program would save many hours of laborious, manual work needed to reset switches and wiring that were required to reprogram the early computers. This increased the speed at which calculations were performed, and led to what many say was the beginning of the computer age.

Von Neumann was born in Budapest, Hungary, in 1903. He studied in Germany at Göttingen University, a prestigious center of mathematical research. He spoke German fluently and even thought in German, translating those thoughts to English.

Friends and acquaintances were baffled by his ability to calculate complex mathematical problems in his head. He had the power of total recall and could recite entire books from memory many years after he had read them. Von Neumann employed this ability to accumulate a vast array of jokes, anecdotes, stories, and risque limericks to amuse his friends. On the other hand, the highways were unsafe with the reckless von Neumann behind the wheel because he was known to drive on either side of the road; once he even asserted that a tree jumped in front of his car, causing an accident. His combination of awe-inspiring creative intellect and personal idiosyncrasies may account for the legends that surround him.

In the 1930s, von Neumann moved to the United States. He went to Princeton and soon immersed himself in studying hydrodynamics—the principles of fluid motion. His knowledge of hydrodynamics, a crucial aspect in designing atomic bombs, enabled von Neumann to produce a mathematical model that showed exactly how bombs would perform. This work apparently appealed to von Neumann as a "problem" to be solved, not a question of lives to be lost.

Was it chance, in 1944, that brought Herbert Goldstine and von Neumann together at a train station? Regardless, it was there that the two mathematicians met and talked about a computing machine that Goldstine was working on—the ENIAC, one of the first operational electronic digital computers. The ENIAC fascinated von Neumann; he now devoted his energies to thinking about something more important than bombs—computers.

While examining von Neumann for a shoulder injury in 1955, doctors discovered he had bone cancer. His life prognosis was six months. Perhaps the radioactivity exposure during the atomic bomb testing was responsible. At any rate, von Neumann's death at 54 was a tremendous loss.

Von Neumann viewed the living brain as more than a highly complicated digital computer, and he doubted that a computer could duplicate its functions. Unfortunately, he did not live to see the miniaturization of parts that may someday make artificial intelligence a reality.

C hapter 2 described main memory, a temporary storage location for data or instructions. This chapter introduces secondary storage, which holds data and instructions permanently, or relatively permanently. You will learn how data are organized and examine several file storage and access methods. Common secondary storage devices and media and their characteristics are described. Additionally, secondary storage problems and solutions are discussed.

Objective 5.1   State the purpose of secondary storage.

What Is Secondary Storage?

Data and instructions are loaded into main memory when they are to be worked on by the CPU. Although this allows very fast access to the data or instructions, main memory is volatile. A computer needs to store data or instructions for extended periods of time. **Secondary storage** provides a nonvolatile means of keeping large amounts of data for permanent or long-term storage. The data in secondary storage can be easily loaded into main memory. Let's examine the hierarchy of data and several methods of storing and accessing data.

Objective 5.2   Describe the basic hierarchy of data organization.

How Are Data Organized?

This section explores some ways data are organized in and accessed from secondary storage. Organization of ideas or tangible objects is the key to productivity. Finding the right wrench in a toolbox is easy if they are laid out smallest to largest rather than scattered. The same logic applies to data stored on secondary storage media.

Why Organize Data in a Structured Manner?

Imagine for a moment that you are the instructor of a class. Assume that there are 30 students in class and you assign grades weekly for tests, homework, and computer lab reports. During each week of a 16-week semester, you collect and grade material from all three sources. When you finish grading each piece of work, you mark the student's name and grade on a piece of paper and toss it onto your desk. Each week you accumulate another 90 pieces of paper. At the end of the semester, the grades are due by noon. You must find over 1,400 pieces of paper, organize them, and calculate a grade for each student. This method is not very productive, is it?

The same haphazard data entry into a computer renders the data virtually useless. To be effective and achieve the most efficiency, you must systematically organize the data. In the example, setting up an organized plan could have prevented many problems. If you keep a gradebook with a row for each student's name and break down the columns following each name to record grades for each test, homework assignment, and computer lab report, at the end of the semester, it would be easy to locate and average the grades.

Data Hierarchy

Data Hierarchy

- Database
- File
- Record
- Field
- Byte
- Bit

The hierarchy of computer data organization, from the most general to the most specific, is database, file, record, field, byte, and bit. A **database** is a cross-referenced collection of files designed to minimize repetition of data. A database could be compared to listing all the gradebooks from all of the instructors together so any of the data contained in them could be accessed from one program.

A **file** is a collection of records (similar groups of data) that fit under one name or heading. An individual gradebook is an example of a file. All data in the gradebook deal with that instructor's students and their grades.

A file may be further separated into records. A **record** is a collection of related data items. Information about a particular student, such as name and test scores, is an individual record. The information in the record pertains to that student only, but all of that information is related to class grades.

In a record, space must be allocated for data. Each individual classification of data stored in the record is called a **field**. Each record may contain one or more fields. Once again, in the instructor example, there are many fields: one for the student's name, one for each test grade, one for each homework grade, and one for each computer lab report grade (Figure 5.1).

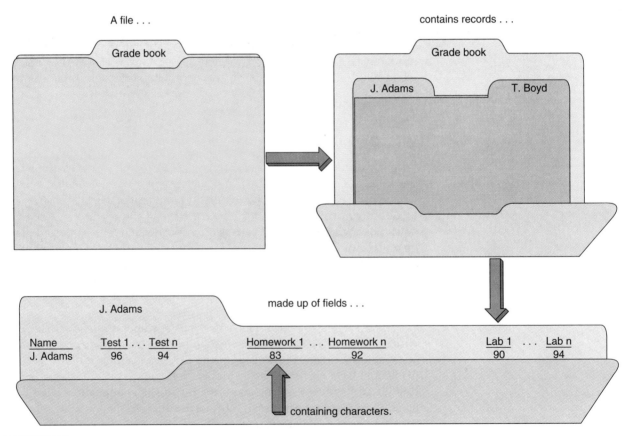

FIGURE 5.1
Organization of data by file, record, field, byte, and bit.

To round out the hierarchy, each character in a field is represented internally to the computer as a byte. Each **byte** is composed of eight bits. The **bit** is the smallest unit of data that the computer recognizes.

Objective 5.3   Contrast three methods of storing and accessing a file.

How Are Files Stored and Accessed?

Application and processing requirements dictate which of the following organizational structures is most appropriate, and the computer professional who designs the system makes that decision. Some of the things to be considered include the resources available, the access time, programming requirements, the software products available, as well as both present and future needs.

There are three primary methods of storing files in and retrieving them from secondary storage. These are (1) sequential-access, (2) direct-access, and (3) indexed file processing.

Sequential-Access File Processing

Sequential-access file processing is a method of storing and retrieving information in sequential order (Figure 5.2). Records in a sequential file appear one after another in the order they were entered into the computer and subsequently stored on the medium. Access to any file requires a program to start reading from the beginning.

Think of finding a song in the middle of a cassette tape. If you were at the beginning of the tape you would have to listen to each song from the beginning before you reached that particular song. A mailing list is an example where sequential processing is appropriate. Usually it would not be necessary to immediately access a name from the middle of the list.

Direct-Access File Processing

Direct-access file processing, also called random-access file processing, is a method in which files or records in a file can be located, retrieved, and updated without reading each preceding file or record, regardless of how they were stored (Figure 5.3). This is done through a key field. A **key field** uniquely identifies each record. Account numbers, employee identification numbers, and Social Security numbers are examples of key fields. Playing a

File-Access Methods

- Sequential
- Direct
- Indexed

FIGURE 5.2
With the sequential-access method, records are stored and accessed in a row (sequentially). When accessing a record, all preceding records in the file must be accessed first. Here, to access Record 4, Records 1, 2, and 3 must be accessed first.

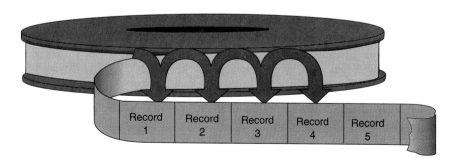

FIGURE 5.3
With the direct-access method, records can be accessed directly without accessing all of the preceding records. Here, Record 4 can be accessed directly, without accessing any other records.

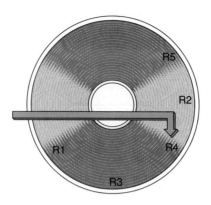

song on a compact disk is an example of direct access. You can program the compact disk player to go directly to a particular song without playing those before it.

Direct access is best used where files or records do not rely on one another, such as with customer data. For example, when a bank customer withdraws money from a savings account, the computer goes to the random file, accesses the record with the customer's account number, and updates the record with an amount withdrawn debit.

Processing data using direct-access files is much faster, thereby making the computer more convenient to use and more vital to a company's performance. In fact, the ability of the computer to instantaneously store and retrieve data via random files has created new businesses and industries whose main function is the dissemination of information. Credit card companies, credit bureaus, travel agencies, airlines, banks, insurance companies, telephone companies, and most government agencies would offer greatly reduced services if they did not have the ability to access files directly.

Indexed File Processing

The third method, **indexed file processing,** incorporates elements of both sequential and direct access. An indexed file can be set up in many ways. Figure 5.4 shows a very elementary view of one type. Basically, the records are stored sequentially when the indexed file is created. When additional records are added to the file, they are stored out of sequence in an overflow area on the disk. In Figure 5.4 the "O" entries are stored out of sequence in the overflow area. Each record has a key field that contains data unique to that record in a file. The key field in the example is indicated by a letter in parentheses. An index of the key fields from each record is kept. Each key field in the index is associated with an address that specifies where the record is stored on disk. The index is usually kept sorted and updated automatically to allow both sequential and direct access. The index then is searched by key field to access a record. When the key field is found, the record can be accessed directly using the address associated with the key field. To search sequentially, the record associated with the first key

FIGURE 5.4
The indexed method allows records to be accessed either sequentially or directly.

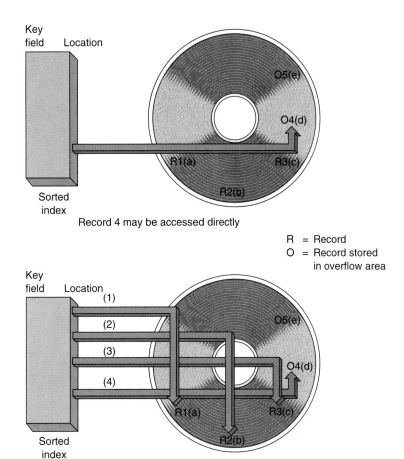

Record 4 may be accessed directly

R = Record
O = Record stored in overflow area

Record 4 may be accessed sequentially

field in the sorted index is accessed followed by the rest of the index in sequential order. The sorted index allows records to be found in sequence no matter where they are physically located on the disk. In practice, there are usually multiple indexes that narrow the location of each record. This type of file access does not work with tape because tape is a sequential-access medium only. This method is analogous to searching the table of contents of a book in order to find exactly where a particular subject matter would be found.

The disadvantage of indexed files is that the process of searching the index for the key creates an additional, time-consuming step. However, even though indexed files are slightly slower for random access than are direct files, their versatility is a significant advantage and makes them a popular form of storage.

Search Methods

To find the appropriate data or information, keys are often used. There can be many keys, with each "pointing" to the location of a particular record.

For the key to find its target information various search algorithms are used. **Algorithms** are finite sets of step-by-step instructions for carrying out a particular task. Search algorithms include the hash search, binary search, and the linear search.

Hash searches use a method called hashing. The key is given a numeric value which is used in calculating the location of the corresponding record. An alphabetic key might be given a numeric value by adding the ASCII values of all the letters in the key. Then, by a prescribed formula, this final value would indicate the proper record. Hash searches allow direct access to the information being sought and are very efficient.

Binary searches use a key value and compare it to values in an ordered (i.e., ascending or descending) list of values of the target information. The key's value is compared to a value in the middle of the ordered list. If the key's value is greater the lower half of the list is discarded. This process is repeated, with the key's value being compared to the middle of the sorted list and again half of the list being eliminated. This continues until the proper information is located.

The *linear search* is the simplest but least efficient of the search algorithm methods. In a linear search the entire list is searched sequentially until the target information is found. The linear search is usually used only on short lists.

Objective 5.4   Identify main types of magnetic secondary storage.

What Are the Main Types of Magnetic Secondary Storage?

Magnetic secondary-storage media used with all sizes of computers are magnetic tapes and magnetic disks. These media are nonvolatile. Desktop as well as smaller portable computers use both tape and disk storage. Because of their size, they have storage capacities much less than their large system computer counterparts. Large system computers use both magnetic tapes and magnetic disks like small computers. The main difference is that the secondary storage media and devices are capable of storing considerably larger amounts of data and handle the data at a much faster rate of speed.

Magnetic Tape

Forms of Magnetic Tape

- Reel-to-reel
- Cassette
- Cartridge

Typically, **magnetic tape** is a one-half or one-fourth inch ribbon of mylar (a plastic material) coated with a thin layer of iron oxide. The **tape drive** is an input/output device that reads and writes data on tape. The tape passes by a read/write head, the electromagnetic component that contains heads that read, write, and erase data on the tape. When the tiny, haphazardly arranged particles of iron oxide are aligned through magnetization, data are stored as magnetized spots. If they are aligned (polarized) in one direction, the particle represents a 1; in the opposite direction, it represents a 0. To read, the drive passes the tape by the read head and the patterns of 1s and 0s are interpreted as pieces of data.

Magnetic tape stores records, or groups of related data, sequentially (one after another). To get to the data you're looking for, a computer must read every preceding record.

You may have heard that expression on TV commercials for different products. You could also apply this saying to computer users as well. How important is it to "pay me now"? Well, take the case of Amoco Research Center in Naperville, Illinois. One day almost 1,000 files were accidentally deleted from the network. They represented a year and a half of data at a cost of over $150,000. But Amoco had paid up front and a backup system was already in place. The information was restored in about 20 minutes. In addition to the on-site backup, Amoco puts the complete backup tapes in a climatized, fireproof vault off-site.

Off-site backup worked very well for Kemper Securities, Inc. Their World Trade Center office found this out one February day in 1993 when a terrorist bomb exploded. Kemper backs up its vital New York office data to computers in Milwaukee every night. The following Monday after the blast, workers in New York were back in temporary offices complete with their customer files intact.

Fortunately, Kemper's data were contained on mainframes and minicomputers. For microcomputer users backup procedures are not automatic. Some users could be seen trying to salvage their PCs from the debris of the World Trade Center explosion. "Pay me later."

Tapes store large quantities of data inexpensively; therefore, they are often used as backup storage media. Magnetic tapes are erasable, reusable, and durable. They can easily be cataloged and stored in a tape library (Figure 5.5). However, magnetic tape is not well suited for data files that are revised or updated often. These files should be stored on a medium that offers faster and more direct access to the data.

Although mainly used with large computers, magnetic tapes can be found with all sizes of computers. They are made in reel-to-reel, cassette, and cartridge forms.

Magnetic tape is generally used with microcomputers for backing up (making copies of) the contents of a hard disk. **Cassette tape** (also called a data cartridge) (Figure 5.6) is one-fourth inch wide and enclosed in a plastic case that resembles the cassette tape used for audio recording. It is relatively inexpensive and has a storage capacity in excess of a gigabyte. One-half inch **cartridge tape** (Figure 5.7) is another form of magnetic tape. Tapes store more data in relatively the same physical space as a disk. A disadvantage, however, is that access to the data is sequential.

Half-inch cartridge tapes and reel-to-reel systems are popular as secondary-storage media for large computer systems. A **reel-to-reel tape** is magnetic tape placed on open reels about 10½ inches in diameter (Figure 5.8). A typical tape is about 2,400 feet long and one-half inch wide. It holds many megabytes of data. Data transfer rates vary from approximately 5,000 bytes per second to over one million bytes per second. Reel-to-reel tapes are relatively inexpensive, durable and hold a large quantity of data. The cartridge tape used for large system computers provides much more storage capacity and is much smaller than its reel-to-reel tape counterpart.

FIGURE 5.5
This magnetic tape library is located in the Santa Fe Railway Computer Center at Topeka, Kansas. (Courtesy of Santa Fe Southern Pacific Corp.)

FIGURE 5.6
Cassette tapes for data storage are similar to cassette tapes used for audio recording. (Merrill Publishing/Cobalt Productions)

Magnetic Disk

A **magnetic disk** is a mylar or metallic platter on which electronic data can be stored. Although disks resemble phonograph records, they do not have the characteristic spiraling groove, even though data are accessed in much the same way as an individual song is selected on a record. Data files on a magnetic disk can be read sequentially, as tape is, or directly. The main advantages of a magnetic disk over magnetic tape include the ability to: (1)

FIGURE 5.7

This tape cartridge is approximately one-half the size of a videocassette and holds about 20,000 pages of information. (Courtesy of BASF Corporation Information Systems)

(a)

(b)

FIGURE 5.8

(a) Magnetic reel-to-reel tape with raw iron oxide. (Courtesy of BASF Corporation Information Systems) (b) Magnetic reel-to-reel tape mounted on tape drives. (Courtesy of U.S. Department of the Navy)

Forms of Magnetic Disk

- Floppy diskette
- Hard disk
    Fixed disk
    Removable
    cartridge

directly access the data stored on it, (2) hold more data in a smaller space, and (3) attain faster data access speeds.

Magnetic disks are used with all sizes of computers. The difference is in the number of disks and the data storage capacity of each disk. Magnetic disks are manufactured in both floppy diskette and hard disk styles.

Floppy Diskette. A **floppy diskette,** also called simply a diskette or disk, is a small, flexible mylar disk on which data are stored. Floppy diskettes are used to load programs into a computer and provide portable secondary storage. The floppy diskette has been around since the early 1970s. Originally, it was 8 inches in diameter; now it is usually found in 5¼ inch or

3½ inch sizes. Microcomputers use 3½-inch microfloppy and 5¼-inch floppy diskettes (Figure 5.9). The smaller disk is the more popular of the two sizes.

The 5¼-inch disks are covered by stiff, protective jackets that have various holes and cutouts (Figure 5.10). The disk drive uses the hub ring to hold the disk for rotation. The elongated read/write window allows the read/write head of the drive to write data on or read data from the floppy disk. The small hole next to the hub ring is the index hole through which the computer determines the relative position of the disk for locating data. The cutout on the side of the floppy disk is the write-protect notch. Covering this opening with a piece of tape protects data on the disk from being erased or written over.

The 3½-inch disks have hard plastic jackets and metal pieces that cover the read/write window when the disk is not in use. The additional protection makes the disk less prone to damage from handling, dust, or other contaminants (Figure 5.11).

Floppy disks for personal computers are available in different capacities. Common for the 5¼-inch floppy disks are 360KB and 1.2MB capacities. For 3½-inch disks, the most common capacities are 720KB, 1.44MB, and 2.88MB. Technology advances are increasing the data storage density on disks.

Flopticals are a high-capacity medium that combine the features of magnetic and optical storage. They look like ordinary 3½-inch disks but have capacities of approximately 21MB. The drives for this medium are called superfloppy drives.

A floppy diskette that contains one and a half megabytes of storage space represents only about 500 pages of text. To compensate for the limited space on the floppy diskette, another type of disk is used—the hard disk.

FIGURE 5.9
Desktop microcomputers use 5¼- and 3½-inch floppy diskettes.

FIGURE 5.10
A floppy disk in a jacket.

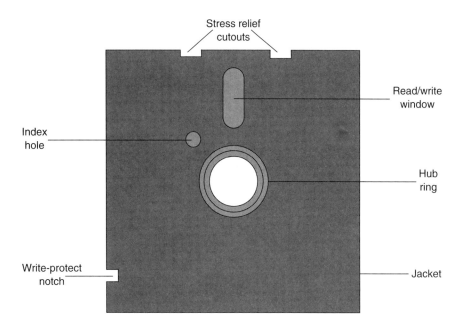

Stress relief cutouts

Read/write window

Index hole

Hub ring

Write-protect notch

Jacket

FIGURE 5.11
A 3½-inch diskette.

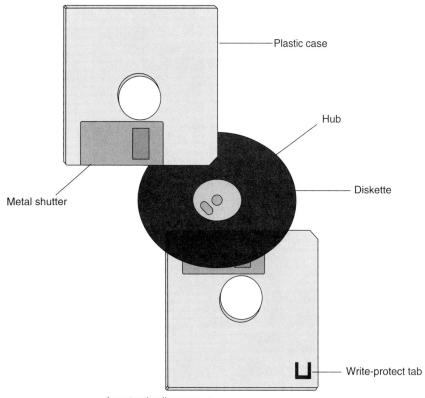

Plastic case

Hub

Diskette

Metal shutter

Write-protect tab

A protective liner covers both sides of the diskette.

Hard Disk. A **hard disk** is made from materials such as aluminum instead of mylar and is hard and inflexible. The input/output device that transfers data to and from a hard disk is a **hard disk drive**. The read/write head of a hard disk drive floats above the surface of the disk at a height of about 50 millionths of an inch (0.00005 inch). In comparison, a human hair is a hundred times larger in diameter (Figure 5.12). Because of the high rotation speed of the hard disk (approximately 3,600 revolutions per minute), if the read/write head runs into any particles of dirt, dust, or even smoke, a **head crash** results. The foreign particle is pushed into the disk, and the head actually bounces and comes into physical contact with the disk. Severe damage can result to the head or the disk and the data stored there can be destroyed.

A hard disk has several advantages over a floppy diskette. The rigid construction of a hard disk allows it to be rotated very fast as compared to a floppy diskette (360 rpm). Thus, data can be transferred much faster to or from a hard disk because it takes less time to find the storage location. Also, because of its hard construction, this disk allows data to be stored more densely. More data can be placed in a smaller area, giving the hard disk more storage capacity than a floppy disk of the same size.

Hard disk drives are available for all sizes of computers, from laptops to mainframe computers. They are also made in two different styles, fixed and removable. A **fixed disk** is enclosed permanently in a sealed case for protection from the elements. **Removable cartridges** are hard disks that are enclosed in such a way that although they still offer the advantages of a hard disk, they are portable. An advantage of removable cartridges is that a user can have a separate cartridge for each application. Other advantages of removable cartridges are that users can store them in a location away from the computer and transport data easily.

FIGURE 5.12
Notice the size of the disk contaminants compared with the distance between the read/write head and the hard disk.

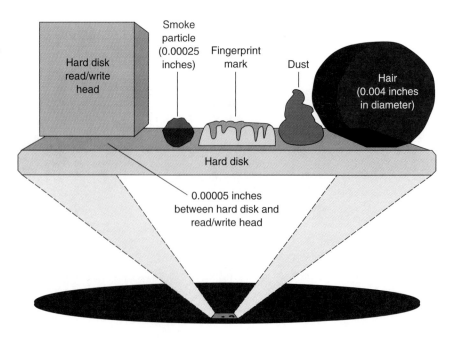

Most of today's larger programs require a hard disk to operate. A hard disk provides not only the storage needed but also allows data to be accessed much more quickly than from a floppy diskette. Hard disks for portable computers are small, ranging from 1.3 inches to 2.5 inches. A hard disk may be permanently installed or may be a removable cartridge that can be withdrawn from the drive. Microcomputers use both fixed and removable hard disk systems. Figure 5.13 shows a typical fixed disk for a microcomputer. Removable cartridges for microcomputers have the same speed and capacity as a system with fixed hard disks. Removable media offer a measure of security because they do not need to remain in the computer when the user leaves (Figure 5.14).

FIGURE 5.13
The case has been removed from this fixed disk to show the hard disk and a read/write head. (Photo courtesy of Seagate)

FIGURE 5.14
The Bernoulli Box is a removable-cartridge storage device. Cartridges can be removed and stored in a secure location.

FIGURE 5.15
An operator installs a disk pack
for mainframe computer storage.
(Courtesy of BASF Corporation
Information Systems)

Magnetic disks for large computers provide storage capacities in the gigabyte (billions of bytes) and terabyte (trillions of bytes) range. Magnetic disk devices are often housed in a separate cabinet. Removable hard disks are available for large systems in the form of disk packs.

A **disk pack** (Figure 5.15) is a removable device in which several hard disks (a common number is 11) are packed into a single plastic case. Disk-pack drives are designed for systems that require large storage capacities. Because a disk pack is susceptible to damage by scratching, the top of the first disk and the bottom of the last disk are generally not used. This leaves 20 sides on which to store hundreds of megabytes. Disk packs can be interchanged, giving a virtually unlimited amount of secondary storage.

Objective 5.5   Identify several different forms of optical secondary storage.

What Types of Optical Storage Are Used?

Optical Storage Media

- Optical laser disk
    CD-ROM
    WORM
    Erasable
- Optical card
- Optical tape

Optical technology involves the use of lasers—highly concentrated beams of light. The word "laser" is an acronym for *l*ight *a*mplification by *s*timulated *e*mission of *r*adiation. Laser beams read to and write data from the optical storage medium. The laser beam is either reflected back to a sensor or scattered due to microscopic pits in the disk. The presence or absence of pits represents a binary 1 or 0. As costs continue to decrease, optical storage may be preferred over magnetic storage because optical storage has much larger storage capacity and greater reliability. However, optical technology is slower when it comes to accessing the data stored on it and is generally read only.

Optical storage is commonly seen in disk format, but it is also available as optical cards and tape. All three forms use laser technology to store data on the media. Figure 5.16 shows a comparison of various storage media.

Media	Approximate Capacity	Cost per Megabyte	Advantages	Disadvantages
CD-ROM	One disk will hold the equivalent of 7 sets of the Encyclopedia Britannica	Varies, average of 50–60 cents	• Removable • Low cost/MB • Very large storage capacity	• Read-only • Slow data access
Hard disk	100MB hard disk will store 1 set of the Encyclopedia Britannica	$1–$5	• Read/write • Fast data access • Large storage capacity	• High cost/MB
Floppy disk	Need over 60 floppies to store one set of the Encyclopedia Britannica	50¢–$1	• Removable • Inexpensive	• Slow data access • Not much storage

FIGURE 5.16
Comparison of some secondary storage media.

Optical Laser Disk

Optical laser disks are metal disks ranging in size from 3½ inches to 14 inches and were originally developed as compact disks for video and audio applications. A typical 14-inch disk can store as much as 20 reel-to-reel tapes. The data are read by a laser beam. Optical disks come in three formats: (1) CD-ROM, (2) WORM, and (3) erasable.

CD-ROM. A common version of the optical disk is the CD-ROM (compact disk, read-only memory). Although not suited to applications where data change, a CD-ROM is convenient for storing data that remain the same (Figure 5.17). The CD-ROM has been around longer than the other forms of optical laser disks, and many applications are available on this medium. For example, Price Waterhouse sent over 15,000 auditing professionals a 40-volume printed packet of information. This was costly and searching for data was almost impossible. Now the auditors access everything on one CD-ROM. Los Angeles County, one of the largest library systems in the country, put more than 5 million titles on a single disk. The search for references is faster than with either a card catalog or microfilm. Boeing uses CD-ROMs to store maintenance manuals for its aircraft. If you were to place the paper manuals end to end they would stretch over 10 feet long. Other applications include annual reports, all types of government statistics, and stock market reports.

WORM. Another type of optical disk is used with a **write once, read many (WORM) drive**. WORM is available in 5¼-inch disks with capacities up to 800MB, and as 12-inch disks that store up to 3 gigabytes for large computer systems. WORM disks are suitable for long-term storage like magnetic tape, but WORM has the advantage of larger storage capacities

FIGURE 5.17
CD-ROM has storage capacities of 500 megabytes and more. This amount of
storage is useful for large volumes of data.

and the ability to access data randomly. Data on WORM cannot be erased.
The only disadvantage is higher cost.

Erasable Drive. Erasable optical drives use a combination of optical and
magnetic principles that allow them to be erased and written to many
times. Although erasable optical drives are relatively expensive compared to
magnetic hard drives, they are making inroads in the small computer
market. In 1988, Steve Jobs's NeXT computer was the first microcomputer
equipped with an erasable optical drive. Erasable optical disks, like other
optical disks, are removable and can hold up to 1 gigabyte or more. Unlike
data on WORM disks, data can be accidentally erased, as can data on any
magnetic medium.

Optical Card

An **optical card,** or laser card, is the size of a credit card and has an optical
laser-encoded strip that stores approximately 4MB of data. These cards have
many potential uses, most notably as credit records or medical histories.

Optical Tape

Continuing developments and refinements in optical technology include optical tape. **Optical tape** is similar to magnetic tape in that it is read sequentially, but data are stored by optical-laser techniques on optical tape. Optical tapes, which are in cassette form, store over 8 gigabytes each. A 15-inch reel of optical tape can store 1 terabyte of data, the equivalent of thousands of ordinary magnetic tapes—about a half billion pages. As optical technology develops, higher densities and expanded uses result.

Objective 5.6   Describe the general characteristics of secondary storage.

What Are the Characteristics of Secondary Storage?

Secondary Storage Characteristics

- **Capacity**
  - Total bytes
  - Density
- **Access time**
  - Data access time
  - Data transfer rate
- **Costs**
  - Fixed cost
  - Cost per megabyte
- **Compatibility**
  - Interface

What should you look for when choosing secondary-storage media and devices? How do you know which secondary storage medium is best? It depends on your needs. First, consider what you are asking secondary storage to do. For example, do you need quick access, or do you plan to store data for a long time? A business user certainly has requirements different from those of a home user. However, whatever your needs, you must consider four main characteristics of all media: (1) capacity of storage medium, (2) access speed, (3) cost, and (4) compatibility with your computer system.

Capacity of Storage Medium

Storage media capacities vary from kilobytes to many gigabytes. The amount of storage is related to the medium's density. **Density** refers to how tightly data are packed and stored on a storage medium. For disk storage, amounts are usually given in bytes, such as 20 megabytes (20MB). When used to describe tapes, density refers to how many bytes per inch (BPI) can be stored. The higher the density the more data can be stored on it. Optical media can store much more data than magnetic media of the same physical size.

As a user you are interested in the storage medium's formatted capacity. To **format** means to prepare the storage medium for use before you can store data or programs on it. Both disks and tapes must be formatted. A disk, regardless of size, is divided into concentric circles called **tracks**. The disk is also divided into pie-shaped wedges called **sectors** (Figure 5.18), which further specify data storage locations. The number of tracks and sectors is usually determined by the operating system of the computer during the formatting operation. The operating system labels each sector of each track with an address. In this way, the computer can go directly to a specific area, rather than start at the beginning, as with magnetic tape.

Many media give their capacity before formatting. For example, a diskette may be listed at a capacity of 2MB, but after formatting have only 1.44MB available.

The amount of data that can be stored on a tape depends on the length of the tape, density of the tape, and the number of interrecord gaps. Not every inch of tape is used for data. Magnetic tapes are formatted with a space called an **interrecord gap (IRG)**. The IRGs identify spaces where

FIGURE 5.18
A diskette divided into tracks
and sectors.

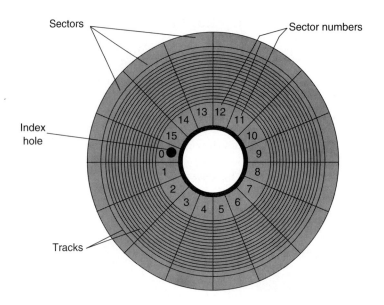

the tape starts and stops. This space allows the tape to attain the proper speed before data are read from or written to it.

When an IRG is located between each record, the tape is referred to as unblocked, and much of the tape is unavailable for data storage because of the space needed for the IRGs. In practice, more than one record is usually stored between two IRGs. The number of records stored between IRGs is referred to as the **blocking factor**. Blocking increases the storage capacity of a tape because it decreases the number of IRGs needed.

Access Time

There are two main speed factors to consider. First, how fast can the data be accessed from a particular medium? This is usually measured in milliseconds, and it varies widely for each device. For example, with a disk drive the read/write head must be positioned to the right track on the disk, then the disk must rotate to the beginning of the right sector.

Second, consider the **data transfer rate**, which is how many characters or bytes can be transferred to or from the storage medium in a given amount of time. Data transfer rates are often listed as kilobytes per second or megabytes per minute and vary widely by the type of medium used and how it is formatted. For example, with magnetic tape, data access is slow because the tape drive has to start and stop between each record. But with a blocked tape the number of IRGs is reduced, thereby increasing the speed of writing data to or reading data from tape.

On disks (especially hard disks) the data transfer rate is affected by the order of the sectors on the disk. Some computer ads talk about the interleave factor. The *interleave* is the physical arrangement of the sequential order of the sectors. Figure 5.19 shows various interleaves for the same 17-sector disk. Why different interleaves? Why not all 1:1? The answer lies in the disk

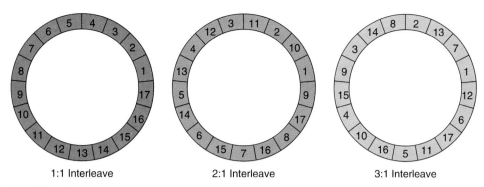

FIGURE 5.19
How sectors are arranged for various interleaves.

drive and its controller. The controller is circuitry that interprets instructions from the CPU to direct the disk drive to read or write to the media.

A hard disk rotates about 60 times per second. Some disk drive controllers cannot direct the disk drive to access and check the data for errors from sector 1 before sector 2 arrives. With a 1:1 interleave the disk would have to rotate another revolution to access sector 2, thus taking more time. Therefore, disk drives are formatted with an optimum interleave. The fastest drives use the 1:1 interleave factor, as do most today.

You might think, "What are a few milliseconds here or there?" But with programs that contain many megabytes, it makes a difference in the performance of the program. Figure 5.20 shows how interleave factors affect data transfer rates.

Costs

There are two ways to look at the costs of secondary storage: (1) fixed cost and (2) cost per megabyte of storage. The fixed cost is simply the cost to buy the particular device or medium. The cost per megabyte is a means of comparing the actual storage costs of two or more methods of secondary storage. For example, a business buying a large amount of secondary storage will be concerned with keeping the cost per megabyte of storage as low as

FIGURE 5.20
Data transfer rates for the same disk with different interleave values.

17-Sector Hard Disk		
Interleave	Sectors Read Per Rotation	Data Transfer Rate (KB Per Second)
1:6	2.8	85
1:5	3.4	102
1:4	4.3	128
1:3	5.7	170
1:2	8.5	255
1:1	1.7	510

possible. A home user or small business user who doesn't have the resources to buy enough secondary storage to substantially decrease the cost per megabyte will be more concerned that the fixed cost falls within a set budget.

Compatibility

As if there weren't enough acronyms, a magazine ad advertises a 170MB IDE hard drive. The price is right but can you use an IDE with your computer system? Well, it depends. As with most components in a computer, not all are interchangeable. For example, your hard drive and its controller must be able to communicate; this is called the interface. There are four basic interfaces caused by such things as competition, improvements, and standardization.

In the 1970s the slow but simple *ST506* interface was developed. In the 1980s, improvements were made by a group of vendors and a new standard was developed called *ESDI (Enhanced Small Device Interface)*. This interface allowed higher data transfer rates and larger capacity drives. But computers have a limited number of expansion slots and more peripherals, in addition to hard drives, are being used, such as CD-ROMs, optical disks, scanners, and tape drives. So another group of vendors developed an "intelligent" interface, the *Small Computer Systems Interface (SCSI)*. This interface allows multiple devices to connect to one "host adapter" while using only one expansion slot. It is standard in Macintosh computers. *IDE (Integrated Device Electronics)* is another interface in which the controller is on the drive itself. This shortened the wiring and improved the data transfer rate.

Without going into more detail, you need to consider compatibility issues so that when you buy additional peripheral devices they will work with your system.

Objective 5.7   Recognize common secondary storage problems and possible solutions.

What Are Some Common Secondary Storage Problems and Solutions?

Each medium has its own niche in the realm of secondary storage. Floppy diskettes make it easy to load new software, hard disks provide increased storage, and tape is often the choice for backup. However, problems do arise, such as lost data, slow access to data, and the necessity for more storage.

Lost Data

So you're sure your data are secure because you used a command to save your file! Think about these scenarios—operator error, system failure, software defects, viruses, theft, vandalism, site destruction, and Mother Nature. Now, do you feel safe? Thankfully, there are ways to protect your data and computer.

Backup. Backing up data on a mainframe computer is standard procedure, whether it is convenient or not. Relying solely on a hard disk, many microcomputer users do not back up their data. But if you ever lose an important file, *backup* is a word you won't soon forget.

Tape backup is reliable, portable, and the least expensive in terms of cost per megabyte. High-capacity hard drives are making tape backup popular for personal computer users. A cassette tape system for personal computers backs up 150 megabytes in 20–30 minutes (Figure 5.21). That amount of storage would require over one hundred 1.2 megabyte floppy diskettes, and copying would take much more time. In addition, you have to continually stop to replace floppies. Some features to look for in a tape drive system include automatic formatting (tapes must be formatted much like disks), unattended backup (you don't have to watch it work), and user and automatic verification (these features make sure the copy matches the original).

Most data are too valuable to be left unprotected. Whether to guard against hard disk failure, operator error, or natural disasters like fire or flood, backing up your work is worth the effort. In fact, many insurance companies require their policyholders to perform regular backup procedures to guarantee coverage.

Data Recovery. It is frustrating to know you saved your data and then not be able to access it. One possible problem is that the storage medium was bad to begin with. The medium should be checked for errors when it is first formatted.

Even if you did not make a backup, there are software programs that recover some data and programs after they have been "erased," or saved on "bad" media. Programs like Norton Utilities provide many programs for

FIGURE 5.21
A microcomputer equipped with a tape drive for backup of data or programs. (Courtesy of Compaq)

It delivers but it's not United Parcel Service. Its cargo is not delivered in cardboard boxes; in fact, it can't be seen. More and more computer users are finding the advantage of protecting their systems with an *un*interruptible *p*ower *s*upply (UPS). A UPS is a device that delivers a constant level of power, or electricity.

Computers at the United Nations headquarters in Mogadishu, Somalia, helped coordinate and oversee a massive relief effort to feed many starving people. Organizations like The Associated Press provided the world with news stories from word processors and photographs delivered by high-speed fax machines. All this computer activity took place in an area where local electric service was unreliable at best. In each case a UPS provided the necessary constant power to enable the agencies to get the job done.

A UPS is not just for remote locations, however. Take the case of General Security, located at the World Trade Center. When the terrorist bomb hit there, all power was immediately lost. The four local area networks (LANs) kept right on working, thanks to the UPS's ability to deliver constant power. The UPS allowed the company time to perform a normal shut-down on the computers and get out of the building safely and without the loss of valuable data.

examining and maintaining your secondary storage media. There are also companies that specialize in recovering data from damaged hard drives.

Electronic Protection. Mother Nature can play havoc with computer systems—ask anyone who has lost power during an electrical storm. Lightning strikes can easily render your computer's electronic components useless. Lesser known, but potentially as damaging, are variations in electrical power levels. These spikes, surges, sags, and brownouts can have devastating effects on both data and components (Figure 5.22).

The best protection against lightning is to unplug your computer. Minor electrical spikes can be eliminated with a *surge protector,* a relatively inexpensive device that all computer users should consider purchasing. For complete protection, although expensive, a *UPS (Uninterruptible Power Supply)* can deliver a constant level of voltage regardless of any variations in line voltage. Be sure that there aren't too many devices running from the same circuit.

Slow Data Access

This is a problem that you may not realize is happening. Through use, data and program storage can become fragmented (stored in parts rather than as one unit) and read/write heads can become misaligned. Both of these problems severely reduce the speed at which data are accessed, and in fact, if the heads are misaligned enough the secondary storage device will be unable to access the data at all. One solution for the user is found in software programs. One, Spinrite, can piece together fragmented files and

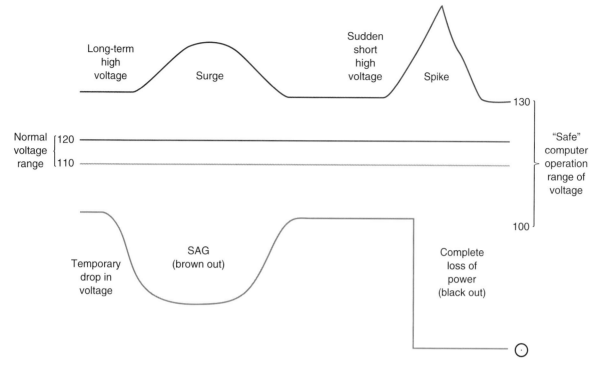

FIGURE 5.22
Voltage variations are harmful to data and electronic components.

help restore your computer to its original performance. Other software products test your drives for proper head alignment, rotational speed, and other drive problems.

Not Enough Storage

Running out of secondary storage space can occur. There are both hardware and software solutions to this problem.

In a network where many computers are tied together, it's easy to build very large files. Technologies like digital audio tape (DAT) use 8 mm tape that can store up to 2.2 gigabytes in a single cartridge. As prices for high-capacity optical devices decrease, they will play a larger role as secondary storage.

Another way to achieve more space on existing secondary storage is with data compression. *Data compression* works by replacing repeated patterns with fewer characters. For example, take a large file in which the word "and" appears 100 times. If you could replace each occurrence with one character your space savings would be 100 characters versus 300. Data compression can be achieved with plug-in hardware boards inside the computer, or with software programs like PKZIP or PC Tools. When the files are loaded back into the computer the hardware or software decompresses the file. Data files have the highest percentage of reduction while program files can be compressed to a lesser degree.

Summary

Secondary storage is the nonvolatile memory used for keeping large amounts of data for permanent or long-term storage. Secondary storage media also store backups, or copies of data and programs.

Data are organized in a hierarchy that includes database, file, record, field, byte, and bit. A database is a group of related files stored together in a logical fashion. A file is a collection of similar groups of data that fit under one category. A record contains data related to one particular item in that category, such as a person's name. A field is the name given to each classification of data in a record. Fields are made up of characters (bytes), which are made up of bits.

The three main storage and access methods are sequential access, direct access, and indexed. Sequential-access file processing accesses and stores records in a file one after another. Direct-access file processing allows a user to retrieve a record without reading each one preceding it. In indexed file processing, an index of key fields allows records to be sequentially or directly accessed.

Three types of secondary-storage media are (1) magnetic tape, (2) magnetic disk, and (3) optical technology. Magnetic tape is a ribbon of mylar coated with a thin layer of iron oxide. It is available in three forms: reel-to-reel, cassette, and cartridge. Magnetic disks are mylar or metallic platters coated with iron oxide. Two types of magnetic disks are floppy diskettes and hard disks. Floppies are manufactured in 3½-, 5¼-, and 8-inch sizes. Hard disks are available as fixed disks, removable cartridges, and disk packs. Optical technology uses a laser to store data on various media. Optical media include optical laser disks, which are available as CD ROM, WORM, and erasable. Optical technology is also used for optical cards and optical tapes.

Four main characteristics of all secondary storage media are (1) capacity, (2) access speed, (3) cost, and (4) compatibility with your current system.

Common areas that may cause problems when dealing with secondary storage are lost data, slower data access time, and lack of storage space on the media. Many problems of this nature can be resolved with software programs or hardware devices.

Backing up data and programs protects them against unexpected losses. Tape is a common medium used for backup.

If you accidentally erase a file or delete a program, data recovery programs can often restore them.

Data compression is a method of reducing the size of a file to create more space on the storage media.

VOCABULARY SELF-TEST

Can you define the following terms?

algorithm (p. 172)	cartridge tape (p. 173)
bit (p. 169)	cassette tape (p. 173)
blocking factor (p. 184)	database (p. 168)
byte (p. 169)	data transfer rate (p. 184)

density (p. 183)

direct-access file processing (p. 169)

disk pack (p. 180)

field (p. 168)

file (p. 168)

fixed disk (p. 178)

floppy diskette (p. 175)

format (p. 183)

hard disk (p. 178)

hard disk drive (p. 178)

head crash (p. 178)

indexed file processing (p. 170)

interrecord gap (p. 183)

key field (p. 169)

magnetic disk (p. 174)

magnetic tape (p. 172)

optical card (p. 182)

optical laser disk (p. 181)

optical tape (p. 183)

optical technology (p. 180)

record (p. 168)

reel-to-reel tape (p. 173)

removable cartridge (p. 178)

secondary storage (p. 167)

sectors (p. 183)

sequential-access file processing (p. 169)

tape drive (p. 172)

tracks (p. 183)

write once, read many (WORM) drive (p. 181)

REVIEW QUESTIONS

Multiple Choice

1. Which one of the following is a reason to use secondary storage, instead of just main memory?
    a. faster access time to data
    b. it comes with the computer
    c. backing up data
    d. it is volatile

2. What is the correct hierarchy of data?
    a. file, database, record, field, byte, bit
    b. database, file, field, record, bit, byte
    c. database, file, record, field, byte, bit
    d. field, file, database, record, byte, bit

3. What is true concerning magnetic tape?
    a. available as reel-to-reel only
    b. records can be accessed directly
    c. used to store large amounts of data
    d. well suited for data that need to be updated often

4. Preparing a disk for use is called _____.
    a. sectioning
    b. tracking
    c. readying
    d. formatting

5. The number of tracks and sectors for a disk is usually determined by the _____.
    a. operating system of the computer
    b. user

        c. disk manufacturer
        d. type of application software
6. Which of the following best describes the storage capacity of a microcomputer hard disk?
        a. kilobytes
        b. megabytes
        c. gigabytes
        d. terabytes
7. CD-ROM is a type of _____.
        a. optical laser disk
        b. main memory chip
        c. magnetic disk
        d. operating system
8. A WORM drive uses a(n) _____ as its storage medium.
        a. magnetic disk
        b. magnetic tape
        c. optical disk
        d. punched tape
9. A sudden short-term increase in voltage is called a(n) _____.
        a. sag
        b. surge
        c. blackout
        d. spike
10. To reduce the size of a file for secondary storage, use _____ software.
        a. data recovery
        b. backup
        c. direct-access
        d. data compression

Fill-In

1. _____ refers to how much data can be stored in a given amount of space.
2. A file contains _____, which are a collection of related data items.
3. The data or programs on magnetic tape are accessed by the _____-access method.
4. Magnetic disk capacities usually are specified in numbers of _____, while magnetic tape capacities are usually described in terms of their _____.
5. The term "laser" is derived from the words _____.
6. Through a(n) _____, a computer determines the relative position of a floppy diskette for locating data.
7. A diskette is divided into concentric circles called _____.
8. The two main sizes of floppy diskettes used with microcomputers are _____ and _____.
9. A hard disk that contains one or more disks permanently enclosed in a sealed case is called a(n) _____.
10. Optical technology uses _____ to write and read data.

Short Answer

1. Describe secondary storage and explain why it is needed.
2. Contrast the three basic methods of file storage and retrieval.
3. Organize the following terms as they would fall under the data hierarchy structure and give a brief explanation of each: record, database, field, file, bit, and byte.
4. What are the advantages of magnetic tape over magnetic disks?
5. In general, how are secondary storage devices for microcomputers different from their larger computer system counterparts?
6. Explain the difference between data access time and data transfer time.
7. What is the purpose of formatting a disk?
8. What might cause a head crash?
9. All fixed disks are hard disks, but all hard disks are not fixed disks. Comment.
10. Briefly describe how data compression is accomplished.

Issues for Thought

1. Some people thought that computers would bring about a paperless society; the opposite seems to be true. Why do you think this is so, especially with the amount of data and information that can be stored on tape or disk in such a small space?
2. "I forgot to back it up!" is an often-heard lament. Do you think that people tend to rely on a computer being able to do everything?

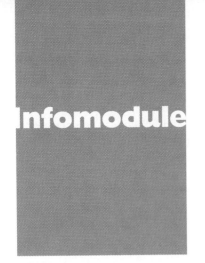

Infomodule
Buying and Caring for a Microcomputer System

HOW CAN I BEST PREPARE TO BUY A MICROCOMPUTER SYSTEM?

Before you think about buying a microcomputer, the first thing you should do is become **computer literate**, that is, learn the terminology associated with computers. You can start the process by reading this book, of course, but there are many other sources of information: magazines, friends, teachers, students, colleagues at work, and computing personnel. Computer magazines such as *PC Today* and *PC Novice* are specially geared to the beginning user. Ask your friends, relatives, teachers, and fellow students how they are using computers. People from work who may have already bought their home system will have hints and advice too. Personnel at computer stores or in your campus computing centers will know what's new on the horizon. They can tell you what system to consider for the future and put you in touch with people nearby who have similar systems.

Once you are familiar with the terms, decide what you want your computer to do. Is it word processing? Then a system with a high-quality printer would be preferable. Is it the ability to create graphs and charts? If so, a system with larger memory capacity and a color monitor would be your choice. Software requirements determine most of the hardware specifications. Although today's first-time buyer knows more than those of ten years ago, you still want to get the most for your money. To do that, it's best to know the questions whose answers will help provide the data required to make an informed decision. Some of the questions you will want to answer follow.

HOW DO I EVALUATE AND SELECT SOFTWARE?

There are well over 100,000 application software programs (those designed for specific computer tasks, like word processing, data management and spreadsheets) available, so you will need to focus on the tasks that you want to accomplish with your system. Seek out the experts: computer magazine reviews, computer stores, people who already use the software you're thinking about. If you are purchasing a household computer, consider all the family members. Not everyone will have the same needs; for example, if there are children in the family, see what programs and equipment are being used at school. Does anyone have a special interest? The more facts you have before you make your decision the better.

The Operating System

The first decision has to do with your operating system environment. The operating system is the set of programs that controls and supervises a computer's hardware and provides services to other system software, application software, programmers, and users. One of the most popular operating systems is Microsoft's Disk Operating System (MS-DOS, or just DOS). Microsoft Windows is a **graphical user interface (GUI);** users choose icons on the screen instead of typing in commands. Windows is not an operating system, but rather a graphical operating environment used in conjunction with DOS. If you choose to use a GUI with your operating system, your computer will have to be more powerful to work efficiently.

Now begin to evaluate the application software. Examine the various features, flexibility, upgradability, price, warranty, and return policy, if necessary, of your programs.

Features

After you have decided on a program, have it demonstrated, using some of your data, if possible. The most expensive program probably has the most features, but it may be more elaborate or complicated than you will require. There may not be a package that does everything exactly as you want, so you may have to choose something that comes close.

Flexibility

Is the program easy to learn? Are the instructions clear? A **menu-driven program** is easier for most beginners to learn because it displays the choices in lists on the screen. A **command-driven program** expects that the user already "knows" or will look up the keystrokes in the user's manual in order to execute the program. The **documentation** is the manual that gives descriptions, either written or graphic, that detail the operation of computer software. Documentation should be clearly written and easy to understand.

Upgradability

Always buy the most recent release of your software; see if upgrades will be available from the manufacturer. System and memory requirements listed on the software package tell you the minimum specifications that your computer system must have to run that particular program.

Price

After you examine all the software programs, price may be the determining factor. You will probably want to get the most program for the least amount of money. Be sure to comparison shop.

Warranty and Technical Support

Most software is sold "as is" with a warranty only if the media prove to be faulty. Technical support, however, varies among manufacturers. Make sure you know not only who gives the support, but who pays for it.

Returns

Some companies accept software returns if the outer package is intact; others charge a fee for restocking their shelves and still others only accept returns for defective media. A sample software buyer's checklist is shown in Table 1. You may want to adapt it to your own situation.

Now you're ready to look for the equipment to run those programs.

WHAT SHOULD I CONSIDER WHEN SELECTING A MICROCOMPUTER?

Before you select a microcomputer there are a number of considerations. Who is your dealer? Does the dealer have repair facilities? Is there a return policy? Is the dealer willing to negotiate price and terms? Are these prices too good to be true? Can I pay by credit card? Is there a warranty? What system do I need? Does the dealer offer technical support? What about upgradability? What's this going to cost? These are a few of the questions you will have to answer before you sign any sales agreement.

Who Is My Dealer?

Verify that the place where you decide to buy is a legitimate business. Check the Better Business Bureau or call a local computer user's group. Working with an authorized dealer is wise for a first-time buyer.

Does the Dealer Have Repair Facilities?

If your dealer also services the products sold, you will know where to take your equipment in case of breakdowns. One way to verify whether your dealer will be able to offer a fast turnaround for repairs is to call them anonymously and ask how long it would take to get something fixed, for example, a keyboard replacement, or a faulty COM port. If there is adequate staff and a supply of parts, turnaround time should be a matter of days. Any longer and you may decide to find another dealer.

Is There a Return Policy?

Beware of a dealer whose policy states: "All sales are final." Your bargaining power is limited; find another

TABLE 1
Software Buyer's Checklist

Application software package: _____
Supplier (retail, mail order, etc.): _____
Price: _____
Includes: _____
Type of operating system: _____
RAM requirements: _____
Other equipment requirements: _____
Features: _____
Documentation: _____
Ease of use (menu vs. command-driven program): _____
Adaptability of program: _____
Upgradability: _____
Warranty: _____
Dealer support: _____
Returnability: _____

dealer. If the dealer prefers to give credit instead of a refund you could be stuck with a limited number of products. This policy could be an indication that the dealer is in financial difficulties. Is there a fee for restocking returned items? This fee can be quite expensive. Look for a 30-day money-back guarantee before you sign anything.

Is the Dealer Willing to Negotiate Price and Terms?

If the dealer doesn't negotiate, try somewhere else. You should ask for 15 percent off the sticker price.

But if you settle for 10 percent that's still a good deal. Visit two competitors to check prices for similar systems. Even after the price is settled, your salesperson may be willing to add other options, for example, software, peripherals such as a mouse, or extra memory.

Are These Prices Too Good to Be True?

If the price seems too low, you are probably not getting a good deal. If the model is merely outdated and you don't particularly need a state-of-the-art package, you may be the beneficiary of a great deal. However, you might find extremely low prices if the dealer is not authorized to sell the products. Always remember the adage of "buyer beware."

Is There a Warranty?

See that *all* components are covered by the warranty. Insist on at least one month on-site free service. Try to negotiate a six-months on-site warranty. Avoid a dealer who indicates that the warranty is covered by the manufacturer. The user who depends entirely on the computer for business uses may be wise to purchase a service contract. You could consider negotiating for it as part of your purchase agreement. However, for most home users a service agreement should not be necessary.

Can I Pay by Credit Card?

Why would I want to pay by credit card? Because buyer protection plans are offered by several major credit card companies (American Express, Visa, and MasterCard, to name a few). You can often double the length of the warranty, stop payment in case you've bought a lemon, and recover the purchase price in case the system is damaged somehow.

What System Do I Need?

Now it's time to investigate the actual components of the computer system that will run the programs that you chose. Here's what you'll need: a system unit (composed of the CPU, memory, expansion slots), hard and floppy disk drives, monitor, keyboard, mouse (optional), and surge protector (strongly sug-

---

Smart Shopping Hints

- **Who is my dealer?**
- **Does the dealer have repair facilities?**
- **Is there a return policy?**
- **Can we negotiate a price?**
- **Are these prices too good to be true?**
- **What about the warranty?**
- **Will they accept a credit card?**

---

gested). Additionally, you may want to have a modem and fax capabilities for communicating with others at a distance. One suggestion for a system follows.

For most everyday home needs, a CPU with a 386 SX microprocessor or higher would be a good choice. There is enough speed and memory to allow you to add applications without causing immediate obsolescence. The most popular operating systems all run well on a 386. Microsoft Windows requires 2 megabytes of RAM; 4 are preferable. If you have plenty of RAM, as new programs are developed you will be ready to run them. Inquire whether you can upgrade RAM later, and at what cost. The more hard disk storage you want, the more money you'll spend. You should probably have not less than 80 MB of hard disk storage. A PC with two diskette drives makes copying files easier. Decide whether you want 5.25- or 3.5-inch disk drives. Many systems come equipped with one of each, which allows you to use each type of disk.

Often a monitor will be included (or "bundled") with your computer. A VGA monitor is more versatile because it also runs CGA- and EGA-compatible software. A 14-inch or larger diagonal screen is best for comfortable viewing. The dot pitch should be .31 mm or less. Monitors require a graphics adapter card. The adapter would be inserted into an expansion slot inside the computer. Find out how many expansion slots are available.

The keyboard is the most popular device for input purposes. It's wise to test the keyboard, see if the keys stick, and experiment with the "feel" of the keyboard. It's important for your hands to be in a comfortable position to help avoid repetitive stress injuries such as carpal tunnel syndrome.

Purchasing a mouse is optional, unless you are using a GUI. Then the mouse is integral as a pointing device for selecting the various commands.

A **surge protector** is a device that protects computers against electrical power-line voltage surges caused by fluctuations in power generation or lightning strikes. At approximately $20, it's an "insurance" deal you shouldn't pass up.

These are the suggested components of a computer system. You may investigate some other options, including a modem or fax. A modem is the device that converts signals from analog to digital and from digital to analog so that computers communicate via telephone lines. There are internal modems found inside the system unit that may be preinstalled or added later into an unused expansion slot. External modems are a separate piece of hardware. Some are battery operated for use with portable computers.

Fax, or facsimile, is a form of electronic mail that copies and sends text, pictures, and graphics over long distances. The fax circuit board could take up another expansion slot.

It's a good idea to have the dealer install these components or plug-in circuit boards before you take your computer home.

Does the Dealer Offer Technical Support?

If your choice is between a low-priced computer with little support and a higher priced computer with good support, choose support. It is best to have someone that you can contact with your questions.

What About Upgradability?

Upgradability is important to prevent obsolescence. That is often a more critical concern to the business user. A modular-based PC is easily upgradable. Although it costs more initially, the modular PC can be changed by replacing processor cards instead of purchasing a whole new computer. The improved programs may require the additional memory, speed, and power of the advanced processors.

What's This Going to Cost?

Remember to negotiate for the best price and try to get extras such as an improved warranty. If you are trying to save money, you may choose a smaller, less complicated system to start with and then if you find that you don't like home computing or are not good at it, you will not have invested a lot of money.

Now that you know what to look for, let's discuss where you'll buy your hardware and software.

> ### Recommended Components of a Microcomputer System
>
> - System unit
>   - CPU (386 SX or higher)
>   - Memory (4MB RAM, preferable)
>   - Hard drive (80MB minimum)
> - Expansion slots, upgradable RAM
> - 5.25- and 3.5-inch disk drives
> - Monitor (VGA or SVGA)
> - Keyboard (usually included)
> - Mouse (may be optional)
> - Surge protector
> - Modem
> - Fax

WHERE CAN I PURCHASE COMPUTER HARDWARE AND SOFTWARE?

There are many places to buy computer hardware and software: direct sales, superstores, value-added resellers, retail stores, mass merchants, mail-order, your college or university computer services, or used-computer outlets. Where you go depends on what you need. Always remember to ask about money-back guarantees. Deals differ from store to store.

Manufacturer Direct Sales

With this method, you order directly from the manufacturer. You save money by avoiding the middleman and get the latest models. Manufacturers offer competitive prices and good technical support. Sales personnel are knowledgeable about their products and support services. When you pay by credit card, orders are usually delivered within two days. Dell is one of the best-known direct sales companies.

Superstores

A **superstore** sells nothing but computers and related items. Prices are usually the lowest with as much as 80 percent off on some items. Because they have a limited focus, salespeople are fairly knowledgeable. You'll be able to see almost everything that's available, but the sheer volume of products may be overwhelming.

The concept was started in the early 1980s with the opening of Micro Center in Columbus, Ohio. Superstores are usually found in highly populated areas. The fastest growing chain of superstores is Comp-USA. They load your software (for a price), train you, give classes on different brands of software, and let you try out software before you buy.

Value-Added Resellers

A value-added reseller (VAR) is primarily used by someone who needs help to design, install, and maintain a business computing system, including computer networks. The VAR will consult, train, and give service, especially to lawyers, doctors, dentists, auto parts stores, accountants, architects, and engineers. Having a single source for assistance is helpful to most businesses.

Retail Stores or Dealers

Dealers or retailers can't compete with the superstore's high volume. But they are usually better at offering a high level of quality and personal service. Stores like MicroAge or Software City can be found in smaller cities and towns. Software City franchises are owner operated and of course each owner wants to be successful. Because of those individual owners, technical support and in-depth consulting vary from store to store. Some dealers like ComputerLand moved to low-rent districts to save money and send their sales representatives to call on clients to make sales and give support.

Discount Warehouse Stores

The discount warehouse stores carry everything. They offer deep discounts but provide no frills or service in order to give their bargain prices. Sam's Discount Warehouse, for example, doesn't have a wide variety of equipment or titles and sotware selections are usually geared toward business users.

Electronics stores such as Radio Shack offer service departments, and often carry as much inventory as computer specialty stores. But for technical advice and custom applications, a full-service dealer may be necessary.

Mass Merchants

Mass merchants include stores like Macy's and Sears. Their sales staff may not be as knowledgeable as computer specialty stores, but they are found everywhere across the country and if you move, you're likely to have a store nearby for support. Additionally, Prodigy, a consumer information service, is a product of Sears.

Mail-Order Houses

When you use a mail-order house you're usually dealing with a third party, not the manufacturer. Some offer good telephone support; others leave you on your own; still others may be disreputable or short-lived companies. As a first-time computer purchaser, you may be better off purchasing locally. Some mail-order houses will refund your money after deducting shipping charges and a restocking fee.

Your College or University

Computer manufacturers offer good prices to colleges and universities and they are usually willing to offer those price breaks to students. The manufacturer thus establishes loyalty to its brand among students. It's easy to sell computers to satisfied student users, and student users become potential buyers of their own computers or computers for their place of employment.

Used-Computer Outlets

Your new computer loses 40 percent of its value the minute you open the box. Full depreciation for tax purposes occurs when the equipment is five years old, but the machine is probably technologically obsolete after the first year or so. Even so, that PC is still sound and fully operable. Very few dealers take your old PC as a trade-in for a newer model. Hewlett-Packard and Digital Equipment Corporation do, though, and often cannibalize them for repair parts, refurbish them if possible, or donate them to charities.

The advantages of buying a used computer include: the system is already configured; the initial problems are fixed; repair parts are easy to find. Because there are few moving parts to break down or wear out a used computer can be a good buy for the alert but wary buyer.

Used PCs can be found in many places: garage or yard sales, newspaper advertisements, used-computer stores, or "outplacements" from companies that are forced to upgrade regularly. One such company is American Airlines. Its SABRE Travel Information Network consists of 70,000 personal computers, of which approximately 5,000 are turned in or "outplaced" every year. The Boston Computer Exchange, founded in 1982, matches buyers with sellers and vice versa for a reasonable fee. The refurbished computers are sold and the purchaser gets seven days to return the item. Buyers can purchase a 90-day warranty for approximately $100. The BoCoEx Index gives the current rates for many used computers and is found on computer networks on both CompuServe and on Delphi in Newsbytes.

Software-Only Stores

A software-only store is usually a small specialty store with a wide selection of programs and knowledgeable employees. Two software-only stores are Egghead Discount Software and Software Etc. They both have computers available so you can try the software before you buy it. Software Unlimited lets you take the software home, try it, and if it doesn't do what you expect, they'll give you a refund.

Other Sources

There are other sources of software: shareware and freeware. **Shareware** is free, copyrighted software that is distributed mainly through bulletin board systems and information services. Users who pay a nominal fee to cover costs and registration will be sent documentation and program updates. **Freeware**, also known as public-domain software, is not copy-protected or copyrighted and is distributed by the author(s) to anyone. You will want to be careful about the potential of a computer virus in software found on some bulletin boards.

Where to Buy Hardware and Software

- **Manufacturer direct**
- **Superstores**
- **Value-added resellers**
- **Retail stores or dealers**
- **Discount warehouses**
- **Mass merchants**
- **Mail-order houses**
- **College or university**
- **Used computer outlet**
- **Software-only stores**
- **Shareware**
- **Freeware**

Superstores, software-only stores, or dealers are most likely to be the best sources for computer novices. Shop around before you buy. A checklist for buying computer systems is found in Table 2. The more you know, the better your chance of getting the "best buy." Remember, before you sign *any* document, read both sides thoroughly, especially anything written in fine print.

When you buy software later, after you have purchased your computer system, remember to bring the specifications of your system: what brand, model, memory, and what microprocessor to ensure compatibility of that new program.

HOW SHOULD I CARE FOR A MICROCOMPUTER?

You should treat your computer as carefully as you do your other expensive electronic equipment. A computer might be able to withstand a minor accident, but don't shake it or drop it on purpose to test this theory. You may avoid a service call through careful maintenance and cleaning policies. There may be specific suggestions in your owner's manual, but here is a short list of things to consider.

TABLE 2
Buyer's Inventory

Software package: _____

Microprocessor: _____

Clock speed: _____

RAM: _____

Hard disk: _____

Drive sizes: _____

Monitor specifications: _____

Dealer: _____

Price: _____

Includes: _____

Dealer support and maintenance: _____

Warranty: _____

Service agreement: _____

Documentation (readability): _____

Printer specifications: _____

    Tractor feed vs. sheet feed: _____

    Daisy/dot matrix/laser: _____

    Carriage size: _____

    Bidirectionality: _____

Where Should I Position My Computer?

Where you put your computer, at home or in the office, is critical. There are many environmental considerations to think about.

Temperature.   Do not put the computer in front of a window, air conditioner, or heat source. Temperatures in excess of 85° F should be avoided. The computer fan's air vents should not be blocked so that the circuits can remain cooled.

Power Surges.   An electrical power surge can occur normally in any electric line. They are common during thunderstorms. Additionally, if your computer is plugged into the same socket as another major appliance a power surge could occur when that other appliance, for example, an air conditioner, is turned on. That resulting surge of electricity can burn up the components in your computer. A surge protection device (costing approximately $20) is worthwhile.

Humidity.   A humidity level between 50 and 70 percent is ideal. High humidity can cause rusting of the computer's metal parts. But low humidity is not good either because it can cause a buildup of static electricity.

Static Electricity.   Static can also be caused by walking across high-pile carpets and opening the shrink-wrapped plastic that your disks come in. Using humidifiers, antistatic mats, rugs and sprays reduces the harmful effects of static electricity.

Magnetic Fields.   Electric motors, appliances, television sets, computer monitors, and, of course, magnets generate magnetic fields and may be responsible for scrambling the electromagnetically encoded data stored on your tapes or disks. Keep those storage media away from magnetic fields.

Dust, Smoke, and Other Deposits.   Microscopic bits of dust can cause mechanical problems for the computer and the software. The tar and nicotine particles in tobacco smoke build up on the computer and monitor, but devastation results when they adhere to diskettes or drives (see Figure 5.12). Other deposits that can cause equipment or disk damage include hair, animal dander, chemical fumes, food crumbs, liquid spills, and even chalk dust. These can cause short circuits, damage the working papers, or harm the computer itself. A hard-disk drive should be **parked** when the computer is not being used. This means that the read/write head is secured away from the disk in case the computer is moved. Many disk drives are self-parking, but you should check with your dealer when you buy to make sure that you don't need to run a parking program yourself. There are several things that you can do to keep your computer, peripherals, and disks clean.

How Should I Clean My Computer System?

Even if you don't eat, drink, or smoke near the computer, and have kept your pets and harmful fumes away from the area, both your computer and its surrounding area will become dirty. Before you begin cleaning, though, unplug the computer system to avoid a 25,000-volt electrical shock. Also remember not to use liquid cleaners or sprays around the computer or keyboard.

System Unit.   Do not turn your computer on before it is plugged in. A power surge can occur and damage your circuits. Cleaning inside a computer should be done carefully because the circuit boards are easily damaged. Dust can be removed by spraying inside with a compressed air canister or by using a crevice-cleaning device with your vacuum cleaner to remove dust around the air vents and other openings, such as the disk drives. Dealers sell cleaning kits with a tiny vacuum and other cleaning supplies.

Environment Considerations

- Temperature
- Power surges
- Humidity
- Static electricity
- Magnetic fields
- Debris

Disk Drives. There is no consensus about cleaning drives. You will find experts divided on whether disk drives should be cleaned twice a year or weekly. Commercial cleaning kits use a special disk and cleaning agent that are inserted into the drive. As it spins, dust and other hazardous particles are cleaned from the read/write head. Having your disk drives cleaned at a computer store is the most prudent method.

Monitor. The screen on your monitor creates static electricity that causes dust to adhere to it. There are experts who suggest that screens can be cleaned with a commercial glass cleaner; others purchase a special product. Whatever you decide, use only a dampened cloth to prevent dripping liquid from falling onto the computer or keyboard. If you leave your monitor on for a period of time it is best to turn the brightness to a low setting or use a screen saver. A **screen saver** is a program that causes random patterns to appear on your screen and thus prevents the unchanging screen from being "burned in" to the phosphor coating inside the CRT. You may find a freeware or shareware screen saver program.

Keyboard. The keyboard is probably the dirtiest part of the computer. Even your clean hands leave dirt and debris in the form of dead skin cells and oily deposits. The crevice device or compressed air canister can remove the dust. Take care not to blow dust off the keyboard and into the disk drive. Once the keyboard is clean, a special dust cover keeps it that way.

Printers. Printers are subject to dust and debris from paper lint and frayed ribbons. The crevice tool or compressed air canister can help here too. Printer paper should be fed using the appropriate line or page-feed options. Motors are responsible for moving the platen and the print head. If you try to move either of them manually you can cause motor damage. A dust cover is important protection when you are not using the printer.

Connections. Contact between your interface cables and ports is important. To keep those connections clean, apply a cotton swab with contact cleaner to the pin connectors, plug screws, and cable ends.

Other Tips

Do not plug your computer into a socket that is controlled from a switch plate near the door. Your work could be lost if someone accidentally turned off the switch when leaving the room. Watch where you step if you plug your computer system components into an electrical strip on the floor near your feet. A cautious owner will unplug the computer in an electrical storm. Each owner must decide about the risks he or she is willing to take. That includes whether or not to purchase insurance coverage or a service contract for your equipment. Some homeowner's policies cover computers automatically, but policies vary, so check with your agent to ensure coverage. Unless you are using your computer in a business situation, a service contract may not be necessary.

HOW DO I PROTECT MY SOFTWARE AND DATA?

Disks should be protected from dust and dirt by keeping them in their protective jackets inside storage boxes. By making two sets of backup copies and keeping each in a different place, you have a better chance of protecting your data. Back up your work every 15 minutes. If you think it takes too much time, think how long it would take you to input the day's work or reconstruct the data. When put into perspective, the interruption every 15 minutes is not particularly troublesome.

Virus Protection

Computers and software are at risk for catching a virus. A virus is a program that gets into a computer to destroy or alter data and spread destruction to other computers. Antivirus programs locate and destroy the virus. They perform three services: prevention, diagnosis, and recovery. By running a monitoring routine these programs can prevent a virus. If you already have a virus, the program can recognize the identifying codes and then help eliminate it.

WHAT IS A WARRANTY?

A **warranty** states the degree of liability that the company is willing to cover. Many warranties are

TABLE 3
Before You Call for Help

Check for loose connections.
Get documentation.
Put phone by the computer.
Print copies of AUTEXEC.BAT and CONFIG.SYS files (see DOS Infomodule in Chapter 3).
Verify product registration.
State the specific problem:
   What is the product (name, version)?
   Was there an error message? What was it?
   What do you think was the cause?
What are the components of your system?
   Brand name
   Model number
   Peripheral devices
   DOS version and manufacturer
   Software version and manufacturer
   Other programs running
Contact your support person (be sure to get his or her name).
Give your name and phone number.
Tell what you have tried.
Be prepared to try other solutions.

voided if someone other than authorized repair staff tries to fix the equipment. Most warranties cover a specific period of time, and state that the company will not cover damage from mishandling, obvious abuse, or accidents.

Article II of the Uniform Commercial Code grants an **implied warranty**, i.e., that the goods sold are merchantable, fit, and of average quality. During the negotiation process, a salesperson may have made claims about the product, thus creating **express warranties**. If you make note of these verbal promises and check guarantees of performance found in advertisements or brochures, these may offer help when repairs are necessary. If negotiations with the company are unsuccessful, you may wish to contact an attorney to discover what other rights you might have.

Software and disks are generally sold "as is." They are not covered by warranties, other than for physical problems that might be found on a tape or disk. It is therefore wise for a first-time buyer to choose programs that have been proven in the marketplace.

Some of the most common warranty mistakes occur when a user:

Attempts to open the computer and tries to fix it.

Exposes the computer/keyboard to liquid, heat, or other environmental hazards.

Fails to return the warranty card.

Loses the receipt.

WHERE CAN I OBTAIN TECHNICAL SUPPORT FOR MY COMPUTER?

Four things to consider when searching for technical support are accessibility, cost, term, and persistence. You will want to know what hours the service is available; naturally 24-hour is preferable. Some fax-back services let you fax your question and receive your answer via fax. Bulletin boards also let you ask and receive answers via a modem and your computer. Costs can vary. A service with toll-free support is preferable. Some make you pay for the call but offer support for free; others charge for both. Check to see whether charges are for a determined period of time, by the call, or even by the minute. Find out for what length of time support is given. An unlimited time or the life of the product is best. Does the technician keep on trying until a solution is found? It is important to find support that is geared to solving problems.

There are other places where you can obtain technical support. The documentation that came with your software will have troubleshooting ideas. You may find helpful hints in newsletters, on-line from services such as CompuServe, the vendor where you purchased your equipment, or a local user group.

If you do find that you need to call for technical help, Table 3 outlines some of the information you should have prepared before you make that call.

WHAT ARE USER GROUPS?

A **user group** is an informal association of owners of similar brand microcomputers who share information about both hardware and software. They are a good source when you are seeking solutions to problems that other users encounter. Others in the group will most likely be able to provide first-hand information about computers and software *before* you buy. The computer dealer, software package, campus computing center, or some of your friends might have contact with a local group using systems and software similar to yours. Don't leave such an important decision to chance.

VOCABULARY SELF-TEST

Can you define the following terms?

command-driven program (p. 195)

computer literate (p. 194)

documentation (p. 195)

express warranty (p. 204)

fax (p. 198)

freeware (p. 200)

graphical user interface (GUI) (p. 194)

implied warranty (p. 204)

menu-driven program (p. 195)

parked (p. 202)

screen saver (p. 203)

shareware (p. 200)

superstore (p. 198)

surge protector (p. 197)

user group (p. 205)

warranty (p. 203)

REVIEW QUESTIONS

Multiple Choice

1. Before you select your computer you should decide:
   a. what you want the system to do
   b. which microprocessor to use
   c. where to buy your system
   d. how much you want to pay
2. A command-driven program _____.
   a. is easiest for beginning users to learn
   b. displays choices in lists on the screen
   c. requires the user to refer to a manual or memorize the choices or options of a particular program
   d. is known as a graphical user interface
3. The written or graphic details of the operation of computer software are called _____.
   a. menu-drive commands
   b. documentation
   c. shareware
   d. warranties
4. A store that sells only computers and related products is known as a(n) _____.
   a. value-added reseller
   b. discount warehouse
   c. superstore
   d. mass merchant
5. The program that prevents the images on the screen from being burned in to the CRT by randomly changing the pattern is known as a(n) _____.
   a. parking program

b. application program
c. surge protector
d. screen saver

Fill-In

1. Learning the terminology that relates to computers is known as _____.
2. An interface, such as Microsoft Windows, where users choose icons on the screen instead of typing in commands is known as a(n) _____.
3. You should be sure to make written notes of the claims that the salesperson makes during a sales pitch because those statements may have created a(n) _____.
4. A hard disk drive that has its read/write head secured away from the disk is said to be _____.

5. An informal association of owners of similar brands of microcomputers who share information about both hardware and software is known as a(n) _____.

Short Answer

1. Tell what to consider before you buy a computer system.
2. Differentiate between shareware and freeware.
3. List five different stores where you might purchase software and/or hardware.
4. Describe advantages and disadvantages of buying computers or software through a mail-order house.
5. Depict three hazardous condition scenarios for your computer or software.

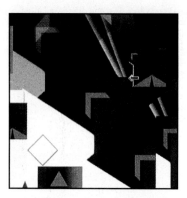

OUTLINE

OBJECTIVES

6.1   Understand the two basic types of software used in the operation of a computer.

6.2   Define operating system, describe its major functions, and discuss several ways it is typically used in the day-to-day operation of a computer.

6.3   Describe several capabilities of operating systems.

6.4   Contrast three types of user interfaces.

6.5   Understand the purpose of a disk operating system and an operating environment, and identify four major microcomputer operating systems and their associated environments.

6.6   Define application software and describe the two broad categories into which application software is grouped.

6.7   Describe the five applications most in demand for microcomputers.

6.8   Define integrated software.

6.9   Identify sources of application software.

6.10 Identify the concerns of those getting started on a new application software package.

Chapter 6

Computer Software

Profile

Peter Norton

Oops! That sound started the rest of Peter Norton's life. Norton, a Southern Californian, appears to be an average, all-American kind of guy. He's in his forties and rather than "dressing for success" his work attire consists of rolled-up shirt sleeves and a tie loosened casually.

Norton lost his job in the late 1970s when the aerospace industry suffered huge cutbacks. He took computer programming jobs to tide him over. Then came the celebrated "Oops" when he deleted an important file accidentally. Now, it's clear that that was a fortunate accident. As a programmer, Norton was sure there must be a better, more efficient way to recover the lost file. He didn't want to have to reenter everything. So he applied his programming skills and successfully created a computer program to recover the data from that lost file.

Peter Norton Computing Inc. (PNCI) was formed in 1982, based on that new program, dubbed Norton Utilities. With the Norton name boldly proclaimed, he felt obliged to deliver the best quality. And since he was the programmer, owner, and sole public relations expert, it wasn't long before he had to hit the road in an effort to market the product. Norton visited computer stores and user groups trying to generate sales. To do this he prepared technical notes and left them for potential buyers. A publisher from Brady Books came across these pamphlets and recognized that Norton had a talent for writing about technical topics in a highly readable form. Shortly thereafter, Norton's first computer book, *Inside the IBM PC,* was published and became an immediate best seller. It has now become an industry standard. In fact, since 1983 Norton's books have been translated into 14 languages and over a million copies have been sold.

The original PNCI offices were in the Norton home. Business hours depended on the family's schedule. Norton finally hired a programmer to help, and he was forced to share work space with Mrs. Norton. At day's end the programmer had to move his files and papers out of the way so the table could be set for dinner.

In 1988 Norton was named "Entrepreneur of the Year" by Arthur Young and *Venture* magazine. Norton's philosophy was to work as long as it was fun; he didn't set out to make lots of money. But PNCI was one of the fastest-growing private companies in America, and in 1990 Symantec Corp., a publicly held software company, worked out a merger deal. Norton's share is estimated at $100 million. The office isn't at the kitchen table anymore, and Norton is much too busy enjoying his family, doing philanthropic work, and collecting contemporary art.

Oops! Is that tomorrow's Picasso?

For many of you, your knowledge of software will be directed at "what" it can do for you. This chapter introduces two types of software: system software and application software. You'll learn how to tap the power of a computer and utilize it for problem solving, decision making, and increased productivity. Other readers may want to develop their own software, or are headed into a computer professional career, and they'll need to know how to design, write, and implement software to meet a user's particular needs. This skill can be complex and requires much expertise. The Infomodule at the end of this chapter gives an introduction to programming languages—the software development tools used to write both system software and application software—and describes how computer programs are developed.

Objective 6.1   Understand the two basic types of software used in the operation of a computer.

What Types of Software Make a Computer Useful?

Types of Software

- **System software**
  Controls hardware
- **Application software**
  Performs specific tasks

Computer hardware cannot perform alone. To accomplish any task, hardware must be given a series of instructions, called **software,** telling it what to do. There are two basic types of software: system software and application software.

System software refers to programs designed to perform tasks associated with directly controlling and utilizing computer hardware. It does not accomplish specific tasks for a user, such as creating documents or analyzing data. Operating systems are the most important system software programs. Operating systems are the focus in this chapter. Other system software includes data management software, computer language–oriented software, and utilities that help users perform various functions. We briefly look at these other types of system software.

Data management software includes database and file management programs that manage data for an operating system. It also includes data center management programs used on large system computers that control program execution, monitor system usage, track system resources and utilization, and bill users accordingly. System software associated with programming languages includes language translators such as assemblers, interpreters, and compilers (discussed in the Infomodule). It also includes program generators (programs that automatically generate program code), debugging and testing programs, as well as other programs that aid in the programming process. Utilities are programs that are purchased as separate products; they perform a wide range of functions. This type of software includes products such as data conversion programs that convert data from one format to another, data recovery programs that restore damaged or accidentally erased data, librarians that log and track the locations of disk or tape program files, security and auditing programs, and merge and sort programs, to name a few.

Application software refers to programs that allow you to accomplish specific tasks, like creating a letter, organizing data, or drawing graphs. Together, system and application software are responsible for directing the hardware to perform the tasks you wish to accomplish with a computer.

FIGURE 6.1
The relationships among system
software, application software,
hardware, and a user.

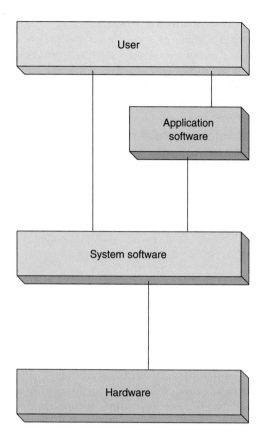

Software acts as a connection, or interface, between you and the hardware. **Interface** is a term that describes how two parts are joined so that they can work together. System software and application software provide an interface to the hardware. Figure 6.1 shows the functional relationship among system software, application software, hardware, and a user.

Objective 6.2   Define operating system, describe its major functions, and discuss several ways it is typically used in the day-to-day operation of a computer.

What Is an Operating System?

When computers were first invented, someone had to program every detail of hardware operation into a computer by setting switches or hard-wiring circuits. This was a long, tedious process that had to be repeated for *each* program executed. The programmer required specific, detailed knowledge about the way a particular computer operated, and the central processing unit (CPU) sat idle while the details were being programmed. Because hardware costs for the early computers were so high, users wanted to increase computer efficiency as well as increase the ease of using them. To accomplish these goals, a type of system software called an operating system was created.

An **operating system (OS)** is a core set of programs that control and supervise the hardware resources of a computer and provide services to other system software, application software, programmers, and users of a computer. Hardware resources include peripheral devices (monitors, printers, etc.), memory, and the central processing unit. Essentially, an OS gives the computer the instructions it needs to operate, telling it how to interact with hardware, other software, and the user. The OS establishes a standard interface, or means of communication, between users and their computer systems.

Before an OS can be used, however, it must be loaded into the computer memory. This happens during the booting process. Booting a computer means starting it. During booting, the OS is automatically loaded and the user has access to it.

The portion of the OS that is in use resides in main memory, so the computer receives and executes the details of an operation at computer speeds. The long delays that existed when humans had to intervene were eliminated. An OS dramatically increases the efficiency of a CPU, because it takes the burden of detailed programming off a programmer or computer user. Today, all computers use an operating system.

Operating System Parts

The OS programs are generally divided into two types: control programs and service programs.

Control programs manage computer hardware and resources. The main program in most operating systems is the supervisor program. A **supervisor program** is a control program that is known in some operating systems as the monitor, executive, or kernel. It is responsible for controlling all other OS programs as well as other system and application programs. The supervisor program controls the activities of all of the hardware components of a computer.

Service programs are external OS programs that provide a service to the user or programmer of a computer. These programs are included in the purchase price of an operating system. However, they must be loaded separately because they are not automatically loaded when the operating system is loaded. They perform routine but essential functions, such as formatting a disk for use and copying files from one location to another.

Operating System Programs

- Control programs
  Manage hardware and resources
- Service programs
  Provide services to users

Major Functions of Operating Systems

The major functions of an OS are resource management, data management, job (task) management, and providing a standard means of communication between the user and the computer.

The resource management function of an OS allocates computer resources such as CPU time, main memory, secondary storage, and input and output devices for use.

The data management functions of an OS govern the input and output of data and their location, storage, and retrieval. For example, it supervises the transfer of characters between the CPU and the keyboard, monitor, printer, and other input or output devices. It also is responsible for storing and retrieving information on disk drives and for the organization of that information on the drive.

The job management function of an OS prepares, schedules, controls, and monitors jobs submitted for execution to ensure the most efficient processing. A job is a collection of one or more related programs and their data.

The OS also establishes a standard means of communication between users and their computer systems. It does this by providing a user interface and a standard set of commands that control the hardware.

Typical Day-to-Day Uses of an Operating System

Operating systems do quite a bit internally, managing resources and routing information inside the computer. How would you use the OS in day-to-day operation of the computer? Here are some common ways that you'll use an OS.

The most common way is for executing application programs. This is typically done by typing in the application program's filename at a prompt, selecting the filename from a menu, or selecting an icon representing the application program from the computer screen. The OS continues to work while the application software is running. It receives requests from the application software for computer resources and carries them out. For example, if you wanted to store data that you entered in an application program onto a disk, you select the "SAVE" option. The application program makes a request to the OS to save the data to disk. It takes over and directs and stores the data to the disk. The OS action is not seen by the user. When software works without additional user direction it is said to be transparent. Much of what the OS does is transparent to the user.

You will also use the operating system to format floppy diskettes. A disk is prepared to store files and data by organizing it so your computer can locate and read data from it. Diskettes must be formatted before the computer can use them.

Another common use of the operating system is setting up directories to organize your files. A directory is a catalog for filenames and other directories stored on a disk. Its purpose is to organize and group the files stored on a disk so that you can locate them easily rather than become overwhelmed by a long list of files. It is a good organizational plan to keep all the files that belong to a particular project together in the same directory.

You will also use the operating system to display a list of files stored on a particular disk. In addition it is useful to verify that there is enough room on a disk to save a file.

A very important function of an OS is protecting and backing up your files by copying them to other disks for safekeeping. This ensures that you won't lose valuable programs or data because of damage to a disk or accidental erasure.

You will also use the OS extensively for computer housekeeping operations. These tasks include erasing old files that are no longer needed, moving files from one directory to another for better organization, and renaming files to make their content more evident.

The OS plays a vital role in your day-to-day computer use. Becoming familiar with it helps you use your computer more efficiently and effectively.

Objective 6.3   Describe several capabilities of operating systems.

How Do Operating Systems Differ?

Operating System Capabilities

- **Number of users**
    - **Single-user**
    - **Multiuser**
        - **Time sharing**
- **Number of tasks**
    - **Single tasking**
    - **Multitasking**
        - **Context switching**
        - **Cooperative**
        - **Time-slice**
    - **Multithreading**
- **Type of processing**
    - **Multiprocessing**
    - **Interprocessing**
    - **Real-time**
    - **Virtual-machine**
    - **Virtual memory**

Capabilities vary from one OS to another. For example, operating systems for larger computers must service and address the needs of numerous (possibly hundreds) of users, application programs, and hardware devices. They also typically perform a host of security and administrative tasks, such as keeping track of and reporting on computer usage to management. Most microcomputer operating systems accommodate only a single user and only a handful of peripheral devices. Therefore, they tend to be smaller and less sophisticated than large computer operating systems.

OS capabilities can be described in terms of the number of users and the type of processing they allow and the number of simultaneous tasks they perform. A particular OS may incorporate one or more of the capabilities discussed below.

Number of Users

A **single-user operating system** allows only one user at a time to access a computer. Most operating systems on microcomputers, such as DOS, are single-user access systems. A **multiuser operating system** allows two or more users to access a computer at the same time. This OS was developed because many computers have much greater computing capacity than can be exhausted by one user. The actual number of users depends on the hardware and the OS design. Although this capability is usually associated with larger computers it is sometimes found in microcomputers.

To facilitate multiuser systems, time sharing is sometimes employed. **Time sharing** allows many users to access a single computer. This capability is typically found on large computer operating systems where many users need access at the same time. The attention of the CPU is shifted among the users on a timed basis controlled by the OS. As long as the computer does not have more users than the OS can handle, it appears that each user has uninterrupted access to the CPU. TSO is a time-sharing operating system used on many mainframes.

Number of Tasks

A **single tasking** operating system allows only one program to execute at a time, and that program must finish executing completely before the next program can begin. Many microcomputer operating systems work like this. The goal of this OS is maximum ease of use and minimum professional support.

In which World Series did Bobby Thompson hit a home run? If you are not a baseball enthusiast this may not seem important to you. But *real* fans know it happened in 1951.

Imagine that you *are* a fan and that you have instant access to over 120 years of baseball facts, trivia, and nostalgia. Wishful thinking? Definitely not. Creative Multimedia Corp. offers just such a product. It has made the best-selling 2,600-page book, *Total Baseball*, available for computers that are equipped to read CD-ROM disks. Data from 1871 to the present on more than 13,000 major-league players are included: batting averages, pitching figures, fielding records—everything that the baseball devotee could wish for. The medium lends itself to fast retrieval and searches can be conducted by player, team, or year. Disks will come out annually so data can be updated with, you guessed it, more statistics.

Images are included too: Hall of Fame greats like Ty Cobb and Cy Young are pictured as are ballparks like Wrigley Field and Ebbets Field. If the CD-ROM drive is equipped with audio output you can even hear sound clips of memorable games and plays.

If only we had a portable computer with CD-ROM drive, we could take *it* out to the ball game.

A **multitasking** operating system allows a single CPU to execute what appears to be more than one program at a time. There are various ways that this is accomplished. **Context switching** allows several programs to reside in memory but only one to be active at a time. The active program is said to be in the *foreground*. The other programs in memory are not active and are said to be in the *background*. Instead of having to quit a program and load another, you can simply switch the active program in the foreground to the background and bring a program from the background into the foreground with a few keystrokes. Some applications allow **cooperative multitasking** in which a background program uses the CPU during idle time of the foreground program. For example, the background program might sort data while the foreground program waits for a keystroke. **Time-slice multitasking** enables a CPU to switch its attention between the requested tasks of two or more programs. Each task receives the attention of the CPU for a fraction of a second before the CPU moves on to the next. Depending on the applications, the order in which tasks receive CPU attention may be determined sequentially (first come first served) or by previously defined priority levels. This processing happens so quickly that to the user the programs appear to be executed simultaneously. This capability can be found on a variety of large computer and microcomputer operating systems. An OS with the capability of **multithreading** supports several simultaneous tasks within the same application. For example, with only one copy of a database management system in memory, one database file can be sorted while data is simultaneously entered into another database file.

Type of Processing

A **multiprocessing** operating system allows the simultaneous execution of programs by a computer that has two or more CPUs. Each CPU can be either dedicated to one program, or dedicated to specific functions and then used by all programs. Many computers, such as mainframes and supercomputers, have more than one CPU and use multiprocessing operating systems.

Interprocessing, also called dynamic linking, is a type of processing that allows any change made in one application to be automatically reflected in any related, linked application. Let's say you wanted to incorporate a spreadsheet graph into a word processing document. Without interprocessing capabilities, if you made a change in the spreadsheet data that affected the graph you would have to generate the new graph, delete the old graph from the word processing document, and then insert the new graph into that document. Interprocessing capabilities enable the word processing document to be linked to the spreadsheet graph. Then each time a change is made in the spreadsheet data that affects the graph in the word processing document, the graph would be automatically updated to reflect the change without further user involvement. In Microsoft Windows this capability is called object linking and embedding (OLE).

In some situations getting a response in time to allow you to correct or modify an event is critical to ensure safe and efficient operations. For example, it would be important to be notified of faulty or defective parts in a space shuttle engine, or of a nuclear reactor that has exceeded a specific temperature, in time to correct the situation. An OS with **real-time processing** capabilities allows a computer to control or monitor the task performance of other machines and people by responding to input data in a specified amount of time. To control processes, immediate response is often necessary; to simply monitor processes, periodic response is adequate. Real-time operating systems usually have fewer functions than do more general-purpose operating systems. Most real-time operating systems are written for an intended application. For example, a real-time system in a large computer might monitor the position of a rocket. In a microcomputer, it might monitor the vital signs of a heart transplant patient.

Virtual-machine (VM) processing creates the illusion of more than one physical machine. The software mimics the performance of different hardware devices, allowing different operating systems to be used concurrently.

VM capabilities permit a computer to run numerous operating systems at one time. Each user chooses the OS that is compatible with his or her intended application. Each operating system appears as just another application program to the VM operating system. Thus, the VM operating system gives flexibility and lets users choose operating systems that best suit their needs. Virtual-machine capabilities are typically used on supercomputers and mainframes.

The advanced operating system capabilities demand that memory be carefully managed. One technique is through virtual memory. **Virtual memory,** also called virtual storage, uses a secondary-storage device as an extension of main memory. A problem experienced on some computers is insufficient main memory to contain an entire program and its data. This problem is common on larger computers where a number of users are vying for the available main memory. Virtual memory resolves this problem. Portions of a program and its data are rapidly swapped between a secondary-storage device and main memory as needed, allowing the computer to function as if the entire program and its data are in main memory.

Objective 6.4   Contrast three types of user interfaces.

How Will I Use an Operating System?

User Interface Types

- **Command-line**
- **Menu-driven**
- **Graphical**

Each OS has a **user interface,** the portion of a program that users interact with—entering commands to direct the operating system and viewing the results of those commands. User interfaces take three forms: (1) command-line, (2) menu-driven, or (3) graphics-based interfaces (Figure 6.2). A **command-line interface** requires a user to type the desired response at a prompt using a special command language. This interface is usually considered more difficult to learn and use because commands must be looked up or memorized. However, once you learn the commands this can be a fast and efficient entry method. A **menu-driven interface** allows the user to select commands from a list (menu) using the keyboard or a pointing device such as a mouse. A **graphical user interface (GUI)** typically includes some or all of the following parts:

- icons, which are graphical images that represent items, such as files and directories
- a graphical pointer, which is controlled by a pointing device, typically a mouse, to select icons and commands and move on-screen items
- on-screen pull-down menus that appear or disappear, controlled by the pointing device
- windows that enclose applications or objects on the screen
- other graphic devices that let you tell the computer what to do and how to do it, for example, option boxes, check boxes, dialog boxes, and buttons

Graphical user interfaces enhance the ease of use of an operating system and have been instrumental in the design of user interfaces with greater human orientation. Human-oriented user interfaces respond to the needs of users rather than the specifics of a computer. A user uses a pointing device, such as a mouse, to point to and select the operation desired instead of typing a command.

Objective 6.5   Understand the purpose of a disk operating system and an operating environment, and identify four major microcomputer operating systems and their associated environments.

What Types of Operating Systems and Environments Are Used on Microcomputers?

There are a variety of operating systems available for microcomputers. Many of the basic functions they perform are similar, but there are some differences. These include the fact that each is designed to run on a specific computer or set of computers; each has a unique user interface; each has its own set of capabilities defining the number of users, the number of tasks, and the type of processing allowed; and each supports a specific set of application software.

FIGURE 6.2
Comparison of (a)
command-line, (b) menu-driven,
and (c) graphical user interface.

```
C:\WP60\BOOK1>dir

 Volume in drive C is MS-DOS_5
 Volume Serial Number is 1ADD-AA42
 Directory of C:\WP60\BOOK1

.            <DIR>      08-28-93   11:38p
..           <DIR>      08-28-93   11:38p
SSP     1       103600  07-25-93    9:54p
SSP     2        68491  06-22-93   11:00p
SSP     3       120981  08-13-93    5:26p
SSP     4       105739  08-13-93    5:28p
SSP     6       117460  08-28-93    3:06p
SSP     7        94761  08-28-93    3:17p
SSP     5        58891  07-29-93   10:52a
        9 file(s)     669923 bytes
                    50098176 bytes free

C:\WP60\BOOK1>
```

(a)

(b)

(c)

Who would have thought that 1992's Hurricane Andrew would have blown anyone any good? But as a result of outstanding journalistic skills and with the help of computer-generated statistics, the *Miami Herald* won the coveted Pulitzer Prize for its three-month investigation of the tragedy, and the area around south Dade County had its eyes opened to the need for changes in the zoning laws.

Stephen Doig, research editor for the newspaper, used an IBM mainframe computer to sort millions of pieces of information. Doig compared records of property damage to tax assessments, to building inspection reports, and to political contributions. Over 60,000 damage reports were combined with tax records in the hope of discovering what variables might have combined to cause the largest amount of damage. In order to depict the data visually, a geographical mapping package was run on a personal computer.

When a map of the neighborhoods with the greatest damage was overlaid by a map showing where the highest winds were recorded, it was clear that the two did not coincide. The newer homes suffered the most damage. But the South Florida Building Code requires structures to withstand wind speeds up to 120 miles per hour. What could have happened? A database of over 17,000 political contributions beginning in 1980 indicated some questionable relationships between builders and elected officials who controlled building codes.

Further statistical analyses were run. Among the irregularities turned up were building inspection reports indicating that one person had completed as many as 80 inspections in one day. It's unlikely that an inspector could make more than 20 in a day. Another interesting computer find was that of the builder of 30 devastated homes who had previously been convicted of bribing roofing inspectors.

Andrew blew the roof off more than the homes of thousands of people.

You may hear the term *disk operating system* when dealing with microcomputers. A **disk operating system (DOS)** is an operating system that allows and manages the use of disk drives for storing and accessing data and programs. All of the following are disk operating systems although only one, DOS, refers to this in its name.

Early operating systems were designed with command-line user interfaces. This made them difficult for the average user to learn and use. User demands and the developers' desire to expand the computer market led to improvements, such as operating environments, that made operating systems easier for users to work with. An **operating environment** is software that enhances the functions of an operating system and improves its user interface. Common functions added include support for larger amounts of main memory, multitasking, and an enhanced user interface that is either menu-driven or graphics-based. Operating environments need an OS as a foundation, because they can't function on their own.

Operating environments often use windows to increase the flexibility of a program. A **window** is a separate area or box on the screen that encloses independent applications. This permits several applications to be displayed on the screen concurrently and data can be transferred among them. The operating environment logically sits on top of the OS (Figure 6.3).

The user interface associated with an OS or operating environment supplies application software developers with numerous user-interface components. Utilization of user-interface components in the development of applications leads to consistently interfaced programs. They are easier to learn and use because key operations (such as printing and file handling) are all accomplished in the same way, no matter what application program is being used.

The most common operating systems for microcomputers include DOS, OS/2, the Apple Macintosh operating system, and various versions of the Unix operating system. We'll look at these and their associated operating environments next.

DOS

Currently, DOS (disk operating system) is the OS in use on IBM and compatible microcomputers. While not officially declared a standard, it has become what is known as a **de facto standard,** that is, DOS is recognized

FIGURE 6.3
The operating environment is an interface between the user and the operating system.

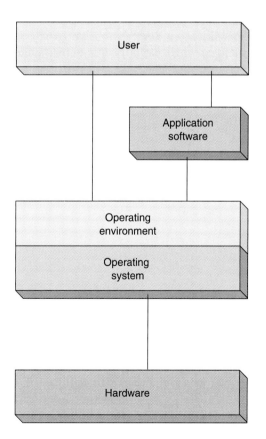

as the most popular and widely used OS. More than one company makes DOS. Microsoft Corp. makes MS-DOS and IBM makes PC-DOS. Through general use both are usually termed just DOS.

DOS was designed as a single-user, single-tasking operating system. That design meant that the computer could accommodate only one user and one application program at a time. DOS uses a text-based, command-line user interface. In other words, to direct the OS to perform a function, a user types a command at the prompt to enter it into the computer. If you want DOS to use a menu-driven user interface you can run the DOS shell command, which also supports a mouse.

If you add an operating environment to DOS, it improves the user interface and ease of use and increases its functionality. Microsoft Windows (see Chapter 4 Infomodule) is the most popular operating environment used with DOS. It adds a GUI to DOS so you are able to access programs and commands using icons, menus, and a mouse. Another popular operating environment for DOS is GEOS from GeoWorks Inc. It also supplies a GUI as well as multitasking and multithreading capabilities.

OS/2

OS/2 (Operating System 2) is an OS created by IBM and made available in 1988. It runs on Intel Corp. 80286 and higher microprocessors, which are found typically on IBM and compatible computers. OS/2 is a single-user, multitasking OS that employs virtual memory and also runs applications made for other operating systems including DOS. However, software designed specifically for OS/2 cannot be run on DOS-based computers. OS/2 comes bundled with a GUI operating environment called Presentation Manager.

Macintosh Operating System

The Apple Macintosh OS, called the System, made its debut with the introduction of the first Macintosh in 1984. It runs on the Motorola 68000 series of microprocessors. Much of this OS is rooted in the Xerox 8010 Star Information System developed at Xerox's Palo Alto Research Center in the 1970s. Many of the well-known user-friendly features of the Macintosh were borrowed from the Xerox computer.

The System has little in common with DOS or OS/2. Early versions of this OS were single-user and single-tasking. Current versions include support for multitasking. The Apple Macintosh OS has always come with an operating environment, called the Finder, which provides a GUI. MultiFinder is a version that allows multitasking. This intuitiveness and the ease of use that it brought to the OS helped make the Macintosh a popular microcomputer.

Unix

Unix is a multiuser, multitasking OS that uses a command-line user interface. It was developed at AT&T's Bell Labs in the late 1960s. Unix was originally designed to run on minicomputers made by DEC. Later, it was rewritten primarily in the C programming language. This rewrite made Unix more portable, i.e., less machine-specific, and thus allowed it to be more easily moved to any size computer that could run C. Unix was moved to microcomputers in 1980.

Many users find Unix difficult to work with because of its structure, including the large volume of commands. Additionally, there is no standard version of Unix. Although several competing versions are available, no version is totally compatible with the others.

Several operating environments are available to give Unix a GUI and make it easier to work with. Popular operating environments for Unix are OSF/Motif and SUN/OpenLook.

Objective 6.6   Define application software and describe the two broad categories into which application software is grouped.

What Is Application Software?

If you head for the computer to write a letter or assemble data for a report, the operating system is no help in performing these specific tasks. Another link is necessary between the operating system and the user. This link makes a computer useful by permitting it to accomplish a particular task. Application software refers to programs that help a user perform a specific task faster, more efficiently, and thus more productively than could be accomplished manually. Application software creates a communication bridge so a user can tell system software how to direct the hardware to perform desired functions.

Application software is written for a specific operating system. So, when you buy application software make sure the version is compatible with your operating system. Some application software is available in several versions for different operating systems; others have specific hardware requirements, such as a particular microprocessor or a minimum amount of main memory.

Application software can be grouped into two broad categories: (1) generalized and (2) specialized. **Generalized application software** is software that can be applied to a wide variety of tasks. The generalized application software programs that are most used on microcomputers by businesses and at home include word processors, electronic spreadsheets, database management systems, graphics, and communications. For example, a generalized spreadsheet program creates one spreadsheet to calculate your household budget and another to calculate your taxes. Chapters 11 through 14 focus on generalized application software.

Specialized application software performs a specific task and cannot be changed or programmed for a different task. For example, a payroll application program is designed exclusively for payroll functions. It cannot do other tasks, such as cost analysis. Popular specialized application programs include business-oriented programs, vertical-market programs, engineering and scientific programs, educational programs, and entertainment programs.

Business-oriented applications include accounting programs (including payroll, accounts receivable, accounts payable, general ledger, budgeting, and financial planning, which are used in almost every kind of business), banking software, financial software, and investment software. Vertical-market software handles the unique needs of specific markets (businesses), such as medicine and health services, legal services, the automotive industry, and property management. Engineering and scientific applications include programs such as computer-aided design (CAD), which automates mechanical drawings; chemical engineering; scientific calculations; and structural analysis. Educational applications include computer-assisted instruction (CAI) that guides a student through a course of study, library services, student services, typing tutors, and grade book programs to assist instructors in the process of recording student scores. Entertainment applications include games, flight simulators, and music programs.

Objective 6.7   Describe the five applications most in demand for microcomputers.

What Is the Most Commonly Used Microcomputer Application Software?

Five application software programs have emerged as the most popular and widely used with microcomputers: word processor, data manager, electronic spreadsheet, graphics, and communications. Each program is available in many levels of complexity, focusing on different users' needs. Some stress ease of use but may have limited features; others are geared toward professionals and contain many advanced features.

Major Microcomputer Application Software

- Word processor
- Data manager
- Electronic spreadsheet
- Graphics
- Communication

Word Processors

At some time you have handwritten or typed a lengthy term paper or similar document; you know how time consuming it is to edit and rewrite—and rewrite—and rewrite—the text. A **word processor** is software that lets you create, edit, manipulate, and print text and makes the job much simpler, easier, and faster. It automates many manual tasks associated with writing in longhand or typing, such as cutting and pasting, centering, and setting margins. For example, this book was written and edited using word processors (Figure 6.4). WordPerfect and Microsoft Word are popular word processors.

Database Management Systems

In business, large volumes of data and information must be organized and accessible in different formats. People's ability to do this manually in a reasonable amount of time was exceeded long ago, creating a demand for machines to take over the task. Thus **database management systems** were developed to store, organize, manipulate, retrieve, display, and print data (Figure 6.5).

Database management systems enable businesses and organizations to keep track of vast amounts of data that must be gathered and stored. For example, a nonprofit organization conducting a fund-raising campaign might use a database management system to store the names, addresses, phone numbers and other pertinent data on thousands of potential donors who must be contacted. Thus, when a fund-raiser makes a contact for a donation or receives a pledge, all pertinent data about that individual donor

File   Edit   View   Layout   Tools   Font   Graphics   Window   Help

CHAPTER SIX

Computer Software

PROFILE: Peter Norton

WHAT TYPES OF SOFTWARE MAKE A COMPUTER USEFUL?

WHAT IS AN OPERATING SYSTEM?

     Operating System Parts

     Major Functions of Operating Systems

     Typical Day-to-day Uses of an Operating System

HOW DO OPERATING SYSTEMS DIFFER?

     Number os Users

     Number of Tasks

     Type of Processing

HOW WILL I USE AN OPERATING SYSTEM?

WHAT TYPES OF OPERATING SYSTEMS AND ENVIRONMENTS ARE USED ON MICROCOMPUTERS?

     DOS

C:\WP51\B1_DE\SSP6.DE   Doc 1 Pg 1 Ln 1" Pos **1"**

FIGURE 6.5
The dBASE database management system can organize different types of data. For example, as shown on this input screen, data for a personal inventory system can be entered. Depending on the user's needs, the data can be manipulated into different formats.

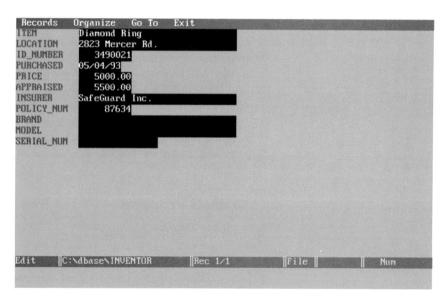

is available on the computer. dBASE, FoxBASE, and Paradox are popular database management systems for microcomputers.

Electronic Spreadsheets

Anyone who must keep track of and manipulate numbers can benefit from a computerized **spreadsheet**, the software that displays, manipulates, and prints rows and columns of data. It is similar to the paper spreadsheet

document used primarily by accountants, in that both have columns and rows in which values and labels are entered (Figure 6.6). The difference lies in the fact that data in an electronic spreadsheet can be easily edited by the user, and all other dependent figures in the spreadsheet are then recalculated automatically and the results stored.

Spreadsheets can perform a wide variety of tasks, from budgeting personal income to financial planning for a corporation. Lotus 1-2-3 and Microsoft Excel are popular spreadsheet programs.

Graphics Programs

Graphics programs display data visually in the form of graphic images. For example, even after using a spreadsheet or database management system to manipulate and organize data, it can sometimes be difficult to see relationships or to interpret that information. Presenting the information visually (graphically) is one way to make this easier.

One type of program extracts and displays data graphically in line, pie, or bar charts. Business managers use graphics programs to visually present statistics and other data to staff or to clients. At home, you could create a bar graph to see if your monthly spending deviated from your budget. Popular independent, or stand-alone, programs include Harvard Graphics and PFS:Graph. Graphics software also may be part of a larger program, such as the graphics in Lotus 1-2-3 (Figure 6.7). Graphics programs are available for artists to create pictures and engineers and architects to create designs.

FIGURE 6.7
Data from a spreadsheet file can be used directly by a graphics program to generate vivid graphics for a meeting or report. Here, a bar chart shows sales projections created from data in a spreadsheet file.

Communications Programs

As more individuals and organizations use computers, the need to transfer data from one to another has increased. Law enforcement agencies exchange information on criminals; home users access information services such as CompuServe; and many individuals and businesses send electronic mail. **Communications programs** allow your computer to "talk" to other computers. But to accomplish communications you need additional hardware: a modem to transmit and receive your data over telephone lines. Popular communications software programs include Crosstalk and PC-Talk (Figure 6.8).

Objective 6.8   Define integrated software.

What Is Integrated Application Software?

The data files of many early microcomputer programs were not always compatible with each other. The programs were not *integrated,* i.e., data usually could not be moved electronically from one program to the other. Transferring data between programs, even when possible, was complex and tedious. Typically, the user's only recourse was to retype all the data into the receiving program, which of course defeated part of the reason for using the computer in the first place: to save time and work. When working with several different programs, users had to learn how each program accomplished a specific task. Many stand-alone programs perform the same task in different ways. Trying to remember how each program accomplishes a task can be difficult and confusing.

    Integrated software is a category of application software that combines a number of applications, such as word processing, database management, spreadsheet, graphics, and communications, into a single application package. The applications are generally integrated in two major

FIGURE 6.8
Communications programs can
be used to connect your
computer to services over
phone lines.

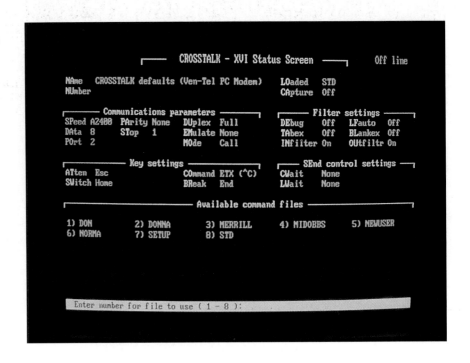

ways. First, data are easily transferred from one application to another. This helps users coordinate tasks and allows them to easily merge data created by the different applications. Second, a consistent interface is provided so that once a user learns a task, such as printing a file, in one application he/she can perform the same task in all the applications without relearning it.

Cost is another reason to use integrated software. It is generally less expensive to buy one integrated software package than to buy each application separately. However, integrated software generally doesn't offer the full range of features that stand-alone applications do. Integrated software packages vary in both the applications they contain and the functionality of those applications.

Common integrated software packages include Microsoft's Works for Windows; Spinnaker Software's PFS:WindowWorks; GeoWorks' GeoWorks Pro; and Lotus Development's LotusWorks.

Objective 6.9   Identify sources of application software.

How Can Application Software Be Acquired?

Application software is created and acquired either as prewritten or as custom-developed software. Each of these methods has advantages and disadvantages. The best alternative will depend on the user's needs and budget.

Prewritten Software

Generally, prewritten software, also called "canned" software, is available for purchase from a vendor, a distributor such as a computer store, or its author. The use of prewritten application software has several advantages:

1. It can be installed quickly, and is ready for immediate use.
2. It is usually less expensive than custom-developed application software.
3. It is available for almost any task required.
4. It has already been tested.
5. Some can be modified to meet a user's special requirements.

The primary disadvantage of prewritten application software is that it may not precisely fit the special needs of a user.

Custom-Developed Software

When prewritten software does not fit the user's need, custom-developed software can be written. Programmers or skilled users sometimes write their own software. The main advantage of custom-developed software is that it can be tailored to exact specifications. A major disadvantage is the cost. Skilled programmers are expensive, and determining precise specifications can be time-consuming and costly.

If the personnel, expertise, time, or money is not available in house for custom development, another option is to contract with a person or group that specializes in developing software. Many firms employ skilled programmers to develop customized software for the specialized needs of their clients.

Objective 6.10   Identify the concerns of those getting started on a new application software package.

How Do I Get Started with a New Application Program?

It is important that you know the application software's system requirements before you purchase it. These are the capabilities your computer must have to run the software, including the amount of memory, type of microprocessor, and the operating system in use. These facts are usually found on the outside of the software package, so check it out before you buy.

When you finally bring an application program home, there are a number of things to do before you start using the application. First, look over the documentation that comes with the program and carefully *read* all materials that apply to getting started and installing the software. The manuals provide you with all the instructions for using and installing the program. You can avoid mistakes by reading first to become familiar with the entire process.

Another important task is learning how to make backup copies of the program disks. Having a backup copy protects your investment if anything goes wrong and the disks are damaged or erased during installation or use. The original set is intact so you can begin again.

When you buy a new program it has to be installed on your computer. To **install** a program means to prepare it to work with your computer. Application programs contain an installation program, typically called INSTALL.EXE. The **installation program** is responsible for getting the application up and running. It guides you through the installation process by presenting a screen menu of setup options. The options to be set may include the type of monitor, printer, or other peripheral device with which

Getting Started on a New Application Software Package

- Determine system requirements before buying
- Read documentation on installing and getting started
- Make backup copies of master disks
- Run installation program
- Load application program
- Use manuals, on-line help, and tutorials to learn program

you work. For example, an installation program typically asks you to identify your printer and then installs the appropriate device driver, the software that allows direct communication with a hardware device. Some operating systems, such as the Macintosh operating system, make the device drivers transparent to the user. The device drivers do not have to be installed by a user because they are standard parts of the OS and are automatically installed.

If you install the program on a hard disk drive the installation program also copies the application program files from the floppy diskettes onto your hard drive. Generally, the files on the master diskettes are stored in a compressed form and require the installation program to convert them and place them on your hard disk.

Once the program is installed and all the appropriate device drivers are in place the program can be loaded. To **load** a program means to place it in main memory. Both system and application software play a role in loading a program. For example, let's say you are using an OS with a command-line interface. If the command to load a word processor is WP, you type in the command WP at the prompt and press the ENTER key. But before anything happens the command sequence WP(ENTER) must be interpreted by the computer. This is the responsibility of a part of the OS called the command interpreter, which identifies symbols typed in from the keyboard as commands and performs the indicated task, in this example, it loads the word processing application program. The command is interpreted, the operating system looks on the disk for the file WP.EXE to bring it into main memory, and the application program takes over loading the rest of the files. You are now ready to be productive. The manuals that come with the application software and any available on-line help and tutorials will help you learn how to use and get the most out of the program.

It takes both system and application software as well as hardware to use the computer to your best advantage. With the emphasis on "user-friendly" interfaces, many software operations are becoming more and more transparent to the user, which in the long run makes the computer an easier tool to use. Chapters 11 through 14 take a closer look at the features and how you can utilize various microcomputer application software programs.

Summary

Software refers to the instructions that direct the operations of a computer. There are two basic types of software: system software and application software. System software performs tasks associated with controlling and utilizing computer hardware directly. Application programs accomplish a task or set of tasks, such as creating a document or analyzing data, for a user.

The most important type of system software is the operating system. It is software that controls and supervises a computer's hardware and provides services to other system software, application software, programmers, and users of a computer.

Operating systems are composed of two major parts: control programs and service programs. Control programs manage computer hardware and resources. Service programs are external operating system programs that provide a service to the user or programmer of a computer.

The major tasks of an operating system are resource management, data management, job management, and providing a standard means of communication between a user and the computer.

Operating systems for large computers are more complex and sophisticated than those for microcomputers because the operating systems for large computers must address the needs of a very large number of users, application programs, and hardware devices, as well as supply a host of administrative and security features. Operating system capabilities can be described in terms of the number of users they can accommodate at one time, how many tasks can be run at one time, and how they process those tasks. An operating system can be designed for single-tasking or multitasking. A multiprocessing operating system allows the simultaneous execution of programs by a computer that has two or more CPUs. Interprocessing, also called dynamic linking, allows any change made in one application to be automatically reflected in any related, linked application. Real-time processing allows a computer to control or monitor the performance of other machines and people by responding to input data in a specified amount of time. Virtual-machine (VM) processing creates the illusion that there is more than one physical machine. Virtual memory, also called virtual storage, allows you to use a secondary-storage device as an extension of main memory.

The user interface of an operating system is the portion of the program with which users interact. The user interface can be command-line, menu-driven, or graphics-based.

A disk operating system (DOS) is an operating system that allows and manages the use of disk drives for storing and accessing data and programs. An operating environment is software that improves its user interface and enhances the functions of an operating system. Operating environments often use windows to allow the display of several applications on the screen concurrently and to facilitate data transfer between them.

Popular microcomputer operating systems include MS-DOS, OS/2, the Apple Macintosh operating system, and Unix. Popular operating environments include Microsoft's Windows for DOS; the Presentation Manager for OS/2; Finder and MultiFinder for Apple Macintosh; and OSF/Motif and SUN/OpenLook for Unix.

Many tasks that people perform manually can be done faster and more efficiently with a computer. Application software are programs that direct a computer to complete tasks for the user. There are two broad categories of application software: generalized and specialized. Generalized application software can be applied to a wide variety of tasks, and it includes such programs as electronic spreadsheets, data managers, word processors, graphics, and communication. Specialized application software performs a specific task. They cannot be changed to perform a different task. Such software includes business-oriented, vertical market, engineering and scientific programs, educational programs, and entertainment programs.

Word processors, data managers, electronic spreadsheets, graphics, and communications are the most popular and widely used applications with microcomputers.

Integrated software allows several programs to share the same user interface and data.

Application software can be prewritten software; in-house, custom-developed software; or outside, custom-developed software.

When getting started on a new application software package, determine the application's system requirements before buying, carefully read the documentation on installing and getting started, make backup copies of the master disks, and run the installation program. Then load the application program and use the manuals, on-line help, and tutorials that are available to learn to effectively use the program.

VOCABULARY SELF-TEST

Can you define the following terms?

application software (p. 211)
command-line interface (p. 218)
communications programs (p. 227)
context switching (p. 216)
control program (p. 213)
cooperative multitasking (p. 216)
database management systems (p. 224)
de facto standard (p. 221)
disk operating system (DOS) (p. 220)
generalized application software (p. 223)
graphical user interface (GUI) (p. 218)
graphics programs (p. 226)
install (p. 229)
installation program (p.229)
integrated software (p. 227)
interface (p. 212)
interprocessing (p. 217)
load (p. 230)
menu-driven interface (p. 218)
multiprocessing (p. 217)

multitasking (p. 216)
multithreading (p. 216)
multiuser operating system (p. 215)
operating environment (p. 220)
operating system (OS) (p. 213)
real-time processing (p. 217)
service program (p. 213)
single tasking (p. 215)
single-user operating system (p. 215)
software (p. 211)
specialized application software (p. 223)
spreadsheet (p. 225)
supervisor program (p. 213)
system software (p. 211)
time sharing (p. 215)
time-slice multitasking (p. 216)
user interface (p. 218)
virtual-machine (VM) processing (p. 217)
virtual memory (p. 217)
window (p. 221)
word processor (p. 224)

REVIEW QUESTIONS

Multiple Choice

1. Programs designed to perform tasks associated with directly controlling and utilizing computer hardware rather than accomplishing a specific application for a user are called _____.

    a. communications software

    b. specialized application software

    c. system software

    d. application software

2. A(n) _____ controls and supervises the hardware of a computer.

    a. operating system

    b. specialized application

    c. database management system

    d. interface

3. Which of the following is not a major function of an operating system?

    a. resource management

    b. providing a means of communication between user and computer

    c. solving specific user tasks

    d. data management

4. This operating system capability allows the use of a secondary-storage device as an extension of main memory.

    a. virtual-machine

    b. time-sharing

    c. multiprocessing

    d. virtual-memory

5. An operating system with _____ capabilities allows a computer to control or to monitor the task performance of other machines and people by responding to input data in a specified amount of time.

    a. real-time

    b. multithreading

    c. multiprogramming

    d. interprocessing

6. A(n) _____ is software that enhances the functions of and changes the user interface of an operating system.

    a. disk operating system

    b. user interface

    c. operating environment

    d. application program

7. Which of the following is a multiuser, multitasking operating system for microcomputers?

    a. Unix

    b. DOS

    c. Macintosh System

    d. OS/2

8. _____ is the software that tells the computer how to solve a problem or perform a particular task; it helps the user work faster, more efficiently and more productively.

    a. Application software

    b. An integrated program

    c. A device driver

    d. An interface

9. Which one of the following would be classified as generalized application software?

a. a payroll program
b. a grade book program
c. a medical office management program
d. a word processor

10. _____ combines several programs into one package so that they share data and a common user interface.
    a. An operating system
    b. Specialized application software
    c. Integrated software
    d. Generalized application software

Fill-In

1. The _____ program is responsible for controlling all other operating system programs as well as other system and application programs.
2. _____ is a capability of an operating system that allows a single CPU to appear to execute more than one program at a time.
3. The operating system capability that allows simultaneous execution of programs by a computer that has two or more CPUs is called _____.
4. A microcomputer operating system that allows and manages the use of disk drives is referred to as a(n) _____.
5. A(n) _____ is software that enhances the functions of an operating system and improves its user interface.
6. Software that can be applied to a wide variety of tasks is called _____.
7. The application software that stores, organizes, manipulates, retrieves, displays, and prints data is a(n) _____.
8. A(n) _____ is the application software that displays, manipulates, and prints rows and columns of data.
9. _____ is a category of software that combines a number of applications in one package and allows them to share data and use a common interface.
10. The _____ program is responsible for configuring a new application program to work with your hardware and copying its files to your hard disk.

Short Answer

1. What is an operating system?
2. Discuss how operating systems differ in regard to the number of users, number of tasks, and types of processing they control.
3. Describe several ways in which you might use an operating system in your day-to-day computer use.
4. Identify and describe three types of user interfaces.
5. Why would you want to add an operating environment to an operating system?
6. List and briefly describe four operating systems commonly used with microcomputers.

7. Identify the two broad categories of application software and give examples of each.
8. Briefly describe the five major microcomputer application software programs.
9. What are the advantage(s)/disadvantage(s) of using integrated software?
10. Identify and discuss the main sources from which software is created or obtained.

Issues for Thought

1. Think about your chosen profession. How might computers and software enhance your productivity? Describe several ways in which you see software changing or affecting your profession.
2. What effect do you think the design of a user interface has on a user? Is the graphical user interface best for both beginners and professionals?

Infomodule
Developing Computer Programs

WHAT IS COMPUTER PROGRAMMING?

Computer programming involves writing instructions and giving them to the computer so it can complete a task. A **computer program**, or software, is a set of instructions written in a computer language, intended to be executed by a computer to perform a useful task. The application packages such as word processors, spreadsheets, and database management systems that you purchase are computer programs. A **programmer** is an individual who translates the tasks that you want a computer to accomplish into a form the computer understands.

DO I NEED TO KNOW ABOUT PROGRAMMING?

You may have no intention of becoming a programmer or of programming your own software. You may be interested only in knowing how to use commercially available application programs. Why, then, should you take the time to learn about programming?

First, your basic knowledge of how a computer works and what it can do will increase. As your understanding increases, computers will become both less intimidating and more useful. Second, the chance that you will have to communicate with a programmer, directly or indirectly, is increasing as computers become more prevalent. Your understanding of a programmer's work and the information needed to do that work will help you work together more effectively. Third, many application programs incorporate macro and special programming languages that can be easily used by nonprogrammers to take greater advantage of a program's power. Understanding basic programming concepts helps you work more efficiently and effectively.

And fourth, FOCUS and other fourth-generation languages (4GL) have been created to make programming and other computer use such as retrieving data from a database readily available to end users. They allow easy development of databases, screens, and programs that can easily be melded into applications. Many noncomputer professionals such as accountants and financial analysts use 4GLs. Knowing the basic concepts of good program design and development can be beneficial when using a 4GL.

WHAT ARE THE QUALITIES OF A WELL-DESIGNED PROGRAM?

A well-designed program should have these characteristics:

■ correct and accurate
■ easy to understand
■ easy to maintain and update
■ efficient
■ reliable
■ flexible

Qualities of a Well-Designed Program

■ Correct and accurate
■ Easy to understand
■ Easy to maintain and update
■ Efficient
■ Reliable
■ Flexible

A correct and accurate program does what it was designed to do without error in accordance with the specifications laid out during program design. The program should be designed so that anyone working with it finds its logic easy to understand. It should also be designed and documented so that program maintenance and updating can be achieved with relative ease. In addition, the program should run efficiently by executing quickly and using computer resources, such as main memory, conservatively.

The reliability of a program is its ability to operate under unforeseen circumstances, such as invalid data entries. For example, if a program expects a yes or no response but you type in a number, the program should recognize the error, inform you of the invalid entry, and indicate the proper form of response expected by the program. Nonetheless, a flexible program operates with a wide range of legitimate input. For example, if a program requests a yes or no answer, it should accept any combination of capital and lowercase letters for the words *yes* and *no,* in addition to the single letters *Y, y, N,* and *n.*

WHAT IS THE PROGRAM DEVELOPMENT PROCESS?

The **program development process** is a series of steps to follow when developing a program. It consists of the following steps: document the program; determine user needs; design the program specifications; review the program specifications; design the algorithm; code the program; compile, test, and debug the program; and get the program to the user.

Document the Program

Although it is listed as the first step, documentation is an important requirement throughout all the steps, each of which will be examined below. **Documentation** is the text or graphics that provides specific instructions about, or records the purpose or function of, a particular step or instruction in a program. Each step throughout the programming process should be documented.

There are two good reasons to document the program development process. First, documentation

---

The Program Development Process

- **Document the program**
- **Determine user needs**
- **Design program specifications**
- **Review program specifications**
- **Design the algorithm**
- **Code the program**
- **Compile, test, and debug the program**
- **Get program to the user**

---

leaves a clear record for someone else to understand what was done. This record is important in a business environment because it is likely that the person who later corrects an error or modifies the program will not be the same person who originally designed or coded it.

Second, documenting the steps as they are developed forces a reexamination of the actions taken. Problems might be discovered early enough to avoid costly alterations later. Documentation is important even if you are programming just for your own use.

Determine User Needs

The first step in the program development process is to determine user needs. In this preliminary step developers and analysts determine what type of program users want or need. They must determine the tasks users need accomplished and the features that will implement them.

Design Program Specifications

Once a clear picture of the needs of the user is obtained it's time to design the program specifications. They are the blueprint that describes what a program is supposed to do. The specification provides a clear plan of what features to incorporate and what it should look like.

Review Program Specifications

The next step in the program development process is to review the design specifications. The design team members, which may include analysts, programmers, and users, need to review the design specifications to make certain they understand what the program is to do. Once everyone understands that, the process proceeds to the next step where the programmer(s) determines how to achieve the desired results.

Design the Algorithm

The programmer now designs the steps that will convert the available input into the desired output. The **algorithm** is the finite set of step-by-step instructions that convert the input into the desired output, that is, solve the problem. These steps are also referred to as program **logic**. There are many aids for designing and documenting an algorithm. Two common ones are program flowcharts and pseudocode.

A **program flowchart** graphically details the processing steps of a particular program. Figure 1 shows some standard program flowcharting symbols. A flowchart is used to:

- clarify the program logic
- identify alternate processing methods available

- serve as a guide for program coding
- serve as documentation

Figure 2 is an example of a program flowchart constructed for a program that checks a client's payment record.

Another tool used to formulate the processing steps of a program is pseudocode. **Pseudocode** uses English phrases to describe the processing steps of a program or module. Pseudocode was designed as an alternative to flowcharts. Often, the phrases resemble the programming language code, consequently the name "pseudo"code.

Processing steps are expressed in a simple straightforward manner so that the pseudocode can be easily converted to program code. Most programming departments establish rules and conventions to be followed when using pseudocode so that others will be able to read and interpret its meaning. Figure 3 is an example of pseudocode as it might be written for the problem in Figure 2.

Designing program logic can be an extremely difficult and complex task. Structured programming techniques, discussed in the next section, were developed to help programmers. After the solution has been clearly formulated, it is time to code (write) the program.

FIGURE 1
Programming flowchart symbols.

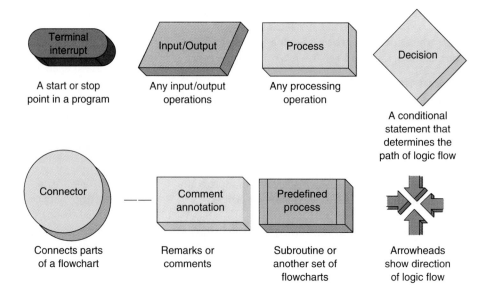

INFORMATION AGE: AN OVERVIEW OF COMPUTING AND COMPUTERS

FIGURE 2
A program flowchart.

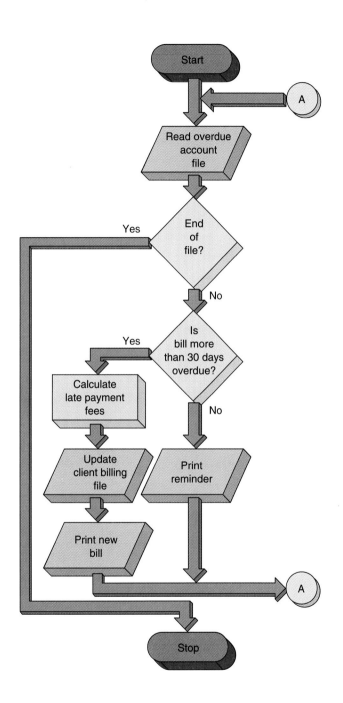

```
Begin
  Read overdue billing file.
  DO WHILE not end of file
    IF bill more than 30 days overdue
    THEN
       Calculate late payment fees.
       Update billing file.
       Print new bill.
    ELSE
       Print payment reminder.
    End-if
    Read overdue billing file.
  End
```

FIGURE 3
Pseudocode for the program in Figure 2.

Code the Program

Coding a program involves actually writing the instructions in a programming language that tells the computer how to operate. Typically coding takes the programmer less time than any of the other steps in the development process and is accomplished usually at a terminal or microcomputer using a program editor. A **program editor** is a program that allows the programmer to type, edit, and save the program code on disk.

Compile, Test, and Debug the Program

The next step requires a language translator program to convert the program code into machine language so it can be executed by the computer. Language translators are discussed in the section on programming languages later in this Infomodule.

Next the program should be tested to ensure that it is correct and contains no errors. It is difficult, if not impossible, to test a complex program for every condition that may cause an error; however, sufficient tests can be made to be *reasonably* sure the program is correct and error-free.

Generally, a programmer tests each module of a program as it is completed. When the entire program is completed it is tested internally and then often is sent to a select group of users for what are called alpha and beta tests. Programmers use feed-

back from each of these tests to modify and improve a program.

Three types of program errors that may be encountered during testing are:

- syntax
- run-time
- logic

The **syntax** of a programming language is the set of rules and conventions to be followed when writing a program; these rules are similar to the grammatical rules of the English language. When these rules are violated, a **syntax error** occurs. All syntax errors must be found and corrected before a program will execute.

A second error that may occur during testing is a **run-time error** and execution of the program is stopped. This happens if invalid data were entered. For example, if the program expects numerical data and alphabetical data were entered instead, a poorly designed program would "crash," i.e., stop executing. A properly written program identifies the problem, prompts the user with an error message, and permits the data to be reentered.

The third error, which is most difficult to find, is the logic error. A **logic error** will not stop the execution of the program; however, the results will not be accurate. With luck, the error will be obvious; usually it is not. Here's a simple example: The problem is to calculate the number of apples by adding 2 apples plus 4 apples. The formula should be $2 + 4 = 6$. But what if the wrong symbol is entered, for example, 2×4? The answer "8" is correct for the formula as entered, but not for the problem to be

---

Types of program errors

- **Syntax**
- **Run-time**
- **Logic**

solved. Finding the logic error in the above example is easy; however, finding a logic error in a complicated program is like trying to find the proverbial needle in a haystack. The process of finding any type of error and correcting it is called **debugging** (Figure 4). After a program has been debugged, all the associated documentation should be finalized so that it accurately reflects the changes.

Get the Program to the User

The final step involves getting the program to the user. In a business setting this involves installing the software on the user's computer and offering training on how to use it. If the software was developed for sale in the commercial market, the master disks are built and duplicated, the documentation is printed,

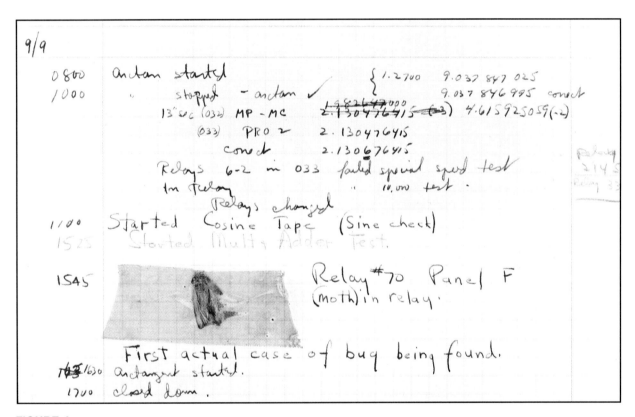

FIGURE 4
Grace Hopper relates the story that in 1945, she and a team of programmers were working on the Mark II when the computer simply quit. They couldn't determine what was wrong. Finally, they looked inside the computer and saw a large, dead moth in one of the signal relays. The moth, the first computer "bug," was removed and saved for posterity in a log book now located at the U.S. Naval Museum in Dahlgren, Virginia. After that incident, when naval officers checked on progress when a computer was not operating, the personnel advised that they were "debugging the program." (U.S. Navy photo)

the product is packaged and then shipped to commercial outlets for sale.

WHAT IS STRUCTURED PROGRAMMING?

In the early days of computers, programming was more an art than a science, and developing a quality program was more a hit-or-miss proposition than a planned goal. Given a task, programmers were left on their own to create a solution any way they could.

But three major problems arose from this free-form method: (1) long development time, (2) high maintenance cost, and (3) low-quality software.

These problems forced a search for solutions and led to development of structured programming. **Structured programming** stresses the systematic design and management of the program development process. Its purpose and overall goals are to:

- Decrease development time by increasing programmer productivity and reducing the time needed to test and debug a program.
- Decrease maintenance cost by reducing errors and making program code easier to understand.
- Improve the quality of delivered software by providing programs with fewer errors.

Structured programming attempts to accomplish these goals by incorporating these concepts:

- top-down design and use of modules
- use of limited control structures (sequence, selection, and repetition)
- management control

Top-down design starts with the major functions involved in a problem and divides them into subfunc-

tions until the problem has been divided as much as possible. Each unit is small enough to be programmed by an individual programmer in the required time frame. This forces an examination of all aspects of a problem on one level before considering the next level. A programmer is left with small groups, or **modules,** of processing instructions, which are easy to understand and code. Thus, a program consists of a **main logic module** that controls the execution of the other modules in the program. Working from the top down (i.e., general to specific) avoids solutions that deal with only part of a problem.

In addition, a program that uses a main logic module to control smaller modules is easier to read, test, and maintain. In structured programming, modules ensure these qualities by:

- having only one entrance and one exit
- performing only one program function
- returning control to the module from which it was received

Control structure determines the *order of execution* of program statements. The most complex program logic can be expressed with just three control structures: sequence, selection, and repetition (also called looping or iteration).

A **sequence control structure** executes statements one after another in a linear fashion (Figure 5). The **selection control structure** presents a number of processing options. The option chosen depends on the result of the decision criterion. Figure 6 depicts some variations of a selection control struc-

---

Goals of Structured Programming

- Decrease program development time
- Decrease program maintenance costs
- Improve the quality of software

Control Structures for Structured Programming

- Sequence
- Selection
- Repetition (looping)

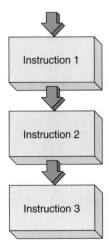

FIGURE 5
A sequence control structure.

ture. A **repetition control structure** executes an instruction(s) more than once without having it re-coded. The two basic variations of this type of structure are DO WHILE and DO UNTIL. If the decision criterion (condition) is placed before the statements (instructions) to be repeated, then it is a DO WHILE loop (Figure 7). A DO UNTIL loop places the decision criterion at the end of the statements to be repeated (Figure 8). In this particular structure, statements are always executed at least once.

A fourth type of control structure commonly used in early programs was the unconditional branch. In many programming languages this structure took the form of a GOTO statement. It allowed program execution to jump indiscriminately to other points in the program. However, programs designed with several of these unconditional branches were confusing and difficult to follow, thereby earning them the name "spaghetti code." Part of the first step toward structured programming methodology was the avoidance of unconditional branching.

When many people are involved in design and development of a large program, different ideas and methods surface. Management control is essential in structured programming. It prevents a project from

being sidetracked, keeps it on schedule, and assures that user needs are met.

The concepts of structured programming are important to follow when using any programming language, whether for business or personal use. A program that adheres to these concepts will be much easier to maintain and modify.

WHAT IS A PROGRAMMING LANGUAGE?

A computer must be told how to accomplish each detail of an operation. For example, to print a file, the computer needs to know how to access the file, initialize the printer, send the data, etc. A **programming language** is a set of written symbols that tells the computer hardware how to perform specified operations.

WHAT ARE THE CATEGORIES OF PROGRAMMING LANGUAGES?

Of the hundreds of different programming languages available, all fit into one of five general categories: (1) machine, (2) assembly, (3) high-level, (4) fourth-generation, and (5) fifth-generation languages.

Machine Language

Machine language is a binary code made up of 1s and 0s, the only programming language that a computer can understand. There is no universal machine language. The arrangement of 1s and 0s to represent instructions, data, and memory locations differs among computers because of different hardware designs.

Machine-language programs have the advantage of fast execution speeds and efficient use of main memory. However, writing machine language is a tedious, difficult, and time-consuming method of programming. Machine language is a **low-level language,** which requires programmers to have detailed knowledge of how computers work, since every detail of an operation must be specified. As you might imagine, it is easy to make an error but very difficult to find and debug it from a machine-language program.

Easier-to-use programming languages have been developed, but they must ultimately be translated into machine language before a computer can understand and use them.

FIGURE 6
Selection control structures.

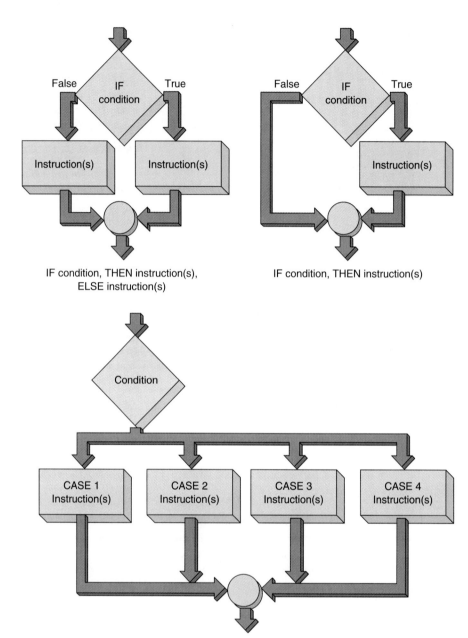

False   IF condition   True

Instruction(s)   Instruction(s)

IF condition, THEN instruction(s),
ELSE instruction(s)

False   IF condition   True

Instruction(s)

IF condition, THEN instruction(s)

Condition

CASE 1 Instruction(s)   CASE 2 Instruction(s)   CASE 3 Instruction(s)   CASE 4 Instruction(s)

CASE condition: CASE 1, CASE 2, CASE 3, CASE 4

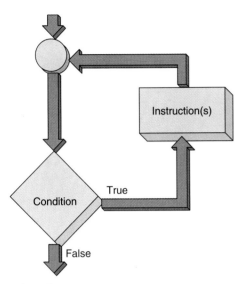

FIGURE 7
A DO WHILE control structure.

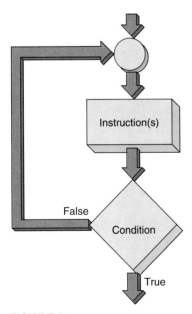

FIGURE 8
A DO UNTIL control structure.

> **Categories of Programming Languages**
>
> - **Machine**
> - **Assembly**
> - **High-level**
> - **Fourth-generation**
> - **Fifth-generation**

Assembly Language

The next higher level is assembly language. It is also classified as a low-level language because detailed knowledge of hardware specifics is still required. **Assembly language** uses mnemonics in place of 1s and 0s to represent the instructions (Figure 9). A **mnemonic** is an alphabetical abbreviation used as a memory aid. For example, instead of using a combination of 1s and 0s to represent an addition operation, a programmer might use the mnemonic *AD*.

Before a computer can use an assembly language, it must translate the assembly language into a machine language. The computer makes this conversion with a language-translator program. A **language-translator program** is a system program that converts programming language code into machine language. The language-translator program used to translate assembly language code into machine language is called an **assembler.**

Assembly languages provide easier and more efficient ways to program than do machine languages. They also produce programs that are efficient, use less storage, and execute much faster than do programs using high-level languages. However, assembly languages are still machine-oriented and require thorough knowledge of computer hardware. Compared with high-level languages, they are tedious and prone to errors.

High-Level Language

A **high-level language** contains instructions that closely resemble human language and mathematical

Assembler code (mnemonics)	Machine-language instructions

```
Assembler code (mnemonics)

sseg                    segment stack
                        db 256   dup (?)
sseg                    ends
dseg                    segment
data                    db "2 x 4 =  "

dseg        ends
cseg                    segment
assume      cs:cseg,ds:dseg,ss:sseg,es:nothing
start       proc far
                        push ds
                        mov ax,0
                        push ax
                        call main
start       endp

main                    proc near
                        cld
                        mov ax, dseg
                        mov ds, ax
                        mov ax, 0b000h
                        mov es, ax
                        mov dx, 0
                        mov bx, 0
                        lea si, data
                        mov di, 32848
                        mov al, 02h
                        mov bl, 04h
                        mul bl
                        or al, 30h
                        mov al,  data+9
msgsb:      mov cx,9
lbl:
                        movsb
                        inc di
                        mov al, 135
                        mov [di], al
                        loop 1b1
main                    endp
cseg                    ends
                        endstart
```

```
Machine-language instructions

0100
110010  100000  1111000  100000  110100  100000
111101  100000  100000
11110
10111000
1010000
11101000
11111100
10111000
10001110  11011000
10111000
10001110  11000000
10111010
10111011
10001101  110110
10111111
10110000  00000010
10110011  00000100
11110110  11100011
00001100  110000
10100000
10111001
10100100
1000111
10110000  10000111
10001000  00000101
11100010  1111000
```

FIGURE 9

This is a comparison of assembly codes (mnemonics) and machine language
instructions for a program that computes and prints out the result of 2 × 4.

notation and do not require the programmer to have detailed knowledge about the internal operations of a computer. High-level languages are much easier to learn and use than either machine or assembly languages. Typically, less time and effort are required for high-level programming because errors are easier to avoid and correct.

A high-level language must also be translated into a machine language before a computer can use it. Two different language-translator programs are used: compilers and interpreters. A **compiler** translates a whole program written in a human-readable high-level or assembly programming language, called the **source code**, into machine language all at one time before the program is executed. Once converted, the program is stored in machine-readable form, called the **object code**. The object code can be executed anytime thereafter. The source code remains intact after the conversion and can be updated and changed as required and then recompiled into object code.

An **interpreter** translates a program into machine language one line at a time, executing each line

---

Types of Language-Translator Programs

- **Assemblers**
- **Compilers**
- **Interpreters**

---

after it is translated. With most interpreters, the machine-readable form is not stored in main memory or on a secondary storage medium; therefore, the program must be interpreted each time it is executed.

Fourth-Generation Language

The different categories of languages are sometimes labeled by generations—from lowest to highest. Machine languages are considered the first generation; assembly languages, the second generation; and high-level languages, the third generation. A **fourth-generation language** is one of a variety of programming languages that require much less effort creating programs than high-level languages. The objectives include increasing the speed of developing programs, minimizing end user effort to obtain information from a computer, decreasing the skill level required of users (they can concentrate on an application rather than the coding and solve their own problems without a professional programmer), and minimizing maintenance by reducing errors and making programs easy to change.

The sophistication of fourth-generation languages varies widely. These languages are usually used in conjunction with a database and include database query languages, report generators, and application generators. A **database query language** permits the user to formulate inquiries that relate to records from one or more files. The appropriate records are printed or displayed in a suitable format. Examples include IBM's SQL and Artificial Intelligence's INTELLECT. (The Chapter 10 InfoModule gives more information on SQLs—structure query languages.)

A **report generator** permits data from a database to be extracted and formatted into reports. Substantial arithmetic and logic operations can be performed on data before they are displayed or printed. NOMAD by NCSS and GIS by IBM are examples of report generators.

An **application generator** allows data entry so a user can specify how to update a database, what calculations or logic operations to perform, and what output to create. A user can build an entire application. Examples include FOCUS by Information Builders and MANTIS by Cincom Systems.

Fifth-Generation Language

Many individuals consider natural languages to be **fifth-generation languages**. **Natural languages** are similar to query languages, but the user or programmer does not need to learn and use a specific vocabulary, grammar, or syntax. A natural language closely resembles normal human speech. For example, if a user enters the command "Get me sales figures for January 1992," a computer that understands natural language interprets this and supplies the desired information.

Because of the complexity of interpreting a command entered in human speech format, natural languages require very powerful hardware and sophisticated software. Although advances have produced computers with enough power, a deficit exists in the development of programming languages and techniques.

WHAT IS THE DIFFERENCE BETWEEN PROCEDURAL AND NONPROCEDURAL LANGUAGES?

Programming languages are classified into two different types: procedural and nonprocedural. **Procedural languages** specify how something is accomplished. Common procedural languages include BASIC, Pascal, C, Ada, COBOL, and FORTRAN. **Nonprocedural languages** specify what is accomplished without going into the details of how. Database query languages and report generators are examples of nonprocedural languages.

The difference between procedural and nonprocedural languages is analogous to giving directions to a taxi driver. With a procedural language, the directions would be specified as: "Drive 600 yards forward. Turn right. Drive 350 yards forward. Turn left. Drive 500 yards forward. Stop." However, with a nonprocedural language, you simply tell the driver what you want: "Take me to the Fairview Hotel."

WHAT IS AN OBJECT-ORIENTED PROGRAMMING LANGUAGE?

There are two main parts of a program: the instructions and the data. A traditional programming language treats the data and instructions as separate entities. A programmer applies programming instructions to data. An **object-oriented programming language (OOPL)** treats a program as a series of objects and messages. An **object** is a combination of data and instructions that works on the data and is stored together as a reusable unit. **Messages** are instructions sent between objects. Basically, what an object-oriented language does is allow a programmer to build programs with preassembled chunks of code instead of individual pieces. It eliminates the need for the programmer to start from scratch every time a new program is coded.

To qualify as an OOPL a language must incorporate the concepts of encapsulation, inheritance, and polymorphism.

The combination of data and instructions into a reusable structure is called **encapsulation,** one of the basic principles of an OOPL. Encapsulation can be thought of as a prefabricated component of a program. For example, if you were building a house using a traditional programming approach you would buy wood for the window frame, paint, glass, putty, appropriate tools and construct and install the window yourself. Using an object-oriented programming approach you buy a prefabricated window and pop it in. The prefabricated window is encapsulated because it is a single entity and not a collection of individual materials.

One of the most powerful concepts of an OOPL is **inheritance**, the ability of the programming language itself to define a new object that has all the attributes of an existing object. To define an object that is similar to an existing object all the programmer needs to do is inherit the existing object and write the code that describes how the new object is different from the existing one. This capability increases code sharing and eliminates the need to write repetitive code.

The third concept of an OOPL is **polymorphism**, the ability of an object to respond to a message in many ways. For example, say you have a circle object and a square object. Each object has the same characteristic of drawing. When a drawing message is sent to the circle object it draws a circle but when the same drawing message is sent to the square object it draws a square. Thus each object has the same characteristic (drawing) but the characteristic is implemented differently.

Object-oriented programming languages provide a number of advantages, including code reuse rather than reinvention and adaptable code. These speed the development and maintenance of applications and reduce costs. Generic functions can be developed to allow easy assembly of applications from prefabricated parts. Users who are familiar with functions from one application quickly and easily learn and work with a new program. Smalltalk, Objective-C, and C++ are examples of object-oriented programming languages.

Major High-Level Languages

- FORTRAN
- COBOL
- PL/I
- BASIC
- Pascal
- RPG
- C and C++
- Ada
- LISP
- Prolog
- Logo

WHAT ARE THE MAJOR HIGH-LEVEL LANGUAGES?

Major high-level languages include FORTRAN, COBOL, PL/1, BASIC, Pascal, RPG, C, Ada, LISP, Prolog, and Logo.

FORTRAN (FORmula TRANslator) was introduced in 1957 and is the oldest high-level programming language. It was designed primarily for use by scientists, engineers, and mathematicians in solving mathematical problems. FORTRAN is well suited to complex numerical calculations. Figure 10 gives a brief example of a FORTRAN program.

COBOL (COmmon Business-Oriented Language) is a widely used programming language for business data processing. It was specifically designed to manipulate the large data files typically encountered in business. Figure 11 is a brief example of a COBOL program.

PL/1, Programming Language One, was created in the early 1960s. It is a general-purpose language that allows powerful computations and sophisticated data structures. PL/1 is largely used in the oil industry today. Figure 12 (p. 252) is an example of a simple PL/1 program.

BASIC (Beginner's All-Purpose Symbolic Instruction Code) was developed at Dartmouth College in the mid-1960s to provide students with an easy-to-learn, interactive language on a time-sharing computer system. It allowed novices to learn and begin programming in a few hours. Because it is easy to learn and use, BASIC has become the most popular language for microcomputers, and it is available for many microcomputers in use today. Figure 13 (p. 252) shows a BASIC program in the Microsoft BASIC language.

In the late 1960s, Niklaus Wirth of Zurich developed **Pascal** and named it after Blaise Pascal, the French mathematician and philosopher who invented the first practical mechanical adding machine. Pascal is suited to both scientific and file processing applications. It was originally designed to teach the concepts of structured programming and top-down design to students. A short Pascal program is shown in Figure 14 (p. 252).

FIGURE 10
A FORTRAN program that computes the sum and average of ten numbers.

```
C    COMPUTE THE SUM AND AVERAGE OF 10 NUMBERS
C
         REAL NUM, SUM, AVG
         INTEGER TOTNUM, COUNTR
C
         SUM = 0.0
C    INITIALIZE LOOP CONTROL VARIABLE
         COUNTR = 0
         TOTNUM = 10
C
C    LOOP TO READ DATA AND ACCUMULATE SUM
      20 IF (COUNTR .GE. TOTNUM) GO TO 30
         READ, NUM
         SUM = SUM + NUM
C        UPDATE LOOP CONTROL VARIABLE
         COUNTR = COUNTR + 1
         GO TO 20
C    END OF LOOP - COMPUTE AVERAGE
      30 AVG = SUM / TOTNUM
C    PRINT RESULTS
         PRINT, SUM
         PRINT, AVG
         STOP
         END
```

FIGURE 11
A COBOL program that computes the sum and average of ten numbers.

```
IDENTIFICATION DIVISION.
PROGRAM-ID.        AVERAGES.
AUTHOR.            DEB KNUDSEN.
DATE-COMPILED.
ENVIRONMENT DIVISION.
CONFIGURATION SECTION.
    SOURCE-COMPUTER. HP-3000.
    OBJECT-COMPUTER. HP-3000.
INPUT-OUTPUT SECTION.
FILE-CONTROL.
    SELECT NUMBER-FILE ASSIGN TO "NUMFILE".
    SELECT REPORT-FILE ASSIGN TO "PRINT,UR,A,LP(CCTL)".
DATA DIVISION.
FILE SECTION.
FD  NUMBER-FILE
    LABEL RECORDS ARE STANDARD
    DATA RECORD IS NUMBER-REC.
01  NUMBER-REC                      PIC S9(7)V99.
FD  REPORT-FILE
    LABEL RECORDS ARE STANDARD
    DATA RECORD IS REPORT-REC.
01  REPORT-REC                      PIC X(100).

WORKING-STORAGE SECTION.
01  END-OF-NUMBER-FILE-FLAG         PIC X(3) VALUE SPACES.
    88  END-OF-NUMBER-FILE                   VALUE "YES".
01  SUM-OF-NUMBERS                  PIC S9(7)V99.
01  AVERAGE-OF-NUMBERS              PIC S9(7)V99.
01  NUMBER-OF-NUMBERS               PIC 9(5).

01  WS-REPORT-REC.
    05  FILLER                      PIC X(2)   VALUE SPACES.
    05  FILLER                      PIC X(17)  VALUE
                                    "Sum of Numbers = ".
    05  WS-SUM-OF-NUMBERS           PIC Z,ZZZ,ZZZ.99-.
    05  FILLER                      PIC X(3)   VALUE SPACES.
    05  FILLER                      PIC X(15)  VALUE
                                    "# of Numbers = ".
    05  WS-NUMBER-OF-NUMBERS        PIC ZZZZ9.
    05  FILLER                      PIC X(3)   VALUE SPACES.
    05  FILLER                      PIC X(21)  VALUE
                                    Average of Numbers = ".
    05  WS-AVERAGE-OF-NUMBERS       PIC Z,ZZZ,ZZZ.99-.
    05  FILLER                      PIC X(8)   VALUE SPACES.
```

RPG (Report Program Generator) was developed in the mid-1960s. Most people at that time had no programming experience, so RPG was designed to be especially easy to learn and use. A programmer uses coding sheets (Figure 15, p. 253) to specify input, output, processing operations, and file specifications. Although RPG is easy to learn, it has limited capabilities. It can produce reports and process files on tape or disk, but it is not well suited to mathematical or scientific applications.

The **C** programming language, developed at Bell Laboratories in the early 1970s, incorporates many advantages of both low-level and high-level languages. Like assembly language, C gives programmers extensive control over computer hardware, but because C uses English-like statements, which are easy to read, it is often classified as a high-level language. C also incorporates sophisticated control and data structures, which make it a powerful but concise language. Figure 16 (p. 254) is a brief C program. **C++** is an object-

FIGURE 11
continued

```
PROCEDURE DIVISION.

100-MAIN-PROGRAM.
      OPEN INPUT   NUMBER-FILE
           OUTPUT REPORT-FILE.
      MOVE SPACES TO REPORT-REC.
      MOVE ZEROS TO SUM-OF-NUMBERS.
      MOVE ZEROS TO AVERAGE-OF-NUMBERS.
      MOVE ZEROS TO NUMBER-OF-NUMBERS.

      READ NUMBER-FILE
        AT END MOVE "YES" TO END-OF-NUMBER-FILE-FLAG.

        IF END-OF-NUMBER-FILE
          NEXT SENTENCE
        ELSE
          PERFORM 200-PROCESS-NUMBER-FILE
             UNTIL END-OF-NUMBER-FILE.

        PERFORM 300-COMPUTE-AVERAGE

        PRFORM 400-PRINT-RESULTS.

        CLOSE NUMBER-FILE
              REPORT-FILE.

        STOP RUN.

200-PROCESS-NUMBER-FILE
      ADD 1 TO NUMBER-OF-NUMBERS.
      ADD NUMBER-REC TO SUM-OF-NUMBERS.

      READ NUMBER-FILE
        AT END MOVE "YES" TO END-OF-NUMBER-FILE-FLAG.

300-COMPUTE-AVERAGE.
      DIVIDE SUM-OF-NUMBERS BY NUMBER-OF-NUMBERS
        GIVING AVERAGE-OF-NUMBERS.

400-PRINT-RESULTS.
      MOVE SUM-OF-NUMBERS TO WS-SUM-OF-NUMBERS.
      MOVE NUMBER-OF-NUMBERS TO WS-AVERAGE-OF-NUMBERS.

WRITE REPORT-REC FROM WS-REPORT-REC.
```

oriented version of C that is popular with software developers.

The **Ada** programming language was developed in the late 1970s with the support of the U.S. Department of Defense. It was named for Augusta Ada, Countess of Lovelace, considered by many to be the world's first programmer. In developing Ada, the goal was to build a very powerful, complete, and efficient structured language for military applications, such as controlling weapon systems. Ada is used primarily by the U.S. Department of Defense. Figure 17 (p. 254) is a brief Ada program.

LISP is a language that processes symbol sequences (lists) rather than numbers. It is a programming language designed to handle data strings more efficiently than other languages. **Prolog** is another language for symbol processing. Both LISP and Prolog are used for artificial intelligence applications.

Logo is an interactive education-oriented language designed to teach inexperienced users logic and

FIGURE 12

A PL/1 program that computes the sum and average of ten numbers.

```
START: PROCEDURE OPTIONS (MAIN);
 DECLARE (N, K) DECIMAL FIXED (2),
          VALUE (N) DECIMAL FIXED (5,2) CONTROLLED,
          SUM        DECIMAL FIXED (6,2) INITIAL (0.0),
          AVERAGE    DECIMAL FIXED (6,3);
 GET DATA (N); ALLOCATE VALUE;
     GET LIST (VALUE);
     DO K = 1 TO N; SUM = SUM + VALUE (K); END;
     AVERAGE = ROUND(SUM/N,3); PUT DATA(N, SUM, AVERAGE);
 END START;

 DATA:

 N=10; 1.0 2.0 3.0 4.0 5.0 6.0 7.0 8.0 9.0 10.0
```

FIGURE 13

A BASIC program that computes the sum and average of ten numbers.

```
10    REM COMPUTE SUM AND AVERAGE OF 10 NUMBERS
20    LET SUM = 0
30    FOR I = 1 TO 10
40      INPUT N(I)
50      LET SUM = SUM + N(I)
60    NEXT I
70    LET AVERAGE = SUM / 10
80    PRINT "SUM = ",SUM
90    PRINT "AVERAGE = ",AVG
999   END
```

FIGURE 14

A Pascal program that computes the sum and average of ten numbers.

```
PROGRAM average(input, output);
{ Compute the sum and average of ten numbers }
VAR num, sum, avg : real;
    i : integer;

BEGIN
    sum:=0.0;
    FOR i := 1 TO 10 DO
    BEGIN
      read(num);
      sum:=sum + num;
    END;
    avg:=sum/10;
    writeln('Sum =',sum);
    writeln('Average =',avg);
END.
```

FIGURE 15
RPG coding sheets.
(Courtesy of International
Business Machines Corp.)

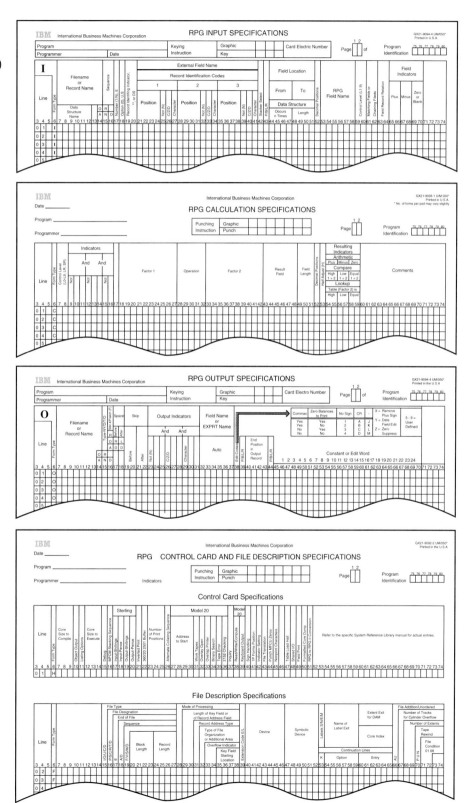

FIGURE 16

A C program that computes the sum and average of ten numbers.

```
#include <stdio.h>

main ()
    {
        int i, num;
        float sum;

        printf("Enter numbers \n");
        sum = 0;
        for (i = 0; i < 10; i++)
            {
                scanf("%d",&num);
                sum = sum + num;
            }
        printf("Sum = %3.1f\n",sum);
        printf("Average = %3.1f\n",sum / 10.0);
    }
```

FIGURE 17

An Ada program that computes the sum and average of ten numbers.

```
PROCEDURE average number IS
    USE simple io;
    num, sum, avg: REAL;

BEGIN
    sum := 0;
    FORiIN 1...10 LOOP
      GET(num);
      sum:=sum + num;
    END LOOP;
    avg:=sum / 10;
    PUT("Sum ="); PUT(sum);
    PUT("Average ="); PUT(avg);
END average number;
```

programming techniques. It includes list-processing capabilities. Logo employs a triangular object called a turtle so users can draw, animate, and color images very simply.

HOW DO I CHOOSE A PROGRAMMING LANGUAGE?

With so many programming languages to choose from, consider these factors before selecting one language for programmer use. First, what is the nature of the problem? Is the programming language designed for this type of problem? For example, CO-

BOL is suited for business data processing, but it is not suited for robotics because it doesn't have the vocabulary or features to control tasks such as robot arm movements.

Second, what is the speed at which the program needs to execute? If the program will be used frequently and requires efficient execution, a language such as an assembly language or C may be necessary to reduce execution time.

Third, what is the expertise of the programming staff? Do the programmers already know the language under consideration? If not, can they learn it in the required time period, and is the additional cost for training justifiable?

Fourth, what is the portability of the language? Will the program have to run on more than one type of computer? Machine and assembly languages are machine-specific and require extensive changes or complete rewrites for new hardware. High-level languages are more portable, and can usually be run on different computers with few if any changes.

Fifth, what is the amount of program maintenance expected? Will the program be subjected to periodic updates and revisions? If so, a structured high-level language may be the best choice.

Sixth, does your organization require the use of a particular programming language? This may be the case to ensure that current and future programs work together as well as for simplification of program maintenance.

VOCABULARY SELF-TEST

Can you define the following terms?

Ada (p. 251)

algorithm (p. 238)

application generator (p. 247)

assembler (p. 245)

assembly language (p. 245)

BASIC (p. 249)

C (p. 250)

C++ (p. 250)

COBOL (p. 249)

coding (p. 240)

compiler (p. 246)

computer program (p. 236)

computer programming (p. 236)

database query language (p. 247)

debugging (p. 241)

documentation (p. 237)

encapsulation (p. 248)

fifth-generation language (p. 247)

FORTRAN (p. 249)

fourth-generation language (p. 247)

high-level language (p. 245)

inheritance (p. 248)

interpreter (p. 246)

language-translator program (p. 245)

LISP (p. 251)

logic (p. 238)

logic error (p. 240)

Logo (p. 251)

low-level language (p. 243)

machine language (p. 243)

main logic module (p. 242)

message (p. 248)

mnemonic (p. 245)

module (p. 242)

natural languages (p. 247)

nonprocedural language (p. 247)

object (p. 248)

object code (p. 246)

object-oriented programming language (OOPL) (p. 248)

Pascal (p. 249)

PL/1 (p. 249)

polymorphism (p. 248)

procedural language (p. 247)

program development process (p. 237)

program editor (p. 240)

program flowchart (p. 238)

programmer (p. 236)

programming language (p. 243)

Prolog (p. 251)

pseudocode (p. 238)

repetition control structure (p. 243)

report generator (p. 247)

RPG (p. 250)

run-time error (p. 240)

selection control structure (p. 242)

sequence control structure (p. 242)

source code (p. 246)

structured programming (p. 242)

syntax (p. 240)

syntax error (p. 240)

top-down design (p. 242)

REVIEW QUESTIONS

Multiple Choice

1. _____ is a set of instructions written in computer language to be executed to perform a useful task.
   - a. A control structure
   - b. A computer program
   - c. Documentation
   - d. Pseudocode

2. Which of the following control structures is not considered part of structured programming?
   - a. selection
   - b. repetition
   - c. unconditional branch
   - d. sequence

3. _____ is the only programming language that a computer can understand.
   - a. BASIC
   - b. Machine language
   - c. Assembly language
   - d. C

4. A(n) _____ translates an entire high-level language program into machine language before the language is executed.
   - a. assembler
   - b. interpreter
   - c. compiler
   - d. syntax

5. _____ is a machine-specific language that uses mnemonics.
   - a. Machine language
   - b. Object-oriented programming language
   - c. High-level language
   - d. Assembly language

Fill-In

1. The _____ is a recommended series of steps to follow when developing a program.

2. A(n) _____ error will not stop the execution of the program; however, the results will not be accurate.

3. A language-translator program that translates an assembly-language program into machine language is a(n) _____.

4. A(n) _____ uses objects and messages to construct programs.

5. The high-level language _____ is used for business data processing.

Short Answer

1. What is computer programming and how can knowledge of computer programming be beneficial to you?

2. List and give details of the steps in the program development process.

3. Specify the goals of structured programming and describe three ways in which it attempts to meet these goals.

4. Discuss the objectives of a fourth-generation language.

5. Describe an object-oriented programming language.

Part 2

Information Systems Concepts

What the world really needs is a better way of handling information, because information is all-powerful. Without information, nothing can happen. But with the right information, virtually anything is possible. And by coming up with the proper information, one can turn want and war into peace and plenty.

David Ritchie, author of *The Binary Brain: Artificial Intelligence in the Age of Electronics*

OUTLINE

OBJECTIVES

7.1 Define data communication and telecommunication, differentiate between analog and digital data transmissions, and describe how modems convert one to the other.

7.2 Describe the basic types and configurations of communication channels, the methods used to share them, the role of front-end processors and common carriers, and the three modes of data transfer.

7.3 Identify the factors that determine the speed at which data are transmitted.

7.4 Define computer network and briefly describe wide-area networks (WANs), local-area networks (LANs), and cellular networks.

7.5 Describe a distributed data processing (DDP) system.

7.6 Recognize some challenges presented by data communications.

Chapter
7

Data
Communication

Profile

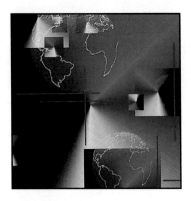

Dennis Hayes

In 1977, Dennis Hayes and his partner, Dale Heatherington, started their business with corporate offices headquartered in Norcross, Georgia, in the Hayes' dining room. Their product was a PC modem. That's the device responsible for converting digital signals to analog signals and vice versa, allowing a computer to send data through telephone lines.

Modems had long been available for the larger computers. But when Hayes saw personal computers coming on the market (the early Radio Shack and Apple models), he also foresaw the potential for a scaled-down modem. Hayes' vision led him to buy out his partner, leaving him as owner of a business with estimated sales of now over $100 million a year. The Hayes modem, built in America, is well known for its high quality. In fact, it is considered the "standard" for networking with personal computers to which other devices are compared.

Hayes cannot rest on his laurels, though. The computer industry is highly competitive and rapidly changing, so these days Hayes Microcomputer Products, Inc. offers more in the way of communications software. Their Smartcom communications program, compatible with Microsoft Windows, configures the modem and allows you to begin communicating as quickly as possible.

Success brought the offices to Atlanta where hopefully Hayes and his designers are hard at work on communication devices for the future. After all, their advertising motto is, "Hayes products have the computer world talking."

D ata communication technology contains solutions to the demand for more power and for data exchange and sharing. This chapter examines some basic concepts related to data communication and introduces computer networks, which enable computer systems to share data, hardware, and software. The Infomodule at the end of this chapter presents a number of ways you can put data communication to work in your personal and professional lives.

Objective 7.1   Define data communication and telecommunication, differentiate between analog and digital data transmissions, and describe how modems convert one to the other.

What Is Data Communication?

Data communication is the process of sending data electronically from one point to another. Linking one computer to another permits the power and resources of that computer to be tapped. It also makes possible the sharing and updating of data in different locations.

Computers that are physically close to each other in the same room, building, or group of buildings can communicate data through a direct-cable link. Computers located far apart use a special form of data communication: **telecommunication,** or teleprocessing, the technique of using communication facilities such as the telephone system and microwave relays to send data between computers.

The Effects of Data Communication

In today's business world, data communication technologies are as important as the computer technologies that support them. Many organizations, including banking and financial firms, could not exist as they do today without data communication. Businesses communicate with a wide variety of individuals—personnel in the same organization, banking and financial services personnel outside the organization, customers, suppliers, shareholders, government officials, consumer groups, advertisers, and more. Communication can take place locally, nationally, or internationally.

Data communication allows users to send and receive data and information in a timely fashion in order to identify and solve problems and make informed decisions. Even a slight delay in today's fast-paced electronic environment means a missed opportunity. However, getting data to a desired destination in a timely manner is not the only concern. Communication systems must transmit the data accurately and in a form that can be understood and used by the receiving system.

One day, you may be faced with decisions concerning data communication, such as which data communication hardware and software options are right for the organization you own or are employed by. These crucial decisions must take into account a number of factors, including cost and performance. In addition, you should consider current or emerging standards so that the hardware and software you select will be compatible with both current and future needs. Even if you never need to select or purchase communication hardware and software, it is essential to understand what data communication can do and how it works to be able to identify opportunities where it could help.

Data communication is important for the home computer user too. It allows access to numerous services that can supply information on countless topics. Through the use of data communication, individuals can also link their home computers to office computers and share data, software, and hardware.

Analog and Digital Data Transmissions

The two forms of data transmission are analog and digital. **Analog data transmission** is the transmission of data in continuous wave form (Figure 7.1a). The telephone system is an example of a process designed for analog data transmission.

Digital data transmission is the transmission of data using distinct on and off electrical states (Figure 7.1b). Remember that data in digital form are represented as a sequence of 1s and 0s. Because computers work in digital form and because digital data communication is faster and more efficient, it would seem that all data communication between computers would be in digital form; however, that is not the case. A completely digital system is possible, but the analog telephone system is used for a great percentage of data communication because it is the largest and most widely used communication system already in place. To avoid the expense of converting to a digital system or running a duplicate digital system over a wide geographic area, a method was devised to transmit digital signals over telephone lines. This method is called modulation-demodulation.

Forms of Data Transmission

- Analog
- Digital

FIGURE 7.1
Analog and digital data transmissions.

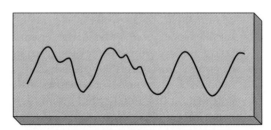

(a) Analog data transmission

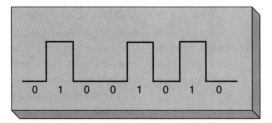

(b) Digital data transmission

Modulation, Demodulation, and Modems

Data in a computer are formatted as digital signals. Because telephone lines were designed to transmit the human voice, they format data as analog signals. For communication between computers to take place over a telephone line, the digital signal must be converted to an analog signal before it is transmitted. After it travels over the telephone lines, the analog signal must then be reconverted to a digital signal so that the receiving computer can use it. The process of converting a digital signal to an analog signal is called **modulation** (Figure 7.2a). **Demodulation** is the process of reconverting the analog signal back to a digital signal (Figure 7.2b). The device that accomplishes both of these processes is a **modem,** short for *mo*dulator-*dem*odulator.

The three basic types of modems used with microcomputers are (1) acoustic, (2) external direct-connect, and (3) internal direct-connect. An **acoustic modem,** or acoustic coupler as it is sometimes called, has two cups into which the handset of a telephone is placed (Figure 7.3). This

FIGURE 7.2
(a) Modulation is the conversion of a digital signal to an analog signal. (b) Demodulation is the conversion of an analog signal to a digital signal.

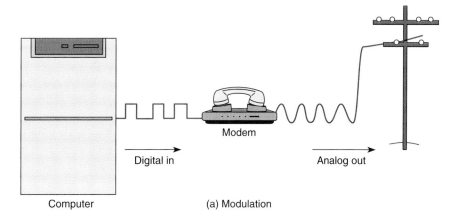

Computer   Modem   Digital in   Analog out   (a) Modulation

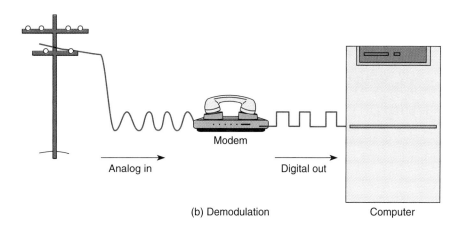

Analog in   Modem   Digital out   (b) Demodulation   Computer

FIGURE 7.3
An operator uses an acoustic modem to send data over telephone lines to another computer. (Photo courtesy of Hewlett-Packard Co.)

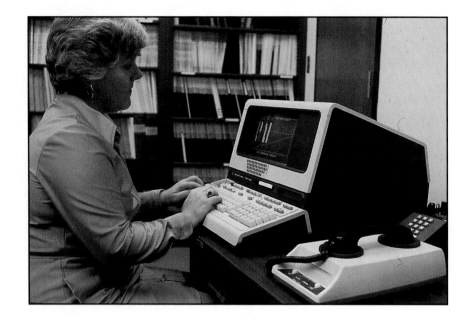

FIGURE 7.4
External direct-connect modems connect to a computer via a serial interface cable and to the telephone line via a modular phone jack. (Photo by Larry Hamill/Macmillan)

modem sends data through the mouthpiece and receives data through the earpiece of the handset. Acoustic modems are not used very often today because their signals are much more susceptible to distortion and the carbon microphones used in a telephone handset limit the rate of data transmission.

An **external direct-connect modem** is external to a computer and connects directly to the telephone line with a modular phone jack (Figure 7.4). The direct connection greatly reduces the distortion of the signals and permits faster data transfer rates. A popular external direct-connect modem is the Hayes Smartmodem. Most external direct-connect modems have a variety of features not found on acoustic modems, including checks of the operating status using status lights and speakers, changes of the speeds at which data are transmitted, automatic dialing and answering of the phone, response to commands from a communication program, and self-testing of their ability to correctly transmit data. Because the specialized circuitry in these modems allows them to perform these and other functions (rather than the computer), they are often called ''smart'' or ''intelligent'' devices.

Both acoustic modems and external direct-connect modems require that a computer be equipped with a communication adapter or other serial port with a connector as a serial interface. A serial interface provides a standard method for serial transmission of data. A modem cable to connect the modem to the serial port is also needed. For example, the RS232C interface is used on most microcomputers. It has 25 pins, called a male connector, where one end of a modem cable is connected, and the modem has 25 receptacles, called a female connector, where the other end of the modem cable is connected.

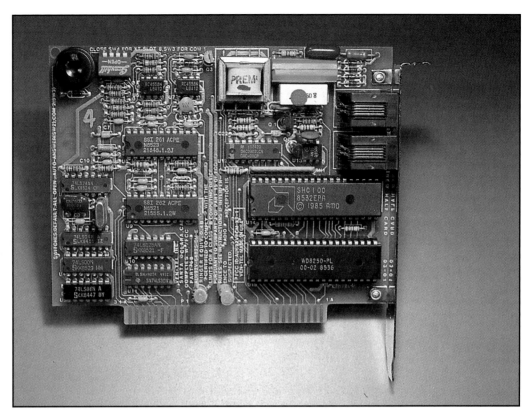

FIGURE 7.5
Internal direct-connect modems contain the necessary serial interface circuitry
and plug directly into the main circuit board of a computer.

An **internal direct-connect modem** has all of its communication circuitry on a plug-in board that fits into one of the expansion slots (empty spaces) inside a computer (Figure 7.5). A separate communication board or an RS232C serial interface board is not needed. Internal direct-connect modems also link directly to telephone lines with modular phone jacks. These modems have many of the same special features that the external direct-connect modems have. In addition, they take up no desk space and are ideal for use in portable computers.

Objective 7.2   Describe the basic types and configurations of communication channels, the methods used to share them, the role of front-end processors and common carriers, and the three modes of data transfer.

What Is a Communication Channel?

A **communication channel** is the medium, or pathway, through which data are transmitted between devices. Communication channels fall into three basic types: (1) wire cable, (2) microwave, and (3) fiber optics.

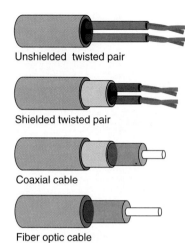

Unshielded twisted pair

Shielded twisted pair

Coaxial cable

Fiber optic cable

FIGURE 7.6
Types of communication channels.

Types of Communication Channels

- **Wire cable**
    Twisted-pair
    Coaxial
- **Microwave**
- **Fiber optics**

Wire cable includes twisted-pair and coaxial cables. **Twisted-pair** lines consist of a pair of wires, each wrapped in a protective coating and twisted around the other. There are two types, shielded and unshielded (Figure 7.6). Because it has been used in telegraph and telephone lines, it is the most common type of data communication channel today.

Coaxial cable consists of a single wire surrounded by both a layer of insulating material and a metal sheath or tube for protection (Figure 7.6). Television cable is a form of coaxial cable.

There are two basic categories of coaxial cables: baseband and broadband. Baseband coaxial cables carry a single digital signal at a rate between 1 million and 50 million bits per second. Multiple devices can use this channel by combining their signals through a multiplexer, which is hardware that permits two or more devices to share a common communication channel. Broadband coaxial cables carry multiple analog signals together (voice, data, and video) at speeds between 20 million and 50 million bits per second. Broadband is the more expensive of the two categories.

Because the extensive wire cable networks that already exist are easier and cheaper to use than the other systems, wire cable channels are the most popular. They are also popular because the technology to transmit data along wire cables is standardized, reducing compatibility problems.

One disadvantage of wire cables is that data must be transmitted in analog form. Conversion of digital data not only requires special hardware but also slows down transmission. Another disadvantage is that wire cables are subject to electrical interference that makes them less reliable than other communication channels. In addition, it is difficult to create the physical links when users are separated by long distances or by natural barriers, such as mountains or large bodies of water.

Another type of analog communication channel is **microwave**. Microwave signals are transmitted through the atmosphere rather than through wire cables, in much the same ways as radio and television signals are transmitted. However, microwave signals must be sent in straight lines because they cannot bend around corners or follow the curvature of the earth. Because microwave transmitter stations must be located about every 30 miles it's probable that in driving any distance you've seen them near the road. The transmitter stations redirect and boost the signals around the curvature of the earth.

Satellites direct microwaves over large, geographically dispersed areas too. A communication **satellite** is an electronic device placed in an orbit around the earth that receives, amplifies, and then transmits signals. Microwave signals are sent from a transmitter station to an earth station and then are beamed to an orbiting satellite (Figure 7.7). Transmission to the satellite is called the uplink. Then they are amplified and beamed on a different frequency back to another earth station if a direct line of sight is possible. When direct transmission is not possible, the signal is transmitted to another satellite that does have a direct line of sight back to an earth station. Transmission from the satellite to the ground station is called the

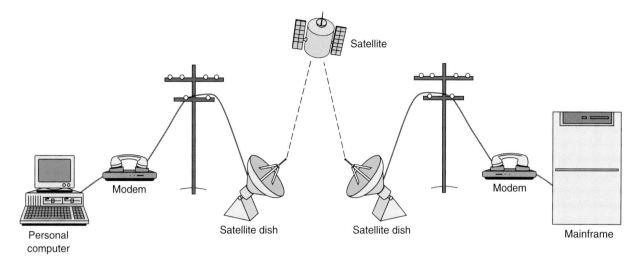

FIGURE 7.7
Data communication is accomplished with the help of computers, satellites, and satellite dishes located at earth stations.

downlink. Only three satellites placed in geosynchronous orbit (seemingly stationary in relationship to the earth) are required to send a signal anywhere on earth.

Compared with wire cable, microwave has a much lower error rate and is more reliable. Also, because there are no physical connections between the sending and receiving systems, communication links can be made over longer distances and rough terrains. One disadvantage, however, is the high cost of ground stations and satellites to support a microwave network.

The third type of communication channel is **fiber optics** (Figure 7.8). Unlike wire cable or microwave, a fiber-optic channel transmits data in digital form. Light impulses travel through clear, flexible tubing thinner than a human hair. Hundreds of tubes can fit in the space of one wire cable.

Fiber optics are very reliable communication channels. In addition, they can transmit data at very high speeds (several billions of bits per second) with few or no errors. Unlike wire cables, fiber-optic cables are not subject to electrical interference. They do, however, require repeaters to read and boost the light pulse signal strength over long distances. Technical developments have driven the costs of installing, using, and manufacturing fiber optics down so they are becoming competitive with traditional cabling. Sprint, a long-distance telephone company, has already converted to a fiber-optic system, and others are in the process of converting.

Channel Configurations

The two principal communication channel configurations are point-to-point and multipoint (Figure 7.9, p. 272). In a **point-to-point channel** configuration, a device (such as a terminal or computer) is connected directly to another device by a dedicated communication channel, giving those devices sole use of that channel. A point-to-point configuration can be inefficient and costly if a terminal is not active enough to keep the channel busy. Large computers that communicate with each other continuously often use point-to-point channel configurations.

An alternative configuration is **multipoint channel configuration,** where three or more devices are connected to one line. A multipoint configuration uses a communication channel more efficiently and reduces the amount of intercabling needed, thus lowering costs. Two methods are used to determine which device gets access to a channel: polling and contention. In **polling,** the computer checks each device, one at a time, to see whether there is a message to send. If the device has a message ready, transmission begins; if not, the computer polls the next device. After all of the devices have been individually polled, the process begins again. A disadvantage to polling is that if there are no messages to send, the processor of a computer being polled will be idle, wasting expensive processor time.

FIGURE 7.8
The tiny fibers of transparent glass in fiber-optic cables transmit data at the speed of light. The beam of light sent through these fibers can be turned on or off about 1 billion times per second. The cables are replacing traditional telephone lines and are used to connect computers in telecommunication systems. (Courtesy of United Telecommunications)

Automakers are incorporating satellite communication technologies to help gain a competitive edge. Using this technology, they can provide their dealers with up-to-date customer records, information about the latest special services, price changes, and other important data. Chrysler Corporation and Toyota Motor Corporation are using very small-aperture terminal (VSAT) dishes in a satellite network that links them to their dealers.

The automakers plan to use the data and video capabilities of the system to offer customers and dealers services not found in most of the auto industry. For example, currently a customer's records are available from the seller only. However, with a national database and the satellite communication system, an automaker can supply on-line information about a customer's car, including its complete maintenance history, to any dealership. In addition, inventory information for both cars and parts can be transmitted. The video capabilities of the system allow an automaker to keep its dealers up to date through live broadcasts from top management, technical service information, and parts announcements.

The drive behind this system is to improve customer service. The automakers, especially those in the higher markets, see service as one way in which a manufacturer can differentiate itself from the competition.

Toyota's system links the dealers for its Lexus LS400 luxury sedan and its main office in Torrance, California. The network includes a hub satellite station and a video broadcasting studio at company headquarters. Each dealer is equipped with a VSAT satellite dish. The hardware for the network and the satellite are provided by Hughes Network Systems in Germantown, Maryland. Each of the Lexus dealers (the network nodes) is equipped with an IBM Application System/400 computer to handle its computing needs. Lexus hopes that the improved customer service gives them a strategic advantage over the competition.

A second method, **contention,** puts the devices in control; that is, each device monitors the communication channel to see whether the channel is available. If it is, the device sends its message. If the communication channel is being used, the device waits a predetermined amount of time and tries again, repeating the process until the channel is available. One problem with this approach is that a single device can tie up the communication channel for long periods of time.

Channel Sharing

Channel-Sharing Devices

- Multiplexers
- Concentrators

Two methods are used to regulate the flow of data from communication channels into a computer: multiplexing and concentration. Their purpose is to increase the efficiency of a communication channel.

Multiplexing. **Multiplexing** is the process of combining the transmissions from several devices into a single data stream that is sent over a single high-speed communication channel. A multiplexer handles the physical

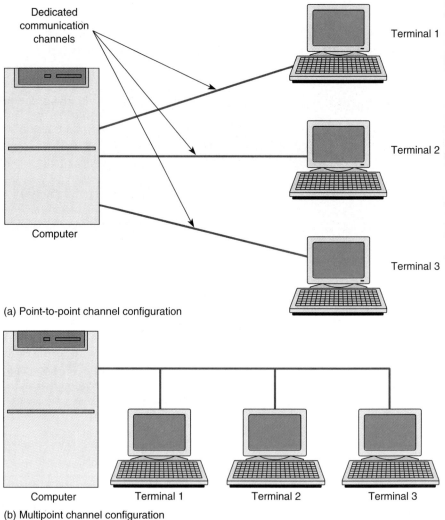

FIGURE 7.9
Communication channel configurations.

Dedicated communication channels

Computer

Terminal 1

Terminal 2

Terminal 3

(a) Point-to-point channel configuration

Computer   Terminal 1   Terminal 2   Terminal 3

(b) Multipoint channel configuration

connections that produce multiplexing. On the sending end, **multiplexers** collect data from several devices and send them over one channel; on the receiving end, they separate the transmissions back to their original order for processing (Figure 7.10). The rationale behind this process is that most communication channels are capable of transmitting more data at a time than a single device can send. Thus, a multiplexer allows a communication channel to be used more efficiently, thereby reducing the cost of using the channel.

Concentration. Frequently, it is necessary to connect more devices to a computer than a communication channel can handle at one time. **Concentration** is the process of connecting and serving these devices. A **concentrator,** often a minicomputer, is the hardware that provides concentration (Figure 7.11). When the number of devices transmitting exceeds the capacity of a communication channel, the data are stored in a buffer for later transmission. Many multiplexers also provide concentration.

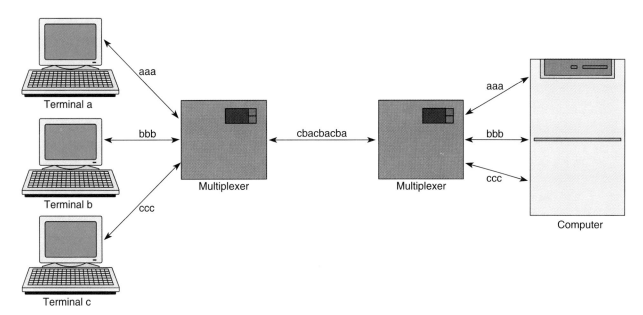

FIGURE 7.10
A multiplexer allows several terminals to share a communication channel.

Front-End Processors

A **front-end processor** is a special-purpose computer that handles all data communication control functions (Figure 7.12). Thus, while the CPU in a front-end processor handles all of the communication tasks, the CPU of a main computer is free to work on other tasks. The two processors interact only to pass data between them. A typical front-end processor might control scores of communication channels of varying types and speeds coming from a number of diverse remote terminals.

A front-end processor can be programmed to perform a variety of functions, such as concentration, error control, code conversion, buffering, and channel sharing, which are activities related to data and message control. Front-end processors can also contain their own secondary storage devices to log (record) the communication activities for billing and audit trails.

Common Carriers

A **common carrier** is a company that is licensed and regulated by federal or state government to transmit the data-communication property of others at regulated rates. There are thousands of licensed common carriers of data communications. Three of the largest are American Telephone and Telegraph (AT&T), Western Union, and General Telephone & Electronics (GTE). All common carriers dealing with communication are regulated by the Federal Communications Commission (FCC) and by various state agencies.

Specialized common carriers and value-added carriers are alternatives to the major common carriers. A **specialized common carrier** is a

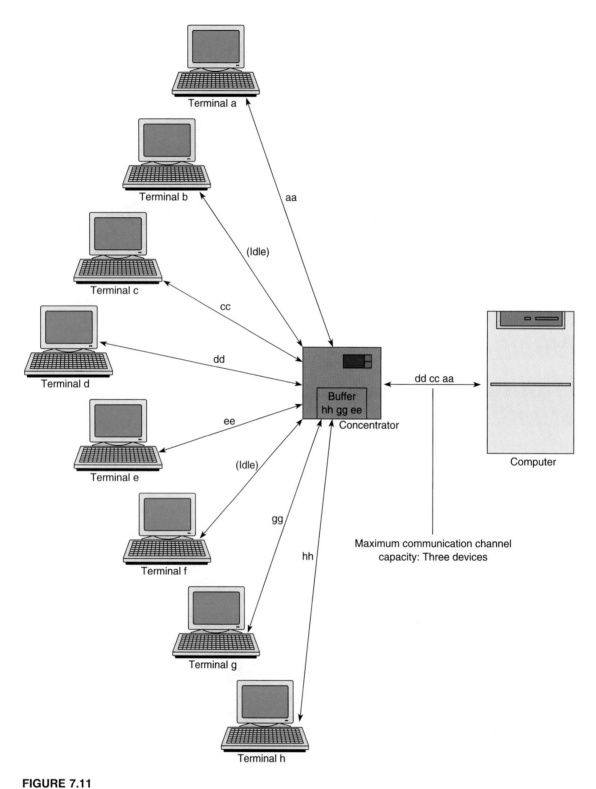

FIGURE 7.11
A concentrator allows connection and service to a number of devices greater than the communication channel is capable of transmitting to at one time.

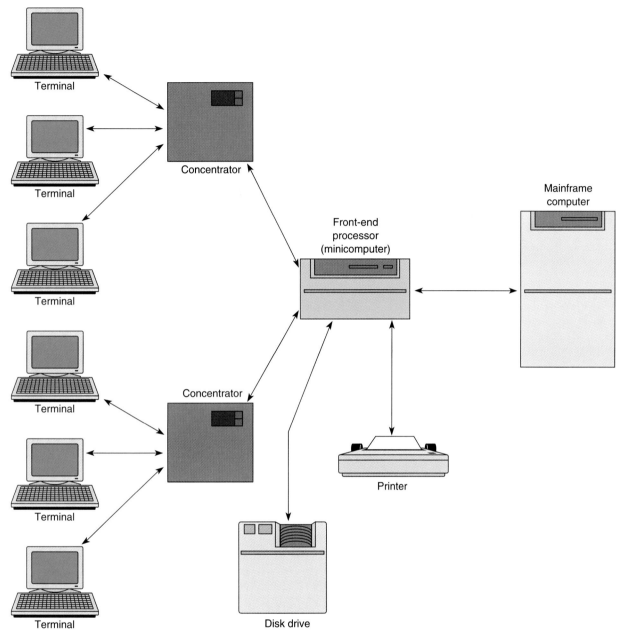

FIGURE 7.12
A front-end processor processes and routes all input and output operations.

company that supplies a limited number of data communication services. It is usually limited to communication in and between selected areas. A **value-added carrier** is a company that leases communication channels from common carriers and adds extra services over and above those that the common carriers provide. Such services include electronic mail, voice messaging, information retrieval services, time sharing, and distributed data processing. Tymnet and Telenet are value-added carriers.

Modes of Transmission

The transfer of data over communication channels occurs in three modes: (1) simplex, (2) half-duplex, and (3) full-duplex. In the **simplex mode,** data can be transmitted in only one direction (Figure 7.13a). A device using the simplex mode of transmission can either send or receive data, but it cannot do both. This mode might be used in a burglar alarm system with the source located in a building and the destination being the local police station. The simplex mode allows no means of feedback to ensure correct interpretation of the signal received. In the burglar alarm example, police officers have no way of knowing whether the alarm had been set off by a test, a malfunction, or a burglar.

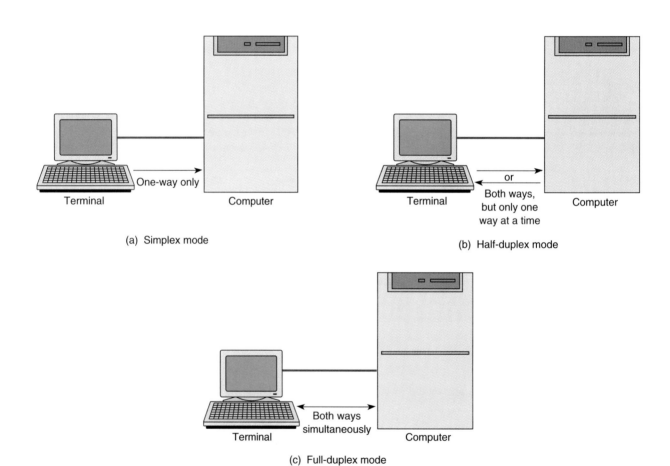

FIGURE 7.13
The transfer of data over a communication line can take place in one of three modes: simplex, half-duplex, or full-duplex.

The **half-duplex mode** allows a device to send and receive data, but not at the same time. In other words, the transmission of data can occur in only one direction at a time (Figure 7.13b). An example of a half-duplex transmission is a citizens band (CB) radio. A user can talk or listen but cannot do both at the same time.

The most sophisticated of the transmission modes is the **full-duplex mode,** which allows a device to receive and send data simultaneously (Figure 7.13c). For example, a telephone system using a full-duplex mode allows the users to talk and listen at the same time. Telephone systems use either the half-duplex or full-duplex mode.

Objective 7.3   Identify the factors that determine the speed at which data are transmitted.

What Factors Affect the Rate of Data Transmission?

The rate at which data are transferred is the **baud rate,** the number of times per second that the transmitted signal changes (modulates or demodulates). Baud is often equated with bits per second (bps); however, this comparison is not entirely accurate because a signal does not always carry one bit.

Although higher speeds are possible, typical data transmission speeds are 1200, 2400, 4800, and 9600 baud. Modems used with microcomputers typically use 1200 or 2400 baud. Large computer systems used by businesses typically transmit data at speeds of 4800 baud or higher using high-speed modems. Factors that determine the rate at which data are transmitted include the bandwidth of the communication channel and the method of data transmission (asynchronous or synchronous).

Communication Channel Bandwidths

> **Communication Channel Bandwidths**
>
> - Narrow band
> - Voice band
> - Broad band

The **bandwidth,** or grade, of a communication channel determines the rate, or speed, at which data can be transmitted over the channel. The term *bandwidth* is often expressed as *band*. There are three bands for communication channels: (1) narrow band, (2) voice band (also called voice grade), and (3) broad band.

The slowest of these is the **narrow-band channel,** which transmits data at rates between 40 to 100 bits per second (bps). A telegraph line is a narrow-band channel. A **voice-band channel** transmits data at rates between 110 and 9,600 bits per second. Telephone lines are voice-band channels. The fastest is the **broad-band channel,** which transmits data at rates up to several million bits per second. Advances in technology will soon allow data to be transmitted on some types of broad-band channels at speeds of more than a billion bps. Microwaves, coaxial cables, and laser beams are broad-band channels.

Asynchronous and Synchronous Transmissions

Asynchronous transmission of data is a method that sends one character at a time. The transfer of data is controlled by start bits and stop bits. Thus, each character is surrounded by bits that signal the beginning and end of the character. They allow the receiving terminal to synchronize itself with the transmitting terminal on a character-by-character basis. Asynchronous transmission, the less expensive of the two methods, is often used in low-speed transmission of data in conjunction with narrow-band and some slower voice-band channels (less than 1200 baud) for which the transmitting device operates manually or intermittently.

In **synchronous transmission,** blocks of characters are transmitted in timed sequences. Rather than having start and stop bits around each character, each block of characters is marked with synchronization characters. The receiving device accepts data until it detects a special ending character or a predetermined number of characters, at which time the device knows the message has come to an end.

Synchronous is much faster than asynchronous transmission. It commonly uses the faster voice-band (greater than 1200 baud) and broad-band channels, and it is usually utilized when data transfer requirements exceed several thousand bits per second. Synchronous transmission is used in direct computer-to-computer communications of large computer systems because of its high data transfer speeds. The equipment required for synchronous transmission of data is more sophisticated than that needed for asynchronous devices.

The special characters used by asynchronous and synchronous transmissions to alert a modem that data are being sent or that transmissions are complete are **message characters**. Before data transmission, however, a set of traffic rules and procedures called a **protocol** must be established. The purpose of a protocol is to perform such tasks as getting the attention of another device, identifying all of the devices involved in the communication, checking to see whether a message has been sent correctly, and initiating any necessary retransmission or error recovery. Protocols vary, depending on the devices being used, but the same protocol must be followed by all devices participating in a communication session. Prearranged signals defining the protocol are sent between computers in an exchange called **handshaking.**

Objective 7.4   Define computer network and briefly describe wide-area networks (WANs), local-area networks (LANs), and cellular networks.

What Is a Computer Network?

One application of data communication technology is the development of computer networks. A **computer network** is created when data communication channels link several computers and other devices, such as printers and secondary storage devices. The connections between computers on a network may be permanent, such as cables, or they may be temporary, made through telephone or other communication links. Computer networks can be small, consisting of only a few computers and related devices, or they can include many small and large computers distributed over a wide geographic area. The purpose of a computer network is to provide users with a means of communicating and transferring information electronically as well as sharing hardware, data files, and programs. The two basic types of networks are wide-area networks and local-area networks. You'll also read about cellular networks in this section.

Wide-Area Networks

Types of Networks

- Wide area
- Local area
- Cellular

A **wide-area network (WAN)** consists of two or more geographically dispersed computers that are linked by communication facilities provided by common carriers, such as the telephone system or microwave relays. This network is often used by large corporations and government agencies to transmit data. Satellites transmit data across large distances divided by geographic barriers, such as oceans or mountains. The National Science Foundation (NSF) in Washington, D.C., has connected six supercomputers in a WAN that eliminates logistical problems and links schools and research centers around the nation to the supercomputers.

Local-Area Networks

A **local-area network (LAN)** consists of two or more computers and related devices directly linked within a relatively small, well-defined area, such as a room, building, or cluster of buildings. The computers and other devices on a LAN are called **nodes** and are connected so that any device can communicate with any other device on the LAN. They commonly encompass microcomputers and peripheral devices such as laser printers and large hard disk drives. Today's LANs support a wide variety of computers and related devices. Chapter 8 takes a closer look at LANs.

Cellular Networks

It's common for people to communicate from their automobiles or other locations within a cellular network via cellular mobile telephones. Cellular phones offer high-quality mobile communication.

In a **cellular network,** transmitters are placed in a checkerboard pattern throughout the system service area (Figure 7.14). The geographical area that each transmitter covers is referred to as a cell. Each cell has frequencies assigned to it that are not available to the other cells in the network. When an individual places a call, the local cell (the one where the caller is) detects it and assigns specific frequencies for transmitting and receiving calls. A computer system monitors the strength of the signal. As a caller moves out of a cell, the signal gets weaker. When the signal strength falls to a predetermined level, the computer detects that the caller has left the cell and checks all of the surrounding cells to determine which cell is picking up the transmission. The call is then taken over by that cell, and the user's telephone is assigned new frequencies for transmitting and receiving. Usually, this handoff between cells happens fast enough that it goes undetected by the user.

Business use of cellular telephones is growing rapidly. Executives who travel by car frequently can stay in touch with their offices and receive last-minute information on their way to meetings. Supervisors and repair technicians who work at remote sites can stay in touch with their offices. Portable computers can be connected to the home office through modems and cellular phones to exchange information conveniently. Terminals are also available to transmit facsimile images over a cellular network. Portable

FIGURE 7.14
A cellular network.

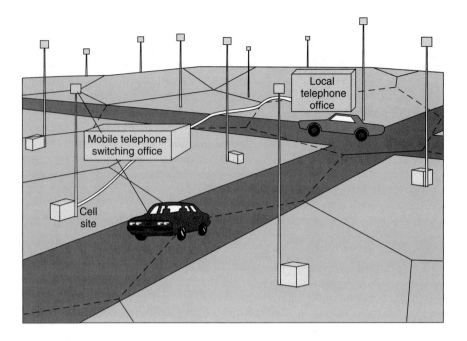

cellular computers transmit data directly over a cellular network without a modem or cellular phone.

Many types of public transportation, such as commuter trains and ferry boats, that cater to a large business clientele are beginning to make cellular phones available to their patrons.

Cellular networks are found in most major cities. Not all of these networks are compatible; however, the trend is toward nationwide compatibility that will facilitate users as they travel across the country.

Objective 7.5   Describe a distributed data processing (DDP) system.

What Is Distributed Data Processing?

DDP Advantages

- Cost efficiency
- User control of computer facilities
- Shared resources

Distributed data processing (DDP) is a concept of dispersing computers, devices, software, and data connected by communication channels into areas where they are used. The computers are distributed by function and geographical boundaries, and they work together as a cohesive system to support user requirements. DDP contrasts with a centralized system, where all data processing resources are in one location. Typically, a centralized system has one large general-purpose computer with many terminals attached. Even though the centralized computer can do many tasks, it may not do them in the most efficient or cost-effective way. A DDP system allows the tailoring of many smaller, more specialized computers to complete a particular task(s) efficiently and cost-effectively.

Three advantages of using DDP are (1) cost efficiency, (2) user-controlled computing facilities, resulting in shorter response time, and (3) shared resources. In the past, hardware costs of computing represented a major argument for not using DDP. However, most components in a computer system have decreased in cost and improved in performance,

Highlight

7.2

Getting on the Right Track!

Some of us have trouble keeping track of our books, assignments, and papers. Imagine the nightmare of keeping track of millions of packages on a minute-by-minute basis. Just how do nationwide shippers like Federal Express, United Parcel Service, and Airborne Express keep track of individual packages? The answer is called tracking software; it gives the ability to find your package in about 30 seconds.

Tracking begins the minute you call asking for a pickup. The package is assigned a number that follows it through the shipping process. A bar code label is generated and affixed to your package. Thereafter scanning devices at various checkpoints report on the progress of each package. Airborne downloads over phone lines several times a day. Other shippers' drivers scan the label and the mainframe is notified immediately by means of radio or cellular links that your package has been picked up. This means that whenever a call comes in to check on the status of that particular shipment, the mainframe should provide an answer within seconds. The tracking process ends when a signature is obtained from the recipient at the appropriate address.

Even with all the "whistles and bells" for tracking, it is estimated that 3–5 percent of packages are not delivered on time. If you know that your delivery was not made within the guaranteed time, you are eligible for a refund. Most people do not pay attention to this detail nor collect their refunds. However, one company cut over 50 percent of its annual $50,000 shipping costs simply by tracking refunds, investigating options for the cheapest rates, and sending larger packages instead of individual shipments to one address. In some cases "lost" packages have been delivered on time, but are found at the loading dock or in the mailroom of the recipient. In these cases, no refund is due.

To follow your own package directly through the shipper's mainframe computer, use UPS' MaxiTrack, Airborne Express' FOCUS, and FedEx Tracking Software. They provide free on-line service, accessible from your computer via modem using toll-free telephone numbers. Customer automation is also offered by the above shipping companies. They provide computers, monitors, printers, and modems that are programmed to prepare the manifest paperwork for each package. The computer creates and prints the correct label and calculates the shipping costs, too. Once you choose to use a particular shipper's computer, you may not get the cheapest rate on a package-by-package basis. But if you or your company ships to the same addresses on a regular basis, you may realize a considerable time savings by not having to look up addresses and prepare the same labels time after time. A company that ships only four or five packages a day realized a savings of approximately an hour and a half each week for one of its employees.

Now we need a tracking system for socks that "disappear" in the washing machine.

while the cost of using communication channels has not decreased as much. Consequently, many organizations have discovered that distributing computers and data storage to local areas can actually save them money by decreasing their use of expensive communication channels. In addition, because a DDP network allows remote sites to share equipment and data, proper management and control of the DDP system reduces redundancy of both.

DDP has also become popular because users gain more control over individual information system needs. They no longer count on a centralized computer staff that attempts to fulfill the needs of everyone. A DDP system typically uses many minicomputers and microcomputers, which are not so complicated and do not require as much maintenance as does a larger, centralized system. Users of the smaller systems access them directly and take advantage of their full power. Nevertheless, for tasks such as managing large and complicated databases, mainframes still play a vital role in many DDP systems.

Response times for many applications are also shorter in a DDP. The concept of distributing management is referred to as decentralized management. When the management of a DDP system is decentralized, the DDP system is often referred to as a fully distributed system. Of course, there are varying degrees of both DDP and decentralized management. As with many things, it is not a simple case of one or the other. Another advantage of DDP is that users share equipment, software, and data with other computers in the DDP system in order to meet their total information needs.

On the other hand, DDP has several disadvantages as well. First, problems can occur with a DDP system if it is not managed properly. If an organization loses control over data processing resources, management will have difficulty controlling costs and maintaining standards throughout the distributed areas of the organization.

A second problem that can develop is a redundancy of resources and data. Without proper management and control, each distributed site may try to develop an information system to meet all of the needs of the site, and several systems that are the same, or nearly the same, may result. This duplicity can lead to higher hardware and software costs than would exist if the distributed sites shared the resources. Uncontrolled data redundancy also can lead to differences in data among the distributed sites, causing discrepancies in reports that are difficult and expensive to resolve.

Third, if the distributed sites do not coordinate their selection of hardware and software, compatibility problems can follow. Different protocols at distributed sites may result in the inability of the hardware to communicate among the distributed sites. Designing software to solve compatibility problems is time-consuming and costly.

A fourth problem occurs if a site falls under the control of untrained and inexperienced users, which may result in poor selection of hardware and software, inferior programming techniques, and little, if any, documentation. This leads to a costly and overly complex system or in some cases to a system that is inappropriate for the job.

Finally, obtaining timely support at some distributed sites can be difficult because they are too far from the support staff of the vendor or organization. However, maintaining a separate support staff at each location may also be too expensive for some organizations.

DDP Disadvantages

- Loss of management control
- Redundancies of resources and data
- Compatibility problems
- Unskilled users
- Support difficulties

DDP is not appropriate for every situation. Large, centralized computing systems are still essential in some cases. However, many applications can be completed more efficiently and cost-effectively with distributed systems. To ensure that DDP meets the needs of an organization, both central management and dispersed users should be involved in the design of the system. Success or failure of the DDP depends on management planning, commitment, and control, as well as user acceptance.

Objective 7.6   Recognize some challenges presented by data communications.

What Challenges Are Presented by Data Communications?

Use of data communication has its challenges. Many computer systems are incompatible with each other and cannot easily establish communication linkages. In addition, data sent over communication channels are subject to various kinds of interference, which may alter or destroy some of the data. Besides ensuring the integrity of data, the privacy of data must also be protected. In this regard, passwords and access codes may be helpful. However, to prevent unauthorized access to highly sensitive data, the data may have to be encrypted, or scrambled, before they are sent. Then, of course, they must be decoded, or unscrambled, when they are received.

The Infomodule following this chapter gives ideas on how to put computer communications to work for you.

Summary

Data communication is the process of sending data electronically from one point to another. Using communication facilities such as the telephone system and microwave relays to send data between computers is a type of data communication often referred to as telecommunication.

Transmission of data takes one of two forms: analog or digital. Analog data transmission is the passage of data in continuous wave form. Digital data transmission is the passage of data in distinct on and off pulses.

Modulation is the process of converting a digital signal into an analog signal. Demodulation is the process of converting the analog signal into a digital signal. A modem (*mo*dulator-*dem*odulator) is the device that converts the signals.

A communication channel is a pathway along which data are transmitted between devices. The three basic types of communication channels are (1) wire cable, (2) microwave, and (3) fiber optics.

Multiplexing is the process of combining the transmissions of several computers or other devices so the transmissions share the same communication channel. Concentration allows a communication channel to be connected to and serve more devices than the capacity of that channel normally allows. A front-end processor is a computer that handles all data communication control functions, freeing the CPU of a main computer to work on other tasks.

Common carriers are companies licensed and regulated to transmit the data communication property of others. Specialized common carriers and value-added carriers are alternatives to the major common carriers for data communication.

Data transfer can occur in three modes: (1) simplex, (2) half-duplex, and (3) full-duplex.

The baud rate of a communication channel is the number of times per second that the transmitted signal changes (modulates or demodulates). The bandwidth, or band, of a communication channel determines the speed at which that channel can transmit data.

Asynchronous transmission transmits data one character at a time while synchronous transmission transmits data as a block of characters in timed sequences. Protocol is the set of rules and procedures defining the technical details of data transfer between two devices.

A computer network is created when several computers and other devices, such as printers and secondary storage devices, are linked together by data communication channels. Each computer or device in a network is called a node. A wide-area network (WAN) consists of two or more computers that are geographically dispersed but are linked by communication facilities provided by common carriers, such as the telephone system or microwave relays. A local-area network (LAN) consists of two or more computers directly linked within a small, well-defined area, such as a room, building, or cluster of buildings. A cellular network permits mobile communication from cellular telephones. Computers can send and receive data over a cellular network through the use of modems and cellular phones. Cellular computers also transmit data directly over a cellular network without the use of modems and cellular phones.

Distributed data processing (DDP) is the concept of dispersing the computers, devices, software, and data that are connected through communication channels into the areas where they are used. The computers are organized on a functional or geographical basis, and they work together as a cohesive system to support user requirements.

Data communication allows computers to share hardware resources and data in spite of the boundaries of time or distance. However, data communication is not without its challenges, including hardware and software incompatibilities that can make establishing communication linkages difficult, interference on communication channels, which may alter or destroy some of the data, and concerns about ensuring the integrity and privacy of the data transmitted.

VOCABULARY SELF-TEST

Can you define the following terms?

acoustic modem (p. 265)

analog data transmission (p. 264)

asynchronous transmission (p. 277)

bandwidth (p. 277)

baud rate (p. 277)

broad-band channel (p. 277)

cellular network (p. 279)

coaxial cable (p. 268)

common carrier (p. 273)

communication channel (p. 267)

computer network (p. 278)

concentration (p. 272)

concentrator (p. 272)

contention (p. 271)

data communication (p. 263)

demodulation (p. 265)

digital data transmission (p. 264)

distributed data processing (DDP) (p. 280)

external direct-connect modem (p. 266)

fiber optics (p. 269)

front-end processor (p. 273)

full-duplex mode (p. 277)

half-duplex mode (p. 277)

handshaking (p. 278)

internal direct-connect modem (p. 267)

local-area network (LAN) (p. 279)

message characters (p. 278)

microwave (p. 268)

modem (p. 265)

modulation (p. 265)

multiplexer (p. 272)

multiplexing (p. 271)

multipoint channel configuration (p. 270)

narrow-band channel (p. 277)

node (p. 279)

point-to-point channel configuration (p. 269)

polling (p. 270)

protocol (p. 278)

satellite (p. 268)

simplex mode (p. 276)

specialized common carrier (p. 273)

synchronous transmission (p. 278)

telecommunication (p. 263)

twisted-pair (p. 268)

value-added carrier (p. 275)

voice-band channel (p. 277)

wide-area network (WAN) (p. 279)

wire cable (p. 268)

REVIEW QUESTIONS

Multiple Choice

1. _____ is the process of using communication facilities such as the telephone system and microwave relays to send data between computers.
   a. Telecommunication
   b. Modulation
   c. Demodulation
   d. Multiplexing

2. A _____ communication channel transmits data in digital form through clear flexible tubing.
   a. wire-cable
   b. fiber-optic
   c. simplex
   d. microwave

3. _____ is a method of determining access to a communication channel where the computer checks with the device to determine if there is a message to send.
   a. Contention
   b. Polling
   c. Multiplexing
   d. Concentration

4. Multiplexing and concentration are two _____.
   a. data transfer modes
   b. communication bandwidths

  c. channel configurations

  d. channel-sharing methods

5. The _____ mode allows a device to send or receive data over a communication channel, but not at the same time.

  a. asynchronous

  b. half-duplex

  c. simplex

  d. full-duplex

6. The _____, or grade, of a communication channel determines the rate, or speed, that data can be transmitted over the channel.

  a. bits per second

  b. baud rate

  c. bandwidth

  d. protocol

7. _____ transmission of data is a method whereby blocks of characters are transmitted in timed sequences.

  a. Asynchronous

  b. Half-duplex

  c. Full-duplex

  d. Synchronous

8. The set of rules and procedures for transmission of data is called _____.

  a. handshaking

  b. protocol

  c. message characters

  d. links

9. A _____ is two or more computers directly linked within a small, well-defined area, such as a room, building, or cluster of buildings.

  a. wide-area network

  b. local-area network

  c. cellular network

  d. network topology

10. Which one of the following is not an advantage of distributed data processing?

  a. user-controlled computing facilities

  b. software and hardware compatibility

  c. cost efficiency

  d. shared resources

Fill-In

1. The process of sending data electronically from one point to another is called _____.

2. A(n) _____ configuration connects one device to another device by a dedicated communication channel.

3. The process whereby each terminal monitors the communication channel to determine whether it is available is called _____.

4. _____ is the process of combining the transmissions from several devices into a single data stream that can be sent over a single high-speed communication channel.

5. The process of connecting more devices to a computer than a communication channel can handle at one time is called _____.

6. A(n) _____ is a special-purpose computer that handles all data communication control functions.

7. A company that is licensed and regulated by federal or state government to transmit the data communication property of others at regulated rates is called a _____.

8. In _____ transmission messages are sent one character at a time and in _____ transmission messages are sent as blocks of characters in timed sequences.

9. A(n) _____ is created when data communication channels link several computers and other devices, such as printers and secondary storage devices.

10. _____ is a concept of dispersing computers, devices, software, and data connected by communication channels into areas where they are used.

Short Answer

1. How does data communication differ from telecommunication?
2. Describe the difference between analog and digital data transmission.
3. When is a modem needed? Why are two needed?
4. Describe the purpose of a communication channel and discuss the three types presented in the chapter.
5. Contrast the processes of polling and contention.
6. List and describe the three modes in which the transfer of data can occur.
7. What are the three bandwidths for communication channels? Recount their differences.
8. Describe the difference between asynchronous and synchronous transmissions.
9. Define computer network and briefly describe wide-area network, local-area network, and cellular network.
10. Discuss the advantages and disadvantages of distributed data processing.

Issues for Thought

1. Various organizations are trying to introduce standards for data communication. Do you think this would benefit communications as a whole, or would it stifle competition and creativity and slow down technical advances?

2. If you were able to work from your home through communication channels connected to your place of employment, would you? What advantages and disadvantages would you foresee? Consider the discipline required for this type of work environment. Should employers monitor the home workers' productivity? How?

Infomodule
Putting Data Communication to Work for You

HOW CAN DATA COMMUNICATION WORK FOR YOU?

Equipping a personal computer with communication hardware and software opens a whole new world of information resources. This section discusses some options available to you, including bulletin boards, electronic mail, facsimile, voice messaging, teleconferencing, commercial on-line services, and gateway services.

Bulletin Boards

One of the easiest and least expensive ways to begin exploring communication capabilities is by using a bulletin board system (Table 1). A **bulletin board system (BBS)** is essentially an electronic equivalent of a conventional bulletin board. Many BBSs are established to let users exchange information about any topic; others are set up for people who own a specific brand or model of computer or who have a common interest. The first electronic BBS was created in 1978 by Ward Christensen and Randy Suess so members of the Chicago Area Computer Hobbyists Exchange could trade information.

Although features vary among BBSs, most provide users with the ability to:

- post messages for other users to read
- read messages posted by other callers
- communicate with the **system operator (sysop)** (the person who operates the bulletin board) to ask questions about the operation of the BBS, report problems, or make suggestions
- post notices of equipment or services for sale
- upload (transfer a file from your computer to another computer) and download (transfer a file from another computer to your computer) programs

Most BBSs currently in operation are noncommercial and free of charge. The telephone company, however, charges for the long distance phone time used when you communicate to a BBS that is outside your local calling area.

There are two basic types of BBSs: message-only and file transfer. Message-only systems permit public or private messages to be sent and received and public bulletin boards to be viewed. BBSs with file-transfer capabilities also allow files to be uploaded and downloaded. These are the most popular because a vast array of free public-domain software can be downloaded, including games, application software, and system utilities.

Most BBSs are operated by individuals interested in computers and communication who have a desire to share information with others. But hardware manufacturers, software publishers, and other businesses have also started bulletin boards. A business might use a BBS for customers or clients to place orders, ask questions, and solve problems relating to its products.

A benefit of a BBS is that it provides an easy and inexpensive way to share information; however, there are some drawbacks. Sysops for the private, individual BBSs donate their own equipment (computers and modem) and software. Because they donate their time as well, the hours of operation vary. Many BBSs handle only one call at a time and impose time limits so that one caller does not tie up the bulletin board for long periods of time.

Electronic Mail

Electronic mail (e-mail) refers to the electronic transmission of messages over a computer network. It is an electronic version of the post office or inter-

TABLE 1

Hints on Using a Bulletin Board System (BBS).

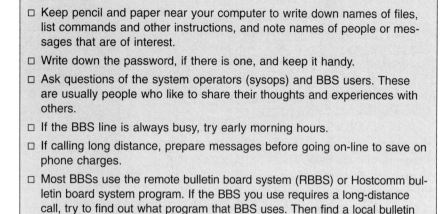

- ☐ Keep pencil and paper near your computer to write down names of files, list commands and other instructions, and note names of people or messages that are of interest.
- ☐ Write down the password, if there is one, and keep it handy.
- ☐ Ask questions of the system operators (sysops) and BBS users. These are usually people who like to share their thoughts and experiences with others.
- ☐ If the BBS line is always busy, try early morning hours.
- ☐ If calling long distance, prepare messages before going on-line to save on phone charges.
- ☐ Most BBSs use the remote bulletin board system (RBBS) or Hostcomm bulletin board system program. If the BBS you use requires a long-distance call, try to find out what program that BBS uses. Then find a local bulletin board that uses the same program to familiarize yourself with the operating environment. This saves money because you do not spend time on a long-distance phone connection learning how that BBS operates.
- ☐ For public domain software, try local BBSs. If the software is not available locally, then try long-distance BBSs.

office mail and it sends messages from one computer or terminal to another computer or terminal on a network. Many businesses use electronic mail systems to reduce paperwork and to lessen the time it takes messages to reach their destination.

An in-house e-mail system connecting all or some of the employees in a business is typically implemented on a LAN. An e-mail system may be implemented on a WAN, which enables people at different locations around the world to be connected. Electronic mail can be sent between subscribers to the same service and some between subscribers of different services. Many e-mail systems on different networks can be linked with the appropriate hardware and software so that messages can be created locally and distributed globally.

E-mail systems differ in features offered. Some provide a text editor to create and edit messages. Many allow users to forward mail, send "carbon" copies, request return receipts, and attach files to a message. Some remain active in the background while you are working on other applications. They can automatically inform you when new messages arrive

and give you the option of viewing them immediately or saving them for reading later.

Messages can be sent to an individual recipient or to a larger group with one action. When messages are sent they are stored in electronic mailboxes assigned to users on the network. Recipients can view, save, or delete a message at their convenience. A typical transmission might proceed as follows:

1. Sender accesses an electronic mail system.
2. Message is keyed into the e-mail editor or uploaded from a message created in a word processor into the e-mail application.
3. Mail box address of recipient(s) is specified telling the computer where to send the message.
4. Sender issues the command to dispatch the message.
5. Message is transmitted to the specified destination.
6. Message is received and can be read immediately at the terminal or placed in the recipient's "mailbox," a file space where it can be retrieved and displayed or printed at any time.

Electronic mail has several notable benefits. First, it is faster than traditional mail and less expensive to prepare and send. Second, a single message can be sent simultaneously to multiple addresses. Third, unlike a telephone call, the receiver of a message doesn't need to be on the line at the same time as the sender. Fourth, a busy person doesn't need to be interrupted to receive the message. Finally, the message can be printed on paper.

Electronic mail does have some drawbacks. It is expensive to set up, and if used indiscriminately, it can be expensive to operate. There is no guarantee that electronic mail systems will be compatible. There is also the problem of privacy and security of electronic mail. It is difficult to ensure that only the recipient reads the mail. Finally, electronic junk mail has emerged.

Facsimile

Facsimile (fax) is the transmission of text or graphics over telephone lines in digital form (Figure 1). A copy of an original document is electronically sent to and reproduced at another location. To send a fax (copy) using a conventional fax machine, you must insert the original document into the unit that is directly connected to the phone lines. The machine scans the document, converts it to a digital form, and sends the document text, graphics, photographs, even handwriting, over telephone lines. A fax machine at the receiving end gathers the electronic signals, converts them, and produces a hard copy duplicate of the original document. Fax machines must be compatible in order to communicate with each other.

Microcomputers can also be equipped with fax boards and software so they can function as a fax machine. Documents created on the computer can be faxed and if a scanner is connected, hard copy documents can be scanned and faxed, just as with a conventional fax machine. Fax/modem boards combine the functions of a fax machine and a modem on a single circuit board that takes up only one expansion slot in your computer. Cellular fax/modem boards are also available and are ideal for those who use portable computers and need to transfer documents.

FIGURE 1
A facsimile (fax) machine sends a document electronically to a branch office in another city.

Through the use of facsimile technology, documents that are urgently needed can now be sent anywhere in the world in a matter of minutes. You could have a contract faxed to your hotel on the beach, sign it, and fax it back, barely missing a single ray of sunshine. Facsimile is rapidly growing in popularity, so much so that "junk fax mail" is considered a problem by many.

Voice Messaging

Even with the introduction of many new forms of electronic communication, the telephone is still the most frequently used device for communicating information between individuals in business. It is simple, efficient, and easy for individuals to understand and use. The telephone can be combined with a computer in a voice messaging system. **Voice messaging systems** are computer-supported systems that allow messages to be sent as human voice without the need for receivers to be present to accept the messages. They can be sent and received from standard pushbutton telephones. When a user prepares a message, the voice messaging system stores it. The user can then review and edit the message before sending it to the recipient's voice mailbox. When the user instructs the computer to do so, it sends the message to the mailbox for storage. When it is convenient, the recipient can then dial his or her mailbox and hear the message. Voice messaging systems have several advantages, including leaving messages for one or more persons, reducing costs from multiple calls when the receiver is not available, using the convenience of pushbutton phones, eliminating concern for time schedules and time zones, and giving the personal touch by sending voice messages.

Teleconferencing

Three or more people have been able to talk on the telephone simultaneously for years in an early form of teleconferencing. Voice teleconferencing does not convey charts and graphs and requires that all participants be present at the same time. Later, video teleconferencing combined voices and images and transmitted them to different locations (Figure 2).

However, equipment is expensive, difficulties arise in arranging the schedules of the participants, and people worry about how they appear on video.

In **electronic teleconferencing**, computer systems are connected by the telephone system and participants enter their conversation on their keyboards. Electronic teleconferencing systems are similar to BBSs, but they are much larger and require large computer systems to run them and store the data. Most BBSs operate on microcomputer systems.

To have a successful conference, participants need not be at their computers at the same time. A question might be asked of a participant and sent to that individual's mailbox. The recipient accesses and reads the message at a convenient time and sends an answer back.

Members of a teleconference can be anywhere in the world. Teleconferencing won't replace business travel; however, it limits trips to only the essentials.

Commercial On-Line Services

A **commercial on-line service** is a business that supplies information to subscribers on numerous topics of interest by using powerful large computer systems that store millions of pieces of data. In some

FIGURE 2
Employees at different locations use video teleconferencing to hold a business meeting where the participants can see and converse with each other. (Courtesy of American Satellite Co.)

ways, commercial on-line services are similar to BBSs; however, they are run on a much larger scale, supply much more information, and operate as businesses for profit.

Commercial on-line services require a subscription and payment of hourly access charges; some require initial sign-on fees. Although a few have limited hours, commercial on-line services usually operate 24 hours a day, 7 days a week. Charges are commonly lower for evening or weekend access. New subscribers are customarily issued a user number and a password to access the service and retrieve information from it.

The topics covered vary among the services from news, sports, and weather, to business, finance, and investment. They also offer computerized shopping; games; teleconferencing facilities; forums on computers and computing; electronic mail and editing capabilities to write messages; airline information; theater, restaurant, and hotel guides; on-line encyclopedias; and computer programs. Some allow you to electronically search millions of articles, abstracts, and bibliographic citations from thousands of books, periodicals, reports, and theses. Commercial on-line services have support in the form of printed catalogs and on-line indexes to help you select the appropriate database or service.

Once you gain access to a database, specific commands and search terms are required to find the data needed. Search terms are the words or phrases actually searched for in a database to help locate relevant data. A good way to begin a search is with general terms or topics. Then, check more specific topics to retrieve records that might have been excluded if you had used a narrower scope originally. Usually, you can preview records, eliminating those you don't need.

Most services use Boolean operators to eliminate specific terms or topics and combine search terms. The Boolean operators AND, OR, and NOT indicate logical relationships among various search terms. For example, to search for information on software copyright laws, you might use "software AND copyright." By searching "software AND copyright," you would locate only references containing both search terms. This search would be the best choice in this case. A

search of "software OR copyright" would find all references that contain the word *software,* all that contain the word *copyright,* and all that contain both words. Thus, it would probably include irrelevant general information about software and copyright. A search of "software NOT copyright" would locate all references containing just the word *software* and not the word copyright. Thus, it would find only software information not related to copyright.

Popular commercial on-line services include CompuServe, Prodigy, America Online, Delphi, Dialog Information Service, Dow Jones News Retrieval, GEnie, and Newsnet. Below are highlights of some of the major topics each covers.

CompuServe provides access to news, weather, sports, health and fitness information, electronic mail, electronic encyclopedias and reference libraries, financial information, travel, entertainment and games, and a host of other topics. Users can also participate in forums on a wide range of topics.

Prodigy features color graphics and provides news and entertainment, educational features such as Academic American Encyclopedia and information and interactive features by National Geographic and Nova, shopping, and more.

America Online offers a GUI and employs color icons to access menu options. It provides computer industry information, news and financial information, message boards, forums on a variety of topics, electronic encyclopedia and reference materials, electronic mail, travel and shopping, games and entertainment, along with a host of other services.

Delphi provides constant access to news wires, business information, entertainment, shopping, and electronic encyclopedias.

Dialog Information Service is one of the largest commercial on-line services and permits users to conduct research on almost any topic with databases that include information from books and periodicals. It covers topics such as agriculture, business and economics, chemistry, current affairs, education, energy and environment, law and government, medicine and biosciences, science and technology, and social sciences and humanities.

Dow Jones News Retrieval offers its users business and financial news covering markets, companies and industries.

GEnie offers access to news, weather, sports, shopping, travel, and stock information in addition to electronic mail and much more.

Newsnet provides information from newspapers across the nation and industry newsletters highlighting products, technology, and trends.

Some commercial on-line services are totally dedicated to special interests and can be subscribed to individually. For example, LEXIS, a specialized database of legal information, is offered by Mead Data Central. They also offer Nexis, which provides general information including ABC news transcripts, files from newspapers across the nation and more.

Some of the large commercial on-line services also offer scaled-down versions of their services. For example, Dialog offers Knowledge Index, which is designed so that people who have little or no experience searching on-line databases will find them easy to use. It has fewer features and simpler commands and offers approximately 25 of Dialog's most widely used databases. Knowledge Index costs less to use, but it is available only during evenings and on weekends.

Gateway Services

A **gateway service** buys large quantities of connect time at wholesale rates from commercial on-line services and then resells the time to its own subscribers at retail rates. With one call to a gateway service, a subscriber connects to several different on-line services and pays no sign-up or monthly minimum fees usually charged by individual services. The gateway service charges only for the actual connect time at the regular rates of the service. The Business Computer Network (BCN) is a popular gateway service; Searchlink is another.

HOW DO BUSINESSES APPLY DATA COMMUNICATIONS?

Data communication has made the computer one of the most vital tools in our information-seeking society. It links two or more computers via communication channels and enables users to send and receive electronic data with little regard for time or distance.

Businesses make extensive use of data communications. One of the earliest and biggest success stories was that of American Hospital Supply Corporation in 1974, with its installation of a computer network that tied order-entry terminals on hospital premises to their organization. Hospitals could enter or check the status of an order at any time, without having to wait for a salesperson.

Today, many businesses use **electronic data interchange (EDI)**, a method that automates and standardizes transactions between retailers and their suppliers. Its purpose is to allow retailers and their suppliers to conduct business transactions electronically, transferring information such as orders and invoices between one computer and another on a network, instead of through the mail or other delivery services. Its goal is to reduce the amount of paperwork, human involvement, and time associated with processing orders manually. Turnaround time on orders has been reduced in some cases by as much as 50 percent.

Electronic funds transfer (EFT), the electronic movement of money among accounts, is a widely used data communication application. A large portion of money in the business and financial communities changes hands through EFT. One popular form of EFT is the automated teller machine. In fact, Society

---

Popular Commercial On-Line Services

- CompuServe
- Prodigy
- America Online
- Delphi
- Dialog Information Service
- Dow Jones News Retrieval
- GEnie
- Newsnet
- LEXIS

FIGURE 3
Federal Express processes over 700,000 packages a day. To make sure that deliveries and pickups are made quickly and accurately, each Federal Express delivery van is equipped with a small microcomputer. The office uses this to communicate with the driver about a package or to direct the driver to a pickup location. When a courier delivers a package, he or she scans the airbill number, adds information about the delivery, returns to the van, and feeds the delivery information into the computer. The information appears in the computers at the Federal Express headquarters in Memphis, Tennessee, within moments. (Larry Hamill/Merrill)

for Worldwide Interbank Financial Telecommunications (SWIFT), the most sophisticated private interbank system in the world, averages 1 million transactions daily for its member banks in numerous countries around the world. Nationally, the Cirrus banking network processes approximately 200 million transactions annually. The network provides services such as cash withdrawals and balance inquiries for checking, savings, and credit accounts and supports more than 6,500 automated teller machines.

Federal Express implemented data communications early to give it a strategic advantage over its competitors. An on-line parcel tracking system known as Cosmos (Figure 3) handles inquiries from remote locations about the status of a parcel. In addition, it locates delayed shipments and automatically sends invoices to customers. The Federal Express delivery vans are equipped with on-board terminals and through telecommunications, drivers can make inquiries of the Cosmos system directly, thereby improving customer service.

On-line reservations systems have also revolutionized the travel industry, from car rentals to hotels to airlines. All of these organizations, as well as travel agencies, send and receive information on reservations and flight schedules through data communication channels. SABRE (American Airlines) and Apollo (United Airlines) are two of the largest reservation systems.

Many of the stories in newspapers and magazines are filed by journalists using portable computers and data communication channels from remote locations. Most supermarket merchants and other retailers are keeping track of inventories because they have linked their cash registers to a large computer in a remote location.

Some companies have adopted a method of employment called **telecommuting**. This technique permits some personnel to work at home and use their computers to communicate with an office computer.

When fully implemented, the **Integrated Services Digital Network (ISDN)** will provide a worldwide digital communications network that computers and other devices can tap into through simple, standardized interfaces. Its goal is to replace digital-to-analog connections in current telephone lines and replace them with totally digital switching and transmitting facilities. It would allow voice, computer transmissions, music, and video to be routed over the same channel. It is expected to provide faster and more extensive communication services to users.

Other data communication services, such as interactive TV, allow you to communicate with and receive immediate response from various shows and services on your TV. These services are being tested in some markets now. Soon we'll all be participating. Changes are happening daily in the world of data communications. Current technologies are evolving and technologies are emerging to offer new and wonderful opportunities for you in your personal and professional lives.

VOCABULARY SELF-TEST

Can you define the following terms?

bulletin board system (BBS) (p. 288)

commercial on–line service (p. 291)

electronic data interchange (EDI) (p. 293)

electronic funds transfer (EFT) (p. 293)

electronic mail (e-mail) (p. 288)

electronic teleconferencing (p. 291)

facsimile (fax) (p. 290)

gateway service (p. 293)

Integrated Services Digital Network (ISDN) (p. 295)

system operator (sysop) (p. 288)

telecommuting (p. 295)

voice messaging system (p. 290)

REVIEW QUESTIONS

Multiple Choice

1. Many businesses employ _____ to reduce both paperwork and time in sending messages to their destinations.
   a. bulletin boards
   b. commercial on-line services
   c. electronic mail
   d. electronic funds transfer

2. _____ electronically sends documents containing text, graphics, photographs, and handwriting over telephone lines and reproduces them at the receiving location.
   a. Voice messaging
   b. Facsimile
   c. A bulletin board
   d. Teleconferencing

3. The telephone can be combined with computers in a(n) _____ system that allows messages to be sent as human voice without requiring the recipient to be present.
   a. voice messaging
   b. bulletin board
   c. electronic mail
   d. teleconferencing

4. A(n) _____ specializes in supplying information on numerous topics of interest to subscribers by using large computer systems that store millions of pieces of data.
   a. bulletin board
   b. commercial on-line service
   c. electronic mail system
   d. electronic teleconferencing system

5. _____ is a method that automates and standardizes transactions between retailers and their suppliers.
   a. Electronic funds transfer
   b. Telecommuting
   c. Integrated Services Digital Network
   d. Electronic data interchange

Fill-In

1. A(n) _____ is responsible for operating an electronic bulletin board.
2. _____ connects participants using computers by the telephone system and allows them to key in their conversations.
3. With one call, a(n) _____ supplies an individual with access to a wide variety of information services.
4. _____ involves the electronic movement of money among accounts.
5. _____ permits some personnel to work at home and use their computers to communicate with an office computer.

Short Answer

1. Describe a bulletin board system and give some advantages and disadvantages.
2. Discuss advantages and disadvantages of electronic mail.
3. How can the use of voice messaging and the various forms of teleconferencing benefit a business?
4. Describe some of the services you might find on a commercial on-line service and identify several popular commercial on-line services.
5. Describe several ways in which businesses are applying data communication technologies.

OUTLINE

OBJECTIVES

8.1 Understand what a local-area network (LAN) is.

8.2 Identify several benefits of using a LAN.

8.3 Describe the components that make up a LAN.

8.4 Define topology and describe three commonly used topologies.

8.5 Identify and describe the three major architectures used for LANs.

8.6 Understand the purpose of a carrier access method and describe two common access methods used for LANs.

8.7 Describe several ways in which applications react to a LAN.

8.8 State the purpose of LAN management software and identify several functions that it performs.

8.9 Discuss the steps involved in using a typical LAN.

Chapter
8

Local Area Networks

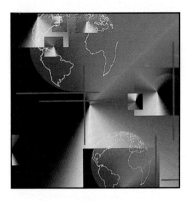

Andrew Fluegelman

A lawyer by training, an editor by profession, and a San Francisco Giants fan by day and night, Andrew Fluegelman left several bright marks on the computer world before his death at age 41. Fluegelman made his first major contribution in the field of data communication when he wrote his own computer program to transfer files between his IBM PC and an acquaintance's North Star computer. The program worked so well that friends and colleagues suggested he publish it.

Because Fluegelman was familiar with the software publishing process, he had some reservations about putting his own program through it. Instead of following this traditional route, which he had little patience for, he tried a new way of getting the program out to users—a way that retained the excitement then being felt about the many promises of computers. The standard way of publishing a program involved the insertion of an element that prevented the software from being copied. However, all of the elements being used at that time for copy protection were easily broken, and Fluegelman did not have the technical skill to create a better form of protection.

After watching a local public television station carry on its fund-raising drive, Fluegelman developed the concept of user-supported software, which is similar to the television station's viewer support of programming. Thus, he began encouraging people to copy his data communication program, called PC Talk, and to send him a voluntary contribution of $35 for each copy. He referred to this process as "freeware." This concept helped promote the use of data communication among early PC users by supplying them with an inexpensive communication software package.

A graduate of Yale Law School, Fluegelman practiced law for five years before turning to book publishing. His new profession made it necessary for him to learn such skills as publishing, distribution, and advertising—all of which he used when he developed and marketed his own software. Fluegelman also became a gifted writer and editor. He co-authored the book *Writing in the Computer Age* and served as editor-in-chief of *PC World* and *Macworld*. Throughout his life, Fluegelman took great delight in baseball, particularly in the fortunes of the San Francisco Giants. He once told a friend that if he ever became disabled, wheeling him out to the ballpark would restore his happiness.

A s a business grows, people need to communicate, data and programs must be transferred among individuals, and more people require access to expensive peripherals. Stand-alone personal computers, each with its own set of peripheral devices, may be too costly or may not get the job done. In this chapter we'll look at local area networks, a solution many businesses are adopting to solve these problems.

Objective 8.1   Understand what a local-area network (LAN) is.

What Is a LAN?

A **local-area network (LAN)** is a data communication network that consists of two or more computers directly linked within a relatively small, well-defined area, such as a room, building, or cluster of buildings. A LAN allows information and computer resources to be shared among its users. Computer resources include items such as mass data storage devices, processors, printers, plotters, and software.

LANs have become very popular with businesses, educational institutions, and many other organizations where there is a desire to share data, programs, and expensive peripheral devices. Let's look at some of the ways in which a LAN can be beneficial.

Objective 8.2   Identify several benefits of using a LAN.

What Are the Benefits of Using a LAN?

Benefits of Using a LAN

- Share information
- Share computer resources
- Reduce hardware and software costs
- Avoid software compatibility problems
- Improve communications
- Increase user productivity
- Enhance security
- Expand on an as-needed basis because of flexibility
- Provide access to wide variety of information sources

When many individuals in a work group or department need to access and update the same files, a LAN permits them to share information. For example, each member in a work group can update a common database, combine spreadsheet information created by multiple users, or access common templates for word processing documents, all from his or her own computer. LANs also expedite sharing and exchanging information. For example, reports are prepared and sent to other departments quickly and easily and databases are maintained so other departments are able to query them at will.

A LAN makes it possible to share computer resources with everyone connected to the LAN. This reduces hardware and software costs. LAN users share expensive peripheral devices such as laser printers, high performance hard disks, tape backup devices, and links to large system computers. In most cases, the cost per user is less with LAN versions of software than if individual copies of the software were purchased for each user. Because everyone works with the same version of the software, it is easier to upgrade everyone at the same time and avoid software compatibility problems.

Because LANs link users in work groups, departments, and throughout an organization they can improve communication among them. A LAN permits the use of electronic mail, which allows the exchange of messages and files with other users, even if they are not at their computer.

LANs also increase user productivity by making it possible for users to do their jobs more quickly and efficiently through sharing information and computer resources. Each user has access to the same files so time is not wasted searching for the most up-to-date information.

LANs can also improve security for your data. Security measures such as access codes and passwords restrict who can read or write to files on the LAN. Many LANs also store their files on redundant hard disks. If one should malfunction your files are still available from the other hard disk. This provides a level of data protection not found in single-user personal computers.

Another benefit of a LAN is the flexibility to expand on an as-needed basis. With larger computer systems you may have to buy more computing capacity than you currently need to avoid outgrowing the system.

A LAN can be linked to other LANS, WANs, and larger computer systems to provide access to a variety of information sources. In many organizations LANs are linked to departmental minicomputers, corporate mainframes, and WANs to form a companywide information system.

There are many benefits in using a LAN, but there are also some drawbacks. First, it can be expensive to install a LAN, train a network administrator and users, and maintain the LAN. Network administrators and users must go through a learning curve before they become comfortable and productive working on a LAN. In addition, there is always the potential for system failures, or crashes. Although most LAN operating systems have built-in protections, they may not prevent data from being lost under every circumstance.

Objective 8.3   Describe the components that make up a LAN.

What Are the Components of a LAN?

A typical LAN contains a number of components including workstations, a server(s), the hardware to connect all the devices on the LAN, and the network operating system. Each is discussed in this section.

Workstations

A **node** is any device, such as a workstation or printer, that is connected to the LAN and is capable of communicating with other devices connected to the LAN. A **workstation**, the input/output device at which a user works, can be either a personal computer or a terminal attached to the LAN.

The most common workstation found on a LAN is the IBM or compatible computer. This is usually the case because these machines were single-user machines before the LAN was installed. Specialized network workstations that resemble PCs, but without disk drives and limited expansion capabilities can also be used at a lower cost. Diskless workstations give added security in a network environment because they prevent users from copying data on floppies and removing them from the site.

Servers

The basic engine of a LAN is the server. A **server** is simply a computer that provides services to LAN users. It can be a personal computer, minicomputer, mainframe, or specialized computer. We'll look at five ways that a server can be configured: file server, database server, print server, communication server, and fax server. Depending on the load requirements of the

---

Components of a LAN

- **Workstations**
- **Servers**
  - File
  - Database
  - Print
  - Communication
  - Fax
- **Connections**
  - Cabling
  - Network interface cards
  - Bridges and gateways
- **Network operating system**

LAN one server may perform all these tasks or there may be a separate server for each.

File Server. A **file server** is a combination of hardware and software that permits LAN users to share computer programs and data. Many LANs have a **dedicated server** whose only purpose is dealing with the shared files on a LAN. Dedicated servers are usually high performance PCs or specialized devices designed for optimal file-serving speed and flexibility. They have extensive hard disk capacity, large memory, and a powerful processor so they can handle the needs of many users. The hard disk of the file server contains most of the applications and user data as well as the network operating system.

Some LANs are configured as a **peer-to-peer network** where every PC on the network acts as a server and shares its resources. A peer-to-peer network is generally used when only basic file and printer sharing capabilities are needed.

After your personal computer has been attached to a LAN you may notice that an additional drive name is available even though no additional hard disks were added to your PC. A **virtual drive**, or network drive, is a drive that can be accessed by a user's workstation even though it is not physically attached. It links a workstation to a subdirectory on the shared hard disk of the file server.

Three important considerations of a file server are its performance, capacity, and reliability or fault tolerance. Performance refers to how quickly a file server can find data and get it back to the requesting user. Performance is affected by a number of factors including the speed of the hard disk, the speed of the network interface card, the type and length of the cable, the type of network operating system, the amount of RAM available, the type of application, and the number of users on the network.

Capacity refers to the amount of storage space on the hard disk drive(s) of the server. Plan for growth when installing a LAN by buying a hard disk with at least twice as much storage space as you currently need or by ensuring that you can add additional hard disks to the file server as your needs expand.

Fault tolerance is the ability of the network to save data from loss in the event of a catastrophe such as electrical power loss, hard disk crash, disk controller failure, or electromagnetic interference. There are different levels of fault tolerance. The simplest is for the file server to read behind every write to the disk to ensure that it was correct. Another is to protect the file allocation table (FAT) by duplicating it and storing it in another location on the disk. If the FAT becomes corrupted the duplicate can locate files on the disk. Many file servers use disk mirroring, which saves data to two different hard disks so if one crashes data can still be read from the other. However, since both hard disks use the same controller in this scheme it does not protect against a disk controller failure. Disk duplexing is a method that avoids this problem by using two hard disks and two disk controllers. In situations where the loss of a file server for even a few minutes causes a devastating problem, shadowing is used. Shadowing involves using duplicate file servers that are attached to the LAN and receive the same information. If one file server fails, the other takes over.

Database Server. A **database server** is a computer that stores a database on disk and makes the data accessible by multiple users. Specialized database software using "client/server" architecture makes the best use of a database server. The software is made up of two components: the client component and the server component. The client component runs on one or more of the LAN workstations where it provides an interface for users to request information or modify records in the database. The server component runs on a central machine where it stores and controls the data. Some of its activities include protecting the data; permitting multiple users to access data; updating and deleting records; and on multiple file server networks, communicating with other file servers.

Using client/server architecture reduces the amount of network traffic, provides faster response time, gives greater data security, and reduces costs because the workstation doesn't need to be as powerful. Also, since the database functions are separated into client and server functions, users can easily run a number of different "front ends" (customized spreadsheets, query languages, etc.), but can still retrieve data from a common database.

Print Server. A **print server** can be a computer and/or program that provides LAN users with access to a centralized printer or a shared printer of a workstation. A LAN user sends output to the print server where it is stored until it is printed.

Print servers use a **spool** (Simultaneous Peripheral Operation On Line), which is hardware, software, or a combination of both to control a buffer that holds data before it is sent to the printer. Most often the buffer is a hard disk on the print server. Here files are stored and placed in a **queue** in a first in, first out order until it's their turn to be printed. Most LANs give the user the option to change or assign specific priorities to print jobs so that they can move up or jump to the head of the queue. Print servers also have a chunk of RAM as a buffer that holds data while the printer and server communicate. This makes the printing process faster since the printer accesses data quickly from RAM rather than waiting while the disk is accessed.

With a print server users don't have to wait for a printer to be available before they send output. Print servers also help defray the cost of expensive printers, such as laser and high-speed printers, over many users. Additionally, fewer printers are able to satisfy more users, reducing the investment in hardware.

What happens when you print on a LAN? After you select the print command in the application, the print job is sent to the local printer port. The network software captures this output and redirects it to the network. The job is sent to the print server where software is ready to handle it. If no other job is being printed, the new job is printed immediately. However, if the printer is busy, the print job will be spooled (i.e., stored in a file on the hard disk of a print server), where it joins the queue waiting to be printed.

Communication Server. A **communication server** gives all nodes on a LAN access to its modems or RS-232-C connections. It provides links to external data networks and to corporate minicomputers and mainframes. The communication server translates packets on a LAN into asynchronous signals that are sent over telephone lines or used in RS-232-C serial communications. A **packet** is a unit of information transmitted as a whole from one device to another on a network.

Fax Server. A **fax server** is a personal computer or a self-contained unit that holds a fax board and the software that gives all users in the system access to it. This permits any user on the network to send a fax from his or her own workstation.

Connections

The hardware components of a LAN must all be physically connected. This is accomplished through the use of cabling and network interface cards. We'll also see how LANs can be connected to other networks by way of bridges and gateways.

Cabling. **Cable** is the medium used in most networks to connect devices. Running cables from desktop to desktop is usually the toughest installation job and often the most expensive part of installing a LAN. The costs include the cable itself as well as the expenses involved in pulling, connecting, and related tasks such as laying false floors or moving walls. Cable is also the largest source of network problems including troubleshooting, installation, and maintenance problems.

There are generally three options for cabling: twisted-pair, coaxial, and fiber optic. Twisted-pair cable is used in nationwide telephone systems and is found in almost every building. In offices where installing additional cable is a problem, existing phone lines can be used to connect the LAN. In many offices the phone lines have excess capacity in the form of unconnected wires bundled with those that carry voice. This is often done in anticipation of future needs. Even if excess capacity is not available, twisted-pair cable is cheap and easy to install and may still be a good option. The distance between computers is limited to about 300 feet using twisted-pair compared to about 2,000 feet with coaxial cable. However, twisted-pair is lighter, thinner, and more flexible than coaxial or fiber-optic cables. Twisted-pair is ideal for offices or work groups without heavy use or electromagnetic interference.

Coaxial cable has a high bandwidth, which means it is capable of transmitting many signals at the same time over numerous channels. Each channel has its own frequency so that it does not interfere with other signals, allowing high-speed networking. Coaxial cable is not particularly susceptible to interference and can carry signals over long distances. It handles video, voice, and data transmissions.

Fiber-optic cable has the largest bandwidth, is immune to electromagnetic interference, sends data over large distances, and carries voice, video, and data. It is ideal for networks with heavy use installed in rough environments.

A few networks implement wireless technologies such as infrared and microwave radio signals that are transmitted through the air. This type of network can be used to cross highways or rivers where cable is inappropriate. They are generally more expensive and less reliable than cable alternatives.

Hewlett-Packard and other companies, including Intel and Zenith, are working on a wireless high-speed communications standard—infrared beams. Use of these beams would allow computers and printers to communicate without cables. This plan, known as Serial Infrared (SIR), sends data at 115,000 bits per second.

The SIR system, as it is known, converts the computer language of 1s and 0s into electromagnetic analog waves and sends them via infrared beams to other devices that are equipped to receive the signals. The receiver then converts the analog signal back into digital form for successful communication.

The devices must be in close proximity and there should be no obstruction to the infrared beam's light path. Now, downloading files from a portable computer to your desktop or sending them to the printer will become much easier.

Network Interface Cards. A **network interface card** is a circuit board that fits inside an expansion slot of a workstation and makes the physical connection to the LAN cable. Its function is moving data both from the workstation to the network and from the network to the workstation.

Bridges and Gateways. A **bridge** is an interface that connects different LANs, allowing communication between devices on each. A bridge simply passes packets back and forth between two networks regardless of the protocols of the individual networks. **Protocol** is the set of rules that enables computers to connect with one another and to exchange data with as few errors as possible. Since a bridge does no translation, the computers on each network must use the same protocol.

Using bridges permits the creation of numerous small, manageable networks that can be connected together to form a larger network, which may be preferable to creating one large, unwieldy network. This approach reduces traffic for individual computers and improves the performance of the network. It also enables a change from one type of cable to another.

A **gateway** is an interface that converts the protocol of one network into a form usable by another network or computer. LANs can be connected to WANs or other minicomputers and mainframes in the organization through the use of gateways.

Network Operating System

Just as stand-alone PCs have operating systems, so do LANs. A **network operating system** is the software that controls the operations and functions of a LAN.

A LAN operating system has numerous functions, including tying the network hardware and software components together; moving data around the network; redirecting data to the appropriate network resource; enabling resource sharing; managing the transfer and updating of shared files; providing security for the LAN by enabling file and record locking; providing passwords and access privileges for each user, and other security features; and performing administrative tasks such as adding, changing, and removing users, computers, and peripherals from the LAN. Many offer internetworking support that ties networks together as well as troubleshooting tools that tell LAN managers what is happening on the network. Popular LAN operating systems include Novell NetWare, 3Com3+Plus, and Banyan VINES.

A network operating system is usually divided into two parts: workstation software and server software. The workstation portion puts the PC or terminal on the network redirecting data over the network when needed. Every workstation must run the software that redirects data because all the workstations put data onto the network. The server portion is responsible for making disks, software, and ports available to other workstations on the network. Only those computers that share their resources need to run the server portion.

You can think of the software on a LAN in terms of layers. The top layer contains application software available to all users such as WordPerfect, Lotus 1-2-3, and dBASE. The next layer is the network operating system such as Novell's NetWare. Next is the host operating system such as DOS, OS/2, or Unix. At the next layer you'll find the link control software. It includes the network transport system that determines how data are put into packets and transmitted. At the core is the media access portion, which is the data path that joins the network hardware together by sensing signals and directing traffic.

Objective 8.4   Define topology and describe three commonly used topologies.

What Are LAN Topologies?

Each network has a particular **topology,** or cabling scheme. The topology does not necessarily describe the placement of workstations and other LAN components but it does describe the arrangement of the cables. Three common topologies are bus, star, and ring topologies.

LAN Topologies

- Bus
- Star
- Ring

Bus Network

A **bus network** is a one-cable topology in which all workstations are connected to a single cable that is terminated at each end (Figure 8.1). A workstation passes information down both directions of the cable to every other node in the network, although only the node that the message is addressed to is supposed to read it. All workstations hear all transmissions on the cable, but select those messages addressed to that particular workstation. A bottleneck may occur if several nodes transmit data simultaneously. Failure anywhere in the line causes all communications to fail. The bus is the simplest and the most commonly used topology. It uses small amounts of cable and components are easily added. This topology works well in situations where all the workstations are relatively close to one another and are not moved very often.

FIGURE 8.1
A bus network.

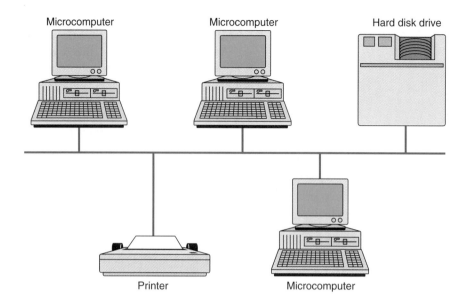

Star Network

In a **star network** each workstation is connected to a single computer location called the hub (the server) using a separate cable (Figure 8.2). The hub computer is usually the only one attached to resources shared by the network and all traffic passes through it. The design of a star network is easy to modify and troubleshooting can be conducted from a central point (the hub). A star network requires a great deal of cable, which increases its expense, and if the hub fails, so does the entire network.

Ring Network

A **ring network** is a closed loop of cable. Each workstation is connected to two other workstations, one that precedes it and one that succeeds it, forming a loop or ring (Figure 8.3). Data are sent from workstation to workstation around the ring in the same direction, passing through workstations until it reaches its destination. Each workstation acts as a repeater, resending the message to the next workstation. The response time of a ring is determined by the number of workstations, i.e., the more workstations, the slower the LAN. Network control is distributed; however, loss of one workstation could disable the entire network. Many ring networks have ways of getting around this drawback by having another workstation take control or physically removing the disabled workstation from the network. The ring topology requires less cable, which reduces costs.

Objective 8.5   Identify and describe the three major architectures used for LANs.

FIGURE 8.2
A star network.

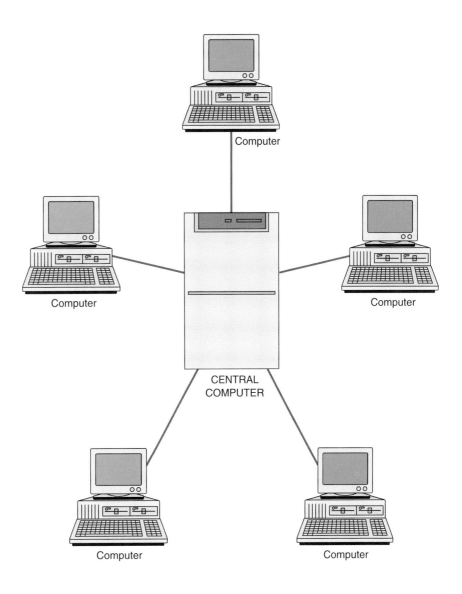

What Are Network Architectures?

Network architecture refers to the structure of the network, i.e., how the components of the system are connected and the protocols and interfaces used for communication and cooperation among the components. There are three major architectures for LANs: Ethernet, ARCnet, and Token Ring.

Ethernet

Ethernet was developed at Xerox's Palo Alto Research Center with the participation of DEC and Intel and has become a network standard. It is one of the most popular LANs in use. It uses a carrier sense multiple access with collision detection (CSMA/CD) access method (protocol). (Access methods are described in the next section.) Ethernet provides access to the network

Network Architectures

- Ethernet
- ARCnet
- Token Ring

FIGURE 8.3
A ring network.

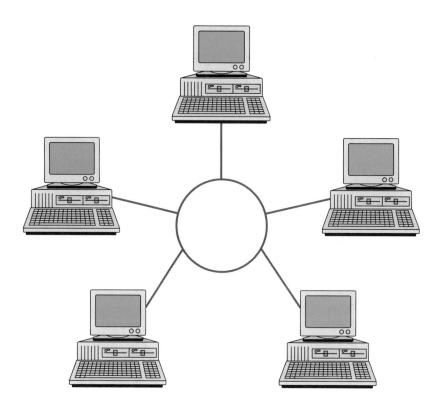

on a transmit-at-will basis. If two transmissions collide, they wait and try again until they get through. Ethernet uses either coaxial cable for a bus topology or unshielded twisted-pair wiring for a star topology. Ethernet permits larger networks to be set up and transmits data faster than other network architectures.

ARCnet

ARCnet was developed by Datapoint Corp. in the early 1970s and derives its name from *A*ttached *R*esource *C*omputer *Net*work. It was one of the earliest networks to be used and experienced a great deal of popularity. ARCnet provides ease of installation and use, and is well documented. It uses a multistar topology in which the hubs of each star are usually connected to form a bus. Having several hubs makes troubleshooting a large network easier. ARCnet uses a token-passing access method (protocol). It primarily uses coaxial cable but some vendors offer twisted-pair as well. ARCnet interface cards are manufactured by many vendors.

Token Ring

The **Token Ring** architecture was introduced by IBM in 1985. It is based on a ring topology forming a closed ring with a number of multistation access units (MSAU) (wiring concentrators) attached to it. Each MSAU supports up to eight workstations in a star-shaped cluster. This architecture is designed to support microcomputers, minicomputers, and mainframes. It uses a token-passing access method and shielded and unshielded twisted-pair cable.

Objective 8.6   Understand the purpose of a carrier access method and describe two common access methods used for LANs.

What Are Carrier Access Methods?

Carrier Access Method
■ Token passing ■ Carrier sense multiple access with collision detection (CSMA/CD)

A **carrier access method** is the protocol, or set of rules, for communicating between computers. The rules govern format, timing, sequencing, and error control. These rules are needed for a computer to make sense of an incoming stream of bits. The access method is how a LAN governs the user's physical (electrical) access to the cable, determining which workstation will be the next to use the LAN. The access method significantly affects the features and performance of the LAN. Two common access methods are token passing and carrier sense multiple access with collision detection (CSMA/CD).

Token Passing

The **token passing** access method uses a special signal called a token, which is passed from station to station around the network. A **token** is a unique combination of bits. Only the station with the token has the right to transmit information. If a workstation receives a token but has no information to transmit, it passes the token on to the next workstation in line. If it has information to transmit the work station seizes the token, marks it as being in use, and attaches the information to it. The marked token is then passed around the network until it reaches its destination, where the information is copied and the token is returned to the sender. The sender removes the attached message and sends the token to the next workstation in line. Since each workstation must wait for the token before transmitting data on the network, collisions caused by transmitting at the same time are avoided.

Carrier Sense Multiple Access with Collision Detection

Using the **carrier sense multiple access with collision detection (CSMA/CD)** access method a workstation transmits data across the entire network. The data are sent as a packet (a unit of information). Only the workstation that the packet is addressed to receives it. Workstations attempt to sense if the network is free before they transmit. If it is not, a collision occurs and only one workstation transmits. The other workstation waits a specified period of time and tries again.

Objective 8.7   Describe several ways in which applications react to a LAN.

What Are LAN Applications?

Applications react differently to a LAN depending on how they were designed. Applications are said to be either LAN ignorant, LAN aware, or LAN intrinsic. **LAN ignorant software** is software designed for stand-alone use. It has no concurrency controls built in so that multiple users can access and update a file at the same time without overwriting the work of other users. A LAN can use the software designed for single-user computers but that software does not take full advantage of the LAN. Single-user software will suffice if you are using the LAN only to share printers and disk drives. Single-user programs by design and by license can be used only by one user at a time.

LAN aware software generally refers to stand-alone programs that have been modified to work on a LAN. They allow multiuser access to applications and files and take better advantage of the peripherals attached to the network. Concurrency controls such as file and record locking are built into the programs, and communication features such as electronic mail are available.

LAN intrinsic software refers to programs designed to share the processing power of several computers, distributing data and computer power across the network. Although there are few LAN intrinsic applications currently available, a database server using a client/server program is an example.

LAN specific software is software that requires a LAN to operate effectively. E-mail and groupware fall into this category. E-mail software sends messages from one user to another instantaneously on the network and was discussed in the Infomodule for Chapter 7. **Groupware** is a broad class of software that allows members of a group of users to work together without all the participants having to be in the same place or available at the same time, for example, several users working to perfect a document. Popular groupware applications include scheduling, document processing, time management, and conferencing.

Objective 8.8   State the purpose of LAN management software and identify several functions that it performs.

What Is LAN Management Software?

LAN management software is used to monitor and diagnose every aspect of a LAN. It includes management functions such as security, performance, accounting (audit trail), fault, configuration, and file and directory.

Security management involves restricting access, recording user activities, auditing data, creating passwords and access codes, and encrypting files.

Performance management entails monitoring network capacity and loading: identifying which applications are being used, how long they are being used, and from which workstation they are being used.

Accounting (audit trail) management covers reporting and allocating the cost of the network to specific network users. An audit trail keeps track of what goes on in the network, who uses what resources at what time, and so on.

Fault management involves troubleshooting, finding, reporting, and correcting failing equipment on the network.

Configuration management includes network installation, booting, and tracking hardware/software configurations.

File and directory management allows you to utilize, change, and manipulate everything stored on the hard disk of the LAN. It also provides

Wouldn't it be exciting if you didn't have to use a keyboard or mouse to input data? What if your thought waves could control the computer?

Japanese researchers from Fujitsu, Ltd. and Hokkaido University are investigating the possibility of "silent speech." They have discovered that the brain sends electrical signals prior to taking action and the voltage from these signals can be measured. By fitting subjects with electrodes, elementary tests are being conducted to determine whether the brain waves indicating "yes" or "no" can be distinguished.

In this country, studies are under way at the Albany, New York, Department of Health to discover if subjects are able to move a cursor on a computer screen by merely emitting brain waves. A mind-controlled typewriter at the University of Illinois is being studied by psychologists. Subjects try to "type" their message by spelling the word (very slowly) in their mind.

Users who are not adept at keyboarding should still keep practicing their typing drills, because this interface is probably decades into the future.

backup utilities. Backup is one of the most important management activities that can be done on a LAN. No matter the type or price of the hardware and software you are using, problems still arise through mechanical failures or more likely human error. You can back up the LAN to disk or tape, but floppy diskettes are not very practical. Many LANs have redundant file servers so if something happens to one the other can take over without any loss of data. However, this is an expensive option. Removable hard disks are also used for backup because they are inexpensive and convenient. Rewritable optical disks with large capacities and durability are also being used; however, they are expensive. Backups only work if you perform them regularly. Files that change should be backed up every day.

Objective 8.9   Discuss the steps involved in using a typical LAN.

What Is It Like to Work on a LAN?

Using a LAN is different from using a stand-alone computer. You depend on equipment that is not on your desktop. You have no control over the version of software or the type of peripheral devices that are available on the LAN. You must learn and remember your access code and password, recall where files and data are stored on the LAN, and remember how to direct your output to the desired printer. In most organizations you'll also be required to learn the E-mail application so that you can communicate with your coworkers effectively. If you are involved in a work group in which several individuals work on the same file simultaneously, you may be required to learn the appropriate groupware applications.

Working on a LAN is not difficult. Typically, the first thing you see on the screen when you turn the computer on is a LAN sign. You enter the access code and a password to gain entry to the LAN. Once approved, you generally find a menu screen that presents a number of options. For example, one LAN offers the following menu options: Software, Tackboard, Fax assist, DOS commands, LAN commands, E-mail, Communication, Personal menu, Telephone directory, and Exit to DOS.

Software provides entry to applications such as WordPerfect and Lotus 1-2-3 that are available on the LAN. Tackboard accesses several bulletin boards including employee information and employee bulletin board. Fax assist permits users to fax directly from their workstation. LAN commands access the LAN commands available to the user such as e-mail, printer functions, file sharing, password update, communications with other computers, send messages, chat with user, list logged in users, address book, select printer, select drive, and change password. E-mail gives direct access to the e-mail application. Communication gives direct access to other computers such as departmental minicomputers and corporate mainframes. Personal menu allows users to customize a menu for applications that they select often. Telephone directory gives access to telephone listings for all employees of the organization. Exit to DOS allows you to quit your current LAN session. When you've finished with your current LAN session you select Exit to DOS and type logoff. Although menu options differ, this example gives you an idea of what you can expect.

Summary

A local area network (LAN) is a data communication network consisting of two or more computers directly linked within a relatively small, well-defined area, such as a room, building, or cluster of buildings.

A LAN allows you to share information, share computer resources, reduce hardware and software costs, avoid software compatibility problems, improve communication, improve user productivity, improve security, have flexibility to expand on an as-needed basis, and access a wide variety of information sources.

A typical LAN includes the following components: workstations, a server(s), the hardware to connect all the devices on the LAN, and the network operating system. A node is any device, such as a workstation or printer, that is connected to the LAN and is capable of communicating with other devices connected to the LAN. A workstation can be either a personal computer or a terminal attached to the LAN.

A server is simply a computer providing services to LAN users. It can be configured as a file server, database server, print server, communication server, or fax server. Depending on the load requirements of the LAN one server may take care of all these tasks or there may be a separate server for each.

Hardware components of a LAN are physically connected using cabling and network interface cards. LANs can be connected to other networks using bridges and gateways.

The network operating system is the software that allows all the components to work together.

A topology is the cabling scheme employed by a network. Three common topologies in LANs are bus, star, and ring topologies.

Network architecture refers to the structure of the network, how the components of the system are connected and the protocols and interfaces used for communication and cooperation among the components. There are three major architectures for LANs: Ethernet, ARCnet, and Token Ring.

A carrier access method is a protocol, or set of rules, for communicating between computers. Two common access methods are token passing and carrier sense multiple access with collision detection (CSMA/CD).

Applications react differently to a LAN depending on how they were designed. Applications are LAN ignorant, LAN aware, or LAN intrinsic. LAN specific software requires a LAN to operate effectively. E-mail and groupware are examples of LAN specific software.

LAN management software monitors and diagnoses every aspect of a LAN. It includes functions of management such as security, performance, accounting (audit trail), fault, configuration, and file and directory.

When choosing a LAN consider objectives and cost.

Using a LAN is not difficult. It requires you to memorize an access code and password. You must learn how to navigate through the LAN menus, use the options available, access LAN specific applications such as e-mail, print to LAN printers, and log off the LAN.

VOCABULARY SELF-TEST

Can you define the following terms?

ARCnet (p. 310)

bridge (p. 306)

bus network (p. 307)

cable (p. 305)

carrier access method (p. 311)

carrier sense multiple access with collision detection (CSMA/CD) (p. 311)

communication server (p. 304)

database server (p. 304)

dedicated server (p. 303)

Ethernet (p. 309)

fax server (p. 305)

file server (p. 303)

gateway (p. 306)

groupware (p. 312)

LAN aware software (p. 312)

LAN ignorant software (p. 311)

LAN intrinsic software (p. 312)

LAN management software (p. 312)

LAN specific software (p. 312)

local-area network (LAN) (p. 301)

network architecture (p. 309)

network interface card (p. 306)

network operating system (p. 306)

node (p. 302)

packet (p. 305)

peer-to-peer network (p. 303)

print server (p. 304)

protocol (p. 306)

queue (p. 304)

ring network (p. 308)

server (p. 302)

spool (p. 304)

star network (p. 308)

token (p. 311)

token passing (p. 311)

Token Ring (p. 310)

topology (p. 307)

virtual drive (p. 303)

workstation (p. 302)

Multiple Choice

1. Which of the following is the best option for sharing data, programs, and expensive peripheral devices between two or more personal computers?
   a. wide-area network
   b. multiuser computer
   c. gateway
   d. local-area network

2. Which of the following is not an advantage of using a LAN?
   a. improve communication
   b. share information
   c. eliminate security and data loss problems
   d. share computer resources

3. A _____ is a combination of hardware and software that allows LAN users to share computer programs and data.
   a. communication server
   b. print server
   c. database server
   d. file server

4. Print servers use a _____ , which is a buffer that holds data before it is sent to the printer.
   a. queue
   b. spool
   c. node
   d. packet

5. Which of the following cable choices has the largest bandwidth, is immune to electromagnetic interference, sends data over large distances, and carries voice, video, and data?
   a. fiber optic
   b. shielded twisted-pair
   c. unshielded twisted-pair
   d. coaxial

6. A _____ is a circuit board used to make the physical connection to the LAN cable.
   a. bridge
   b. protocol
   c. network interface card
   d. gateway

7. Which topology uses a single cable that is terminated at each end to which all workstations are connected?
   a. star network
   b. local-area network
   c. ring network
   d. bus network

8. Which of the network architectures uses a carrier sense multiple access with collision detection (CSMA/CD) access method?
   a. ARCnet
   b. Ethernet

    c. token passing

    d. Token Ring

9. A stand-alone program that has been modified to work on a LAN by including concurrency controls such as file and record locking is an example of _____ .

    a. LAN intrinsic software

    b. LAN aware software

    c. groupware

    d. LAN ignorant software

10. The _____ portion of LAN management software restricts access, records user activities and audits data, creates passwords and access codes, and encrypts files.

    a. configuration management

    b. security management

    c. performance management

    d. accounting management

Fill-In

1. A(n) _____ is either a personal computer or a terminal attached to the LAN.

2. Any computer that is attached to a LAN that provides services to the LAN users is known as a(n) _____ .

3. A(n) _____ is a drive, not physically attached to a user's workstation, which is accessed to link the workstation to a subdirectory on the file server's shared hard disk.

4. A computer and/or program that provides LAN users with access to a centralized printer or a printer shared with a workstation is called a(n) _____ .

5. A(n) _____ is a unit of information transmitted as a whole from one device to another on a network.

6. The software that controls the operations of a LAN enabling it to perform its functions is known as a(n) _____ .

7. A(n) _____ describes the arrangement of the cabling in a network.

8. _____ refers to the structure of the network, that is, how the components are connected, and the protocols and interfaces used for communication and cooperation among the components.

9. The unique combination of bits that is passed around a network from station to station that gives the right to transmit when it is received is called a(n) _____ .

10. _____ monitors and diagnoses every aspect of a LAN.

Short Answer

1. Define a local-area network and state some of the benefits of using one.

2. Differentiate between a dedicated file server network and a peer-to-peer network.

3. Describe the functions of a communication server and a fax server.

4. State the medium used to connect devices in most networks and describe three options for that medium.

5. What is the difference between a bridge and a gateway?
6. Describe several functions of a network operating system.
7. Define topology and describe three common topologies used with LANs.
8. Define network architecture and describe the three major architectures used for LANs.
9. State the purpose of a carrier access method and describe two common carrier access methods used with LANs.
10. Describe how the design of an application affects the way it reacts to a LAN.

Issues for Thought

1. LANs allow users to easily send messages to coworkers through e-mail. They also make it easy for management to secretly monitor and read messages sent between employees. While not illegal, do you think this is ethical? Does management have a right to know how its employees are using their time and equipment provided by the company? If personal information is discovered in an e-mail message, such as an admittance to a coworker of a dependency problem, should management be able to use this information?
2. In many organizations LANs tie into departmental minicomputers and corporate mainframes. This can increase the chances of unauthorized users gaining access to sensitive corporate and personal data. What should an organization do to minimize unauthorized access? If appropriate measures were taken to attempt to avoid unauthorized access, what should the responsibility of the organization be to the individual(s) whose personal data had been compromised?

Infomodule Microcomputer Communications

In the past when a buyer purchased a microcomputer system, modems and associated communication software were luxuries or extras. Today, alongside spreadsheets, databases, and word processors, communication software is becoming important to a complete system. This Infomodule examines communication software for microcomputers.

WHAT IS COMMUNICATION SOFTWARE?

Communication software is a program designed to control communication between two computers. Communication software:

- Establishes and maintains communication with another computer.
- Tells the computer how to send data (i.e., sets the communication parameters).
- Directs outgoing data from the keyboard or disks through the communication port and into a modem, and directs incoming data from the communication port to the screen or disk.

There are many communication programs with a wide variety of options. Popular microcomputer communication software includes Crosstalk, PC-Talk, and Smartcom. No matter how sophisticated or how basic the program, it must be able to set essential communication parameters. These parameters are discussed later in this Infomodule.

HOW DOES COMMUNICATION SOFTWARE AFFECT OUR ACCESS TO INFORMATION?

Because of its ability to communicate and share data with other computers, the microcomputer has become an important tool for research, data gathering, and information exchange.

Purposes of Communication Software

- **Establish and maintain communication with another computer**
- **Set the communication parameters**
- **Direct outgoing and incoming data**

Much of our society revolves around the acquisition, manipulation, and use of information. The traditional approach to gathering information meant hours of research to find the appropriate sources, and then more time to pore over the vast amounts of data to extract pertinent material. Today, however, many commercial on-line services have large databases that provide data, in a fraction of the time needed for manual research. Databases are available for practically any topic—medicine, science, finance, weather, sports, and so on. Communication software establishes the necessary link between a microcomputer and the computers that contain all this information in their databases.

In addition to providing information, services such as shopping and banking can be accomplished using communication software. It allows you to follow your favorite stock through many of the financial services found on-line.

Communication software lets you keep in touch and exchange ideas with other professionals or with users of the same type of computer equipment through bulletin boards and electronic mail. (See the Chapter 7 Infomodule for more information on bulletin boards and electronic mail.) Exchanging files from computer to computer means that information can be sent and retrieved in seconds or minutes instead of days.

Telecommuting, which allows your computer at home to access and process information from the computer at your workplace, has offered an alternative work style for many.

WHY "CONFIGURE" COMMUNICATION SOFTWARE?

Computers communicate following much the same logical sequences as people making a telephone call. First, someone initiates the call; second, the call must be received and answered. Once the connection is made, conversation must take place in the same language for the information exchange to be meaningful, whether between two people or two computers. If you do not understand what the other person has said, the message can be repeated. Similarly, the computer can acknowledge an error in transmission and retransmit. Finally, when all is said and done, the communication link is broken by hanging up.

In most cases, the computer doing the calling is responsible for matching the characteristics of the computer receiving the call. For communication software to work it must be "in sync" with your hardware and the computer system with which you are trying to communicate. Configuring communication software involves setting **communication parameters** that synchronize it with your hardware and that of the **host computer**—the computer with which you want to communicate.

To set the necessary parameters, access the setup screen for the program. This screen varies from program to program. Most offer some type of help function to guide in setting the parameters. Some that must be set include: COM port, transmission speeds, parity, word size and stop bit, emulation, duplex, and mode.

COM Port

The COM port is the location where data will be coming into and going out of your computer. This parameter must match the COM port on your computer. A computer typically has one to four COM ports. Depending on the available port this parameter is set to 1, 2, 3, or 4. You need to tell the communications software which COM port is to be used.

Transmission Speeds

You need to set the transmission speed to define how fast your modem will transmit or receive data. Hardware and software must agree on the transmission speed, which is measured in baud rates. The **baud rate** is the number of times per second that the signal being transmitted changes (modulates or demodulates). Typical baud rates used by most modems are 300, 1200, 2400, and 9600. The higher the baud rate, the faster the transmission of data. The baud rates of the modem for the two communicating computers must match.

Parity, Word Size, and Stop Bit

The parity, word size, and stop bit settings refer to how individual bytes of data are interpreted. These settings must be agreed upon by the sending and receiving parties.

Parity. **Parity** is a type of error-checking procedure used in communications. The **parity bit** checks for transmission errors. Three parity-checking options are generally used with microcomputer communication: even, odd, or none. In even parity the number of 1s in each set of bits that were successfully transmitted must be even. In odd parity the number of 1s in each set of bits that were successfully transmitted must be odd. When none is selected no parity bit is used. Parity settings are usually indicated by typing E for even parity, O for odd parity, and N for no parity.

The computer receiving the data adds all the "one" bits to see if they total an odd or even number. If the parity setting is odd and the bit total is odd, or the setting is even and the bit total is even, the computer assumes the data were sent correctly. If the parity setting is odd and the bit total is even, or the setting is even and the bit total is odd, the computer is alerted that an error in data transmission has occurred. Many programs allow the user to choose how a parity error is handled. For example, the user may set the program to signal that an error has occurred or to ignore the error.

Parity checking is an elementary form of error checking. It cannot detect errors such as the loss of an entire character or larger block of data. For successful communication, both sending and receiving, computers must use the same setting.

Word Size. The **word size** refers to the number of data bits that make up a character. In microcomputer communication, characters are made up of either seven or eight bits. There must be agreement between the sending and receiving computers on the word size.

Stop Bit. Each word contains one or two **stop bits,** which allow the receiving terminal to synchronize itself with the transmitting terminal on a word-by-word basis. Most systems use one stop bit for speeds of 300 baud and above. Two stop bits are generally used for 110 baud.

Emulation

The emulation parameter sets the type of terminal your communication software will emulate. If the computer you are calling uses cursor positioning and clear screen codes for a particular type of terminal, you will need to use this setting. Typically this parameter is used if you want your personal computer to act as a terminal for a minicomputer or mainframe. This parameter is set to "none" for most commercial on-line services. Typical terminals that can be emulated are Televideo 910/920, IBM 3101, ADDS Viewpoint, DEC VT-52, DEC VT-100, and the TI-940. For example, if the host is a Digital Equipment Corporation (DEC) VAX system, it may expect to see a DEC VT-100 terminal. In the terminal emulation mode, your microcomputer can be configured to appear to the host as a DEC VT-100 terminal.

Duplex

The duplex parameter is set to either full, which turns local echo off, or half, which turns local echo on. In full duplex mode there is simultaneous two-

way communication between the participating computers. If a host computer is echoing the data you type, this parameter is set to full. If you are typing and do not see anything on your screen the host computer is not echoing the data and this parameter should be set to half. Most dial-up computer systems require that the duplex be set to full. Typically, communication software will default to full duplex when in a call mode and half duplex when in an answer mode.

Mode

The mode parameter tells your communication software whether it will be making a call or answering a call. You select the call mode to make a call to another computer and the answer mode to answer a call from another computer.

HOW DO I MAKE THE CONNECTION?

Now let's find out how computers talk to each other using communication software.

To accomplish the transfer of data, both the transmitting computer and the receiving computer must have a modem. The modem converts analog signals to digital signals, and digital signals back to analog signals, so that communication can take place between the computers. As noted, two computers must speak the same language to successfully complete a communication link. Once the communication parameters are set, the link can be established.

Communication Parameters

- **COM port**
- **Transmission speeds**
- **Parity, word size, and stop bit**
- **Emulation**
- **Duplex**
- **Mode**

Log On and Log Off Procedures

When you connect to another computer system you'll hear a screech from your modem. This indicates that your modem is about to "shake hands" with the host modem. During this hand-shaking procedure the modems exchange information about what parameters, among other things, they are using to ensure that they are in synch.

Once a connection is made you typically **log on** (also called login or sign in) usually by entering an access code and password. Most programs let you automate the log-on procedure using a script. A **script** is a file your communication program uses to automatically type in information such as your log-on procedure. This saves time and long distance telephone charges since procedures like log on can be performed quickly, reducing the time you spend on the call. When you are done, you need to **log off** or disconnect from the host computer. This is typically done by typing log off, quit, or bye.

Command Mode

Most communication programs have at least two modes, a command mode and a data transfer (or conversation) mode. In the **command mode,** whatever is typed at the keyboard is interpreted as a command. These commands vary among programs.

Data-Transfer Mode

In the **data-transfer mode,** communication actually occurs. Most programs automatically switch between the command and data transfer modes without disconnecting the communication link. The mode-switching feature allows you to temporarily leave the data-transfer mode and enter the command mode (for example, to display a disk directory, delete a file, or activate a printer), and then to reenter the data-transfer mode. To transfer data, however, one computer initiates the call and the other computer receives it. The computer that initiates the call must be in the "call" mode so that settings like entering the phone number and typing the command to initiate the dialing process are made. To complete the connection, the receiving computer must be turned on and ready to receive the call. To receive a call, the computer must be in the "answer" mode, in which it is alerted to watch for an incoming signal from the modem.

Automatic Dialing

Automatic dialing dials the phone number of another computer, using information stored in a directory. A directory can contain names, telephone numbers, and communication parameters. It can also hold the log-on sequence, which is the series of keystrokes, account numbers, and passwords needed to access a computer or on-line service. With one or more keystrokes, the program automatically dials and connects to the specified computer, using the information stored in the directory. If a particular communication session is described only once and saved it can be easily accessed over and over again.

Programs differ in the amount of space available for each directory entry and for the total number of directory entries. Some provide enough space for access numbers, account numbers, and passwords. In addition, they permit programming the function keys to enter a particular log-on sequence automatically. Many communication programs furnish the log-on sequences for some of the popular commercial on-line services already programmed. You simply supply the account number and password to the file to make it usable.

Autoanswer

When the computer is on, the **autoanswer** feature, in conjunction with the appropriate modem, automatically answers calls from other computers. It creates a bulletin board file and receives electronic mail even when the user is not present.

Automatic Message Transfer

The **automatic message transfer** feature dials a specified computer and leaves a message at a preset time.

Pacing Option

Sometimes the rate at which one computer sends data and the rate at which the other computer receives data are not the same. Also, some receiving computers require the transmitting computer to wait for a special prompt before sending data. These situations often occur in microcomputer-to-mainframe communications. The **pacing** feature allows you to determine a specified time to wait between sending instructions. It also instructs a program to wait for a specified character that prompts the transmitting computer to begin sending data.

WHAT IS DATA CAPTURE?

Data capture is the process of retrieving data from a remote computer and storing it in your computer's main memory or secondary storage. A **data buffer** is an area set aside in main memory to temporarily store data. Many communication programs provide a data buffer that allows you to capture data and review, search, and edit it before saving on a disk. Or, it gives the option of discarding the contents of the buffer without saving it. A data buffer conserves disk space by allowing you to select and save only useful data.

Data received after a disk is full may either be saved in a buffer or may be lost, depending on the program. Some communication programs provide a status indicator that tells how much buffer space is left. If this indicator is ignored, however, the buffer may become full and any data that overflows will be lost. With better programs, when the buffer becomes full, overflow data are automatically saved on a disk. Other programs issue a warning when the disk is full so that you can change disks or erase files from the current disk to make room. Data stored in the buffer are volatile. If the computer is turned off or data are erased before storing them on a disk, they are lost.

Another data-capturing capability in some programs is the option to send data directly to a printer as they are received. They also are usually displayed simultaneously on the screen. The printer must be able to print at the same rate that data are being sent, or the data will be lost. However, use of a buffer allows communication at higher baud rates than the printer would normally handle. Print spoolers (a type of buffer) allow data to be temporarily stored and sent to the printer at the proper rate.

WHAT IS FILE TRANSFER?

Communication programs allow transmission and reception of files between computers. This procedure is called uploading and downloading. **Uploading** occurs when data from a disk are sent to another computer, and **downloading** occurs when data are received from another computer and saved on disk. Almost all communication programs will upload and download data; otherwise, the program's usefulness would be very limited.

You can create a file on a disk before going on-line, and then upload it and send it from that disk. This procedure significantly reduces editing time spent on-line, thus lowering the cost of a communication session. Downloading lets you receive data on a disk; the data can then be read or edited off-line afterward. This process dramatically reduces the cost of using information services such as CompuServe and Prodigy where charges are based on actual on-line time.

Transferring a File

In addition to capturing data, communication software allows transfer of complete files from one computer to another. Entire files are not transferred at once, but in blocks. A **block** is a preset number of bytes transferred as a unit. For example, if the block size is 512 bytes, those 512 bytes sent by one computer must be received by the remote computer before the next block of data is sent. If there is an error, sending a file in blocks requires only the defective block to be resent, rather than the entire file. The block format is used for sending or requesting a file.

Transmitting a File.   When a file is sent from your computer to another, you are transmitting a file. A file may be transmitted between compatible computers—those using the same communication software—or may be transmitted between incompatible computers or systems using different communication software.

Transfer of files between dissimilar computers or computers with different software is usually much slower than between compatible computers and software. This can be caused by the systems operating at different speeds with different capabilities.

Requesting a File. In addition to transmitting a file, the caller may also request a file from the remote computer. The ability of the caller to initiate a file request eliminates the need for both computers to hang up and reestablish contact. Built-in safeguards usually prevent the caller from roaming freely in the remote computer's files.

Whether files are sent or received, they can be checked for errors using a communication protocol.

File-Transfer Protocols

File-transfer protocols are sets of rules that ensure error-free transfer of data. They are usually supplied as built-in options that can be selected as needed. Some programs let you define a specific protocol.

Both computers in the link must use the same protocol for data transfer to take place. Because some protocols employ extensive error-checking, their use can increase data-transfer time. Some common protocols offered by communication programs include XON/XOFF, Xmodem, Zmodem and Kermit.

The **XON/XOFF protocol** controls the transfer of text data. An XOFF signal tells the transmitting computer to stop sending data until it receives an XON signal to resume. In some programs, this protocol is invoked directly from the keyboard to stop data transmission temporarily. In others, it is automatic. This procedure prevents overflowing the data buffer.

The public-domain **Xmodem protocol** is widely used with microcomputers for sending and receiving nontext (binary) files between dissimilar systems. Files are sent in 128-byte blocks. If the protocol detects an error, the entire block is resent. If the block cannot be sent successfully, the Xmodem protocol terminates the transfer rather than send erroneous data. This termination warns that problems exist, either in the data or communication link. **Zmodem protocol** is an enhanced version of the Xmodem protocol that handles larger data transfers with less chance of error. One enhancement allows it to re-start an interrupted transmission at the point of interruption rather than at the beginning.

The **Kermit protocol,** developed at Columbia University, is popular for transferring information between microcomputers and mainframes. It allows file transfer among many different types of systems. Data are sent in variable-length packets normally up to 96 bytes long. Each packet is checked for transmission errors.

A flexible communication program allows both text and nontext files to be sent and offers several protocols. Often, a screen appears to show the file transfer in progress (Figure 1).

WHAT ARE SOME ADDITIONAL FEATURES?

Among other useful features often contained in a communication package is the ability to create macros, file protection, error handling, character stripping, break signals, and time on-line status.

Macros

If you use the communication program to call the same number, some programs allow you to create a macro file (sometimes called a command file). The macro stores the log-on sequence of commands,

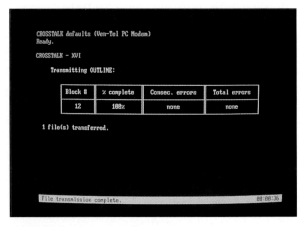

FIGURE 1
Crosstalk XVI transmitting screen.

such as the phone number and baud rate. You then call up only the command file, which performs the log-on sequence automatically.

Another type of macro is the script file, a group of commands written in the communication package's own programming language. Script files automate the sequence of activities once the communication link is established.

File Protection

A **password** feature lets you create passwords to protect files, dialing directories, and other portions of the communication program from unauthorized access. This feature is valuable if sensitive data are involved, or if several people access the communication program.

The **encryption** feature creates an unreadable version of a file before it is transmitted. A decrypt feature then recreates the readable version of an encrypted file after it is received. This feature ensures the confidentiality of a file as it is sent over communication lines.

Error Handling

There are many different ways a program can alert you to your own errors. The methods vary among programs, but a good program should indicate what the error is and, if possible, suggest steps to recover from the error.

Character Stripping

This feature lets you inspect, change, or delete any character as it leaves or enters the computer. For example, if an incoming text file contains special control characters (for example, those used to format a document or control the printing) that are incompatible with your word processor, the program deletes those characters or changes them to compatible codes.

Break Signal

The **break signal** tells the receiving computer to stop or interrupt current operation without disconnecting the communication link. However, if the standard DOS break sequence (the Ctrl-Break sequence

on IBM PCs and compatibles) were used, the danger would be extremely high of terminating the communication program, the communication link, or both.

Time On-Line Status

Some programs monitor and display the time spent on-line during a communication session. This helps you budget the cost incurred for each communication session.

VOCABULARY SELF-TEST

Can you define the following terms?

autoanswer (p. 322)

automatic dialing (p. 322)

automatic message transfer (p. 322)

baud rate (p. 320)

block (p. 323)

break signal (p. 325)

command mode (p. 322)

communication software (p. 319)

communication parameters (p. 320)

data buffer (p. 323)

data capture (p. 323)

data-transfer mode (p. 322)

downloading (p. 323)

encryption (p. 325)

file-transfer protocols (p. 324)

host computer (p. 320)

Kermit protocol (p. 324)

log off (p. 322)

log on (p. 322)

pacing (p. 323)

parity (p. 320)

parity bit (p. 320)

password (p. 325)

script (p. 322)

stop bit (p. 321)

REVIEW QUESTIONS

Multiple Choice

1. Which of the following is not a function of communication software?
   a. Directs incoming and outgoing data
   b. Establishes communications
   c. Corrects errors in incoming data
   d. Sets communication parameters
2. Which of the following parameters determines the rate at which the modem operates?
   a. emulation
   b. parity
   c. baud rate
   d. duplex
3. Sending a file from your computer to a host computer is called _____ .
   a. uploading
   b. downloading
   c. capturing
   d. pacing
4. To ensure error-free transfer of data between two computers, the proper _____ must be set.
   a. voltage
   b. spooler
   c. protocol
   d. break signal
5. If you wanted to transmit private data in unreadable form so that unauthorized people could not use it, you would use the _____ feature.
   a. validation
   b. password
   c. encryption
   d. verification

Fill-In

1. The _____ is the number of times per second that a signal being transmitted changes (modulates or demodulates).
2. The _____ is the mode in which anything typed at the keyboard is interpreted as a command.
3. A computer that is watching the modem for a signal is in the _____ mode.
4. The caller has the option of two file-transfer functions—to send or _____ a file, and to ask for or _____ a file.
5. The sets of rules for the transfer of data are called _____ .

Short Answer

1. What is the purpose of a communication package?
2. List the basic parameters that a communication program establishes.
3. Describe the function of the parity bit and list three parity-checking options commonly available for microcomputer communication.
4. What does it mean to log on and log off?
5. What is the purpose of transferring a file in blocks?

OBJECTIVES

9.1 Define the term information system.

9.2 Understand the importance of learning about how information systems are used and developed.

9.3 Describe the different levels of management and the types of information each needs.

9.4 Describe the basic types of information systems and explain their uses.

9.5 Describe the four major phases of the SDLC and discuss the importance of each.

9.6 Define prototype information system and describe its effect on the SDLC.

9.7 Describe the purpose of computer-aided systems engineering (CASE) software.

9.8 Define end-user computing and summarize its effect on an organization.

Chapter 9

Information Systems and the System Development Life Cycle

Profile

Grace Murray Hopper

Most retirees stay retired. But not Grace Murray Hopper.

In 1966, the U.S. Navy suggested that Commander Hopper was ready for retirement at the age of 60. Although the Navy at first thought she was too old, within seven months she was recalled to duty in the Reserves. Rear Admiral Hopper's second retirement, from the Naval Data Automation Command in 1986, led to her employment at Digital Equipment Corporation as a senior consultant.

Hopper, born in New York City, came to the Navy by way of Vassar, having received her master's and doctorate degrees from Yale University. Hopper's work life spanned academics, business, and the military.

Admiral Hopper joined the U.S. Naval Reserve and earned her reputation with the computers of the 1940s, having worked on programming the Mark I, Howard Aiken's large-scale digital calculator. It was capable of doing six months of manual calculations in one day. Additionally she was instrumental in developing the programming language COBOL. Hopper also helped develop the program that translated other programs into machine language for the UNIVAC I. She was senior mathematician for Eckert-Mauchley Computer Corporation and system engineer and staff scientist in system programming at Sperry Corporation.

Most of Hopper's military service was spent keeping the Navy as current on the emerging computer technology as she could. The computers she was involved with were primarily nonweapon systems. The Data Processing Management Association chose Hopper as its first Computer Science "Man of the Year" in 1969. She was as proud of her service in the U.S. Navy.

During Hopper's lecture tours she could be counted on to stress the importance and the value of information to students and industry representatives. One phrase that Hopper never liked to hear anyone say was: "We've always done it that way."

Hopper's final retirement came with her death in 1992.

E very day, people buy goods and services from businesses. Who buys what? Why? How much does it cost to make? How much should it be sold for? How much inventory is left? The answers to these and many other questions produce enormous amounts of data for businesses.

By using computers, businesses can collect and store vast amounts of data. To turn data into useful information and to manage all of that information, successful businesses develop information systems. In this chapter you'll learn about the basic types of information systems and look at the system development life cycle. You'll also find out about prototyping and its effect on information system development, computer-aided systems engineering (CASE) software, and end-user computing.

Objective 9.1   Define the term information system.

What Is an Information System?

As you learned in Chapter 1 an **information system** is a set of people, data, procedures, hardware, and software that works together to achieve the common goal of information management. Information management includes gathering data; processing them into reliable, accurate, and usable information; and distributing the information in a timely fashion for use in decision making, problem solving, and control.

Objective 9.2   Understand the importance of learning about how information systems are used and developed.

Why Learn About Information Systems?

No matter what your career path, you will likely be responsible for identifying and solving problems, controlling people and procedures, and making decisions. Some decisions may be inconsequential, and others may have monumental impact on you and your organization. To ensure that the decisions you make are in the best interests of your organization, you must understand how to recognize, acquire, and manage the appropriate information.

Information systems have been a primary force in enabling people to collect, process, and manage information needed for problem solving, control, and decision making. They have become the foundation of most businesses. The ways in which information systems are used will profoundly affect the growth, productivity, and profitability of an organization. Thus, you must be aware of and understand how to use computers and information systems to their best advantage.

Businesses depend on information systems for productive operation. Because the success or failure of an information system can make or break a business, it must be carefully designed and developed. You may never develop an information system yourself, but because you operate the system, you will undoubtedly eventually work with system professionals in developing one. The more you know about how information systems are developed, the better you will be able to work with them in designing a system that will meet your needs.

Objective 9.3   Describe the different levels of management and the types of information each needs.

What Types of Information Do Managers Need?

In business, managers at all levels make decisions. Each level has its own needs for specific types of information to handle its problems. Before defining the different levels of management, this chapter describes what managers are and what they do.

The Roles of Managers

A **manager** is a person responsible for using available resources—people, materials/equipment, land, information, money—to achieve the goals of an organization. Managers are the key decision makers and problem solvers in organizations. In order to perform most efficiently and effectively, managers must receive the information they need in a timely manner.

Managers work toward goals through five major functions: (1) planning, (2) staffing, (3) organizing, (4) directing, and (5) controlling resources. Planning is the future-oriented process of developing courses of action to meet the short-term and long-term goals of an organization. Staffing is assembling and training personnel to achieve the goals. Organizing provides resources and a structure in which personnel are responsible and accountable for working toward the goals. Directing supplies leadership in supervising personnel. It works through communication and motivation. Controlling involves development of procedures to measure actual performance against goals and to make any adjustments necessary to ensure that the organization is moving toward its goals.

Management Levels and Information Needs

Management is divided into three basic levels: (1) strategic (top-level) managers, (2) tactical (middle-level) managers, and (3) operational (low-level) managers (Figure 9.1). Although all three levels of management work toward organizational goals and are involved to varying degrees in all five of the management functions, each level requires different types of information.

Strategic Managers. **Strategic (top-level) managers** make decisions involving the long-range, or strategic, goals of organizations. Of the five major management functions, top-level managers spend most of their time planning and organizing. They need summarized information that covers past and present operations as well as future projections. Information drawn from internal sources gives them broad views of the internal situations of their companies. Information drawn from external sources permits them to evaluate industry trends, world economic trends, government regulations, and other outside activities that influence the business health of corporations. A strategic manager such as the chief executive officer of an automotive company might be required to decide whether a new plant should be opened or a new sports car produced.

Tactical Managers. **Tactical (middle-level) managers** divide their time among all five functions of management. They are concerned with short-term, tactical decisions directed toward accomplishing the organizational

FIGURE 9.1
Levels of management, types of decision making, and information needs.

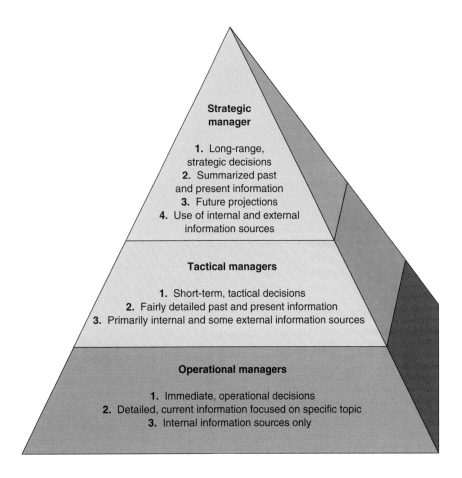

Strategic manager

1. Long-range, strategic decisions
2. Summarized past and present information
3. Future projections
4. Use of internal and external information sources

Tactical managers

1. Short-term, tactical decisions
2. Fairly detailed past and present information
3. Primarily internal and some external information sources

Operational managers

1. Immediate, operational decisions
2. Detailed, current information focused on specific topic
3. Internal information sources only

goals established by the top-level managers. Middle-level managers work on budgets, schedules, and performance evaluations and need information that is fairly detailed to permit them to compare present and past results and make adjustments where necessary. Middle-level managers require mainly internal information but also use some external information. A tactical manager for an automotive company might decide how long to advertise a new car on television in a particular state. Many organizations are using computerization to reduce the number of tactical managers and cut costs.

Operational Managers. **Operational (low-level) managers** are directly involved with the day-to-day operations of business. They are responsible for seeing that the tactical decisions of middle-level managers are implemented by personnel at the operations level. The information of operational managers must be detailed, current, and focused. It comes from such sources as inventory lists, historical records, and procedures manuals. An operational manager for an automotive company might decide to use a newer and less expensive method for cleaning paint-nozzle jets.

Objective 9.4   Describe the basic types of information systems and explain their uses.

What Are the Basic Types of Information Systems?

Several types of information systems exist to accommodate the differences in information needs of individuals in an organization. These include operational information systems, management information systems (MISs), decision support systems (DSSs), executive support systems (ESSs), expert systems, and office information systems. Each is described below.

Operational Information Systems

A **transaction** is a business activity or event. Transactions include buying a product such as a shirt at a department store or a service such as cable television from the local cable company. The information system that records and helps manage these transactions is known as an **operational information system,** or a **transaction processing system (TPS).** Certain transaction processing systems are commonly seen in business organizations: accounts payable, order entry, accounts receivable, inventory control, payroll, and general ledger. These systems are grouped into one broad category—accounting information systems.

Transaction processing systems provide information on past transactions. They perform routine record-keeping functions to provide information for operational management personnel who manage the day-to-day activities of an organization. A TPS performs several functions, including data collection, input validation, information processing, updating computer records, and output generation.

Management Information Systems

During the early days of computers in business, routine record keeping of an accounting nature was the only activity that a computer performed. Later, the realization that computers could be used for purposes other than simple transaction processing led to the introduction of management information systems.

The purpose of a **management information system (MIS)** is to provide information to managers for use in problem solving, control, and decision making. They are used for situations that recur and are highly structured where the information requirements are known in advance.

Often, a TPS feeds information to MISs. For example, an MIS can use the sales information gathered by an order entry TPS over several years to forecast the sales for the following year. The transaction processing system provides the actual sales performance, but the MIS furnishes the sales prediction. With the sales forecast, a manager attempts to detect and solve any problems regarding the purchase of materials, plant capacity, manpower requirements, and the like.

MISs are used in all areas of activity, including planning, marketing, finance, manufacturing, human resources, and project management. They are used primarily by tactical management. Tactical (middle) managers are concerned with short-term planning decisions directed toward accomplishing the organizational goals established by the strategic (top-level) managers. An MIS not only makes internal operations more efficient, but also extends its impact to external operations, such as customer and vendor relations, to make them more efficient and beneficial.

An MIS provides information in the form of management reports and on-line retrieval. Reports are hard-copy printouts containing information in a predetermined format, whereas on-line retrieval generates information as a result of inquiries from managers.

An MIS presents information to a user only in a predetermined form. It cannot provide any other views of the information or incorporate new information without being reprogrammed. To give users greater flexibility in entering, retrieving, and analyzing the data they need, decision support systems are used.

Decision Support Systems

A **decision support system (DSS)** is an interactive information system that helps users solve semistructured or unstructured management problems. An **interactive system** allows a user to communicate with a computer through dialogue. Unstructured problems are those without any clear-cut solutions, such as problems that do not repeat or problems that cannot be predicted in advance. Structured problems have well-known solutions and are repetitive, whereas semistructured problems fall between structured and unstructured problems.

DSSs contain a set of related programs and data to help with analysis and decision making in an organization. At a minimum, a DSS includes a database relating to the types of decisions being made, the capability to state problems and questions, and modeling software (e.g., a spreadsheet) that can test alternative solutions. More powerful modeling software such as Integrated Financial Planning System (IFPS) and graphics software are often included.

Although different levels of management benefit from decision support systems, they are used predominantly by tactical management for creating models to assist in analysis and decision making. A DSS can present several tentative solutions for one problem. It permits the user to enter, retrieve, and analyze data in an *ad hoc* manner. The user does not have to rely on the systems department to change the program, create new relationships among existing data, enter new data, or analyze the data in a new way. As a result, information is available almost immediately. A DSS does not make decisions for users, but it does support them in their decision making. The user first evaluates the solutions proposed by a DSS, then uses his/her judgment, intuition, and experience to reach a decision.

There are numerous DSS applications in business organizations. Some of the most important and widely used applications are in financial planning, manufacturing, mergers and acquisitions, new product development, plant expansions, and sales forecasting. In financial planning, banks use DSSs for budgeting and analyzing the impact of changes in money market rates, financial regulations, and interest rates. Manufacturing firms use DSSs to study the impact that different combinations of production processes, labor rates, and machine capacities have on production costs. DSSs are important in new product development to analyze the impact that different marketing strategies and competitive actions have on the success of a new product. In plant expansions, application of DSSs involves analyzing the effect of different expansion alternatives on cost and production. Sales forecasting incorporates DSSs to evaluate various estimates of the profit of a company being considered for acquisition.

Executive Support Systems

Executive is usually synonymous with strategic or top-level management. An executive has the responsibility of setting long-range planning goals and a strategic course for an organization for the years ahead. An information system that caters specifically to the special information needs of executives, such as managerial planning, monitoring, and analysis, is called an **executive support system (ESS).**

An ESS incorporates large volumes of data and information gathered from the external environment of an organization, i.e., from sources outside itself. That information is used in conjunction with the information generated by MISs within functional areas (e.g., marketing, accounting, production, etc.) of the organization to accommodate the specialized information needs of executives. An ESS plays a vital role in summarizing and controlling the volume of information that an executive must read. An executive assigns values to the various sources of information from which data for an ESS are drawn in order to place emphasis on sources deemed most important. Thus, ESSs can be tailored to meet the specific needs of each executive in an organization.

Expert Systems

An **expert system**, also called a knowledge-based system, is a type of application program used to make decisions or solve problems in a particular field. It uses knowledge and analytical rules defined by human experts in a field. It is called an expert system because it depends primarily on the knowledge of human experts. It functions like an expert in a discipline, solving problems that require knowledge, intelligence, and experience. Expert systems are a key part of many decision support and executive support systems.

The two major components of an expert system are a knowledge base and an inference engine. A **knowledge base** contains the accumulated body of knowledge of human experts in a particular field. The knowledge is a combination of data and rules to be applied to that data. The knowledge base is the most important component of an expert system. The performance of an expert system is a function of the size and quality of that knowledge base. The **inference engine** is the software that applies the rules from the knowledge base to the data provided by the user to draw a conclusion.

A number of commercial tools are available to build expert systems, making it unnecessary to create such systems from scratch. These tools are known in the industry as shells, or **expert system shells.** Most shells contain all of the components of an expert system except the knowledge base. Thus, buyers need to add only a knowledge base to create their own expert systems.

Many businesses have been using knowledge-based systems to provide quicker and easier problem detection as well as assistance in problem solving and decision making, thereby improving productivity and reducing the costs of operation. They are used in offices, hospitals, research laboratories of various types, industrial plants, manufacturing shops, repair shops, oil wells, and the like.

MYCIN is a landmark expert system used to diagnose infectious diseases and suggest possible therapies. The system was developed by Edward Feigenbaum and Edward Shortliffe, both of Stanford University. It has a knowledge base that contains expert knowledge about diagnoses. Each rule has a probability figure associated with it to indicate its level of certainty. MYCIN's performance is almost as good as that of physicians, an indication that this technology has practical business applications. EMYCIN, or essentially MYCIN, is an expert system shell; it is MYCIN without the knowledge base and is marketed as a shell to be used with other knowledge bases.

Office Information Systems

In the past 20 years computers have exerted a powerful effect on the office environment and the way in which offices operate. In fact, with the acceptance of computers and communication technology, the whole concept of office work and the business workplace changed in the 1970s and 1980s. Computers and communication technology made possible the concept of office information systems (OISs).

An **office information system (OIS)** helps knowledge workers manage the preparation, storage, retrieval, reproduction, and communication of information within and among business offices. A **knowledge worker** is a person who creates, processes, and distributes information. In the Information Age these activities are the predominant tasks of most business workers, making an office information system extremely important to the efficient management of information in today's business world. An OIS makes the production and flow of information more efficient, cheaper, and faster.

OISs incorporate a variety of technologies. Word processing is the most widely adopted of all the office technologies. Computer technology has also changed the way data are processed, stored, and retrieved in a business office. Computerized equipment automates and in many cases separates data-processing activities from general office activities. Most of a company's records are now stored electronically in separate data-processing departments. Some records need to be stored for many years; electronic media, such as tapes and disks, take up much less space than traditional file cabinets. OISs link data-processing departments electronically to other department offices, permitting secretaries, managers, executives, and others to access relevant data and information while remaining at their desks.

A business often needs to create duplicate images of documents for distribution to users who require that information. Several technologies that

Could a chocolate chip cookie be part of an information system monster? In the case of Mrs. Fields Cookies, the answer is a resounding "yes."

The reason behind the monstrous information system success story at Mrs. Fields was found in its standardized automated management systems. The system involved little user training and supplied consistency throughout the franchise stores. It worked well.

But Park City Group, formerly Fields Software Group, improved that good idea even further. In mid-1993 they promised a virtually paperless operation. Standard corporate forms are created and delivered to each franchise by means of electronic mail. Everyone gets the same information simultaneously. There are 25 software modules that can be mixed and matched. Time sheets, attendance records, production reports, and auditing forms are among those available. Inventory reports, profit and loss statements, and forecasting plans are all submitted between franchises and corporate headquarters in an expected format. Many of the forms that are created trigger updates to specific database files. Employees are not bogged down in paperwork, but are free to sell cookies—which, after all, is the point of their business. Park City wants other companies to try the paperless management system. It's appropriate for businesses with approximately 50 outlets. They say each outlet can obtain about a dozen modules for between $3,000 to $4,000.

When you ask, "What's cookin'?" at Mrs. Fields, you might be surprised at the answer.

work toward those ends are office copiers, scanners, and desktop publishing systems.

Some of today's copiers can be linked directly to a computer or LAN tying them in to an OIS network. Information can then be sent directly from a computer to a copier, where multiple documents can be printed without waiting for the computer system to print out the original. These devices are sometimes referred to as intelligent printers.

Many components of an office information system are concerned primarily with the communication of information. These include electronic mail, facsimile, telephone and voice messaging, electronic teleconferencing, and telecommuting. These technologies were discussed in the Infomodules for Chapters 7 and 8.

OISs also incorporate a number of applications that assist users to better organize many of their daily office activities. They typically include an electronic calendar and time manager, tickler files, and electronic scratchpad files. Such systems also include electronic mail, word processing, and document storage and retrieval. These applications increase individual efficiency by reducing reliance on telephones, standard mail, and written documents. OISs greatly reduce the time spent preparing, sending, and receiving information among individuals.

An office is not really fully automated until all electronic elements are joined. Office information systems link, or integrate, all of the equipment and people within and among offices so that they can communicate electronically, using all of the electronic data and hardware resources of an organization.

Objective 9.5   Describe the four major phases of the SDLC and discuss the importance of each.

What Is the System Development Life Cycle?

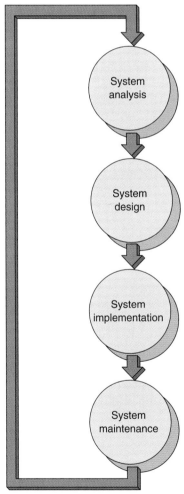

FIGURE 9.2
System development life cycle.

The **system development life cycle (SDLC)** is the structured sequence of operations required to conceive, develop, and make operational a new information system. The term *cycle* stresses that a newly designed system will not last forever; ultimately, it will need replacement, and the development cycle starts again. The cycle may begin in response to a problem in a current information system that is not performing well or in response to a new opportunity for which no information system currently exists. The system development life cycle can be broken into four major phases—(1) analysis, (2) design, (3) implementation, and (4) maintenance (Figure 9.2).

Developing an information system throughout the SDLC involves continual and clear communication among the users and system personnel—the professionals responsible for designing and implementing the information system.

A **user** is a person who will utilize an information system once it's been installed. Users include the operators who run computers and individuals who require information from the system. System personnel include system analysts, system designers, and programmers. A **system analyst** works with users to determine their information-processing needs. A **system designer** is a specialist who designs a system to fulfill the users' information needs. A **programmer** codes the instructions in a programming language for a computer to solve a problem. In large organizations, these positions are usually separate; however, in some cases, particularly in small companies, one person may do all or several of the tasks.

To make the communication process easier and more efficient, a project management team is often established. **Project management** is the structured coordination and monitoring of all activities involved in a one-time endeavor, or project. Three basic functions are required for the management of an information system project: (1) planning, (2) monitoring, and (3) resource control. During planning, detailed task lists are developed to specify timing, sequencing, and responsibilities. During monitoring, all project tasks are measured periodically to determine progress, in terms of both time and costs. During resource control, planned progress is compared with actual progress to determine whether to make resource or schedule adjustments. A project management team usually consists of a project manager and, depending on the size of the project, users, system analysts, programmers, and other specialists (Figure 9.3).

The role of user involvement cannot be overemphasized. Users are the ultimate consumers of an information system and must accept the system if it is to be successful. The best way to ensure this acceptance is close

FIGURE 9.3
A project management team composed of system personnel and users must agree on the nature and scope of a problem. (Courtesy of Honeywell, Inc.)

communication between the team and the users throughout the development process.

A project manager is responsible for planning and coordinating the tasks to be accomplished by a team. The project manager breaks a project down into small tasks that have specific end points. The manager assigns each task a time frame in which to be completed by specific team members. Then the manager monitors the tasks to ensure that they are on schedule.

Accurate and complete documentation throughout the cycle is important. **Documentation** is a written or graphic record of the steps carried out during the development of an information system. System personnel are responsible for accurately documenting each task they perform. Then a system librarian compiles the documentation, maintains it, and makes it available to other personnel. Keeping accurate and complete documentation is important for several reasons. First, many persons may be involved in the development of an information system, and many tasks rely on work already completed by other members of a development team. Documentation allows system personnel and management to review what was previously done and understand why it was done. A second reason is that many system development projects extend over a long period of time. During that time, there are generally personnel changes or additions to the team. New personnel can review documentation to understand what is going on and be able to contribute valuable ideas even in the middle of a project.

System Analysis

System analysis includes identifying a system problem or new opportunity, analyzing the current system in light of the problem or new opportunity, and justifying the development of a new system or modification of an

<table>
<tr><td>

System Analysis Stages

- Problem definition
- Requirements analysis
- Project justification

</td></tr>
</table>

old system to meet the needs of users. It can be divided into three stages: problem definition, requirements analysis, and project justification. Many of you will one day become part of management in an organization. Managers control the system analysis process and make the final decision of whether or not to proceed to the next phase of system design. Managers must understand what should take place during system analysis so that they are able to make sound decisions.

The system analysis phase is crucial in developing an information system that will satisfy the information needs of users. Users must work with system personnel to identify the true nature of a problem or opportunity and develop a system to provide the information required for solving that problem or maximizing that opportunity. If a problem or new opportunity is not correctly analyzed, the resulting information system may be useless or even detrimental to an organization.

Problem Definition.   The first stage in the system analysis phase is **problem definition.** System analysis is initiated with the recognition of a problem or new opportunity that the current information system cannot handle. A problem or new opportunity, however, does not always mean that the present system must be scrapped. It may simply mean that new features are needed or that currently no system exists to perform the functions needed. The initiation of a new system or a major system modification is costly and time-consuming. During the problem definition stage, facts should be carefully gathered to determine the nature, scope, and seriousness of any alleged problem with an information system. A preliminary problem report is written by the system analyst and submitted to management. If management approves the report the next stage of system analysis is performed.

Requirements Analysis.   The second stage in the system analysis phase is **requirements analysis.** In this stage, a system analyst determines how the present information system performs, how the best possible system might perform, and what new system might bridge the gap between the two performance levels. A system analyst uses many graphic and tabular tools to describe a system, and typically interviews a number of information system users. An analyst might choose other methods to support the interviewing process. Among the more common techniques are surveys, document reviews, policy and procedure reviews, and direct observations.

The analyst consolidates the interviews and other material into a composite picture of the ideal information system for the user group. The composite portrait must, of course, be approved by key management personnel within the user group. Often compromises must be made. For example, although a top-of-the-line system would be very fast and have tight security, its cost might exceed the limits set by management. In such a case, a system analyst must identify alternative information systems to balance the needs of the users with the constraints of management and technology.

Project Justification.   The third and last stage of the system analysis phase is **project justification.** In this stage, an analyst systematically compares alternative information systems and decides which of them to propose to management. It is a critical stage because it ends with the approval or rejection by management. The project justification stage includes cost/benefit analyses of alternate systems, selection of the best system, preparation of a system study for submission to management, and management's final go or no-go decision.

Cost/benefit analysis is often referred to as a feasibility study. The objective of cost/benefit analysis is to compare the costs to the benefits of alternative new information systems and the current system to determine which information system to recommend to management.

A **system study** is an extensive report sent to management that is generally accompanied by a formal oral presentation. It incorporates the results of the previous steps to justify the recommendation of the system analyst.

At this point, management must decide whether or not to accept the analyst's recommendations. That decision is often referred to as the "go/no-go" decision because it determines whether or not the analyst is given authority to go ahead with designing a replacement information system. The project justification stage ends with the analyst continuing the SDLC, abandoning the project entirely, or polishing the project for another presentation to management at a future date.

System Design

<table>
<tr><td>

System Design Stages

■ Logical system design
■ Physical system design

</td></tr>
</table>

The **system design** phase includes the logical system design stage and the physical system design stage.

Logical System Design Stage. **Logical system design** shows the flow of data through an information system. It can be thought of as the information system blueprint. Much like an architect's blueprint, a logical system design is a series of charts, graphs, and data layouts. These describe the input documents that the information system will process and the precise way these documents will look; the computer records needed to store data generated by the input documents; output documents and reports required by users of the information system including how the output will look (format), who receives the output (distribution), and how often the output will be produced (frequency); and the sequence and method by which documents are input and used to update computer records and then to produce user-desired output documents and reports.

Logical design tasks must be carefully planned because the remaining stages in the SDLC are dependent on the logical design stage. Even the smallest error in this stage can be magnified throughout the cycle so that it becomes a major problem when the new system is implemented. In addition, design errors identified early in this stage can be corrected much quicker and at less expense than later.

Physical System Design Stage. The purpose of the **physical system design** stage is to convert the system blueprint into the specific hardware and computer programs that transform the logical design into a working information system. It is during this stage that acquisition of the hardware takes place.

The programs that make up the information system are also created during this stage. A typical business information system is comprised of hundreds of thousands of lines of program code. Each line represents a separate operation for the computer to perform. Many programmers are needed, and their efforts must be coordinated.

System Implementation

The **system implementation** phase of the SDLC includes testing, installation, and training steps. During this phase, an information system is transferred to the users, and managers must ensure that systems are thoroughly tested and as free from errors as possible to build confidence and acceptance in users. Frequently, managers must also budget the type and amount of training that information system users should have.

Testing Stage. In **testing,** a new information system is checked to ensure that all of its parts are correct. Testing is one of the most important activities in the development of an information system. Any system—whether a bridge, a piece of equipment, or an information system—can cause disastrous results for its users if it is not thoroughly tested and found to be satisfactory. Development of an information system incurs a huge expenditure of money and is often critical to the success of an organization, so a system should not be delivered to the users without thorough testing.

Installation Stage. After the successful testing of an information system, installation is performed. During **installation,** a system is made operational. This is a significant component in the development of an information system, and it may require considerable capital to support both people and equipment. In some cases, the cost of installation exceeds the cost of system design. However, the ultimate success of an information system may depend on how well the various parts of this task are carried out.

Planning is the first subtask to be completed for the installation of an information system. Many information systems cause significant changes in the operating procedures of a business organization. Change can cause technical and human problems. For an installation that is as free of trouble as possible, careful planning is essential.

A team that consists of the users, system developers, and managers should prepare a plan for installation. The plan should include the various tasks to be completed, the completion dates for those activities, and the individuals responsible for their completion.

Conversion is the replacement of an existing system with a new information system. Four basic approaches to conversion are: (1) direct, (2) parallel, (3) phased-in, and (4) pilot conversion (Figure 9.4).

With **direct conversion** (also called crash conversion), an existing information system is replaced by a new information system as of a certain date; the old system is no longer used. With **parallel conversion,** both new and old information systems are used for a certain period of time, after which the old system is no longer used. With **phased-in conversion,** the new information system is installed in phases, or segments. As individual

FIGURE 9.4
Conversion strategies for
information systems.

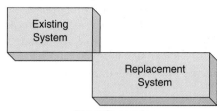

Direct Conversion
End existing system and begin replacement system immediately.

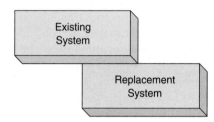

Parallel Conversion
Existing system and replacement system are both run for a specified
period of time and then the existing system is dropped.

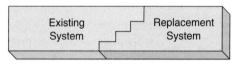

Phase-In Conversion
Gradually phase out existing system as replacement system is gradually phased in.

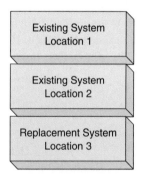

Pilot Conversion
Replacement system is installed in one location and tried out
before being installed in other locations.

segments of the system are developed, they are installed and used. If an
information system is to be used in multiple locations, **pilot conversion** may
prove safe and economical. With pilot conversion, a new system is installed in
one location and tried there before it is installed in other locations.

Training Stage. **Training** involves one of the most important tasks in the
implementation of a new information system. The primary purpose of
training is to make users and others familiar with the system so that they

can work with it effectively. Training is normally provided for three levels of employees: (1) users, (2) operators, and (3) managers.

User training is provided to employees who work with the new system on a regular basis. User training must be hands-on and may last several days or weeks. The purpose is to make users thoroughly familiar with the operation of the new system.

Operators are employees who work in the computer center of an organization and who are responsible for running the computer system. Operator training communicates operational details to the people who will run the computer system.

Whereas user and operator training deal with operational details, management training deals with an overview of the new system. The main purpose of this training is to familiarize managers with the major strengths and weaknesses of a system and the effect of the system on an organization.

System Maintenance

System maintenance is the last phase in the SDLC of an information system. After a system has been tested and installed and the users trained, it enters the maintenance phase. Information systems are maintained by a special group of programmers known as **maintenance programmers.** After an information system is installed, it is handed over to maintenance programmers. Most college graduates with a degree in information systems or related disciplines start their careers as maintenance programmers. The maintenance of a system may span several years, during which time the changing requirements of users lead to minor modifications to the system. Most often, the maintenance costs of an information system are considerably higher than the development costs. Eventually, the system reaches a point where routine maintenance is no longer sufficient and the SDLC begins again.

Objective 9.6   Define prototype information system and describe its effect on the SDLC.

What is Prototyping and How Does It Affect the SDLC?

A **prototype information system** is defined as a working information system that is built economically and quickly, with the intention that it will be modified. In the system analysis phase, prototyping is used to help users who aren't certain determine what they really want in an information system. In the system design phase, a system analyst uses a prototype for varied reasons. For example, to fine-tune system specifications, users are given copies of system output so that they can make any desired changes before any further effort is put into programming output. With a prototype, users can be trained earlier in the development process. A prototype involves users so that they have a sense of system ownership, hopefully generating tolerance of minor faults after the new system is operational. Finally, a prototype demonstrates the system to management so that key personnel can see how a long and expensive information system project is progressing.

How do you find out if your information system is safe? System developers as well as managers have concerns about the security of their data. There are at least two options available to check out your system.

One is offered by highly respected companies such as Price Water-house's Management Consulting Services. Their team of three or four people attempts to break into your mainframe, minicomputer, or desktop system for a fee ranging from several thousand to over a hundred thousand dollars. These experts generally use four approaches: as a totally uninformed outsider, a totally uninformed insider, an insider with standard company information, and an insider bent on destructive purposes. Sometimes these "insiders" are disgruntled employees or former employees who, for whatever reason, want to sabotage the system.

The team looks for any weak spots. Many times it's as simple as gaining access through the account of a user who continues using the default password. In other cases a user chooses an easy-to-guess password, for example, a combination of letters in his or her name. After completion of the team's review, a security plan is recommended.

Another choice is offered by those computer experts who look at the possibility of accessing a "secure" information system as a challenge to their expertise. Most of these users are fascinated by the intricacies involved in entering the systems of others. Some have even been caught doing this illegally. The object remains the same: Try to successfully break into the client's system. Some approach this task by searching through trash bins looking for scraps of paper that may contain passwords or other sensitive information critical to their purpose or share tricks of the trade with less scrupulous users on electronic bulletin boards.

No matter which expert you employ, you must be very sure that the operation is conducted with the highest level of ethical behavior. And, as always, *caveat emptor!*

A typical prototyping effort might follow these steps:

1. A business user identifies the need for a new information system, perhaps to accomplish some specific task.
2. The user communicates that need to a prototyper, who is a systems expert in the design of quick, cheap systems that a user can change easily to accommodate specific needs.
3. The prototyper quickly designs a model for the user to examine.
4. The user suggests changes to the first version of the prototype. The changes are made, and the user experiments with the second version. More changes are made, and more versions of the prototype are quickly produced.
5. Finally, the user likes a prototype, and that model becomes the working blueprint from which the new information system will be developed.

The concept of prototyping is not new. It has been used in other fields for many years. Models of aircraft have been tested in wind tunnels since the 1920s, and architects have constructed scale models of buildings for centuries. In the information system field, however, it took the advent of microcomputers and fourth-generation languages (4GL) for prototyping to become an efficient development tool. Effective use of prototyping cannot substantially change the tasks that must be accomplished to produce a new information system, but it can significantly decrease the time generally taken to develop such a system. The growing use of prototyping promises to streamline the development of information systems in general and the system analysis and system design phases in particular.

Objective 9.7   Describe the purpose of computer-aided systems engineering (CASE) software.

What Is Computer-Aided Systems Engineering Software?

Until recently, system analysts were in a bizarre situation regarding the tools they used. These analysts were designing large, complex computer information systems with pencils and paper. In other words, the automators were not automated.

In recent years, automated system analysis and design programs have been marketed to run on microcomputers. These programs automate many of the system analyst's trivial but time-consuming tasks. The approach is similar to that of computer-aided design (CAD) in aiding architects and computer-aided manufacturing (CAM) in helping production designers. The entire class of software that automates system development tasks is referred to as **computer-aided systems engineering (CASE).** CASE products offer the following automated capabilities:

- Graphics to produce and change automatically such analysis tools as data flow diagrams, as well as system and program flowcharts
- Integration of other productivity tools, such as word processors and spreadsheets
- Quality assurance functions that evaluate graphs and other CASE products for completeness, consistency, and accuracy
- Data sharing, which allows system analysts to use several different microcomputer workstations to create graphics and data
- Rapid prototyping, which allows quick and automatic generation of user input screens and output reports and forms

The use of CASE products has the potential to make the design of business information systems faster, easier, and better.

Objective 9.8 Define end-user computing and summarize its effect on an organization.

What Is End-User Computing?

Traditionally, most users of computer-generated information had no control over the computers and applications that produced the information they needed. Information system design, development, and use were controlled by the systems department. The complexity and expense of the hardware and software made it impractical for users to have control over their own processing needs. The advent and geometric growth of microcomputers and associated software applications has reduced the complexity and cost of computing to the point where it is now feasible for end users to have some control of their own processing activities. Most people have the capability to use these computing systems with a modicum of effort. They like the immediacy of the results and the feeling of control over their own processing activities.

The use of microcomputers and associated software gave rise to the concept of end-user computing. **End-user computing** supports the notion that the person who is responsible for the computing output should be the person who is going to utilize that output. In other words, the person who needs the information should be the person who obtains it from the system. Similarly, the end user who is responsible for obtaining the correct output should be actively involved in the development of the information system that supplies it.

Different organizations have taken this concept to disparate levels. One way is for users to acquire their own prewritten application packages and use them to generate the desired output with little or no help from the systems department. Another way is for end users to develop their own applications with the assistance of a system analyst and software tools. On the extreme end is end-user development of applications without any assistance from system analysts.

Problems with End-User Computing

Although many information system managers accept and encourage the idea of end-user computing, many new problems are created by this emerging practice. End users must be given the resources necessary to complete their own activities—the hardware and software as well as extensive training, support from systems experts, and freedom to use the information resource. If end users are to be successful, they must have unlimited access to the data files and/or information required to do the job.

There is the possibility that users in different departments will develop redundant applications and that data integrity and security problems could occur. It also may not be in the best interest of an organization to have a highly paid professional spending time developing an application that could be more economically developed by the systems department.

End users who develop applications on their own must be adequately trained in system analysis techniques to help ensure that their applications will meet the standards of the organization for application development. These problems provide significant challenges for organizations.

Benefits of End-User Computing

End-user computing has solved some of the problems associated with application development using the traditional SDLC.

One of the biggest problems is the slow turnaround time from user request to implementation of an application, often months or years, caused by the large backlog of projects facing most systems departments. Because organizations are dynamic and constantly changing, by the time a user receives an application it may be obsolete. End-user computing can significantly speed up development time.

Allowing end users to develop applications in which they have expertise helps remove some of the backlog from the systems department. Because of the high cost of labor, most organizations cannot afford to keep enough programmers and system analysts on staff to meet user needs in a timely fashion. The nature of the traditional SDLC requires significant time to perform the required tasks. Reducing the time and personnel required to develop information system applications helps to decrease the cost of development.

The Information Center

In order to facilitate end-user computing many organizations employ an information center. An **information center** in an organization distributes information, provides instruction in the use of information systems, allocates computing hardware, and provides information systems experts and other useful functions in a support role. Information centers were first described by IBM as a way of distributing information system resources throughout a firm. Generally speaking, the information center is responsible for overseeing many different activities.

- Technical support—helping end users with software, hardware, communications, and other technically related processes
- Education—training end users on new software and hardware
- Systems consulting—helping end users define and solve their systems problems
- Resource allocation—carrying out the functions of software, hardware, and information distribution
- Evaluation—looking at the possible applications of new products
- Marketing—promoting the services of the information center to the potential users

Information center services should be provided to all employees of a firm. The major function of an information center is to encourage the use of distributed processing and end-user computing throughout the firm. Clearly, these activities create an even greater need for good management of information resources.

Summary

An information system is a set of people, data, procedures, hardware, and software that works together to achieve the common goal of information management. Because end users rely on information systems for information and are often asked to participate in their development it is important to understand how they are used and developed.

Managers are the key decision makers and problem solvers in an organization. Managers are responsible for using the resources available to achieve organizational goals. The five major functions of a manager are (1) planning, (2) staffing, (3) organizing, (4) directing, and (5) controlling in order to get others to accomplish desired objectives. There are three basic levels of management: (1) strategic (top-level), (2) tactical (middle-level), and (3) operational (low-level). Each level has specific information needs.

Several types of information systems exist to accommodate the different information needs of individuals in an organization. Operational information systems, also called transaction processing systems (TPS), record and manage transactions to provide information to operational management who manage the day-to-day functions of an organization. A management information system (MIS) provides information to managers for use in problem solving, control, and decision making for situations that recur and are highly structured. A decision support system (DSS) is an interactive information system, composed of a set of related programs and data, that helps users solve semistructured or unstructured user problems. An executive support system (ESS) is an information system that caters to the special needs of executives. An expert system is a type of application program used to make decisions or solve problems in a particular field. It uses knowledge and analytical rules defined by human experts in a field. Its two major components are a knowledge base and an inference engine. An expert system shell consists of all the components of an expert system except a knowledge base. An office information system is used to help knowledge workers to manage the preparation, storage, retrieval, reproduction, and communication of information within and among business offices. Individuals who create, process, and distribute information are known as knowledge workers.

The system development life cycle (SDLC) is the structured sequence of operations required to conceive, develop, and make operational a new information system. The SDLC consists of four major phases: analysis, design, implementation, and maintenance. A project management team facilitates communication between users and the system personnel. Project management is the structured coordination and monitoring of all activities involved in a one-time endeavor, or project. It is important that accurate and complete documentation be kept throughout the SDLC.

The system analysis phase includes identifying a system problem or new opportunity, analyzing the current system in light of the problem or new opportunity, and justifying the development of a new system or modification of an old system to meet the needs of users. System analysis is divided into three stages: problem definition, requirements analysis, and project justification. A cost/benefit analysis, or feasibility study, is performed to compare both the costs and the benefits of the alternative information systems to the current information system to see which should be recommended to management. The system study is an extensive report sent to management to justify the recommendations of the system analyst.

The system design phase is broken down into the logical system design stage and the physical system design stage. The logical system design shows the flow of data through an information system. It is composed of a series of charts, graphs, and data layouts and can be thought of as the system blueprint. During the physical design stage the logical system design is converted to the specific hardware and computer programs required to transform the logical design into a working information system.

During the implementation phase an information system is transferred to the users. This phase includes testing, installation, and training stages.

Testing ensures that all the parts of an information system are correct. The installation stage involves making an information system operational and putting it to work. Conversion is the process of replacing an existing information system with a new information system. There are four basic conversion methods: direct, parallel, phased-in, and pilot. Training involves making users and others familiar with an information system.

During the maintenance phase maintenance programmers make minor modifications to the information system in response to changing user requirements.

A prototype information system is a working information system built economically and quickly, with the intention that it will be modified.

Computer-aided systems engineering (CASE) software automates system development tasks.

End-user computing supports the notion that the person who needs the information should be the person who obtains it from the system and should be actively involved in the development of the information system that provides it. Information centers support end-user computing through the distribution of hardware, software, training, support, and consulting resources. Problems with end-user computing include the distribution of and access to the required hardware, software, and information resources; development of redundant applications; data integrity; and data security. Benefits include quicker turnaround time from request to delivery of an application and lower development costs.

VOCABULARY SELF-TEST

Can you define the following terms?

conversion (p. 343)

computer-aided systems engineering (CASE) (p. 347)

cost/benefit analysis (p. 342)

decision support system (DSS) (p. 335)

direct conversion (p. 343)

documentation (p. 340)

end-user computing (p. 348)

executive support system (ESS) (p. 336)

expert system (p. 336)

expert system shell (p. 336)

inference engine (p. 336)

information center (p. 349)

information system (p. 331)

installation (p. 343)

interactive system (p. 335)

knowledge base (p. 336)

knowledge worker (p. 337)

logical system design (p. 342)

maintenance programmers (p. 345)

management information system (MIS) (p. 334)

manager (p. 332)

office information system (OIS) (p. 337)

operational information system (p. 334)

operational (low-level) managers (p. 333)

parallel conversion (p. 343)

phased-in conversion (p. 343)

physical system design (p. 342)

pilot conversion (p. 344)

problem definition (p. 341)

programmer (p. 339)

project justification (p. 341)

project management
   (p. 339)

prototype information system
   (p. 345)

requirements analysis (p. 341)

strategic (top-level) managers
   (p. 332)

system analysis (p. 340)

system analyst (p. 339)

system design (p. 342)

system designer (p. 339)

system development life cycle
   (SDLC) (p. 339)

system implementation (p. 343)

system maintenance (p. 345)

system study (p. 342)

tactical (middle-level) managers
   (p. 332)

testing (p. 343)

training (p. 344)

transaction (p. 344)

transaction processing system (TPS)
   (p. 334)

user (p. 339)

REVIEW QUESTIONS

Multiple Choice

1. A(n) _____ records and manages transactions.
   a. management information system
   b. transaction processing system
   c. expert system
   d. decision support system

2. A(n) _____ provides information for situations that recur and are highly structured where the information requirements are known in advance.
   a. decision support system
   b. executive support system
   c. transaction processing system
   d. management information system

3. That set of related programs and data that are used to solve semi-structured and unstructured problems is called a(n) _____ .
   a. management information system
   b. transaction processing system
   c. decision support system
   d. expert system

4. Which of the following information systems is designed to cater to the needs of strategic (top-level) management?
   a. executive support system
   b. expert system
   c. decision support system
   d. management information system

5. A(n) _____ manages the preparation, storage, retrieval, reproduction, and communication of information within and among business offices.
   a. transaction processing system
   b. expert system

c. office information system

d. decision support system

6. The structured sequence of operations required to conceive, develop, and make operational a new information system is called _____ .

    a. project management

    b. a system development life cycle

    c. a system analysis

    d. a system blueprint

7. _____ includes problem definition, requirements analysis, and project justification.

    a. Implementation

    b. System design

    c. System analysis

    d. Maintenance

8. During which stage does the system analyst compare alternative information systems to decide which one to propose to management?

    a. requirements analysis

    b. project justification

    c. system design

    d. problem definition

9. The flow of data through an information system is shown in the _____ .

    a. system study

    b. logical system design

    c. physical system design

    d. layout forms

10. An information system is made operational and put to work during the _____ stage of the implementation phase.

    a. testing

    b. installation

    c. physical design

    d. training

Fill-In

1. A(n) _____ is a set of people, data, procedures, hardware, and software that works together to achieve the common goal of information management.

2. A business activity or event is called a(n) _____ .

3. A(n) _____ allows a user to communicate with a computer through dialogue.

4. A(n) _____ uses knowledge and inference procedures to solve problems that require significant human experience.

5. An individual who creates, processes, and distributes information is called a(n) _____ .

6. _____ is the structured coordination and monitoring of all activities involved in a one-time endeavor, or project.

7. Identifying problems with a current system or a new opportunity, analyzing the problem or opportunity, and justifying the modification

of an old system or development of a new system takes place during _____ .

8. During the _____ , the system blueprint is converted into the hardware and computer programs that comprise the information system.

9. _____ involves making minor changes in an information system in response to changing user requirements.

10. The entire class of software that automates system development tasks is referred to as _____ .

Short Answer

1. Why is it important to understand how information systems are used and developed?
2. Identify the five major functions of a manager and describe the information needs of each level of management.
3. Recount several uses of a decision support system.
4. Identify several components of an office information system.
5. Describe why it is important to accurately and completely document each phase of the system development life cycle.
6. What is the purpose of the system analysis and system design phases?
7. List and describe four types of conversion.
8. Tell how the use of a prototype information system affects the system development life cycle.
9. What is the purpose of CASE software?
10. What is meant by end-user computing?

Issues for Thought

1. Summarize some effects that a poorly tested transaction processing system might have on an organization.
2. Information systems gave us the ability to collect and process tremendous amounts of data. What problems does this cause for managers of organizations? What problems do you foresee for society in general?

Infomodule

Applications of Information Systems

The acceptance of information as a strategic corporate resource together with competitive pressure have forced many businesses to expand the use of computers in their information systems. In this Infomodule you'll see how information systems have affected businesses. Let's examine where information systems are being used in several of the more common functional areas of business, as well as how they are being used in selected industries.

WHAT ARE APPLICATIONS OF INFORMATION SYSTEMS IN FUNCTIONAL AREAS OF BUSINESS?

This section looks briefly at some ways in which information systems are used in several of the more common functional areas of business. Remember that these are typical descriptions and are by no means

the only ways that information systems are organized and named. Figure 1 shows an organizational chart of the functional areas to be examined—accounting, finance, marketing, production/operations, and human resources. Each area may be supported by its own information system, although there can also be sharing of information among them.

Accounting Information System

An **accounting information system** uses primarily transaction processing systems to record operations that affect the financial status of the organization. These systems are referred to as operational accounting systems and they maintain a historical record of the transactions. These systems also produce reports, such as a balance sheet and income statement, that give a financial picture of the organization.

FIGURE 1
Several functional areas of business.

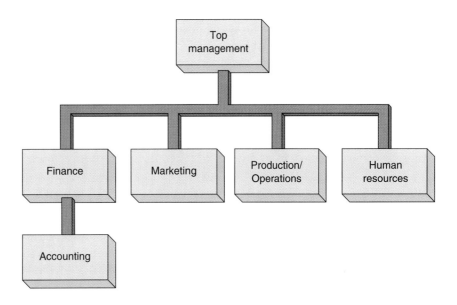

Accounting was one of the first functional areas to incorporate computer-based information systems; the nature of accounting readily lends itself to computerization for several reasons. Accounting transactions generate large amounts of data that need to be regularly processed and stored, accurately and quickly. The processing required is relatively simple and easy to implement on the computer, and management can establish appropriate controls and error-checking procedures to ensure the security and accuracy of the data. In addition, accounting systems are designed to maintain an audit trail, which enables data stored in the system to be traced back to the original transaction. Computers can easily handle tasks with these requirements.

Accounting systems also use some MIS and DSS applications. Management accounting systems usually involve projections and estimates of the future to help in developing budgets and plans. Accounting information systems are made up of a number of subsystems. Several of the more common ones include accounts receivable, accounts payable, payroll, and general ledger systems.

Financial Information System

A **financial information system** provides information concerning both the acquisition of funds to finance business operations and on the allocation and control of the financial resources of the organization. Whereas an accounting information system focuses on recording data generated by the daily operation of a business, financial information systems focus on planning and control. In doing so, they rely heavily on DSSs, which in turn draw much of their data from the transaction processing systems of the accounting information system.

Financial information systems are excellent candidates for computerization. Many financial calculations are complex, requiring large numbers of variables with numerous possible interactions. The calculations often need to be repeated numerous times with minor data changes to answer what-if questions. A computer speeds up the recalculation process. Financial information systems are less concerned with absolute accuracy than accounting information systems

are because many of the financial variables are future-oriented and difficult to predict precisely.

Financial information systems are also made up of numerous subsystems. Several common ones include requirements analysis, planning, cash management, credit management, and capital expenditure systems.

Marketing Information System

A **marketing information system** involves gathering details about day-to-day sales transactions, managing and controlling marketing operations, and planning sales and strategies for the future. A marketing information system deals with existing products and markets and plans for future products and markets. To accomplish these goals, it relies equally on transaction processing systems, management information systems, and decision support systems.

A marketing information system can be broken into two subsystems: a sales system and a marketing system. The sales system records data about day-to-day sales transactions—for example, customer names, item numbers, quantities ordered, and billing and shipping addresses. This information is recorded using a transaction processing system. The sales system must be capable of processing a high volume of data accurately and thus is an ideal candidate for computerization.

The marketing system focuses on planning and control and relies on MISs and DSSs. The MISs use data generated by the sales system to provide information on how well products and sales staff are performing. Management may use this information to adjust activities to meet organizational goals. DSSs help plan for the future by assisting in tasks such as forecasting sales, planning pricing, and designing promotional strategies. Since the marketing system must process complex calculations of many variables with numerous possible interactions, it is also an ideal candidate for computerization.

Marketing information systems are also composed of numerous subsystems. Some of the more common subsystems include order entry, customer profile, product management, sales management, sales forecasting, advertising, and market research systems.

Production/Operations Information System

The **production/operations information system** gathers and processes data about all of the activities involved in producing goods and services. That information is then used to plan, monitor, and control the production/operations process. Such a system enables an organization to produce goods and services more efficiently. Production scheduling can be planned better and the workload balanced with the available production capacity. Production/operations information systems also enable continuous monitoring, feedback, and control of production/operations, resulting in stricter quality control and leading to better products and greater productivity. They can also reduce the costs of carrying inventories by enabling better control of raw materials and finished goods and fewer occurrences of depleted inventories.

The production/operations information system is also composed of a number of subsystems. Several of the more common include the master production schedule, materials requirement planning, capacity planning, engineering, production control, plant maintenance, process and numerical control, and physical distribution systems.

Human Resources Information System

The **human resources information system** in most organizations involves recruitment, placement, evaluation, compensation, and development of employees. The goal of the system is enabling the effective and efficient use of the human resources of an organization by its management. The information should permit the personnel needs of a business to be appropriately met and should create effective personnel policies and programs.

The human resources system is also made up of a number of subsystems. Some of the more common include payroll and labor analysis; personnel records; personnel skills inventory; recruitment, training, and development analysis; compensation analysis; and human resource requirements forecasting systems.

WHAT ARE APPLICATIONS OF INFORMATION SYSTEMS IN SELECTED INDUSTRIES?

Applications for computers and information systems proliferate in numerous industries as more and more business people recognize the advantages of having computers do a wide variety of tasks. Now you will learn some of the ways that computers and information systems are used in the manufacturing, banking, investment, retail, and health care industries.

Manufacturing

A manufacturing firm is one that transforms raw materials into finished goods. It relies on engineering activities, such as the planning and design of new products, and depends heavily on information from MISs and DSSs. A manufacturer is also concerned with the procurement of raw materials, which may be finished goods from another manufacturer. This area of manufacturing relies on TPSs to monitor inventories and generate purchase orders when needed. It also relies on MISs and DSSs in the planning and control of inventories and orders. Scheduling the efficient use of facilities to maximize productivity is another function of a manufacturing firm, one for which MISs and DSSs are also important in planning and control. Finally, a manufacturing firm is involved in the fabrication of finished goods, which requires making or acquiring components and assembling them into finished products. TPSs gather data about the fabrication process. MISs supply management with information to help control the fabrication process. And expert systems help diagnose problems with machinery in some firms.

Most manufacturing companies realize that they must computerize their factories—either partially or fully—to be competitive. The use of computers to control machines in the manufacturing process is called **computer-aided manufacturing (CAM).** To be fully automated and integrated, a company must link all the different parts of the manufacturing process with all other aspects of the company. An information system that automates and integrates the entire manufacturing enterprise results in **computer-integrated manufacturing (CIM).** With CIM, companies not only link product design to the manufacturing process, but also link those processes to the company computers that handle project management, general accounting, inventory control, order processing, factory-floor scheduling, and all other operations in the factory itself (Figure 2).

Only a few companies have fully implemented CIM. To integrate all computer-controlled operations and make sure that each piece of equipment communicates with all others, equipment manufacturers must agree on communication links. The industry standard in communication links was developed by General Motors and is called **manufacturing automation protocol (MAP).** Although developed by an automaker, MAP standards can be implemented in other manufacturing environments.

Because the computer has become more powerful over the years, it is now capable of handling more sophisticated tasks than the simple processing of numerical data. As modern manufacturing plants are built, or older ones are remodeled, they are incorporating computer-controlled machinery into their overall information system. Computers are used for very practical reasons: to increase productivity and to reduce costs.

Computer-Aided Design. If you had walked into a design work area just a few years ago, you would have seen numerous drafting tables with designers or engineers hovering over them. Planning and drawing a proposed new product was a pencil-and-paper operation. If you walk into that same room today, you will probably see a different scene. The room contains design and drafting workstations, plotters, and graphics tablets. The computerized tools used to design and draw the various items may be either individual microcomputers or terminals connected to a large computer system of the company.

Computer-aided design (CAD) is the integration of the computer and graphics to aid in design

FIGURE 2
Technicians and assemblers at the Convair Division of General Dynamics Corporation in San Diego are using a "paperless" factory system that replaces up to 90 percent of manufacturing paperwork in the final assembly area of the Tomahawk cruise missile. Accessing the system through bar codes, assemblers receive instructions at their workstation computers. The system maintains configuration control and is being adapted to other factory areas to maintain high quality and reduce the cost of manufacturing. Convair produces the Tomahawk cruise missile for the U.S. Navy and the U.S. Air Force.

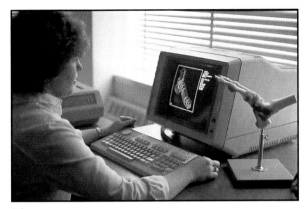

(a)

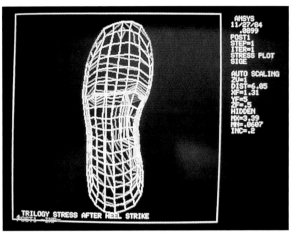

(b)

(c)

FIGURE 3
(a) A computer-generated model of the human foot is used to help design athletic shoes. (b) A computer generates a three-dimensional, finite-element model of an athletic shoe midsole that can be tested for stress points. (c) A two-dimensional cross-section of an athletic shoe midsole.

and drafting. A manufacturer such as Brooks Shoe, a maker of footwear, uses CAD systems to design running shoes (Figure 3). The advantages of this application of computers are twofold:

1. It makes the designing and drafting easier, more accurate, and better planned.
2. It increases productivity because design and drafting time are significantly shortened.

Designers find this drawing method much easier than the pencil-and-paper method because mistakes can be corrected easily and designs can be redone many times until they are just right. Designers move, copy, mirror, or erase sections or entire images—all without eraser marks, of course. And drawings can be scaled to any size and plotted on all sizes of paper.

The use of a CAD system reduces production time because the initial drawing can be done more easily and quickly. Repetition of drawing is avoided since each design can be filed and used later to create different products. Often-used items or images can be stored in libraries and simply retrieved whenever needed and inserted into a current drawing.

Automobile designers at Ford Motor Company use CAD to draw the many prototypes of a new car before creating solid models (Figure 4). CAD systems are used by clothing manufacturers to design the patterns and fabrics for their apparel lines.

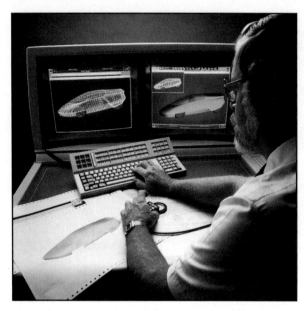

FIGURE 4
An engineer at Ford Motor Company uses a CAD system to assist in designing new automobiles.

Computer Numerical Control (CNC). Manufacturing techniques have been through a tremendous transformation in recent years. A common task in the manufacturing process is the milling of parts. In the past, all operations of this sort were controlled by individual machine operators, and the quality of the end product was often directly related to the skill of the operator. Today, many of these milling operations have been turned over to **computer numerical control (CNC),** a system in which an operator programs a computer that controls the milling apparatus. The actual machine is not attended by a human being. A computer-controlled drill bit, for example, can perform the same task precisely, over and over again. This ability is particularly beneficial in forming repetitive parts.

CNC devices make it possible to cut more difficult parts and to operate with greater precision. The computer-controlled machines are even becoming easier to use. When programming is required, the commands usually appear as simple English words rather than complex computer codes.

In addition, the computer with a CNC machine can be programmed to change drill bits during a cutting operation. Operators no longer have to stop the manufacturing process to change drill bits and are therefore free to perform other duties. Often a CNC machine is connected to a CAD workstation. By watching the monitor, the CNC operator views the part as it is being made by the machine.

Robotics. **Robotics** is a branch of engineering devoted to creating and training robots. Many people think of robots as walking, talking androids or highly intelligent machines capable of carrying out all kinds of unusual stunts. Those are the robots of science fiction and modern-day movies rather than reality. "Robot" as defined by the Robotics Institute of America is "a reprogrammable, multifunctional manipulator designed to move material, parts, tools, or specialized devices through variable programmed motions for the performance of a variety of tasks." More simply put, a robot is a machine that can be programmed to do a variety of useful tasks.

Although some experimental robots are made into humanlike forms, most industrial robots resemble nothing of the sort and would be impractical in that form. Far from being intelligent, robots are capable of completing only preprogrammed instructions. But they can be programmed to do some rather complicated tasks, and they can turn out products in a factory with unsurpassed precision.

Robots are used in manufacturing mainly to reduce costs and increase productivity. They are excellent at repetitive tasks, which humans find boring; robots never tire. They are also ideal to replace humans on hazardous jobs.

The first industrial robots were simply computer-controlled mechanical arms performing a single, simple task. Today, industrial robots are still used primarily for assembly-line tasks, but some can do multiple tasks and move along on wheels or a track or belt system. Many robots have elementary senses of touch and vision that give them more precision.

Robots are generally delegated to three types of jobs: operating tools, lifting and handling materials or parts, and assembling parts. The operation of tools is the most common application of robots. Spot or arc welding and spray painting of automobile parts are typical tasks (Figure 5). The robots at Fey Manufacturing in California weld bumpers for small trucks. The drilling of hundreds or thousands of rivet holes in aircraft components is another natural task to assign to robots, and General Dynamics does just that.

The lifting and handling of materials are also fairly uncomplicated tasks for robots. Most robots are of the "pick and place" variety. They simply pick up an object, such as a piece of metal, and place it somewhere else, as in a stamping machine.

Assembly is still difficult for robots, although inroads have been made in some areas. Some companies use robots to insert electrical components of standard shapes into printed circuit boards destined for many types of electrical equipment. IBM not only sells robots that can handle this type of assembly task, but also uses them to assemble products in its computer and terminal plants.

As computer capabilities grow, so do the applications for robots. Robots can now be adapted with sensors that help the robot "see" and "feel" its way around the workplace. An elementary sense of sight is accomplished with digital-imaging cameras or by bouncing infrared or microwave signals off the object. These signals are received by a robot's computer and matched with previously stored images for the purpose of identification and inspection.

Robots can be programmed to pick up heavy objects or objects as delicate and lightweight as an egg without damaging either. The sense of touch, tactile sensing, is in its elementary stages of development, but robots can now distinguish many different shapes, handle each appropriately, and perform various operations. These tasks are possible because the robot's "hands," called end effectors, are available in many varieties and are often interchangeable.

Programmable Controllers. Two important aspects of running an industrial plant are monitoring and controlling the activities of the machinery. These jobs are being taken over by the **programmable controller,** which is a computer-regulated unit consisting of a microprocessor, an input and output module, and a power supply (Figure 6). A programmable controller controls the on/off functions of switches and relays and controls processes (process control).

The microprocessor of a programmable controller is programmed with a keyboard that can be attached when needed. After programming is complete, the keyboard is removed and the programmable controller is functional. A programmable controller can be programmed to reflect any desired cause-and-effect relationship (e.g., throwing Switch 1 starts Motor 2).

FIGURE 5
Robots are used for welding automobile parts at this Honda plant.

FIGURE 6
The Babcock & Wilcox Company's Loose Parts
Monitoring System III, a programmable controller, uses
sophisticated computer-analysis techniques to
evaluate the metal-to-metal impact of loose parts
caught in the high-velocity flows of nuclear steam
systems. The controller provides real-time estimates of
the location and damage potential of loose parts.

The programmable controller can also be reprogrammed if any changes are necessary.

Process control is monitoring and controlling of
various processes in a system's operation (Figure 7).
For example, a programmable controller can play an
important part in regulating the furnace temperature
for melting glass. Basically, a "set point," such as a
specific temperature, is programmed into the programmable controller for the glass-melting furnace.
The furnace sends temperature data signals back to
the programmable controller, where these signals are
compared to the preprogrammed set point. If the

signals do not match, the programmable controller
signals a control element that adjusts the furnace
temperature accordingly. One programmable
controller can control many process-control systems,
a more complex task than controlling on/off
operations.

Because of fierce worldwide competition more
factories are incorporating the latest computer technologies into their information systems. Factories
need to keep their costs down, and with the aid of
computers the productivity of each person can be
increased. In addition, the precision of computer-
controlled machinery reduces product defects, which
also affect operating costs.

Banking

Banking is the most computer-intensive industry in
the United States because of the repetition of the
transactions, the accuracy required, and the speed
needed to handle the great volume of daily transactions. Transaction processing systems are heavily used
throughout the banking industry. In addition, computers and information systems help banks plan and control their accounting and reporting operations and
enable them to provide new and improved services.

The most widely used computer application in
banking is demand-deposit, or checking account
banking. This transaction processing system generates
monthly customer statements and supplies information to management on checking account activities.

Computers and information systems also make
real-time banking possible, where customer accounts
are immediately updated after a transaction. Each
teller station has a terminal and operates on-line
when accessing accounts to cash checks or make
deposits (Figure 8). Most banks and branch offices
also have automated teller machines (ATMs), where
cash is dispensed to customers any time of the day
or night (Figure 9).

Lending activities have also been able to take advantage of computer-based information systems. Consumer, commercial, and mortgage loans are all analyzed by computers. Sometimes an expert system is
used to evaluate the credit worthiness of a customer.

FIGURE 7
Process control can be integrated with plant data. The system used by this factory offers touch-screen access to thousands of terminals along the plantwide reporting network.

The information system generates customer statements and numerous management reports, such as loan analysis, interest, and tax reports. Many banks also offer credit card services and trust management, which are handled by computers.

In addition, the banking industry uses computers and information systems to provide electronic funds transfer (EFT), a computerized method of transferring funds from one account to another. Many of an organization's funds are moved in this way.

Besides providing new or better services to customers, computers have created new business opportunities for banks. Many banks now promote their computer facilities and expertise by offering computer services to other banks, financial institutions, businesses, and other organizations.

Investment

The investment industry has traditionally used computer-based information systems to record transactions, process billing information, and prepare monthly statements. Computers are now used in the stock market to keep track of the stocks being traded on the floor of the New York Stock Exchange (Figure 10). The average volume of shares traded daily is over 140 million, far beyond the capacity of the old ticker-tape machines. In 1975 the designated order turnaround (DOT) system was implemented to handle orders. Although some transactions are still completed by specialists, the turnaround time for a market order processed by a computer is approximately 75 seconds. This system greatly facilitates the exchange of information between involved parties.

FIGURE 8
A bank teller's computer terminal and printer are linked to the bank's mainframe computer to process customer transactions.

FIGURE 9
Automated teller machines are linked to a bank's mainframes and offer individuals easy and convenient access to their bank accounts.

People who invest in the stock market need current facts about the financial condition of their investments. Computers permit the quick and easy retrieval of financial statistics through on-line information services. Services like Dow Jones News Retrieval give traders the instant financial data they need for making decisions on stock trading. Others include Standard and Poor's Compustat, Wharton's Econometric, and Data Resources, Inc. (DRI).

Security analysis has also benefited from the use of computers. Improved forecasts on the market prices of securities can be obtained by computer analysis of the numerous variables that affect the financial position of a firm. Many brokers use computers to help them analyze their decisions to buy, sell, or hold securities for the portfolios of their clients. Interestingly, the computer has been blamed for aiding the stock market disaster of October, 1987. Critics claim that the ability of the computer to offer automatic trading fueled the fire of the panic in the market.

Retail Sales

The area of retail sales includes many repetitive transactions that lend themselves to computer technology. Although each sale is different, the basic recording process remains the same. Consequently, retail stores use TPSs to record transactions. In addition to basic applications such as accounting and customer billing, computers are used in forecasting sales, analyzing sales, and merchandising. Retail purchases made with credit cards also involve computers. The computer stops consumers who attempt to charge over their approved credit limits.

A growing computer application is the point-of-sale system (POS). A POS system typically consists of cash register-like terminals that are on-line to a computer in the store or to a unit that stores and transmits data over communication lines to a computer at a regional center. A POS terminal with a laser scanner reads sales data from items containing a product code (Figure 11). A POS system allows management to analyze the effects of sales and advertising quickly and more accurately.

FIGURE 10
The New York Stock Exchange is a busy place where trade decisions are based on the most current data available. Computers are also important in individual offices, where stockbrokers keep clients informed of late-breaking developments.

Many businesses, including grocery stores, are automating inventory using hand-held computerized input devices, which save information read from the bar codes on the products. These data can later be entered directly into the main computer system.

Computers can also spur sales by simulating products and services. Three L. S. Ayres department stores in the Midwest tried a leased system called Magic Mirror, programmed with a Liz Claiborne spring collection. While standing in front of the mirror, the customer could see her own face, but the computer projected a comparable body image wearing as many different outfits as she wanted to try. The simulation concept proved to be quite a sales promotion; Claiborne's sales increased more than 700 percent in one week.

FIGURE 11
Supermarkets use optical scanning systems to read sales data from a product code and speed the checkout process.

Health Care

The health care industry uses computer-based information systems for traditional data-processing operations such as patient billing, accounting, inventory control, calculation of health care statistics, and maintenance of patient histories. In addition, the industry uses such systems for more challenging tasks, such as scheduling lab times and operating room times, automating nurses' stations, monitoring intensive care patients, and providing preliminary diagnoses. Expert systems often assist physicians in making diagnoses because the expert system "remembers" more facts than the doctor can.

Many physicians and medical researchers enter their fields of specialty not only with a knowledge of physical science, but also with skills in using computers. In addition to helping with the usual record-keeping and administrative tasks in pharmacies, doctors' offices, and hospitals, this combination of knowledge and technology enables doctors and other health care technicians to (1) test for and diagnose diseases and illnesses faster and more accurately; (2) design prostheses and reconstruction models; (3) build and use devices to monitor vital signs and

other bodily functions; (4) design and test pharmaceuticals; and (5) offer choices in lifestyle and job selection to people who are physically challenged.

Some computerized methods that aid physicians in diagnosing diseases and illnesses include digital subtraction angiography, sonography, computed tomography, and computerized lab testing. Digital subtraction angiography (DSA) creates a clear view of a flow or blockage of blood. Pictures are first made by a digital X-ray scanner. Then an injection of a contrasting agent (iodine) is introduced into the body, and a second image is made. The computer subtracts the first image from the second and leaves an image that shows what has changed.

In sonography, beams of high-frequency sound waves penetrate a patient's body, and the computer translates the rebounding echoes into an image that the doctor can read. Sonograms view internal organs—such as the heart, liver, and gall bladder—and help monitor the growth and condition of a developing fetus.

Computed tomography (CT) scanners view different sections (or slices) of the body from many angles by moving X-ray tubes around the body. The scanner converts the X-ray pictures into a digital code to create high-resolution images. Three-dimensional pictures can be created by combining the cross sections, thus giving surgeons a total picture when planning reconstructive surgery.

Computerization of laboratory tests, such as blood typing and testing sugar levels, leads to faster and more accurate reporting of test results and, therefore, more timely and accurate diagnoses. During biopsy procedures surgeons need reports quickly to determine whether further surgery is required. If such processes are computerized, the results can be sent automatically to the operating room, printed and forwarded to the patient's physician, placed in the main file, and updated in the billing files, all simultaneously.

Computer technology is also important for programmers and engineers who work closely with physicians to design prostheses and create models for reconstructive surgery. Some orthopedic surgery requires the creation and implantation of artificial limbs and other replacement parts, such as hip joints. By using diagnostic scanning procedures, technicians can digitize an accurate picture of damaged bone and visually compare it with a prosthesis design for fit and function. Then the actual prosthesis is built, usually with the help of computer-aided manufacturing machinery to ensure that precise measurements are met.

Computer-controlled devices are another important area of medical technology for patients who need constant monitoring, such as those in intensive care units, postoperative recovery rooms, and premature baby nurseries. Premature infants, especially babies whose birth weight is under 3 pounds, are at high risk for death from strokes caused by high blood pressure. These babies' vital signs, blood gases, and head movements can be computer-monitored, with measurements taken up to 32 times per minute. It would be physically impossible for nurses to obtain the same volume of data and it could be hazardous for the infant to undergo the amount of physical contact that such data gathering would require. Researchers are hopeful that the causes and possible prevention of sudden infant death syndrome (SIDS) can be learned from these computer monitoring tactics.

Other computer-controlled medical devices have also been developed. One device frees diabetics from hypodermic needles by automatically dispensing the proper doses of insulin from a reservoir implanted in the patient's body.

Pharmaceuticals are another area influenced by computerization. Development of a new drug is time-consuming and costly, involving years of research and experimentation and costing millions of dollars. Thousands of compounds have to be made and tested before a new drug can be released for production and human use. Computer graphics techniques save drug researchers time by simulating, in 3-D, the shapes of molecules. Because the shape of a molecule usually determines its behavior, biochemists can accurately predict how various molecules should be combined. In addition, some computers are programmed to simulate various attributes of test animals so that toxicity can be checked or the safety of certain procedures can be verified by computer simulation without endangering human or animal life.

For individuals with movement deficits, devices that stimulate muscles to move (with patterned electrical stimulation) continue to be improved. The computer stores a signal of brain-wave muscle patterns, reads the signal, and gives an electrical stimulation to the appropriate muscle group to cause movement. Tendon injuries are being treated in this way, and improvement has been shown in patients paralyzed by strokes, accidents, or cerebral palsy. Dr. Jerrold Petrofsky at Wright State University in Dayton, Ohio, is one of the most widely recognized researchers using this type of computer technology. Some of his patients, whose damaged spinal nerves caused paralyzed limbs, are able to walk and ride bicycles by using attached electrodes and adapted equipment.

Other requirements of physically challenged individuals are being addressed in computer design. The Kurzweil Reading Machine scans printed words and then speaks them aloud through a speech synthesizer. The Versabraille is a laptop computer that some blind people use to write letters or take notes. There are also braille keyboards, keyboards adapted for those with limited muscle control, and keyboards that can be activated merely by eye movement.

Computers and information systems have had, and continue to have, a tremendous and far-reaching effect on nearly all aspects of the business community.

VOCABULARY SELF-TEST

Can you define the following terms?

accounting information system (p. 355)

computer-aided design (CAD) (p. 358)

computer-aided manufacturing (CAM) (p. 357)

computer-integrated manufacturing (CIM) (p. 358)

computer numerical control (CNC) (p. 360)

financial information system (p. 356)

human resources information system (p. 357)

manufacturing automation protocol (MAP) (p. 358)

marketing information system (p. 356)

process control (p. 362)

production/operations information system (p. 357)

programmable controller (p. 361)

robotics (p. 360)

REVIEW QUESTIONS

Multiple Choice

1. A(n) _____ primarily uses transaction processing systems to record transactions that affect the financial status of the organization.
    a. human resources information system
    b. accounting information system
    c. marketing information system
    d. production/operations information system

2. The information system that gathers and processes data about all of the activities involved in producing goods and services is called a(n) _____ .
    a. accounting information system
    b. financial information system
    c. production/operations information system
    d. marketing information system

3. An information system that automates and integrates the entire manufacturing enterprise results in _____ .
    a. manufacturing automation protocol (MAP)
    b. computer-aided manufacturing (CAM)
    c. computer-aided design (CAD)
    d. computer-integrated manufacturing (CIM)

4. The integration of the computer and graphics to aid in design and drafting is called _____ .
    a. process control
    b. computer-aided design (CAD)
    c. computer numerical control
    d. computer-aided manufacturing (CAM)

5. "... a reprogrammable, multifunctional manipulator designed to move material, parts, tools, or specialized devices through variable programmed motions for the performance of a variety of tasks" is one organization's definition of a(n) _____ .
    a. robot
    b. end effector
    c. machine controller
    d. programmable controller

Fill-In

1. A(n) _____ is designed to provide information concerning the acquisition of funds to finance business operations.

2. _____ is the process of automating and integrating an entire manufacturing organization.

3. The process of programming a computer to control a process such as milling is called _____ .

4. A(n) _____ is a computer-regulated unit that controls on/off functions of switches and relays and processes.

5. The monitoring and controlling of various processes in a system is called _____ .

Short Answer

1. How does an accounting information system differ from a financial information system?

2. How have robots influenced the manufacturing industry?

3. Describe several ways in which information systems are used in the banking and investment industries.

4. Explain how information systems are used in the retail sales industry.

5. Summarize ways in which information systems are used in the health care industry.

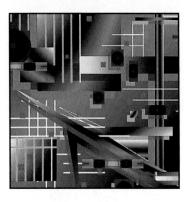

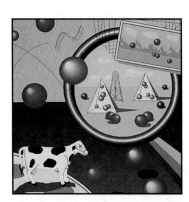

OUTLINE

OBJECTIVES

Chapter

10

Managing Data: Files and Databases

Profile

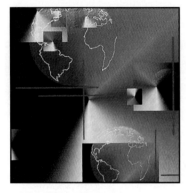

E. F. Codd

Experience is one of life's best teachers. Most of us can see how something can be done by doing it. Some, however, can see how something is done and devise a new and better way of doing it. So it was with Edgar F. Codd, the creator of the relational database structure. Codd received his master's degree in mathematics from Oxford University in England in 1949. Later, he incorporated the mathematical concepts he learned there to develop his strategy for a database management system. This development did not happen overnight, for Codd had 20 years of computer experience before proposing his ideas on a relational database model.

Codd, who was born in England and served as a pilot for the Royal Air Force in World War II, was employed at IBM in 1949. He helped design IBM's first stored-program computer, the IBM 701. Codd also lived briefly in Canada, where he managed the computer center for the Canadian Guided Missile Program. A short time later he returned to and became a citizen of the United States.

Twenty years later, Codd found himself at a seminar on database management systems where he saw something amiss. Finding data was a potentially complex process under the current structure. Codd reasoned that by using sound mathematical principles, called predicate logic, the database could be simplified into tables. In mathematical terms, these tables were called relations. Codd's idea thus became known as a relational database structure.

New ideas are not always welcomed, and Codd struggled for years to persuade IBM to accept his concept. In fact, it took until 1981 before IBM announced its first relational database product. Still, perseverance paid off for Codd, as the relational model became the standard for databases.

The battles were not over, though. Codd had to fight to recover from a serious fall that left him in a coma. Although he eventually retired from IBM in 1985, Codd was not one to rest on his laurels. He and a friend formed a company, Codd and Date Consultants, to continue improving the relational database model. New fronts on the battlefield arise from the proponents of object-oriented databases, who say the relational system is outmoded. But don't count Codd out just yet.

Personal and professional lives involve gathering data and organizing them into information required for decision making and problem solving. For example, a salesperson closes a deal, the production department needs access to the engineering specifications for a new product, a friend gives you a new address and telephone number, or you contact a travel agent about flight information to your favorite vacation spot. Computers enhance many of our data-gathering and information-processing tasks and are essential for other tasks because they easily store and access data from storage media. This chapter looks at two general types of programs for managing data: file management systems and database management systems. It explores several different types as well as the functions of database management systems. Later, in Chapter 12, we'll look specifically at microcomputer database management systems (DBMS).

Objective 10.1   Explain what a file is and describe the use of flat files and file management systems.

What Is a File?

A **file** is a structure used to store data that are composed of related records. Each of these records is composed of fields that relate to the record (Figure 10.1). Flat files are the oldest and simplest way to manage data. A **flat file** is a file that has no relationship to or integrating structure with any other file. It cannot be cross-referenced with other files. The software that manages the storage, access to, retrieval from, and use of files is called a **file management system (FMS)**. Because an FMS defines no relationships between files, it accesses and manipulates only one file at a time (Figure 10.2). An FMS is the simplest type of program used to manage files.

Advantages of an FMS include low purchase price, ease of operation and maintenance, and low vulnerability to data error caused by hardware failures and software errors because only one file is accessed and used at a time. It can be an easy, low-cost solution to managing flat files that contain data rarely, if ever, cross-referenced with data in other files. An FMS meets the needs of individuals who simply want to store lists of data, such as inventories of personal assets.

FIGURE 10.1
A file is composed of records and fields.

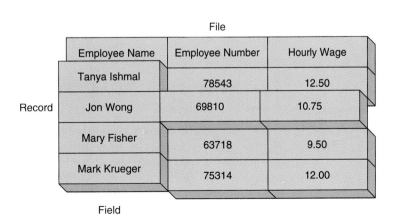

FIGURE 10.2
A file management system can
access only one file at a time.

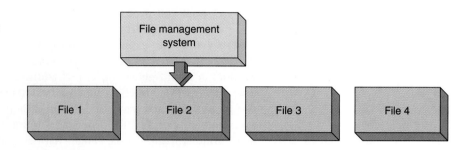

File management systems do have some major limitations for data storage and access. These disadvantages result from the fact that data are often related. The disadvantages include the following:

- Flat files are independent and are not integrated.
- The same data are often duplicated in multiple flat files. If the data change, all occurrences of the data must be located and updated in the appropriate files.
- Programs are dependent on the arrangement of the fields in the records, called the file format. The data in a file must be stored in the exact format that the program expects.
- Programs to manage data in multiple flat files at the same time are difficult to create and maintain. Some file management systems, called **programmable file management systems**, allow users to enter programming commands for cross-referencing of multiple flat files. However, users are responsible for creating the code to do this, and such users must have a great deal of programming knowledge.

Because the data used by businesses are often related, an easier and more efficient way to store and manage data was developed: databases and database management systems.

Objective 10.2   Define database and identify the structures used to store data in a database.

What Is a Database?

To remedy some of the pitfalls in standard flat file structures, many users rely on databases. A **database** is a collection of related and cross-referenced data designed and created to minimize repetition and ease manipulation of data.

How Data Are Stored in Databases

The data in a database are stored in one of three types of data structures: (1) files, (2) tables, or (3) objects. You already know that a file contains records and fields. A table contains rows and columns. The rows are tuples (rhymes with couples), and the columns are domains (Figure 10.3). Tables contain related tuples, just as files contain related records. A file in a database may correspond to one or more tables in a database that uses tables. In a table, each row contains the same number of columns, and data in the columns

FIGURE 10.3
A relational database table.

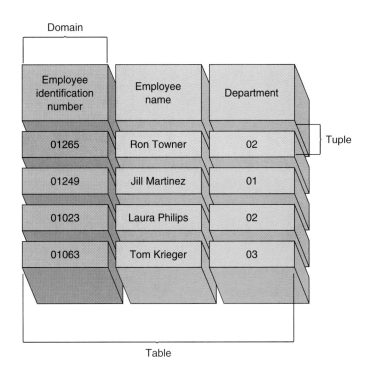

are of the same type (character or numeric, etc.) and size. An object consists of both data and programming instructions that act on the data (Figure 10.4).

Objective 10.3   Describe the advantages and disadvantages of a database.

Why Would You Use a Database?

Although a database has advantages and disadvantages, the former greatly outweigh the latter. Following are the major reasons to consider a database.

Advantages

A database *reduces data redundancy.* For example, a customer's name and residence may appear only once in a database. Some redundancy in a database can be tolerated, and even encouraged, to support data manipulation tasks; however, in independent file processing, each file needs the name and address of the customer. In an independent file system, therefore, a customer's name and residence information may appear in 20 to 30 files. Whenever a customer address changes, updating all of the affected files is both time-consuming and prone to error.

A database *improves data integrity.* Since a particular piece of data appears in only a limited number of locations, future reports are more apt to reflect any change or addition. For example, if a customer notifies the bank of an address change and the address is stored in only one location, then all other files—checking account, savings account, outstanding loans, bank-issued credit card, tax reporting, and solicitation—will reflect the new address.

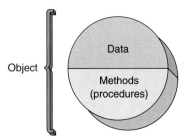

FIGURE 10.4
An object.

A database *maintains data independence.* The structure of the database requires that data be independent; i.e., deleting or changing selected data does not affect other data in the database. If a manager quits his/her job, for example, data concerning his/her office furniture, telephone number, travel expenditures, and other nonsalary items are not destroyed when the manager is deleted from the current employee database. Also, data dependency between the data and the application software is eliminated. A database stores data independently of the programming language or file access method used to access the database. Therefore, if these factors change, the database does not have to be changed.

A database *improves data security.* Since most database systems maintain their own security and all of the data are in one place, security is easier to maintain. Ensuring security for redundant data in standard, multiple files stored on several disks or tapes is difficult.

A database *maintains data consistency.* The kind, type, and size of data are consistent for all applications. For example, the size of a specific field is the same for all applications using the database.

A database allows more *powerful manipulation of data.* Because the data stored in a database can be cross-referenced and integrated, users can perform much more sophisticated data manipulations than with an independent, unrelated file system.

In a database, data are *easier to access and use.* Since data are available for all applications, the data do not have to be duplicated or repeated.

Disadvantages

There are several disadvantages to using databases. First, mainframe databases are highly complex and require specialized designers and programmers to implement. Second, mainframe databases are expensive in terms of the hardware and software needed and the personnel required to design and maintain them. Third, even though databases provide increased security, massive damage to a database can occur if an unauthorized person penetrates the system. Fourth, since all data are in one location, databases are vulnerable to hardware failure or software errors. The large size of databases may make recovery from a disaster time-consuming and costly. Making a backup copy of an entire database poses problems and challenges for a data-processing staff, particularly if the database spans several disks, each of which contains multiple gigabytes of disk space.

A database system is not a necessity for everyone. A small company or an individual with simple needs and relatively few files may not need one. However, many companies could not exist or could not function efficiently without a database.

Objective 10.4   Describe the purpose and basic functions of a database management system.

What Is a Database Management System?

A **database management system (DBMS)** is software that manages the creation, storage, access, updating, deletion, and use of a database. A DBMS can access and manage multiple files, tables, or objects at the same time,

What effect does a hydroelectric dam have on fish—specifically salmon and steelheads—their migration patterns, and their hatcheries? Are there implications for irrigation and logging? These are typical problems for engineers and biologists in various agencies in Oregon, Idaho, Washington, and Montana.

In 1980, Congress charged the Northwest Power Planning Council (NPPC) with keeping these things in mind while developing plans for building dams along the Columbia River system. Some of the other variables that had to be considered included the ability to identify several fish species as well as process geological and archeological information. All these restrictions resulted in a database of 300,000 records with each record containing about 7,500 characters. Additionally, the Endangered Species Act expected data about threatened species of salmon, such as tracking the river in which they were found, the hatchery from which they came, and counts from each dam. And, while you're at it, would it matter if that dam was modified slightly when it is being repaired?

A Digital Equipment VAX 4300 using a CompuServe 1032 database management system was the solution for this monumental tracking problem. Now the system quickly screens each request to build or modify a dam by cross-referencing it to the protected areas. This screening process prevents licenses from being issued before the environmental concerns are considered. The database menu system is easy enough so that even novice end users are able to create their own applications.

This is one fish story that you can believe.

linking them together if needed. Mainframe DBMSs are dominated by IBM's DB2 (DataBase II). Minicomputer DBMSs include Oracle, Sybase, and Gupta. Typical microcomputer database management systems include Paradox, dBASE, and RBASE.

The routines and programs in a DBMS perform a variety of tasks and have numerous features that make the product attractive to businesses. A typical DBMS makes it possible to:

■ Create the databases and their structures, using information furnished by the database designer. It defines the data, their relationships, and the way they will be maintained.

■ Control and administer the data in the database. It controls security by setting the level of access for each user. For example, read access allows a user to read only, write access allows a user to change the contents of a database, and administrative access allows a user to change the structure and relationships, as well as the contents, of a database.

■ Access, enter, modify, and manipulate the data in a database by users and application programs.

■ Generate reports. Users can design and name reports to be extracted from the contents of a database. Once created, the reports can be generated with a simple command using the latest data available.

- Obtain information from the database quickly using *ad hoc* query facilities. For instance, you might ask how many customer accounts in your database are past due by more than 90 days, or how many of your customers live in Ohio.
- Provide reports to management on who accessed the database and what activity was performed.
- Provide reports to operators on hardware utilization, the status of current users, and other monitoring data.
- Back up and recover data in the database. Routines restore data to a known state if hardware, power failures, or human error cause the data to be lost or corrupted.

Many microcomputer-based DBMSs lack several of these features because they are not multiple-user systems. The needs of a single user with a microcomputer system are different from those of multiple users with a mainframe system.

Multiple-user DBMSs present several challenges. One is decreased system performance. As more people and applications become active on a computer system, performance levels decrease until response time at terminals becomes intolerable. When system performance decreases substantially, major changes in hardware, software, and database structure may be necessary. Other challenges include controlling concurrent access of data, maintaining security, and administering the database.

Objective 10.5   List and define the four database models.

What Are the Different Database Models?

Database Models

- Hierarchical
- Network
- Relational
- Object-oriented

There are four types of database models: (1) hierarchical, (2) network, (3) relational, and (4) object-oriented. The hierarchical and network models have been available since the early 1970s. They use standard files and provide structures that allow them to be cross-referenced and integrated. The relational model became popular in the early 1980s, and it is used extensively. It uses tables to store data, provides the ability to cross-reference and manipulate the data, and provides for data integrity. The object-oriented model began making its mark in the late 1980s. It uses objects and is expected to increase in popularity for applications that require complex data.

Hierarchical Model

In a **hierarchical database,** data relationships follow hierarchies, or trees, which reflect either a one-to-one relationship or a one-to-many relationship among record types (Figure 10.5). The uppermost record in a tree structure is called the **root record**. From there, data are organized into groups containing parent records and child records. One parent record can have many child records (called siblings), but each child record can have only one parent record. Parent records are higher in the data structure than are child records; however, each child can become a parent and have its own child records.

FIGURE 10.5
Hierarchical data relationships.

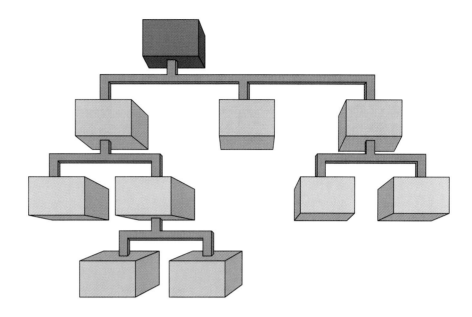

Network Model

A **network database** is similar to a hierarchical database except that each record can have more than one parent, thus creating a many-to-many relationship among the records (Figure 10.6). For example, a customer may be called on by more than one salesperson in the same company, and a single salesperson may call on more than one customer. Within this structure, any record can be related to any other data element.

The main advantage of a network database is its ability to handle relationships among various records. Therefore, more than one path can lead to a desired data level. The network database structure is more versatile and flexible than is the hierarchical structure because the route to data is not necessarily downward; it can be in any direction.

In both the network structure and the hierarchical structure, data access is fast because the data path is predefined. However, any relationship between data items must be defined when the database is being created. If a user wants to retrieve or manipulate data in a manner not defined when the database was originally created, it is costly and time-consuming to redesign the database structure. This limitation led to the development of the relational database model.

Relational Model

A **relational database** is composed of many tables in which data are stored, but a relational database involves more than just the use of tables. Tables in a relational database must have unique rows, and the cells (the intersection of a row and column—equivalent to a field) must be single-valued (that is, each cell must contain only one item of information, such as a name, address, or identification number). A **relational database management**

FIGURE 10.6
Network data relationships.

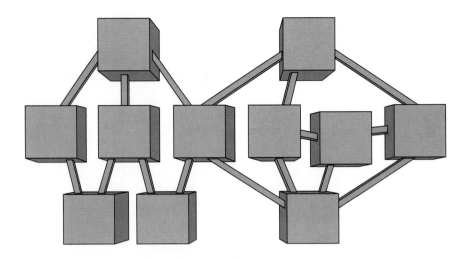

system (RDBMS) allows data to be readily created, maintained, manipulated, and retrieved from a relational database.

In a relational database, data relationships do not have to be predefined. Users query a relational database and establish data relationships spontaneously by joining common fields. A **database query language** acts as an interface between users and a relational database management system. The language helps the users of a relational database to easily manipulate, analyze, and create reports from the data contained in the database. It is composed of easy-to-use statements that allow people other than programmers to query the database.

Two basic query styles are used in a relational database: (1) query by example, and (2) structured query language. In **query by example,** the database management system displays field information and users enter inquiry conditions in the desired fields. For example, if a user wants to list all of the employees whose salaries are greater than $25,000 and sort the items in ascending order by department number, the screen might appear as in Figure 10.7.

Structured query language (SQL) is the standard database query language used with relational databases. Using structured query language the inquiry in Figure 10.7 would appear as it does in Figure 10.8. This tells the database management system to use the fields EMPNAM, EMPNUM, DEPTNUM, and SAL from each record in the employee file (EMPF) if the employee's salary is greater than $25,000 and to sort that list by department number.

Object-Oriented Model

Although the relational model is well suited to the needs of storing and manipulating business data, it is not appropriate for the data needs of certain complex applications, such as computer-aided design (CAD) and computer-assisted software engineering (CASE). Business data follow a defined data structure that the relational models handle well. However,

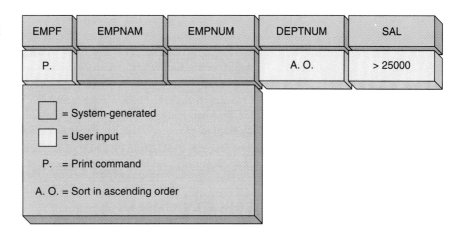

FIGURE 10.7
A database query language that uses the query-by-example approach.

EMPF	EMPNAM	EMPNUM	DEPTNUM	SAL
P.			A. O.	> 25000

☐ = System-generated

☐ = User input

P. = Print command

A. O. = Sort in ascending order

FIGURE 10.8
A database query language that uses the structured query language approach.

```
SELECT      EMPNAM, EMPNUM, DEPTNUM, SAL
FROM        EMPF
WHERE       SALARY > 25000
ORDER       BY DEPTNUM
```

applications such as CAD and CASE deal with a variety of complex data types that cannot be easily expressed by relational models.

An **object-oriented database** uses objects and messages to accommodate new types of data and provides for advanced data handling. An **object-oriented database management system (OODBMS)** permits objects to be readily created, maintained, manipulated, and retrieved from an object-oriented database.

An OODBMS provides features that you would expect in any other database management system, but there is still no clear standard for the object-oriented model. OODBMSs are expected to evolve and be used for applications with complex data needs. They are not, however, expected to replace relational databases. Instead, they work in tandem, each suited for different tasks.

Objective 10.6   Identify some basic considerations in the design of a database and define logical database design, physical database design, schema, and subschema.

What Is Involved in Designing a Database?

Most database design is done by programming staff, usually by a senior system analyst or, in larger companies, by a database designer or a database administrator. The designer must consider the needs of each department's users, the type of DBMS software already in use, the training of the staff, and the availability of system resources. Also, the requests of each department must be compatible with the long-range plans.

A feasibility study, usually performed by a system analyst, identifies the needs and wants of the users. The analyst identifies what data are needed, how to capture the data, and how to merge the data into the framework of the existing databases. An analyst also designs procedures and standards for the maintenance and sharing of the data. Because a database restricts access to sensitive data, such as an employee's salary or a customer's medical history, an analyst may have to consult with other departments, upper management, or company attorneys to guarantee security. After analyzing user needs and understanding data requirements, the analyst begins database design.

Logical Database Design

A **logical database design** is a detailed description of a database in terms of the ways in which the data will be used. During this phase, an analyst performs a detailed study of the data, identifying how the data are grouped together and how they relate to each other. An analyst also determines which fields have multiple occurrences of data, which fields will be keys or indexes, and the size and type of each field.

Physical Database Design

After identifying all of the data to be included, an analyst enters a description into a **data dictionary,** which is a data file containing a technical description of the data to be stored in the database. The dictionary includes the field names; their type (such as alphanumeric or numeric), size, and descriptions; and their logical relationships. A data dictionary is a tool that a developer uses to communicate with other members of the development staff about a database description. A dictionary also provides a way of standardizing the names and lengths of data within a database structure.

An analyst, a database designer, or a database administrator then transforms the logical design into a **physical database design,** the actual structure of the database, to match the DBMS software already in use. If multiple database management systems are available, the feasibility study should have identified which DBMS is to be used for the development of the application. An analyst designs the database according to the structure (hierarchical, network, or relational) of the recommended DBMS.

Schema and Subschema

DBMS software must know the structure of the database and the relationships among the data. Consequently, a database administrator, who has the primary responsibility for providing this information, creates a schema and subschema for the database. A **schema** is a complete description of the content and structure of a database. It defines the database to the system, including the record layout; the names, lengths, and sizes of all fields; and the data relationships. A **subschema** defines each user's view, or specific

Highlight

10.2

FBI Database Expansion Seen as Threat to Civil Rights

The Federal Bureau of Investigation (FBI) maintains the National Crime Information Center (NCIC) database. Housing the hardware necessary to operate the system requires a room half the size of a football field. The NCIC database consists of 12 main files and a total of about 19.4 million individual files. These files contain information on criminal arrests and convictions, missing persons, individuals with outstanding warrants, stolen vehicles, and individuals suspected of plotting against high-level government officials.

Law enforcement officials access the NCIC files more than 700,000 times a day, checking on everything from routine traffic violations to information on felony suspects. The database is a valuable resource for law enforcement, but many groups and individuals are worried that violations of civil rights may result from storing inaccurate or false information in such databases. Even the FBI, which spends $1 million a year auditing the system, admits "a lot of things can happen" with so many queries being made each day.

Such was the case of a Michigan man who was arrested five times for crimes he did not commit after his wallet was stolen. He was even mistaken for a murder suspect who had used his identification. Eventually he received a settlement from the city of Los Angeles for failing to remove his name from its database, but his fate could have been much worse.

Another worry is that the FBI cannot provide adequate security for the information stored in the NCIC. For example, if the FBI's listing of drug informers fell into the wrong hands, it could be devastating. The computer virus that brought the Internet computer system to a standstill several years ago was a further reminder that most computer systems have serious security vulnerabilities. Maintaining large databases of any kind poses significant challenges for the security and privacy of the data as well as for assurance that only valid, correct data are entered into the database.

parts of the database that a user can access. A subschema restricts each user to certain records and fields within the database. Every database has only one schema, but each user must have a subschema.

Objective 10.7   Describe several concerns of managing databases.

How Are Databases Managed?

When considering the management of a database, the following objectives should be met:

- Avoid unnecessary redundancy.
- Provide access flexibility.
- Provide reliability.
- Maintain data independence.
- Allow for growth and changes in needs.
- Preserve data integrity.
- Ensure data security.

Administrating a Database

Databases are managed by a **database administrator (DBA),** who may be one person or a group of people. A DBA should be trained in the specific DBMS software package and in the construction of databases. A skilled DBA coupled with DBMS software should provide efficient database management. If a company has multiple DBMS packages, there is usually at least one DBA for each DBMS package.

The main functions of a database administrator are:

- *Implementing the database.* A DBA coordinates the input of the intended users of a database. He or she works with the users and a system analyst to create an effective and efficient database structure.
- *Providing security for the database.* A DBA is responsible for designing and implementing security standards and controlling both who uses a database and what data are available. A DBA works with middle and top-level management to create corporate goals and guidelines for long-term usage of a database.
- *Monitoring performance.* A DBA continually oversees the performance of a database, fixes problems when they develop, and consults with a system team or a DBMS technical support team when necessary. If database performance declines, a DBA makes recommendations for modifying software or purchasing additional hardware and software.
- *Designing standards.* A DBA creates, distributes, and enforces standards and procedures for using a database. In addition, a DBA distributes any literature, memos, and other documents on changes or modifications associated with a DBMS to users and the programming staff.
- *Providing backup and recovery.* A DBA establishes controls and procedures for the systematic backup of a database and plans and implements disaster recovery.

Appointing a Database Administrator

The DBA of each DBMS maintains and coordinates the use of the DBMS. After a company acquires a DBMS, it must select an administrator. The vendor company trains the selected person to use and manage the DBMS. Usually, this initial training lasts from one to three weeks. In an ongoing educational program, a DBA attends conferences, seminars, and user support groups on the DBMS. These groups consist of other users of the same product, who exchange suggestions with each other and the DBMS vendor. When a vendor releases a new version, a DBA is the first to attend workshops.

Maintaining a Data Dictionary

Some companies maintain a file that contains the entire description of the data to be stored in a database. This data dictionary is a tool that many DBAs, database designers, and system analysts use to coordinate the activities of application development. Developers access the data dictionary to find out about any field—its name, type, size, editing criteria, structure, and so on.

However, maintaining a data dictionary to include any and all changes in data descriptions is time-consuming and costly. One DBMS that has a data dictionary as an integral part of the product is IDMS/R's Integrated Data Dictionary. When an active data dictionary is not included, a user company must purchase or license one from another vendor. Unfortunately, many of the data dictionaries on the market today do not fulfill all programming needs, such as charting data relationships and automatically inserting data changes into the software. For that reason, many companies do not install an active data dictionary. For a data dictionary to be of value, it must describe all of the records in a database. But for some installations that have had a product for a long period of time, it is not worthwhile to try to enter years of database designs into a dictionary after the fact.

Validating Input

One of the critical challenges associated with data entry is entering error-free data into the system. For hierarchical and network databases, programmers write codes containing edit routines to monitor the entry of data. An edit routine captures invalid data before they are stored in a database. However, with relational databases, users can access and change the database without programmer involvement. In addition, since most users do not write edit routines, the data they enter may not be electronically edited by a program. Thus trash, or garbage, may enter the database through unedited data entry. *Garbage* refers to any database data that are invalid (such as 12TY4 for a zip code or 12345YY77 for a Social Security number).

To solve some of the editing problems, many relational DBMSs permit a programming staff to write procedures to ensure data integrity and then attach those procedures to the data description. Thereafter, all data entering the DBMS pass through those routines, which are transparent, or invisible, to users but guarantee the validity of the data.

Providing for Backups

All databases have backup procedures to guarantee the recovery of data in case things go wrong with the system. For most DBMSs, the database is removed from active status before the backup procedure starts so that additional processing cannot occur. Such backups are usually made during nonpeak work hours, i.e., on second and third shifts, to minimize interference with regular company business.

Other products provide automatic backups during real-time operation. In other words, when a transaction enters a database, the DBMS makes an immediate backup of the data affected. The advantages of a transaction-by-transaction backup are that the system does not have to be taken off-line, so 24-hour operations are possible, and transactions can be reposted electronically to a backup copy of the database in the event of data contamination.

Providing Security and Privacy

Security for a computer system is handled through a log-on process in which each user enters an account number and a password. Generally, security specialists handle the security for a system; however, once a user accesses DBMS software, a subschema controls security for the database. A DBA manages the security framework for a DBMS, writes the subschema for each user, and indicates what data are available to which users. Thus, it is the responsibility of the DBA to identify sensitive data and restrict access via subschemas. If a DBA fails in this endeavor, sensitive data become vulnerable. The personal ethics of the user and the corporate philosophy have a tremendous impact on whether mistakes are identified and management informed about existing or potential problems.

Controlling Concurrent Operations

On real-time systems, many users access the same database at the same time. Occasionally, two or more users may attempt to access the same data simultaneously, creating a situation called **concurrent access**. If both are simply viewing the data, the system should allow simultaneous use. However, if one user wants to change the data, the system must temporarily lock the data from further access until the change occurs or the access is abandoned. Consider a typical college registration process in which each class added or dropped changes the number of available seats. While one student is adding or dropping a class, other students must be locked out of the database; otherwise, the class might be overloaded or a student might be turned away when a seat exists. To handle this potential problem, programming staff place locking instructions in the codes they write. In addition, most DBMSs permit a DBA to write locking strategies into schemas or subschemas and permit a user to temporarily lock data.

Objective 10.8   Discuss the advantages and disadvantages of a distributed database.

What Is a Distributed Database?

Distributed data processing is accomplished through a network of decentralized computers, possibly with a central, or host, computer. Databases can also be distributed. A **distributed database** exists in the following forms: (1) the database can be on-line at the host computer in a central location but also available to remote locations, (2) part of the database at the host computer can be duplicated and placed in a remote computer, a type of distributive database processing called *segmentation,* or (3) copies of the entire database and DBMS can be situated at each remote location, a type of distributive processing called *replication.* Any of these methods might be used with an inventory database for various units of a large chain department store.

The cost benefits associated with distributed databases vary, depending on many factors in a company. For example, a database on a computer system in Atlanta that contains only data used by a San Francisco office will incur considerable data transmission expense. In addition, the differential in time zones may require the host site to keep the DBMS on-line during second-shift operations, thus affecting the resources available for other processing at the central site. Furthermore, keeping key personnel (such as a system team, DBA, and programmer) on-site in Atlanta for extended hours may be expensive in terms of both money and loss of key personnel for other activities.

The expense of duplicating a DBMS at a remote site includes buying additional hardware, purchasing or licensing software for multiple sites, and maintaining key personnel at the remote site. As microcomputers and minicomputers become more powerful, mainframe DBMS vendors are making products available. As costs decrease, many businesses may find distributive database processing an economical option.

Summary

A file is a data structure made up of records and fields. Flat files have no relationship or integrating structure with any other file. A file management system is software that manages the storage, access to, retrieval from, and use of flat files. A file management system has the advantages of being low in cost, easy to operate and maintain, and low in vulnerability to data error due to hardware failures and software errors. However, disadvantages include the fact that flat files are independent, not integrated, and the same data are often duplicated in multiple flat files. Each occurrence of any data must be located and updated each time they are changed, programs are dependent on the arrangement of the fields in the records, and programs to manage data in multiple flat files are difficult to create and maintain. Programmable filers are file management systems where users enter programming commands to allow cross-referencing of multiple flat files.

A database is a collection of related and cross-referenced data designed to minimize repetition and improve ease of manipulation of the data. Data can be stored in a database in file, table, or object form.

Database processing has the following advantages: redundancy is reduced, integrity is improved, data independence is maintained, security is improved, consistency is maintained, more powerful manipulation of data is allowed, and data access and use are easier. Disadvantages of databases include: they are highly complex and require specialized designers and programmers to implement them; they are expensive in terms of the hardware and software needed and the personnel required to design and maintain them; massive damage to a database can occur if an unauthorized person penetrates the system; and all data are in one location, which makes databases vulnerable to hardware failure or software errors.

A database management system (DBMS) is software that manages the creation, storage, access, updating, deletion, and use of a database. A typical DBMS creates databases and their structures; provides the vehicle for the control and administration of the data in the database; provides the vehicle for users and application programs to access, enter, modify, and manipulate the data in a database; provides a report generator; provides "ad hoc" query facilities; provides reports to management on who accessed the database and what activity was performed; provides reports to operators on hardware utilization, status of current users, and other monitoring data; and provides automatic backup and recovery routines for the data in databases.

Multiple-user databases present several challenges including decreasing system performance as the number of users increases, controlling concurrent access of data, maintaining security, and administrating the database.

There are four database models: (1) hierarchical, (2) network, (3) relational, and (4) object-oriented. The hierarchical and network models use files for storing data. Data relationships in the hierarchical databases follow hierarchies, or trees, which reflect either a one-to-one or a one-to-many relationship among the record types. Data relationships in network databases follow a many-to-many relationship among the records. The data relationships must be defined at the time that a hierarchical or network database is created. Relational databases use tables for storing data. The data relationships can be dynamically determined by the users and do not have to be defined when the database is created. A relational database uses a database query language for users to access and manipulate data in the database. Query by example and structured query language are two database query languages. Object-oriented databases store data together with procedures in objects.

A logical design is a detailed description of a database in terms of the ways data will be used. In a logical design, a data dictionary, which is a data file containing a technical description of the data to be stored in the database, is created. A physical design details the actual structure of a database. A schema is a complete description of the content and structure of a database. The subschema defines the specific parts of a database that each user can access.

The objectives of managing databases include avoiding unnecessary data redundancy, providing for access flexibility, providing data reliability, maintaining data independence, allowing for growth and changes in needs, preserving data integrity, and ensuring data security. A database administrator manages and oversees database operations. It is important that data are validated and that there are provisions for backing up the data stored to prevent their loss if things go wrong with the system. Adequate security and privacy of data must be provided to protect both the data and the individuals or organizations about whom data is contained in a database. Finally, concurrent access (access by more than one user to the same data) must be controlled to protect data.

A distributed database is one that (1) can be on-line at the host computer in a central location but also available to remote locations, (2) has part of the database at the host computer duplicated and placed in a remote computer, a type of distributive database processing called segmentation, or (3) has copies of the entire database and DBMS at each remote location, a type of distributive processing called replication.

VOCABULARY SELF-TEST   *Can you define the following terms?*

concurrent access (p. 386)

database (p. 374)

database administrator (DBA) (p. 384)

database management system (DBMS) (p. 376)

database query language (p. 380)

data dictionary (p. 382)

distributed database (p. 386)

file (p. 373)

file management system (FMS) (p. 373)

flat file (p. 373)

hierarchical database (p. 378)

logical database design (p. 382)

network database (p. 379)

object-oriented database (p. 381)

object-oriented database management system (OODBMS) (p. 381)

physical database design (p. 382)

programmable file management system (p. 374)

query by example (p. 380)

relational database (p. 379)

relational database management system (RDBMS) (p. 379)

root record (p. 378)

schema (p. 382)

structured query language (SQL) (p. 380)

subschema (p. 382)

REVIEW QUESTIONS

Multiple Choice

1. A(n) _____ is a file that has no relationship or integrating structure with any other file and cannot be cross-referenced with other files.
   a. table
   b. object
   c. database
   d. flat file

2. Which of the following is not an advantage of file management systems?
   a. ease of operation and maintenance
   b. cross-referencing
   c. low purchase price
   d. low vulnerability to data error due to hardware failures and software errors

3. A collection of related and cross-referenced data designed and created to minimize repetition and ease manipulation of data is called a(n) _____.
   a. flat file
   b. object
   c. master file
   d. database

4. Which of the following is not an advantage of a database?
   a. Data integrity is improved.
   b. Data are more difficult to access and use.
   c. Data redundancy is reduced.
   d. Data consistency is maintained.

5. A(n) _____ is the software that manages the creation, storage, access, updating, deletion, and use of a database.
   a. file management system
   b. database management system

    c. flat file

    d. application

6. The database model that allows each record to have more than one parent, creating a many-to-many relationship among the records, is called a(n) _____.

    a. network database

    b. hierarchical database

    c. object-oriented database

    d. relational database

7. A(n) _____ database allows users to query a database using a database query language.

    a. object-oriented

    b. network

    c. hierarchical

    d. relational

8. A(n) _____ defines each user's view or specific parts of a database that a user can access.

    a. subschema

    b. schema

    c. object

    d. logical design

9. A _____ contains a complete description of all data fields in the database and is used by many DBAs, database designers, and system analysts to coordinate the activities of application development.

    a. schema

    b. logical design

    c. data dictionary

    d. physical design

10. A(n) _____ allows part of a database located at a host computer to be duplicated and placed in a remote computer.

    a. relational database

    b. object-oriented database

    c. hierarchical database

    d. distributed database

Fill-In

1. A file that has no relationship or integrating structure with any other file is called a(n) _____.

2. A(n) _____ is software that manages the creation, storage, access, updating, deletion, and use of a database.

3. In the _____ model, data relationships follow hierarchies, or trees, which reflect either a one-to-one or a one-to-many relationship among record types.

4. The _____ model is composed of many tables in which data are stored.

5. _____ is a database query language that displays field information and allows users to enter inquiry conditions in desired fields.

6. A(n) _____ uses objects and messages to accommodate new types of data and provide for advanced data handling.

7. A(n) _____ is a detailed description of a database in terms of the ways in which the data are used.

8. A complete description of the content and structure of a database, including the record layout, the names, lengths, and sizes of all fields, and the data relationships, is called the _____.

9. The person who is responsible for managing a database is called a(n) _____.

10. _____ is a situation in which two or more users attempt to access the same data simultaneously.

Short Answer

1. Discuss the advantages and disadvantages of a file management system.

2. Describe the different structures in which data can be stored in a database.

3. Identify the advantages and disadvantages of database processing.

4. What is a database management system, and what are its main functions?

5. Identify and describe the four database models presented.

6. Explain the difference between a logical database design and a physical database design.

7. What limits a user's access to a database?

8. Describe the functions of a database administrator.

9. Identify the objectives of managing a database.

10. What is a distributed database?

Issues for Thought

1. Multiple-user databases increase the potential that an unauthorized user may gain access to sensitive or personal data. You've noticed that a coworker left out a note that contains the code and password required to access the payroll compensation data for your organization. Disclosure of compensation data often leads to tension and jealousy among workers and to poor performance by disgruntled employees. Given the possible consequences, how should this incident be treated? Should you talk directly to your coworker? Should you go straight to management? How should management react? How should your coworker react?

2. You have always paid your bills and maintained good credit. However, a credit bureau mistakenly updates your file with data from someone else's file who happens to be a poor credit risk. As a result, you are denied a loan. What implications does such an incident have for the credit bureau? Although it was not done maliciously, what are the responsibilities and rights of the credit bureau? What about your rights and responsibilities as the person denied the loan?

Infomodule

A Structured Query Language (SQL) Primer

In this Infomodule you'll learn the definition of structural query language, why it's important to the world of databases, and what the most common features of SQL do.

WHAT IS STRUCTURED QUERY LANGUAGE?

There used to be a number of database languages, each specific to the computer system on which it was being used. A user had to learn a different set of commands for each computer system. Imagine if each town used different colors in their traffic signals. As long as you didn't go out of town, obeying the traffic laws would be easy. A standardized database language is like having a standard traffic signal; it's easier to move around. A language for database management systems (DBMS) was needed that made machine specifics irrelevant. The same commands could retrieve data regardless of the computer system being used. This database language is called structured query language.

Structured query language (SQL) (pronounced "sequel" or "S-Q-L") is a standard database language used to query, update, and manage relational databases. It allows users to create and operate sets of related information that are stored in tables. SQL is part of a DBMS, not a separate stand-alone software program that you can buy in a store.

History of SQL

SQL became popular in part because it fit into Edgar Codd's (see Profile) definition of the relational database. He saw the goal of relational databases as one where there was a simple way to view data, where data items were independent of one another, and where the database could be easily administrated.

In the early 1970s, researchers at IBM's San Jose Research Laboratory created a database language called Sequel (Structured English Query Language) because it was a sequel to another database query language. Eventually, "English" was dropped from the name and it became Structured Query Language. These early attempts at developing a query language for relational databases evolved into what is now called SQL.

It took many years before SQL became commercially viable. Now most relational database management systems use it to some extent. SQL could be used across a wide variety of computer systems, but many companies began to develop their own versions. The need for standardization became evident.

Many database vendors have established a coalition to standardize SQL commands. The SQL Access Group (SAG) includes companies such as Borland, Novell Inc., and WordPerfect Corp. This may mean that new standards will be set. If you have specific questions, it's best to consult your database manual.

Is SQL Standard?

The American National Standards Institute (ANSI) defined a standard to which all SQL products should conform. However, because so many products existed before the standard there are some discrepancies among the various SQL products. Therefore, the standard is fairly limited; as a result, it has become a minimum standard. Many database vendors have added features beyond the ANSI standard and others have not found the minimum standards to be the most useful so they implemented some features contrary to the ANSI standard.

Most vendors attempt to conform to the ANSI standard without compromising their product to allow a degree of transferability of SQL from one system to the next. Knowing one version of SQL makes it much easier to learn another. Despite the lack of a universal standard, SQL is still accepted as the standard for relational database languages.

Understanding SQL in depth can be a difficult undertaking. Because product variations exist, and because SQL involves many areas of database use that the novice user has never examined, this Infomodule introduces you to the basics of SQL.

What Are the Basics of SQL?

SQL is a database language, but it is not a programming language in the same sense as BASIC, COBOL, or other high-level languages. Those languages are highly structured and use specific artificial syntax to define a sequence of instructions to be processed and executed by the computer. SQL is not a complete programming language like Pascal or FORTRAN because it lacks a rigid structure and uses English-like words to create more natural, written statements.

SQL can be used as a part of a programming language, embedded into it, or used with a DBMS to formulate interactive queries. Its features make it usable by technical and nontechnical users.

Embedded SQL

High-level languages were not specifically developed to be used by themselves in a database setting. These languages can be enhanced, however, with subsets of the SQL language that extend the high-level language for database access. This is called *embedded* SQL, which means that the SQL statements interact with the other languages. The SQL statements are specialized for database management tasks. With embedded SQL the user needs to know how the SQL statements interface with the high-level language.

Interactive SQL

The nonprofessional computer user, as most of you will likely be, will work with DBMSs that contain interactive SQL. With *interactive* SQL, the statements are part of the DBMS. They are "built in" so the user does not have to be concerned with how the statements interface with another language. The SQL statements are entered at the program's command prompt.

What Is a Query?

The core of SQL is its flexibility in querying a database. A **query** is a directive given to the DBMS to retrieve specified information from its tables. It is the process of requesting data and receiving the results from a database, without changing the data stored there.

Table Properties

Users benefit from SQL because of the flexibility in retrieving data. This flexibility is possible because of the manner in which data are stored in a relational database. Data are stored in tables that have specific properties. These properties include: (1) one or more named columns, (2) the data in each column are of the same type, (3) zero or more rows (zero rows occur when the table is defined but no data are entered yet), (4) every row is unique, (5) a single data value is contained in the intersection of any column and row, and (6) the order of the columns and rows does not matter.

Figure 1 shows the customer table, which includes the named columns CUSTNUM (customer number), NAME, and COMPANY. Each customer is in its own row, thus avoiding duplication of data. The table contains a column designated as a primary key, which holds values unique to each row, such as the customer number.

In Figure 2 the invoice table contains the invoice number, INVNUM, CUSTNUM, and DATE columns. CUSTNUM is sometimes called a foreign key because it refers calls back to a primary key in another table. This permits information in the customer table to be linked to information in the invoice table without duplication.

CUSTNUM	NAME	COMPANY
1	BROWN	ABC
2	SMITH	XYZ
3	WHITE	ALPHA
4	JONES	ABC

FIGURE 1
A customer table. CUSTNUM is the primary key.

INVNUM	CUSTNUM	DATE
6	2	01-18-94
8	3	02-14-94
14	4	02-16-94
23	1	03-07-94

FIGURE 2
The invoice table. INVNUM is the primary key, CUSTNUM is the foreign key.

Finding Data with SQL

There are two basic schemes in which data are retrieved from a database: set orientation and record orientation. Each method has advantages and disadvantages.

A **set-oriented** database allows the user to focus on the characteristics of the data rather than the physical structure of the data. The user works with data in groups, or sets, of tables rather than as individual tables. It is easier to write a query, because the user does not need to understand the format in which the data are stored (Figure 3). DBMSs that use SQL such as SQL Server, Oracle, and SQL Base are set-oriented. It is harder to access successive rows of data in a table, which is a disadvantage in set orientation.

Record-oriented databases access data based on the physical structure of data and indexing (Figure 4). A record pointer permits the user to maneuver

through a table one record at a time. It is easy to access successive rows or records in a table. However, the developer of the database management system must write the programming code such that it will loop through every record requested, which is a disadvantage. Examples of DBMSs that use a record-oriented approach are dBASE and Clipper.

HOW IS SQL USED TO RETRIEVE DATA?

This section gives some SQL commands for retrieving data. Only the basics are given so you can see the ease and versatility of a query using SQL. Many other commands and modifiers are not presented.

CREATE TABLE Command

Tables can be defined easily using SQL commands. Column names and the type of data to be stored there are defined. Data can be of various types, for example, a person's name, employee number, or dollar amount, to name a few. The minimum ANSI SQL data types supported are numeric, decimal, integer, small integer, floating point, real, double precision, and character. The exact data types that each SQL version supports varies. Other common data types include graphics, date, time, and text. Column names are required to identify the columns and to provide a handle by which to retrieve the data.

There are many different number data types because there are many different applications, each of which requires varying degrees of accuracy. For ex-

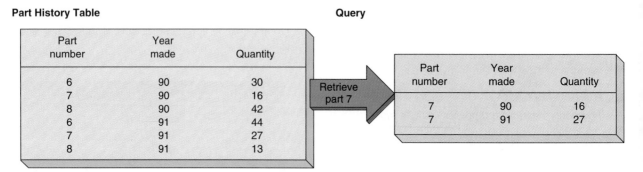

FIGURE 3
With set orientation a simple query can retrieve the pertinent data.

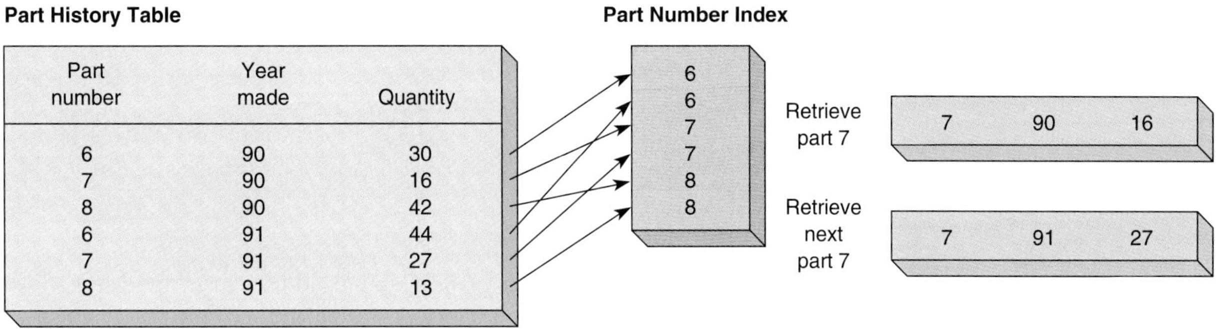

Part History Table

Part number	Year made	Quantity
6	90	30
7	90	16
8	90	42
6	91	44
7	91	27
8	91	13

Part Number Index

```
6
6
7
7
8
8
```

Retrieve part 7

7	90	16

Retrieve next part 7

7	91	27

FIGURE 4

With record orientation the parts history table is first opened, then the part number index is opened, then the requested parts records are retrieved.

ample, employee numbers are not used in calculations and are not handled with decimal place accuracy whereas interest rates, percentages or other monetary units are.

A table is created using the CREATE TABLE command. Proper syntax with interactive SQL includes ending each command with a semicolon and repeating parts of the command with a comma. Column names, data types, and length of fields are also specified. The SQL command sequence to create the customer table in Figure 1 is as follows:

```
CREATE TABLE customer (
custnum NUMERIC,
name CHARACTER (15),
company CHARACTER (15));
```

Rules regulating the length of table and column names vary among SQL versions, but generally they are up to 18 characters with some as many as 31 characters. The name cannot begin with a digit and there is no distinction between upper- and lowercase letters. In the example above, the names are shown in lowercase to distinguish them from the SQL statements. The number of characters shown in parentheses gives the length of the name.

SELECT Command

The SELECT command is used to request data. It is followed by the columns that are to be retrieved.

The SELECT command produces a new table with only those requested columns of data. The table may be saved, but it does not alter the original table. To retrieve the customer number and name columns you would enter:

```
SELECT custnum, name
```

To select all the columns, either specify them in the query or use an asterisk as shown below:

```
SELECT *
```

The SELECT command is not used alone, however. You must also describe the table from which the columns will come. This is accomplished with the FROM command.

FROM Command

The FROM command specifies the table from which to search for the columns of data. The name of the table follows the word FROM. The SELECT and FROM commands are always used in conjunction when querying the database. The following command retrieves all the data in the customer table:

```
SELECT * FROM customer;
```

Multiple requests from different tables are possible with the FROM command. For example, all the columns from both the customer and invoice tables can

FIGURE 5

Table produced from the query:
SELECT * FROM customer,
invoice;.

CUSTNUM	NAME	COMPANY	INVNUM	DATE
2	SMITH	XYZ	6	01-18-94
4	JONES	ABC	8	02-14-94
3	WHITE	ALPHA	14	02-16-94
1	BROWN	ABC	23	03-07-94

be retrieved at the same time. The results are stored
in a new table (Figure 5). The query to accomplish
this would look like this:

```
SELECT * FROM customer, invoice;
```

When the database has searched the customer
and invoice tables for the data requested, it produces
a new table including that data. However, the data
columns won't be arranged in a particular way. In
fact, the same command executed on the same data
at different times may not produce the same order.
In most cases, the retrieved data are listed in the
order in which they were found in the tables.

WHERE Command

Using only the SELECT and FROM commands limits
how narrow a search may be. For example, in the
customer table it would not be possible to select the
names of only those people who are customers of
the ABC company using the previous two commands.
You would have to select the entire company column.
The WHERE command narrows the search to those
specific data items that you want from each column
rather than the entire column.

The WHERE command follows the FROM command in the SQL query. For example, to retrieve
only those customers from the ABC Company, the
query would be as follows:

```
SELECT * FROM customer
WHERE company = 'ABC';
```

The WHERE command above limits the row selection to only those customers from ABC Company.
This is indicated by the apostrophes placed around
the text ABC.

The WHERE command uses many modifiers.
You can query on varied and multiple search conditions. The WHERE command chosen below searches
and retrieves those employees from the sales table
who generated more than $20,000 in sales in
Region 1:

```
SELECT * FROM sales
WHERE sales > 20000 AND region = 1;
```

Some of the special search conditions used in the
WHERE command are: equal to, not equal to, greater
than, less than, equal to or greater than, equal to but
less than, AND, OR, NOT, BETWEEN, and LIKE.

Updating with SQL

Data in tables are often dynamic, that is, they change.
You may need to add a customer, remove a customer, or change an address. The SQL commands
that perform these functions include INSERT, DE-
LETE, and UPDATE.

To add a row to a table, for example, when you
add a new name to the customer table, you must
specify the table, indicate the columns, and list the
new values that are to be added to the table. For
example:

```
INSERT into customer (custnum, name,
company) values ( 5, 'Baker', 'PDQ');
```

Be careful when removing data so that only data
that you want deleted is actually erased. The DELETE
command by itself removes all rows in a table. The
following command deletes all customers:

```
DELETE FROM customer;
```

To remove one or a specific group of customers, the DELETE command is used with the WHERE command as shown below:

```
DELETE FROM customer
WHERE name = 'Jones';
```

The UPDATE command works much like the DELETE command in that all rows of a column will be updated if you don't use a WHERE command. For example, Ms. Smith recently changed her name and that change needs to be reflected in your customer table. SET indicates which column to update. The command sequence looks like this:

```
UPDATE customer SET name = 'Green'
WHERE name = 'Smith';
```

This command looks at the customer table, finds the name Smith, and changes it to Green. However, any other customers who have the last name Smith will also be changed. In order to change only the desired field in the record for Ms. Smith, you would want to include a unique field in the WHERE clause to identify the specific record. The following statements would accomplish that:

```
UPDATE customer set name = 'Green'
WHERE name = 'Smith' AND socnum =
'555-55-5555';
```

VIEW Command

Data retrieved with a query can be saved as a new table and given a new name. Retrieving the data and naming the new table are accomplished with the VIEW command. The new table is created from data pulled from existing tables. For example, if you need to create a new table called "bonus" containing the names of all the staff who exceeded sales of $15,000 for the first quarter:

```
CREATE VIEW bonus AS
SELECT * FROM sales
WHERE sales > 15000 AND quarter = 1
```

CREATE TABLE and CREATE VIEW both name a table but treat the data differently. The CREATE

TABLE command initially creates a table to provide a physical place for data. A table named with the CREATE VIEW command does not physically store any data; only the definition of the data is stored.

Performing Mathematical Functions When Querying Data

Mathematical functions can be performed when you query data, but commands vary depending on your version of SQL. Basic arithmetic functions include addition, subtraction, division, multiplication, and exponentiation. Functions available in standard SQL include minimum, maximum, counts, averages, and sums. For example, the query to retrieve products from a parts table and list them reflecting a 10% price increase would look like:

```
SELECT product, 1.1 * cost,
FROM parts;
```

Imagine a table called numbers with columns A and B. Column A contains the numbers 2, 6, and 8; Column B, the numbers 4, 16, 36. The query below retrieves the table shown in Figure 6. It shows how you could write a query using some mathematical functions (i.e., maximum, minimum, sum and square root).

```
SELECT MAX(A), MIN(B), SUM(A),
MAX(SQRT(B)),
FROM numbers;
```

The SQL language provides services to the relational database management system in addition to those described in the previous sections. The database management functions of data definition, data

MAX(A)	MIN(B)	SUM(A)	MAX(SQRT(B))
8	4	16	6

FIGURE 6
This table returns the maximum value of column A, minimum value of column B, sum of column A, and the maximum square root value of column B.

retrieval, and data manipulation were observed through the commands above.

Data definition was accomplished when the original tables were created. Data retrieval with SQL can be as simple as retrieving an entire table or more complex through commands such as WHERE. The data stored in a table can be manipulated in a variety of ways. Tables may have rows added or deleted, or their contents changed. Through a VIEW new arrangements and new tables may be developed.

WHAT OTHER DBMS FUNCTIONS DOES SQL CONTROL?

SQL also takes charge of other database functions such as data integrity, access control, and data sharing. Because each one is important a brief definition will follow.

Data Integrity

Data integrity refers to database constraints that prevent it from accepting bad data. A data integrity check that limits the range of value of accepted data is called **values integrity**. For example, to make sure that a view will only accept correct, valid data during an update, a range can be described in the WHERE command and a WITH CHECK OPTION can be added. The WITH CHECK OPTION is used to limit any changes to a column outside of a range determined by a WHERE command. In the following example any update to the cost column in the parts table with less than zero would be rejected.

```
CREATE VIEW new_price AS
SELECT * FROM parts
WHERE cost < 0
WITH CHECK OPTION;
```

Data integrity can also take the form of **referential integrity**. Referential integrity involves comparing columns that are common to more than one table in that they contain the same values. A primary key in one table may be a foreign key in another table. Queries often use a key in one table to link or reference data in another table. If the two tables did not contain the same values, some rows of data may not be retrieved in a query using both keys.

Access Control

Access control restricts access to data so that only authorized users are permitted to retrieve or update data. In SQL, security is maintained by the granting authority. Authority may be granted to an entire database, certain tables, or certain commands. A database administrator must have access to the entire database so that it can be maintained properly, while a user generally needs access to specific tables or parts of tables. For example, a person might have access to a personnel table but not to the salary column in that table.

The following SQL command sequence gives a user access to the database if the correct password is given.

```
GRANT CONNECT TO jones
IDENTIFIED BY codeword
```

A user can be limited to only certain commands. The following SQL command sequence allows the user to update only the department number of the personnel table.

```
GRANT UPDATE(dept_num)
ON personnel TO jones
```

Data Sharing

Data sharing occurs when more than one person has access to the data tables concurrently. Data-sharing SQL techniques protect the database from erroneous data. Automatic locking procedures can be implemented in a system that uses SQL to prevent data corruption caused by multiple users sharing data.

Locking can be exclusive, i.e., an unauthorized user cannot have any access to a row of data in a table. Locking may also be shared. Shared locking means a user has access to a particular row of data to view it but not update or change the data.

Although all the commands and functions of SQL are not covered here, you can see that it is a powerful database language. It gives the user a means to easily and creatively access data, and provides the database administrator with the tools to manage the entire database.

VOCABULARY SELF-TEST

Can you define the following terms?

query (p. 393)

record-oriented (p. 394)

referential integrity (p. 398)

set-oriented (p. 394)

structured query language (SQL) (p. 392)

values integrity (p. 398)

REVIEW QUESTIONS

Multiple Choice

1. SQL evolved from a database language called
   _____.
   a. PASCAL
   b. BASIC
   c. Sequel
   d. FORTRAN
2. When SQL is part of the DBMS it is said to be
   _____.
   a. embedded
   b. standard
   c. interactive
   d. ANSI
3. Which one of the following is not a property of a
   relational table?
   a. one or more named columns
   b. columns can contain variable data types
   c. each row is unique
   d. order of columns and rows does not matter
4. When a table is originally defined the _____
   command is used.
   a. CREATE TABLE
   b. SELECT TABLE
   c. FROM TABLE
   d. CREATE VIEW

5. Which one of the following does not update a
   table?
   a. UPDATE
   b. INSERT
   c. SELECT
   d. DELETE

Fill-In

1. Minimum SQL standards were set by the
   _____.
2. When SQL is used to enhance a programming
   language by providing database functions to that
   language it is known as _____ SQL.
3. A(n) _____ is a statement or statements
   used to retrieve data from a table.
4. A(n) _____ oriented database accesses data
   based on the physical structure of the data and
   indexing.
5. In order to select columns you must also use the
   _____ command to reference the table.

Short Answer

1. Define structured query language.
2. How does SQL differ from programming languages
   like BASIC or COBOL?
3. Briefly describe the difference between set-
   oriented and record-oriented databases.
4. How does CREATE TABLE differ from CREATE
   VIEW?
5. Write a query to retrieve the columns PRICE and
   TOTAL_COST from the PURCHASE table. Retrieve only items whose price is greater than one
   dollar.

Part 3

Microcomputer Application Software

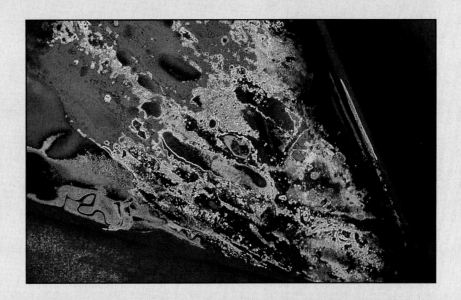

If technology use is somehow connected with bringing people closer to each other to form a community ... then it's very good.

Mitch Kapor, founder of Lotus Development Corporation

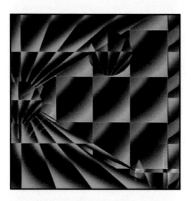

OUTLINE

OBJECTIVES

11.1 Define the terms "word processing" and "word processor."

11.2 Describe the benefits of using a word processor.

11.3 Summarize the basic functions of a word processor.

11.4 Describe several features that add significant power to a word processor.

11.5 Understand what is meant by the term "desktop publishing."

11.6 Describe the benefits of desktop publishing.

11.7 Contrast desktop publishing and word processing.

11.8 Understand the limitations of desktop publishing.

Chapter 11

Document Preparation: Word Processing and Desktop Publishing Software

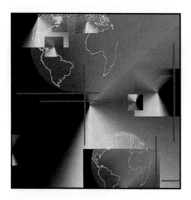

Profile

Alan C. Ashton and Bruce W. Bastian

"We're perfect!" Well, that's what it might sound like when people at the Orem, Utah–based offices of Word-Perfect answer the phone. Today sales are in the hundreds of millions of dollars and the word processing software for IBM PCs and compatibles is offered in approximately 20 languages found in more than 80 countries of the world. More people use WordPerfect than any other word processing software.

The WordPerfect story began in the late 1970s when Alan C. Ashton, a computer science professor at Brigham Young University, developed a program so a computer could produce organ music. During this time, the Wang computer was popular; it was a computer specifically dedicated to word processing tasks. After reviewing the manual that described the functions of the word processor, Ashton felt confident that with his musical editing expertise, he could create a more efficient program. So he did. However, Ashton did not promote his ideas at that time; the specifications lay dormant.

A BYU music student, Bruce Bastian, was trying to computerize marching band formations as part of his graduate project. As the venture became more involved, it was clear that a computer science advisor would be helpful. Enter Ashton, who ultimately encouraged Bastian to forsake music and pursue a computer science degree.

They went into business after Bastian's graduation and called themselves Satellite Software International (SSI). One of the first problems the budding entrepreneurs faced was a scarcity of funds. Thus begins a series of exciting coincidences. During the late 1970s, Orem City was looking into the purchase of a computer, specifically the Data General minicomputer. However, they also wanted the ability to accomplish word processing with that equipment. Unfortunately the software was not available. It was time to resurrect Ashton's word processing specifications. Now Bastian's background and creativity in music played an instrumental (pardon the pun) part. He wrote the clear and concise programming code for the program that would be called the SSI word processing program (SSIWP). By March 1980, the software was being sold to other Data General minicomputer users.

The developers wanted to make their program available for other computer users, but there was no standard machine to adapt to. Until 1981, that is, when the IBM PC appeared on the scene. By November, 1982, an IBM version of SSIWP was released. Because there was some name confusion with MultiMate (a competitive PC word processor now part of Ashton-Tate Corp.), who also used the acronym SSI for Software Systems, Inc., the new name Word-Perfect was coined. It's been part of our vocabulary since early 1986.

Most of you won't be required to know much technical information about computers. However, many of you will be expected to understand and use application software to accomplish a specific task or solve a problem.

Because microcomputers are a productivity tool for both business and personal use, and because people are most likely to use microcomputers rather than large computer systems, our discussion focuses on application software for microcomputers.

In this chapter you'll learn about two types of application software used to prepare documents: word processors and desktop publishing software.

Objective 11.1   Define the terms "word processing" and "word processor."

What Is a Word Processor?

At some time almost everyone needs to write something—a personal letter, business letter, memo, term paper, or perhaps a manuscript for the great American novel. Several methods are available. You might use pen and paper; however, editing and producing clean, legible copy can be tedious and time-consuming. This is especially true for those of us whose handwriting is indecipherable. The typewriter eliminated the problem of poor penmanship, but editing meant significant retyping. It was still a chore.

Technology has helped. With the arrival of computers a method of writing called word processing evolved that greatly reduced the tedium involved in writing, editing, and printing all forms of written work. **Word processing** is the term that describes the act of entering, editing, and printing text with a word processor. A **word processor** is application software that creates, saves, edits, formats and prints text-based documents. It can be compared to an electronic equivalent of the typewriter. Anything you previously wrote with a typewriter, or pen and paper, you can write with a word processor. However, as you will discover, the capabilities of a word processor go far beyond those of the typewriter. In fact, many of you probably have already been introduced to computers through their word-processing functions. Popular word processors include WordPerfect, Microsoft Word, Ami, and PC-Write.

Word processors were one of the first software packages available for personal computers. Today, they are the most popular generalized application software for microcomputers. Anyone who regularly works with words can benefit from using a word processor. So pervasive is the technology that almost every current document you read originated on a word processor.

Word processing has a broad appeal to practically everyone. Word processors are versatile in business operations. Users write business letters, individualized form letters, memos, reports, proposals, advertising copy, contracts, or other text-based documents.

In schools teachers type lesson plans and tests. School secretaries prepare school board minutes and reports, cafeteria menus, letters to parents, and activity lists with word processors. Scholars and scientists find that using a word processor makes typing research papers much easier.

You might use one at home to type personal correspondence, lists, term papers, homework assignments, books, articles, and newsletters.

Objective 11.2   Describe the benefits of using a word processor.

How Does a Word Processor Help?

> **Benefits of Using a Word Processor**
>
> ■ Speed and efficiency
> ■ Concentrate on sub-
> ject matter rather
> than mechanics

People who use word processors find that they have two significant advantages over using a typewriter: (1) speed and efficiency in creating documents, and (2) freedom to concentrate on the subject without concern for the mechanics of writing and typing.

With a word processor, revisions are made electronically in the document until it is exactly right, and in a fraction of the time it took on a typewriter. With a typewriter the page would have to be rekeyed manually after editing. The many editing features found in word processors are responsible for the speed difference in creating documents. In a handwritten or typed document, to move or delete a word or a letter meant messy manual corrections or starting over with a clean sheet of paper. It was even more time-consuming to rearrange whole sentences and paragraphs. Consequently, the document writer often spent as much time typing the paper as completing the research and preparing the draft.

With a word processor it is not necessary to retype pages or use correction fluid to cover words or lines. Typographical errors can be corrected and editing changes can be made on the screen before the text is ever printed. Words and paragraphs can be moved anywhere in the text, and characters can be changed, inserted, or deleted with a few keystrokes. Even spelling can be automatically checked. The final printed document is clean and neat, with no corrections visible.

Word processors offer an enormous advantage over typewriters because they allow you to type as fast as you are able without worrying about typographical errors. Corrections can be made later. This process is ideal for those whose minds work much faster than they can type. It is easy to lose your creative thought if you are worried about typing properly. Once the thought has been captured, it is easy enough to edit and polish the writing later. With a word processor, the writer concentrates on the subject and getting the point across to the reader rather than on the physical aspects of writing or typing.

Objective 11.3   Summarize the basic functions of a word processor.

What Does a Word Processor Do?

The three basic functions common to all word processors are (1) text entry and editing, (2) formatting, and (3) printing the document.

Entering and Editing Text in a Document

If your task is to write a term paper with a word processor, you must first load the software into the computer. Then, depending on the word processor, you will either be in an edit window or be given menu choices from which you can select the edit window. The **edit window** is the work area for entering and editing a document. An empty edit window is analogous to a clean sheet of paper in the typewriter. Text is entered through the keyboard, stored electronically in the computer, and displayed on screen in the edit window. Most documents contain more text than will fit in the edit window. To see text that is not currently in the edit window you can use the cursor movement keys to scroll through the document.

The cursor, which marks the point of present activity on the screen, is found in the edit window. This point indicates where the first (or next) character will be entered, or where the next operation begins. Depending on your system, the cursor is controlled by either cursor-movement keys or a mouse. If you learn and memorize the ways in which the cursor can be moved, it is possible to speed up the editing process.

Many word processors allow more than one window to be displayed. For example, a user could view two portions of a document at the same time, or see portions of two separate documents (Figure 11.1). The window in which the cursor currently resides is called the **active window**. A keystroke or key combination moves the cursor between the windows, giving you access to more than one document at a time.

The **status line** provides information about the current document and the system and is found at the top or bottom of the display screen (depending on which word processor you are using). It may include the disk drive being used; the name of the document; document number; page, line, and column position on which you are working; amount of available memory; and current mode of operation (Figure 11.2). This information is helpful if you are switching back and forth between documents.

Before you begin typing on a typewriter, you had to insert and align the paper and set margins, tab spacing, and line spacing. Word processors

FIGURE 11.1
Many word processors have a windowing capability so that a user can see and edit two or more different parts of the same document or two or more different documents at the same time. This photo shows WordPerfect's multiple document windows opened in WordPerfect.

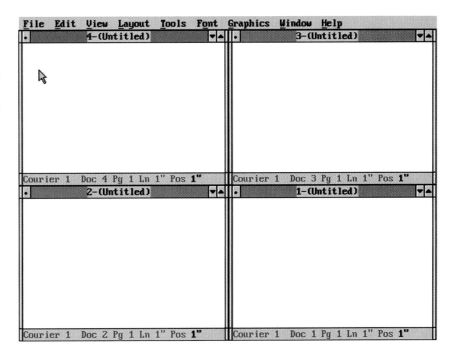

FIGURE 11.2
WordPerfect's edit window and status line.

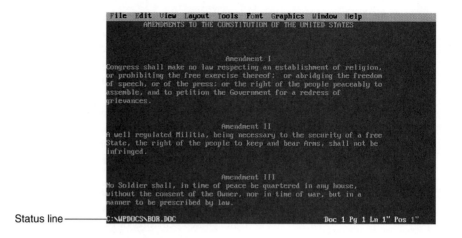

File Edit View Layout Tools Font Graphics Window Help

AMENDMENTS TO THE CONSTITUTION OF THE UNITED STATES

Amendment I
Congress shall make no law respecting an establishment of religion, or prohibiting the free exercise thereof; or abridging the freedom of speech, or of the press; or the right of the people peaceably to assemble, and to petition the Government for a redress of grievances.

Amendment II
A well regulated Militia, being necessary to the security of a free State, the right of the people to keep and bear Arms, shall not be infringed.

Amendment III
No Soldier shall, in time of peace be quartered in any house, without the consent of the Owner, nor in time of war, but in a manner to be prescribed by law.

Status line — C:\WPDOCS\BOR.DOC   Doc 1 Pg 1 Ln 1" Pos 1"

incorporate default settings for parameters like margins, tab settings, line spacing, and page length. **Default settings** are values used by a program unless the user gives other instructions. Default settings allow you to start typing immediately. However, you can choose different parameters.

One of the headaches of typewriter use is remembering to add a carriage return at the end of a line of type. If you are concentrating on your handwritten notes as you type, you may not be aware that the end of the line is getting closer. With a word processor it is not necessary to keep an eye on the right margin. You just continue typing, and the program performs a **wordwrap**, automatically putting the words on the next line and continuing until you press Enter (Return). Then the cursor moves to the next line and begins a new paragraph. You don't worry about typing past the margin. If the text is not supposed to go to the end of the line—e.g., in a typed column of names—just press the Enter (Return) key after typing each item in the list. When you press the Enter key, it creates a "hard return." When the software forces a wordwrap, it is called a "soft return."

Once the first draft of your document is entered, it should be saved to a disk to avoid accidental erasure by power outage, elecrical surge, human error, or other problem. Saving to disk protects your document and allows you to retrieve it again to edit or reuse it later. As a rule you should save your work often. Whether you do this every 5 minutes or 15 minutes depends on how difficult it would be for you to recreate any lost work. It is important to give your document a descriptive name so that it can be easily identified. Now editing can begin.

Even the best typist makes an occasional mistake, and usually after reading through a document you may need to add or remove some text. Characters, phrases, or blocks of text can be inserted into the existing document. If the program is in the **insert mode**, the existing text automatically shifts to make room for the new text. If it is in the **typeover mode**, entries strike over and replace existing text. Most word processors automatically default to the insert mode when loaded.

Characters, phrases, or blocks of text can also be deleted from the document either with the Backspace key or the Delete key. The remaining text automatically shifts left to fill the space of the deleted text.

Your document may present its point more appropriately if you move some of the text or clarify certain portions by deleting text. This editing creates a lot of work for a typewriter, but not for a word processor. Block actions called **block editing** permit units of text—characters, words, sentences, paragraphs, sections, or even pages—to be moved, copied, deleted, saved, or altered as a unit (e.g., changing print style to boldface, underline, or italic). First mark the entire text to be changed. The whole block of text is then manipulated according to further instructions (Figure 11.3).

Suppose you have just finished a 20-page report and discover that you misspelled a proper name throughout. It would be tedious and time-consuming to search through the entire document to correct the spelling, and there is no guarantee that you would find all the occurrences. Word

FIGURE 11.3
Block editing. (a) Text is marked to be moved. (b) Text is moved to a new location.

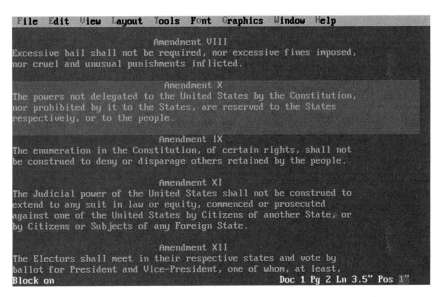

(a)

(b)

processors offer a **search and replace feature** that easily finds text and makes corrections throughout an entire document with only a few keystrokes.

In a "simple search," the program looks for a specified string of characters (the misspelled name, in this case), highlights it, and stops. You decide whether to correct it, remove it, or move on. In a "conditional search," the user specifies a replacement string; the program searches for and locates all occurrences of a particular string of characters and inquires at each instance if the existing string should be replaced with the new one. If so, the program replaces the string with the change or correction that was specified. In a "global" search and replace, the program searches the document so that when each instance of a specified string is found it is automatically replaced.

Here's an example of using the search and replace feature to save time. If your term paper quoted Dr. Emerson Gorfsnorben numerous times, instead of typing the whole name each time, you could type a short version such as "deg." By searching and replacing the text "deg" with "Dr. Emerson Gorfsnorben," you would only have to type the full name one time.

Formatting a Document

The **format** of a document refers to the way it looks on the screen or after it is printed, and is controlled through the use of various formatting features of a word processor. Some are typically specified before keying in the document (e.g., margins), others during entering and editing (e.g., boldface), and still others after the document is completed but right before it is printed (e.g., headers and footers). One attraction of a word processor is that the formatting options can be changed easily at any time.

Not all format characteristics appear on the screen as they will when printed. Some word processors indicate formatting through embedded codes. These codes are communicated from the computer to the printer before printing starts. When they are used most word processors provide a preview feature so you see what the document will look like when it is printed (Figure 11.4). Adjustments can be made, if they are needed.

Perhaps you have some statistics that you've tried to arrange in a table, but when the page is printed you see they are not aligned under one another. This usually occurs when a proportional type font is chosen. It allocates space differently; for example, the letter "i" takes up less space than the letter "m." Using the space bar to align the text is not successful because proportional fonts are not always displayed on the screen, but their actual alignment can be viewed with a WYSIWYG feature. Many word processors that contain a graphical interface have a **WYSIWYG (What You See Is What You Get)** capability so that you see on the screen how the document will look before it is printed. A fixed font does not cause misalignment because each letter is the same width.

Several formatting features that change the appearance of your document include margin settings, justification, tab settings, line spacing, page breaks, automatic page numbering, centering, headers and footers, and character enhancements (Figure 11.5).

FIGURE 11.4
Preview screen showing how document will look when printed.

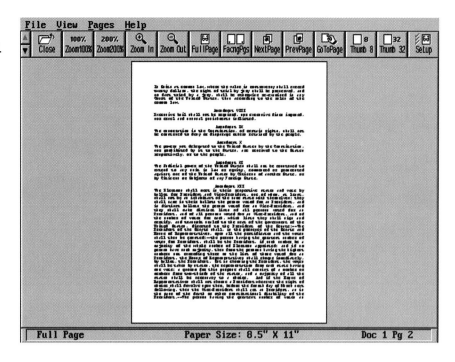

Often there are specific requirements on how much white space, or margin, is to be left around the text. **Margin settings** are the specifications that allocate space on the left, right, top, and bottom of a printed document. You might choose to have the text justified. **Justification** is the feature that aligns the text flush with the left margin (i.e., left justified); or flush with the right margin (i.e., right justified); or centered between both sides (i.e., same left and right margin) (see Figure 11.6). When you choose full justification, the text on your screen *may* not appear to be justified, but it will print appropriately. Examples of justified print can be seen in magazine articles as well as this text.

Just as a traditional typewriter indents paragraphs (usually 5 or 6 spaces from the margin), a word processor also provides **tab settings** to make indentations. Most word processors also have a sophisticated tab feature that automatically aligns columns around the decimal points.

Traditionally, word processors measured margins, tabs, and other positions on the screen by character positions. Today, many—even those that use a text interface—measure margins, tabs, and other positions on the screen in graphic terms, that is, in inches rather than by character position on the screen. For example, one word processor might set a left margin at 1 inch, and another might set it at 12 character spaces. Using the measurements in inches allows more precise placement of text and graphics in a document.

You have probably had to submit a report typed in double-spaced format. This makes a document easier to read and provides space for written corrections or comments. A word processor gives you a range of

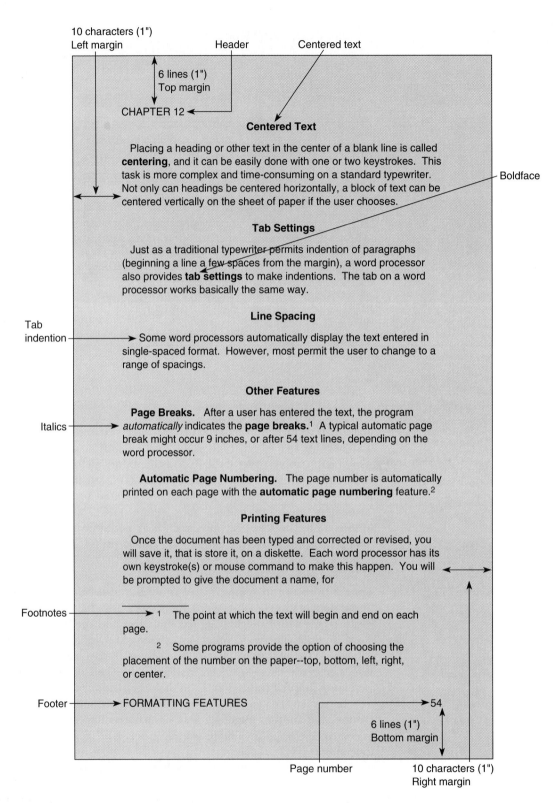

10 characters (1")
Left margin

Header

Centered text

6 lines (1")
Top margin

CHAPTER 12

Centered Text

Placing a heading or other text in the center of a blank line is called **centering**, and it can be easily done with one or two keystrokes. This task is more complex and time-consuming on a standard typewriter. Not only can headings be centered horizontally, a block of text can be centered vertically on the sheet of paper if the user chooses.

Boldface

Tab Settings

Just as a traditional typewriter permits indention of paragraphs (beginning a line a few spaces from the margin), a word processor also provides **tab settings** to make indentions. The tab on a word processor works basically the same way.

Line Spacing

Tab indention

Some word processors automatically display the text entered in single-spaced format. However, most permit the user to change to a range of spacings.

Other Features

Page Breaks. After a user has entered the text, the program *automatically* indicates the **page breaks.**[1] A typical automatic page break might occur 9 inches, or after 54 text lines, depending on the word processor.

Italics

Automatic Page Numbering. The page number is automatically printed on each page with the **automatic page numbering** feature.[2]

Printing Features

Once the document has been typed and corrected or revised, you will save it, that is store it, on a diskette. Each word processor has its own keystroke(s) or mouse command to make this happen. You will be prompted to give the document a name, for

Footnotes

[1] The point at which the text will begin and end on each page.

[2] Some programs provide the option of choosing the placement of the number on the paper--top, bottom, left, right, or center.

Footer

FORMATTING FEATURES

54

6 lines (1")
Bottom margin

Page number

10 characters (1")
Right margin

FIGURE 11.5
Document showing format features.

FIGURE 11.6

Justifying the text in a document changes its appearance. (a) Left justified, ragged right; (b) Right justified, ragged left; (c) Both left and right justified.

Left Justification. The feature that aligns the text flush with the margin is called justification. It is used to make the right margin evenly aligned, the left margin evenly aligned, or both. The justification of the text may not show on the screen, but will when the document is printed. This style of blocking text can be seen in commercially generated books and magazines.

(a)

Right Justification. The feature that aligns the text flush with the margin is called justification. It is used to make the right margin evenly aligned, the left margin evenly aligned, or both. The justification of the text may not show on the screen, but will when the document is printed. This style of blocking text can be seen in commercially generated books and magazines.

(b)

Full Justification. The feature that aligns the text flush with the margin is called justification. It is used to make the right margin evenly aligned, the left margin evenly aligned, or both. The justification of the text may not show on the screen, but will when the document is printed. This style of blocking text can be seen in commercially generated books and magazines.

(c)

line spacings, for example, half space, single space, double space, or triple space. These choices can be set for the entire document or be applied to certain text in the document.

A word processor automatically indicates the page breaks, that is, the point where the text ends on one page and begins on the next. This is called a **soft page break**. Unless you indicate otherwise, the program generally expects that you are printing on 8½ × 11″ sheets of paper, so a soft page break might occur at 9 inches, or after 54 text lines, depending on the defaults of the word processor. You can override the soft page break and indicate where you want the text to stop on one page and begin on another by choosing a **hard page break**. This feature forces selected text to be printed on a new page, for example, title page, table of contents, index, or bibliography.

Automatic page numbering automatically prints the page number on each page. Some programs provide the option of deleting the page number from certain pages or choosing the placement of the number on the paper—top, bottom, left, right, or center.

Term papers and other written materials often have a title page where headings are usually centered. Placing a heading or other text in the center of a blank line is called **centering**. You know how tedious and time-consuming it can be to center headings using a typewriter. On a word processor, this task can easily be accomplished with one or two keystrokes.

Sometimes specific text is to be included at the top or bottom of each page. For example, a report's title and the author's name could be printed at the top or bottom of every page. A **header** is a line (or lines) of text repeated at the top of each page. A **footer** is text that appears at the bottom of each page. The information in the header or footer is keyed in just one

You should know that the book *Just This Once* was written by a computer. No, not by someone sitting at a computer keyboard using word processing software—the computer actually "wrote" the book. First, however, the computer had been programmed to "think" like the late author, Jacqueline Susann. An expert system was created by Scott French, who used passages obtained from Susann's previous novels, *Valley of the Dolls* and *The Best of Everything,* to provide the data required for the knowledge base. The best-selling author's use of verb tense and sentence structure, the ratio of dialogue to action, even the length of time between passionate love scenes were analyzed.

Susann's style was matched so well that one reviewer indicated that the book was indistinguishable from her previous works. Watch your local bookstores for more books written by expert systems. Unless this time "once" happens to be enough.

You may want to try your own hand! Did you ever dream about writing the next *Star Wars?* A screenplay isn't your style? How about a novel? Even if you haven't the foggiest idea of where to begin, there is software to the rescue.

Utilizing the ability of one of Hollywood's best screenwriter instructors, John Truby, StoryLine takes you through the creative process of writing. A template guides your story and the software keeps it credible with proven building blocks. It helps you keep track of as many as ten characters in a scene at a time. If you stray too far from the plot, StoryLine warns you and offers suggestions through examples from classic films such as *The Godfather.*

Is the great American novel waiting inside you—or your computer?

time for the entire document rather than page by page; the program automatically inserts the appropriate text on the specified pages. The header and footer usually appear on the document when it is printed, but do not appear on screen.

You may want to place specific emphasis on certain words or phrases in some documents. Most word processors permit **character enhancement** to the text style when it is printed. Typically they include **boldface** or *italics,* underlining, or a ***combination***.

Printing a Document

The bottom line in using a word processor is to produce a printed document. You will generally be presented with several print options from which to choose (Figure 11.7). For example, you might tell the program to print only the first page, several specific pages, or all of the pages. You can also specify sections (blocks) or paragraphs to be printed. More than one copy of the same document can be printed. Many word processors permit choosing paper sizes other than the standard 8½ × 11″, assuming the printer is capable of handling different sizes. Popular sizes of paper are 11 × 17″

FIGURE 11.7
Example of printing options.

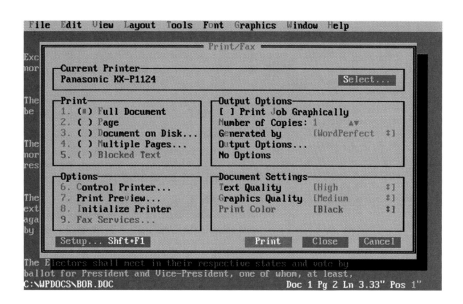

(legal), envelopes, and mailing labels. Other options include choosing the printed quality of the type such as draft or near-letter quality.

Developments of laser printers in the last few years have made near-typeset-quality printing affordable so many small businesses produce their own newsletters, magazines, and brochures. The results often look as good as those done by a commercial printer. Because the trend is for word processors to include more and more page-layout features, laser printers are becoming more popular. Some laser printers come equipped with a special page description programming language, such as PostScript, that gives you precise control over nearly every detail of a printed page. Modern laser printers offer an almost unlimited variety of type styles, called fonts, in a wide range of sizes. A font includes all the letters, numbers, and symbols of one style of type, in one size. A collection of all available sizes of one font is called a typeface. Laser printers have several fonts built in, and cartridges are available to provide additional fonts. Although in some fonts the characters appear on the computer screen, the printer may not be capable of printing that character in that font. This will result in a blank space.

Objective 11.4   Describe several features that add significant power to a word processor.

What Additional Features Contribute to a Word Processor's Power?

Developers of word processors make them as versatile as possible for a broad spectrum of users. Some common features that add significant power to a word processor are described below.

Checking for and correcting spelling errors has always been a tedious aspect of writing. A typist would have to stop in the middle of a sentence to look up the correct spelling in the dictionary. Many word processors have a **spelling checker** to quickly and easily locate misspelled words and typographical errors in a document. The checker compares each word in a document to those in the dictionary of the word processor, usually between

20,000 to over 100,000 words. The spelling checker highlights the words on the screen that are misspelled or not in its dictionary. Options for the correct spelling are presented. The user decides whether or not to replace the word with the recommendation of the spelling checker.

However, a spelling checker cannot detect *misused* words that are correctly spelled. For example, in the sentence "I placed the book over their," the spelling checker cannot know that the word "their" is *used* incorrectly; it merely recognizes that the word is *spelled* correctly.

Sometimes writers get stuck using the same word over and over again. Many word processors contain a **thesaurus** to suggest alternative words that offer more variety or precision than those used originally. Usually, the thesaurus is accessed by highlighting the word to be replaced. With the correct command or keystrokes, a list of synonyms (and often antonyms) is presented on the screen. Sometimes even the synonyms have lists of synonyms (Figure 11.8).

Forgetting to put a period at the end of a sentence is easy to do when you're trying to finish your work on time. Some word processors have a **grammar and style checker** to point out potential problems with punctuation, grammar, sentence structure, and writing style. They point out mistakes such as using the wrong verb tense.

A particularly useful option for business users is the **mail merge** feature, which permits a form letter to be addressed and personalized automatically to any number of addressees. With mail merge, a form letter is created containing specially coded characters that tell the word processor where to insert variables such as names and addresses. Once the process is complete, the computer merges the form letter with the variables to produce multiple "original" letters. With mail merge, each recipient's name appears in the body of the text. And, even though hundreds or thousands of these letters may have been sent, each looks and sounds personal. Such mass customizing would have been impossible without refinements in word processing.

FIGURE 11.8
Thesaurus in use. Here we highlighted the word "alters" in order to find a more appropriate word from the thesaurus. The thesaurus presents several possibilities, including "convert." When we prompted the computer to seek synonyms for "convert" it gave synonyms for that word, too.

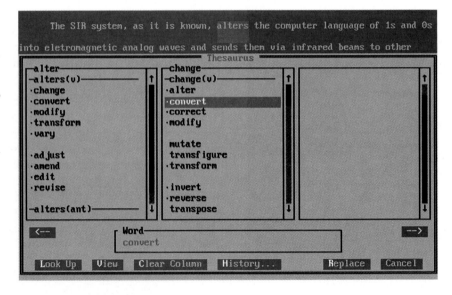

A math function that performs simple calculations is helpful to users who create documents that are mainly text, but that include some columns and rows of numbers. With this feature, calculations can be done automatically while creating a financial report or an accounting statement.

As our language has developed, it has created certain conventions about the ways written information should be presented for maximum effectiveness. Readers have come to expect visible signals that alert them to a change of topic, or to a particularly important passage. Thus, document preparation involves more than merely putting together a series of sentences.

Although writers still need to know when to apply these conventions, word processors make them easy to include either as the document is being written or after the first draft has been completed. Most word processors include features for creating footnotes, endnotes, and subscript/superscript notations. In addition, writers mark segments of text to be used for other purposes—for example, to indicate words and phrases in the text to automatically generate an outline, a table of contents, or an index. These are slow, tedious, and error-prone tasks when performed manually, but with a word processor, these functions are automated and are completed faster and easier.

Page layout features are included in many word processors so that businesses or personal users can type, design, and publish professional-looking newsletters, brochures, fliers, or pamphlets in the office. One feature creates newspaper-style columns. When the first column is full, the type flows to the top of the next column and begins to fill that column. Several options of type faces, styles, and sizes are usually available with a program, assuming your printer can accommodate them. Many word processors also allow graphic images to be combined with text. Separate page-layout software is available for more complex publishing efforts. This topic is discussed in more detail below.

Objective 11.5   Understand what is meant by the term "desktop publishing."

What Is Desktop Publishing?

Desktop publishing is a concept that combines the use of microcomputers with word processing, page composition software, and high-quality laser printers. Page composition software, typically called desktop publishing software, permits placement of graphic elements in the document where desired, and then "flows" the text around the photo, chart, or illustration. Popular desktop publishing software programs are PageMaker and Ventura Publisher.

You can use desktop publishing to create and publish documents. Large corporations that want to publish in-house, managers of small businesses, and writers who decide to self-publish use this software to produce booklets, brochures, newsletters, and annual reports. Figure 11.9 shows an example of a document produced using desktop publishing.

Graphic elements to be included in the document are produced in one of three ways: (1) generated at a computer, using desktop publishing software or paint and draw programs and a mouse; (2) digitized, using a scanner; or (3) copied from proprietary clip art on a disk.

Creating Graphic Elements for Desktop Publishing

- Computer generation
  Page composition software
  Paint and draw programs
- Digitizing (scanners)
- Clip art

FIGURE 11.9
A document produced using
desktop publishing.

Desktop publishing software can enhance the document by incorporating lines in a variety of widths and lengths. Paint and draw programs, such as MacPaint, PC Paintbrush, Adobe Illustrator, and others, allow you to create original artwork directly on the monitor with a drawing device such as a mouse. These programs have enhanced the eye-appeal and readability of documents through company logos or letterheads, cartoons, or other graphic illustrations.

A scanner can "read" a photograph or other graphic representation and then convert the image into a pattern of electronic digits. This data is then stored in a file and can be imported into the document.

A common and cost-effective method of adding visual interest to desktop publishing documents is through clip art. **Clip art** consists of pictures on floppy disk or CD-ROM available from a variety of publishers. Clip art is also included with some desktop publishing software. The user selects appropriate illustrations from these files, imports them into the desktop publishing software, and positions them on the screen.

Objective 11.6   Describe the benefits of desktop publishing.

The English language consists of 26 letters—they're relatively easy to arrange on the keyboard. What about people using computers in other cultures? For example, each Chinese word is formed by an elaborate combination of pen strokes as opposed to letter by letter, as in English. This causes a problem for creation of a simplified input system for the Chinese written language. Chinese word-processing functions are slow, because each character must be created through artificial methods. One method requires the computer user to spell the Mandarin Chinese word with English letters, phonetically. This is called Pinyin.

James Monroe, a Canadian inventor, created a computer program that conquered that problem. His program used a keyboard to simulate the brush strokes of handwritten Chinese. Using Monroe's method, an operator makes the characters by hitting a maximum of five keys on a nine-by-nine layout of 81 keys. The first company to incorporate Monroe's system into an electronic typewriter, China Business Machines, Inc., says that anyone who knows Chinese can learn the keyboard in ten minutes and ultimately can touch type as fast as in English.

A Chinese phonetic keyboard. (Courtesy of International Business Machines Corp.)

What Are the Benefits of Using Desktop Publishing?

To fully appreciate the benefits of desktop publishing, it is necessary to understand the traditional process of preparing professional-looking documents using typography and a printshop. The first step is creating the basic text using a typewriter or microcomputer. Second, decisions must be made about type styles and sizes, headlines, borders, and other elements that make the document more attractive or readable. A professional typesetter then rekeys the document and produces "galley proofs," which are returned for proofreading by the author. After checking for errors, the text is corrected and cut-and-pasted according to the design layout. In addition to "pasting up" the text in columns, space must be left to accommodate photographs and other illustrations. Finally, this document is ready for the printer's camera to make printing negatives. It is said to be "camera-ready" and is sent to a commercial printer who prepares a photographic plate and prints the finished document on a press. The cost for a commercially printed document runs between $50 and $250 per page.

By contrast, desktop publishing allows the computer user to create high-quality documents in less time and at a significantly lower cost. The unique qualities of a desktop publishing system lie in the **page composition software**. It is basically visually oriented or graphics-oriented and involves positioning and aligning text, graphics, and other elements of the document page entirely on the screen.

Besides the time and cost savings, desktop publishing helps the originator control the creative process from start to finish, thus preventing errors and misunderstandings due to poor communication among originator, typesetter, and printer. It assures consistency of appearance and quality in the case of documents that need to conform to a specific layout, such as newsletters and reports, which are produced on a regular basis.

Objective 11.7   Contrast desktop publishing and word processing.

How Does Desktop Publishing Differ from Word Processing?

As word-processing programs have become more sophisticated, some blurring has occurred between the capabilities of word processors and desktop publishing. High-end word processors such as WordPerfect, Word, and AmiPro now incorporate many desktop publishing features. However, many mid- and low-end word processors remain substantially different, as outlined below.

Desktop publishing differs from basic word processing in its ability to handle graphics, typographical control, and column control. Desktop publishing software is far superior in permitting text and graphics to flow around each other in a document. You can easily curve text around irregular shaped objects.

Second, desktop publishing provides greater control over layout of the document through changing or mixing type styles (incorporating several on the same page); increasing or decreasing the size of letters; kerning (stretching or squeezing text); creating headlines; adding, removing, or substituting one illustration for another; creating decorative special effects like headlines and borders; and merging all these elements quickly and with a minimum of effort. In short, desktop publishing software is used to design the "look" of the document page.

Third, desktop publishing gives the user much better control over the text in columns even though some word processors allow columns. This is important since many of the applications for desktop publishing involve documents such as newsletters that incorporate many columns.

Although most desktop publishing programs have provisions for creating and editing text, this step is often performed using word-processing software because of its specialized and sophisticated text creation features.

The text document is imported into the desktop publishing document and then manipulated to include the graphic elements.

A desktop publishing system requires more advanced hardware than most word processors. The computer requires greater amounts of main memory and disk storage to work efficiently with graphics and text. A high-resolution monitor is recommended. Most require a mouse to direct operations and to manipulate elements on the screen quickly. Scanning devices allow desktop publishing programs to import photographs, drawings, and other visual elements into a document. Professional-quality documents would be impossible without laser printers, which produce high-resolution copy. On the other hand, system requirements for word processing are considerably less expensive.

Objective 11.8   Understand the limitations of desktop publishing.

Will Using Desktop Publishing Ensure an Effective Document?

No. New users of desktop publishing software should realize that even the most sophisticated program is at best a very limited substitute for typographic experience and design ability. These skills come from training and practice. More than one purchaser of a desktop publishing system has been disappointed to discover that the first document was not as attractive or professional-looking as those illustrated in the advertising promotional material. Desktop publishing maximizes the creative abilities of users who are responsible for producing professional-looking documents and who are willing to learn. If in doubt, seek the advice of an experienced graphics artist before distributing your document to the public.

Summary

Word processing is the process of using a word processor to enter, edit, and print text. A word processor is application software that manipulates text-based documents. Word processors are used extensively in business, schools, and homes to produce a wide variety of text-based documents.

Word processors improve the speed and efficiency of creating a document and allow the user to concentrate on the subject rather than the mechanics of writing and typing.

A word processor has three basic functions: text entry and editing, formatting, and printing.

The edit window is the work area for entering and editing text. Most word processors allow multiple windows. The window containing the cursor is the active window. A status line provides information about the current document and system. Unless otherwise instructed a word processor uses default settings for adjusting parameters like margins, tabs, and line spacing so you are able to begin typing immediately.

Wordwrap is the feature that automatically moves text that is running past the right margin down to the next line. You should save your document often to avoid accidentally erasing or losing the text.

Text can be entered in one of two ways: through the insert mode where existing text automatically shifts to the right to make room for the new entry, or through the typeover mode where entries strike over and replace existing text.

The search and replace feature allows you to find text and make corrections throughout a document. Block editing permits units of text to be acted on as a single component.

The format of a document refers to how it looks on screen or after it is printed. Formatting features may appear on the screen as embedded characters or be displayed as they will print in a WYSIWYG environment.

Several frequently used formatting features include margins, justification, tabs, line spacing, page breaks, automatic page numbering, centering, headers and footers, and character enhancements.

Word processors provide a variety of print options including the number of copies, choice of which pages to print, and quality of print.

Word processors also include a number of additional features that add to their power. These include a spelling checker, thesaurus, grammar and style checker, mail merge, math functions, endnotes, footnotes, subscripts/superscripts, outline, table of contents, index generator, and page-layout features.

Desktop publishing is a concept that combines the use of microcomputers with word processors, page composition software, and high-quality laser printers. Page composition software, typically called desktop publishing software, permits placement of graphic elements in a document where desired and allows text to be flowed around photos, charts, or illustrations. Benefits of desktop publishing include reduced time and cost of preparing a document and the ability to maintain control over the process.

Graphic elements used in desktop publishing are created in one of three ways: computer generated, digitized, or pulled from a clip art disk.

While word processing and desktop publishing software are becoming closer in capabilities most desktop publishing programs allow more immediate interaction between text and graphics. Users of desktop publishing software should be aware that designing effective documents requires the right software and skill and experience in page layout.

VOCABULARY SELF-TEST

Can you define the following terms?

active window (p. 407)

automatic page numbering (p. 413)

block editing (p. 409)

centering (p. 413)

character enhancements (p. 414)

clip art (p. 418)

default settings (p. 408)

desktop publishing (p. 417)

edit window (p. 406)

footer (p. 413)

format (p. 410)

grammar and style checker
   (p. 413)

hard page break (p. 413)

header (p. 413)

insert mode (p. 408)

justification (p. 411)

mail merge (p. 416)

margin settings (p. 411)

page composition software
   (p. 420)

search and replace (p. 410)

soft page break (p. 413)

spelling checker (p. 415)

status line (p. 407)

tab settings (p. 411)

thesaurus (p. 416)

typeover mode (p. 408)

word processing (p. 405)

word processor (p. 405)

wordwrap (p. 408)

WYSIWYG (What You See Is What You Get) (p. 410)

REVIEW QUESTIONS

Multiple Choice

1. Which application software is best suited for manipulating text-based documents?
    a. desktop publishing
    b. word processor
    c. graphics software
    d. database management system

2. For writing a business letter a user could best be helped by which software?
    a. database management system
    b. desktop publishing program
    c. communications program
    d. word processor

3. Which of the following is not a benefit of using a word processor?
    a. documents can be created quicker
    b. writer concentrates on subject rather than mechanics of writing and typing
    c. allows faster and more creative data analysis
    d. documents can be created more efficiently

4. A(n) _____ is a line (or lines) of text repeated at the top of each page. It usually doesn't appear until you print the document.
    a. header
    b. footer
    c. wordwrap
    d. index

5. _____ features are used to control how a document will look when it is printed.
    a. Editing
    b. Text entry
    c. Formatting
    d. Printing

6. A(n) _____ gives the user a list of synonyms that might replace a word in a document.
    a. spell checker
    b. editor
    c. thesaurus
    d. footer

7. Complex documents that combine numerous graphic elements and text can best be produced using which of the following?
    a. word processor
    b. desktop publishing software

    c. graphics software

    d. paint and draw software

8. Photographic images can be incorporated into a desktop publishing document through the use of _____.

    a. a scanner

    b. clip art

    c. a painting program

    d. a drawing program

9. Kerning is a capability of desktop publishing software that _____.

    a. colors text

    b. squeezes and elongates text

    c. draws graphic images

    d. imports drawings

10. Predrawn art on floppy disk or CD-ROM available from a variety of publishers is called _____.

    a. text

    b. scanner art

    c. clip art

    d. desktop art

Fill-In

1. The act of entering and editing text with a word processor is called _____.

2. A(n) _____ is used to manipulate text-based documents.

3. The _____ feature allows text that extends past the right margin to be placed on the next line.

4. The _____ is located at the top or bottom of the display screen and provides information about the current document and the system.

5. The _____ allows existing text to automatically shift to make room for new text.

6. The word processor automatically indicates the page break known as a(n) _____ page break, while a(n) _____ page break occurs when the user overrides the computer.

7. To make all the text align against the left or right margins is called _____.

8. The way a document looks on screen or after it is printed is called its _____.

9. A(n) _____ locates misspelled words and typographical errors in a document.

10. The concept of combining microcomputers with word processing software, page composition software, and laser printers is called _____.

Short Answer

1. Contrast the terms word processing and word processor.

2. Discuss the benefits of using a word processor.

3. Describe the difference between the insert mode and the typeover mode.
4. Describe the three options of the search and replace feature.
5. What is block editing?
6. Compare the functions of a spell checker to a thesaurus.
7. Briefly describe the mail merge function of word processing.
8. Describe the benefits of desktop publishing.
9. Describe three ways in which graphic elements are created for use in desktop publishing.
10. In what basic ways does desktop publishing differ from word processing?

Issues for Thought

1. Desktop publishing software and many word processors incorporate graphics into a document. Scanners allow you to easily scan any available graphic. Should you scan artwork created by someone else, modify it, and use it in your own document? Should permission or credit be given for the original artist's inspiration and work that led to the modified version used in your document?
2. Using desktop software does not guarantee that the document produced will convey the message you want. Have the class break into small groups to design a one-page flier enticing people to buy a product. Discuss each design and comment on the different layouts.

Infomodule Document Design

WHAT IS DOCUMENT DESIGN?

A Chinese printer, Bi Sheng, invented movable type in 1045. But it wasn't until Johannes Gutenberg modified a wine press into a printing press and hand-fashioned movable type characters in the fifteenth century that the technology became widely used. This was the beginning of the art of **typography**, or setting up pictures and printed words so that they are pleasing to look at as well as functional. Typography is a learned art and although we cannot give you all the "tricks of the trade," it's important that you know some basic considerations when designing a document. **Document design** is the methodology used to combine text and artwork or graphics into a final product.

Today's desktop publishing packages combine a microcomputer with graphics-oriented page composition software, word-processing software, and printers, usually high-quality laser printers, to create nearly professional-quality products. Many businesses use desktop publishing (DTP) to create their own publicity brochures, fliers, manuals, newsletters and even technical journals with tables, charts, and graphs, rather than have an external source prepare them. The user, as originator, has control over the typographical aspects. Two of the more sophisticated desktop publishing programs are Pagemaker by Aldus and Ventura Publisher by Ventura Software.

Some features in word processors rival the options of the first DTP programs. Microsoft Word and WordPerfect both let the user import graphics and when used with laser printers can create professional-looking resumes, attractive term papers, and eye-catching newsletters. But, remember, the computer is merely a tool to display your artistic capabilities.

Although using a computer is not a prerequisite for designing documents these examples are given with the presumption that you are a computer user. In any case, it will be helpful to know some fundamentals before you design anything.

WHAT ARE SOME FUNDAMENTALS OF DOCUMENT DESIGN?

It's essential to have a plan in mind and take into consideration the tools you have available to implement that plan.

Planning

Before the first word is written, plan a general idea of the layout by sketching your proposed design. Decide what message, what look, what market you want to reach and what facts, data, or graphic devices you need to include to present that information. These and other variables need to be considered because each decision focuses your attention on the document being prepared. The best advice is to keep your design as simple and uncluttered as possible.

Then assemble a style sheet. The **style sheet** for a document is like a blueprint or master plan. It sets out specifications, such as what typeface and point size will be used; what spacing will be inserted between letters, lines and paragraphs; what margins and paragraph indentation to set. For longer documents or reports, you must look at page numbering and the possibility of using headers or footers (the words that appear at the top or bottom of the page; they are often included with pagination). A style sheet maintains continuity for your document(s).

You may be adding lines, shapes, and possibly colors. So, some elementary design principles are important factors to consider: repetition, harmony, contrast, rhythm, and unity.

Repeating a line, shape, or color generates a feeling of harmony. However, too much repetition produces boredom. You must strike a balance. Balance can be either symmetrical, where identical shapes in a design are placed equidistant from the center of the page; or asymmetrical, where shapes are neither identical nor are they placed equidistant from the center; or you could choose a visual balance, where color and shape create a harmonious design. Contrast in color, shape, or size also adds appeal to a design. A sense of rhythm or movement is achieved by using wavy lines or patterns in contrast to fixed lines or patterns. A good design has unity, which suggests that all the elements function collectively.

Equipment

Next you need to decide what equipment is required to execute your document design. If you are handwriting your document, the equipment is certainly different than if you are using a DTP program or a word processor. Your computer program should offer WYSIWYG (wizzy wig), that is, "what you see is what you get." This concept means that the screen shows exactly what the printer will produce. Even with WYSIWYG, because the hard copy is produced on a different medium, it may have a different look. The impact on the reader may be different once it is printed. In addition to the computer and software, a laser printer is probably essential to get a high-quality printed product.

Now you've planned the basics and you know what you need to execute that design, let's examine some of the components of typography—white space, type, and graphics.

HOW CAN WHITE SPACE BE USED EFFECTIVELY?

White space is not always "white"; you may be using colored paper. In any case, white space, also called blank space, offers the reader's eye a resting place. It contrasts with the print or graphics found on the remainder of the page. The margins at the top, bottom, and sides of the page are considered blank spaces. But the area at the indentation for paragraphs, between columns, around a headline, as well as spaces and lines between words and letters are also considered white space. Readability specialists and psychologists advise that uniform spacing between words creates a document that is easiest and fastest to read. There are two ways to ensure this uniform spacing: leading and kerning.

Leading (rhymes with wedding) refers to the amount of space between lines. The terminology comes from the early days of typesetting when a metal strip, called a lead, was placed between lines to prevent text from being set in that place. **Kerning** is a method for adjusting the space between characters. A font that is not proportional allocates the same space to each letter. However, when a proportional font is used, letters, especially capitals, are not the same size (larger letters take up more space) so they appear to be spaced too far apart, for example, the letters W and M when placed next to I. Kerning decreases the space between those combinations that are not equal.

Hyphenating words at the ends of lines also adds white space. A higher reading rate is achieved if words are hyphenated properly. For example, if you

---

Elementary Design Principles

- **Repetition**
- **Harmony**
- **Contrast**
- **Rhythm**
- **Unity**

White Space

- **Margins**
- **Paragraph identation**
- **Between column space**
- **Around headlines**
- **Between letters and words**

hyphenate a long word at the end of a smaller word that it contains, the reader usually has trouble grasping the meaning and may have to reread the sentence. Most DTP programs have a large number of words in their dictionaries and they may give you choices of both the preferred and less-preferred hyphenation choices. Whenever a word is hyphenated, there should be at least two letters on each line, and there should be no more than three lines in a row ending with hyphens.

HOW CAN COLOR ENHANCE A DOCUMENT?

White space is important, but color also conveys a message. Adding color was a process handled strictly by professionals operating specialized equipment, with costs for color stripping running from $700 to $2,000 per page. Now many DTP programs apply color. There are two color-separation processes: spot color and four-color printing.

Spot color is available on both Ventura and Page-Maker, so no additional software is required. It adds color for borders, headlines, or other areas where a page full of print needs an interest break. Usually there are only two colors involved, one for print (often black) and then another color. Of course, the printer has to have the capacity for color printing. If not, you may have to take the diskette containing your document to a specialty shop for this type of printing.

Four-color printing offers thousands of colors by combining cyan, magenta, yellow, and black. Additional programs must be purchased to use the four-color separation process. Some DTP programs offer add-on packages capable of two- and four-color separation that can correct color distortions. Color printer prices range from several hundred to well over ten thousand dollars, so you can decide how much money you want to invest to make your statement.

Even if you do not choose to add color to your document, another method of adding interest is through different typefaces and font sizes.

WHAT ARE TYPEFACES AND FONTS?

A **typeface** refers to the design of a set of characters; it is a representation of the type. Some examples of common typefaces include Helvetica, Courier, and Times Roman (Figure 1). Typefaces have various qualities such as serif or sans serif, pitch, weight, type, and orientation. The characters in a serif typeface have finishing decorations, called feet and hats. These typefaces are appropriate for the main text of a document, for example, Times Roman, Garamond, and Baskerville. The characters in a sans serif typeface have no decorative feet or hats. They are often found in headings rather than the main body of text and include, for example, Helvetica. A typeface can set the mood for your document. Some are suitable for personal use; others present a more professional look.

Pitch refers to the horizontal spacing between characters. In a fixed-pitch typeface each character takes up the same amount of space. In a proportional typeface, spacing depends on the width of each particular character; for example, the letters M and W take up more space than I and J. The **weight** of a typeface refers to the width of the characters and can be light, medium, or bold. **Orientation** refers to the direction the letters print on the paper. In portrait orientation the characters print across the width of the paper. In landscape orientation the characters print lengthwise down the paper.

A **font** is a set of alphanumeric characters that all share the same characteristics. As noted earlier, Times Roman is an example of a typeface and 12-point Times Roman is an example of a font, as is 12-point bold Times Roman or 10-point italic Times Roman. A **point** is a measurement of a font's size. The American Point System measures the height of

This is an example of Helvetica
This is an example of Courier
This is an example of Times Roman

FIGURE 1

type or the length of lines of type. Common point sizes are from 6 to 72 points. One point is 0.013837", which equates to approximately 72 points per inch. Character height is measured from the ascender (i.e., in the lowercase letter h, it would be highest part of the left straight line) or the descender (i.e., in the lowercase letters j or y, the lowest part of the letter that appears below the line). Therefore in a 72-point font, each character would be one inch tall. An "em" space or "en" space is equal to the width of the lowercase letter "m" or "n" respectively in the typeface being used. Generally an en dash (–) is set the width of a capital letter N while an em dash (—) is set the width of a capital letter M. Most fonts include standard letters and numbers as well as symbols for language, mathematical, monetary, and legal use. However, some fonts consist entirely of symbols for scientific or mathematical uses. The typeface of this book is ITC Garamond Book using a font size of 10 points.

There are two types of font technologies, bit maps and outlines. In a **bit-mapped font** each character is composed of dots within a grid pattern. Since each character is a fixed pattern of dots each bit-mapped font comes in only one size. A new set of characters is needed for each size. This requires a great deal of memory for storage of the fonts. An **outline font** is only one set of characters that can be enlarged or made smaller to fit the desired point size. This is referred to as a scalable font. This is possible because outline fonts are stored as a mathematical representation instead of a predefined grid pattern of dots. The outlines are converted to the desired point size and then filled with dots. Outline fonts require less storage space than bit-mapped fonts.

There are other options from which to choose for printing typefaces. They include shadow, outline, or underlined text. A script typeface resembles handwriting because the lowercase letters are joined together. Italic letters are printed at a slant toward the right. Book and magazine titles as well as names of newspapers are usually printed in italics. Sometimes the style is used to add emphasis to a word or group of words. Condensed type has narrower characters, but it still maintains the characteristics of its design

Type
■ **Serif**
■ **Sans serif**
■ **Pitch**
Fixed
Proportional
■ **Weight**
■ **Orientation**

style. This also means that more words can be printed in a smaller space. Printed text can also have different alignments.

Text can be aligned in one of four different ways: justified, flush left, flush right, or centered. **Justified text** is aligned at the left and the right margins giving the text the appearance of a block. The left-hand margin in **flush left** alignment is all the way to the left with the right margin being different lengths (also called ragged right). Text that is aligned **flush right** is lined up along the right margin. **Centered text** is in the middle of the paper equidistant between the margins that have been set.

HOW CAN GRAPHICS ENHANCE A DOCUMENT?

Graphics can add high interest to a document. A graphic as simple as a bullet (•) enhances entries in a list of items. Borders around the paper's edge or lines drawn around text to form boxes offer easy, high-interest graphics. There are other graphic elements that you can use in document designing. Word processing programs have many of their own graphics that can be used in your document design. But there are drawing and painting programs that allow you to create your own graphics and then import them into a DTP program. Scanners can "read" a graphical image directly into your computer where you can adapt it to your design. Yet another source of graphical images is contained in clip art. Found in other software packages, clip art depicts graphics for special occasions, holidays, even borders. But do not offer too many distractions from the text or message that you are trying to relay.

Moderation is a good rule of thumb. When you start putting the white space, text, and graphics together to finalize your document, consider the following guidelines: balance, unity, and sequence. Good balance is achieved if the placement of each element gives a sense of stability. You may place the elements on the page so they appear to be unbalanced, but the design can still give a sense of stability in placement. Unity is achieved if a single theme carries the message. Your design should encourage the reader along a definite reading path in order to make your point. You want the reader to comprehend the message you are sending through your design.

HOW DOES PAGE DESIGN AFFECT READABILITY?

Professionals have devised tests to determine the readability of documents. **Readability** is measured on various indices, the end result being that the person reading understands and can use what has been written. In fact, most textbooks have been evaluated by readability experts. Results of testing done by Donald Paterson and Miles Tinker at the University of Minnesota during the 1940s is found in Table 1. Some of the factors that affect readability are the level of language used, the length of sentences, the style of writing, and the way the type appears on the page. For easiest readability, type should be consistent, well laid out, and proportioned on the page.

TABLE 1
How Design Affects Reading Comprehension

Upper- and lowercase letters are preferred by 94% of people.
Margins should leave a minimum of ¼″ white space around the text.
Most books are set in 10- and 11-point type.
Variation from these sizes resulted in a 5–6% slower reading rate.
Serif typefaces can be read 2.2% faster than sans serif.
Use of all capital letters reduces the reading rate by 11.8%.
White printing on a black background reduces reading speed by 10.5%.

TABLE 2
Examples of Text Alignment

JUSTIFIED: This sample of typing illustrates a fully justified text. You can see that the letters fill the entire line from the left margin all the way to the right margin on each line.
FLUSH LEFT: This sample of typing illustrates flush left, also known as ragged right text. The letters all begin at the left margin and the right margin is of differing lengths.
FLUSH RIGHT: This sample of typing illustrates a flush right margin. The letters align at the right margin and the margin at the left side is ragged.
CENTERED: This sample of typing illustrates a centered margin.
All the letters in each line are centered on the page.

Consistency

Choose one typeface and point size throughout the main part of the document. Introduction of too many typefaces creates a lack of harmony. Titles or headlines should be varied in weight and style so that they stand out from the remainder of the text. For the highest readability levels avoid long blocks of text using italics, script, bold, or all capital letters.

Design

When you are laying out your document, refer to your draft design plan. Remember also that vertically rather than horizontally set type is extraordinarily hard to read. Widow and orphan lines also defeat readability. A so-called **orphan line** occurs when one line of a paragraph begins at the bottom of a page. The **widow line** results when a paragraph ends with only one line at the top of the next page.

You may have to experiment with various strategies before obtaining the "look" you're after. But the fundamentals of design to remember are: Be subtle and keep your concepts simple.

VOCABULARY SELF-TEST

Can you define the following terms?

bit-mapped font (p. 429)

centered text (p. 429)

document design (p. 426)

flush left (p. 429)

flush right (p. 429)

font (p. 428)

justified text (p. 429)

kerning (p. 427)

leading (p. 427)

orientation (p. 428)

orphan line (p. 431)

outline font (p. 429)

point (p. 428)

readability (p. 430)

style sheet (p. 426)

typeface (p. 428)

typography (p. 426)

weight (p. 428)

white space (p. 427)

widow line (p. 431)

REVIEW QUESTIONS

Multiple Choice

1. The art of setting pictures and words so they look good is called _____.
   a. document design
   b. graphic arts
   c. typography
   d. design methodology
2. A font's size is measured in _____.
   a. weight
   b. fonts
   c. pitch
   d. points
3. A good design has _____, which suggests that all the elements function collectively.
   a. unity
   b. color
   c. a theme
   d. conflict
4. The set of alphanumeric characters that all share the same characteristics is known as a(n) _____.
   a. characteristic
   b. orientation
   c. typeface
   d. font
5. Which of the following is inappropriate for document readability?
   a. consistent type
   b. colorful
   c. script type
   d. in proportion on the page

Fill-In

1. The technique of combining text, art work or graphics into a final product is known as _____.

2. The _____ of your design can be thought of as a blueprint or master plan.
3. The place on the paper that gives the reader's eye a place to rest is known as _____.
4. The method of adjusting space between lines is referred to as _____; _____ is the method for adjusting the space between characters.
5. The design of a set of characters is known as its _____.

Short Answer

1. Identify at least five kinds of documents that could benefit from the page layout capabilities of desktop publishing software.

2. Recount some of the elementary design principles that you should consider for your document.
3. Give examples of white space and describe how it affects readability.
4. Explain what might influence WYSIWYG so that your hard copy might not "look" the same as the screen.
5. Summarize the qualities associated with typefaces, i.e., serif or sans serif, pitch, weight, type, and orientation.

OUTLINE

OBJECTIVES

12.1 Describe the microcomputer
database management system.
12.2 Explain the functions of a
microcomputer database
management system.
12.3 Understand how you ensure the
validity and maintain the security of
data in a database.
12.4 Define how an image database
differs from a text-based database.

Chapter 12

Managing Data: Database Management Systems

Profile

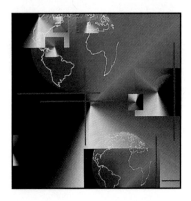

C. Wayne Ratliff

You would probably be surprised by the number of products in everyday use that have been developed by backyard or basement tinkerers rather than by large corporations. Many of these people who develop products don't do it for money but for the love of the project itself. Some see a need and try to fill it, whether it be a personal need or a widespread business need.

C. Wayne Ratliff, the original author of dBASE, a microcomputer data manager, was one of those do-it-yourself individuals. As an engineer at Jet Propulsion Laboratories in Pasadena, California, Ratliff was no stranger to writing programs. His credits include writing a database management system for a NASA Viking space program called Lander Project. This project was small potatoes, however, to what was to come.

In his spare time Ratliff liked to analyze football pools. In the mid-1970s the space required for the data essential to make the correct picks began to take over his living area. A better storage system had to be found. For Ratliff, the better way was yet another do-it-yourself project.

Like most entrepreneurial projects, the beginnings were humble.

The first formal offering of the program, originally called Vulcan, was in January, 1978. Ratliff's first buyers were fellow computer hobbyists who acquired the program through mail order from advertisements placed in a national computer magazine. The program started selling fairly well and put an extra burden on Ratliff. He kept his regular job and handled the Vulcan business by himself, just like many basement inventors. He personally copied the software and assembled software manuals for each buyer.

Ratliff wanted to concentrate more on the program development itself and eventually left the marketing to an upcoming computer software marketing firm called Ashton-Tate, a firm he later joined. Because the Vulcan name was already being used, the name of the data manager was changed to dBASE. It went on to become one of the most popular programs for microcomputers. Ratliff left Ashton-Tate in 1986 and is a founding partner in another business endeavor called Queue Associates.

As for football, Ratliff was so busy that he never did get to use the program to analyze the football pool.

Today's society thrives on information. To meet our increasing demand for information, we require more and more data to be gathered, stored, and manipulated. In fact, many people require so much data that it has become impossible to manually manage and extract the information needed in a timely fashion. To solve this problem, microcomputers have been called upon to help manage and store the data gathered. Recall in Chapter 10 we discussed the basics for using files and databases for managing data. In this chapter you will read about microcomputer database management systems, a type of application software used to manage data.

Objective 12.1   Describe the microcomputer database management system.

What Is a Microcomputer Database Management System?

A microcomputer **database management system (DBMS)** is the software that allows a user to store, organize, and retrieve data from a database. It is the interface among programs, users, and data in the database. Database management systems for microcomputers include Paradox, R:BASE, and dBASE.

Basically anyone who needs to organize any sizable collection of data finds it helpful to use a database management system to electronically store and retrieve information (Figure 12.1). Typical users include librarians, stockbrokers, and small business owners, among others. A librarian might use a database management system to manage special collections of books, records and CDs, or maps. Stockbrokers might use one to keep track of clients and prospective clients. A small business owner might use a database management system to control inventory, organize employee records, or gauge the responsiveness of mailing lists.

One of the most popular applications is in accounting and involves integration of several different files. These files include the general ledger, accounts receivable, accounts payable, and payroll files. Other applications that require integration of several files—and thus are well suited to a database management system—include financial management, travel agency management, medical office management, and real estate management.

At home you might use a database management system to record personal information for tax or insurance purposes. You might also use it to organize names and addresses, your CD collection, your coin collection, and so on.

A database management system provides the user a method to easily access data as well as protect the integrity of the data. It provides a means of developing applications through the database software. Networking is becoming more and more fundamental in business. For the business or corporate environment the microcomputer database program should accommodate multiple users.

Objective 12.2   Explain the functions of a microcomputer database management system.

What Does a Microcomputer Database Management System Do?

The exact features of a microcomputer database program vary. Most, however, contain features that allow them to perform basic functions of a database, including creating a database, maintaining the database, organizing the database, querying the database, generating reports, creating customized database applications, and connectivity with other programs.

FIGURE 12.1
In 1974, approximately fifty-five zoos in North America and Europe began pooling data on their animals. By the end of 1986, over 70,000 living specimens from over 200 zoos in sixteen countries had been cataloged. From this database, reports covering census, breeding, age and sex distribution, and population trends are routinely generated and distributed to participating zoological facilities. Personnel at the Columbus Zoo record pertinent data about their tiger population. (Kjell B. Sandved. Insets: Merrill Publishing/Cobalt Productions)

Creating a Database

Functions of a Microcomputer Database Management System

- Entering data
- Maintaining data
- Organizing data
- Querying the database
- Generating reports
- Creating customized applications
- Connectivity

The first step in creating a database is to define the problem that you want the database to solve. For example, let's say you maintain all your customer contacts on a paper Rolodex system. Now you want a list of all regular customers in each region so that you can send promotional and special sales notices to them. You'll need to generate mailing labels for this material. First, decide what information the database should provide. In this case, it is the customer's name and address. Each piece of data should be contained in its own field. The individual data items would include title, first name, middle initial, last name, street address, city, state, zip code, and telephone number.

Before any data can be entered the organization, or *structure*, of the data must be defined. By defining the data structure you tell the program how to treat the fields in each record. This includes naming the field, determining the data type (e.g., character, numeric, date, etc.), setting the length of the fields, and in some cases specifying additional information such as the number of decimal places or the format for a date entry.

A field is given a name that identifies the data stored in that field; for example, CUSTNAME could identify the field that contains the customers' names. The type of data stored in a field must also be identified. For example, if a field contains the price of a product that will be used as part of a calculation, such as multiplying the price times a number of items, the field must be designated as numeric.

The structure of a database file is created using the **database design screen**. The database design screen is where names, types, width, and other factors for each field in a database file are defined. Figure 12.2 shows an example of a data structure for the mailing list file.

Fields can be designated as key fields when defining the data structure. **Key fields** uniquely identify a record in a file. For example, when extracting information from the database, customer names may be arranged

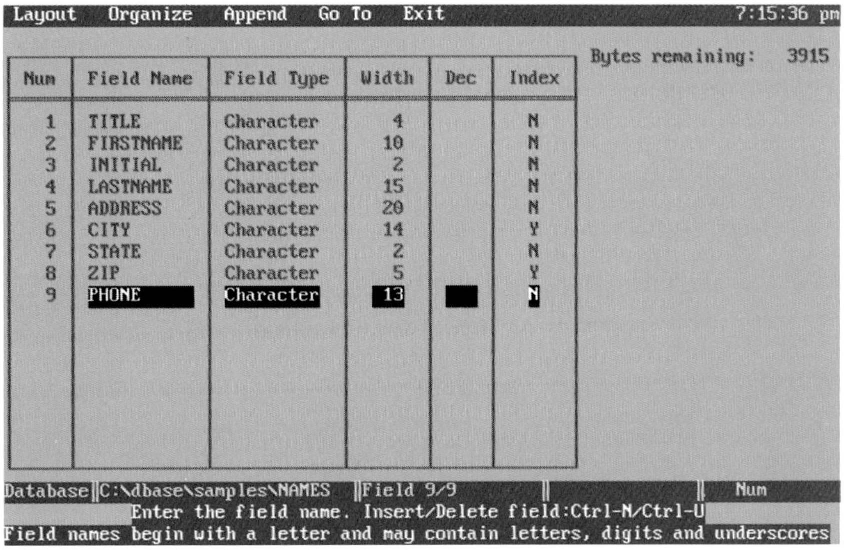

FIGURE 12.2
In the dBASE IV data structure for a database file is created using the database design screen.

Num	Field Name	Field Type	Width	Dec	Index
1	TITLE	Character	4		N
2	FIRSTNAME	Character	10		N
3	INITIAL	Character	2		N
4	LASTNAME	Character	15		N
5	ADDRESS	Character	20		N
6	CITY	Character	14		Y
7	STATE	Character	2		N
8	ZIP	Character	5		Y
9	PHONE	Character	13		N

Layout   Organize   Append   Go To   Exit   7:15:36 pm

Bytes remaining: 3915

Database C:\dbase\samples\NAMES   Field 9/9   Num
Enter the field name. Insert/Delete field:Ctrl-N/Ctrl-U
Field names begin with a letter and may contain letters, digits and underscores

in alphabetical order by the key field LASTNAME. Once the data structure has been defined you can begin entering data.

Database management systems allow users to customize the input screen used for entering data by defining a screen form. A **screen form** describes the layout for entering data into a record. The fields are positioned according to the user's preference and serve as an output screen where field alignment is determined for printing (Figure 12.3).

Maintaining a Database

The contents of a database rarely stay the same; they are changed often. The change may be to a field in an individual record, or it may involve an entire record within the file. In the mailing list file, for example, you may add a new customer or change the address of an old customer. Maintenance functions most likely utilized are updating data in a record and adding or deleting records from your file.

Updating is the process of changing the content of a record or records in a file. It may involve adding to, deleting from, or changing the contents of an existing record—for example, entering a new address or telephone number for a person in your mailing list file. You can keep the data current by accessing records in a file and changing the field contents.

To change the data, most database management systems provide two methods for accessing and viewing the records. An **edit mode** typically shows you the contents of an individual record and allows you to edit each field (Figure 12.4a). The **browse mode** typically shows an entire screen full of records and permits you to edit each field (Figure 12.4b).

Adding to a file means to add an additional record or records to an existing file—for example, entering a new person to a customer file or a new employee in a personnel file. Some programs append the added

FIGURE 12.3
Most DBMS's allow more than one screen form to be created to display the field names and data. The user selects which screen form will be used.

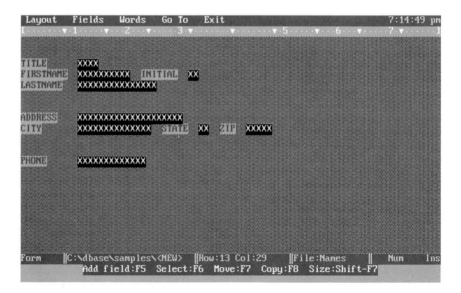

"I think this shot calls for a five iron." Swoosh! There it goes, but unfortunately there goes my back with it. So where do you turn, the local doctor, the caddy, your wife's uncle? No, try the computer.

That's right, the computer. The Centinela Hospital Fitness Institute has developed a computer application that tracks golf stars like Arnold Palmer, among others, on the PGA and the Senior PGA Tour. Through the use of dBASE IV, a microcomputer database program, the hospital employs a mobile medical unit to follow the golfers around, gathering statistics about injuries, strength and flexibility, and physiological data.

The database program allows the hospital to store, organize, and update the information gathered in a timely and efficient manner. The hospital correlates this information with its research in the field of biomechanics. These data can then be used to analyze the golfers' techniques and come up with training suggestions that will improve the game or reduce the chance of injury.

Called the Amateur Golfer Improvement Program, it combines the sciences of computer engineering and medicine. While the medicine part is best left to the doctors, the fact that this application was developed using microcomputer software helps make it more user-friendly for the hospital employees and less costly than if it were run on a mainframe.

Other clients of the hospital who will require their own specialized programs include the Los Angeles Dodgers and Harlem Globetrotters.

records at the end of the file; others place them in a spot vacated by previously deleted records; still others make it possible to insert a new record at any point in the file.

Deleting involves removing records from a file. A record may be deleted in direct response to a delete command prompt or may be a two-step process in which the records are first "marked" for deletion. Once marked, the records are later removed from the file. Individual fields within a record can also be deleted.

Extra care should be taken when deleting data to avoid removing a field or record unintentionally because after the data are deleted, they are no longer available. Often, a prompt such as ARE YOU SURE? (Y/N) will appear on the screen before the deletion takes place. It is wise to keep a backup copy of the file in case of accidental deletion.

Organizing a Database

Usually, it is easier to read and make sense of data if they are arranged in a previously designated order. For example, data could be arranged alphabetically by last name or numerically by invoice number.

There are two methods of organizing the records in a file—sorting and indexing. Both methods are similar in that they order records numerically or alphabetically, and in ascending or descending order. However, they differ

FIGURE 12.4
(a) The contents of one record in the dBASE IV edit mode. (b) Records are displayed one screen at a time in the dBASE IV browse mode.

(a)

(b)

in the way the sorted records are stored. So in the mailing list database you would request that the address labels be printed in order by zip code. You could receive substantial discounts from the post office for bulk mailings that have been presorted.

Sorting reorders records in a file according to a desired condition, after which the original file is saved in the sorted order. A sort "physically" reorders the records and creates a new file with the sorted data. However, if you sort a file in several ways, naming each new file, valuable disk space is quickly consumed.

The process of **indexing** creates a file that contains the user's sorted data conditions. Unlike sorting, where the entire file is stored in sorted order, the index file is saved separately so that the original file remains the same. Indexing allows many different sort orderings without affecting the integrity of the original file and consumes much less disk space since the index file contains only the conditions on which the file was sorted. A simple index may be created in which ordering of data takes place according to the contents of one field. Complex indexing orders the records according to the content of multiple fields. For example, you might index the records by last name and state. This would list the records alphabetically by the customer's last name, from A to Z for customers in Alabama, then by name from A to Z for customers in Alaska, and so on.

Querying a Database

Probably the most important function in the use of a database program is the ability of the user to query the database. A **query** is the process of extracting data from a database and presenting it in a requested format. Queries are accomplished through the use of a database query language. A **database query language** acts as an interface between users and a database management system. It helps users easily manipulate, analyze, and create reports from the data contained in the database. It makes it easy for people other than programmers to use a database management system. The quality of the query process determines how fast and efficiently the data is retrieved. This is where the performance of a database is either made or broken.

The relational database structure is used more than any other in today's powerful microcomputer databases. As we saw in Chapter 10, the two basic query styles used in a relational database are query by example and structured query language.

Generating Reports

For the majority of cases, data extracted from the database will be communicated to others through a paper report. These reports may be simple or custom-created in the database program.

Sometimes it is necessary to print only the raw data rather than to arrange the output into a more formal report. Database management systems allow you to print the screen contents at any time. Data in a record can be sent to the printer in the same format as it appears in the screen form.

Many times, however, you want to customize your output to meet particular needs. This customizing is possible by using a report generator. A **report generator** defines how the output is to appear when printed. In addition to customizing the placement of fields, most report generators allow you to incorporate headers, footers, formatting, and mathematical and statistical functions.

The header section of a report is found at the top of the report page and contains items such as date, page number, column headings, or perhaps a company logo. The footer, like the header, is a separate section of the report, found at the bottom of the page. The footer may contain page numbers, the user's name, or other relevant information. Formatting features give you control over the way a report looks by setting margins, justifying text, and indicating page lengths and spacing between lines. Most report generators contain features that perform mathematical and statistical functions such as calculating column subtotals, grand totals, averages, and counts.

Creating Customized Database Applications

Any of the microcomputer database programs will probably fulfill all the needs for a typical home user. In business, however, there is often a need to create custom applications to manage a task efficiently. There are two basic methods included in many microcomputer database management systems that allow development of customized applications: through a database programming language or through an application generator.

A **database programming language** is a language specific to the database that allows you to create applications customized to your needs. The database language commands let you create and control how data are entered, processed, and retrieved from the database. The programmer is responsible for coding all menus, data entry screens, output forms, and all the features that tie the database program together.

An **application generator** is a separate program that removes some of the burden of coding an entire custom application. The user inputs to the program what it should do through a series of questions and answers. The application generator simplifies customizing by generating much of the program code. This makes it easier to develop an application. An application might display a start-up menu of choices, or provide instruction screens to guide a user. You don't need to be a programmer to take advantage of the power of an application generator. Templates for database applications, such as accounting systems, can be purchased.

The application must first be compiled. Most database management systems are available with compilers to perform this task. Once compiled an application can be loaded and run on its own without having to first load the database management system.

Connectivity and the Database

Microcomputer database programs are available as both single-user and multiuser products. Single-user programs cannot be used by multiple users in a network environment. Multiuser microcomputer database programs can be purchased in file/server architecture or client/server architecture. Basically, with the file/server arrangement, the database program runs entirely on the user's system and the network server merely stores the data files that are shared among the different users. This method does not take advantage of the computing power of the server. In a **client/server architecture**, the processing of an application is split between a "front-end" client and a "back-end" server. The client portion is the user's microcomputer, which typically controls user interaction with the database management system. The server portion can be another microcomputer, minicomputer, or mainframe, which performs tasks such as data management, information sharing between clients, and sophisticated network administration and security features. Using the processing power of both the client and the server computers increases the processing power available and the efficiency with which it is used.

In addition to multiuser support, many microcomputer database programs allow the user to integrate data from other applications. Examples include writing a letter using a word processor and importing (bringing) it into the database program to perform a mail merge with the data contained in the mail list file; or exporting (sending out) data from the database to be used in a graph in a spreadsheet program. Another desirable feature is for the database program to work with different data file formats from other database programs.

Objective 12.3   Understand how you ensure the validity and maintain the security of data in a database.

How Can Data Integrity Be Maintained?

Data Integrity and Security

- **Validation**
    Format checks
    Range checks
    Accuracy checks
- **Security**
    Data encryption
    Passwords
    File locking

A business depends on its ability to acquire the right data at the right time. The data must be accurate and untainted. This means ensuring careful data entry and protecting against unauthorized use.

Since most data errors can be traced back to their point of entry, the microcomputer database programs provide a method for detecting them at this point through validity checks. Checking data for appropriateness and accuracy is called **validating**. Data-entry checks can be built into the data manager to prevent invalid data from being entered. These checks are often set as the data structures are being defined. Validity checks may be accomplished in the microcomputer database program by:

- Format checking—determining if data are in the correct format, e.g., numeric or text
- Range checking—determining if the data fall within an acceptable chosen range, e.g., greater than 100 but less than 500
- Accuracy checking—making sure that an entry is possible, e.g., cross-checking a product number with the product numbers in an inventory file

Data stored in a file are often sensitive or confidential in nature. Therefore, a user may want to restrict access to the computer and data only to authorized personnel. This is especially true in a multiuser environment. Data **encryption** is a way to code data so they appear as a scrambled display of alphanumeric characters if retrieved by unauthorized persons. Database software provides features built into the software itself that limit or prevent access.

The database can be designed so that a password grants access to only certain files or to the entire database. A **password** may be a letter, number, or a combination of both designed to prevent access unless the exact entry code is used. It can be designed so that the user needs one password to view the file and another password to change, add, or delete anything in the file.

When NASA launches a shuttle, do you think of tax dollars or possible technological breakthroughs? Many people, unfortunately, only think about the astronomical costs of going into space. NASA realizes this and developed a program to inform the public of the applications of developments in space technology as they are applied to everyday life.

The Spinoff Technology Application Retrieval System (STARS) is an interactive multimedia database found at the Virginia Air & Space Museum in Hampton, Virginia. The purpose of the system is to help people understand how NASA's research contributes to our economy. Through touch screens visitors are able to access a variety of topics such as how research has affected industry, products, and services in areas such as aerodynamics, computers, electronics, health care, robotics, and textiles. Don't think of NASA as only that group that sends up rockets. They are involved in much more than that, and the STARS database will shed some light on that mystery.

Data security is especially critical when the database is run on a network, where more than one person has access to the files in the database at the same time. Sometimes, however, unintended deletions, additions, or changes occur when two people work with the same file in a data manager. Errors occur because one person does not know what the other is doing; therefore, one person's update may be accidentally deleted by the other. A data manager can restrict access or lock the file to prevent accidents like this from happening. **File locking** is a procedure that permits only one user to access a file at a time. The file cannot be manipulated by another person until it is released by the first person.

Objective 12.4   Define how an image database differs from a text-based database.

What Is an Image Database?

An **image database** is database software that allows storage of both pictures and text (Figure 12.5). Images comprise large volumes of data and require large amounts of storage and long transmission times to bring the pictures to the screen. For these reasons, until recently, microcomputer databases only stored text.

However, recent enhancements in data storage techniques paved the way for color images to be stored in a database much like text. The technique is called compression technology. Compression technology reduces the file size to a small percentage of the original without significantly reducing the quality of the picture. For example, an E-size ($34'' \times 44''$) color drawing might require 10 megabytes of memory. With compression technology, the file could be reduced to approximately one megabyte.

Image databases require a video camera or graphics scanner, an image capture and compression circuit board that plugs into the computer, and the appropriate image database software.

FIGURE 12.5
An image database allows the storage of both text and graphic images.

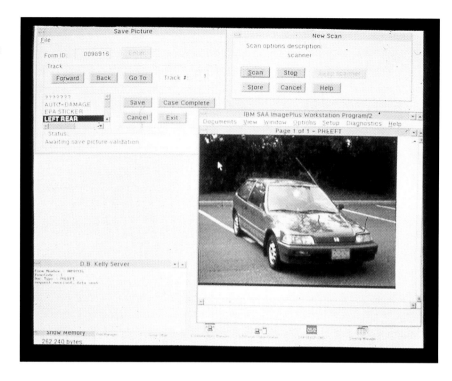

FIGURE 12.6
An image database used in the real estate business.

Data compression has created many applications for image databases. These include picture inventory files for museums and insurance companies. Seng Jewelers of Louisville, Kentucky, uses an image database to maintain inventory control, provide a record of repairs done for clients (before-and-after pictures), and aid in appraisals. Databases of maps and satellite images use geographic information systems (GIS). Picture security systems are another application of image databases. Image databases in the real estate business allow prospective buyers to browse through full-color pictures of homes without leaving the agent's office (Figure 12.6).

Summary

A database management system is software that allows the creation, manipulation, and retrieval of data from a database. It acts as the interface among programs, users, and data in the database. A database management system is helpful for businesses or others to organize any sizable collection of data. The database management system allows quick and easy access to quantities of data, sorts large numbers of records, generates reports, and creates customized applications.

The basic functions of a database management system include creating the database, maintaining the records, organizing the data, querying a database, generating reports, and creating customized applications.

When creating a database you first need to define the problem, decide what information you want the database to supply, and determine the data items needed to produce the desired output. The user should pay particular attention to entering data by carefully defining the data structure, that is, telling the program how to create the fields in each record. The data structure is created using the database design screen. Screen forms can be designed to define the layout for entering data into a record.

A database management system permits the user to update data, add data, and delete data from a database. It also allows you to sort and index data to place them in a specified order.

Database management systems allow you to query the database, that is, make a request for information. This is done through the use of a database query language. The two basic query styles are query by example and structured query language (SQL).

Database management systems provide report generators, which let you define how the output would appear when printed.

Database programming languages allow you to create customized applications to give control over input, processing, and output of data. Application generators take some of the detail of coding the program off the user.

Database programs work in single- and multiuser environments. The ability of the database program to import or export files gives it greater flexibility. In a file/server architecture, the database program runs entirely on the user's system and the network server merely stores the data files that are shared among the different users. In a client/server architecture, the processing of an application is split between a "front-end" client and a "back-end" server. Using the processing power of both the client and the server computers increases the processing power available and the efficiency with which it is used.

Security and validity are concerns of every user. Many database programs have built-in features that protect the integrity of the data as well as ensure the confidentiality of the data.

An image database is database software that stores both pictures and text.

Can you define the following terms?

application generator (p. 444)

browse mode (p. 440)

client/server architecture (p. 444)

database design screen (p. 439)

database management system
    (DBMS) (p. 437)

database programming language
    (p. 444)

database query language
    (p. 443)

edit mode (p. 440)

encryption (p. 445)

file locking (p. 446)

image database (p. 446)

indexing (p. 442)

key fields (p. 439)

password (p. 445)

query (p. 443)

report generator (p. 443)

screen form (p. 440)

sorting (p. 442)

updating (p. 440)

validating (p. 445)

REVIEW QUESTIONS

Multiple Choice

1. A librarian who wants to keep track of a special collection of books easily and efficiently would use _____.
   a. desktop publishing software
   b. database management software
   c. a word processor
   d. a scanner

2. Updating, adding, and deleting are all types of _____ functions.
   a. maintenance
   b. retrieval
   c. utility
   d. security

3. TEXT, NUMERIC, DATE, and YES/NO are different kinds of _____ that the user must specify before data can be entered.
   a. design forms
   b. validation methods
   c. data managers
   d. data types

4. Changing the contents of a record in a file is called _____.
   a. browsing
   b. updating
   c. indexing
   d. sorting

5. _____ is a data organizing method where the reordered records are stored in their reordered sequence.
   a. Sorting
   b. Manipulation
   c. Ordering
   d. Indexing

6. Which one of the following is a method of querying a database?
   a. DBMS
   b. SQL
   c. asking
   d. indexing

7. A _____ is used to define how the output of a database management system will appear when printed.
   a. database programming language
   b. database query language
   c. report generator
   d. data structure

8. Headers and footers are features used when _____.
   a. deleting a record
   b. creating a sort
   c. calculating a field
   d. creating a report

9. Checking to see if data fall within acceptable limits is called _____.
   a. range checking
   b. accuracy checking
   c. file locking
   d. format checking

10. An image database differs from a text database because of its ability to store and retrieve _____.
    a. words
    b. data
    c. reports
    d. graphics

Fill-In

1. Before data are entered into the database, the data _____ must be defined.
2. To look through an entire screen full of records a user would typically be in a(n) _____ mode.
3. Fields specially designated to be used when retrieving data are called _____ fields.
4. A(n) _____ is created to define the layout for entering data into a record.
5. A(n) _____ is a request for information from a database.
6. Format checking, range checking, and accuracy checking are all methods of _____ data entry.
7. A(n) _____ allows you to create database applications to control input, processing, and output of data.
8. When more than one person has access through more than one computer to a data manager it is known as a(n) _____ data manager.
9. To bring in a file from another program is to _____ the file.
10. A type of database that incorporates pictures and text is called a(n) _____ database.

Short Answer

1. What is the purpose of a microcomputer database management system?
2. Name three applications that are well suited for a relational database management system.
3. Why must care be taken when initially defining the data structure?
4. Describe the difference between the edit mode and the browse mode.
5. Contrast sorting and indexing.
6. Describe the difference between file/server and client/server database architectures.
7. What is a validity check? Describe three types of validity checks.
8. What can be done to ensure data confidentiality?
9. What does it mean to import a file? Export a file?
10. What is the importance of using compression technology with image databases?

Issues for Thought

1. The proliferation of microcomputers and database management systems enables employees to create their own databases. What problems do you see in allowing individual users to create and maintain personal databases of business information?
2. Databases maintained by companies of their customers' names and addresses are subsequently sold to others. There is potential for misuse. You probably have received unsolicited mail because of this practice. Discuss the benefits and drawbacks of this practice.

Infomodule

Hypertext and Multimedia

WHAT IS HYPERTEXT?

While reading an article on the history of aviation, your interest is piqued as you come across the section on aircraft of World War II. You put that book down to find a book on World War II aircraft. While reading this material you wonder how gliders were used. Wasn't there more information on gliders in that recent magazine article? While reading about gliders you need more information about aerodynamics, and so on.

Most of you have acted out a scenario similar to this at one time or another on one topic or another. If you haven't, it might be because to do so would be too time-consuming. Imagine if all that information could be found in one place. What if it were stored in a computer, cross-referenced, and available at the click of a button? Sounds like a database, right? Well, in its simplest form hypertext resembles a database, but hypertext is itself a software program. **Hypertext** is graphic-oriented software that contains data that are related; however, data are not stored in traditional files or records. They are stored as objects that can be arbitrarily linked together and accessed rapidly in innumerable ways.

Imagine hypertext as a stack of index cards, each card containing one concept or idea. Those concepts may be in the form of text, graphics, or pictures, unlike a text database. You can move from one card to another, either browsing through all the cards or moving to a specific card anywhere in the stack with the click of a mouse.

Hypertext software incorporates components of a database, text and graphics editors, and employs a mouse to move through windows, click on icons, and access pull-down menus (Figure 1).

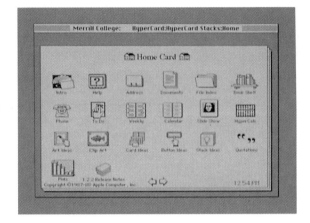

FIGURE 1
Icon representation of features available in HyperCard.

How Did Hypertext Evolve?

Hypertext actually is a fairly recent implementation of a much older concept. In fact, conceptual visions of a hypertext system can be traced back to the 1940s. President Roosevelt's science advisor, Vannevar Bush, conceived a system that combined drawings, photographs, and notes in an on-line text and retrieval system. In his system there would be links between any two points of data, which could then be accessed and retrieved.

These postwar visions enlightened two 1960s thinkers, Douglas Engelbart (see Chapter 3 Profile) and Ted Nelson. Engelbart developed a system for storing information on-line. The mouse provided a means to increase the speed at which input could be made into the computer. Ted Nelson coined the term "hypertext" and developed a hypertext system called Xanadu to store and cross-reference all types of literary works.

Today's microcomputer hypertext programs are a result of foresight and the increasing interest in acquiring information. Owl International, Inc., introduced Guide, the first personal computer hypertext software for the Macintosh, in 1986. Since then Apple has included its HyperCard with each Macintosh it sells. In 1987, Guide was made available for the IBM. Every year more and more hypertext products and applications are becoming available.

WHAT ARE SOME HYPERTEXT APPLICATIONS?

Hypertext programs may be implemented on single- or multiuser systems. At first hypertext was used only on workstations, but now it is being used more and more on personal computers. Compared to other software products, there are relatively few commercial hypertext applications created for a mass market. Most are developed by a user for a specific purpose. As more companies (as well as individual users) learn how to set up hypertext applications, there will be more products available in the stores.

One of the more prominent areas for a hypertext application is in education. A hypertext product called The Bone Box teaches students about the skeletal system and its terminology. The student chooses a particular bone from the skeletal system and sees different views of that bone.

At the University of Southern California, music and text are integrated into a hypertext that teaches scales and film scoring and the application provides for student improvisation.

Reference books and other voluminous manuals are suited for hypertext. For example, Ford Motor Company mechanics use a hypertext developed on Guide that provides easy access to their service and parts manuals.

Hypertext applications fall into one of several categories. On-line browsers are those hypertext products whose main purpose is to permit the user to look through the information. These are used for products such as reference manuals whose contents are altered little, if at all. They provide the user with quick on-line information, but they usually limit the amount of customizing that can be done.

Most microcomputer-oriented hypertext falls into the category of general-purpose or user-defined products. These include HyperCard, Guide, and HyperPad, in which the user defines the data and how they are to be linked together.

Hypertext products can be combined with expert systems as part of a problem-solving process. These are usually implemented in a workstation environment.

WHAT ARE THE BASICS OF HYPERTEXT?

Although more and more hypertext applications are becoming available, microcomputer users will probably have to develop programs to meet their individual needs. But before you can develop your own application you need to understand some basic concepts of hypertext.

Cards and Stacks

Organization is the key to creating a successful hypertext application. The data must be broken down into small, discrete units. These units of data usually fill one computer screen. HyperCard calls these units cards, HyperPad calls them pages, and Guide calls them guidelines. We'll refer to these units as cards, each of which contains text fields to store alphanumeric data. The cards may also contain graphics or pictures.

A collection of related cards under one name is called a stack; related pages are called a pad. (Notice the relationship of hypertext concepts to everyday objects: a stack of index cards; a pad of paper contains many pages.)

All the cards in a stack may contain the same elements, or background. For example, if the stack were used for security identification, each card might contain an outline where a picture is placed, or boxes where a name and other fields of data will be inserted. Each individual card would contain only the information for one person. A background is like a screen form in a text database.

Linking Cards

To move from card to card in a stack, or page to page in a pad, the individual cards or pages must be linked together. Linking is the method by which the user moves about in a stack or pad. For the most part, the links established depend solely on the user. Since you are creating the hypertext program, only you see how the data are related. Hypertext card arrangements can take many forms. They may be simple, straight line links, simple or complex hierarchical structures, or may be in random order.

To sort through the cards you would click on a "button." A button can be a few descriptive words or an icon that describes the link. Buttons may be user- or program-defined icons (Figure 2). By clicking on a button a new card is immediately brought to the screen. Buttons can also be defined to perform functions such as activating a video disc player or dialing a phone. For example, if you created a stack of cards on the birds of North America, the card might contain a button to activate a video disc player with a map showing the range of the bird and also provide an audio recording of the call that the bird gives.

User Levels

The user has the option of working at various levels within the hypertext program. The level depends on

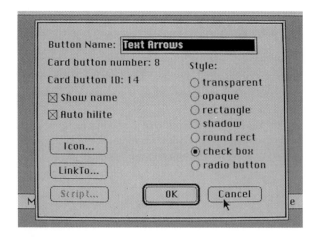

FIGURE 2
HyperCard menu for creating a button.

what you are trying to accomplish. Some hypertext products contain all the levels, some do not. In general the user level options are browsing, typing, painting, authoring, and scripting.

Browsing. At the browsing level you move through individual cards or move from stack to stack. Browsing is usually limited to viewing and printing cards. Once the hypertext application is fully developed you will spend most of your time at this level looking up information. Many systems contain a graphical browser that shows you where you are in the stack with an on-screen map. It keeps you from getting lost in a complex card structure.

Typing. In addition to the capabilities of the browsing level, the user can edit text and add new cards to the stack. Higher levels usually contain the features of the preceding levels.

Painting. Cards are customized at the paint level. Here you alter the look of the cards by adding or changing the images. This can be accomplished for each individual card or for the background. There are usually a number of paint tools available to create pictures or art may be copied from another card.

Authoring. At the author level the user acquires more control over the program. You can change the objects, such as move and redefine the buttons, change the placement and size of the text fields, and change the background graphics on a card. At this level no programming knowledge is necessary. The authoring functions are accessed through menus and dialog boxes. This level is where the applications are set up or authored.

Scripting. Scripting provides the maximum in user control of the program. It is programming in the hypertext language. HyperCard's script language is called HyperTalk. Script languages, like programming languages, must follow syntax rules, but they tend to be written more like English sentences. For example, if you wanted to insert the date in a card after a field called "date," the script could read:

```
put the date after field ''date''
```

Advantages

Once it is set up, hypertext is relatively easy to use. Buttons simplify the process of moving between cards to access the right information. Hypertext has the potential to enhance learning by combining text, pictures (both still and motion), and sound into one complete presentation. Much of learning and understanding takes place visually. Could you describe da Vinci's Mona Lisa in words only? It would be more effective to see the painting as you read about the artist than merely to read the text.

Although hypertext is not the final word in computing applications, it has potential for sophisticated uses like artificial intelligence.

Disadvantages

Because hypertext is a graphically oriented program, it has large memory requirements, usually a coprocessor and graphics plug-in cards. A modestly equipped personal computer will not be able to run hypertext programs. The computer systems that run hypertext are usually more expensive.

A potential problem with hypertext is created by the user who authored the application. If a user devises obscure and meaningless links, the program is rendered useless.

WHAT IS MULTIMEDIA?

Multimedia is the integration of high-quality sound, still and motion video, text, animation, and graphics in a computer system. That is true, but a better description might be one word—communication. That's what it truly is, an exciting way to stimulate the senses, a means to address many levels of comprehension. Multimedia enables the user to read text about a subject and to "see" the topic. Because of the interactive environment of multimedia, educators have found that many students learn and retain information. The biggest drawback to multimedia was its cost. However, this is no longer the barrier it once was, so there are more applications using multimedia today.

In the next sections you will read about the major components of a multimedia system: audio, video storage, and software. Major applications that use multimedia are also described.

WHAT ARE THE COMPONENTS OF A MULTIMEDIA SYSTEM?

Integrating text, graphics, audio, and video requires certain qualities of hardware and software (Figure 3). There are two ways to acquire a "multimedia system." One is to purchase the entire system from a vendor. The other is to upgrade with add-ons to bring your system up to multimedia standards. There are no consistent standards that define multimedia; therefore, make sure that components fit the requirements of the application you will use.

Audio

The main focus in multimedia development used to be video. Now, however, audio (sound) is as important as any other component. There are two basic types of sounds: analog and digital.

Your voice is an example of analog sound. These sounds must first be converted to digital form to be stored by the computer. Through a process called sampling, the sound is "grabbed" in small increments. The higher the sampling rate, the more parts of the analog signals are grabbed and the better the quality of the resulting digital sound. Sounds initially generated by the computer are already in digital form. This is called synthesized audio.

To produce sound, you must have two other pieces of hardware, a sound board or card, and speakers. Sound cards are the plug-in electric circuits that enable your computer to generate audio signals. They are available in 8-bit and 16-bit versions, with the latter delivering better quality sound.

Musical Instrument Digital Interface (MIDI) is often a component of multimedia. Although mainly used for musical applications, it can be used in a variety of ways. MIDI is a communication protocol used to communicate between the computer and other peripheral devices that are MIDI controlled. A MIDI interface makes control and response between a computer and an instrument a two-way street.

All the money spent on high-quality equipment is wasted unless you can reproduce the sound effectively. Speakers are very important to this process. External computer speakers are different from your home or car speakers. Because of the close

FIGURE 3
Multimedia equipment.

proximity to the computer they must be magnetically shielded to protect the monitor from interference. Speaker systems are available in stereo and surround sound, which give your multimedia applications dramatic impact.

Video

Most users consider video the most important part of a quality multimedia application. Multimedia video includes full motion, stills, graphics, and animation. Many applications use more than one at a time.

In order to see a video image, you must have a means for recording that image. There are numerous ways to capture video, both full motion and still. Videotape and a camcorder are probably the easiest and most popular method for taking motion video pictures. Video cameras use a variety of different tape formats depending on the level of quality. Usually for videotape, the wider the tape the better the resolution of an image. As with sound, tape formats record an image in analog format that must be converted to a digital representation for use by the computer.

Video cards are available that perform many different functions. Some, called multimedia cards or multifunction boards, combine video and audio functions on one card. Data compression technology like that used in image databases reduces the storage demands for video images. New technologies further reduce the storage space needed. General Electric and RCA developed a compression technology (later purchased by Intel) called digital video interactive (DVI) that reduces a file to as much as 1 percent of its original size.

Still video cameras come in analog and digital versions. Analogs use still video players or video floppy disks so that the computer can access the image. They generally have a higher resolution than digital still video cameras. Photo compact disc (CD) players permit storing of images on disc for playing on the monitor. Compact disc-interactive (CD-I) players play back the images on a television screen instead of the monitor. A digital camera sends the image directly into the computer through a serial port.

Another way images enter the computer is through scanners. Flatbed scanners are fairly inexpensive for mid-range quality models and are available in both black and white and color. Slide scanners capture the images from 35mm films or slides.

Once the images are entered, a screen is required for viewing. For one person, the monitor of the computer is sufficient. The monitor should be VGA, but Super-VGA is a better choice. For multimedia business presentations, other types of display devices would be required.

Overhead projection systems permit viewing even in a large auditorium by a group of people. High-end users can afford to choose the expensive LCD-based projectors, some of which cost tens of thousands of dollars. A less expensive option is the cathode-ray type (CRT) projectors.

An alternative to the computer screen is Video Information System (VIS) by Tandy. The VIS disc player displays multimedia applications directly to the television set without requiring a computer.

Storage

Storage was a major stumbling block to desktop multimedia. Both audio and video take a tremendous amount of storage with full motion color video requirements of about 40MB per minute. Usually much of the information is compressed. However, even text data, in the amounts used by some applications, takes a large amount of storage space. Compact Disc–Read Only Memory (CD-ROM) was the technology that made multimedia available to the PC user. The typical 5.25″ floppy diskette holds approximately 1.2MB, while a CD-ROM disk holds 650MB or more.

Because files used in multimedia applications can be very large, removable secondary storage media is a good choice. Hard disk storage can be used, preferably at 200MB or more, but it leaves little room for additional applications. Removable media allow the applications to be transported to other multimedia stations.

One drawback to CD-ROM is that it is read-only media. Another storage method is available that allows the user to edit multimedia applications. Magneto-optical media combines the benefits of magnetic and optical technology to give the user a high-capacity disk that can be rewritten as well.

Software

Multimedia software can generally be classified as authoring or prewritten. Authoring software such as QuickTime by Apple Computer gives the ability to incorporate animation, video, and sound into a document. Multimedia can be an effective tool for use in training employees. Sales presentations take on a new aura when enhanced by a multimedia presentation. An impressive desktop video presentation of a report at a board meeting could boost the career of the savvy user. One must be careful, however, to prevent the show from overshadowing the product or process being presented.

Multimedia can use hypertext programs. Often the combination of hypertext and multimedia devices is referred to as hypermedia. Animation software like Autodesk's Animator produce motion. Individual pictures are drawn and then displayed quickly one after another to simulate motion. Overlays are used to place animation and text on top of video images.

For full motion and animation applications the computer must be able to quickly retrieve and send a picture to a screen with enough speed (frames per second) to prevent it from appearing jittery. Potential multimedia uses are in animation, simulation, teleconferencing, education and training, engineering, and medical imaging.

WHAT ARE SOME MAJOR MULTIMEDIA APPLICATIONS?

The majority of prewritten multimedia applications are found in educational settings, specifically reference and training materials. Reference materials such as encyclopedias are commonly seen and heard. The Presidents by the National Geographic Society gives information about all the presidents of the United States and lets the user hear them "speak." The CD Sourcebook of American History is a collection of over 600 documents representing approximately 20,000 pages of text, including the Declaration of Independence as well as Patrick Henry's famous "Liberty or Death" speech.

Multimedia has the potential to help students learn. The California State Board of Education adopted a seventh-grade science multimedia application called "Science 2000." This nontextbook curriculum actively engages students in the learning process. Teachers personalize the software by adding their own knowledge. Other states are incorporating more multimedia applications into their school systems; for example, the Texas Learning Technology Group course in Chemistry I.

Gateway Stories, from the Center for Applied Special Technology, Inc. is multimedia software that scans books, adding sound and speech. These stories can then be "read" by disabled students who ordinarily would not have access to the mainstream materials.

Hearing-impaired students and those who are learning English as a second language are using Sounds of English from Irvine Interactive Inc. The student sees how the lips and tongue are positioned to form the words and hears a voice pronounce them properly. The student learns by comparing his own recorded voice to the correct pronunciation.

Show and Tell for Kids by Digispeech, Inc. is an authoring tool for children aged 7 to 14. A short tutorial describes how they can combine voice, sound, graphics, and text to create their own slide presentations.

Many companies offer interactive job training by means of multimedia applications. United Airlines adopted this type of system to educate its flight attendants about aircraft equipment, emergency preparedness, world geography, and cultural awareness. More touch-screen devices are being incorporated into the newer aircraft, so the touch-screen formats of the program also help attendants become familiar with this technology. Because there are training locations throughout the world employees are able to take their discs as they travel, learning at their own pace.

Nissan is another company that offered multimedia training. In 1989, to prepare for the introduction of the Infiniti, mechanics from 62 dealerships were brought to Scottsdale, Arizona, for intense instruction. They learned how to service this new model via interactive videodiscs, along with more traditional lectures as well as hands-on training.

In April, 1993, a multimedia museum of memories opened in Washington, D.C. These memories from 1933 through 1949 are depicted in the world's largest networked multimedia system—the faces, voices, and stories of the Holocaust. Visitors are able to track someone of their age and gender through this time via 24 IBM 486-based personal computers that access a network that contains the compressed digital information.

New applications for multimedia are steadily appearing as it finds its way into the marketplace.

VOCABULARY SELF-TEST

Can you define the following terms?

hypertext (p. 452)

multimedia (p. 455)

REVIEW QUESTIONS

Multiple Choice

1. The basic unit of data in HyperCard is called a
   _____.
   a. page
   b. pad
   c. stack
   d. card

2. A device the user activates to perform a link to another card is a _____.
   a. linker
   b. stacker
   c. button
   d. script

3. Hypertext concepts can be traced back to the _____ when _____ described a system for on-line text and retrieval.
   a. 1960s, Ted Engelbart
   b. 1980s, HyperCard
   c. 1960s, Ted Nelson
   d. 1940s, Vannevar Bush

4. _____ are used to place animation and text on top of video images.
   a. Browsers
   b. Scripts
   c. Overlays
   d. Data compressors

5. A typical CD can store much more _____ than _____.
   a. text, video
   b. video, text
   c. audio, text
   d. video, audio

Fill-In

1. Hypertext programs that are used for reference manuals fall in the classification of on-line _____.
2. Most microcomputer hypertext falls in the category of general-purpose or _____ products.
3. Creating multiple drawings and rapidly displaying them one after another is called _____.
4. Multimedia software that allows the user to develop the application is called _____ software.
5. The majority of multimedia software is used in the field of _____.

Short Answer

1. In your own words, describe hypertext.
2. Summarize the five basic user levels in hypertext.
3. Write a short definition of multimedia.
4. Describe an application that would use hypertext and multimedia.
5. Contrast analog and digital sound.

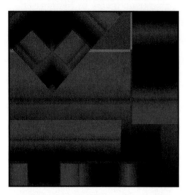

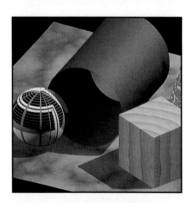

OUTLINE

OBJECTIVES

13.1 Understand what spreadsheet software is.

13.2 Describe several benefits of spreadsheet software.

13.3 Explain several ways in which spreadsheet software is used.

13.4 Identify and summarize the basic functions of spreadsheet software.

13.5 Describe the three types of programs commonly integrated with spreadsheet programs.

Chapter 13

Manipulating Numeric Data: The Spreadsheet

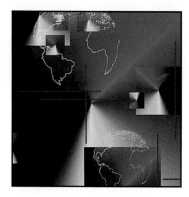

Mitchell Kapor

How does a self-described "nerd" make it big in the world of business? Mitchell Kapor did it by combining an interest in personal consciousness, antiwar activism, and interdisciplinary study of linguistics, psychology, and computer science at Yale University.

After college, Kapor entered the working world as a stand-up comic, disk jockey, and teacher of transcendental meditation. Instead of following the usual path toward corporate success by earning an MBA degree, he took his master's in psychology and became a counselor in the psychiatric unit of a small hospital.

Still, Kapor, who grew up in a middle-class Brooklyn family, was on his way to becoming a multimillionaire. Kapor first veered toward computer entrepreneurship when he came across an Apple II. While at Yale, he had found that working with mainframe computers was extremely frustrating. On campus, mainframes were often inaccessible, and they required special programming skills and punched cards for both the instructions and data. This was not so with microcomputers; they were easy to use and program. Kapor was captivated.

The microcomputer was the perfect tool for turning loose his creative instincts. He began doing freelance programming in the BASIC language for other new owners of microcomputers. His first programming job was to create a small database of patient information for a doctor.

This simple beginning led Kapor to an alliance with Jonathan Sachs, a former Data General Corporation programmer. The two devised an electronic spreadsheet that was sophisticated enough to appeal to the business world, yet could be run on a microcomputer. (A spreadsheet, as you will learn in this chapter, is a device for keeping track of and manipulating rows and columns of numbers.) The two developers called their program Lotus 1-2-3. Their spreadsheet, designed for the IBM Personal Computer and compatibles, could make projections, display results, and sort data. The documentation for Lotus was clear and concise, and the program did what it promised. Moreover, it was fast.

Lotus 1-2-3 revolutionized accounting on small computers in much the same way word processors changed writing with typewriters. Spreadsheet programs convinced the business community of the value of the relatively new microcomputer, and were the impetus that sent IBM PC sales soaring. With an alluring product, the powerful thrust of IBM's sales, and Kapor's expertise, all the elements for success were in place. First-year sales projections for Lotus were $3 million, but actual sales were $53 million. Kapor proved to be a master of marketing and a genius at advertising.

Kapor resigned as chief executive officer of Lotus in 1986 to spend time with his family, to continue his study of linguistics at MIT, and to consult at Lotus. Kapor's "retirement" did not last long, however, and now he is the chairman of the Electronic Frontier Foundation, a nonprofit, public-interest organization based in Washington, D.C. He has signed with Disney's Hyperion Division to write a book entitled *Cyberspace Manifesto*, scheduled for release in the fall of 1995.

The earliest methods that humans used to keep track of items included tying ropes in knots, marking notches on sticks, and similar crude devices. Then came the abacus, a wooden frame with wires and beads for calculating. Gradually, as numbering systems were developed, the paper-and-pencil approach started. Each item to be counted was assigned a number, and the numbers could be added, subtracted, multiplied, and divided.

As time went on, a sophisticated means of tracking and manipulating these numbers was devised. For ease in manipulating, numbers and dollar amounts were written on paper that had been divided into rows and columns; the paper was called a *spreadsheet*.

Today, users equipped with microcomputers and spreadsheet software manipulate numbers in rows and columns faster, more accurately, and more reliably than ever before. Spreadsheet users—including small business owners, teachers, students, and especially corporate accounting giants—are asking for, and getting, still faster programs with even more capabilities, including a spreadsheet in three dimensions!

Objective 13.1   Understand what spreadsheet software is.

What Is Spreadsheet Software?

A **spreadsheet** is simply a means of tracking and manipulating numbers—organizing them into rows and columns. The paper version of a spreadsheet is a form with horizontal and vertical lines that separate each row and column of numbers. You may have seen paper spreadsheets similar to the one in Figure 13.1. Your checkbook ledger is also a type of spreadsheet. A spreadsheet can take other forms, too; each user can adapt a spreadsheet to various applications and formats.

With the development and advancement of the computer and its capabilities, the paper spreadsheet was converted to a computerized

FIGURE 13.1
A paper spreadsheet.

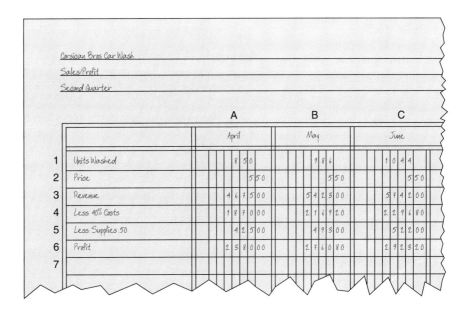

format. The program is called **spreadsheet software**, or an **electronic spreadsheet**. The spreadsheet software instructs the computer to manipulate rows and columns of numbers, make calculations, and evaluate algebraic formulas. Figure 13.2 illustrates an electronic version of the paper spreadsheet shown in Figure 13.1.

Of course, merely loading spreadsheet software into a computer cannot guarantee either the accuracy or effectiveness of any spreadsheet you create. It must be organized logically so that changes in one part will not adversely affect other parts. You will see later how critical organization can be when algebraic formulas are entered to solve problems. The Infomodule at the end of this chapter takes a closer look at spreadsheet design.

The first electronic spreadsheet programs operated on large computer systems. The cost of such systems limited availability of the new technology, so most businesses and individuals still used paper spreadsheets. The development in 1979 of VisiCalc, the first electronic spreadsheet created especially for microcomputers, gave everyone easy and affordable access to this powerful tool.

VisiCalc was rather crude by today's standards, because it was severely limited in the volume and size of jobs it could handle. But with the continuing development of more sophisticated hardware and software, programs improved to such an extent that most of today's computer spreadsheets allow at least 256 columns and as many as 32,766 rows, for a possible total of over 8 million spaces for entries. A paper spreadsheet of only 65 columns and 254 rows stretched out would be over 3½ feet long and more than 5 feet wide. Now consider that some spreadsheets allow as many as 32,000 columns and 32,000 rows—over one billion cells! Can you imagine how unmanageable that paper document would be?

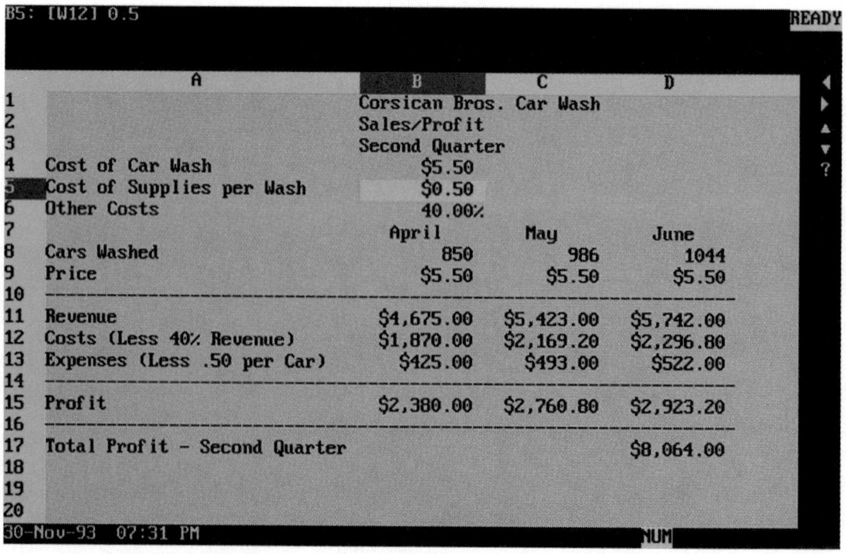

FIGURE 13.2
A screen of the paper spreadsheet as it appears when created electronically.

B5: [W12] 0.5				READY
	A	B	C	D
1		Corsican Bros. Car Wash		
2		Sales/Profit		
3		Second Quarter		
4	Cost of Car Wash	$5.50		
5	Cost of Supplies per Wash	$0.50		
6	Other Costs	40.00%		
7		April	May	June
8	Cars Washed	850	986	1044
9	Price	$5.50	$5.50	$5.50
10				
11	Revenue	$4,675.00	$5,423.00	$5,742.00
12	Costs (Less 40% Revenue)	$1,870.00	$2,169.20	$2,296.80
13	Expenses (Less .50 per Car)	$425.00	$493.00	$522.00
14				
15	Profit	$2,380.00	$2,760.80	$2,923.20
16				
17	Total Profit - Second Quarter			$8,064.00
18				
19				
20				
30-Nov-93 07:31 PM				NUM

In addition to the standard spreadsheet, which contains only rows and columns, some spreadsheet software allows you to work with multidimensional spreadsheets. A **multidimensional spreadsheet** helps you visualize spreadsheet cells as solids having three dimensions, rows, columns, and depth. Imagine the capability of a file that can contain 256 separate layers. This 3-D capability helps users to divide large applications into more manageable units, to consolidate information from many separate spreadsheets, to create a centralized database, and to summarize results on multiple worksheets that have identical layouts. The speed, power, and attributes of such 3-D programs will continue to suggest new applications to their users.

Objective 13.2   Describe several benefits of spreadsheet software.

What Are the Benefits of Using a Spreadsheet?

Today, instead of writing and calculating each entry by hand on a paper spreadsheet, you can sit at a computer keyboard and use spreadsheet software to make the entries. Data can be easily moved, copied, and deleted without messy erasures or using correction fluid. It is important that a spreadsheet be neat and legible. A paper spreadsheet is only as neat and legible as the handwriting of its creator. Even extremely neat entries may lose clarity if there are many erasures. Spreadsheet software, on the other hand, can simply be revised and reprinted.

One of the most powerful benefits of a spreadsheet is its ability to recalculate formulas. The speed and power of the computer allow the spreadsheet to make accurate calculations and recalculations in fractions of a second. Because data in a spreadsheet are usually dependent on other data, changes made in one value often result in changes in numerous other related values. This can require time-consuming and tedious manual recalculations in a paper spreadsheet. Spreadsheet software provides automatic recalculation of all dependent values. You no longer have to worry about which values are dependent or how long or difficult it will be to make all the changes manually. Simply type in a new value and the spreadsheet does the rest. This ability allows a spreadsheet to answer "what-if" questions posed by a user.

What-if analysis involves changing entries on a worksheet, viewing the outcome, and comparing it to the original worksheet to determine the effect. It allows you to see how an increase or decrease in one or more entries might affect the end result. Make sure you keep a copy of the original plan for comparison. For example, what if you decided to buy a used car at a certain price? How would that choice affect other areas of the budget, such as car insurance, loan payments, automobile repair expenses, and other living expenses? What if you buy this year's model instead, and the payments are higher? A spreadsheet can analyze the effects on all these areas so that the purchase can be more closely evaluated (Figure 13.3). The spreadsheet capability of analyzing many different situations will show ramifications of each choice so that the best course of action can be taken.

Like other applications, spreadsheet software provides you with reusable data. Recreating even relatively simple paper spreadsheets each month can take many hours to prepare the paper forms and handwrite the entries. Valuable time is wasted in rewriting the same column and row labels

FIGURE 13.3
This woman uses spreadsheet
software to analyze long-range
effects before making important
business decisions.

from month to month on blank paper forms. With spreadsheet software, a **template,** or blank form, can be created for the required report. The template contains any standard information that doesn't change. You simply load the template, make minor modifications as needed, and then enter your data.

The clerk who prepares monthly reports for the company president could create a template including headings for standard expenses such as rent, utilities, insurance, and payroll. When the report is due, the clerk simply calls up the template form and enters the name of the new month and the amounts of expenses incurred for that month. Even small companies save time by not having to handwrite or reenter all the standard parts of these reports each time.

Spreadsheet software often requires repetitive keystrokes or commands, and the speed and power of the macro are especially useful. In addition, the data in the spreadsheet can also be used to create graphs and charts to represent the data visually. (Business and analytical graphics are discussed in the Infomodule for Chapter 14.)

There are many spreadsheet programs available for almost any brand of computer. Spreadsheet processing is one of the most popular computer applications; it brings the shortcuts, speed, and accuracy to accounting functions that word processors bring to writing.

Objective 13.3   Explain several ways in which spreadsheet software is used.

What Are Some Common Uses of Spreadsheets?

A problem is a candidate for an electronic spreadsheet if it has the following characteristics:

- Can be written in mathematical terms
- Is repeated regularly
- Will be edited or revised

- Is made up of both variable and fixed information
- Must be neat and legible

Accountants and businesspeople maintain important information, such as sales, expenses incurred, costs of doing business, inventory control, and projections of profits or losses, through spreadsheet programs. They make sales forecasts, analyze competitors' statistics, compare discounts and markup costs, and prepare financial information, such as profit/loss statements and income statements for their banks.

Bankers use spreadsheet programs to track all the day-to-day monetary transactions, create loan amortization schedules, make interest rate computations, and evaluate potential customers' loans, among other tasks.

With spreadsheet information easily accessible, managers can make decisions about future expenditures, plan for expansion of products or services, or formulate pricing strategies using the most comprehensive information available. Then, creative managers can display this spreadsheet information in graphic format.

Engineers, scientists, and technical users store empirical data, perform statistical analysis, build complex graphs, and prepare complex mathematical models using spreadsheet programs.

Personal uses of spreadsheets include tracking cash flow, preparing household budgets and personal financial statements, and figuring annual income taxes, among others (Figure 13.4). People who sell items such as

FIGURE 13.4
An accounting student uses a laptop computer and a spreadsheet software
program to complete his assignments at home.

household products, beauty aids, and cleaning supplies from their homes use a spreadsheet program for orders, inventory, and accounts payable and receivable. A spreadsheet created in a table format could help young students learn mathematical facts. Other applications are limited only by your imagination!

Objective 13.4   Identify and summarize the basic functions of spreadsheet software.

What Are the Basic Functions of Spreadsheets?

The basic functions of any spreadsheet software include creating and saving a worksheet, editing a worksheet, formatting a worksheet, manipulating a worksheet, and printing a worksheet.

Creating and Saving a Worksheet

Figure 13.5 shows what the spreadsheet program displays first: a relatively blank screen used for entering and organizing your data. This is the beginning of a **worksheet**, the name often given to a data file created by a spreadsheet program. At this stage the screen is hardly impressive, but once the data are entered on the worksheet, the true power of the electronic spreadsheet can be demonstrated.

The numbers down the left side of the screen constitute the **row** grid, and the alphabetic characters at the top of the screen are the **column** grid. Using a combination of these labels identifies specific points on a worksheet. The point where imaginary row and column grid lines intersect is the **coordinate,** or the address of that particular point. In Figure 13.6, Coordinate B5 is the point where a line down Column B intersects a line across Row 5.

The box formed by the imaginary lines at each coordinate is a **cell.** The highlighted box in Figure 13.7 is the **cell pointer;** it indicates the **active cell,** or "current" cell. The cell pointer's size changes to reflect the width of the column it is marking. A flashing dash inside the cell pointer is the **cursor;** it indicates the position where the next character typed will

FIGURE 13.5
The typical worksheet screen.

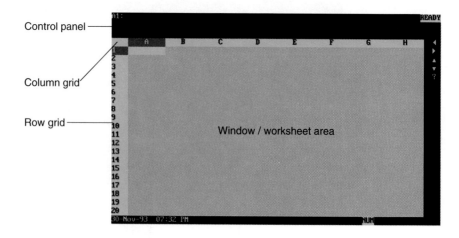

FIGURE 13.6
The cell at Column B, Row 5 is the active cell.

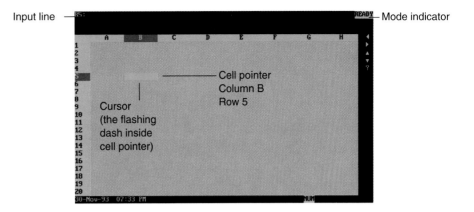

appear or the next entry will occur. (We'll describe what kinds of data are entered and how the data get into each cell later.)

The worksheet has two main parts: the **window,** the area on the display screen where the entries will be visually displayed; and the **control panel** and **status line** areas that provide valuable information about activity on the worksheet.

The worksheet control panel often found at the top of the screen provides specific information about the worksheet. Typical information provided includes the coordinates where the cursor is positioned, the cell width, whether the cell is protected from unauthorized change, any contents or entry in the cell, and the current spreadsheet mode. Spreadsheet modes are discussed below.

A status line may include other information about the worksheet. For example, the status line in Lotus 1-2-3, at the bottom of the screen, gives the current date and time, error messages, and other status indicators such as NUM (number lock on), CAPS (all caps selected), or a prompt indicating that the worksheet should be recalculated.

Modes. Spreadsheet programs have two basic modes of operation: a command (or menu) mode, and a ready/entry mode. When the spreadsheet is in the **command mode,** you are offered menus from which to make command selections. Usually, this is done by moving the cursor or mouse pointer to the desired option and selecting it. Some commands may be invoked by various keys or key combinations.

Commands are generally selected from a main command menu. Often, there are submenus listed under menus because some spreadsheets have as many as several hundred or more commands from which to choose. For example, a spreadsheet program may have a menu that contains a "format" command that, when selected, presents another menu that contains more explicit choices, i.e., setting dollar signs and the option of listing decimal points and zeros with number entries. Formatting choices let you change the look of the worksheet, or make the entries more readable.

The **ready/entry mode** indicates that the program is ready for data entry. The program automatically shifts from the ready mode to the entry mode as soon as the first character is typed.

FIGURE 13.7
The cell pointer is positioned to show (a) an example of a text entry; (b) an example of a number entry; and (c) an example of a formula entry.

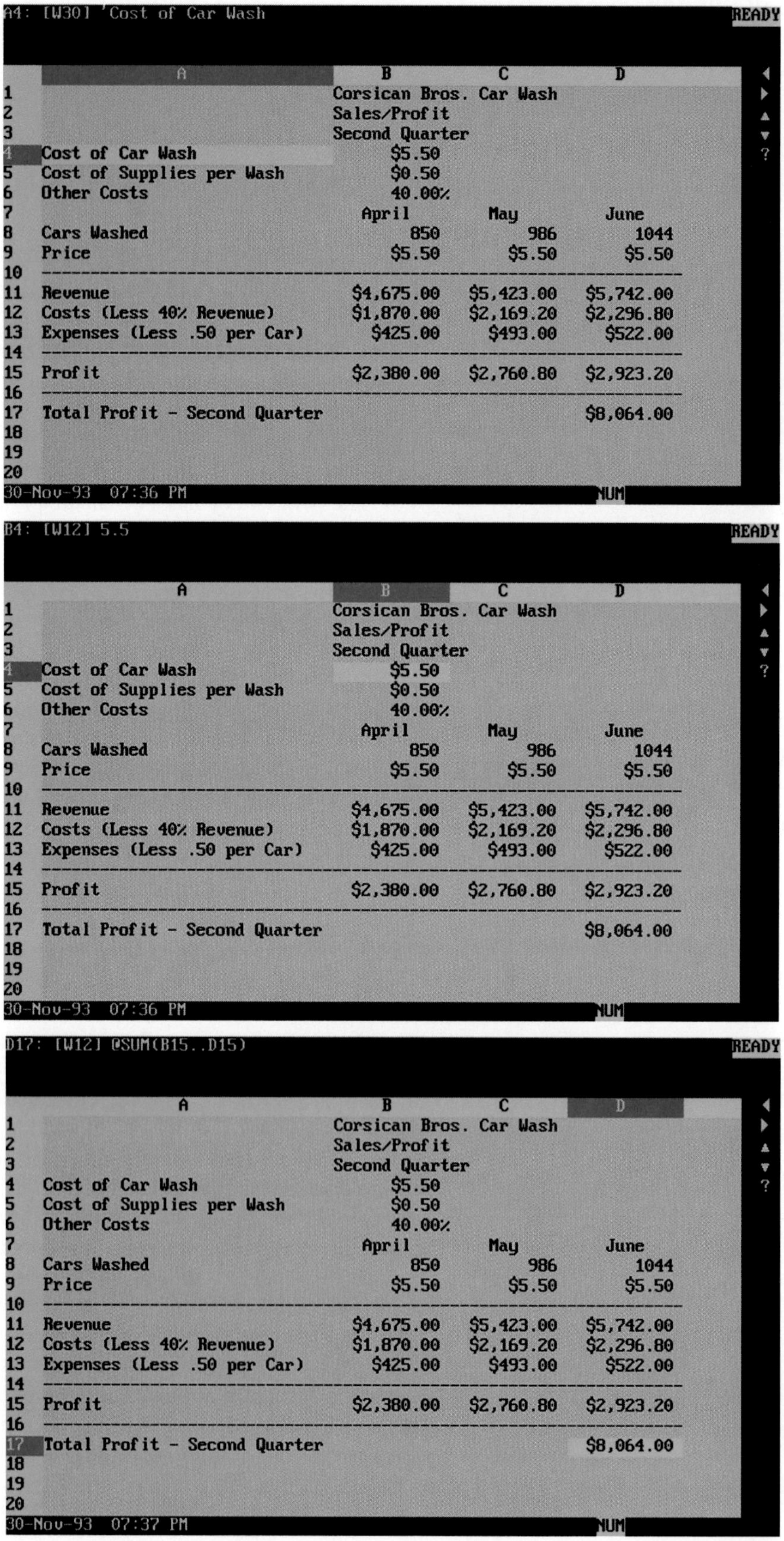

(a)

(b)

(c)

At least you're not retiring yet! However, sooner or later you will retire and the sooner you prepare for that event, the better.

The good news is that the personal computer can be instrumental in planning your financial future. The purpose of investment and retirement planning software is making more money instead of just keeping track of the money you have. The Securities and Exchange Commission (SEC) has even registered software such as Smart Investor as an "investment advisor."

In order to plan for retirement the "advisor" needs data: how old are you now, at what age would you like to retire, what income will you need, how much are you saving toward that retirement, what rate of return is required to meet those needs, how much risk are you willing to take with your capital, and other matters concerning investment philosophy. The "advisor" then suggests particular types of investments to explore. With answers to these and other questions the "advisor" uses on-line information services such as CompuServe and Prodigy to let you examine stocks, mutual funds, bonds, commodities, and money market holdings. Predictions of future values for each investment strategy can be compared. Once you decide what investments to make the software tracks the ups and downs of your individual portfolio. Charts and graphs of a particular stock or bond help you visualize the history of each holding. This advisor doesn't charge fees for each transaction.

Many programs offer "what if" analyses to help you prepare for contingencies such as the purchase of a home, payments for your children's education, weddings, or unexpected occurrences.

Although many of you are still planning your career(s), preparing now for your retirement is important to provide the "gold" you'll need in those golden years.

Moving Around the Worksheet. Because the window lets you see only a small portion of a worksheet at any time—approximately 80 spaces across and 20 lines down—you must scroll the cell pointer "off the screen" to view the rest of the worksheet. The cell pointer can be scrolled past the right-hand margin and below the bottom of the monitor screen. For example, to reach coordinate Z100, you would scroll to the right 25 columns, and downward 99 rows. The cursor movement keys are used to do this.

The arrow keys move the cell pointer in the direction that the arrow points—e.g., the down arrow moves the cell pointer downward one cell at a time. By using various keys and key combinations (such as Home, End, PgUp, PgDn), you move the cursor over larger distances quickly instead of one cell or row at a time. Another method of moving rapidly is by using a "go to" feature where you designate which coordinates are needed and use appropriate keystrokes to move the cursor automatically to that particular cell coordinate.

Defaults. Although default settings vary among spreadsheets, and can be reset by the user, some common ones are:

- The columns are all the same width—every column is a certain number of spaces wide.
- All entries that begin with a letter will be left-justified in the cell.
- All entries that begin with a number will be right-justified in the cell.
- The worksheet is automatically recalculated whenever a number is changed.
- Numbers appear without commas and dollar amounts appear without ending zeros.

Entering Labels, Values, and Formulas. Different types of data can be entered into the cells. You must know what type of data are being entered, because the computer views entries based on identifying characteristics. The three types of entries are labels, values, and formulas.

A **label** is text that identifies some aspect of the spreadsheet—Figure 13.7a. A label placed at the top to indicate the contents of a worksheet might appear like this:

Bookcase Company
Profit and Loss Statement
for the period January to March

Other entries that require labels include the column and row headings, and any other words or text necessary to identify or clarify the spreadsheet information. Some programs automatically recognize as a label any entry that begins with an alphabetic character or certain special characters. If a label begins with numbers or other special characters that normally indicate a value—e.g., a street address or a year—specific keystrokes are required to tell the computer that the entry is a label, not a value. Many programs include an **automatic spillover** option; if the cell label is too long to fit the column width, the text continues on, or spills over, into the next cell.

A **value** is a constant that can be entered by itself into a cell or as part of a formula. In Figure 13.7b the upper-left part of the screen indicates that the value 5.5 is entered in cell B4. **Formulas** are the mathematical equations entered into the spreadsheet program to perform calculations. Formulas may contain constants, cell references that do not contain labels, built-in functions, and range names.

Cell references refer to the contents in another cell. For example, if cell B3 contained the value 200 a formula created in cell D10 could use that value by referencing the cell address as follows: +B3 * .15. This formula commands the spreadsheet to multiply the value found in cell B3 by the constant .15.

In Figure 13.7c, the formula +B15 + C15 + D15 is shown for cell D17. The computer understands that the entry in that cell is the total of those cells. Therefore, $8064.00 appears in the cell, but the formula (not the total) for the cell entry is shown above the input line. The computer completes the calculation and enters the result where specified. Remember, formulas cannot include cell references that contain labels.

Cell Entries

- Labels
- Values
- Formulas

To identify a cell reference such as B3 that begins a formula as a value and not as a label, a special character entry is usually required. The plus sign (+) character is a common example, used to indicate that the entry following it is a value, not a label. Therefore, to indicate that the entry in cell D17 is a formula it should be preceded by the appropriate keystrokes—in this case a + sign.

Some programs let you toggle, or switch, between label and value entries just by using certain keys. This option is handy when a number, such as a date or address, needs to be entered and recognized as a label. For instance, the numbers in the year 1995, street addresses, and zip codes would ordinarily be construed as values because they begin with numbers. These entries have to be specifically identified as labels, or the computer recognizes them as values.

Built-In Functions. Most spreadsheets have **built-in functions** where formulas for solutions to certain standard problems have already been created and stored in the program. These functions provide shortcuts for many common tasks, typically mathematical, statistical, financial, date, string, logical, and tabular. Table 13.1 describes these built-in functions.

TABLE 13.1
Built-In Functions

Mathematical function	Performs a mathematical transformation on a single value and returns a single value—for example, a SQRT(x) determines the square root of a value.
Statistical function	Accepts a list of values and provides summary statistics about those values (for example, an average function returns the average value from a list).
Financial function	Calculates the effect of interest rates on sums of money over time (for example, a payment function calculates the payment that will pay off the principal of a loan borrowed at the specified interest rate after the specified number of payments have been made).
Date function	Calculates with dates and times (for example, it can automatically enter the date and time in a report).
String function	Performs operations on text (for example, a length function indicates the number of characters in a string).
Logical function	Tests the condition of cells or performs comparisons to determine what value should be entered in a cell (for example, an IF function enters one value in the cell if the condition is true and another value in the call if the condition is false).
Table function	Retrieves an entry from a table (for example, a "value look-up" function can search an income tax table that has been entered into the spreadsheet to find a specific number).

Most spreadsheets have dozens of built-in functions, and their names vary from program to program. The spreadsheet reference manual and on-line help that come with the software detail the functions offered by that spreadsheet. Common built-in functions include SUM, SIN, and MAX, which automatically total, find the sine, and determine the maximum value in a list of numbers.

Defining and Naming a Range of Cells. Designating a **range of cells** is a method of selecting specific contiguous cells. The range can consist of only one cell or two or more cells. A range of cells containing more than one cell must be square or rectangular in shape (Figure 13.8). A designated range can be copied, moved, deleted, saved, printed, or otherwise treated as a unit. This feature is a time-saving device when a large worksheet is in use.

Although spreadsheet programs vary, the usual method to identify a range of cells is to type the coordinate of the upper-left cell first, then a delimiter—usually two periods (..) or a colon (:)—followed by the coordinate of the lower-right cell. For example, if a column of numbers starting at C1 and continuing through to C200 needs to be added, by entering the range of cells the drudgery of keying each separate row's cell label under column C is avoided. Merely keying SUM C1..C200 (or a similar formula, in most cases) directs the computer to give a total of the entries in that column. A mouse can also be used to designate a range of cells by clicking and dragging the mouse pointer over the desired block of cells.

A range of cells can be named for ease in identification. Using a range name makes formulas more readable and understandable. Going back to Figure 13.7b, the cell containing the cost of the car wash (B4) could be named COST. Then the formula at cell C11 for finding how much revenue was made could be stated as the number of cars washed times the cost, or +850 * COST.

FIGURE 13.8
A range must always be square or rectangular in shape; a single cell can be considered a range.

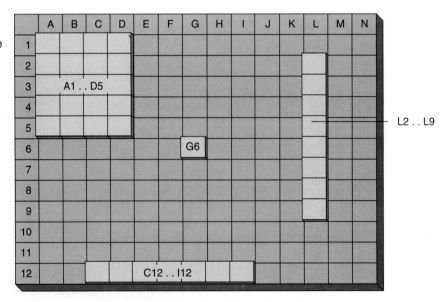

Names can be added, revised, and even deleted when they are no longer useful. In large worksheets, identifying various ranges by name can also speed up the process of scrolling from one portion of the worksheet to another. Most spreadsheets allow you to specify the range name and the program jumps directly to that area.

Order of Calculation.   Most spreadsheet programs solve the formulas that are entered using the normal order of mathematical operations. That is, they assume that operations enclosed in parentheses are done first, exponentiation next, then multiplication and division before addition and subtraction.

Some spreadsheets may be programmed to read and solve equations left to right. The order of operations procedure affects formulas. Therefore, it is important to know which method your program uses, because answers can vary drastically depending on the method of solution. As an example, use the simple formula 10 + 10/2. If the rules of the normal order of operation were followed, the division operation would be performed first, then the addition; the answer would be 15. But if this equation were solved from left to right, the addition operation would be performed first, then the division; the answer would be 10.

Saving a Worksheet.   The save feature stores a created worksheet on a disk. You can then recall the file from computer memory at a later time and continue working on or editing that particular worksheet.

The exit feature quits a worksheet without saving it. An existing worksheet can be loaded and changed to answer various "what-if" questions, and then exited without overriding the original data stored on the worksheet. However, some programs automatically save programs as they exit. If this happens, any changes made to answer the "what-if" questions are saved and the original worksheet is permanently altered. In this case you would want to create a duplicate, or second copy, to make "what-if" analyses. A number of copies could be made so that many scenarios could be performed.

Retrieve or Open are typical spreadsheet commands to access an existing worksheet that has been saved on a disk. You select the retrieve command or its equivalent from a menu and enter the name of the desired worksheet or select it from a list.

Editing a Worksheet

From time to time you will want to update or change labels, numbers, or formulas in a worksheet. You may need to correct a typographical error, or correct an incorrect number or an erroneous formula. To avoid inaccurate results you should always carefully check the numbers and formulas entered in a worksheet; never assume they are correct. Labels, numbers, and formulas can be easily edited to correct or update them by either completely retyping the entry for a cell and reentering it or using a spreadsheet's edit mode to correct specific characters in an entry. It is such editing chores that give headaches to accountants who work on a paper spreadsheet.

However, changing a number or formula often affects numerous other dependent cells in a worksheet. Most spreadsheets have an **automatic recalculation** feature as a default, which automatically recalculates the entire worksheet after a new figure is entered. Many also allow you to turn off automatic recalculation and offer a manual recalculation mode in which you make a menu selection to recalculate the worksheet. Recalculation that occurs while other operations are in process is known as the **background recalculation mode**. Some programs offer **intelligent recalculation** whereby only cells affected by a change are recalculated. This greatly speeds the recalculation process for large worksheets. This ability to quickly edit and recalculate a worksheet is the basis for one of the spreadsheet's most powerful uses—the "what-if" analysis.

Formatting a Worksheet

The **formatting** process includes various instructions and techniques that change how the contents of the cells are displayed. Format changes can be made in one of two ways: (a) globally, which affects the entire worksheet, or (b) individually, which affects an individual cell or range of cells.

Attributes. The characteristics or formatting commands available in most spreadsheets are called **attributes**. Attribute commands can:

- Change column widths
- Set precision of numbers (the number of decimal places)
- Set justification (usually left, centered, or right)
- Determine number formats, or how the number will appear (some common number format choices are shown in Table 13.2)
- Establish character attributes (boldface, underline, italics)
- Set data types (text or value)
- Change how negative values appear—in parentheses; or preceded by DB (debit) or CR (credit); or in red
- Lock cells (prevent cell entries from being changed)
- Hide cells (the contents of the cell are not displayed on screen)

TABLE 13.2
Common Number Format Choices

Integer	Whole number
Dollar	Dollar sign ($) and two decimal places
Floating point	Decimal point followed by specified number of places
Exponential	Scientific notation
Commas	Numbers displayed with commas
Leading $	Leading dollar sign ($) placed before any other format
Percent	Displayed using a percent (%) sign
Foreign currency	Displayed using foreign currency symbol, such as DM for Deutsche marks (German money)

Titles. The **titles** feature freezes rows or columns so they stay in the window when the rest of the worksheet is scrolled. This feature is especially helpful when there are many rows and columns of numbers to scroll through and review. When the titles scroll off the window, it is difficult to remember what the numbers represent. However, the "titles" command freezes the titles so they remain on the screen and identify the data no matter the row or column of the worksheet.

Insert and Delete Rows/Columns. There are many other formatting choices. One that improves readability is inserting or deleting blank rows and columns. Rows can be added to increase space between headings and numbers in the spreadsheet. Underlines or other characters can be inserted by creating a blank row and using a repeating character label to insert a line or column width of a specified character, for example, an underline or a row of asterisks. New columns can be created to accommodate entries not originally planned, for example, if a company added a new product line.

Figure 13.9 shows how a spreadsheet looks before adding some formatting instructions. Figure 13.10 shows the same spreadsheet after formatting.

Manipulating a Worksheet

Electronic spreadsheets have many features that make them more efficient and effective than paper spreadsheets. For example, portions of a spreadsheet can be quickly and easily moved or copied and mathematical formulas that are entered are calculated by the computer. Spreadsheet features allow you to present and manipulate values in many ways. We'll look at some features below.

Copying. The copy feature selects an existing cell (or range of cells) and replicates it in other cells of the worksheet. To copy labels or numbers,

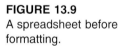

FIGURE 13.9
A spreadsheet before formatting.

```
A14: [W30] 'Total Profit - Second Quarter                              READY

              A                    B          C          D           ◀
1                          Corsican Bros. Car Wash                    ▶
2                          Sales/Profit                               ▲
3                          Second Quarter                             ▼
4    Cost of Car Wash           $5.50                                 ?
5    Cost of Supplies per Wash  $0.50
6    Other Costs                40.00%
7                            April       May        June
8    Cars Washed                 850        986       1044
9    Price                     $5.50      $5.50      $5.50
10   Revenue                $4,675.00  $5,423.00  $5,742.00
11   Costs (Less 40% Revenue) $1,870.00  $2,169.20  $2,296.80
12   Expenses (Less .50 per Car) $425.00    $493.00    $522.00
13   Profit                 $2,380.00  $2,760.80  $2,923.20
14   Total Profit - Second Quarter                 $8,064.00
15
16
17
18
19
20
30-Nov-93  07:40 PM                                          NUM
```

FIGURE 13.10
A spreadsheet after formatting.

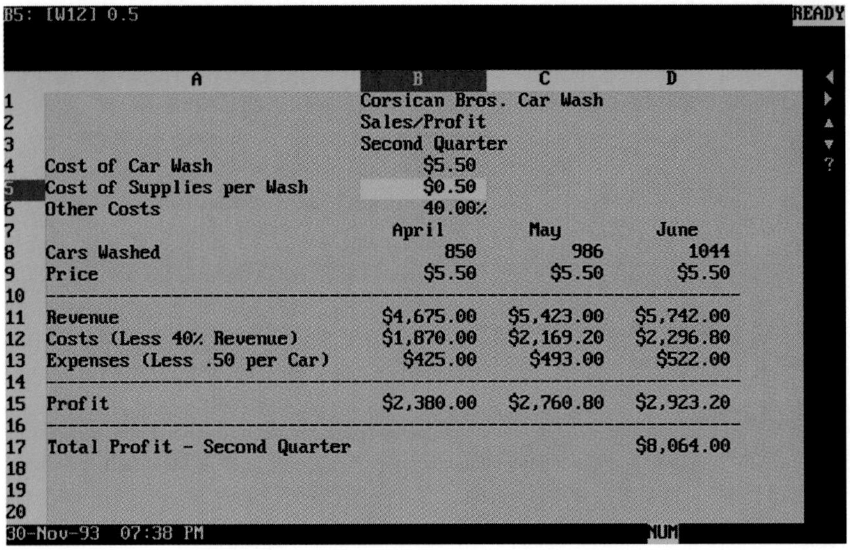

```
B5: [W12] 0.5                                                          READY

                   A                  B          C          D          ◄
 1                              Corsican Bros. Car Wash                 ►
 2                              Sales/Profit                            ▲
 3                              Second Quarter                          ▼
 4    Cost of Car Wash              $5.50                               ?
 5    Cost of Supplies per Wash     $0.50
 6    Other Costs                  40.00%
 7                                April       May       June
 8    Cars Washed                    850       986       1044
 9    Price                        $5.50     $5.50      $5.50
10    ----------------------------------------------------------
11    Revenue                  $4,675.00  $5,423.00  $5,742.00
12    Costs (Less 40% Revenue) $1,870.00  $2,169.20  $2,296.80
13    Expenses (Less .50 per Car) $425.00   $493.00    $522.00
14    ----------------------------------------------------------
15    Profit                   $2,380.00  $2,760.80  $2,923.20
16    ----------------------------------------------------------
17    Total Profit - Second Quarter                  $8,064.00
18
19
20
30-Nov-93  07:38 PM                                             NUM
```

simply identify both the range of cells to be copied and the range of cells into which they should be copied.

Copying formulas is a bit more involved. Sometimes you will want exactly the same formula using exactly the same cell references in both places. In this case, the computer must be instructed to copy the formula using **absolute cell reference.** For example, if the formula in cell D1 in Figure 13.11a is copied to cell D2 using absolute cell reference, it appears exactly the same and evaluates in both instances to 10 (5 + 5).

Usually, however, you will want a similar calculation but different cell references. Then you instruct the computer to copy the formula using **relative cell reference.** For example, if the formula in cell D1 of Figure 13.11b is copied to cell D2 using relative cell reference, it changes to B2 + C2 and evaluates to 6 (3 + 3).

There may also be times when you will want some references in the same formula to be relative and others to be absolute. In this case, you would instruct the computer to copy the formula using **mixed cell reference**. Each cell reference is specified as either absolute or relative. For example, if the formula in cell D1 in Figure 13.11c is copied to cell D2 using relative cell reference for cell B1 and absolute cell reference for cell C1, the formula in cell D2 will be B2 + C1, which evaluates to 8 (3 + 5).

Moving. The move feature allows repositioning of the contents of individual cells or ranges of cells from one location to another. You can redesign the appearance or layout of the spreadsheet. When a range of cells is moved, any formula in the spreadsheet that will be affected by the move must be corrected. For example, if the content of cell B2 is moved to cell B10, and the formula in cell E2 is 2 * B2, then the formula in cell E2 will have to be edited to be 2 * B10 to obtain the same results.

Copying Formulas

- Absolute cell reference
- Relative cell reference
- Mixed cell reference

FIGURE 13.11
Cell references: (a) absolute; (b) relative; and (c) mixed.

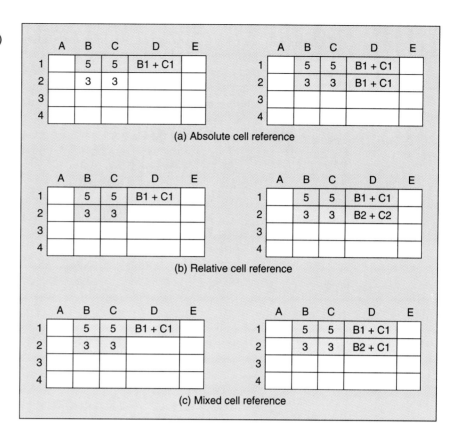

(a) Absolute cell reference

(b) Relative cell reference

(c) Mixed cell reference

Sorting. Many spreadsheets can sort information by rows or columns, alphabetically or numerically. This feature gives many choices, including allowing a search for specific numbers or labels, arranging the spreadsheet in date order, organizing in ascending or descending dollar amounts, and so on.

Printing a Worksheet

Printing the spreadsheet produces a hard (paper) copy. To print a spreadsheet, you usually access a special print menu and indicate the size of paper, number of copies, and margin parameters. The row-and-column grid designation lines can be deleted at this point to give the printed spreadsheet a more formal appearance.

A printer that can print wider than 8½″ standard paper is often desirable. Some programs print sideways, i.e., across the length of the paper, thereby offering more space to print additional columns side by side.

Objective 13.5   Describe the three types of programs commonly integrated with spreadsheet programs.

Imagine high finance and high tech on a family cattle ranch in the Nebraska panhandle! Millenium Genetics, owned by the Cunningham family, runs a cow-calf operation using computers, spreadsheets, and other financial software. They buy cows, breed them, raise calves to sell, and eventually liquidate the herd. Their operation requires lots of investment money, and they don't want to make huge interest payments for the use of that money.

Millenium has found a way to avoid the higher costs associated with borrowing directly from banks by selling Securities and Exchange Commission (SEC) registered investments to individuals. Limited partnerships, secured notes, and other investment opportunities are available to potential investors. Typically investors buy an interest in a particular herd for a specified number of years. Millenium uses Tax Solver software, a program that works directly with spreadsheet programs such as Lotus 1-2-3 and Microsoft Excel. Keeping track of deferred income for the multiple limited partners and preparing the appropriate tax returns, depreciation schedules, and business income and expense reports for each partner caused voluminous amounts of paperwork and required additional clerical staff, especially for year-end summary preparation. Millenium was able to cut accounting expenses by not having to hire extra help while still providing required tax information to investors in a timely fashion. Now they file more professional-looking reports with both the SEC and the IRS.

Regular accounting software tracks the expenses incurred for buying stock and feed, paying veterinarian bills, hiring stock hands, and estimating quarterly taxes, as well as calculating the profits due each partner.

These "limited" partnerships appear to have unlimited possibilities.

What Additional Features Do Spreadsheets Have?

Spreadsheet programs vary, but some common additional features are described below.

Graphing Functions

The data entered and saved in a worksheet can be the basis for generating graphics—pictorial representations such as pie charts, line charts, and bar charts. The data to be graphed must be identified, the type of graph chosen, titles specified, and legends explained. Many spreadsheet programs require that the graph be saved as a worksheet file so that it can be recalled later with the settings intact. (Chapter 14 contains more specific information on graphics.)

Database Functions

You may want to analyze the data in a worksheet, for example, compute the average, count cells, find the largest and smallest number, determine standard deviation, find the sum, and discover the variance. In order to accomplish this type of function easily, the worksheet data may be set up as

TABLE 13.3
Database Functions

DAVG	Computes the average
DCOUNT	Counts the nonblank cells
DMAX	Indicates the largest number
DMIN	Indicates the smallest number
DSTD	Computes the standard deviation
DSUM	Computes the total
DVAR	Computes the variance

a database. Each row is equivalent to a record and each cell, a field. Typical functions are listed in Table 13.3. Each item listed is preceded by the letter "D" to indicate that it is a database function.

Desktop Publishing Functions

Many spreadsheet programs come integrated with numerous desktop publishing features that allow for the production of high-quality reports. You can print using a wide variety of fonts; add emphasis with lines, boxes, shades, and colors; and incorporate graphs into a report. The availability and relative low cost of laser printers has brought about the addition of these features.

Summary

A spreadsheet is a paper tool on which to track and manipulate rows and columns of numbers. Spreadsheet software uses a computer and special software to do those same manipulations faster, more accurately, and more reliably. A multidimensional spreadsheet allows cells to be visualized as solids with dimensions of rows, columns, and depth.

Spreadsheet software makes editing and recalculating tasks easy and fast. It provides the capability to easily perform "what-if" analysis, develop reusable templates, and create graphs and charts to visually view data.

A spreadsheet application is appropriate if the problem can be stated in a mathematical format, and if the problem is to be repeated, edited, revised, made up of both variable and fixed data, and required to be neat and legible.

Worksheet is the name often given to a data file created by a spreadsheet program. The numbers down the left side are the row grid and the alphabetic characters across the top are the column grid. At the intersection of an imaginary line drawn from any point on each grid lies the coordinate, or the address of a point on the worksheet. The box thus formed is called a cell. The cell pointer identifies the cell that is available for use called the active cell, or current cell. The cursor, usually a flashing dash, is inside the cell pointer.

The worksheet display on a computer monitor includes the window (where entries are displayed) and the control panel and status line areas (where useful information about the worksheet is typically displayed).

A spreadsheet has two basic modes of operation: command mode, where the action choices are listed, and ready/entry mode, where the program is ready for the user to move the cursor and begin making entries.

There are three types of entries: labels, values, and formulas. A label is text used to identify some aspect of the spreadsheet. A value is a constant that can be entered by itself into a cell or as part of a formula. Formulas are the mathematical equations entered into the spreadsheet program to perform calculations. Formulas may contain constants, cell references that do not contain labels, built-in functions, and range names.

Spreadsheets include built-in functions containing solutions to commonly encountered problems: mathematical, statistical, financial, date, string, logical, and tabular functions. Most spreadsheets have dozens of built-in functions that offer shortcuts; users do not have to write formulas for these built-in functions.

A range of cells can be selected to be edited or acted upon; it may be one cell or a specified portion of the spreadsheet. Naming a cell or a range of cells offers ease in identification when the range is moved from one place on the spreadsheet to another, copied, or specified for use in a calculation.

Mathematical operations are performed following standard rules of operation, i.e., values in parentheses, exponentiation, multiplication and division, addition and subtraction.

The save feature stores a worksheet on a disk. The exit feature quits a worksheet without saving it.

Typographical errors and wrong values are corrected by editing the spreadsheet. Recalculation of totals can be automatic, background, or intelligent.

Formatting, or changing the look of the worksheet, is accomplished globally or on a range of cells. Attributes that can be set include changing column widths, setting precision of numbers, setting justification, determining number formats, establishing character attributes, setting data types, changing how negative values appear, and locking and hiding cells.

Other formatting features include the titles feature that freezes rows or columns so they stay in the window when the rest of the worksheet is scrolled and the ability to insert rows and columns in the worksheet.

Data entered into a worksheet are easily manipulated by copying, moving, sorting, and editing cell entries and recalculating formulas. Formulas that are created can be copied to other cells, but they must be referenced in one of three ways: absolute cell reference, relative cell reference, or mixed cell reference.

A worksheet is printed so that a hard copy of the information can be distributed and used.

Spreadsheet software is often integrated with graphing, database, and desktop publishing functions.

VOCABULARY SELF-TEST   *Can you define the following terms?*

absolute cell reference (p. 478)

active cell (p. 468)

attributes (p. 476)

automatic recalculation (p. 476)

automatic spillover (p. 472)

background recalculation mode (p. 476)

built-in functions (p. 473)

cell (p. 468)

cell pointer (p. 468)

column (p. 468)

command mode (p. 469)

control panel (p. 469)

coordinate (p. 468)

cursor (p. 468)

electronic spreadsheet (p. 464)

formatting (p. 476)

formulas (p. 472)

intelligent recalculation (p. 476)

label (p. 472)

mixed cell reference (p. 478)

multidimensional spreadsheet (p. 465)

range of cells (p. 474)

ready/entry mode (p. 469)

relative cell reference (p. 478)

row (p. 468)

spreadsheet (p. 463)

spreadsheet software (p. 464)

status line (p. 469)

template (p. 466)

titles (p. 477)

value (p. 472)

what-if analysis (p. 465)

window (p. 469)

worksheet (p. 468)

REVIEW QUESTIONS

Multiple Choice

1. A _____ is software that manipulates rows and columns of numbers.
   a. database management system
   b. word processor
   c. design program
   d. spreadsheet program

2. The numbers at the left of a worksheet screen are the _____.
   a. control panel
   b. row grid
   c. column grid
   d. cell coordinates

3. The highlighted box, also called the _____, indicates the active cell.
   a. cell
   b. cursor
   c. coordinate
   d. cell pointer

4. A data file created by a spreadsheet program is called a _____.
   a. database
   b. document
   c. template
   d. worksheet

5. A _____ is the text that identifies various aspects of the worksheet.
   a. label
   b. value

    c. cell

    d. formula

6. Which of the following cannot be contained in a formula?

    a. labels

    b. cell coordinate

    c. built-in functions

    d. constants

7. Changing entries on a worksheet, viewing the outcome, and comparing it to the original worksheet to determine the effect is called _____.

    a. "what-if" analysis

    b. intelligent recalculation

    c. manual recalculation

    d. formatting

8. _____ features change the look of the worksheet or make it more understandable.

    a. Scrolling

    b. Editing

    c. Formatting

    d. Windowing

9. _____ is the feature that freezes the rows and columns and keeps them visible on the screen, even when you scroll across or down the spreadsheet.

    a. Windows

    b. Titles

    c. Hold

    d. Copy

10. Selecting specific contiguous cells in a worksheet is known as _____.

    a. setting defaults

    b. entering a label

    c. defining a range

    d. designating titles

Fill-In

1. A spreadsheet that allows you to work in rows, columns, and depth is referred to as a(n) _____.

2. A worksheet form containing standard information that doesn't change and can be called to the screen to have new data entered is known as a(n) _____.

3. The _____ is the flashing symbol inside the cell pointer; it indicates the position where the next character typed will appear or the next entry will occur in a worksheet.

4. The _____ mode indicates that the spreadsheet is ready for data entry.

5. SUM, SIN, and MAX are examples of _____ functions in a spreadsheet program.

6. In a worksheet, the entry C4..D10 indicates a(n) _____.

7. _____ , _____ , and _____ are the three types of entries that can be made in a worksheet.
8. In _____ , only cells affected by a change are recalculated.
9. A(n) _____ format change affects the entire worksheet.
10. _____ and _____ programs are commonly integrated with spreadsheet programs.

Short Answer

1. What factors indicate that a spreadsheet may be useful in solving a problem?
2. Describe several benefits of spreadsheet software over a paper spreadsheet.
3. List several professional and personal uses of spreadsheets.
4. Give examples of the three types of entries that can be made in spreadsheets.
5. Describe how a worksheet cell's coordinate, or address, is derived.
6. What is the standard order of mathematical operations? Explain why knowing the order of operations of a particular spreadsheet program could be critical.
7. Describe the difference between a label, value, and a formula.
8. Give two ways that errors in the cells of a worksheet can be corrected or edited.
9. Describe the advantages of the ability to pose "what-if" questions in an electronic spreadsheet.
10. Identify possible ramifications to consider before copying formulas in a worksheet and describe the three types of cell references.

Issues for Thought

1. Your job requires using spreadsheets designed and created by others. Before relying on the information generated by these spreadsheets to make decisions, what questions do you think you should ask concerning their design?
2. When designing spreadsheets for use by more than one person, what are some of the concerns?

Infomodule

Spreadsheet Design

WHAT IS SPREADSHEET DESIGN?

The design of a spreadsheet has much to do with its success, and some time spent planning up front can save headaches later. **Spreadsheet design** refers to the way the values, labels, and formulas are arranged in the rows and columns of a spreadsheet. Two basic methods for spreadsheet design are a free-form approach and a structured-block design approach.

As its name suggests, in a **free-form approach** values, labels, and formulas are entered without any preplanned structure. This approach is often employed by people who are learning how to use a spreadsheet program. The free-form approach can be useful for small spreadsheets where the data are not changed and the developer is the only user of the spreadsheet.

However, as spreadsheets grow larger and more complex and the number of users grows, a **structured block design approach** improves the design, understandability, and usefulness of the spreadsheet, because the design of the spreadsheet is planned in advance. The block approach to spreadsheet design is discussed later in this Infomodule.

No matter which approach or variation thereof you use, there are certain basic design guidelines to be followed. They are presented throughout the discussion of block design, but can be applied to free-form spreadsheets as well.

It is important to test your spreadsheet design and question the assumptions used in its construction before you use the information generated to make decisions or solve problems.

WHAT ARE THE CHARACTERISTICS OF A WELL-DESIGNED SPREADSHEET?

The most obvious characteristic of a well-designed spreadsheet is that it accomplishes the goal(s) for which it was designed. It also exhibits the characteristics of accuracy, readability, and consistency. An accurate spreadsheet is free of errors in both the source data and the formulas. The readability of a spreadsheet is determined by how easily a user can ascertain a spreadsheet's purpose, assumptions, and any important information about the values and formulas in the spreadsheet. Factors that affect readability include the visual appearance, the organization of the content, the length of the words and sentences used, how complex it is, and how well it takes into account the knowledge and needs of its users. A spreadsheet makes consistent use of spreadsheet design elements such as using standardized terminology in headings, labels, and documentation. Careful planning before entering data into the program ensures that your spreadsheet will exhibit these characteristics.

WHAT SHOULD I CONSIDER WHEN PLANNING A SPREADSHEET?

The first step in planning a spreadsheet involves answering a few basic questions. First, who will use the spreadsheet? Will it be used only by you, the developer, or will it be used by others? How you answer this question will have an impact on how you design the spreadsheet. If a spreadsheet is to be shared with others, it usually requires a more structured and formal design. Assumptions used to develop the spreadsheet should be clearly spelled out. The type and form of data to be entered by the user needs to be clearly indicated. Factors such as the technical expertise and level of experience of the users should be considered.

A spreadsheet for your own use does not need to be as formal. However, it is suggested that you follow the guidelines for a well-designed spreadsheet discussed in this Infomodule. Using an organized structure and following standard design guidelines make it easier to adapt the spreadsheet as your needs change or expand.

What is the purpose of the spreadsheet? The purpose(s) should be clearly defined to determine what data are essential to realize the goal(s) of the spreadsheet. You'll need to identify the kinds of data required and determine their form. Most spreadsheets contain fixed and variable data. If the variable data are entered into a common area they can be easily updated. You'll need to decide on standard conventions for the units of measure to be used so that cells can be formatted to display data appropriately (i.e., should it be displayed as percent, currency, or integer, etc.).

After you've answered these questions, it's time to sit down with paper, pencil, and calculator and create the basic block design for your spreadsheet indicating where the various parts will be entered and how they will work. It's important to know how your spreadsheet will look and work before you start entering the values, text, and formulas. This step can save you the time, work, and frustration associated with redesigning a spreadsheet and reentering data halfway through the development.

WHAT IS THE BLOCK DESIGN APPROACH?

Block design involves defining and positioning a number of blocks of cells, each with a specific purpose, within the limits of the spreadsheet. The blocks are positioned to meet the objectives of a particular spreadsheet. When using the block design method or creating large and complex spreadsheets, you will want to first sketch it on paper. Once you have gained some experience, it may be just as easy to develop the block design on the monitor for small, less complex spreadsheets. A number of basic guidelines are discussed here to help you create an accurate, readable, and concise spreadsheet. Most of them can be applied to free-form or loosely structured spreadsheets. There are two basic block designs, single block design and multiple-block design.

Single Block Design

Many spreadsheets that you create, such as those used for record keeping or simple calculations, only require a single block design. A **single block design** contains headings at the top of the block identifying the title and other pertinent information about the spreadsheet. Below this is a range of cells containing the data and formulas.

The biggest design concern is what data should be contained in the rows and what data should be contained in the columns. This decision affects the efficiency of the spreadsheet. Because most spreadsheets have more rows than columns, you should use rows for the dimension that is most likely to expand. Consider an inventory spreadsheet in which one dimension holds the inventory items and the other holds details about the items such as inventory number, description, unit price, and the amount in stock. The number of inventory items is more likely to expand than the details about each item. Therefore, rows should be used to enter inventory items and columns to enter the details about the inventory items. This structure allows room for your list of inventory items to expand.

If you don't expect your spreadsheet to expand, use a vertical block design in which rows are used for the larger of the two dimensions. For example, if one dimension takes up 40 cells and the other dimension takes up 10 cells, the spreadsheet should contain 40 rows and 10 columns. This design allows for easier scrolling and vertical printing.

Of course, for some spreadsheets established practices determine which data appear in rows and which in columns. For example, in financial spreadsheets, the financial items such as revenue and expenses appear in rows and the time periods appear in columns. When there are no overriding factors, rows should be used for the dimension containing the longer labels, because the width of columns is generally set to the width of the data they contain. To make the spreadsheet clear and readable, column labels should fit within this limit. The row label columns can be expanded to fit the longest label.

Multiple Block Design

For many spreadsheets, for example, those used for financial statement calculation, capital budgeting, and financial analysis, the simple layout of a single block design is not sufficient. A **multiple block design** that uses a number of standard spreadsheet blocks is used. These include the documentation block, input block, calculation block, output block, and macro block. Each of these is examined below. A spreadsheet may use all or some of these blocks. The names and contents of the blocks can be easily adapted to fit each spreadsheet.

Documentation Block.   The **documentation block** supplies information about a spreadsheet, but does not contain the actual data. It is typically located at the upper left corner of a spreadsheet so that it is immediately available when the spreadsheet is loaded. Documentation is important to any spreadsheet, even if it is for your use only.

Basic documentation that is helpful includes the title, the filename under which it is saved, the date it was prepared, the date of the last revision, the name of the person who developed it, and the name of the user or users.

A title should inform the user of the content and purpose of the spreadsheet as well as include any relevant time periods, activities, or departments covered. It should be written as clearly and concisely as possible. Long titles should be split into a title and subtitles. A short form of the title is often placed in cell A1 as a quick reference to the contents and purpose of the spreadsheet.

The filename should give as much information about the spreadsheet as possible, but your operating system limits the maximum length of a filename. Standard conventions should be developed to reduce confusion or duplication of filenames. If you organize and store your spreadsheet files in directories it will be easy to find the one you need (see Infomodule to Chapter 3).

Another important element is the date indicating when the spreadsheet was originally prepared and when it was last revised. These dates identify the time period during which certain assumptions were made and when changes took place. It is also helpful to include a date function in a header or footer so it is reflected when the spreadsheet is printed.

It is useful to identify the developer. If there are any questions, the user knows who to contact. For example, a user may want to know the source and currency of data, why and how certain formulas were developed, and so on. The documentation should also identify the intended user.

Many larger or more complex spreadsheets require detailed program documentation that gives the user information about the spreadsheet's design and how its various parts work. Typical program documentation might include the names and locations of the blocks of data that make up the spreadsheet, the assumptions used in designing the spreadsheet, identification of named ranges, how data are to be input, the location of the output, descriptions of critical or complex formulas, the location and operation of macros, and so on.

Input Block.   The **input block** is the portion of the spreadsheet set up to contain variable data used in formulas. For example, the interest rate and loan amount that change are entered into cells in the input block and formulas that use these values refer to the cell address where the data are contained.

There are several benefits to using an input block rather than embedding the data in formulas. When the data change, you change only one cell in the input block instead of locating and changing every formula that contains that data. This improves the accuracy of the spreadsheet since you are assured that all formulas requiring that data are using the current value. Using input blocks as a standard part of any spreadsheet design supplies a consistent means of entering data. It also clarifies what variables can be changed when performing what-if analyses or forecasts.

Data can be entered into the input block through a simple input screen, the range of cells that includes the labels and cells for entering the data. A user locates the cell in the input block that contains the variable data to be changed and enters the new data directly into the cell. Some spreadsheet programs allow the creation of data-entry forms and dialog boxes that prompt the user for the appropriate input data. The user enters the data into the data-entry form or dialog box and it is automatically entered into the correct cell. Following are some guidelines that will help ensure error-free input.

When setting up the input screen form, or dialog box, the layout and wording should closely match any paper form from which the input data are transcribed. This reduces the risk of error since the user doesn't have to rearrange the data. If no paper form is used, the input screen should reflect the natural flow of information. Input cells should be preformatted so that they reflect the type of data they require. For example, if an input cell requires a dollar amount it should be formatted to display a dollar sign, thousand comma, and decimal point when data are entered. The same holds true for entries in a data-entry form or dialog box. This helps a user visually identify entry errors. In addition, the unit of measure required should be clearly indicated so that the data are entered in the appropriate form. Error-checking routines should be used when users other than the developer will be entering data values into the spreadsheet and where erroneous data can result in costly mistakes.

Calculation Block. The **calculation block** is the area of the spreadsheet that includes formulas and fixed data. It may consist of one block or it may be divided into several blocks each serving a particular function. For example, the calculation block for a financial statement spreadsheet may be divided into separate calculation blocks for the balance sheet, income statement, and statement of retained earnings. Fixed data are data that are unlikely to change and are therefore included here rather than in the input block. Formulas that perform calculations on the spreadsheet data are also found in this block. The entries here should all be clearly identified with row and column labels to identify the contents of the cells and show the relationships among them.

Each value contained in a cell should also be formatted to identify its unit of measure. If a value represents a percentage, the cell should be formatted to display the percent (%) sign. If a value is a dollar

amount the cell should be formatted to display it with a leading dollar sign ($), embedded commas to specify thousands, and decimal points to specify cents. However, if all the values in a column represent dollar amounts it is an accepted practice to show the dollar sign only in the first and last value.

When developing formulas there are several guidelines to keep in mind. First, and most important is to keep the formulas simple. This reduces the chance of error and makes the spreadsheet easier to maintain. If a formula becomes too long and complicated, break it down into intermediate calculations, clearly labeling each step.

Excessive use of parentheses makes a formula too complicated and difficult to understand. Use a spreadsheet's built-in functions to make a formula simple, more readable, and easier to modify. These functions are predetermined formulas that perform a specific calculation or operation. Typical functions include arithmetic (rounding and square roots), financial (investment and annuities), logical (IF and CHOOSE), statistical (means and standard deviation), and trigonometric (sine and cosine).

Deciding how to handle common data used by more than one formula is another consideration when designing formulas. To illustrate, let's imagine that you have eight formulas throughout your spreadsheet that use the current interest rate. If the interest rate value is included in each formula, you would need to locate and change it in all eight formulas whenever this value changed. If only one formula gets overlooked, calculations will be made using an invalid rate. To reduce errors and make the process of changing common data values easier, those values should be extracted from the formulas and placed into a common data area that is clearly labeled. Each formula that requires that data references the cell that contains it; therefore changing the data in one cell ensures that all formulas dependent on that data use the correct value without changing each and every formula.

It is common practice to precede subtotals by a ruled line and totals by a double-ruled line to indicate that the value represents a sum of the values above the lines.

The chapter introduced absolute, mixed cell, and relative references. The following guidelines will help you decide when to use them. If a reference to a cell must stay constant regardless of where a formula is copied, then an absolute cell reference must be used. If a reference to a certain row or column, rather than a specific cell, must stay constant when a formula is copied, then a mixed cell reference is used. In all other cases a relative reference should be used.

Named ranges can simplify a formula and make it more readable and understandable. The following formula calculates the total royalty payable on sales recorded in cells D4 to D10, applying the royalty rate stored in cell B4.

@SUM(D4:D10)*B4

The range D4 to D10 could be named SALES and the value in cell B4 could be named ROYALTYRATE (Figure 1). These named ranges could be used in the formula to make it more readable and easier to understand, as follows:

@SUM(SALES)*ROYALTYRATE

Range names should only be used for key data values. Overuse causes confusion as to the meaning of the range name and the location of its cells. Range names should be short and indicate the precise meaning of the cell(s). They should not include blank spaces or characters (i.e., + - * / ^) since these could be mistaken for part of a formula. Additionally, names that could be mistaken as cell names or functions should not be used. A list of the named ranges, their meanings, and their corresponding cells should be included in the documentation block.

Output Block. The **output block** is the portion of a spreadsheet where the results of the calculations are displayed. In a free-form approach, the results of calculations are often displayed across the spread-

FIGURE 1
Named ranges can be used in a formula to make it more readable and easier to understand.

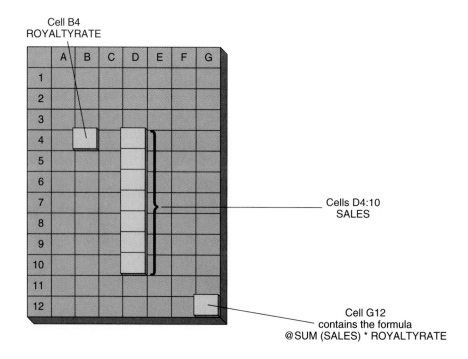

Cell B4
ROYALTYRATE

Cells D4:10
SALES

Cell G12 contains the formula @SUM (SALES) * ROYALTYRATE

sheet. Even when the results are arranged in an orderly and consistent style under the columns they can still be difficult to find and read. An output block allows you to summarize the output in one place so you don't have to look through the entire spreadsheet, which may consist of numerous pages.

The output block can be located wherever it is the most convenient to view the output. Often it is placed close to the input block so that when changes are made to input variables the results can be easily and immediately viewed in the output block.

Macro Block. Macros automate various operations such as printing portions of a spreadsheet. The **macro block** is the portion of the spreadsheet where the macros are located. It should be located in a part of the spreadsheet that will not be affected by changes made elsewhere. Two common locations are in the far right columns of the spreadsheet as far away from the input and calculation blocks as possible or in the top left of the spreadsheet immediately following the documentation block. Each line of a macro should be documented with a comment line. You should also include information about the location, purpose, and any cautions about the use of the macro in the documentation block.

Figure 2 shows a block design for a capital budgeting spreadsheet. The purpose of this spreadsheet and how it is used are described in the documentation block. The input block would include the assumptions used in the spreadsheet and the input variables such as cost of capital, initial investment costs, and cash inflows and outflows. The output block would contain key results from the calculation block. It can be set up to contain the information needed by a manager to make budget decisions. In this case it is placed next to the input block so that the manager can immediately see the results of changes in assumptions and input variables without having to scroll all over the spreadsheet. The various calculations required for capital budgeting decisions, such as calculated payback period, net present values, and internal rates of return, are contained in the calculation block. The macro block may contain macros used in printing various portions of the spreadsheet for review and reports.

WHAT ARE THE LIMITATIONS OF SPREADSHEET DESIGN?

The spreadsheet design you create on paper must be feasible on the screen. Common limitations of spreadsheet programs include window size, presenting data in row and column format, cell formatting, spreadsheet capacity, and complexity.

The size of the spreadsheet window is limited by your display screen, so only a certain number of rows, typically 20 to 24, can be viewed at once. The number of columns that can be viewed in the spreadsheet window depends on their width. A typical monitor displays a maximum of 80 characters, so a standard column width of 9 characters allows a matrix of 20 rows by 8 columns to be displayed. Plan your spreadsheet so that the area in which a user works fits these dimensions. A spreadsheet can be difficult to read and prone to error if the user has to scroll back and forth.

If the data you need to work with cannot be adequately presented in the row and column format then an alternate means of processing those data should be sought. Certain data are better handled by other programs such as database management systems and word processors.

Some spreadsheets are limited in the cell formatting options offered. Make sure that the formats you need are available. For example, if your spreadsheet is to be used by a European client, be sure that it can format dates, units of measure, and currency appropriately.

A spreadsheet model is a numeric representation of a real-world situation. If a model is very large, the spreadsheet program may not accommodate it because of the physical limitation of the number of rows and columns available. Also, if there are many formula calculations, it may take a spreadsheet model longer to process than if the model were developed using a programming language.

Calculations that require complex logic, mathematical formulas, logical comparisons, or decision branches might be accomplished more efficiently using a programming language or a database management system.

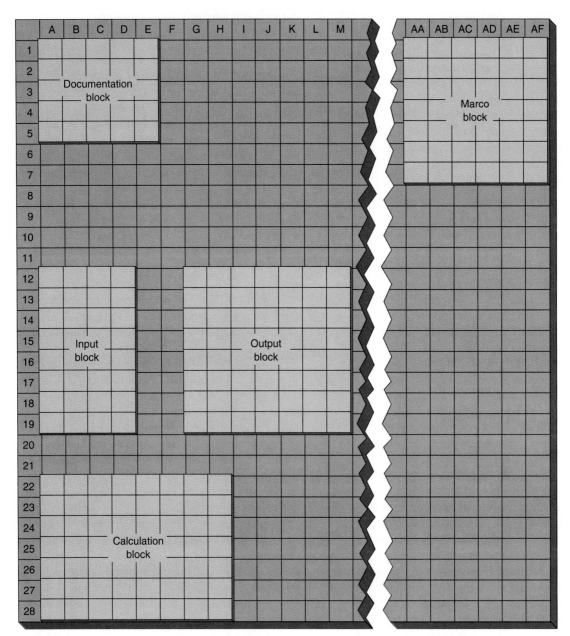

FIGURE 2
A block design for a capital budgeting spreadsheet.

VOCABULARY SELF-TEST

Can you define the following terms?

block design (p. 487)

calculation block (p. 489)

documentation block (p. 488)

free-form approach (p. 486)

input block (p. 488)

macro block (p. 491)

multiple block design (p. 488)

output block (p. 490)

single block design (p. 487)

spreadsheet design (p. 486)

structured block design approach (p. 486)

REVIEW QUESTIONS

Multiple Choice

1. _____ refers to how the values, labels, and formulas are arranged in the rows and columns of a spreadsheet.
   a. Block design
   b. Spreadsheet design
   c. Spreadsheet planning
   d. Documentation

2. A single block design is appropriate for which of the following spreadsheet applications?
   a. keeping a record of inventory items
   b. financial analysis
   c. capital budgeting
   d. financial statement calculation

3. Which of the following blocks is used to enter variable data into a spreadsheet?
   a. documentation block
   b. calculation block
   c. input block
   d. macro block

4. Formulas and fixed data are included in the _____ block.
   a. macro
   b. input
   c. documentation
   d. calculation

5. The _____ block is the area where the results of the spreadsheet calculations are displayed.
   a. calculation
   b. output
   c. macro
   d. documentation

Fill-In

1. Values, labels, and formulas are entered into a spreadsheet without any preplanned structure in the _____ design approach.

2. The _____ block supplies information about a spreadsheet.

3. Data that change should be extracted from formulas and placed in the _____ block.

4. The most important guideline in developing formulas is _____.

5. The _____ block is the portion of the spreadsheet where the macro is located.

Short Answer

1. Describe the characteristics of a well-designed spreadsheet.

2. What factors should you consider when designing a spreadsheet?

3. For a single block design, describe several guidelines that determine which dimension occupies rows and which occupies columns.

4. List the various spreadsheet blocks and describe some design guidelines associated with their use.

5. Identify several limitations of spreadsheet design.

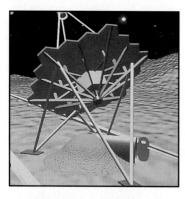

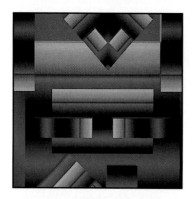

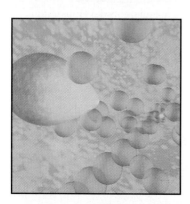

OUTLINE

OBJECTIVES

14.1 Understand what constitutes
     computer graphics and what
     graphics software is.
14.2 Contrast vector and raster graphics.
14.3 Describe the main types of graphics
     software.
14.4 Discuss how graphics enhance
     various professions.
14.5 Identify graphs and charts used to
     represent business data.
14.6 Describe some typical features in
     graphics programs.

Chapter 14

Data Presentation and Graphics Software

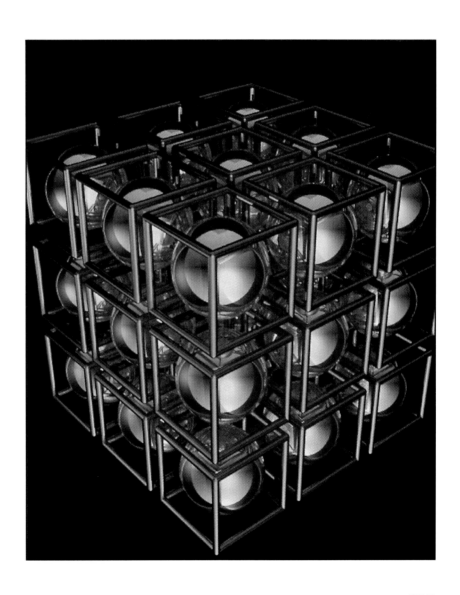

Profile

Augusta Ada,
Countess of
Lovelace

The Countess of Lovelace, as Augusta Ada, daughter of the famous poet Lord Byron, was later to be known, seemed destined for greatness from the start. Early in her life Augusta displayed a penchant for the study of mathematics, which her mother, Annabella Milbanke, encouraged and supported.

She was an accomplished linguist. This expertise with languages led to her being employed by Count Luigi Frederico Menabrea, who had written an article on the analytical engine, a predecessor of the computing device designed by Charles Babbage. The fact that she undertook the assignment of translating the articles from Italian into English is not remarkable, but what she did with those papers is.

Augusta became great friends with Charles Babbage. She had the ability to really understand his designs. She actually worked out most of the theoretical principles and the programming behind Babbage's analytical engine and added her own notes and observations. She suggested that for storage, the binary system would be more suitable than the decimal system. She also included looping as part of the design of the analytical engine.

The Countess died in 1852, and although it took a while, she has finally been recognized for her accomplishments. Her immortality emerged from her love of mathematics. The other title (besides Countess) bestowed on Augusta Ada is "first programmer." She has also been recognized by the United States Department of Defense, which named its most complex and far-reaching computer language "Ada."

Someone once said, "A picture is worth a thousand words." Indeed, a picture can often clear up the meaning of muddled verbal descriptions. Computer software developers have been incorporating more "pictures" into their applications. Computer graphics is one of the fastest growing areas of microcomputer applications that cover many areas of study from aerospace to zoology. The focus of this chapter is on the type of graphics software programs that prepare graphs, charts, and other documents for business presentations.

Objective 14.1   Understand what constitutes computer graphics and what graphics software is.

What Are Computer Graphics and Graphics Software?

Although a graphic image can be created in many ways, this chapter concentrates on those that are created with a computer. **Computer graphics** are those images that are newly created or modified through the combination of the computer, software developer, and the user. The images produced may be text, still pictures, animations, or combinations thereof.

Your computer system needs to be equipped with a large storage capability in order to process graphic files. State-of-the-art microprocessors are required to provide fast access to main memory and cache memory, essential components for animation.

The role of the software developer is in creating the graphics software. **Graphics software** is the program that permits the computer and the user to create, manipulate, and output computer graphic images from simple line drawings to complex 3-D images.

The role of the user is in providing the intelligence and creativity to use the computer that controls the software to produce the graphic images that will communicate ideas to the intended audience.

The focus of the data determines the type of software to produce the required graphics output.

Objective 14.2   Contrast vector and raster graphics.

What Is the Difference Between Vector and Raster Graphics?

Computer-generated graphic images use either vector or raster methods. Images that are created as a set of lines are called **vector graphics**. They are generated through mathematical formulas that determine the length, position, and orientation of an object. A vector graphic such as a circle is handled as a single entity. These images can be scaled and they retain their shape; however, shading is more difficult. Vector graphics are also called **object-oriented graphics**.

In contrast, a **raster graphic** is a collection of dots arranged to form an image. The image is stored in memory locations that correspond to pixels on the screen. Raster graphics are better able to control the shading of colors. A disadvantage is that the image may appear to have jagged instead of smooth edges. These graphics are also called **bit-mapped graphics**. Let's see how the main types of graphics software are used.

Objective 14.3   Describe the main types of graphics software.

What Are the Main Types of Graphics Software?

Graphics software for microcomputers can be divided into four main types: paint and draw programs; design programs; chart/graph and presentation graphics programs; and image-editing programs.

Paint and Draw Programs

For many of us, drawing a straight line or a round circle without the proper tools can be a disaster. Fortunately there are graphic programs especially created for this purpose, called paint and draw programs. They contain the tools used by artists, illustrators, advertising agencies, and businesses to create original art and illustrations, business forms, logos, and letterheads. Whether you use a draw program or a paint program depends on the type of graphic chosen: vector or raster. Some programs combine aspects of both (Figure 14.1).

Draw programs use vector graphics to create both freehand and line drawings. Instruments with which to draw are selected from menus or chosen by clicking on representative icons. A pencil often represents freehand drawing. Drawing tools consist of lines, squares, circles, and text, among others. These drawing objects can be shaped, scaled, colored, and otherwise manipulated to create the final picture. CorelDRAW, CA-Cricket Draw, and IntelliDraw are popular drawing programs.

Paint programs provide better color editing and create detailed graphics. Paint programs handle graphics as rasters. In addition to creating pictures as with a draw program, paint programs contain "artist" tools like a paint brush, spray can, air brush, and paint roller, all capable of producing different textures and shades of color (Figure 14.2). Paint programs, because they work with bit-mapped graphics, allow you to blend, smooth, and sharpen the outlines of one image into another (Figure 14.3). The colors and types of tools in a program are part of its *palette*. The number of colors available is determined by how many bits represent a pixel. For example, if one bit (0 or 1) is used, there are two colors. If two bits (00, 01, 10, or 11) are used, four colors are possible. Four bits mean 16 colors, and so on. PC Paintbrush, CA-Cricket Paint, and BrushStrokes are examples of paint programs.

Design Programs

Design programs aid in applications involving the development of products or structures. These programs are generally vector-based and permit the user to complete the designs much faster and with greater flexibility than with traditional pencil and paper. There is no need to manually erase or redraw.

Computer-aided design (CAD) is software for designing and drafting. CAD programs are found primarily in the fields of engineering, industrial design, and architecture. Figure 14.4 shows one step in the design process, called a wire-frame drawing. Figure 14.5 shows a rendered version of the wire-frame drawing.

Types of Graphics Software

- Paint and draw
- Design
- Chart/graph and presentation graphics
- Image editing

FIGURE 14.1
Paint and draw programs are
used to (a) draw illustrations or
(b) create original art.

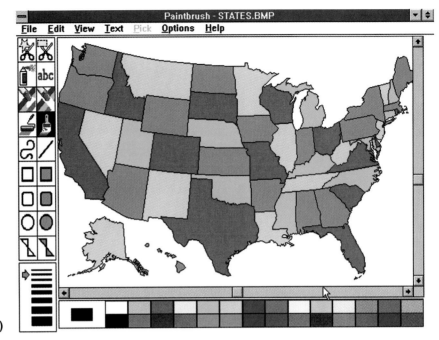

(a)

(b)

FIGURE 14.2
You can almost "feel" the texture on this computer-generated basketball. (Courtesy of Image Software)

FIGURE 14.3
Paint programs incorporate such "tools" as brushes, pens, paint cans, and opaque and transparent paint to create images like this. (Courtesy of Lasergraphics LFR)

CAD programs can also be used in **simulations**, that is, artificially creating an environment for testing products or processes (Figure 14.6). For example, a skyscraper design can be tested to see if it would withstand the forces of an earthquake, without actually having to construct the building first.

FIGURE 14.4
A wire-frame drawing. (Courtesy
of Ralph Semrock)

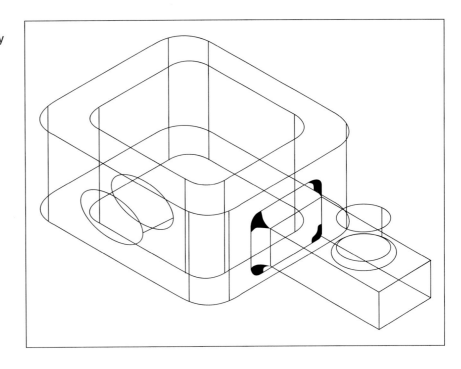

FIGURE 14.5
A rendering of the wire-frame
drawing in Figure 14.4.
(Courtesy of Ralph Semrock)

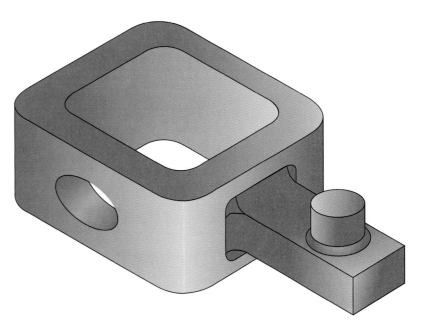

Chart/Graph Programs and Presentation Graphics Programs

A **chart or graph program** is used mainly to display numerical data in graphical form. These programs are created by the computer as bit-mapped images. The data are represented in a variety of chart or graph types, including bar, line, pie, scatter, stacked-bar, three-dimensional, and surface graphs.

FIGURE 14.6
CAD software is used here to analyze and simulate how a robot will move in its factory-floor environment. The operator can check work-cell design elements, such as interference in the motion of the robot or "hand," with other work-cell components. (Reprinted with permission from Calma Co., a wholly owned subsidiary of General Electric Co., U.S.A.)

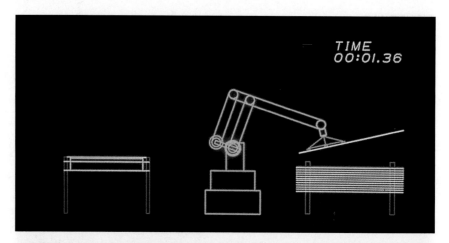

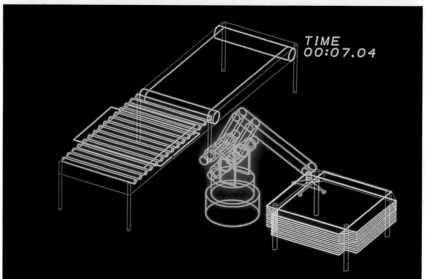

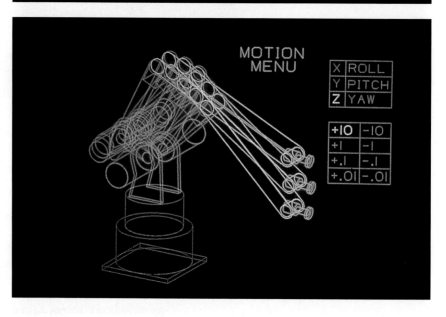

FIGURE 14.7
(a) A simple bar graph. (b) An
enhanced bar graph. (Courtesy
of Lasergraphics LFR)

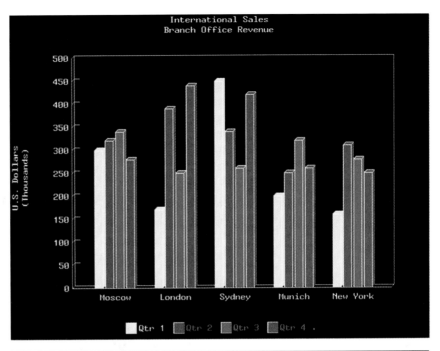

(a)

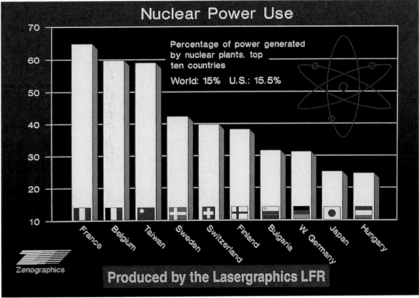

(b)

The chart or graph programs may be separate, stand-alone software or
they may be part of another program, often a spreadsheet program. Unlike
using a paint or draw program, however, the user does not actually draw
the graphs. The user decides what type of graph format the data should
take. Figure 14.7a shows a simple bar graph; Figure 14.7b shows a bar graph
that is embellished. Pictorial representation makes it easy to compare data
or to spot trends that might otherwise be difficult to see from a printed page
of numbers.

Each of the preceding graphics programs has its own niche; however, when it is necessary to prepare a formal presentation of business data they may fall short. You could probably use selected parts from each program but that would be tedious. To prepare data in graphic form for business use, a single program could be used. A **presentation graphics** program combines the features of paint programs and chart programs. In addition to basic drawing and graph creation it contains features to help create, organize, and sequence a slide presentation, create audience handouts, and produce overhead transparencies, speakers' notes, and flip charts. The presentation graphics program can sequence and present a slide show on a monitor with 35mm slides, or show them on a large-screen projector (Figure 14.8). Popular presentation graphics programs include Harvard Graphics, Freelance Plus, and Aldus Persuasion.

Image Editing Programs

Image editing programs allow the user to modify a graphic or photographic image. The image editing programs are often part of a paint and draw program or they may be stand-alone programs. Photographs, pictures in a magazine, or any other scannable image can be edited. For example, you could scan a photograph of the company headquarters, crop it (for example, cut out the background), and place it in a different background. With image editing you can improve a bad photograph by enhancing color, altering shading, and changing the brightness and contrast. Image editing programs include CA-Cricket Image, Image Assistant, and Picture Publisher.

Objective 14.4   Discuss how graphics enhance various professions.

FIGURE 14.8
The graphic image can be output not only to the monitor screen but also can be projected to a large screen without converting the image to a slide or overhead transparency. (Courtesy of Electrohome Limited)

Where Are Computer Graphics Used?

You may think of graphics as charts and graphs that represent numerical or statistical data. However, the ability of the computer to display graphical images extends far beyond business graphs. Although the focus of this chapter and its Infomodule is on business graphics, this section shows how graphics can aid other professions.

Design and Testing

Computer-aided design and computer-aided manufacturing (CAD/CAM) use graphics programs that allow engineers to design new parts or systems much faster than with manual drafting. The computer allows changes to be made on screen to one part of a drawing without having to scrap the entire drawing. Chemical engineers in Alaska use CAD to redesign oil well piping systems. Electronic engineers use it to draw circuit schematics; civil engineers draw bridges, houses, and other structures; and mechanical engineers draw machine parts. By experimenting with various computer-aided designs, engineers create different models to test under varying conditions. A graphic design makes it easier to envision how a product will look (Figure 14.9).

The yacht hulls of many of the America's Cup entries are designed by computer. These designs can be computer-tested under all kinds of simulated water, wind, and weather conditions before being transformed into models and finally into real vessels with multimillion-dollar construction costs (Figure 14.10).

FIGURE 14.9
3D-CAD enables engineers and designers to explore design alternatives and to test a product before manufacturing. (Courtesy of CADKEY Inc.)

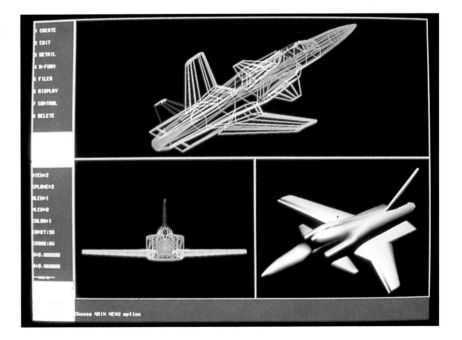

Simulation and Training

Dangerous situations can be minimized for operators who normally work in hazardous conditions by training them in a safe environment. This can be done by a computer simulation of the workplace. The simulations mimic routine operations as well as occasions when things go awry. Graphic simulations allow a trainee to learn from situations that would ordinarily be too costly or too dangerous to recreate.

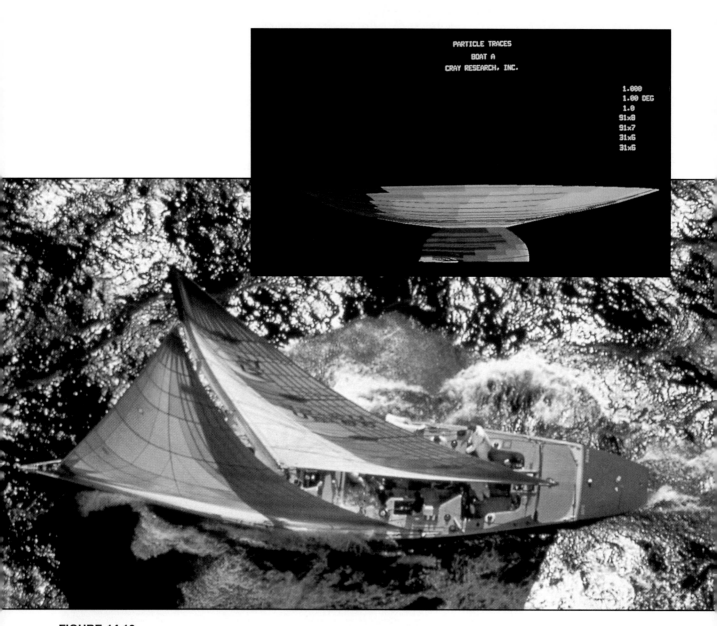

FIGURE 14.10
Supercomputers analyzed millions of pieces of data before coming up with the optimum design for the hull of the *Stars and Stripes,* the 12-meter sailing yacht that won the America's Cup race held in Australia. Plausible designs were suggested and tested (by simulation) for seaworthiness and speed until the winning hull was identified. Onboard computers charted the best course and suggested sail trims. (Leo Mason/Image Bank. Inset: Courtesy of Cray Research, Inc.)

Real-life training is important when it comes to operating lake or ocean-going vessels. Having a mishap with an 800 ft. ship would not appear on a list of "things to do today." However, personnel need to be trained on a variety of ships that sail to different ports. It is impractical and expensive to train staff in each situation and location. One solution is to use a simulation program that uses state-of-the-art graphics.

Computer simulators involve sophisticated programs that offer this training at the Maritime Training & Research Center in Toledo, Ohio. The simulators make it possible to receive training not only in the local harbor, but (through the use of geographical databases) in a variety of harbors, including Los Angeles, Long Beach, Tampa Bay, Jacksonville, Beaumont, Halifax, the St. Lawrence River, and the Strait of Canso.

The marine simulator includes many ship models that can be used by deck officers and engineers who require advanced training to maintain their current licenses or to move up in rank. The integration of the proper computer hardware and software, especially databases and graphics, allow the user to model many situations. Running a ship onto a sandbar is a lesson best learned in a classroom.

Pilot trainees are put into realistic mock-ups of plane cockpits. The computer graphics simulate all sorts of takeoffs, flying, combat, and landing conditions. A crash here is not fatal. Errors can be reviewed and situations tried again. A commercial airline pilot might fly for dozens of years and hundreds of thousands of miles and never experience what it is like to be caught in a wind shear or face the terror of losing all engine power. However, a computer simulation that creates these conditions gives the trainee some degree of readiness should the actual situations ever occur.

Analysis

The ability of the computer to store and retrieve graphic images in real time allows many different professionals to employ the computer as an analysis tool. Through graphical representations, climatologists can "see" temperature variations. When comparisons are made over time they can analyze the data and correlate changes in the environment with changes in temperature. Hurricanes and other violent weather, when graphically animated, permit meteorologists to study their origins.

Medical personnel diagnose diseases through computer graphics. Linked with a scanner, a computer renders a three-dimensional image of the patient's brain so doctors are able to examine the organ in great detail from every angle, without performing invasive surgery. Black and white X-rays that are computer-enhanced and produced in color reveal more information about the examination area. In the field of biology, computers create molecular models to demonstrate nature's building blocks in visible form

FIGURE 14.11
This researcher is using
a CAD system to design
pharmaceuticals. (Courtesy of
G.D. Searle & Co.)

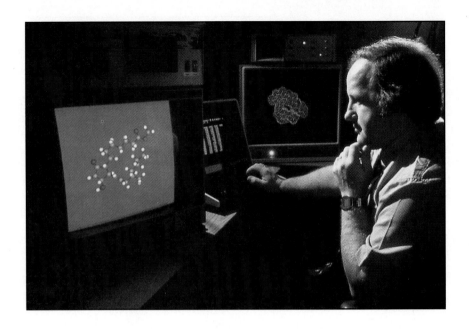

(Figure 14.11). Veterinary science students dissect computer images rather than actual laboratory animals.

Objective 14.5   Identify graphs and charts used to represent business data.

What Types of Graphs and Charts Are Used in Business?

Clear representation of data is the goal in any business presentation. Depending on the message you wish to convey, different methods of displaying those data are used. These include bar, line, and scatter graphs, and pie, organizational, and flowcharts.

Chart/Graph Types

- Bar graph
- Line graph
- Scatter graph
- Pie chart
- Organizational chart
- Flowchart

Bar Graphs

Bar graphs show comparisons or relationships among data items. Data are shown using rectangular bars. Figure 14.12 shows several different types of the many variations of bar graphs.

Line Graphs

Line graphs show trends and emphasize the movement and direction of change over time. Points are plotted on the graph and then connected by straight or curved lines (Figure 14.13). Line graphs that have the area between the lines or curves shaded or filled in are called **stacked-line** or **area** graphs (Figure 14.14).

Scatter Graphs

A **scatter graph** shows the correlation between sets of data. If one set of data increases and the other set decreases relative to the first set, the

FIGURE 14.12
Several types of bar graphs.

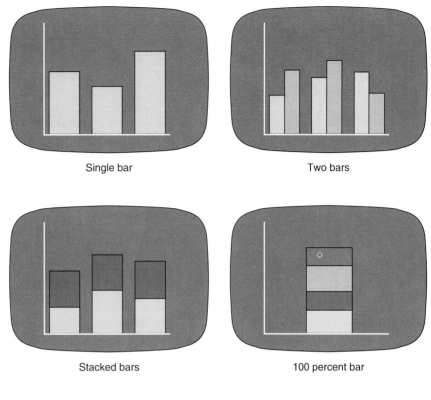

Single bar

Two bars

Stacked bars

100 percent bar

FIGURE 14.13
Line graph connected by both straight and curved lines.

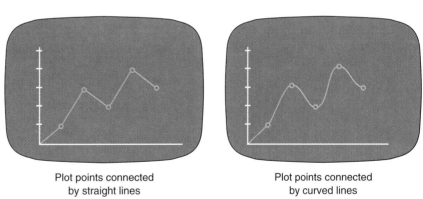

Plot points connected
by straight lines

Plot points connected
by curved lines

FIGURE 14.14
Stacked-line graph or area
graph.

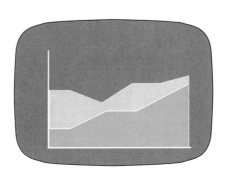

correlation is negative. If both sets of data increase (or decrease) at the same rate, the correlation is positive (Figure 14.15). If there is no relationship between the two sets of data, the correlation is zero.

Pie Charts

A **pie chart** displays part-to-whole relationships. The entire amount is represented by a circle, or pie, and individual wedges represent parts of the pie. Often these wedges indicate a percentage of the whole pie (Figure 14.16). Individual segments of the pie may be colored differently or exploded to draw attention to or highlight that particular wedge.

Organizational Charts

Organizational charts display a hierarchy of data. They are often used to display supervisory levels describing how company departments are laid out (Figure 14.17).

Flowcharts

Flowcharts display how events are sequenced. They may include how much time is involved or merely represent order; what must be done first, second, and so on (Figure 14.18).

Objective 14.6   Describe some typical features in graphics programs.

FIGURE 14.15
Scatter graphs. (a) Positive correlation. (b) Negative correlation. (c) Zero correlation.

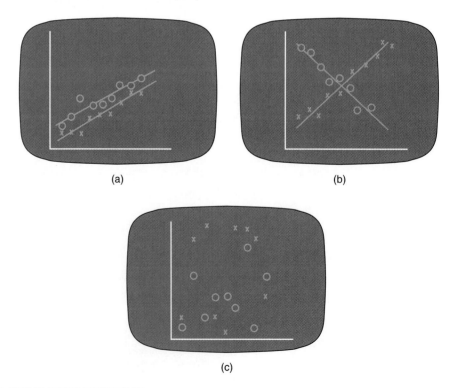

(a)

(b)

(c)

FIGURE 14.16
Pie chart.

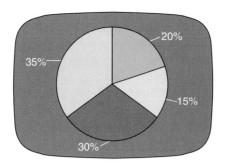

FIGURE 14.17
An organizational chart.

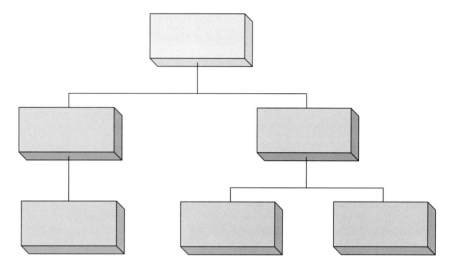

FIGURE 14.18
A flowchart.

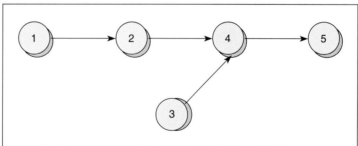

What Are Features of Graphics Software?

Graphs and charts can be developed from spreadsheet data and output through a graphics component of the spreadsheet. They may also be developed through inputting data into a stand-alone graphics program. This section presents common components of graphics programs.

File Formats

Data are input and output in different formats by separate spreadsheets and graphics programs. A feature of many programs is that they accept and

The phrase takes on new meaning when you consider that a personal computer animation package can recreate the scene of the crime. The Anite Group, a ballistics consultant group based in Pinole, California, has successfully done just that.

The consultant firm was called in to produce evidence for a murder trial. Artie Mitchell was allegedly shot by his brother Jim. Eight shots were fired in just over a minute. The jurors would have had a hard time tracking those eight shots. Each shot would have been painstakingly described in detail: the height of the gun, the angle of trajectory, where the bullet landed, and the time each was fired, etc. It would have been extremely difficult for anyone to keep track of all that action.

How could the prosecution make its case? To enact the scene of the crime would have been too dangerous. The solution in this case came through animation. Traditionally a skilled animator created animation one cell at a time. However, the software used in this case was known as a path-based type of program where the user controlled movement through tools such as mapping and lofting. In less than two weeks the ballistics consultant created an animation outline that showed top, front, and side views of the shooting scene. The path of each bullet could be viewed from different angles as well.

Imagine what fun Perry Mason would have had with this kind of evidence!

convert data in varied file formats. For example, this allows data from a spreadsheet to be imported to a graphics program, then exported to a word processing program for inclusion in a report. Many programs offer **clip art,** images such as trees, animals, houses, borders, backgrounds, and business and industry icons that are selected from a menu and incorporated into a drawing. Clip art can be sold as a package separate from your drawing program. The clip art drawings must be in a format that is compatible with your graphics program. If it isn't, there are graphics conversion programs available.

Editing Graphics

You are either very skilled or very lucky if your graphic image or chart comes out exactly right the first time. Usually there is some editing required. The availability of editing features depends on the program, but in general they contain the following aspects.

Selecting an Entity. In order to edit an entity, also called a graphic object, you must identify the object to be selected. It may be selected individually or an entire group can be selected at one time. To select a group of entities a window is required. A **window** is created with a pointing device such as a mouse or digitizer to identify the corner points of a rectangular area in which all the entities are to be selected.

Positioning Entities. An entity can be relocated in the drawing without altering its shape. Methods of moving objects include copying, cutting and pasting, superimposing, and rotating. With the **copy** feature, the original object selected is left in position and a replica of it is placed in the new location. For objects that appear more than once, copying eliminates the need to draw each object separately.

Objects are moved through cut and paste. **Cut and paste** erases or cuts an object from the graphic and places it in a buffer so that it can be inserted or pasted in another location in the graphic. Once an object is cut it may not be visible on the screen until it is pasted. Some programs feature a drag option, however. The **drag** feature lets you watch the object as it moves across the screen as if it were actually being dragged. The objects may be **superimposed**, which means that one object moves over another object, or portion of that object, without erasing either one. When separated, both images remain intact.

The **rotate** feature turns an object so that it can be viewed from other angles, or pivots it from its original orientation when it was placed in the drawing.

Altering Entities. The shape of an entity may be altered. This takes the form of changing the scale of the object or aspect ratio, or mirroring it.

The **scale** feature permits the user to increase or decrease the relative size of the object, that is, change its dimensions. Individual objects or an entire drawing may be scaled to fit the needs of the user. When an object is scaled, the height and width change size equally. If the object is doubled in size both the height and the width are doubled. This creates an object with the same shape but different size.

Objects can be reshaped by altering the ratio of their height and width. The **aspect ratio** is the relationship between the width and the height of an image. For example, a square can become a rectangle by altering only the height. A circle is seen as an ellipse if the aspect ratio is changed (Figure 14.19).

While not actually altering the shape of an object the **mirror** feature produces a mirror image of an object. Drawing time can be reduced if an object is symmetrical by drawing half of it and completing the object by

FIGURE 14.19
The effect of changing the aspect ratio.

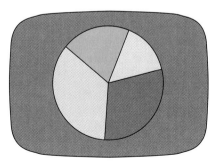

Normal circle as
drawn on screen

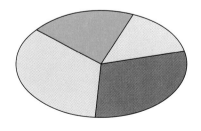

Disorted circle is
printed when incorrect
aspect ratio is used

mirroring it. Often you have the option to retain the orientation of any text or have it mirrored.

Changing the View. To see an object or part of a drawing better, most programs have the ability to enlarge sections of the drawing or to shift it over. To **zoom** means to center on part of the drawing; to view an enlargement of that portion. This permits detail that could not be seen at the original magnification. The **pan** feature moves the whole drawing from side to side so the user can create and view a graphic that is wider than the computer screen. Objects that are close to the border of the screen can be temporarily panned to the center of the screen so that work on them can be completed easily.

Graph and Chart Appearance Features

The effectiveness of a graph or chart is often a function of its appearance rather than the data it contains. A number of fairly standard appearance features are found in most stand-alone and spreadsheet graphics programs. Often included are the following features.

Templates. A **template,** or blank form, can be created for the required graph or chart. The template contains any standard information that doesn't change. You simply load the template, make minor modifications as needed, and then enter your data.

Text. Text is found in titles, labels, and footnotes. All graphs and charts should have a title that describes the main idea. Titles are typically centered. Text labels are used to indicate the meaning of an axis, its units, and the graphic elements that denote the data, such as lines, bars, columns, or pie slices.

Footnotes or other annotations provide additional information about the graphic. Typically, they appear below the main part of the graphic.

The text styles and fonts can be changed to a limited extent in order to add impact to the graph or chart. Another example of altering text is kerning. **Kerning** improves the readability by adjusting the space between certain pairs of letters, giving the illusion of equal spacing between them.

Representing Data. Data may be represented simply or elaborately. Enhancements that embellish the graph or chart include color, patterns, line width, and types and grids that make the data stand out in a graph.

The color scheme of the background, labels, and the graph or object can be changed in most programs. Color is an important factor in graphics presentation. It highlights a portion of a graph for emphasis, to give meaning, or to enhance images created with paint and draw and design programs.

Colors and fill patterns can be set and changed to highlight or show comparisons of data. Color differentiates the various elements of the graphic. The **fill pattern** is the way the bars, columns, pie slices, and area graphs are depicted; they may be solid, open, or crosshatched.

Line graph widths and types of lines can be changed to distinguish data. Each graphics program offers selections such as solid, dotted, dashed, or other line types.

A **grid** is a pattern of horizontal and vertical lines on the display screen. The grid lines help to visualize, pinpoint, or enter specific coordinates. Tick marks may be more appropriate for some types of graphs. A tick mark is a small symbol depicting a value at a precise point. Other symbols such as tiny circles or squares mark data points.

Other Graphics Features

Additional features that may be available to enhance a presentation are slide shows, animation, and 3-D.

Slide Show. A **slide show** displays a series of graphics on the monitor in a predetermined order for a predetermined time period. This produces the same effect as using 35mm photographic slides and a slide projector. The slide show feature helps the user produce a script and graphs, as well as specifies the sequence, timing, and slide transitional effects (such as "fade" and "wipe") of a presentation.

Animation. **Animation** is the ability to simulate motion. This feature links and sequences a series of individual graphics to create a "desktop video." Engineers see how various parts of an object, normally hidden from view, interact. Animation can also serve as a teaching tool showing students how the moving parts of an internal combustion engine operate.

3-D. Some programs display images so they appear to be **three-dimensional (3-D)**. By viewing from various angles and shading the object, it appears to have depth as well as length and height.

Summary

Computer graphics are the images and pictures created by computers and people. Graphics software are the programs employed to create, edit, display, and print those images.

Computers create graphics in different ways. Bit-mapped, or raster, graphics are comprised of individual pixels; vector, or object-oriented, graphics are mathematically defined.

There are four basic types of graphics programs: paint and draw; design; chart/graph and presentation graphics; and image editing. Paint and draw features are sometimes combined into one program, but they are also available as separate programs. Presentation graphics have been prepared for use in a formal presentation along with other materials. Image editing programs allow the user to alter graphics and scanned images such as photographs.

Graphics software contains a variety of features, including different graph types, numerous image manipulation options, color, fill patterns, grid, template and many more.

VOCABULARY SELF-TEST

Can you define the following terms:

animation (p. 515)   aspect ratio (p. 513)
area graph (p. 508)   bar graph (p. 508)

bit-mapped graphics (p. 497)

chart/graph program (p. 501)

clip art (p. 512)

computer-aided design (CAD) (p. 498)

computer graphics (p. 497)

copy (p. 513)

cut and paste (p. 513)

design program (p. 498)

drag (p. 513)

draw program (p. 498)

fill pattern (p. 514)

flowchart (p. 510)

graphics software (p. 497)

grid (p. 515)

image editing program (p. 504)

kerning (p. 514)

line graph (p. 508)

mirror (p. 513)

object-oriented graphics (p. 497)

organizational chart (p. 510)

paint program (p. 498)

pan (p. 514)

pie chart (p. 510)

presentation graphics (p. 504)

raster graphic (p. 497)

rotate (p. 513)

scale (p. 513)

scatter graph (p. 508)

simulation (p. 500)

slide show (p. 515)

stacked-line graph (p. 508)

superimpose (p. 513)

template (p. 514)

three-dimensional (3-D) (p. 515)

vector graphics (p. 497)

window (p. 512)

zoom (p. 514)

REVIEW QUESTIONS

Multiple Choice

1. _____ graphics are generated by a computer as a series of dots.
   a. Presentation
   b. Raster
   c. Object-oriented
   d. Vector

2. _____ are vector-based, so the user can create illustrations and line art.
   a. Draw programs
   b. Paint programs
   c. Presentation graphics programs
   d. Chart programs

3. _____ programs are bit-mapped programs that let the user create images simulating the texture of a brush stroke.
   a. Draw
   b. Paint
   c. Film graphics
   d. CAD

4. _____ programs are employed by business people for making formal presentations.
   a. Draw
   b. Paint

    c. Presentation graphics

    d. Design

5. As an architect, which program would you choose to draw the plans for a client's new home?

    a. draw program

    b. paint program

    c. presentation graphics

    d. design program

6. Training an airline pilot with a device using computer graphics is an example of _____.

    a. animation

    b. simulation

    c. manipulation

    d. conditioning

7. When used by the medical profession as a(n) _____, the computer, linked to a scanner, provides a 3-D image of a patient's brain.

    a. word processor

    b. analysis tool

    c. cutting tool

    d. number cruncher

8. The graphics program feature where the user specifies the sequence and timing of a series of graphics is known as _____.

    a. undo

    b. word chart

    c. rotate

    d. slide show

9. A library of already-drawn pictures, for example, trees, houses, and business icons, is called _____.

    a. clip art

    b. simulation

    c. draw and paint

    d. copy

10. Use of the _____ feature means that a "flipped-over" image will be drawn.

    a. rotate

    b. copy

    c. mirror

    d. pan

Fill-In

1. Bar graphs are used to show _____.

2. A(n) _____ graph shows the correlation between two sets of data.

3. A(n) _____ chart shows the relationship of the parts to a whole.

4. The collection of ready-drawn art known as _____ is accessible to newspapers for display advertisements, among other applications.

5. The _____ -ratio is the relationship of the width to the height of an image.

6. Hierarchy of data can be displayed with a(n) _____ chart.
7. Adjusting the space between letter pairs is called _____.
8. A(n) _____ is a pattern of horizontal and vertical lines that aid the user in entering, visualizing, and pinpointing data.
9. The _____ feature of a graphics program displays a series of graphs on the monitor in a predetermined order.
10. The ability to simulate motion is called _____.

Short Answer

1. Define computer graphics and graphics software.
2. How do vector (object-oriented) programs differ from raster (bit-mapped) graphics?
3. List and contrast the four basic types of graphics programs.
4. Give examples of how graphics play a role in design and testing.
5. Describe instances of graphics playing a role in simulation and training.
6. How can a graphic image aid in medical diagnosis?
7. List and briefly define the types of graphs and charts presented in this chapter.
8. Why is knowledge about the file format of a file important?
9. Describe ways in which entities are positioned in graphics software.
10. How might a grid pattern help you read a graph?

Issues for Thought

1. What applications, in addition to those already discussed, could benefit from the graphics capabilities of microcomputers? Explain your answer.
2. Should patents be issued for software? If they are, what do you think this will do to innovation? If not, how can companies protect their investment in software development? How should the courts decide which software products get patents and which don't?

Infomodule Creating Business Graphs and Charts

A significant study done by the Wharton Business School's Applied Research Center demonstrated that graphics make the point faster and more persuasively in a presentation. It also showed that people who create and use visuals in their business presentations were perceived to be more professional and more interesting than those who did not.

Developers of graph and chart software and presentation graphics software try to create programs that reinforce the rules of good design. They make it easy for the amateur to create good graphs and charts by including suggestions on the type of graph you should use, color, and various other features. However, users still need to plan their graphs carefully.

WHAT FACTORS ARE IMPORTANT FOR CREATING BUSINESS GRAPHS AND CHARTS?

Sometimes, a basic graph with no frills will suffice. But to be most effective in a formal presentation, the user should design a dynamic graph that will impress the point on an audience. Attention to proper design is important. A poorly designed chart or graph can be very dull, or worse, misleading.

Since many of you are headed into managerial positions and because of the importance of graphics in the business environment, we've included some basic concepts of creating business graphs and charts.

In general, a good presentation graph should:

- Be simple
- Be accurate and easy to interpret
- Make a visual impact on the intended audience

Simplicity

Keep the graph simple. Too much information can make it difficult to grasp the meaning of the graph. A

> **Good Business Graph Design**
>
> - **Simplicity**
> - **Accuracy**
> - **Visual impact**

graph should not show finite details or figures, but rather should focus on general ideas such as trends, comparisons, and movement. Keeping a graph simple increases its clarity and effectiveness.

Accuracy

The data used to create the graph must be accurate or the graph may not have the intended meaning. Also, the use of appropriate scales makes it easier to interpret a graph. Poorly designed scales on the horizontal or vertical axis may cause a curve to appear more or less pronounced than it really is. When two graphs are to be compared, the increments between grid marks should be the same on the horizontal and vertical axes of both. Changing the distance between grid lines for a portion of a graph may cause identical data to appear different, or vice versa (Figure 1).

Visual Impact

Several factors should be considered when trying to make a visual impact on the audience.

- Balance—Maintain proper balance and spacing of the elements. Elements in a graph should fill the available space and balance with the other dimensions. Bars and columns should be wider than the space between them (Figure 2).

FIGURE 1
Correct versus distorted scale.

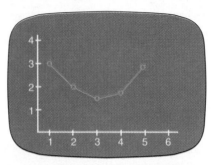
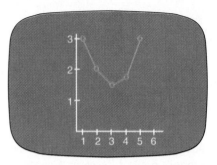

Equal distance between grid marks on horizontal and vertical axes gives the graph a smoother, more realistic appearance.

Contracted and uneven grid marks make the curve appear to have a severe dip.

FIGURE 2
Balanced versus unbalanced bar graph.

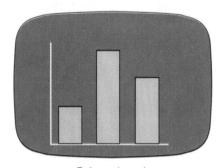
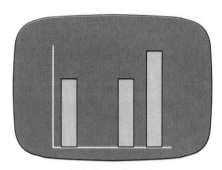

Balanced graph

Unbalanced graph

- Emphasis—Choose design elements such as color, shape, and texture carefully. They can alter the visual effect of a graph. Emphasize important elements of a graph. For example, a segment of a pie chart can be exploded, or a bar might be colored or shaded differently from other bars to make it stand out (Figure 3).
- Color—When shades of colors and textured patterns are used, they should move from darker in the foreground to lighter in the background because darker colors tend to recede and lighter colors tend to "jump" forward. Blues and greens are generally considered good background colors for graphs. In business situations, it is usually recommended to avoid red (it suggests failure to most business people) unless failure is what is being conveyed. Also, if the colors red and green appear next to each other, a person with red-green color blindness will see only brown. This affliction affects approximately 4 percent of males in the U.S.
- Texture—Avoid using textures or patterns that can cause distortion. For example, solid bars stand out more than outlined bars and vertical lines in a horizontal plane make the surface appear higher.
- Line thickness—Plot lines, the lines that connect the data points in a graph, should be of varying thicknesses, or weight. The plot lines should be the heaviest, grid lines the lightest. Use color shades or textures to differentiate between plot lines. Grid lines should not overlay solid areas on the charts.
- Text—Numbers and titles should be large enough to read. Titles should be horizontal whenever possible for easier reading.

FIGURE 3
Exploded pie chart and colored
bar graphs.

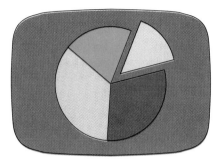

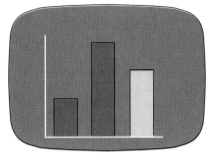

Exploded pie chart   Colored bar for emphasis

All these factors influence where the viewer's attention will be focused and what part of the graph will be perceived as the most important. Not all programs, however, give the user control over every aspect of creating a graph. Some allow more flexibility in graph design than others.

WHAT TYPE OF GRAPHS OR CHARTS WORK BEST?

Choosing the right graph or chart type is very important. If the wrong type is used it may do more to misinform than to explain the data. Keep in mind the suitability of the data to a particular type and why the data are being used. In this section you will look at how the axis and scales should be set up. The main emphasis is on the various graph and chart types and the most appropriate situations for each.

Axis and Scales

Graphs that rely on placing data values on an axis must be done correctly to prevent misrepresenting the data. The X-axis is reserved for an independent variable. The Y-axis is used for a dependent value; that is, the Y-axis values depend on the quantity graphed on the X-axis. For example, sales dollars would be graphed on the Y-axis and time graphed on the X-axis. A second Y-axis is used when two related data items depend on the same units of time or X-axis values. All axes must be labeled and indicate the units of measurement.

To prevent distorted representation of data, scale increments should be consistent. This is especially critical when multiple graphs are shown in close proximity to one another. Scales may be linear, logarithmic, or semilogarithmic. Log- and semilogarithmic graphs are used when graphing extremely large ranges or when displaying rates of change. When possible use whole numbers for the scales. Standard intervals make it easier to interpret the data.

Line Graphs

Line graphs are used to show changes in a quantity over an extended period of time. Multiple trends can be shown but you need to use different line types or a legend that clearly identifies each line. Line graphs provide a better means of showing continuous data items. A drawback to line graphs is that they may be intimidating to an audience unfamiliar with the topic.

Bar Graphs

Bar graphs are probably one of the most commonly used graph types. They come in a variety of forms and are best used to show comparisons of distinct categories. A nontechnical audience is best served by this type of display.

Bar graphs with vertical bars are sometimes called column graphs. Column graphs are best used to show how data vary over time, while horizontal bar graphs show how values compare at a given time. Clustered bar graphs, where multiple bars are side by side, allow you to compare several items at once. The X-axis may be sales periods in a year. For each sales period you might compare three different salespersons.

Stacked Bar Graphs

Stacked bar graphs, both horizontal and vertical, are good alternatives. They combine the features of bar graphs and pie charts. They let you show side-by-side bar comparisons and also how the parts of a single bar compare. Often, as in the case of the 100 percent bar graph, percentages of a whole are shown.

For best appearance when using a stacked bar graph put the most important variable at the bottom of the column. Use the darkest color or shade at the bottom of the column and go lighter as you move up the column.

Area Graphs

Area graphs combine the features of line graphs and stacked bar graphs. They resemble a line graph with the area shaded below each line. Like stacked bar graphs their appearance should follow the same guidelines. In addition to showing trends, they also can show the importance of one data item over another at a given time. The area graph provides an alternative if there is too much data to plot on a stacked bar graph.

Scatter Graphs

Scatter graphs are also called X-Y graphs. Earlier it was mentioned that the X-axis is used for independent data and the Y-axis for dependent data. The scatter graph is an exception to that rule because you are looking to see if any correlation exists between two categories of data. When using scatter graphs use more tick marks on the axes to help determine any relationship.

In statistical graphing programs a regression line may be graphed with the data to show the general correlation among the data.

High-Low Graphs

High-low graphs are special types of line graphs that are used to plot minimum and maximum values over time. They are often used to plot stock market prices or temperature variations. The marks for the high and low data points are usually of different types.

Pie Charts

Pie charts are very simple yet can be very effective. They are used to show parts to a whole and generally display this as a percentage. Avoid cluttering the pie with too many wedges; five or six is a maximum. If you find yourself with too many categories, consider combining categories. A second pie chart could be used to detail the combined wedge. Often to highlight a particular segment of the pie the wedge is exploded.

WHAT IS THE BEST WAY TO PRESENT YOUR GRAPHS AND CHARTS?

Once you have assembled your graphs and charts you may need to present them at a meeting. Choose your presentation medium according to the size of your audience and the size of the room. Popular presentation methods include overheads, 35mm slides, on-screen computer presentations, and video.

Overheads

Overhead transparencies are best used when the audience size is no more than thirty or forty people. This method is suited to a situation that uses audience interaction as part of the presentation. If you need the lights on in the room overheads also work well. Overheads are used more for informal settings such as a training session or a sales meeting.

35mm Slides

When you have a large audience 35mm slides are useful. They work well because they retain their clarity, sharpness, and color even when projected on large screens.

On-Screen Computer Presentations

The on-screen computer presentation is the newest and most versatile way of presenting data. The data to be displayed come directly from the computer. A small group of up to four or five persons can gather around the computer screen. For larger groups, up to forty or fifty people, you can use a liquid crystal display (LCD) that connects to the computer and shows your graphs on a pull-down screen. For even larger groups graphic data can be displayed right from the computer using an overhead projection system. This is a good alternative when you don't have time to produce overheads or slides and still want to retain high-quality graphs.

Video

Video presentations are good for stand-alone presentations. However, video is a passive type of medium. The presenter must be careful not to rely solely on the video in his or her presentation, but has a greater responsibility to produce viewer interest. Video is good in that you can pause, rewind, and review your data easily.

Sometimes a combination of the above methods can be used to create a dramatic presentation.

REVIEW QUESTIONS

Multiple Choice

1. A study at the Wharton Business School's Applied Research Center demonstrated that _____.
    a. 35mm slides and slide projectors are seldom used in formal business presentation
    b. graphics make the point faster and more persuasively in a formal business presentation
    c. paint and draw programs are the most popular type of graphics program
    d. design programs are the most popular type of graphics program
2. Ordinarily the _____ variable is on the _____-axis.
    a. dependent, X
    b. independent, X
    c. dependent, Z
    d. linear, X
3. Which one of the following is not a type of graph scale?
    a. linear
    b. semilinear
    c. semilogarithmic
    d. logarithmic
4. Which one of the following graphs does not use dependent and independent axes?
    a. scatter graph
    b. bar graph
    c. column bar graph
    d. stacked bar graph
5. The _____ presentation allows you to use an LCD to project your graphs from the computer screen.
    a. overhead
    b. 35mm
    c. on-screen computer
    d. video

Fill-In

1. Simplicity, accuracy, and visual impact are qualities of a good _____.
2. When deciding on colors to use in a graphic, keep in mind that _____ colors tend to "jump" forward and _____ colors tend to recede.
3. The scale on a graph should be in _____ numbers to make it easier to read.
4. A(n) _____ graph plots minimum and maximum values.
5. _____ transparencies are best used when you want an interactive session and the lights may be on.

Short Answer

1. List three factors to consider when trying to create a good presentation graph.
2. Explain how simplicity affects a graph.
3. Why is accuracy important when creating a graph?
4. Briefly outline the factors you should consider for visual impact.
5. List and describe the benefits of using overheads, 35mm slides, on-screen computer presentations, and video.

Part 4

Implications of the Information Age

The problem is not the technology, but to change our perspective of what it's for. Who would believe [in the 1850s] that you could have an empty intersection and because the light's red you stop?

Douglas Engelbart, developer of the mouse

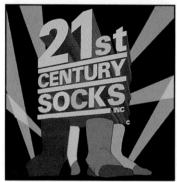

OBJECTIVES

15.1   Discuss how the field of computing relates to a global society.

15.2   Describe challenges facing the United States for competition in the global market.

15.3   Understand ways the United States can compete with other nations.

15.4   Describe how information systems can benefit a particular geographic region.

15.5   List and briefly describe obstacles to computing on a global level.

15.6   Understand how events in one part of the world affect computing elsewhere.

15.7   Explain why joint ventures are popular in the computer industry.

15.8   Describe how information networks affect a developing nation.

15.9   Describe services available through the global network Internet.

15.10   Identify trends in information systems use.

15.11   Understand how technology developments affect hardware, software, communications, and the user.

15.12   Explain how green computing affects the environment.

15.13   Recognize how computers are changing careers.

Chapter 15

International Computing and Trends in Technology

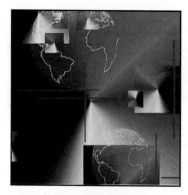

Alan M. Turing

"Can machines think?" Alan Turing spent much of his life being intrigued by this question.

Turing, a brilliant mathematician who was born in London in 1912, received his education at Cambridge University and later Princeton. He and his colleagues were responsible for developing the first (arguably) operational computer in 1940. The machine, known as Robinson, was instrumental in breaking Nazi codes. Turing's decryption methods have remained secret. For all we know, they may still be in use somewhere.

After the war, Turing authored papers entitled "Intelligent Machinery" and "Computing Machinery and Intelligence." Because his theory compared the human brain to a machine, he wondered if the machine could also "think." He is responsible for creating the Turing test as a model to determine whether a machine is intelligent. Turing hypothesized that if a person *thought* a machine was intelligent, then it *was*. With reference to machine intelligence, Turing said, "... it is possible that one man would consider it as intelligent and another would not." Turing would most likely be highly involved in the study of what is known today as "artificial intelligence."

You might have heard or read about the Turing test that was conducted at the Boston Computer Museum as part of the first Loebner Prize Competition in November, 1991. Ten human judges using only keyboards were charged with determining whether they were interacting with a terminal (there were eight) or a human (there were two). Each judge had to decide whether a program or a person was answering their inquiries. Judges were restricted to preselected topics, among them women's apparel, Shakespeare, and martini making. Turing most likely would not have liked the idea of these restrictions. However, several programs were identified as "human," or having human intelligence. In other words, they passed the Turing test. The winning program, PC Therapist, lets users vent their emotions.

Such a program might have been helpful to Turing, who in spite of all his scientific success apparently committed suicide at home. Evidence that the 41-year-old mathematical marvel may have ingested cyanide was found near his body.

This chapter examines some ways in which computing influences the global community and is itself influenced by global events. Technology has given rise to increased use of new developments for manipulating and communicating information. In this chapter you will read about aspects of computing that are moving from the "gee whiz" realm into everyday applications. You will also read how environmental as well as world concerns affect computing and how computers and computing affect careers.

Objective 15.1   Discuss how the field of computing relates to a global society.

What Are the Global Implications for Computing?

Should you concern yourself with the global implications of computer technology? Can it affect your job, the way business is conducted, or have social-political ramifications? Consider that by some estimates over 60 percent of all jobs in the industrialized countries of the world will be related to computers and the exchange of information by the turn of the century. Electronic data interchange, electronic forms of insurance, and banking are but a few application areas involved in acquiring and sharing information globally. Increasingly, businesses recognize the necessity of competing in the global market. This global competition fuels the importance of information technology and global networking through telecommunications.

To be competitive in the global marketplace, information systems and the technology to implement them must take high priority for organizations. Enterprises operating in world markets must be prepared to do business on a 24-hour basis, to mesh with working schedules in different time zones. Global networks have affected electronic trading. One company that provides a method for world markets to do business around the clock is Globex. Developed by the Chicago Mercantile Exchange, the Chicago Board of Trade, and Reuters PLC, Globex is moving to become an international electronic trading service.

Computers and computing influence international monetary transactions, information gathering, strategic communications, and the way that information reaches individuals—even those under less-than-democratic governments. For example, the Berlin Wall and the Iron Curtain began to disintegrate when the governments behind them could no longer keep their citizens in the dark about what was happening in the world outside. Telecommunications was more than a channel for conveying political news; it became an actual part of the political process. Computer technology and communications kept people informed during the break-up of the former Soviet Union in the early 1990s. Computers can empower a Third World nation by providing the data necessary for water and crop management.

International corporate telecommunications is increasing by 15–20 percent per year. Companies that specialize in telecommunication equipment are looking for new ways to compete, including upgrading equipment and technology, such as using digital switching, installing fiber-optic lines, and implementing voice and data networks. This fierce competition for subscribers will undoubtedly result in technological developments and applications as yet unknown. In subsequent sections you will look at the United States and its involvement in global computing, the problems associated with global computing, and what some nations are doing on the global front.

Objective 15.2   Describe challenges facing the United States for competition in the global market.

Where Is the Global Challenge in Information Technology?

Historically the United States was the leader in almost every area of computer research, development, and use. In the past decade or so the balance began shifting to overseas competition.

Large corporations in the United States are becoming more multinational. Much of this global shift is due to increased competition from abroad. Two major factors have stimulated the need for increasing a global presence for U.S. businesses: the challenges from Asian countries like Japan and Korea; and the European Community (EC).

Asia

Until 1983, all the world's supercomputers were American made. The U.S. had also been the leader in innovation and design of microprocessors. But many computers and computer components began to be manufactured in Japan and Taiwan. A world leader in printers (with Epson and NEC), Japan owns many of the robots in the world and moved to the front line in robotics. Japan also leads in the technology for flat-panel displays for laptop computers.

Taiwan, which had been primarily a manufacturer of computers, is more involved in product engineering. New Taiwanese products such as "green" monitors, high-speed modems, and image compression programs offer competition to U.S. firms. In the information industry, survival is often dependent on the design and production of new and innovative products.

Certain Asian computing centers such as Hong Kong, Singapore, Taiwan, and South Korea rely heavily on exports. To keep and expand their markets in Europe, many have located and merged with companies in the EC. They are preparing for the future by recognizing the value of information and global networks. Singapore built a strong supply of educated programmers and computer science professionals and has become a world leader in electronic data interchange (EDI). Singapore created a network called TradeNet that links trading companies with the government agencies that issue permits for the movement of goods. This network is responsible for processing documents in minutes where it used to take days.

The European Community

Europe is emerging as one of the largest computer markets in the world. In the early 1990s many European firms began developing networks to manage services, when it seemed evident that some form of single European economy would exist. For example, West Germany was the first supplier of a line of components for transmitting data, voice, and video over the same communication channels. Great Britain and France are moving ahead in artificial intelligence research. A Dutch-based company is exploring using LCD keys on the keyboard so that any layout can be programmed to display on the keyboard. For example, multinational executives in a foreign country could switch the keyboard to a layout corresponding to their native language.

The EC saw the need for information networks and developed strategies to implement them more fully. The Treaty of European Union called for strengthening social and economic bonds through development of a trans-European network for telecommunications, transportation, and energy. It has been proposed that a common band of frequencies for digital European cordless telecommunications be adopted. Development of satellite communications is also a priority of the EC. By realizing the importance of information systems, other countries have put the U.S. on notice that they are not waiting for us.

Objective 15.3   Understand ways the United States can compete with other nations.

What Can the United States Do to Respond to Global Challenges?

Growing European and Asian markets put new demands on computer engineers. American manufacturers will have to meet international standards and integrate foreign language and cultural differences. The United States leads the world in most communication technology and programming, hardware such as fiber-optic cables, microprocessors, and networking; but the prospect of losing its technological leadership has been recognized by the U.S. government.

Developing Information Policy

Both Japan and Europe had an advantage over the U.S. because they had national policies for public communication networks. However, in 1993 President Clinton sent an initiative to Congress to invest upward of $20 billion in computing technology. The plan includes money for private research and development, investment tax credits, and relaxed technology export controls. Emerging products are conceived as the result of research and development.

Developing a Global Mentality

Many U.S. companies generate a substantial portion of their income from overseas sales. To better understand these markets, some companies are hiring executives from abroad to help run their businesses. Recruiters stress the need for leaders with international qualities, such as fluency in more than one language, residency in a foreign country, or being employed in more than one country. Such managers may offer a global approach and have a long-term focus that keeps them on the cutting edge. This is especially important in new markets, such as the former Eastern Bloc countries, as they opened up their borders to international trade.

It wasn't too many years ago that computing was confined to the office, that is, before technology brought us portable computing. Now, of course, a computer goes everywhere.

Richard Bangs, an author and explorer, demonstrated just how far you can take one. When you are away from the computer everything must be hand written and later typed into the computer. Ideas can be lost when trying to decipher your own scribbled handwriting or brief notes. So Bangs took his notebook computer along. Not particularly remarkable, until you consider that where he went was to the top of Mount Kilimanjaro in Africa to conduct research for a book on the world's ten highest mountains. From the relative warmth at the base of the mountain to the extreme cold of the summit, the computer went along.

Mother Nature still regulates technology, however. Ordinarily a single battery charge lasts for about three hours, but at 19,000 feet, the minus 40 degree Fahrenheit temperatures reduced that time to only 15 minutes.

Trading for the Future

American companies that export goods generally are in favor of reduced tariffs on their products. This allows them to compete freely in a foreign market. There are pros and cons to these agreements between countries. The North American Free Trade Agreement (NAFTA) was a much-debated agreement between the United States, Canada, and Mexico. It was favored by many computer professionals. In fact, Bill Gates, the head of Microsoft, made a commercial endorsing it. He gave the computer industry's support for the reduction of the 20 percent tariffs of computer goods going to Mexico. Without the agreement, he said, Japan and Europe would grab yet another market for selling their products. There are many such agreements being proposed worldwide.

Restrictions on trade exist for many reasons. Because of Cold War restrictions set by the Coordinating Committee for Multilateral Export Controls, computer companies were not permitted to sell "high-end" computers or parts to many countries, like China. Potential sales in the Chinese market are great because only 1 in about 6,000 people have a computer whereas 1 in 4 people in the U.S. do. Lifting some restrictions has helped American companies account for over 60 percent of the Chinese market.

In many ways, the economies of nations have always been connected, and computers will be instrumental in making the long-talked-about "global village" a distinct possibility. Because of computer and communication technology, worldwide communication is immediate.

Objective 15.4   Describe how information systems can benefit a particular geographic region.

How Can You Prepare for the Future with Information Networks?

Cities or countries with the ability to facilitate telecommunications will have an advantage over those that do not. Countries with free markets or those that have liberalized their postal-telegraph-telephone (PTT) agencies are reaping the benefits of global communication.

The end of the PTT monopoly in Britain provided many benefits for London businesses. Major banks set up high-speed communication systems that allow up-to-the-minute access of updated data for automatic fund control and other financial services. Because of their global networks, London handles about half of the foreign exchange transactions in the world.

Information systems technology has been instrumental in making The Netherlands the major trading center in Europe. Deregulation provided the impetus to develop information systems that allow cargo to clear customs rapidly, resulting in a dramatic increase in import and export business. Federal Express chose Belgium as one of its main distribution centers largely because of its communication networks.

Although Germany is one of the strongest countries in the EC, it has a strongly regulated PTT. Many banks have moved their data centers to other countries that provide lower prices and better network service.

Europe and Asia certainly do not have a monopoly on using information networks and electronic data interchange to foster growth. Qantas Airlines of Australia is a world leader in using information systems for on-line real-time information networks. Australia is also home to one of the top five electronic banking firms in the world.

Borland, Lotus Development Corp., and Symantec Corp. have been encouraged to locate development offices in Ireland. Some Irish incentives include the fact that corporate profits are taxed at only 10 percent, inexpensive skilled labor is available, and telecommunications are carried over one of the most modern fiber-optic networks in the world.

Any country that hopes to compete on the world playing field or even on a local level needs to develop viable information networks. In the United States an example of this can be seen in Omaha, Nebraska. With low telephone call charges because of its extensive fiber-optic networks, they garnered a large portion of the 800-number telephone services. These services are alluring to credit card companies and businesses that require reservations, such as airlines and hotels/motels. Heathrow, Florida, became the new location of the Automobile Association of America because it had the foresight to install a fiber-optic network to handle telecommunications.

On a smaller scale individual businesses are integrating various aspects of information technology into their products. A chain of photocopy stores, Kinko's, added the capability of video conferencing to its list of services. A small booth is provided complete with computer, fax, and scanner so that a user who contacts a business associate or colleague across the country has the ability to share data and files.

It is clear that information networks hold the key to building a strong economy both now and in the future.

Objective 15.5   List and briefly describe obstacles to computing on a global level.

What Are Some Obstacles to Global Computing?

Many perils exist to going on-line with an information network in a global environment. They include language barriers, different standards, software piracy, and finding skilled labor. Yet those who develop products that make use of global networks easier will surely gain market share.

Language Barriers

The EC is divided by over a dozen languages, and as other countries such as Poland and Hungary enter, the problem does not get easier.

The International Association for Machine Translation wants to provide translation programs so that users have access to computers and applications in their native languages. The demands for linguistic support have grown astronomically. Consider that translation of the nine official languages of Europe actually involves interpretation of each language into all of the others—72 translations for just these nine. Some U.S. computer manufacturers sold their computers in Europe because of their awareness of these differences. Cultural awareness is important in global trading. For example, Chrysler Corporation sold many more Jeeps in Japan after it manufactured them with right-hand drive. The English keyboard arrangement is called QWERTY. However, France uses an AZERTY arrangement. Sinclair, which produced a special version of its computer with the AZERTY keyboard, sold very well in France where others did not.

Software can pose problems if differences in language are not taken into account. Many foreign word equivalents are much longer and will not fit into the same space as the English words. A programmer coding a menu structure cannot simply leave a blank space where the English words were. This is just one example of problems found by programmers.

Global communication means interacting with a variety of cultures and languages. One way for dealing with international language barriers is being developed by Advanced Telecommunications Research Institute International of Japan, Carnegie Mellon University, Karlsruhe University, and Siemens of Germany. They used a system of workstations to create a computer translator phone system that translates a spoken English, German, or Japanese sentence into the other two languages. One computer converts speech into text, another translates the text into the one required at the receiving end. The text is sent via modem and international phone lines where the translated text is synthesized into speech. The system was limited to about one thousand words, but within the next 20 years fully fluent systems are expected to be available.

With the importance of global economies, companies realize that they must be able to develop products that reflect a multinational environment. The 8-bit ASCII code represents only 256 characters and does not include characters for languages with non-Roman alphabets. So one organization, Unicode Inc., which includes Apple Computer Inc., Microsoft Corp., and IBM, developed an extension of that code. The newer 16-bit code represents 65,536 characters and allows all international language characters to be represented. This innovation makes it easier to exchange data between international applications.

Because the Middle East is a fast-growing market for computers, it is particularly noteworthy that technology exists that enables the use of the Arabic language, which is written from right to left. Some Arabic characters are connected, some have different shapes depending on their location in the word, and still others require diacritical marks. The ASCII code requires approximately 65 new characters to accommodate Arabic. The first Arabic spell checker program was developed by a Cairo company called al-Alamiah.

Defining Standards

Global computing infers that you coexist with other countries, which necessitates dealing with a variety of standards. This creates numerous obstacles when quality and availability of hardware and software are not the same. International standards for products have to be defined to accommodate international cultures. Data are often accessed from the same database, but from different worldwide locations. Data definition standards are the key to using information networks on a global level. Electronic data interchange standards have been developed through cooperation of the American National Standards Institute and the United Nations. Ultimately, standards may be set by the countries or companies that emerge as the world leaders in a particular technology.

Software Piracy

The world software market is an approximately $25 billion market. The greatest profit margins lie in computer software. U.S. companies estimate over $400 million in losses annually because they don't receive royalties from pirated software. Piracy can be a problem, but there are solutions.

Japan has traditionally put more emphasis on developing hardware than producing software. Most Japanese companies purchase custom software, which is time-consuming and costly to develop and problematical for software vendors. Software piracy is four times as high in Japan as in the United States. Foreign software developers (primarily American firms) control approximately 50 percent of Japan's $1 billion wholesale business software market, so piracy can be costly. With some Japanese companies starting to develop software, it is hoped that piracy will decrease. For example, Ichitaro is a Japanese-language word processing software developed by Justsystem. Some experts suggest that Japan will be the site of future program development because of their ability to work in small group teams, which promises to be conducive to better programming. Some Japanese software firms use Chinese labor to design software.

Software piracy is a problem in the former Soviet Union with 68 percent of all software being pirated, primarily because of high cost, poor maintenance, and shortage of copies. Microsoft's MS-DOS is the most popular operating system, but most copies there are pirated. Microsoft hopes that by employing some of the pirates, illegal copying will diminish and it will prove to be more beneficial than prosecuting the bootleggers.

They are hopeful of implementing copyright laws. Nantucket Corporation has a joint effort with a foundation in Russia for disabled children. Nantucket supplies microcomputers and legal copies of its Clipper software. In return, the foundation pays the salaries of programmers who work as the support staff. By providing support service they place importance on owning legal copies of software.

The New Labor Pool

A trend in software production is emerging. Many companies and even some countries use Third World labor pools to develop programs. This came about because of the diminished labor pool in Western nations (fewer U.S. students are following the technical career track) and the availability of low-cost labor elsewhere. Labor costs are kept low because workers are paid in their native currency, which is usually much weaker than in industrialized nations.

India has the second-largest technical workforce that speaks English. Their programmers are renowned for their mathematical abilities. India hopes to export $1 billion in software by 1996.

The computer software industry is one of the only industries doing well in the economy of the Philippines. This is primarily because of the easy availability of inexpensive, highly skilled labor. Equidata Philippines, Inc. doubled its business in 1990. Another computer industry leader, Pact Group, turned an original investment of $5,000 into a business that generated sales of $5.5 million annually.

In the former Soviet Union (FSU) many programmers are eager to sell their services to Western countries. Although the FSU suffers from high inflation, poor telecommunications, and unsophisticated banking systems, programmers have experience in object-oriented programming, expert systems, and power plant control software.

Because of its skilled labor force Israel is attracting many overseas computer firms. They boast more Ph.D.'s per capita than any other country in the world. The only Intel 80386 microprocessors that were not manufactured in the U.S. were built in Israel. Digital Equipment Company (DEC) located a research center there.

Objective 15.6   Understand how events in one part of the world affect computing elsewhere.

How Can World Events Influence the Computer Industry?

Events in other parts of the world can have a dramatic effect on supplies and prices of goods in the U.S. Natural disasters, political upheaval, and internal national interests are among the many uncertainties that play a part.

In July of 1993 there was an explosion and fire at the Sumitomo Chemical Company in Japan. It was significant in that 60 percent of the world's supply of epoxy resin, used in the packaging of chips, is produced there. This had the effect of doubling the price of dynamic random access memory (DRAM) chips, which in turn increased the price paid for computers. The price increase was expected to be in effect until early 1994.

A few years ago some Korean computer chip manufacturers were charged by the U.S. Commerce Department with dumping chips on the U.S.

market. The penalties, in the form of additional duties, raised prices by as much as 20 percent.

The rise and fall of international currencies can have a dramatic effect on products sold by U.S. manufacturers. For example, in one six-month period in 1993 the price of an imported Apple computer fell by over 25 percent. This occurred because of the increased value of the yen over the dollar, which made imported merchandise in Japan cheaper and foreign markets more competitive.

Closed societies also preclude the global community from conducting business. In Brazil until the early 1990s, only Brazilian-made computers were allowed to be used; all foreign models were confiscated. Sometimes the only way to survive to compete another day is by working together. This can be seen in the proliferation of national and international joint ventures.

Objective 15.7   Explain why joint ventures are popular in the computer industry.

Why Is Cooperating in a Global Society Necessary?

Competition and the rising cost of research and development have prompted many companies to join with overseas firms to collaborate on projects. In the past few years many U.S. companies have moved into strategic relationships with Japanese firms. For example, IBM and Toshiba Corporation have a joint venture for color displays, Tandy Corporation and Matsushita for notebook computer manufacturing, and Apple Computer and Sony Corporation are co-designers of Apple's PowerBook computer.

The U.S. is not the only country that recognizes the importance of being competitive and responding to challenges from abroad. The European Commission recognizes that by the year 2000 the main economic focus will switch from automobiles to information industries in its member nations. Siemens Nixdorf Informationssysteme (Germany), Cie. des Machines Bull (France), and Ing. C. Olivetti (Italy) formed a joint venture to attempt to catch up with U.S. and Japanese companies. The TransEuropean Information Systems joint venture will mainly work on applications for health care, environmental protection, and governmental applications. They also attempted to control the bidding from outside companies on the European Community computer network.

Cost of research and the risks in new development are skyrocketing and many companies realize the benefits of joint ventures to defray the costs. Normally competitors, IBM, Siemens of Germany, and Toshiba of Japan entered into a partnership to develop new 256M-bit memory chips. The semiconductor industry is increasingly becoming a global enterprise. Although much U.S. production was taken over by the Japanese back in the 1980s, companies such as IBM still provide the role model for new chip technologies.

Advanced Micro Devices Inc. and Fujitsu Ltd. have joined together to share the costs of developing computer chips and Texas Instruments and Hitachi have collaborated to research memory chips since 1988.

Objective 15.8   Describe how information networks affect a developing nation.

How Do Information Networks Affect Developing Nations?

The global economy is gradually shifting toward more reliance on information systems to spur the continuing development of nations. Developing countries are often further alienated from their more prosperous neighbors in spite of efforts to introduce information technology. For example, the U.N. International Telecommunication Union was pressured by Third World nations to allocate a satellite orbiting position and a bandwidth of frequencies for communications to all nations. When people in your country are wondering where the next meal is coming from, information technology usually receives low priority. Third World countries often end up working with outdated equipment.

Many of the applications for information technology involve dealing with large corporations and not many of these transactions are in Third World tongues. If the information is old or if literacy rates are low, what good is information? Many poor countries are agrarian-based; they find it prohibitive to invest monies in technological hardware.

Although basic needs must be met, ultimately the real power for developing countries is in acquiring knowledge. This is being attempted through agencies such as UNESCO and the International Labor Organization (ILO), among others. These and other regional agencies plan to bring technological and scientific information systems to developing countries to deal with similar problems. Information systems are necessary components of finding or maintaining effective water supplies and implementing sanitation, agricultural, and other crucial activities. Information systems were used in Mogadishu, Somalia to coordinate food distribution during famine conditions in 1993.

Often the first information systems created are those for library or university use. This allows access to a basic storehouse of knowledge that can be used for research and development and to provide a means to gain world information. In the Slovak and Czech republics, connection to computer networks is a recent development. Much of the funding for the networks is done through involvement and donations from outside the republics. The Federal Educational and Scientific Network (FESNet) is a plan to give access to academic networks such as Internet and the European Academic and Research Network (EARN).

Hungary is typical of a country in transition. The Information Infrastructure Development Project and other programs were launched to help Hungary adjust to increased privatization, a banking system overhaul, and other reforms by developing a nationwide networking infrastructure. The goal of the project was to provide a means to connect people in education, research, and administration to information available on the international networks. DEC and IBM helped connect universities to networks such as EARN, in part thinking that when the people are well educated and informed, they become potential customers.

Telecommunications and information networks help developing countries operate in the global community by providing them a means to coordinate development projects, pursue scientific study, and conduct business. Accessibility, accountability, and democracy in developing countries are all benefitting from information technology.

Objective 15.9   Describe services available through the global network Internet.

What Is the Internet?

Internet, which is comprised of thousands of computer networks linked together, can be accessed worldwide. Originally, Internet was used primarily by academia and the scientific community for conducting research. However, as services increased, the demand for access has risen to over 15 million users with some estimates of potential for growth at 1 million users per month.

Internet services include electronic mail, complete with your own Internet address. Users can join any of over 2,000 mailing lists to share information with others. Data are available on just about any subject, from job listings, stock prices, sports trivia, library catalogs, Supreme Court rulings, government documents, to scientific data, among others. Specific topics can be found using the Gopher menu system on Internet to search through thousands of computers around the world. A user can transfer files around the world and have access to literally thousands of newsgroups or Internet bulletin boards.

Businesses use Internet to connect with remote personal computers in other offices or to a mainframe or supercomputer without traveling to those locations. Industries such as health care, manufacturing, finance, and retail trade use Internet to connect with purchasers and suppliers around the world.

Users connect to Internet through organizations like the International Internet Association or through a gateway provided by on-line services including Prodigy, CompuServe, GEnie, and America Online. Users who need very high speed links to Internet use services offered through Sprint, AT&T, and Microelectronics and Computer Technology Corporation (MCC). Costs range from a few dollars to thousands of dollars a month depending on the connections and services used.

Objective 15.10   Identify trends in information systems use.

What Are the Trends in Information Systems Use?

Information systems are evolving to provide better standard access to information and greater ease of use. The goal is for a user to be able to quickly and easily access and use information systems to generate or retrieve information. Many improvements in information systems come from advances in hardware, software, user interface, and communication technologies. As these components become faster, more powerful, and easier to use, the overall performance of an information system also improves. Some examples are the development of more powerful processors and faster access to memory; development of operating systems that better handle real-time data analysis; improved user interfaces that offer users easier and more intuitive access to information; and "smarter," more feature-laden electronic mail programs that play a greater role in corporate communication.

As costs decline and performance and ease of use rises, LANs play a bigger role in corporate information systems. A trend termed "rightsizing" has organizations examining their information system applications to determine if they are running on the most efficient and economical equipment, also known as the computer platform. Many applications that once resided on mainframe or minicomputers have been transferred to more economical microcomputer servers on LANs. There has also been a trend to develop applications on a LAN using a client/server architecture. This allows the application to take advantage of the computer power of both the server and the LAN workstations.

More organizations are incorporating document-imaging technologies into their information systems. This involves converting documents contained on paper, microfilm, microfiche, and other electronic data into digital images. The digital images can then be faxed, printed, or viewed on the monitor by the appropriate individual(s). This makes the document readily available, reduces paper and hard copy file storage, and saves money. It often improves productivity. Connecticut Mutual Life Insurance Company uses document-imaging technology to reduce the time to process death claims from three weeks to three days, and the time for titles and beneficiary changes from days to seconds.

Moving documents through a business can be very time-consuming, much of it spent locating the relevant office or the appropriate person to respond. Work flow automation management software is a concept whereby a business examines how information travels through its organization. This exercise forces examination of procedures and elimination or reduction of untimely or unneeded steps. Once this procedure is set, work flow automation software tracks the information and gets it to the right place instantly.

Multimedia applications have been incorporated into some information systems. Accident reports for insurance companies and real estate sales are ideal applications. Data are easier to interpret when presented as a combination of sight, sound, and motion. As prices decrease, more multimedia applications will appear.

Objective 15.11   Understand how technology developments affect hardware, software, communications, and the user.

What Are the Emerging Directions in Technology?

While predicting the future is difficult, some technological advances and trends are recognizable. It is easy to predict that computers and related equipment will get faster, smaller, and cheaper. Computer technology will find new applications and computer manufacturers will strive to make computing easier. This section looks at recent advancements and speculates what's in store for the next few years in the areas of hardware, software, communication, and user interface.

Hardware

As can be expected, most hardware components will get smaller and faster, which means computers become smaller and can do more. Small computers such as the new personal digital assistants may give way to the portable office as more and more people work on the run. To keep up with the demand for increased performance, researchers have to look for alternatives to semiconductor technology for providing speed and power.

Personal Digital Assistants. Personal digital assistants (PDAs) such as Casio/Tandy's Zoomer and Apple/Sharp's Newton introduced a new era in computing. PDAs weigh about one pound, run on batteries, and fit in the palm of your hand. Applications include organizer functions like date book, address lists, and notebooks. For an additional cost, some have fax capabilities. Users combine text with handwritten messages on a single page. However, the 5-inch display size may limit the availability of traditional business applications. Data that you key into a PDA can be downloaded to your personal computer. Subsequent generations of PDAs may eventually boast capabilities comparable to the first supercomputers.

The smaller size of notebook and pen-based computers contributed to many advances and challenges to technology. These computers offer 2½-inch disk drives and VGA-quality LCD displays. Unfortunately, batteries have not kept up, but battery technologies such as zinc-air and lithium ion look to extend the time between recharging.

Some low power processors operate on 3.3 volts instead of 5 volts. Large volumes of power are consumed by magnetic rotating disks. Smaller disk drives (look for 1.8-inch drives) permit development of even smaller computers with the capability of running eight hours or more. Another solution to the power problem is flash memory. **Flash memory** is a type of silicon chip or card that retains its memory even when the power is turned off. These flash cards can be used as removable hard disks, but are more durable. However, they are more expensive than hard disks. The Fujitsu FMR-Card notebook computer that weighs only two pounds and runs for 100 hours uses this technology.

Chip Technologies. To increase the speed and power of computers, developments in how chips are made and what they are made of will probably shape the future of computing. These include the use of optics, superconductors, different materials, increased use of parallel processing, and new ways to store and access data.

Some experts think that the secret to the next generation of computers is in new chip designs to increase speed, power, and memory, rather than trying to squeeze more circuitry into smaller spaces. One option is found in optics (the use of light energy) instead of electricity for processing and storing data. An **optical computer** uses laser beams instead of electrical signals to perform the on/off switching. Photons, or light particles, move at ten times the speed of electrons and light beams can cross each other without causing interference—a common problem with electrical signals. The refinement of optical computers offers the possibility of robots with "eyesight." Potential uses are in high-speed graphic processing, where it could replace a supercomputer and many hours of work.

A working model, called a Bit Serial Optical Computer, was developed at the University of Colorado's Optoelectronic Computing Systems Center. The relatively simple machine gave credence to the feasibility of more complex parallel optical computers. Future optical computers will contain millions of switches connected by light using mirrors and holograms. They will truly be supercomputers on the desktop. Holographic technology, which stores bits of data at the molecular level, is being developed by IBM.

Superconducting materials may dramatically improve the speed of computers. The key feature of **superconductors** is the ability to work at low temperatures—near absolute zero (-473°F)—where there is little resistance to electricity. This lack of resistance means that on and off switching operations occur about 1,000 times faster than with silicon transistors. However, producing this switch is costly and if materials that become superconductors at higher temperatures could be used, this type of computing would be more feasible.

In a joint effort, Sandia National Laboratories, AT&T Bell Laboratories, and Conductus Inc. developed memory chips that can be accessed 10 times faster than those in current personal computers. There may be specialized applications, especially in digital communications, by the mid to late 1990s. Chips with this technology have tested clock speeds of 120G hertz, which is about 2,000 times faster than current personal computer clock speeds.

Other materials that are considered as replacements for the silicon that is used in most computer chips include gallium arsenide, ceramics, and synthetic diamonds. Gallium arsenide is made by combining arsenic and gallium and was the material used for Cray-3 supercomputer chips. Electrons move through gallium arsenide five times faster than through silicon. It has been used for more than fifteen years on a small scale in applications where silicon is too slow—transistors and small circuits in high-frequency microwave radio and satellite communication systems.

Semiconducting oxides, basically ceramics, are made from inexpensive elements, such as calcium and lutetium. The ceramic oxides become superconductors at higher temperatures without adding resistance.

Another discovery mixes methane and hydrogen in a simple and inexpensive process to produce a thin, synthetic diamond coating for use on chips as the base for circuitry. Electrons move faster through this material than through silicon.

The clock speed of most computer devices is determined using a quartz crystal. Quartz crystals work for today's computer speeds, but as faster speeds are required, quartz crystals begin to develop variations in their oscillations at their upper limits. Bellcore has developed a method that uses semiconductor lasers the size of a grain of sand to replace the traditional quartz clock. This technique may result in speeds ten times faster than computers with quartz crystal clocks.

Parallel Processing. Another promising technique for increasing computer speed and power is a combination of hardware and software. **Massively parallel processing (MPP)** links many processors so that greater volumes of data are processed simultaneously instead of in sequence, as with single-chip computers. Massively parallel processing was previously available only in supercomputers, but microprocessor improvements have brought parallel processing to personal computers, although on a smaller scale.

Parallel processing is accomplished in two basic ways. *Single instruction multiple data (SIMD)* machines operate on the same instructions but on different data (Figure 15.1). These are best suited for uniform

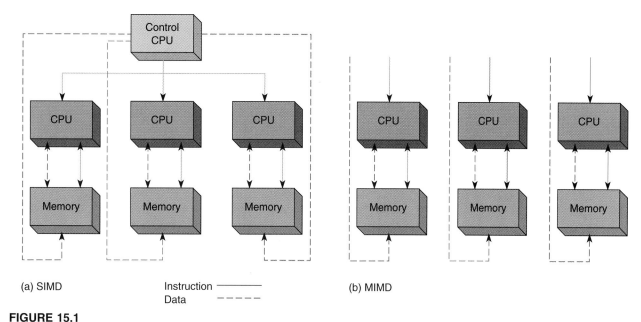

(a) SIMD   Instruction ———————   (b) MIMD
            Data   – – – – –

FIGURE 15.1
Parallel processing is accomplished in two basic ways. (a) Single instruction
multiple data (SIMD) machines operate on the same instructions but on different
data. (b) Multiple instruction multiple data (MIMD) machines assign different
portions of a single program to various processors and use different data.

and structured applications. *Multiple instruction multiple data (MIMD)* machines assign different portions of a single program to various processors and use different data. Applications for these machines include complex database searches that require more flexibility.

Mobil Oil uses a massively parallel processing system to create 3-D seismic images to locate energy reserves in the ocean. The computer contains 128 processors and reduces the time needed for certain seismic applications from 30 weeks to 10 days. Applications for MPP are limited by available software and are found mostly in commercial data processing and scientific and engineering fields. Some people believe that using millions of processors, all communicating with each other, it could be possible to create a computer with the ability to simulate human thinking processes.

Some scientists employ biomolecular technology with hopes of creating a biochip. **Biochips** are tiny circuits grown from the proteins and enzymes of living material. The circuits use oxygen and send signals similar to those sent and received by the human brain.

Storage Technology. Magnetic storage is a viable option for a long time. However, manufacturers are producing high-capacity superfloppy drives with large storage capacities using new materials such as metal particle and barium ferrite. New disk-drive technology includes the wet disk and the glass disk. The wet disk separates the disk drive heads from the rotating disk with liquid instead of air. The glass disk uses glass platters instead of aluminum. These methods allow data to be more densely written, thereby increasing the storage capacity. However, they are both more expensive than current technology.

AT&T Bell Laboratories developed new ways of storing data at much higher densities than are currently available on magnetic storage. The technology utilizes lasers and fiber optics and allows storage of 2 billion bits per inch—about 300 times more than magnetic storage and 100 times more than CD-ROM storage. Applications for this technology include high definition television and multimedia.

Reading to and writing from hard disks may take a giant leap soon with developments from IBM's Adstar subsidiary. They found a practical way to use giant magneto-resistance, a discovery made by French scientists in 1988, in a read/write head. Predictions are that by the year 2000 densities of 10 billion bits per inch are possible. This means a 3.5-inch disk drive could contain the equivalent of 10,000 300-page books.

Hardware add-in boards for CD-quality sound, high resolution graphics, and digital video are available for the desktop user. Hardware advances also spawn growth in noncomputer devices. Televisions and computers are expected to merge into one device offering interactive television programming. Copiers are equipped with storage devices for image capturing, and disk drives are found in printers, facsimile machines, and other document-imaging equipment.

Software

Software generally lags behind hardware development. It is often difficult to write and meet the demands of users. From the time the software is conceived, tested, retested, and offered for sale, what was originally a powerful package may be obsolete. Software development is taking a new turn, however. Instead of adding new features, new approaches are sought to deliver those features.

Computers have taken on some traditional paper and pencil applications. By the 1996–97 school year, students will take the Graduate Record Examination (GRE) on a computer. Scores will be available immediately instead of six weeks later.

One trend seen is the transition from application-based computing to document-based computing. With document application programming the user has all the necessary tools: spreadsheet, database, word processing, among others, all available in a single document. With this program, the type of document to be created is defined after the user is in the program rather than deciding which program to initially load as with application-based computing. This approach results in less duplication of program code than with separate application programs. Examples of this approach are seen with object-oriented products such as Microsoft's Object Linking and Embedding (OLE) and Apple's Open Collaborative Environment (OCE).

Operating Systems. To facilitate document-based programming, operating systems are moving toward object-oriented operating systems (OOP). Operating systems will take more responsibility for applications. The OOP will play an integral part in giving the user more control over how data are linked and shared. Evidence of the importance of OOP operating systems is found in the joint venture by Apple and IBM to develop a microprocessor-based object-oriented operating system.

New operating systems will focus on object linking, message passing, and data sharing. Object linking was first used in NewWave by Hewlett-Packard. Microsoft's object linking and embedding technology allows data and code to reside (i.e., be embedded) in another application and was first used in Excel 3.0. It is expected that applications will become objects that can be linked into new user-defined applications. The operating system will take on a new role as message passer between the objects.

Pen-based and other small computers' operating systems have become more portable. Data accumulated in the field using a portable computer may later have to be dumped (i.e., entered) into any number of desktop computers; therefore, operating systems will need to be compatible.

To handle the increased load, powerful 32-bit operating systems such as OS/2 and Windows NT incorporate multitasking capabilities. These are competing with and edging out more traditional DOS-based operating systems, especially in high-end microcomputing.

Interoperability. **Interoperability** is referred to as using hardware and software from different vendors interchangeably. For end users, it means not having to learn machine-specific operating system commands. Application programs would "look and feel" the same on any system and data from one application could be readily linked to the next. Interoperability should lead to increased productivity and competitiveness for businesses. We've seen a beginning of this concept with the introduction of the Power PC computers in 1994.

Local-Area Networks. As local-area networks (LANs) increase in popularity, software packages are required in both single-station and multiuser network versions. The goal is better and more universal data access. More access often leads to security problems and has proven to be a boon to developers of antivirus and security software.

Visualization. In part because of advances in microprocessor speed and power, and availability of large amounts of memory, visualization software is finding more applications on microcomputers. Some applications, such as heat mapping, where much numerical data is gathered, is best interpreted in graphical form. Data visualization provides the benefits of analyzing numeric data graphically, comprehending complex information more obviously, and viewing data multidimensionally.

Three-dimensional representations aid in understanding and diagnosing of many problems. In Canada, doctors at the University of Saskatchewan use three-dimensional visualizations of ovarian follicles to study ovarian cancer. The computer analysis of a tumor structure allows them to determine if it is malignant or benign. Visualization applications extend beyond science and medicine. For example, foreign exchange traders at Chemical Bank use it to quickly determine the relative strength of foreign currencies.

Software capabilities will see developments in artificial intelligence, expert systems, natural language processing, neural networks, and fuzzy logic.

Artificial Intelligence. **Artificial intelligence (AI)** is the capability of computers to simulate the functions of the human brain. Programs that use

1998, 1999, 2000! "I expect there will be some who aren't going to notice until it happens." What Peter Weinberger, director of software and system research at AT&T Bell Laboratories, is referring to is how computers will be prepared to handle the change of dates from 1999 to 2000.

When computers, especially mainframes, were first used memory conservation was very important. One area where conservation was thought to be appropriate was excluding the first two numbers of the year, i.e., 1950 simply became 50. The possible ramifications for the year 2000 didn't enter into many people's minds. After all, that was a long time in the future. But now the time's arrived and there may be big problems for many businesses.

Software written for computers that use two digits instead of four for the date take the larger number to be the later date. This means many programs will interpret 99, or 1999, as a later date than 00, or 2000. This could have disastrous outcomes—for example, compounding bank account interest, sorting data by dates, and computing ages by deducting the year of birth (a smaller number) from this year (a larger number). In the year 2000, your age will register as a negative number! And imagine the problems created by a check written in 1999; the bank could misread the date and assume that it was 99 years old.

Some companies sell software to test your computer system to see how it handles the change of dates. It may sound trivial but changing a database or other program everywhere a date is used is not an easy task. It won't be done overnight, and the costs worldwide, including design, could approach $75 billion.

Torrington Co., a division of Ingersoll-Rand Co., has been working on the century date change issue since 1991. An internal group discovered that 30 percent of its programs and 25 percent of its files and databases would be affected. Correction costs could range from as little as $35,000 to as much as $3.5 million.

A Brooklyn, New York, newsletter, "Tick, Tick, Tick," makes subscribers aware of many of these problems. They even ran a contest seeking the Worst-Case Scenario. Hopefully, that won't be the case when the millennium changes. Tick. Tick. Tick.

AI do not use step-by-step procedures (algorithms) to solve problems; they operate on values that infer uncertainty. For example, how far is far when you say, "Sue lives far away?" Because the AI program does not rely on answers preprogrammed by a human, the software determines the outcome. AI incorporates parts of other concepts such as expert systems, natural language processing, neural networks, and fuzzy logic.

Expert Systems. Software programs that store the knowledge of a human expert and then serve as consultants in particular fields are called **expert systems.** NASA increasingly relies on expert systems and advanced computers to prepare for retirement of experienced personnel. Thus, when current scientists and engineers retire, the agency will maintain the same quality of decision making and train new personnel simultaneously. Expert systems in medicine are instrumental in diagnosing illness while service/repair technicians use them in analyzing equipment malfunctions.

Natural Language Processing. **Natural language processing** is the capacity of a computer to "understand" human language and translate it into instructions upon which to act. For example, you could request a list of customers from a database by typing, "Print a list of customers with an outstanding balance greater than $500." It is expected that future systems using language-processing software will understand language input in any form, from any speaker, and translate it into any other language.

Neural Networks. Another way to give machines human "intelligence" is through neural network computing. A regular computer processes information in a chainlike preprogrammed sequence, but **neural networks** are organized like a grid where information is shared and tasks are performed simultaneously—just as the brain does. Research on biological neural networks provides models for developing "intelligent" computers.

A neural network differs from an expert system in that the expert system is fed only data that allow it to make a conclusion about a relatively narrow subject. It follows the "If this is so, then what?" pattern of reasoning, and it does not increase the size of its database by its own actions. A neural network, however, handles broader topics and adds to its database.

Neural networks and expert systems can work together. As one scientist differentiated them, "A neural network tells the difference between an [enemy] tank and a [friendly] tank and an expert system tells whether to shoot."

Fuzzy Logic. Traditionally programmers break up conditions and processes into distinct "either" or "or" divisions, for example, the choices of on or off, odd or even, and black or white. This approach doesn't address situations in which conditions change rapidly. **Fuzzy logic** provides the ability for a computer to make "decisions" based on varying data much the same way as a human would. It is a simple matter to program a computer to turn up the heat when the room temperature is at a certain level and turn it off when the temperature is above that level. This is an example of an on or off decision. It doesn't take into account humidity, efficient use of fuel, the number of people in the room, or their level of activity. All of these factors affect the amount of heat required.

To program a computer according to fuzzy logic involves many more variables than traditional programming. It is a valuable addition to artificial intelligence technology, where computers simulate the actions of the human mind. So far, Japanese scientists have made the most of fuzzy logic, applying it to subway systems, transmission and braking mechanisms, stock market investment programs, and automobile traffic controls. Spreadsheet programs such as FuziCalc from FuziWare Inc. use fuzzy logic algorithms to perform scenario analysis. Users enter a range of data into each cell and perform multiple scenario calculations giving a range of results.

Communication

Computer communication involves hardware, software, services, and the ability to integrate all three in a productive manner. The ability of a computer to communicate is one of its most powerful characteristics. One of the most exciting developments is wireless computing.

Wireless Computing. **Wireless computing** implements the technologies of cellular, infrared, and radio frequencies so that computers communicate without a conducting medium such as copper wire. Although cellular is the most popular, radio frequency (RF) modems will become more prevalent with the Federal Communications Commission (FCC) standardization of frequencies for data communications. Portable computers are most likely to use wireless communications. A portable system from GO Corp. recognizes the presence of a wireless LAN and transmits messages to the pen-based computer that you hold in your hand as you walk into the room. Rearranging an office would be easier if the devices did not require rewiring.

In response to the rapid development of wireless communication, the FCC in late 1993 made the decision to auction parts of the frequency spectrum for Personal Communication Services (PCS). Many frequencies will go to common carriers, but some are destined for private use so businesses can create their own wireless data networks. The PCS frequencies are much higher than cellular and use a different transmission technique. Transmission on PCS frequencies reduces interference between services and increases data security. In addition, because PCS is a digital system, it will be easier to maintain data integrity. By the end of this century it is estimated that there will be over 15 million users on wireless computing networks.

While applications such as sending text manuals over the digital highway might save trees, the real potential lies in the ability to transmit voice and full motion video cost effectively over the airwaves.

Teleconferencing. Existing satellite technology allows the networking of computers and their stored information—not just among companies and organizations but among nations. Information can be sold, shared, and traded to open new markets for products and services. Advances in satellite communication and interactive capabilities made teleconferencing an important method for conducting business and education. This fueled the home market by facilitating interactive television. In Birmingham, Michigan, families use the Interactive Channel on cable television to communicate with teachers and review homework assignments or other school projects. Television is more than a one-way medium.

On-line service products are easier to access and use. To attract customers, services will be more interactive so users can obtain the information and get off-line quickly to save money. New developments in technology allow faster data transfer and bring applications such as multimedia to on-line services.

Advances in video compression and transmission over a network brought teleconferencing to the desktop. Components required include hardware and software for video capturing, compression, cameras, speakers, microphones, and software for sharing computer applications.

Information Highway. In 1993 President Bill Clinton sent an initiative to Congress to invest upward of $20 billion to create an "information highway." It included money for private research and development, investment tax credits, and relaxed technology export controls. The Telecommunication Infrastructure Act of 1993 proposed to lower costs of video conferences, real-time telecommunications, and real-time multimedia applications. A billion-dollar market is expected for these services.

The National Information Infrastructure (NII), as the information highway was dubbed, planned to bring information to those who need it. Applications involve acquiring information for health care, education, electronic commerce, telecommuting, entertainment, and information access in general.

The NII is conceptual and when it is to be implemented is as yet unknown. However, the need for this information sharing has been recognized and it will provide benefits to all who avail themselves of the electronic superhighway.

User Interface

User interface begins as soon as you turn on the computer; it is probably the most important part of computing, especially to the novice user. Macintosh always implemented a GUI, and because of the emergence of Windows, MS-DOS computers do too. A GUI reduces the learning curve for new users and gives a consistent look across applications.

The greatest progress for users is expected to be in the way data are entered into the computer, including pen-based computers, pointing devices, and speech input. Pen-based computers allow users to enter data by writing on the screen rather than using a keyboard. They are small enough to carry and some are equipped with screens of embedded intelligence called **smart paper**. The user enters "2 × 5 =" and the answer "10" appears on the smart paper. Spelling is checked and corrected as it is entered and a rough sketch of a square object can be converted into a perfect square.

New pointing devices are built into computers. The Isopoint, found in Grid laptops, controls the cursor through a thumb-manipulated roller tube. Minijoysticks are built into the J-key of the keyboard, an important innovation for portable computers where space to use a mouse is at a premium.

Voice Recognition. Voice input gives the greatest freedom for computer users. Kurzweil and Dragon Systems make devices that recognize thousands of words. These systems are being used by physically challenged individuals and professionals in the field of medicine. The ability to recognize the voice of the speaker using ordinary conversational speech has proven to be a major stumbling block, but greater advances in speech recognition systems are expected as microprocessor technology continues to expand.

Voice recognition will find applications in telephone services. Nynex, AT&T, and U.S. West plan to use voice recognition technology for operator-assisted calls, dialing, messaging, and other features. Complex software allows the user to "converse" with a computer rather than a live operator through a series of standard questions. Answers are recognized regardless of stammers, pauses, or grammatically incorrect responses. This may displace thousands of operators, but companies hope to place most workers in other jobs.

Major companies like IBM and Microsoft are introducing sophisticated voice recognition software and hardware for personal computers. IBM's Speech Server Series allows a user to enter data and control the PC by voice. Developments in digital-signal processing help voice recognition in applications where dictation plays a large part, such as medicine, law offices, and police work.

Japan is responsible for most of the speech translation software, but researchers at Carnegie Mellon have developed a prototype application that allows a person wearing a data glove to make American Sign Language hand signals and arm movements that are subsequently translated, synthesized, and spoken through computer equipment.

Virtual Reality. Applications in virtual reality are also on the horizon. **Virtual reality** is the integration of color, sound, and animation in a "wrap-around" environment that offers the capability of three-dimensional applications. Virtual reality systems allow the user to "step into" the animated environment and to sense the position of an object (x, y, and z coordinates) and its orientation (pitch, roll, and yaw) to the position of the user's head. Virtual reality devices include goggles through which the user can see in 3-D, and a glove to manipulate the 3-D entities.

Some systems add virtual sound as an enhancement of the experience. Sounds seem to emanate from a stable point. In other words, if you turn your head to the right the sound doesn't move as it does when you wear a headset. Instead the sound appears to be coming from the same point as when you were facing it. You get the feeling of moving away from the sound.

Experiments using virtual reality can be conducted without encountering the costly or destructive trial-and-error process that occurs in real-life situations. A common example is found in the flight simulator where pilots learn to deal with conditions such as fuel loss, engine failure, low visibility, insufficient runway space, or other potential calamities. Everything looks terrifyingly real. The pilot works the controls properly and "saves" the craft, or improperly and "loses" it. Happily, none of the mistakes are fatal—or expensive. Applications for virtual reality are seen in the fields of finance, science, education, architecture, and aviation, to name a few. NASA used it to train astronauts to repair the Hubble space telescope.

Virtual reality is moving from the realm of video games to everyday applications. Most business applications are found in architecture, design, and training. BioControl Systems in California developed a device called the Biomuse, which permits interface in a virtual environment through use of eye, muscle, and brain signals rather than a traditional mouse or joystick. One young quadriplegic used the Biomuse to "fly" in the virtual environment by puffing his cheeks and twitching his forehead. Hospitals are exploring the Biomuse for use in applications such as medical rehabilitation and minimally invasive surgery.

Virtual reality research was given support through President Clinton's VR Technology Task Group, which recognizes the possibilities of virtual reality. Early in 1994 the committee recommended that the government provide funding for virtual reality research at major laboratories and universities.

Surgeons from Brigham and Women's Hospital in Boston and General Electric scientists are working to develop 3-D images that can be consulted during brain surgery to aid in diagnosis by providing data on the size and weight of a tumor. The 3-D images are developed from magnetic resonance images and can be rotated, pivoted, and layered to expose various parts of the brain.

A virtual reality application called Wheelchair VR from Prairie Virtual Systems allows architects to see how patients in wheelchairs will be able to move around in a new building before it is constructed.

User Concerns Now and in the Future. Other factors that affect users include technophobia, accessibility, and computer-related injuries. Technophobia, or fear of technology—in this case, computers—causes sweaty palms, heart palpitations, and headaches for as many as one-third of the approximately 14 million college students in the United States, according to some researchers. These fears can be learned from parents, teachers, friends, or caused by a stressful introduction to new equipment. It was expected that the generation of students who grew up playing hand-held video games would be less likely to be technophobic, but the phenomenon persists.

Assuming that you are *not* a member of the technophobic student population, you may still have problems with computers—access to equipment on your campus. Often labs are crowded, have short hours, lack support staff, or are not hooked into networks. Solving these problems should be a priority of higher education administrators to improve the learning environment.

If access is no problem and you work at a computer any time you want for as long as you want, you may suffer computer-related injuries such as eye strain, stiff necks, and lower-back pain. Additionally, when people use keyboards they often stay in the same position for long periods of time. Their wrists and fingers are subjected to repetitive-motion injuries. Typewriter users had to hit carriage returns and they had to stop typing occasionally to reload paper, use correction fluid or lift-off tape and before that erasers, so they were less likely to be affected by these problems. Many injuries are not curable, so be sure to take preventative measures. Maintain an ergonomically designed work space and divide typing assignments into smaller segments so you are not typing continuously for large blocks of time. Give yourself an opportunity to stretch, rest your eyes, and finish other tasks in between.

An eightfold increase in trauma disorders such as carpal tunnel syndrome occurred over the last ten years. This led to a dramatic increase in the number of health-related computer items such as new keyboard designs and wrist and elbow rest pads. No doubt this will fuel developments in alternative methods of input.

Objective 15.12   Explain how green computing affects the environment.

What Is Green Computing and How Does the Computer Affect the Environment?

After April of 1993, the federal government was directed to buy only "green" computers. **Green computers** are those computers and related equipment that fit an ecological profile set by the Environmental Protection Agency (EPA) Energy Star Computers Program. Following are some guidelines. Computers and monitors cannot use more than 30 watts of power each when idle. The equipment must be able to "power down" or automatically go into an idle or low-power mode when not being used. These computers have no fans, have lower power microprocessors, and are equipped with power-management software, thus requiring less demand for power. Computers without fans are less noisy and monitors with low emissions reduce radiation risks. Since the U.S. government is the largest purchaser of computers in the world, manufacturers have a real incentive to produce green computers.

The EPA estimates that computers use about 5 percent of commercially consumed power. Use of green computers could cut energy consumption by half according to their estimates—enough to power Maine, Vermont, and New Hampshire annually. The EPA also estimates that the equivalent carbon dioxide emissions of five million cars could be saved because of the reduced production of electricity. Green computers are identifiable by the Energy Star logo—a star with the word "energy" written in script part way through it (Figure 15.2). The greening of the computer industry includes replacing nonbiodegradable packing materials with recyclable packaging materials and printing manuals on recycled paper. Although green computers may cost more money, savings for the environment are worthwhile.

Peripheral equipment is going green. Kyocera Electronics, Inc. substituted the laser printer toner cartridge with a silicon drum. Because it never needs replacing, waste deposited in landfills is reduced. A company called

FIGURE 15.2
The Energy Star logo identifies a "green" computer. (Courtesy IPC Technologies, Inc.)

Greendisk recycles old floppy diskettes. Software firms such as Autodesk Inc., which previously threw out hundreds of thousands of floppy diskettes that contained old versions of their software, are sending them to Greendisk where they are reformatted and sold as recycled diskettes. The environment wins because of less trash, and consumers win with lower diskette prices.

Objective 15.13   Recognize how computers are changing careers.

How Are Computers Affecting Careers?

No matter what your chosen career, it will likely involve computers. Even if you are not a system analyst, programmer, or other computer specialist, your job will probably require that you use a computer. This section describes computer occupations as well as other professions in which computers will play an important role. In fact, you may start out by using a computer, on-line services, and software to help you find a job.

Computer Professional Careers

Computer professional careers are directly involved with computers. Most of these occupations require higher education with a minimum of a bachelor's degree.

System analysts are strategists and planners who design and improve information systems. They analyze the problems of the current system, decide how to solve them, determine which data to collect, and ascertain the processing steps needed to get the information to the user. This process results in the criteria for an algorithm.

A **programmer** codes the instructions that tell the computer how to solve a problem. Programmers code the algorithm, designed by the system analyst to solve a problem, into a programming language making sure that it all works. In a small organization, the jobs of programmer and system analyst are sometimes combined and called programmer/analyst. Application programmers write programs for users to solve problems; system programmers write programs that run the computer.

The increase in the number and size of databases in government and business creates a need for someone to coordinate all the elements. **Database administrators** design, implement, and maintain the database. They monitor users and data security and direct and plan all the elements required to maintain a database. Database administrators consult with others in the organization to determine their information needs and decide the best ways to access that information. They also help other managers plan the collection, storage, and organization of the data.

The **information system manager** plans and oversees all the information resources in an organization. This is one of the higher level computer positions, although the title may vary depending on the size and structure of the enterprise. The title might be management information system (MIS) director, information system manager, or data processing manager. This person needs technical knowledge about the system development process as well as managerial and leadership skills to oversee and motivate the programmers, system analysts, and computer operators in a data processing or MIS department. This person must be familiar with the overall goals and information needs of the business.

Many other jobs developed from and relate to the computer industry, including:

- Service technicians who install and repair computers and equipment, e.g., damaged disk drives, tape drives, keyboards, and circuit boards
- Sales representatives who sell computer equipment and software
- Technical writers with experience in a particular specialized area who explain in nontechnical terms how to use the equipment and software; they write user manuals, operator manuals, and software documentation
- Security personnel who specialize in techniques to protect the computer room, hardware, programs, and the data and information stored
- Electronic data processing (EDP) auditors who monitor and evaluate computer operations to ensure that there are no incidents of fraud or misuse of the system
- Hardware developers who formulate new ideas using the latest technology to design computer hardware and chip circuitry
- Software engineers who create and write new system programs (e.g., operating systems) and new application programs for business (e.g., word processors, spreadsheets, database management software) or for entertainment (e.g., video games)
- Network designers, telecommunication specialists, who design and improve computer networks

How Computers Affect Other Jobs

It is likely that utilizing computers or handling information will be necessary to perform your job. Here are some of the ways computers affect noncomputer careers.

- A graphic artist designs logos for television programs or art for music videos with computers and graphics software. Movie and television producers and special-effects creators produce unusual scenes with computer images and simulations.
- Journalists enter news stories from computer terminals or PCs. Copy editors revise text on a computer and transmit it via telecommunications to publishing personnel who typeset it electronically and print the final story on computer-controlled presses.
- Physicians prescribe diagnostic tests for their patients by computer-controlled tools, and most coordinate their office management by computer.
- Technicians in hospital laboratories operate computerized testing equipment, store the results in a computer, and retrieve them upon request.
- Secretaries use computers for word processing; some also implement financial applications to handle budgets and keep expense records.
- Automobile mechanics employ computer diagnostics to pinpoint engine troubles.

- Teachers use computers to expedite research, design learning materials, and keep student records, and also encourage students to use computers as study aids.
- Managers retrieve information from a database in the form of reports; they send messages and schedule appointments using computers.

Opportunities to use computers abound in all careers. Almost every occupation needs specialists with knowledge of that field, and the skills and knowledge to know how computers can enhance their positions.

Using Computers to Find a Job

Computers can help you find a job. Job-hunting software falls into two major categories, those that help you in advance, such as resume preparation, and on-line services that advertise career positions.

Some software packages contain various templates for cover letters, eliminating the problem of formatting the letter yourself. Resume-writing software often includes different types of resume templates designed for specific jobs, i.e., engineering or business. Programs such as Career Directions by Cambridge Career Products help determine where your professional interests lie. Many programs analyze specific career objectives.

Job hunts can be conducted using on-line computer services and bulletin boards like the Career Network, an on-line employment service. These services are used by people looking for work, employers, and college placement offices. In addition to specialized services, CompuServe and Prodigy allow a version of a help wanted ad. Operated by the Professional Association of Resume Writers, the National Resume Bank is a service where subscribers electronically post their resumes.

It's clear that this introduction to computers is just the beginning. You will see that computers are widespread in your school, your country, and throughout your world.

Summary

The power of the computer extends beyond the United States. Computers and computing influence international monetary transactions, information gathering, strategic communications, and allow information to reach individuals under difficult government situations. The U.S., Japan, the European Community, and the rest of the world are key participants in an ongoing race for computer and information technology leadership.

Obstacles when computing across nations are solvable. Cooperation among nations is essential to deliver productive worldwide communication networks. The information brought by these networks can have a lasting impact on developing nations as well as the rest of the world.

Trends in information systems involve new methods to facilitate the dispersal of information. These include better and more standardized access to information, better user interfaces, and better connectivity. Many advancements that make information systems better come through improvements in hardware, software, communication, and user interface technology.

Hardware developments include pen-based computing, smaller disk drives with more capacity, new chip-making techniques, and methods to improve processing power and speed such as light energy and holographic technology.

Software developments include object-oriented programming and GUIs. Other software developments will be in artificial intelligence, expert systems, natural language processing, neural networks, and fuzzy logic.

Interoperability is referred to as using hardware and software from different vendors interchangeably. End users do not have to learn machine-specific operating system commands. Interoperability should increase productivity and competition for business.

Communication developments are highlighted by wireless communication abilities. Communication on-line services will be easier to access and interact with. Televisions and computers are expected to merge into one device offering interactive television programming. Some families communicate with teachers and review homework assignments or other school projects with computers.

Most computer interaction will occur through a GUI. New devices spurred by pen-based computing alter the way data are entered into the computer. These technologies include handwriting capabilities, smart paper, minijoysticks, voice input, and virtual reality.

Green computing focuses on environmental issues. Using less electricity and producing less waste are goals toward which computer manufacturers strive.

Other factors affecting users include technophobia, accessibility, and computer-related injuries. Fear of technology causes sweaty palms, heart palpitations, and headaches. It can be learned or caused by a stressful introduction to new equipment. Familiarity with video games has not radically diminished the phenomenon. Accessibility to computers is a problem—labs are crowded, have short hours, lack support staff, or are not hooked into networks.

Computer-related injuries such as eye strain, stiff necks, lower-back pain, and repetitive-motion injuries are prevalent for users who stay in the same position for an extended time. Ergonomic design of work space and shorter periods of time spent on continuous typing tasks are ways to avoid injuries.

Many jobs are directly related to and in fact came about because of computers. Most other jobs are dependent on the computer.

Job applicants use computers to search for a job through software programs designed to help the applicant write a cover letter or a resume. On-line computer services provide a method for electronically posting resumes or looking through help wanted ads.

VOCABULARY SELF-TEST

Can you define the following terms?

artificial intelligence (AI) (p. 545)	expert system (p. 546)
biochip (p. 543)	flash memory (p. 541)
database administrator (p. 553)	fuzzy logic (p. 547)

green computers (p. 552)

information system manager (p. 553)

interoperability (p. 545)

massively parallel processing (MPP) (p. 542)

natural language processing (p. 547)

neural network (p. 547)

optical computer (p. 541)

parallel processing (p. 542)

programmer (p. 553)

smart paper (p. 549)

superconductor (p. 542)

system analyst (p. 553)

virtual reality (p. 550)

wireless computing (p. 548)

REVIEW QUESTIONS

Multiple Choice

1. One drawback to portable computers is their _____ .
   a. CPU speed
   b. disk drives
   c. battery life
   d. weight

2. Tiny circuits grown from living matter are called _____ .
   a. superconductors
   b. ceramics
   c. biochips
   d. glass disks

3. Which of the following is not a method of wireless computing?
   a. cellular
   b. radio frequencies
   c. infrared
   d. coaxial

4. The capability of computers to "think" like humans is called _____ .
   a. future shock
   b. multiple processing
   c. artificial intelligence
   d. robotics engineering

5. The software that stores data and knowledge for later use as a consultant in a particular field is called _____ .
   a. an expert system
   b. fuzzy logic
   c. a knowledge base
   d. a knowledge program

6. _____ is the ability of the computer to understand and translate everyday language.
   a. Multiple processing
   b. Artificial intelligence
   c. Parallel processing
   d. Natural language processing

7. The integration of color, sound, and animation in a "wraparound environment" is called _____ .
    a. virtual reality
    b. pen-based computing
    c. natural language processing
    d. an expert system
8. A green computer must power down when idle to less than _____ watt(s).
    a. 1
    b. 5
    c. 10
    d. 30
9. Some people suggest that _____ are the breakthrough to propel computer technology into the next generation of computers.
    a. virtual reality
    b. further miniaturization of chips
    c. artificial intelligence
    d. new chip designs
10. _____ uses hardware and software from different vendors interchangeably.
    a. Operability
    b. Robotics
    c. Interoperability
    d. Flexibility

Fill-In

1. Silicon memory that retains its contents when the power is turned off is called _____ .
2. Document imaging technology converts documents contained on paper, microfilm, microfiche, and other electronic data into _____ .
3. Embedded intelligence in a screen is called _____ .
4. Low voltage chips decrease the _____ requirements in portable computers and make battery life longer.
5. _____ computers use multiple processors to process data and instructions.
6. A new type of data storage being developed works by storing data on the molecular level called _____ technology.
7. An operating system that combines data and code into an object is called a(n) _____ operating system.
8. Wireless computing is accomplished through three basic technologies: _____ , _____ , and _____ .
9. The standards for green computers are set by the _____ , an agency of the U.S. government.
10. The _____ is in charge of designing, implementing, and maintaining a database.

Short Answer

1. Briefly describe how global events affect computing.
2. Describe how an organization might develop a "global mentality."
3. Describe three obstacles that may hinder global computing.
4. What is a joint venture? Give a reason why one is formed.
5. How can information networks help a developing nation?
6. What are some areas where research is being conducted to give machines "intelligence"?
7. What is wireless computing?
8. What types of applications do you think could benefit from developments in virtual reality?
9. How does fuzzy logic differ from traditional step-by-step programs?
10. Briefly relate what is meant by green computing.

Issues for Thought

1. Discuss emerging technologies and theorize which ones will become most widely used and which might fall by the wayside.
2. Are you involved in green computing? Your school? Your employer? Discuss the benefits and drawbacks of being ecologically concerned.

Infomodule

A History of Computers

As soon as humans domesticated animals and started to carry on trade with others, they needed to keep track of numbers. First, people used their fingers. Then they used notches on sticks, counting stones, and even knots tied in ropes. The abacus, a rudimentary computing device, evolved in different cultures at about the same time. This simple device, which uses beads to represent digits and wires to hold places, is still used today.

PEOPLE AND THEIR CONTRIBUTIONS

As early as the seventeenth century, mathematicians and other scholars were eager to create a machine that could add, subtract, multiply, and divide numbers. Initially, the evolution of computing devices proceeded slowly. Yet an interesting thing happened with numbers. John Napier, a Scotsman, discovered a way to manipulate numbers that would reduce multiplications and divisions to additions and subtractions—logarithms. Then Robert Bissaker invented the slide rule, which helped solve complex problems relatively quickly.

Blaise Pascal, a French mathematician and philosopher, invented the first mechanical digital calculator, which could perform addition and subtraction on whole numbers. The Pascaline (Figure 1), developed around 1640, was a financial failure. It was cheaper to have human labor perform the calculations, workers feared losing their jobs, and only Pascal could repair the machine. However, Pascal's concept of a decimal counting wheel using gears with ten teeth and one

FIGURE 1
The Pascaline. (Courtesy of International Business Machines Corp.)

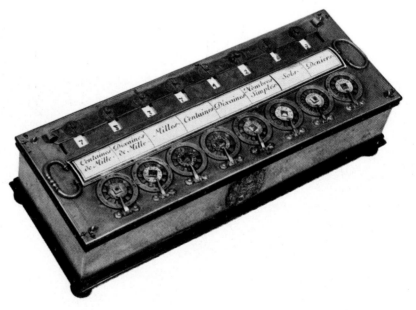

carrying tooth wasn't made obsolete until the development of the electronic calculator. A programming language, Pascal, was later named to honor his contributions.

Nineteenth-Century Technology

In 1804, the French inventor Joseph Marie Jacquard built an automated punched-card machine (Figure 2) that was used to operate weaving looms. Jacquard's invention used data coded on cards joined to create a series of instructions to automate weaving. This use of programmed instructions was a concept of great importance to modern computers. However, workers in the mills feared this kind of automation would cost them their jobs.

In the 1800s, a British inventor and mathematician, Charles P. Babbage, designed an all-purpose problem-solving machine, the difference engine (Figure 3), which had a mechanical memory to store results. He also designed, but never built, an analytical engine that would have required half a dozen steam engines and would have taken up the space of a football field. Babbage's concepts led to the modern computer and earned him the title "father of the computer."

Babbage's confidante and partner, Augusta Ada, the daughter of poet Lord Byron and later Countess of Lovelace, understood Babbage's ideas, recognized their great value, and in the 1840s translated and wrote scientific papers defining them for others. She suggested using a binary system rather than the

FIGURE 2
Jacquard's loom. (Courtesy of International Business Machines Corp.)

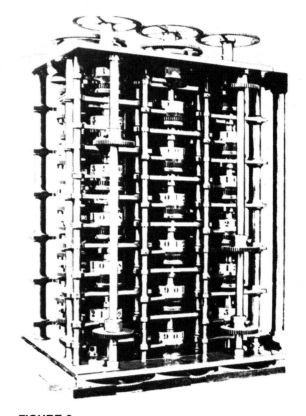

FIGURE 3
Babbage's difference engine. (Courtesy of International Business Machines Corp.)

decimal system for storage. Lady Lovelace is sometimes called the first programmer because she also refined the design of the analytical engine to include the automatic repetition of a series of calculations—the loop. This looping procedure is extremely valuable to today's programmers.

George Boole, a self-taught English mathematician of the 1850s, realized that complex mathematical problems could be solved by reducing them to a series of questions answered either affirmatively or negatively. The binary system of 1s for positive answers and 0s for negative answers is thus implemented. This theory of Boolean logic became fundamental to the design of computer circuitry.

Later, in the 1880s, Dr. Herman Hollerith built the first electromechanical punched-card data-processing machine (Figure 4), which tabulated and sorted the data from the 1890 census. His Tabulating Machine Company was one of the companies that later became IBM.

Early Twentieth-Century Technology

There is a time gap in the computer's history after Hollerith. Progress was being made, but nothing spectacular was reported. However, by 1931, at Massachusetts Institute of Technology (MIT), Vannevar Bush and his colleagues created, modified, and perfected a differential analyzer, which was an electronic machine that solved simple differential equations. Although the mechanism resembled a giant dishpan with projecting steel rods, it was a mechanical analog computing device. It performed calculations by the rotation of various shafts.

George Stibitz, a research mathematician at Bell Telephone Laboratory, tinkered with the idea that Boolean logic provided a natural language for electromechanical circuits. His device, created in 1937 from batteries, flashlight bulbs, wire, and tobacco-can strips of metal, controlled the flow of electricity. The Complex Number Calculator machine was a binary

FIGURE 4
Hollerith's punched-card machine. (Courtesy of International Business Machines Corp.)

adder—a basic requirement for all future digital computers. In 1940, Stibitz and his colleague Samuel Williams successfully demonstrated that this device could send calculations over a distance of 250 miles using teletype machines.

In Iowa in 1939, John Atanasoff and Clifford Berry collaborated to build the Atanasoff-Berry Computer (ABC). The ABC (Figure 5), the world's first general-purpose electronic digital computer, did not generate a lot of interest in the scientific community even though its purpose was to solve simultaneous linear algebraic equations. In fact, when Dr. Atanasoff contacted IBM about his machine, the company said that it would never be interested in an electronic computing machine.

Vacuum Tube Technology

In 1941, during World War II, Konrad Zuse built the first operational general-purpose computer in Germany. His machine used binary logic even though Zuse had not heard of George Boole. Zuse proposed an updated model that used vacuum tubes instead of electromechanical relays to increase the speed a thousandfold and suggested that the machine be used by the military to compare and evaluate aircraft designs and to break wartime codes. But Adolf Hitler

FIGURE 5
The Atanasoff-Berry Computer (ABC). (Courtesy of Iowa State University)

refused funding, saying that the war would be over before the two years Zuse needed to finish the machine.

Fortunately for the Allies, the Polish secret service smuggled a replica of the German message-scrambling device, Enigma, to the British. Alan Turing, an eccentric English genius, unraveled the mysteries of the Enigma. In 1943, Turing and his colleagues capitalized on the vacuum-tube technology that Zuse had wanted to pursue. The British machine could process 25,000 characters per second. In 1950, Turing also constructed the Automatic Computer Engine (ACE), which was touted as the first (arguably) programmable digital computer.

Most of the industries in the United States rallied to support the war effort. Thomas J. Watson, president of IBM, offered to supply thousands of punched-card sorting machines. Watson also knew about and offered IBM's support to Howard Aiken, a Harvard mathematician who wanted to build a general-purpose programmable computer that could calculate cannon shell trajectories. This device was similar to that which Babbage had proposed.

In 1944, Aiken completed the first automatic sequence-controlled calculator, the Mark I. It calculated with electromechanical relays and used electricity rather than muscles, effectively replacing Hollerith's gear mechanism. The Mark I was 51 feet long and 8 feet high (Figure 6) and contained over 750,000 parts strung with 500 miles of wires. It used paper-tape input and punched-card output. Calculations of 23-digit numbers took only 3 seconds. With the Mark I, 6 months of manual calculations could be completed in 1 day.

Technology advanced rapidly, and many people worked on similar ideas simultaneously. As a result, some dates, discoveries, and claims overlap in the history of the computer.

In 1941, John Mauchly, a physicist at the University of Pennsylvania's Moore School of Engineering, visited Atanasoff in Iowa, where the ABC computer was still in the early stages of construction. Mauchly was impressed with the possibilities of the machine. In 1942, Mauchly and another Moore School colleague, J. Presper Eckert, proposed to build a machine that would

FIGURE 6
The Mark I. (Courtesy of International Business Machines Corp.)

FIGURE 7
The ENIAC. (Courtesy of International Business Machines Corp.)

compute artillery firing tables for the government. This device was called the Electronic Numerical Integrator and Computer (ENIAC).

At 80 feet long and 18 feet high (Figure 7), the ENIAC was twice as big as the Mark I. Instead of gears or mechanical relays, the 30-ton device contained over 100,000 electronic components, including 17,468 vacuum tubes. Although the vacuum tubes took up a great deal of space, their use increased the speed of calculations a thousandfold. The ENIAC operated on the decimal system, which allowed the punched-card output to be read easily by humans. However, changing programs or operations was extremely difficult because the instructions had to be wired into the circuitry manually. Since it could take the operators as long as two days to manually replug the hundreds of wires involved when changing from one operation to another, the ENIAC was not a particularly efficient general-purpose computer. (Mauchly and Eckert claimed the ENIAC was the first general-purpose electronic digital computer, but on October 19, 1973, a court settlement declared that the Atanasoff-Berry Computer was entitled to that honor.)

The ENIAC was obsolete almost before it was completed, and Mauchly and Eckert planned a successor machine called the EDVAC (Electronic Discrete Variable Automatic Computer). Completed in 1949, EDVAC stored its instructions electronically, using the binary system for instruction coding and input. The EDVAC was one of the first two stored-program computers. It consisted of five units: (1) arithmetical, (2) central control, (3) memory, (4) input, and (5) output. Improvements over the ENIAC included reduction of the number of tubes, increased memory, and increased ease of use, including an easier, faster way to set up new problems.

The stored-program concept has been claimed by many. However, the definitive paper outlining this and other differences in design features has been credited to John von Neumann, the special consultant hired by the Moore School for the EDVAC project. Presented in the mid-1940s, John von Neumann's paper "First Draft of a Report on the EDVAC" served as a blueprint for future stored-program computers.

At the same time, Maurice V. Wilkes of Cambridge, England, incorporated von Neumann's stored-program concept into the EDSAC (Electronic Delay Storage Automatic Computer). The EDSAC was available just before the EDVAC.

The term "bit" as an abbreviation for binary digit was coined by John Tukey in 1946.

Around 1949 at Harvard, An Wang, founder of Wang Laboratories, developed magnetic-core memories. When current flows through wires inside a mag-

netic core, the electricity magnetizes the core in different directions. The direction of magnetization indicates certain data representation to the central processing unit. Subsequently, Jay Forrester at MIT discovered a way to organize magnetic-core memories into a grid, providing a more practical application than the previous serial connections. Computers became faster and more reliable, as well as capable of containing larger memories. Magnetic-core memory has given way to newer technologies, including semiconductor memories.

In 1951, Mauchly and Eckert formed their own company to create a commercially usable general-purpose computer, the UNIVAC I (Figure 8). Remington Rand bought the company when Mauchly and Eckert fell upon hard times. The UNIVAC I was the first general-purpose computer designed specifically for business data-processing applications. Previously, computers had been used solely for scientific or military applications. The U.S. Census Bureau immediately installed UNIVAC I, using it for over 12 years. In 1954, the General Electric Company in Louisville, Kentucky, used UNIVAC I to process the first computerized payroll. Before long, other companies, including Burroughs (now called UNISYS), Honeywell, and IBM, realized the commercial value of computers and began offering their own machines.

From 1950 to 1952, the U.S. Navy and the Digital Computer Lab at MIT developed the Whirlwind computer, another early vacuum-tube stored-program computer. One of the students involved in the Whirlwind's development was Ken Olsen, later the founder of Digital Equipment Corporation (DEC). The Whirlwind simulated high-performance trainer aircraft, contained self-diagnostics, and performed 50,000 operations per second, but it was only about 85 percent accurate.

Chip and Computer Technology

Other innovators appeared on the scene in the late 1950s. Both Jack Kilby, at Texas Instruments, and Robert Noyce, at Fairchild Semiconductor, discovered that resistors, capacitors, and transistors could be made from a semiconductor material at the same time and that any number of transistors could be

FIGURE 8

The UNIVAC I correctly predicted that Dwight Eisenhower would defeat Adlai Stevenson in the 1952 presidential election. A young Walter Cronkite confers with J. Presper Eckert, Jr., and the computer operator. (Courtesy of UNISYS Corp.)

FIGURE 9

Comparison of size between vacuum tubes and an integrated circuit. (Courtesy of National Semiconductor Corp.)

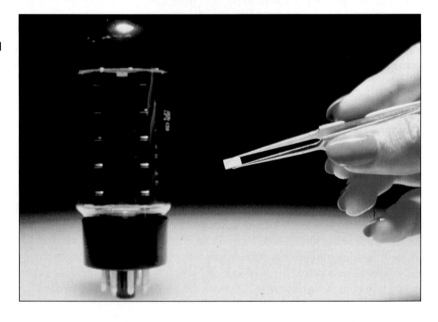

etched on silicon. Thus, the integrated circuit was born and refined (Figure 9). During this time, the integrated circuit was christened a chip. These 1959 discoveries were finally mass produced in 1962 and were included in the computers of the mid-1960s.

Gene Amdahl's revolutionary IBM System/360 series of mainframe computers were also introduced in the 1960s. They were the first general-purpose digital computers using integrated-circuit technology. The IBM System/360 was a "family" of computers. This meant that small but growing companies could start with a relatively inexpensive, small computer system and then, as the company grew, add larger, more powerful computers from the same family. Because the software was compatible, a company could share programs among all the computers in the family. Later, in his own company, Amdahl built a competitive computer that was less expensive, smaller in size, and faster.

Miniaturization, which had come about through various technological innovations, coupled with the commercial success of computers led Ken Olsen and DEC to produce the first minicomputer, the PDP-1, in 1963. Its successor, the PDP-8, was the first commercial minicomputer. It was considerably less expensive than a mainframe, and small companies could afford it to computerize their operations.

However, miniaturization was not the only direction for computers. Computers were also becoming more powerful. In fact, the ILLIAC IV was a supercomputer first used at the Ames Research Center in 1972 for solving aerodynamic problems that were too large and complicated for other systems.

Meanwhile, in the mid-1950s, advances were being made in the field of high-level English-like programming languages. FORTRAN (FORmula TRANslator) was developed by John Backus and a group of IBM engineers as the first problem-oriented algebraic programming language. Therefore, its orientation was more toward mathematicians and scientists than computer specialists.

Rear Admiral (ret.) Grace Murray Hopper was instrumental in developing COBOL (COmmon Business-Oriented Language) as the first programming language designed for business data processing. Hopper also helped develop the UNIVAC I's compiler, a program that could translate other programs into machine language, the 1s and 0s that computers understand.

During the mid-1960s, Dr. John Kemeny (a mathematics professor and president of Dartmouth) and his colleague Dr. Thomas Kurtz developed the computer language BASIC (Beginner's All-purpose Symbolic Instruction Code). They later developed a version called True BASIC, which uses structured

programming tools to make programs easier to read, debug, and update. Today, numerous other high-level languages, including Pascal, C, and Logo, are in use.

Douglas Engelbart introduced a hand-held device that could roll across a flat surface on wheels and cause a corresponding movement on the computer screen. This device was called a "mouse" because its electric cord looked like a tail. This mouse roared and revolutionized the input process.

By 1970, Intel had created a memory chip that could store a kilobit of information. A kilobit translates into roughly 25 five-letter words. Another innovation at Intel came from Ted Hoff, who further improved the integrated circuit by compressing twelve chips into four. Thus, the arithmetic and logic functions of several chips could be contained on one chip, called a microprocessor. This microprocessor, called the Intel 4004 (forty-oh-four), made the development of the small computer, or microcomputer, a possibility. The first chips could handle only four bits of data at a time. However, eight-bit microprocessor chips were developed and used in early microcomputers.

The earliest microcomputer, the Altair 8800, was developed in 1975 by Ed Roberts. Roberts, who has been called the "father of the microcomputer," founded a company called Micro Instrumentation Telemetry Systems (MITS). He developed the Altair to be sold in kit form to consumers (mainly hobbyists) for $395. This computer used an early Intel microprocessor and had less than 1 kilobyte of memory. In 1977, competition for the Altair appeared in the form of Tandy's TRS-80 Model 1, which was available from Radio Shack stores, and the Personal Electronic Transactor (or PET) from Commodore Business Machines.

The focus was not on microcomputers only. Supercomputers were being developed, too. In 1976, Seymour Cray's Cray-1 supercomputer was delivered to the Los Alamos Scientific Laboratory in New Mexico, and a Control Data Corporation CYBER-205 was used by the Meteorological Service in the United Kingdom for weather predictions.

The first commercial computer store appeared in 1975 in Santa Monica, California. ComputerShack, a retail franchise group selling computer equipment, opened for business in 1977 in Morristown, New Jersey. It was to become the leading hardware and software outlet known today as ComputerLand.

The market for software was also growing. In 1974, Bill Gates and Paul Allen developed Microsoft BASIC, a high-level language for microcomputers. The language was used by the MITS Altair in 1975. IBM adopted Microsoft BASIC for its personal computers in 1981, a move that turned Microsoft into a thriving company. Most popular microcomputers—including the Apple II, Commodore 64, and Commodore PET—use Microsoft BASIC. Other successful Microsoft products include PC-DOS and MS-DOS, the operating system software that runs millions of personal computers.

The application software industry got its initial boost because Dan Bricklin, a Harvard Business School student, was not fond of the tedious mathematical calculations involved in the preparation of financial planning sheets—part of the assigned work. Preparing the worksheets was repetitive, requiring numerous hand calculations and recalculations to obtain meaningful results. At times, erroneous calculations in the middle of the worksheet affected other numbers, which had to be recalculated. This method was time-consuming and frustrating.

Bricklin thought that an electronic spreadsheet would be practical for businesspeople and other microcomputer owners. He teamed up with friend Bob Frankston and together they developed and marketed an electronic spreadsheet. The product, called Visi-Calc, was the first of its kind in 1979 and stayed a best-selling package until 1983. At that time, lawsuits prevented timely upgrades from being issued to include 16-bit technology. Eventually, Bricklin sold the company and the rights to VisiCalc to Lotus, Inc., a name recognizable for its spreadsheet package, Lotus 1-2-3. It would become the best-selling program for the personal computer.

Many microcomputer companies have come and gone, but one of the great rags-to-riches stories is Apple Computer, Inc. It was founded by Steven Jobs and Stephen Wozniak on April Fool's Day, 1976. The partners' first headquarters was located in Jobs's ga-rage. Wozniak, the technical expert, made a micro-computer affordable for both the individual and the small businessperson. Because Jobs knew very little about circuitry or coding, he provided the marketing impetus for the small company. The first Apple computers came on the market in 1977. The Apple II was the first PC capable of generating color graphics.

The microcomputer's microprocessor history evolved through a series of competitions primarily between Intel and Motorola. Of course, there are other microprocessing companies, but these two have been battling since Intel's 8088 came out in 1979. In 1981, the Intel 8088 was selected as the central processing unit for IBM's personal computer—a microprocessor coup. Then Motorola's 68000 microprocessors were chosen not only by Apple but also by companies that were building workstations. Microprocessors have changed drastically, moving from the 80286 in 1982 to an 80386 in 1985 and subsequently to the 80486 of 1989. With the 80386, a 32-bit microprocessor, Motorola and Intel ended up tied for sales in 1988. With the introduction in 1993 of the Pentium chip, it appears that the 486 is now history in some people's books. It's almost as if even before the chip hits the market, its successor is in production.

Printers have evolved rapidly over time. The first Epson dot-matrix printer, the TX-80, appeared in 1978, followed by the Hewlett-Packard Laser-Jet in 1984. The following year, the Apple LaserWriter incorporated page description languages so the parameters for the printed page could be specified.

D.C. Hayes and Associates introduced the Hayes microcomputer modem 100 in 1978. Since then Hayes has set the standard for modems and most today are said to be Hayes-compatible. The modem was a necessary device for accessing the popular on-line information service, CompuServe, that was founded in 1979.

Another benchmark in the microcomputer revolution was the introduction of the Apple Macintosh in 1984. The Macintosh was visually oriented, and its mouse made it remarkably easy to use. It was praised for its ability to produce graphics and to print text of near-typeset quality using Apple's LaserWriter. Logitech obtained mouse technology rights and began producing the popular input devices in 1983.

In 1979, WordStar, a word processing program produced by MicroPro International, became available. The popular microcomputer word processing software package WordPerfect was introduced in 1980. By 1993, a 6.0 release was on the market. Word was introduced as the Microsoft entry into the word processing arena in 1983. Release 5.1 appeared in 1993 too.

Even though business was booming, total sales of microcomputers were still fewer than 1 million units until IBM came along. Table 1 shows how rapidly sales have increased. IBM had been in the business of manufacturing and marketing office equipment and larger computer systems for years. In 1981, IBM presented the IBM Personal Computer (IBM PC), which used a 16-bit microprocessor. That year, other computer giants, Xerox and Digital Equipment Corporation, also entered versions of microcomputers. Sony, Hewlett-Packard, NEC, North Star, Zenith, and others now have microcomputers on the market.

Adam Osborne introduced a truly portable microcomputer in 1981, the Osborne 1. It weighed only 24 pounds, had memory capacity of 64 kilobytes, and cost approximately $1,795. It could be manufactured in just over one hour's time, using only 40 screws to put together the easy-to-find parts.

Time magazine annually honors someone who during the year has made a difference in the world. In 1982, *Time* chose the computer as its "Man of the Year." That same year, Peter Norton produced the popular file recovery program called Norton Utilities for the IBM PC.

By 1984, the IBM PC had become the *de facto* industry standard (that is, the most popular and widely used computer), with hundreds of companies designing software for it. IBM did not stay at the top of the heap for long, however. Because it was the most popular microcomputer, almost every microcomputer manufacturer presented a version. These are called IBM PC compatibles, or clones—machines that run the IBM PC software and work with other IBM PC equipment. Some compatibles are made by Leading Edge, Tandy, Epson, Kaypro, and Compaq.

In 1986, the Compaq DeskPro 386 computer, the first to use the powerful 32-bit Intel 80386 microprocessor, was introduced. Compaq became the biggest competition for the corporate market of IBM. The even more powerful 80486 microprocessor first appeared in 1988. In 1987, the OS/2 operating system was announced. It had multitasking and multiuser features that made headlines in networking. New network applications, however, were developed more slowly than initially hoped for.

The year 1987 also saw the introduction of PageMaker from Aldus Corp. The program incorporates both type and graphic images on a page. Multimedia applications that integrate video, animation, sound and text began appearing in 1989.

The NeXT computer was introduced in 1988 as a computer system for educators. Deliveries began in 1989. That year also saw NEC Technologies, Inc.'s UltraLite laptop computer weigh in at just over four pounds. IBM had produced a laptop computer in the mid-80s that was less than a hit. The following year the first pen-based PC was completed, the GRIDPAD.

The late 1980s also saw Lotus bring suit against other spreadsheet software developers, claiming that their packages infringed on the Lotus copyright, that the competitors' packages looked like Lotus, and that they operated like Lotus. Thereby, these actions earned the nickname "look and feel" lawsuits.

TABLE 1
Total Computers in Use in the U.S.

1978	500,000 units
1980	1,000,000 units
1983	10,000,000 units
1983	500,000 IBM PCs in business alone
1986	30,000,000 units
1989	100,000,000 units
1991	60,000,000 IBM PCs in business alone

A nondestructive worm was introduced into the Internet network in 1988, bringing thousands of computers to a halt.

Windows 3.0, a graphical user interface product released in 1990, sold over 3 million copies. It offered pull-down menus and icons to identify its functions.

Today's history can, of course, be found in computer and noncomputer magazines, newspaper headlines, nightly news, and probably your own classroom.

Table 2 lists many of the major contributors to the development of computers.

TECHNOLOGICAL EVOLUTION OF COMPUTERS

Over time, computers changed. They improved in speed, power, and efficiency. The changes are recognized as a progression of generations, each characterized by specific developments.

First Generation (1951–1959)

First-generation computers were powered by thousands of vacuum tubes. The UNIVAC I and others like it were large because of the massive number of tubes that were required. The **vacuum tubes** themselves were large (the size of today's light bulbs). They required great amounts of energy, and they generated much heat. The computer's memory was stored on magnetic-storage devices, primarily magnetic tapes and magnetic drums. Most of the data were entered into the computers on punched cards similar to those used in Jacquard's process. Output consisted of punched cards or paper. Binary (machine) language and assembly languages were used to program the computers. Operation was under human control; that is, a human operator had to physically reset relay switches and wiring before a program could be run.

Second Generation (1959–1965)

The device that characterized the **second-generation computers** was the transistor. **Transistors** were made of a semiconducting material and controlled the flow of electricity through the circuits.

Transistors were a breakthrough technology that allowed computers to become physically smaller but more powerful, more reliable, and even faster than before. The transistor was developed at Bell Labs in 1947 by William Shockley, J. Bardeen, and W. H. Brattain. It was displayed for the public in 1948, and it won a Nobel Prize in 1956; however, it was not used in conjunction with computers until 1959.

Transistors were less expensive and smaller, required less electricity, and emitted less heat than vacuum tubes. Also, fewer transistors than tubes were required to operate a computer. Transistors were not so fragile as vacuum tubes, and they lasted longer. Because the components were substantially smaller, computers became considerably smaller.

Although magnetic tape was still the most commonly used external storage medium, magnetic-disk storage was used so that data could be located more rapidly. MIT developed magnetic-core storage in which each core stored one bit of information. Contrasted with tape and drum storage, in which the location of data had to be found first, magnetic-core storage made data instantaneously available. Punched cards and magnetic tape were the primary means for input, and punched cards and paper constituted the output.

Programming languages also became more sophisticated. High-level languages resembling English were developed, including FORTRAN, COBOL, BASIC, and PL/I. Like the first-generation computers, second-generation computers were primarily under the control of human operators.

Third Generation (1965–1971)

Integrated circuits signified the beginning of **third-generation computers.** Again, computers were smaller, more efficient, and more reliable than their predecessors. Unlike transistors and circuit boards that were assembled manually, **integrated circuits (ICs)** were single, complete electronic semiconductor circuits contained on a piece of silicon, sometimes called chips. ICs could be manufactured by machinery, which ultimately resulted in a lower cost.

Memory technology improved. By 1969, as many as 1,000 transistors could be built on a chip of sili-

TABLE 2

Major Contributors to Computer Development

Date	Person	Contribution
1642	Pascal	The first mechanical digital calculator, the Pascaline.
1804	Jacquard	Used punched cards with weaving loom.
1822	Babbage	"Father of the computer." Invented the difference engine with mechanical memory to store results.
1840s	Augusta Ada	"The first programmer." Suggested binary system rather than decimal for data storage.
1850s	Boole	Developed Boolean logic, which later was used in the design of computer circuitry.
1880s	Hollerith	Built first electromechanical, punched-card data-processing machine, used to compile information for 1890 U.S. census.
1939	Atanasoff and Berry	Built the ABC, the world's first general-purpose, electronic digital computer to solve large equations.
1943	Turing	Used vacuum-tube technology to build British Colossus, to counteract the German code scrambling device, Enigma.
1944	Aiken	Built the Mark I, the first automatic sequence-controlled calculator; used by military to compute ballistics data.
1940s	von Neumann	Presented a paper outlining the stored-program concept.
1947	Mauchly and Eckert	Built the ENIAC, the second general-purpose electronic digital computer; used to compute artillery firing tables.
1949	Wilkes	Built the EDSAC, the first stored-program computer.
1949	Mauchly, Eckert, and von Neumann	Built the EDVAC, the second stored-program computer.
1949	Wang	Developed magnetic-core memory.
1949	Forrester	Organized magnetic-core memory to be more efficient.

continued on next page

TABLE 2
continued

Date	Person	Contribution
1950	Turing	Built the ACE, which some consider to be the first programmable digital computer.
1951	Mauchly and Eckert	Built the UNIVAC I, the first computer designed and sold commercially, specifically for business data-processing applications.
1950s	Hopper	Developed the UNIVAC I compiler.
1957	Backus	One of a group of IBM engineers to develop FORTRAN.
1959	Kilby and Noyce	Developed and perfected the integrated circuit to be used in later computers.
1960s	Amdahl	Designed the IBM System/360 series of mainframe computers, the first general-purpose digital computers to use integrated circuits.
1961	Hopper	Instrumental in developing the COBOL programming language.
1963	Olsen	With DEC produced the PDP-1, the first minicomputer.
1965	Kemeny and Kurtz	Developed BASIC programming language; True BASIC followed later.
1970	Hoff	Developed the famous Intel 4004 microprocessor chip.
1975	Roberts	"Father of the microcomputer." Designed the first microcomputer, the Altair 8800 in kit form.
1976	Cray	Developed the Cray-1 supercomputer.
1977	Jobs and Wozniak	Designed and built the first Apple microcomputer.
1978	Bricklin and Frankston	Designed VisiCalc, an electronic spreadsheet.
1981	IBM	Introduced the IBM PC with a 16-bit microprocessor.
1986	Compaq	Released the DeskPro 386 computer, the first to use the 80036 microprocessor.
1987	IBM	Announced the OS/2 operating-system technology.
1988	Compaq	Introduced the 80486 microcomputer.
1988	Steven Jobs	Introduced NeXT computer.

con. Magnetic disks were improved and were used more for storage. Monitors and keyboards were introduced for data input and output. Punched cards lost their preeminence as input and output devices.

A new program controlled the computer and its resources and used them more effectively. This new program was the operating system. It meant that human operators were no longer required, and processing could be done at computer speeds rather than human speeds. High-level programming languages continued to be developed, including RPG and Pascal.

Another phenomenon of this third generation was the concept of families of computers. Businesses that bought computers and programs found that almost before a system was fully adapted, it was outdated or unable to grow with their needs. IBM recognized this problem and created an entire product line, the IBM/360 series, which allowed necessary upgrading or expansion. Programs written for one computer were compatible with any of the machines in the line. Businesses could upgrade or expand their data-processing operations as necessary.

Digital Equipment Corporation introduced the first minicomputer in November, 1963. Its PDP-1 was substantially cheaper than a mainframe, thus making smaller computers available to yet another business market.

Fourth Generation (1971–Present)

The significant distinction for **fourth-generation computers** lies in the techniques of implementation of integrated circuits by using **large-scale integration (LSI)** of chips with several thousand transistors. In the mid-1970s the development of **very-large-scale integration (VLSI)** produced a chip containing a microprocessor. VLSI made the microcomputer possible. The Intel 80386 microprocessor followed. The Intel 80386 is faster and more powerful than its predecessors.

Magnetic disks became the primary means of internal storage. The proliferation of application programs for microcomputers allowed home and business users to adapt their computers for word processing, spreadsheet manipulating, file handling, graphics, and much more.

Fifth Generation (Future)

Although many people disagree on the start of the **fifth-generation computer** technology, some say that it will begin with the creation and use of a computer with **artificial intelligence (AI).** AI indicates the ability to perform humanlike thinking and reasoning. The unofficial original goal was a thinking machine by 1990. Although expert systems are already being used for specialized applications, true artificial intelligence, or computers that can think, are still merely concepts. Table 3 lists the generations of computers and their respective characteristics. The future remains to be seen, of course, but since you will be part of the future, you may have some ideas or innovations of your own.

TABLE 3
Generations of Computers and
Their Characteristics

First Generation (1951–1959)

- Vacuum tubes
- Magnetic tape for external storage—some magnetic drum
- Punched cards for input
- Punched cards and paper for output
- Machine and assembly languages
- Human operators to set switches
- UNIVAC I typical example

Second Generation (1959–1965)

- Transistors
- Magnetic-core storage
- Magnetic tape most common external storage, but magnetic disk introduced
- Punched cards and magnetic tape for input
- Punched cards and paper for output
- High-level languages—FORTRAN, COBOL, BASIC, PL/I and others
- Human operator to handle punched cards
- Honeywell 200 typical example

Third Generation (1965–1971)

- Integrated circuits
- Improved disk storage
- Monitors and keyboards for input and output
- More high-level languages, including RPG and Pascal
- First complete operating systems meant less involvement for human operators.
- Family of computers introduced allowing compatibility
- Minicomputers used commercially
- IBM System/360 typical example

Fourth Generation (1971–Present)

- LSI and VLSI
- Magnetic disk most common external storage
- Introduction of microcomputer
- Fourth-generation languages emerged and application software for microcomputers became popular
- Microcomputers used—Compaq DeskPro 386 typical example
- Burroughs B7700 and HP 3000 (minicomputer) typical examples

Fifth Generation (Future)

- True artificial intelligence

VOCABULARY SELF-TEST

Can you define the following terms?

artificial intelligence (p. 573)

fifth-generation computer (p. 573)

first-generation computer (p. 570)

fourth-generation computer (p. 573)

integrated circuit (IC) (p. 570)

large-scale integration (LSI) (p. 573)

second-generation computer (p. 570)

third-generation computer (p. 570)

transistor (p. 570)

vacuum tube (p. 570)

very-large-scale integration (VLSI) (p. 573)

REVIEW QUESTIONS

Multiple Choice

1. The _____ generation of computers was characterized by vacuum tubes.
   a. first
   b. second
   c. third
   d. fourth

2. The second generation of computers was characterized by _____ .
   a. magnetic cards
   b. artificial intelligence
   c. transistors
   d. transformers

3. Integrated circuits signified the beginning of the _____ generation of computers.
   a. first
   b. second
   c. third
   d. fourth

4. The advancement that allowed several thousand transistors to be placed on a single chip is known as _____ .
   a. artificial intelligence
   b. large-scale integration
   c. first-generation efficiency
   d. vacuum-tube technology

5. Some experts say that artificial intelligence represents the entry of the _____ generation of computers.
   a. second
   b. third
   c. fourth
   d. fifth

Fill-In

1. First-generation computers are characterized by _____ technology.

2. _____ are made of a semiconducting material and are primarily characteristic of the second generation of computers.

3. The _____ generation of computers is characterized by the use of integrated circuits.

4. _____ is the incorporation of several hundred thousand transistors onto a single chip.

5. _____ is the ability of fifth-generation computers to think and reason.

Short Answer

1. What characteristics delineate the first and second generations of computers?

2. Distinguish between the third- and fourth-generation computers.

3. What characteristics will appear in the fifth generation of computers?

4. Write a thumbnail sketch of someone you found interesting in this Infomodule.

5. What invention or innovation do you think is most responsible for making the computer a successful product? Defend your choice.

Glossary

Absolute cell reference   A method of copying in which the exact formula is repeated, using the same cell references; used with spreadsheets.

Accounting information system   An information system using primarily transaction processing systems to record transactions that affect the financial status of an organization. It maintains a historical record of the organization's transactions and is used to produce reports that give a financial picture of the organization.

Acoustic modem   Also called an acoustic coupler; a type of modem with two rubber cups into which the standard telephone receiver is placed to send and receive data.

Active cell   A cell in a spreadsheet that is currently being used for data entry or data manipulation; usually indicated by the cursor position.

Active-matrix display   A type of LCD screen that uses one set of transistors for each LCD element. This produces a better image than the passive-matrix display.

Active window   In an application, the current window in which you are working.

Ada   A programming language developed for the U.S. Department of Defense for use in military applications. Ada includes powerful control and data structures and a specialized set of commands that allow it to directly control hardware devices.

Address bus   Unidirectional pathway used to locate instructions or data in memory.

Algorithm   The finite set of step-by-step instructions that convert the input into the desired output, that is, solve the problem.

Analog data transmission   The transmission of data in a continuous wave form.

Analog-to-digital port   See game port.

Animation   A feature of some graphics packages that rapidly displays drawings that progressively change slightly, thereby simulating motion.

Application generator   A fourth-generation language that allows users to enter data and specify how the data are to be manipulated and output.

Application software   Software that allows you to perform a specific task or set of tasks.

ARCnet   A type of network developed by Datapoint Corporation.

Area graphs   See stacked-line graphs.

Arithmetic-logic unit (ALU)   The part of the central processing unit (CPU) that performs all arithmetic and logic functions.

Artificial intelligence (AI)   The ability of computers to perform humanlike thinking and reasoning.

Aspect ratio   In a graphics program, the relationship between the height and width of an object. The aspect ratio may be altered to change the shape or proportions of an object.

Assembler   A language-translator program that translates assembly-language code into a machine-language code.

Assembly language   A low-level language that uses mnemonic codes instead of 1s and 0s.

Asynchronous transmission   A method of data transmission in which characters are sent one at a time over a communication channel. Each character is surrounded by a start-and-stop bit that controls the transfer of that character.

Attributes The set of characteristics used to describe a data entry field or the appearance of output. These are often set by a user to fit a particular situation.

Autoanswer A feature of a communication package that automatically answers calls from other computers. A computer with this feature can create a bulletin board file and receive electronic mail without anyone being present at the computer.

Automatic dialing A feature of a communication package that allows previously stored numbers to be accessed and automatically dialed to access another computer.

Automatic message transfer A feature in a communication package that automatically dials a computer at a preset time and leaves a message on that computer.

Automatic page numbering An application software feature that automatically places a consecutive number on each page.

Automatic recalculation When a new data entry is made some spreadsheet programs automatically recalculate all cells that are affected by the new value.

Automatic spillover A spreadsheet option in which a cell label is allowed to continue, or spill over, into the next cell.

Background recalculation mode Mode in which recalculation of a worksheet occurs while other operations are ongoing.

Band printer A line-at-a-time impact printer similar to a chain printer but using a band containing characters instead of a chain.

Bandwidth A characteristic of a communication channel that determines the rate, or speed, at which data can be transmitted over that channel.

Bar code A series of thick and thin black bars and spaces of various widths that represent data; seen on many consumer products.

Bar graph A graph using a fixed scale to compare data in simple and compound relationships. Data may be represented as either vertical or horizontal bars.

BASIC (Beginner's All-purpose Symbolic Instruction Code) A high-level language developed at Dartmouth College as an easy to learn and use language for beginning programmers.

Batch file A file that contains a series of commands that when executed automatically performs all those commands as if each were typed and executed individually.

Batch input Involves the collection of data on source documents, for a specified period of time, which are grouped into "batches" and entered at one time into the computer and stored until they are to be processed.

Batch processing Involves processing data entered through a batch input process without user intervention.

Baud rate The number of times per second that a transmitted signal changes (modulates or demodulates).

Binary system The base-2 numbering system using the digits 0 and 1. Computer data can be represented by this numbering system.

Biochip A newer technology for designing integrated circuits; uses living protein and enzymes to grow circuits.

Bit A binary digit; the smallest piece of data that can be recognized and used by a computer.

Bit-mapped font In word processing, a character composed of dots in a grid pattern. Each bit-mapped font comes in only one size.

Bit-mapped graphics Graphics created with pixel-oriented images.

Block A preset number of bytes that are transferred as a unit.

Block design In spreadsheets, defining and positioning a number of blocks of cells for a specific purpose.

Block editing A word processor feature that allows a user to edit large portions of text as a unit.

Blocking factor The number of records stored between a pair of interrecord gaps.

Break signal In a communication program, a feature in which a signal is sent to stop the current operation between two communicating computers without disconnecting the communication link between them.

Bridge An interface that connects different LANs allowing communications between devices on each LAN.

Broad-band channel A communication channel, such as microwaves or fiber optics, that transmits data at rates as high as several megabits per second.

Browse mode In database managers, the mode in which the user can view an entire screen full of records.

Buffer A temporary holding place for data; may be part of a CPU or part of an input or output device.

Built-in function A function that is contained within an application program and that automatically performs a mathematical or logic function without manually entering a formula.

Bulletin board system (BBS) Electronic equivalent of a conventional bulletin board. A BBS is part of a communication network where users can post messages, read those posted by other users, communicate with the system operator, and upload or download programs.

Bus An electrical path from point to point in a circuit.

Bus architecture Characteristics of a bus, which include speed of data transfer and amount of data handled at one time.

Bus network A computer network arrangement in which each device is connected to a single communication cable by an interface. Each device can communicate directly with every other device.

Byte A group of eight bits. The basic unit of measuring quantity of computer data, such as amount of memory or size of a file.

C A programming language that uses English-like statements; uses sophisticated control and data structures, which make it a very concise, powerful language.

C++ An object-oriented version of the C programming language; popular with software developers.

Cable A medium used to connect computing and communication devices.

Cache memory A high-speed memory logically located between the CPU and main memory. Used to increase the speed of retrieving data by storing only the most frequently used data.

Calculation block The area of a spreadsheet that includes the formulas and fixed data.

Carrier access method A protocol for communication that sets format, timing, sequencing, and error control of signals.

Carrier sense multiple access (CSMA) A local-area network access method in which a device listens to a channel to sense whether that channel is in use.

Carrier sense multiple access with collision detection (CSMA/CD) The carrier sense multiple access (CSMA) method with collision detection capabilities.

Cartridge tape A form of magnetic tape similar to cassette tape but with a much greater storage density; used mainly with large computer systems.

Cassette tape A form of magnetic tape about one-quarter inch wide; generally used for secondary storage with microcomputers.

Cathode-ray tube (CRT) A type of display that uses an electron beam to illuminate a phosphor-coated screen to form characters.

Cell A data entry point in a spreadsheet, defined by its row and column coordinate.

Cell pointer A highlighted box that shows the active cell.

Cellular network A network in which transmitters are placed in a checkerboard pattern throughout the system service area to enable mobile communication.

Centered text Text that is aligned equidistant between the left and right margins.

Centering A feature in application software that automatically places a word(s) in the center of a defined space, such as a spreadsheet cell or a document page.

Central processing unit (CPU) The name given to the processing unit of a computer; contains the arithmetic-logic unit (ALU) and control unit, used to decode and execute instructions.

Chain printer A line-at-a-time impact printer that uses a rotating chain containing all the characters.

Character enhancements Features in application software that allow a user to alter text style, for example, by boldfacing or italicizing.

Character printer A type of printer that prints one character at a time, as opposed to line or page printers.

Chart or graph program Software used to create charts and graphs; used for pictorial representation of data.

Chip Another term for microchip; see integrated circuit.

Client/server architecture The processing of an application is split between the client's, or user's computer, and a separate server.

Clip art Predrawn art available on separate disks or built into a program; the user can select individual images to bring into a document or publication to enhance its appearance or to illustrate a point.

Coaxial cable Communication channel consisting of a single wire surrounded by a layer of insulation and shielding.

COBOL (COmmon Business-Oriented Language) A high-level language used in business information processing; specifically designed to manipulate large data files.

Coding Refers to actually writing the program instructions in a programming language that tells the computer how to operate.

Color dot-matrix printer A dot-matrix printer that uses a color ribbon and makes multiple passes to produce colored characters.

Color ink-jet printer An ink-jet printer that uses colored ink and can produce 16 million colors by combining sprays of color.

Color laser printer The highest quality color images are produced using dry ink electro-photographic technology.

Color wax thermal printer Prints characters by melting colored wax onto paper. Produces higher quality images than colored dot-matrix or ink-jet printers.

Column In a spreadsheet the alphabetic ordering from left to right that, along with the numeric row designation, locates the position of a cell.

Command-driven program A program in which commands must be typed to be entered and executed. Contrast menu-driven.

Command-line interface A user interface that requires a user to type the desired response at a prompt using a special command language.

Command mode (1) A mode of operation in which application program commands can be selected. (2) In communications, when typed characters are interpreted as commands and not data. Contrast with menu-driven program.

Commercial on-line service An on-line computer service in which users may access large databases of information. Like information services, these are subscriber services, but they contain information on more specialized topics.

Common carrier A company licensed and regulated by federal or state government to carry the data communication property of others at a regulated rate.

Communication channel The medium, or pathway, through which data are transmitted between devices. This pathway may be wire cable, microwave, or fiber optics.

Communication parameters The boundaries within which devices are able to communicate with each other. Four essential components are the baud rate, the number of bits used to create each character, the number of stop bits, and the type of parity checking used.

Communication server The computer that gives each node access to a communication device such as a modem.

Communication software An application program that allows the exchange of data between computers.

Communications programs Software that allows your computer to "talk" to other computers.

Compiler A language-translator program that translates a whole high-level language program at once into machine language before it is executed.

Completeness check A type of validity checking that determines if all the required input data are present.

Compressed print Low-quality print formed by tightly spacing characters using a minimum number of dots or lines.

Computer An electronic device that can accept input, process it in a prescribed manner, output the results, and store the results for later use; a tool used to process data into information.

Computer-aided design (CAD) The integration of computers and graphics to aid in the design and drafting processes.

Computer-aided manufacturing (CAM) The use of computers to control machines in the manufacturing process.

Computer-aided systems engineering (CASE) An entire class of programs (software) that automates systems analysis tasks.

Computer-assisted retrieval system (CARS) The integration of micrographic technology and computers in a system that allows random and fast retrieval of information stored on microforms.

Computer-based information system A set of people, data, procedures, hardware, and software that work together to achieve the common goal of information management.

Computer crime A crime in which computers and software are used with illegal intentions.

Computer ethics A set of rules that govern the standards or conduct of computer users; principles used with computers and the information they produce.

Computer graphics Images and pictures generated by a computer, software, and the person using it.

Computer-integrated manufacturing (CIM) The linking and integration of manufacturing and all other aspects of a company by computers.

Computer literacy Possessing knowledge and understanding of computers and information systems in combination with the ability to use them effectively.

Computer network The linking of two or more computers, thus making it possible for data to be shared and updated at different locations.

Computer numerical control (CNC) The controlling of milling or cutting operations by a computer.

Computer output microform (COM) Hard copy in the form of photographic images recorded on microfilm or microfiche.

Computer programming The writing of instructions and giving them to the computer so it can complete a task.

Computer programs The instructions, written in a computer programming language, that direct the operations of a computer and cause the hardware to do the work.

Concentration The process of connecting and serving more devices on a communication channel than that channel was designed to handle.

Concentrator A hardware device, often a minicomputer, that controls the process of concentration.

Concurrent access An attempt by two or more individuals or groups to use the same data simultaneously.

Consistency check A type of validity checking that verifies if the input data conform to certain formats, boundaries, and other parameters.

Contention A method for determining device access to a communication channel. With this method each device checks a channel to see whether it is free before sending data. Once a device begins transmission, it maintains sole control of that channel until it completes its transmission.

Context switching A type of multitasking that allows several programs to reside in memory but only one to be active at a time.

Control bus Unidirectional pathway for all timing and controlling functions.

Control panel An area in an electronic spreadsheet that displays information about the current file and the command or activity being performed.

Control program The computer program in an operating system that manages the computer's hardware and resources, such as CPU time, primary storage, and input and output devices.

Control unit That part of a central processing unit that controls the sequence of events necessary to execute an instruction.

Conventional memory In an MS-DOS–based system, the first 640k bytes of main memory.

Conversion The replacement of an existing system with a new information system.

Cooperative multitasking A type of multitasking in which a background program uses the CPU during idle time of the foreground program.

Coordinate The intersection of a row and a column in a spreadsheet; used to define a cell's position in a spreadsheet.

Copying (1) The process of making a duplicate file from an existing file. (2) The process of duplicating text or graphics on the screen for placement elsewhere while leaving the original text or graphics intact.

Copyright infringement   Occurs when the appropriate royalty payment is not made for use of the protected work.

Cost/benefit analysis   Part of the project justification stage of the system development life cycle, often referred to as a feasibility study; compares both costs and benefits for alternative new information systems and the current system to determine which system should be recommended to management.

Current drive   The drive on which DOS will put any files or search for any filenames or commands you type unless it is instructed to look elsewhere.

Cursor   An on-screen indicator, such as a blinking underline or rectangle, that shows where the next keystroke will appear when typed.

Cut and paste   An application software feature that "cuts" (erases) an object from a graphic or text and places it in a buffer, so that it can be "pasted" (inserted) in another area of the graphic or document, or in another document.

Daisy-wheel printer   A type of printer that uses a print wheel resembling a daisy. At the end of each "petal" is a fully formed character.

Data   Numbers, letters, characters, or combinations thereof that can be entered and processed by a computer. Raw facts before processing.

Database   A cross-referenced collection of files designed and created to minimize repetition of data.

Database administrator (DBA)   One person or a group of people who manage a database. A DBA is specially trained in the DBMS software package being used on a system and in the construction of database structures.

Database design screen   A screen in which the structure, including names, types, widths, and other features for each data field are defined.

Database management system (DBMS)   Software that works with a database storing, organizing, manipulating, retrieving, displaying, and printing data from multiple files, tables, or objects. It is the interface among programs, users, and the data in the database.

Database programming language   A language specific to the database that allows the user to create customized applications.

Database query language   A fourth-generation language used in conjunction with a relational database; acts as an interface between a user and a relational database management system to facilitate easy access to data without use of complex programming code; permits the user to formulate inquiries that relate to records from one or more tables.

Database server   The computer that stores the database in the network which is available to multiple users.

Data buffer   An area set aside in main memory to temporarily store data.

Data bus   Bidirectional pathway where data transfer takes place.

Data capture   Retrieving data from a remote computer and storing it in main memory or secondary storage.

Data communication   The process of sending data electronically from one point to another.

Data dictionary   A data file containing the technical description of the data to be stored in a database; it includes the field names, types (e.g., alphanumeric, numeric), size, descriptions, and logical relationships.

Data entry   The act of entering data and instructions into a computer.

Data manipulation   In a computer crime, refers to a user altering data in the computer without proper authorization (sometimes called "data diddling").

Data processing   Refers to the input, processing, output, and storage steps associated with converting data into information.

Data stealing   Occurs when a user steals information that has been gathered for a legitimate purpose.

Data-transfer mode   In a communication package, the operational mode in which actual data transfer takes place between communicating devices.

Data-transfer rate   The number of characters or bytes that can be transferred to storage media in a given amount of time.

Debugging   The process of finding any type of error in a program and correcting it.

Decimal system   The base 10 system, composed of the numerals 0 through 9.

Decision support system (DSS)   An information system that is designed to allow managers
to interact directly with a computer for assistance with relatively unstructured decisions.

Dedicated server   A server whose purpose is to
deal with shared files on a LAN.

De facto standard   Software or hardware that is
recognized as the most popular and widely
used but whose status has not been officially
declared by a recognized standard setting
organization.

Default entry   A value that the computer uses if
you don't supply another value.

Default settings   In application software a parameter that is automatically entered unless
changed by the user.

Demodulation   The process of converting an
analog signal into a digital signal.

Density   The amount of data that can be stored
in a given area of a storage medium. The higher
the density, the more data are stored.

Design program   A graphics program that is
used as a design tool to create and/or alter the
image of an object.

Desktop   In Microsoft Windows the background
screen area.

Desktop computer   A microcomputer that can
fit conveniently on a standard business desk.

Desktop publishing   A concept that combines
the use of a microcomputer with page-
composition (graphics-oriented) software and
high-quality laser printers.

Device driver   The software that allows peripheral devices to communicate with the
computer.

Dialog box   A box displayed on the screen from
which commands or other information can be
set or selected.

Digital data transmission   The transmission of
data as distinct pulses, or on/off electrical states.

Direct-access file processing   A file accessing
method in which files can be retrieved or
stored regardless of the order. Also, random-
access file processing.

Direct conversion   A type of changeover in
which an existing information system is replaced with a new information system as of a
certain date; also called crash conversion.

Directory   A structure for holding files that lets
you organize them into convenient groups so
they can be easily located on disk.

Disaster recovery teams   Experts whose job it
is to help recover data that may have been destroyed by fire, flood, or virus attack.

Disk operating system (DOS)   An operating
system that allows and manages the use of
disk drives for storing and accessing data and
programs.

Disk pack   A removable, hard-disk storage device
containing multiple hard disks in a plastic case;
provides increased storage capabilities for large
computer systems.

Distributed database   A database that exists in
one of the following forms: (1) on-line at the
host computer in a central location but also
available to remote locations; (2) partially duplicated at the host computer and placed on a
remote computer for processing, called segmentation; (3) entirely copied for processing, called
replication, at each remote location.

Distributed data processing (DDP)   The concept of dispersing computers, devices, software,
and data connected through communication
channels into areas where they are used.

Documentation   (1) The written or graphic
record of the steps involved in developing or
maintaining an information system. (2) Written
or graphic descriptions detailing the purpose
and the operation of software.

Documentation block   In a spreadsheet, it supplies information about a worksheet but does
not contain any actual data.

Document design   The methodology used to
combine text and art work or graphics into a
final product.

Dot-matrix printer   A type of impact printer
that uses a print head containing pins, usually 9
to 24, that produce characters by printing patterns of dots.

Dot pitch   A measure of the size of the dots that
make up an image, measured in millimeters. The
smaller the dot pitch, the sharper the image.

Downloading   The process of receiving a file
from another computer. Contrast with uploading.

Drag   A graphics package feature that allows
moving (dragging) an object around the drawing area.

Draw program A vector-based graphics program displaying high-quality dots and lines. Users may also draw, fill shapes, and change color while creating illustrations.

Drum printer A line-at-a-time impact printer that uses a rotating drum of 80 to 132 print positions, with each print position containing a complete set of characters.

Dumb terminal A stand-alone keyboard and display screen that can send or receive data but cannot process those data because it does not contain a microprocessor.

Dye sublimation printer Very high resolution color printers capable of producing photographic quality images. Uses special paper on which dye is heated onto the paper.

Edit mode In a database manager, the mode in which the user can view the entire contents of a record.

Edit window The main window in a word processor; the work area for entering and editing a document.

Electronic data interchange (EDI) A communication protocol that automates and standardizes communication that allows retailers and their suppliers to conduct business transactions electronically.

Electronic funds transfer (EFT) A method of data communication that uses a communication channel to transfer money between accounts.

Electronic mail (e-mail) Any mail or messages transmitted electronically by computers using communication networks.

Electronic spreadsheet An application software program that displays, manipulates, and prints data in a row and column format; computerized version of the paper spreadsheet. Also, spreadsheet software.

Electronic teleconferencing A method of communicating via computers connected through a telephone system. Each user or group of users participates in the conference by keying in their conversations.

Encapsulation In an object-oriented programming language, the combination of data and instructions into a reusable structure that act on that data.

Encoding system A system whereby alphanumeric characters are represented by patterns of 1s and 0s so that they can be recognized and used by a computer. The American Standard Code for Information Interchange (ASCII) and Extended Binary Coded Decimal Interchange Code (EBCDIC) are the two most widely used encoding systems.

Encryption A data-coding scheme that converts data into unintelligible characters so that they cannot be read or used by unauthorized persons.

End user A person who uses computer hardware and software to perform a task.

End-user computing The concept that supports and embraces the notion that the person who is responsible for the output of computing should be the person who is going to utilize that output.

Ergonomics The study of people in their work environments. It involves examining the physical characteristics of people and the way they function in relationship to the furnishings and machines at work.

Ethernet A network protocol; permits large networks to be set up and transmits data faster than other network architectures.

Execution time The time during which an instruction is decoded and executed by the ALU.

Executive support system (ESS) An information system that specifically caters to an executive's special information needs in managerial planning, monitoring, and analysis.

Expanded memory Paged memory. Additional memory accessed through swapping pages of memory into the reserved memory area.

Expansion ports External connection ports that allow the computer to be physically connected to peripheral devices. Also, input/output ports.

Expansion slots Internal sockets where additional computer boards can be plugged in.

Expert system (also called a knowledge-based system) is a type of application program used to make decisions or solve problems in a particular field using knowledge and analytical rules defined by human experts.

Expert system shell A general-purpose inference engine and a skeleton of the knowledge base into which users can add their own special data.

Express warranty   A claim, either written or verbal, about a product.

Extended memory   Additional memory beyond the first 1 megabyte of main memory.

External commands   In MS-DOS, commands that are in separate files stored on a hard disk or diskette which must first be loaded into main memory before they can be executed.

External direct-connect modem   A type of modem that is external to a computer and connected directly to a telephone line. This type of modem reduces distortion and allows for faster data transmission than the acoustic type permits.

Eye trackers   A pointing device that uses a video camera to track the position of the eye's pupils and translate that data into a screen coordinate, thus enabling the eye to point to and select items on the screen.

Facsimile (fax)   A form of electronic mail that copies and sends text and graphics over long distances.

Facsimile (fax) machine   A communication device that allows a user to digitize text, graphics, and photos and send them to another location electronically.

Fax server   A server in a network that contains the fax hardware and software.

Fiber optics   A type of data communication channel in which data are transmitted and received as digital pulses of light.

Field   An individual classification of data stored in a record.

Fifth-generation computer   The next generation of computers, which will incorporate artificial intelligence.

Fifth-generation language   One of the next generation of programming languages that will include natural languages.

File   A collection of related records in which each record contains related data fields.

File locking   A file-protection procedure that allows only one user to access a file at a time.

File management system (FMS)   An application program that can manage (manipulate, store, retrieve, and print) data in separate files. In this system only one file can be accessed at one time.

Filename   A name given to a file to indicate the contents and to distinguish it from other files.

Filename extension   An optional portion of a filename used to identify a file's type. It can be from one to three characters long and is separated from the filename by a period.

File server   A combination of software and hardware that permits local area network users to share computer programs and data.

File-transfer protocol   A set of rules for the transfer of data. Communicating devices must use the same protocol to make possible the transfer of data.

Fill pattern   The way a bar, column, pie slice, or area graph is depicted. They may be solid, open, or crosshatched.

Financial information system   A system designed to provide management with information concerning the acquisition of funds to finance a business and the allocation and control of the organization's financial resources.

Firmware   A term used to represent the contents of read-only memory.

First-generation computer   Computers developed and used before 1960 which employed vacuum tube technology.

Fixed disk   A hard disk storage system of one or more hard disks protected in a permanently sealed case.

Flash memory   Silicon memory that can retain data even when its power supply is turned off.

Flatbed scanner   A type of scanner that resembles a photocopy machine and is suited to scanning full-page documents.

Flat file   A file having no relationship or integrating structure with any other file.

Flat-panel display   A type of display that does not use a picture tube to display characters; includes liquid-crystal display (LCD) and gas plasma.

Flicker   The shimmering effect of pixels being turned off and on caused by the refresh rate.

Floppy diskette   A flexible, mylar magnetic diskette commonly used with microcomputers for magnetic storage of data.

Flowchart   A type of chart that displays how events are sequenced by time or order.

Flush left   Text that is aligned at the left margin with the right margin being different lengths (also called ragged right).

Flush right   Text that is aligned at the right margin with the left margin being different lengths (also called ragged left).

Font   A collection of all the letters, numbers, and symbols of one style of type in one size.

Footer   Text that appears at the bottom of a page; often a page number.

Format   (1) The setting of parameters such as margins or tabs that control the appearance of text or the setting of attributes to describe how data are to be displayed. (2) A term used to describe the preparation of a disk or diskette for use.

Formula   A mathematical or logical equation from which data values are calculated.

FORTRAN (FORmula TRANslator)   A high-level language designed for scientists, engineers, and mathematicians to solve complex numerical problems.

Fourth-generation computer   Computers developed and in use from 1971 to the present, which use large-scale integration (LSI).

Fourth-generation language   A class of programming language in which users need very little programming knowledge to write computer instructions; e.g., database query languages, report generators, and application generators.

Free-form approach   In application program design, the entry of values, text, or formulas without regard to a preplanned structure

Freeware   Also, public domain software. A software program not protected by copyright law; available for public use.

Front-end processor   A special-purpose computer that controls the input and output functions of a main computer.

Full-duplex mode   A method of transferring data over a communication channel; permits data to be transmitted and received at the same time.

Fuzzy logic   A method of computing in which the computer makes "decisions" based on changing conditions rather than two states such as on or off.

Game port   A port used to connect joysticks or paddles to the computer. Also, analog-to-digital port.

Garbage in, garbage out (GIGO)   Refers to a situation in which incorrect input produces incorrect output.

Gas-plasma display   A flat-panel display that uses ionized gas to form images on the screen. These types of displays do not create flicker.

Gateway   An interface that converts the data codes, formats, addresses, and transmission rates of one network into a form usable by another network.

Gateway service   A service whereby computer time is bought from many information and commercial database services at wholesale rates and sold to subscribers at a retail rate. A gateway service provides users with the convenience of accessing many services through one central communication line.

Generalized application software   Software that can be applied to a wide variety of tasks. Category includes word processors, electronic spreadsheets, database management systems, graphics, and communications.

Grammar and style checker   A software program that locates grammar, sentence structure, writing style, and punctuation errors in a document.

Graphical user interface (GUI)   A type of user interface that includes some or all of the following parts: icons, a graphical pointer, on-screen pull-down menus, windows that enclose applications or objects on the screen, and other graphic devices that let you tell the computer what to do and how to do it, for example, option boxes, check boxes, dialog boxes, and buttons.

Graphics adapter card   A circuit board that converts electrical signals sent by the computer into a form usable by the monitor. The graphics card determines the monitor display type.

Graphics programs   (see Graphics software) Programs that display data visually in the form of graphic images.

Graphics software   An application program that allows a user to create, edit, display, and print graphic images; may be a separate software program or integrated into another software program.

Graphics tablet   A device that consists of a flat plastic rectangle that contains electronic circuitry below its surface to detect when an object makes contact with the tablet. Used in conjunction with pointing devices such as the stylus and the puck. Also called a digitizing tablet.

Green computing Computers and related computer equipment that fit an ecological profile set by the Environmental Protection Agency's Energy Star Program.

Grid A pattern of horizontal and vertical lines (sometimes just the dots representing the intersection of these lines) providing a visual aid to help enter or find data at specific coordinate positions on the screen.

Group In Microsoft Windows, a collection of applications that can be run under Windows.

Groupware Software that allows members of a group of users to work together without all participants having to be in the same place at the same time.

Half-duplex mode A method of transferring data over a communication channel; permits data to be transmitted and received but not at the same time.

Handheld scanner A type of scanner that can be held in the hand. They are best suited for scanning smaller images such as photos.

Handshaking The process of sending prearranged signals specifying the protocol to be followed when transmitting or receiving data.

Hand-tracking device A special purpose input device that converts the movements of a hand into digital signals used to control various functions such as the movement of a graphically produced hand displayed on the screen.

Hard copy A form of relatively stable and permanent output; for example, paper or computer output microform. It can be read immediately or stored for later use.

Hard disk A hard metallic disk used for magnetic storage of data. Because of its rigid construction, it can be produced with higher storage densities than floppies, allowing more data to be stored. Data can also be accessed faster than they can with a floppy diskette.

Hard disk drive The input/output device that transfers data to and from a hard disk.

Hard page break When a user manually inserts a page break starting text on a new page.

Hardware The physical components of a computer system, such as the computer itself, input devices, output devices, and data communication devices.

Head crash The result of the read/write head of a hard-disk drive coming into contact with the hard disk; results in severe damage to the head, disk, or both.

Header Text that appears at the top of a page; often a title.

Head position trackers A pointing device that uses a headset that emulates a mouse, and a control unit that sits on top of the computer, which measures the change in the headset's angular position and translates this change into cursor movements. The headset also contains an attached mouth tube into which the user can lightly puff to select an item, such as a letter to be entered into a word processing document from a keyboard that is displayed on the screen.

Hexadecimal system The base 16 system, composed of the numerals 0 through 9 and the letters A through F.

Hierarchical database A database structure in which data relationships follow hierarchies or trees, which are either one-to-one or one-to-many relationships among record types.

High-level language A programming language using instructions that closely resemble human language and mathematical notation. BASIC and Pascal are examples.

Host computer The computer with which you establish communication.

Human engineering The design of furnishings and machines to meet the needs of people. See Ergonomics.

Human resources information system A system designed to provide management with information involving the recruitment, placement, evaluation, compensation, and development of employees.

Hypertext Graphically oriented software in which data are stored as objects that can be arbitrarily linked and accessed. Hypertext software incorporates components of a database, text editor, and graphics editor, and uses a mouse to move through windows, to click on icons, and to pull down menus.

Icon An onscreen graphical representation of items such as programs or instructions.

Image database Database software that allows the storage of pictures.

Image editing programs   Programs that allow the user to modify a graphic or photographic image.

Impact printer   A type of printer that produces characters by using a hammer or pins to strike an ink ribbon against a sheet of paper.

Implied warranty   A product warranty which implies that the goods are reasonably fit and of average quality.

Indexed file processing   A file processing method that incorporates elements of direct and sequential access. An index is created that is searched sequentially; upon finding the appropriate value the file or record is then directly accessed.

Indexing   The process of creating a file of a sorted database. The index file is saved separately, allowing the original database to be left unchanged.

Inference engine   The component of a knowledge-based (expert) system that uses the rules from the knowledge base together with the data provided by a user to draw a possible conclusion.

Information   Data that have been processed into an organized, usable form and are meaningful to the recipient for the task at hand.

Information center   An area within a firm that distributes information, provides instruction in the use of an information system, distributes computing hardware, and provides information system experts and other useful functions in a support role.

Information literacy   Being able to judge the value of information and use the information wisely.

Information processing   Refers to the input, processing, output, and storage steps associated with converting data into information.

Information system   A set of hardware, software, people, data, and procedures that work together to manage the acquisition, storage, manipulation, and distribution of information.

Information system manager   A person who plans and oversees all information resources in an organization.

Inheritance   In an object-oriented programming language, the ability of the programming language itself to define a new object that has all the attributes of an existing object.

Ink-jet printer   A type of nonimpact printer that forms characters on paper by spraying ink particles in character forms.

Input   (1) The data and instructions entered into a computer for processing. (2) The act of entering data and instructions.

Input block   A portion of a spreadsheet set up to contain variable data used in formulas.

Input device   Hardware that allows instructions and data to be entered into the computer for processing, e.g., keyboard and mouse.

Input form   A structured document in which spaces are reserved for specific information.

Input/output (I/O) device   Devices that can transfer and receive data and instructions to and from the computer.

Input/output (I/O) ports   See Expansion ports.

Insert mode   A condition in an application package in which the addition of new text results in all text to the right being moved over to make room for the new text.

Install   In application software the process of preparing the program to work with your computer.

Installation   The second task in the system implementation phase of the system development life cycle, during which an information system is made operational by being put to work for the users.

Installation program   The program responsible for getting the application up and running, guiding the user through the process by presenting a screen menu of set-up options.

Instruction cycle   The instruction time and execution time steps in the process of performing an instruction.

Instruction set   The group of instructions that defines the basic operations of a computer, that is, the arithmetic, logical, storage, and retrieval functions.

Instruction time   Time required to fetch an instruction from memory and place it into a register.

Integrated circuit (IC)   A single, complete, electronic semiconductor circuit contained on a piece of silicon; also called a microchip or chip.

Integrated Services Digital Network (ISDN)   Worldwide digital communication network using standardized interfaces. This communication will be entirely digital when fully implemented.

Integrated software   A category of application software that combines a number of applications, such as word processing, database management, spreadsheet, graphics, and communication, into a single application package.

Intelligent recalculation   Recalculation controlled by the spreadsheet program.

Intelligent terminal   A stand-alone keyboard and display screen that can send or receive data and that incorporates a microprocessor, enabling it to process data independently.

Interactive processing   Type of processing associated with on-line input that involves the user in a command and response mode with the computer in a more or less continuous participation.

Interactive system   A system that allows a user to communicate with the computer through dialogue.

Interface   Describes how two parts are joined so that they can work together.

Interface cable   The cable that connects the computer to the peripheral device.

Interlaced screen   A method of scanning a screen in which all the even lines are scanned, then all the odd lines. This method increases flicker.

Internal commands   In MS-DOS, commands that are part of the COMMAND.COM file and are stored in main memory so that they execute immediately after you type them and press Enter.

Internal direct-connect modem   Similar in function to the external direct-connect modem; has all the circuitry on one circuit board, which fits into an expansion slot inside the computer.

Interoperability   Refers to using hardware and software from different vendors interchangeably.

Interpreter   A language-translator program that translates a high-level language program into machine code one line at a time. Each line is executed after it is translated.

Interprocessing   An operating system capability that allows any change made in one application to be automatically reflected in any related, linked application. Also called dynamic linking.

Interrecord gap   The section of magnetic tape between individual records that allows the tape to attain the proper speed for reading or writing.

Joystick   A pointing device that uses a lever to control cursor movement.

Justification   A feature of application software that allows a user to move text flush to the right, left, or centered between the margins.

Justified text   Text that is aligned at the left and the right margins, giving the text the appearance of a block.

Kermit protocol   A set of rules used for sending and receiving nontext files; popular on large computers.

Kerning   In text composition or typesetting, selectively nudging letters together to improve spacing; gives the illusion of equal spacing between letters.

Keyboard   An input device that resembles a typewriter keyboard on which you press individual keys or combinations of keys to send data to the computer for processing.

Key field   A field used to uniquely identify each record.

Knowledge base   The component of a knowledge-based (expert) system that contains a collection of facts and the rules by which those facts relate.

Knowledge workers   The people who create, process, and distribute information.

Label   An alphanumeric designator that describes the contents of an area or device, such as a title or a heading for a report.

LAN aware software   Stand-alone programs that have been modified to work on a LAN.

Language-translator program   A program that translates a programming language into machine code for execution by a computer.

LAN ignorant software   Software designed for stand-alone use only.

LAN intrinsic software   Programs designed to share the processing power of several computers, and distribute data and computer power across the network.

LAN management software   Software used to monitor and diagnose the LAN.

LAN specific software   Software that requires a LAN to operate effectively.

Laptop computer   A microcomputer that can run on both AC and batteries and weighs around 10 to 15 pounds.

Large-scale integration (LSI) The process of putting the equivalent of several thousand components on a single chip.

Laser printer A nonimpact printer that produces images on paper by directing a laser beam onto a drum and leaving a negative charge to which positively charged toner powder will stick. The toner powder is transferred to paper as it rolls by the drum and is bonded to the paper by hot rollers.

Leading In word processing, refers to the amount of space between lines.

Letter-quality print Print of fully formed characters, similar to typewriter print.

Light pen A light-sensitive pointing device used to select an entry or indicate position; when touched to the display screen, it detects the presence or absence of light.

Line graph A graph that represents data as a series of points connected by straight or curved lines; used to show trends and emphasize movement and direction of change over a period of time.

Line printer A printer with a print mechanism capable of printing an entire line at a time; also called a line-at-a-time printer.

Liquid-crystal display (LCD) A type of flat-panel display that produces images by aligning molecular crystals.

LISP A language used to process symbol sequences (lists) rather than numbers; used frequently in artificial intelligence.

Load Refers to placing a program in main memory.

Local-area network (LAN) A type of computer network in which two or more computers of the same or different sizes are directly linked within a small, well-defined area, such as a room or building.

Local bus Type of bus in which video devices are connected directly to the CPU bus, allowing data transfer to take place at the CPU's speed.

Logic In a program the finite set of step-by-step instructions that convert the input into the desired output, that is, solve the problem.

Logical database design A detailed description of a database, based on how the data will be used.

Logical system design The blueprint phase of designing a new information system. Descriptive tools (graphs, charts, and tables) are used to describe what the inputs, outputs, and files of a new system will look like. The products of this step are turned over to application programmers, who convert a conceptual information system blueprint into an actual working system.

Logic error A computer program error caused by improperly coding either individual statements or sequences. It does not stop program execution, but will produce inaccurate results.

Logo An interactive education-oriented language designed to teach inexperienced users logic and programming techniques.

Log off The process of disconnecting from the host computer.

Log on The process of entering into a system an account number followed by a password to control user access to the system.

Low-level language A programming language, such as machine language or assembly; requires a programmer to have detailed knowledge of the internal workings of the computer.

Machine language A programming language that a computer understands; based on electronic on/off states represented by the binary number system of 1s and 0s.

Macro block The part of the spreadsheet where the macros are located.

Magnetic disk A mylar (floppy diskette) or metallic (hard disk) platter on which electronic data can be stored; suitable for both direct-access or sequential-access storage and retrieval of data.

Magnetic-ink character recognition (MICR) A source-data input technique in which data are represented by magnetic ink characters that can be read either by humans or directly into a computer via a scanner.

Magnetic strip A thin band of magnetically encoded data used on the backs of many credit cards and automatic banking cards.

Magnetic tape A strip of mylar coated with iron oxide and used to store data magnetically; a sequential storage medium.

Mail merge   The process of combining two documents into one. For example, a form letter can be merged with a file containing names and addresses, in order to personalize the letter.

Mainframe computer   A large-scale computer with processing capabilities greater than those of a minicomputer but less than those of a supercomputer.

Main logic module   The portion of a program that controls the execution of the other modules in the program.

Main memory   Storage where the instructions in a computer program and the data they work on must be stored to be executed. Main memory consists of both RAM and ROM.

Maintenance programmer   A special type of programmer responsible for the maintenance of an information system.

Management information system (MIS)   A system that supplies managers with information to aid in decision-making responsibilities.

Manager   A person responsible for using available resources (people, materials/equipment, land, and money) to achieve an organizational goal.

Manufacturing automation protocol (MAP)   A communication link developed by General Motors that allows different types of computers to communicate with each other.

Margin settings   Specifications that describe the blank spaces around the left, right, top, and bottom of a document.

Marketing information system   An information system designed to gather details about day-to-day sales transactions, management and control of operations, and sales and marketing strategies for the future.

Massively parallel processing (MPP)   See parallel processing.

Mechanical mouse   A type of mouse that has a device on the underside that detects the direction and speed of its movement across a flat surface. This device is usually a ball that is rolled along the surface. The rotation of the ball is translated into a digital signal that controls the movement of the cursor.

Menu   In application software a screen listing of commands, actions, or other alternatives from which a user may select at a particular point in a program. A menu selection may perform an action or bring up another menu.

Menu bar   A line of available commands or functions, usually located at the top of a window. Accessing the menu bar reveals additional commands or functions available.

Menu-driven interface   A type of user interface that allows the user to select commands from a list (menu) using the keyboard or a pointing device such as a mouse.

Menu-driven program   A program that uses on-screen menus to access commands and functions.

Message characters   The start and stop bits of asynchronous transmission and the synchronizing characters in synchronous transmission that signal when data are being sent and when a transmission is finished.

Messages   In an object-oriented programming language, the instructions sent between objects.

Microchip   An integrated circuit; chip.

Microcomputer   A computer that is built around a single-chip processor called the microprocessor; relatively small in size.

Microprocessor   A single chip that contains both the arithmetic-logic unit (ALU) and the control unit.

Microsoft Disk Operating System (MS-DOS)   A microcomputer operating system. It is the most commonly used operating system for IBM and compatible microcomputers.

Microsoft Windows   A graphical environment for DOS-based systems created by Microsoft Corporation. It creates a GUI consistent from one application to the next.

Microwave   A type of data communication channel in which data are transmitted through the air as analog signals for reception by satellites or microwave transmitting stations.

Millions of instructions per second (MIPS)   A measure of computer speed; the number of instructions completed per second.

Minicomputer   A computer in the large-scale category that has less processing capability than a mainframe computer.

Mirror   A graphics feature that allows a mirror image of an object to appear as a user draws the original.

Mixed cell reference   A method of copying a formula in a spreadsheet; requires that each cell reference be specified as either absolute or relative.

Mnemonic   An alphabetic abbreviation used as a memory aid.

Modem   Acronym for modulator-demodulator; the device that converts signals from analog to digital form and from digital to analog form.

Modulation   The process of converting a digital signal to an analog signal.

Module   A small group of related processing instructions that are easy to understand and code; part of a larger program.

Monitor   A televisionlike device used to display data or information.

Mouse   A popular pointing device that controls the cursor position on the screen. It is designed to be easily gripped in your hand and contains one or more buttons on the top which are used to select items and choose commands.

Mouse driver   The software that enables a program to use a mouse.

Mouse pointer   An object such as an arrow that shows the position of the mouse on the screen.

Mouse port   Serial port designed especially for a mouse.

MS-DOS command prompt   An onscreen indicator that consists of the current drive letter and the symbol > used to denote the current drive.

Multidimensional spreadsheet   An electronic spreadsheet capable of showing ranges of cells as solids (three-dimensional objects). This form allows for organization of complex worksheets.

Multimedia   The incorporation of the peripheral devices necessary to integrate text, graphic images, audio, and video.

Multiple block design   In spreadsheet design, using a number of predesigned blocks in the construction of a worksheet.

Multiplexer   A hardware device that performs the multiplexing process.

Multiplexing   The process of combining the transmission from more than one device, character by character, into a single data stream that

can be sent over a single communication channel.

Multipoint channel configuration   A type of communication channel configuration in which three or more devices, connected together, share the same communication channel.

Multiprocessing   An operating system capability that allows the simultaneous execution of programs by a computer that has two or more CPUs.

Multisync monitor   A type of monitor that supports VGA and higher resolutions.

Multitasking   An operating system capability that allows a single CPU to execute what appears to be more than one program at a time.

Multithreading   An operating system capability that allows the execution of several simultaneous tasks within the same application.

Multiuser information system   An information system designed to be used by many users.

Multiuser operating system   An operating system that allows two or more users to access a computer at the same time.

Narrow-band channel   A communication channel, such as a telegraph line, that transmits data at 40 to 100 bits per second.

Natural language   A computer language that can understand and translate a natural language, such as English, into commands that perform a specific operation.

Natural language processing   The ability of a computer to understand and translate a natural language, such as English, into commands to perform a specific operation.

Near-letter-quality (NLQ) print   High-quality print formed by the print head making multiple passes over each character.

Network architecture   The structure of the network, that is, how the components are connected, and the protocols and interfaces used for communication.

Network database   A database structure in which data use a many-to-many relationship among the records.

Network interface card   Circuit board that connects a computer to the LAN cable.

Network operating system   The software that controls the operations and functions of a network.

Neural networks A method of making computers "think" more like humans by organizing processing into a grid in which information is shared and tasks are performed simultaneously, as in the human brain.

Node Each computer or device in a computer network system.

Nonimpact printer A type of printer that produces characters without physically striking the paper.

Noninterlaced screen A method of scanning in which every line is scanned on the screen sequentially. This reduces the flicker.

Nonprocedural language A programming language that describes the task to be accomplished without specifying the approach.

Notebook computer A microcomputer that is about the size of an 8½ × 11 inch notebook, uses both AC and battery power options, weighs around 6 to 8 pounds, has a display screen from 7 to 10 inches, and a keyboard that is smaller than desktop microcomputers.

Object In an object-oriented programming language, a combination of data and instructions that work on the data and are stored together as a reusable unit.

Object code A machine-readable form of a program that can be executed by the computer.

Object-oriented database A database model that uses objects and messages to accommodate new types of data and provides for advanced data handling.

Object-oriented database management system (OODBMS) A database management system that allows objects to be readily created, maintained, manipulated, and retrieved from an object-oriented database.

Object-oriented graphics See vector graphics.

Object-oriented programming language (OOPL) A programming language that treats a program as a series of objects and messages. Three important principles of an OOPL are encapsulation, inheritance, and polymorphism.

Octal system The base 8 system, composed of the numerals 0 through 7.

Office information system (OIS) An information system that includes a number of subsystems integrated together to perform office functions more efficiently and productively.

Off-line (1) Refers to a device that is ready for use and can communicate with or be controlled by a computer. (2) The condition in which no communication link is established.

On-line (1) Refers to a device that cannot communicate with or be controlled by a computer. (2) The condition in which a computer is linked to and communicating with another computer.

On-line input Involves the immediate capture and entry of data into the computer for processing.

On-line real-time processing Involves the immediate processing of data upon input to the computer. Order-entry systems and airline reservation systems typically use on-line input and on-line real-time processing.

Operating environment Software that enhances the functions of an operating system and improves its user interface.

Operating system (OS) The core set of programs (provided by the developer of the operating system) that controls and supervises a computer's hardware and provides services to other system software, application software, programmers, and users.

Operational information system An information system that records and helps manage a transaction.

Operational (low-level) managers A manager running day-to-day operations of a business, mainly directing other personnel in implementing the tactical decisions of middle-level management.

Optical-bar recognition (OBR) A data-input method that reads and interprets bar codes.

Optical card A small card that stores data on a strip of special material that is similar to a magnetic strip. However, the data on an optical card are encoded by a laser rather than magnetically.

Optical-character recognition (OCR) software Software that translates images captured with a scanner into text files that can be used by programs capable of manipulating text.

Optical computer A computer that uses laser beams instead of electrical signals to perform on/off switching. This enables faster computing.

Optical laser disk A type of storage medium on which data are stored and read by a laser. Optical-laser disks have much higher data densities than their magnetic disk counterparts.

Optical-mark recognition (OMR) A data-input method in which a series of pen or pencil marks on a special form are scanned and their position is translated into machine-readable code, e.g., computer-scored test answer sheets.

Optical mouse A type of mouse that detects light reflected off a pad containing a very precise set of grid lines to track the mouse's movements and convert these into a digital signal to control an on-screen cursor.

Optical recognition The process of using light-sensing equipment to scan paper or other sources and translate the pattern of light and dark, or color, into a digital signal that can be used by the computer.

Optical scanner An input device that uses light to sense the patterns of black and white (or color) on paper or other medium and convert them into a digital signal that can be manipulated by graphical software or optical character recognition (OCR) software. Often simply called a scanner.

Optical tape A storage medium that is similar in appearance to magnetic tape but that stores data with optical-laser techniques.

Optical technology The technology that uses lasers as a means of storing and retrieving data.

Organizational chart A type of chart that displays a hierarchy of data.

Orientation In word processing, refers to the direction the letters print on the paper.

Orphan line The first line of a new paragraph that stands alone at the bottom of a page.

Outline font One set of characters that can be enlarged or made smaller to fit a desired point size. Also, scalable font.

Output (1) The process of retrieving stored information, converting it into human-readable form, and displaying that information in a form understandable to a user. (2) The result of processing.

Output block The part of the spreadsheet where the results of the calculations are displayed.

Output device A peripheral device that translates machine-readable codes into a form that can be used by humans or other machines.

Pacing In communication, a feature that allows a user to designate the amount of time between data transmissions; often used when two communicating devices send and receive data at different rates.

Packet A unit of information transmitted as a whole from one device to another in a network.

Page-composition software Graphic-oriented software used in positioning and aligning text, graphics, and other elements of a document page on the screen.

Page description language (PDL) The set of codes that dictates the character size and font style, among other attributes, that the printer can print.

Page printer A type of printer that prints an entire page at a time, as opposed to character or line printers.

Paint program A microcomputer graphics program that allows a user to "paint" an image by using an input device, such as a mouse, as the brush. The user can also draw, fill shapes, and change the color and texture of a painting. Paint programs handle graphics as rasters.

Palmtop computer A microcomputer that weighs less than one pound and fits easily into your pocket; provides quick access to the data wherever you need them.

Pan A graphics package feature that moves the entire graphic content on the screen from side to side, allowing users to create and view images wider than the screen.

Parallel conversion A conversion approach in which both new and old information systems are used for a certain period of time, after which the old system is discontinued.

Parallel port Ports that transmit data over eight wires eight bits at a time. Often used for printers and called printer ports.

Parallel processing A data-processing method in which a computer accesses several instructions from the same program at once and works on them at the same time, using multiple CPUs; much faster than traditional serial processing techniques.

Parity A type of error-checking procedure used in communication.

Parity bit   The bit used to check for errors in a transmitted signal. It may be even, odd, or none.

Parked   In a computer with a hard disk drive, moving the read/write head away from the disk and "parking" it to prevent its bouncing on the disk and damaging the disk surface (and therefore data) if the computer is bumped or moved.

Pascal   A high-level language originally designed to teach structured-programming concepts; suited for both file processing and mathematical applications.

Passive-matrix display   A type of LCD monitor that uses one set of transistors for each row and column on the screen.

Password   An alphanumeric code that restricts data access to those with knowledge of the correct password.

Path   Tells MS-DOS where you want it to look for a file; can consist of a drive name, directory names, and the name of the file you want to find.

Peer-to-peer network   A LAN in which each personal computer acts as a server and shares its resources.

Pen-based computer   A microcomputer that can use a penlike device to input data.

Peripheral devices   Hardware that is externally attached to the system unit.

Personal computer (PC)   A microcomputer designed to be used primarily by a single individual.

Personal information system   An information system designed for use by an individual user.

Phase change printer   High-quality color printers; unlike wax thermal printers they require no special paper, but spray the melted wax directly onto the paper.

Phased-in conversion   A conversion approach in which a new information system is installed in phases, or segments.

Physical database design   The actual structure based on the database management system software on the system.

Physical system design   A stage of the system design phase of the system development life cycle during which a logical (paper) design is transformed into an actual working system.

Pie chart   A graph that uses a circle (pie) divided into segments to show the relationship of data to the whole.

Pilot conversion   A conversion approach in which a new system is installed in one location and tried there before it is installed in other locations.

Pixel   The smallest part of a display screen that can be individually controlled.

PL/1 (Programming Language One)   A high-level language that allows powerful computations and sophisticated data structures. It was designed to replace FORTRAN, ALGOL, and COBOL and is used largely in the oil industry.

Plotter   An output device especially designed to produce a hard copy of graphics.

Point   In word processing, a measurement of a font's size.

Pointing device   An input device that controls an on-screen cursor or creates drawings or graphical shapes. Often used for actions such as choosing menu items, "pressing" on-screen "buttons" in dialog boxes, and selecting text or other values.

Point-of-sale (POS) terminal   A device that reads data at the source of a transaction and immediately translates them into usable information.

Point-to-point channel configuration   A type of communication channel configuration that directly connects a computer to a single device, giving those two entities sole use of the channel.

Polling   A method of determining which device needs to access a communication channel. The main computer checks, or polls, each device on the channel, one at a time, to see whether it has any data to send. Only one device can use that channel at a time.

Polymorphism   In an object-oriented programming language, the ability of an object to respond to a message in many ways.

Portable computer   A microcomputer that is small enough to be carried easily from place to place.

Portable printer   A printer that is generally smaller, lighter, and more rugged than desktop printers; most are battery powered so they can be taken anywhere.

Presentation graphics   Graphics suitable for a formal presentation.

Primary storage   Type of storage in which the instructions in a computer program and the data they work on must be stored to be executed. More often called main memory.

Printer   An output device that produces hard copy, usually consisting of text but sometimes including graphics as well.

Printer driver   Software that informs the computer what type of printer is connected and its capabilities.

Print server   The computer that provides LAN users with access to a centralized printer or a shared printer of a workstation.

Problem definition   The first stage of the system analysis phase of the system development life cycle, which begins when a problem with the current information system is detected and is serious enough to lead to the question, "Should we start planning for a new system to replace the current system?"

Procedural language   A programming language that specifies how a task is accomplished.

Procedures   The instructions that tell a user how to operate and use an information system.

Process control   Monitoring and controlling an operation.

Processing   The steps performed to convert data into useful information.

Production/operations information system   An information system designed to gather and process data about all activities involved in producing goods and services.

Program development process   A series of steps to follow when developing a program consisting of the following steps: documentation; determining user needs; designing the program specifications; reviewing the program specifications; designing the algorithm; coding the program; compiling, testing and debugging the program; and getting the program to the user.

Program editor   A program that allows a programmer to type, edit, and save program code on disk.

Program flowchart   A design aid that graphically shows the processing steps of a computer program.

Programmable controller   A computer-controlled unit consisting of a microprocessor, input and output modules, and a power supply; used to monitor and control machinery and processes.

Programmable file management system   A file management system that allows a user to enter programming commands to cross-referenced multiple flat files.

Programmer   An individual who translates the tasks a user wants a computer to accomplish into a form the computer understands.

Programming language   A set of written symbols that tells the computer hardware how to perform specified operations.

Project justification   A stage of the system analysis phase of the system development life cycle in which the information system personnel perform cost/benefit analysis of the various alternative information systems that could bridge the gap between the current and the ideal information systems and select one system to recommend to management.

Project management   The structured coordination and monitoring of all activities involved in a one-time endeavor, or project.

Prolog   A language used to process symbol sequences (lists) rather than numbers; used extensively in artificial intelligence.

Protocol   A set of rules and procedures for transmitting and receiving data so that different devices can communicate with each other.

Prototype information system   A real, working, and usable system, built economically and quickly with the intention of being modified.

Pseudocode   A code that uses English-like phrases to describe the processing steps of a program or a module.

Puck   A pointing device, often used with a graphics tablet, that has a mouselike shape with buttons for selecting items or choosing commands and a clear plastic piece with cross hairs printed on it that extends out from the body.

Query   A series of statements instructing the database management system to retrieve specific information.

Query by example   A query-language style in which the user inputs query conditions in the desired fields.

Queue In printing, the storage place for files while waiting to be printed, usually first in, first out.

Random-access memory (RAM) A type of memory into which data and programs can be written and from which data and programs can be read. Data stored in RAM are erased when the computer's power is shut off.

Range of cells In a spreadsheet a method of selecting specific cells by identifying the upper-left cell and the lower-right cell; permits large blocks of cells to be manipulated together.

Raster graphic Graphic images drawn from a collection of dots.

Readability A measure of the appropriateness and understandability of a document.

Read-only memory (ROM) A type of memory, the contents of which are entered during manufacturing. The contents can only be read; they are permanent and cannot be changed.

Ready/entry mode A mode of operation in which a spreadsheet program indicates that it is ready to receive information. When a character is entered, the program automatically switches to the entry mode.

Real-time processing An operating system capability that allows a computer to control or monitor the task performance of other machines and people by responding to input data in a specified amount of time.

Record A collection of related data items.

Record-oriented A type of database based on the physical structure of data and indexing.

Reel-to-reel tape Magnetic tape, usually one-half inch wide, wound on reels. Typically used with large computer systems to provide greater amounts of secondary storage at a comparatively modest cost.

Referential integrity Comparing columns that are common to more than one table in that they contain the same value.

Refresh rate The number of times a screen is scanned, measured in hertz.

Register A temporary holding place for data or instructions that are to be worked on immediately; part of a CPU.

Relational database A database that is composed of many tables in which data are stored, having unique rows.

Relational database management system (RDBMS) The database management system that allows data to be readily created, maintained, manipulated, and retrieved from a relational database.

Relative cell reference A method of copying in which the formula is the same but the cells referenced in that formula are different; used with spreadsheets.

Removable cartridge A hard disk storage system that utilizes a cartridge containing one or more hard disks. The cartridge can be removed from the hard disk drive and replaced with another cartridge at any time.

Repetition control structure Also called looping; a programming control structure that allows a series of instructions to be executed more than once without being recoded.

Report An organized presentation of information.

Report generator A fourth-generation language that allows data to be extracted from a database and formatted into a report.

Requirements analysis A stage of the system analysis phase of the system development life cycle that involves the analysis of a current system's performance to determine what the ideal system would be. The gap between the current system and the ideal system is explored to determine which system will best close the gap.

Resolution The quality of a monitor's screen, measured by the number of pixels the screen contains.

Ring network A computer network arrangement in which each computer or device is connected in a closed loop by a single communication channel. Communication between the source and the destination must flow through each device in the ring.

Robotics The area of study dealing with the design, construction, and operation of robots.

Root record The topmost record in a tree structure.

Rotate A graphics package feature that allows turning (rotating) an object on the screen.

Row In a spreadsheet, the numeric ordering from top to bottom that, along with the alphabetic column designations, locates the position of a cell.

RPG (Report Program Generator) A programming language designed for producing reports and processing files.

Run-time error An error that causes a program to stop executing.

Satellite An electronic device placed in orbit around the earth to receive, amplify, and transmit signals; used in wide-area networks.

Scale A feature in graphics software that lets a user change the dimensions of an image, e.g., reduce or enlarge it.

Scanner See Optical Scanner.

Scatter graph A graph in which two sets of data points are plotted; used to show the correlation (if any) between the data sets.

Schema A complete description of the content and structure of a database.

Screen form A layout form created for the purpose of defining the position of data fields and providing an entry point for the data in a data manager.

Screen saver A program that causes random patterns on the screen to prevent images from being burned into the screen.

Script In communication, a file used to automatically log on.

Search and replace An application software feature that allows a user to look for a word or phrase in a file and determine whether it should be replaced. One option permits it to be automatically replaced.

Secondary storage Nonvolatile storage typically used for long-term storage or for large quantities of data or programs.

Secondary storage device Hardware that provides permanent or relatively permanent storage of data and instructions, e.g., hard disk drives and floppy disk drives; nonvolatile.

Second-generation computer Computers developed and used between 1959 and 1965 that used transistors to control internal operations.

Sectors A pie-shaped division of each magnetic-disk track, which further identifies the storage location of data.

Selection control structure A programming control structure that selects a processing option based on the result of decision criteria.

Sequence control structure A programming control structure that executes statements in order, one after another.

Sequential-access file processing A file processing method in which information is stored and retrieved in sequential order, that is, one after another.

Serial port A port in which data are transmitted over one wire one bit at a time.

Serial processing A processing method in which a single CPU finishes executing one instruction before starting the next.

Server A computer that provides services to a local-area network.

Service program An external operating system program that provides a service to a user or application program; it must be loaded separately.

Set-oriented A type of database that focuses on the characteristics of data rather than the physical structure of the data. The user works with data in sets.

Shareware Software program available to the public; the author may request a donation if you use the program.

Simplex mode A method of transferring data over a communication channel in only one direction. Simplex mode devices can transmit or receive but not both.

Simulation A method of creating computerized models of real-life situations; also a method of computer instruction.

Single block design In a spreadsheet, contains the headings at the top of the block identifying the title or other information.

Single tasking An operating system capability that allows only one program to execute at a time, and that program must finish executing completely before the next program can begin.

Single-user operating system An operating system that allows only one user at a time to access a computer.

Slide show In a graphics program, a feature that allows individual graphics files to be displayed in a predetermined order for a predetermined amount of time, similar to a slide projector and slides.

Small computer system interface (SCSI) port A fast versatile parallel port that allows multiple peripheral devices to be connected together to one port.

Smart paper Embedded intelligence in a computer screen.

Soft copy   A form of volatile output, usually a screen display.

Soft page break   When the word processor or other application program automatically inserts a page break to indicate the end of one page and the beginning of the next.

Software   The instructions, written in a computer programming language, that direct the operations of a computer and cause the hardware to do the work.

Software piracy   The unauthorized duplication of copyrighted computer programs.

Sorting   The process of arranging data in numeric or alphabetic sequence, either in ascending or descending order.

Source code   A program written in a human-readable high-level or assembly programming language.

Source data entry   The data collection method wherein data generated at a source are entered directly into a computer in machine-readable form.

Source document   The original document, such as an employee timecard, on which data are recorded.

Specialized application software   Application software developed for a specific use; for example, a payroll package.

Specialized common carrier   A common carrier that offers only a limited number of services, usually within only a specific area.

Speech coding   A type of voice output. The computer uses stored sounds to build sentences or phrases to be spoken.

Speech recognition   The ability of a computer to accept input by understanding the speech of a user.

Spelling checker   Also called a dictionary; a word processor program that locates misspelled words or words not in its dictionary.

Spool (Simultaneous Peripheral Operation On-Line)   The hardware, software, or combination of both used to control a buffer that holds data before they are sent to another device.

Spooling   The process of sending output to a buffer for temporary storage before printing.

Spreadsheet   A paper form, divided into rows and columns, that can be used to keep track of and manipulate numeric data. The computerized version is called an electronic spreadsheet.

Spreadsheet design   The arrangement of values, text, and formulas in the rows and columns of a spreadsheet.

Spreadsheet software   An application software program that displays, manipulates, and prints data in a row and column format; computerized version of the paper spreadsheet. Also, electronic spreadsheet.

Stacked-line graph   Line graph in which the areas between sets of data are shaded or filled in. Also called area graph.

Standard-quality print   Print made from dots that is suitable for most informal applications; of lower quality than near-letter-quality print. Also called draft-quality print.

Star network   A computer network arrangement in which each device is connected to one centralized computer. All communications must be routed through the central host computer.

Status line   One or more lines located at the top or the bottom of a display screen; provides information about the current file or operation in progress.

Stop bit   In communication, the bit used to synchronize the receiving and transmitting terminals on a word-by-word basis.

Storage   Refers to the computer's ability to maintain data or information for use at a later time. Two primary means of storage are internal storage (called main memory, or primary storage) and external storage (called secondary storage).

Strategic (top-level) managers   Managers who make long-range, strategic decisions. Most top-level managers' time is spent in planning and organizing.

Structured block design approach   In application programs, the preplanned layout method that improves the design, understandability, and usefulness.

Structured programming   A method of writing computer programs that emphasizes the systematic design, development, and management of the software development process. This type of programming increases programmer productivity, improves the quality of programs, and makes them easier to read.

Structured query language (SQL)   A query language that allows end users to make inquiries into a database.

Style sheet   A formatting feature in word processors that automates text repetition and certain formatting functions by providing a built-in collection of documents or the basic forms for documents.

Stylus   A pointing device that can be used with a graphics tablet or pen-based computer. It is pressed against the graphics tablet or computer screen to draw, point, or enter data. Also called a pen.

Subdirectory   A directory within another directory.

Subschema   Defines each user's view or specific part of a database; a security envelope that restricts each user to certain records and fields within a database.

Supercomputer   The most powerful type of computer; used primarily by government agencies and organizations that process vast quantities of data.

Superconductors   The flow of electricity through certain materials with no resistance; occurs at very low temperatures.

Superimpose   A graphics feature that allows a user to place one object over another without erasing either one.

Superstore   A type of store that specializes in selling computers and related items.

Supervisor program   Also called monitor, executive, or kernel; the main control program in an operating system responsible for controlling all other OS programs as well as other system and application programs.

Surge protector   Device that protects computers against power-line voltage surges caused by fluctuations in power generation or lightning strikes.

Synchronous transmission   A method of data transmission in which blocks of characters are sent in timed sequences. Each block of characters is marked by special synchronizing characters. This method is much faster than asynchronous transmission.

Syntax   The rules and conventions by which a programming language is governed.

Syntax error   An error that occurs when a programming language's rules are violated in the coding of a computer program.

System analysis phase   The term applied to the first three stages of the system development life cycle: problem definition, requirements analysis, and project justification.

System analyst   A specialist who works with users to determine their information needs, and then designs a system to fulfill those needs.

System clock   Control circuitry that sends out electrical pulses to synchronize all tasks in the CPU; instrumental in determining the speed of a processor.

System design phase   A phase of the system development life cycle that is comprised of two stages: (1) the logical design, during which the paper blueprint for the new system is developed, and (2) the physical design, during which that blueprint is translated into the specific programming logic that will cause the new system to operate as planned.

System designer   A specialist who designs a system to fulfill the information needs of users.

System development life cycle (SDLC)   A structured sequence of operations required to conceive, develop, and make operational a new information system; includes a system analysis phase, a system design phase, a system implementation phase, and a system maintenance phase.

System implementation   The phase of the system development life cycle during which a completely new system or replacement system is introduced into the workplace; includes testing, installation, and training.

System maintenance phase   The fourth phase in the system development life cycle, during which an information system is continually modified to meet the changing requirements of its users.

System operator (sysop)   In an electronic network, a person in charge of operating a bulletin board system.

System software   Software that directly controls and monitors the operation of the computer hardware.

System study   An extensive report that is prepared by a systems analyst at the end of the system analysis phase; sent to management to promote a chosen information system.

System unit   The housing that contains the major components and controls of the computer.

Tab settings   An application software feature that sets indentations in a file and aligns columns and decimal numbers.

Tactical (middle-level) managers   Managers generally concerned with short-term tactical decisions; they allocate time to staffing, planning, organizing, directing, and controlling.

Tape drive   The input/output device that reads and writes data on tape.

Telecommunication   Also called teleprocessing; the process of using communication facilities, such as the telephone system or microwave relays, to send data to and from devices.

Telecommuting   A method of working whereby a person uses a computer and a communication channel to establish a link with a remote office computer. With a personal computer (or terminal) connected to a company's computer, an off-site employee can communicate with the office.

Template   In an application program, a screen form that contains only entries that do not change. A template may be used as an input form as well as an output form.

Terminal   The combination of a monitor and a keyboard used to view output and to enter and check input; also called a video display terminal (VDT).

Testing   The activity through which a new information system is checked to ensure that it is correct.

Thesaurus   A software program that provides alternative words (synonyms) for a given word in a document; also provides antonyms.

Third-generation computer   Computers developed and used between 1965 and 1971 which first used integrated circuits (ICs).

Three-dimensional (3-D)   In computer graphics, an image that appears to have depth as well as length and height.

Time bomb   A program put into a computer that is set to disrupt operations and destroy data either at a certain time or after a specified number of times the program is run.

Time sharing   An operating system capability that allows many users to access a single computer; typically found on large computer operating systems where many users need access at the same time.

Time-slice multitasking   A type of multitasking that enables a CPU to switch its attention between the requested tasks of two or more programs.

Title bar   A graphic element of a window to identify its contents.

Titles   (1) A feature in a graphics package that allows a user to enter text information, such as a title, into the drawing. (2) A feature in a spreadsheet package that freezes row and column titles so that they remain stationary as the spreadsheet is scrolled.

Token   A string of bits that is passed around a network.

Token passing   An access method that utilizes tokens in a local-area network. A device must wait for and hold a token in order to transmit a message and then release the token when finished transmitting.

Token Ring   A network architecture based on token ring topology designed to support microcomputers, minicomputers, and mainframes.

Top-down design   A structured programming design concept that starts with the major functions and divides them into subfunctions until a problem has been subdivided as much as possible.

Topology   The arrangement by which a computer or a device is connected in a computer network.

Touch screen   An input device that allows a user to enter data or show position by touching the screen with a finger or other object.

Trackball   A pointing device that uses the movement of a hand-rotated stationary sphere to control cursor movement.

Tracks   The concentric circles of a magnetic disk where data are stored; used by a computer to identify where data are stored.

Training   The third task in the system implementation phase of the system development life cycle; intended to make users and others familiar with a system so that they are able to work with it.

Transaction   A business activity or event—for example, the receipt of an order or the sale of a product.

Transaction processing system (TPS)   An information system that processes data about transactions or other events that affect the operation of a business. Also, operational information system.

Transcription error   A type of input error that occurs when the wrong characters are entered.

Transcriptive data entry   The data collection method in which data generated at the source are written on an input form that must be later transcribed to a computer-readable medium.

Transistor   Device made from a semiconducting material, such as silicon, to control the flow of electricity through circuits.

Transposition error   A type of transcription error that occurs when two characters are reversed.

Trojan horse   A program that disguises itself as a legitimate program, but once it is installed the rogue program does its damage—garbling data, destroying indexes, or erasing all the data in the computer.

Twisted-pair   Communication channel consisting of a pair of wires twisted around each other.

Typeface   The design of a set of characters.

Typeover mode   A mode in application software; when new text is entered, it takes the place of, or overwrites, any existing text occupying that same space.

Typeset-quality print   Top-of-the-line print; produced by computer-driven typeset machines. Examples can be seen in magazines and high-quality books.

Typography   The setting of words and pictures in a document.

Updating   The process of altering the data that are stored in a computer through adding, deleting, or changing.

Uploading   The process of sending a file from one computer to another. Contrast with downloading.

User   A person who uses computer hardware and software to perform a task.

User group   A formal or informal organization of users to solve problems or exchange software or hardware information.

User interface   The portion of a program that users interact with—entering commands and data and viewing the results of those commands. When an operating environment supplies the key elements of the user interface, programs are easier to learn and similar operations are handled the same way among applications.

Vacuum tube   Device used to control the flow of electricity through circuits in early computers.

Validating   The process of checking data for appropriateness and accuracy as they are entered.

Validity checking   A type of program control designed to determine if the input data are consistent and complete.

Value-added carrier   A type of carrier that specializes in leasing services from common carriers and then adding extra services beyond the leased services for their customers.

Value of information   A determination of how meaningful and useful information is as determined by each user on a case-by-case basis; should be reevaluated periodically and viewed in terms of its incremental value and user benefit.

Values   Any numbers or formulas that are used to represent data in a program.

Values integrity   A data integrity check that limits the range of values of accepted data.

Vector graphics   A way of depicting characters and images on a computer screen by describing them as vectors; images are mathematically defined and stored as geometric descriptions. Also called object-oriented graphics.

Very-large-scale integration (VLSI)   The process of putting the equivalent of several hundred thousand components on a single chip.

Video port   A port into which the monitor is connected to the computer.

Virtual drive   In a network, a drive that can be accessed by a user workstation even though not physically attached.

Virtual-machine (VM) processing   An operating system capability that creates the illusion of more than one physical machine. The software mimics the performance of different hardware devices allowing different operating systems to be used concurrently.

Virtual memory   An operating system capability that uses a secondary-storage device as an extension of main memory. Also called virtual storage.

Virtual reality   The integration of sound, color, and animation in a wraparound environment. It gives the illusion of computing in three dimensions.

Virus   A program that can get into a computer to destroy or alter data and spread itself to other computers.

Voice-band channel   A communication channel, such as a telephone line, that transmits data at 110 to 9600 bits per second.

Voice messaging system   A combination of a telephone and a computer to create a computerized system that allows a message to be sent in human voice without the receiver needing to be present at the same time to receive the message.

Voice output   Soft copy output in which the computer mimics the human voice.

Voice recognition   The ability of a computer to accept input by understanding the speech of a user.

Voice synthesis   The capability of a computer to electronically reproduce the human voice in a recognizable manner.

Volatile   When applied to computer memory it means that the contents of memory are lost when power is turned off.

Warranty   A document that states the degree of liability that a company is willing to cover.

Weight   Refers to the width of a character.

What-if analysis   In spreadsheets, involves changing data entries in a worksheet to show how it would affect other entries.

White space   In word processing, an area of the document containing no text or graphics.

Wide-area network (WAN)   A computer network in which the computers are geographically dispersed and linked by communication facilities provided by common carriers.

Widow line   The last line of a paragraph that stands alone at the top of a page.

Wildcard   In MS-DOS, a character that can represent a character or characters in a filename. The wildcard ? represents one character in its position in the filename. The wildcard * stands for one or more characters in the filename.

Window   (1) Separate, defined areas on a computer screen that can be used to display data, menus, or other software packages. (2) In a graphics program, the rectangular area for selection of entities.

Wire cable   A type of data communication channel; includes telegraph lines, telephone lines, and coaxial cables.

Wireless computing   The use of cellular, infrared, or radio frequencies to transmit and receive data without a conducting medium such as copper wire.

Word   The number of adjacent bits that can be stored and manipulated as a unit by the computer.

Word processing   The activity of entering, viewing, storing, retrieving, editing, rearranging, and printing text material using a computer and a word processor.

Word processor   An application program that creates, edits, manipulates, and prints text; generally used for writing documents such as letters and reports.

Word size   In communication, the number of bits that make up a character.

Wordwrap   A word processor feature that automatically continues a sentence on the next line without the user's pressing the return key at the end of the first line. Any words that extend past the right margin are moved down to the next line.

Worksheet   The blank spreadsheet form used for entering and organizing numeric data; a paper form in a noncomputerized spreadsheet and a screen form in an electronic spreadsheet.

Workstation   (1) A category of powerful stand-alone computer whose base price includes a 32-bit processor, very large main memory, considerable calculating and graphics capability, and all of the hardware and software needed to connect it to a network. (2) In a LAN it is one of the nodes.

Worm   A surreptitious program that issues false or misleading commands. Occupies computer memory and spreads quickly as does a virus—stopping normal computer operation.

Write once, read many (WORM) drive   The hardware device used to read data from and write data to a WORM optical disk.

Write once, read many (WORM) optical disk   An optical disk that allows a user to write data to the disk once. After part of the disk has been written to once, it can only be read from.

WYSIWYG   An acronym for "What You See Is What You Get" (pronounced "wizzy-wig"). This feature implies that what is seen on the display screen is exactly how the output will look when printed.

Xmodem protocol   A public-domain, data-transfer protocol used with microcomputers to send and receive nontext files.

XON/XOFF protocol A protocol that enables software to control data transmission. An XOFF signal instructs the transmitting computer to stop sending data; an XON signal tells the computer to begin sending data.

Zmodem protocol An enhanced version of the Xmodem protocol that handles larger data transfers with less chance of error.

Zoom A graphics package feature that allows enlargement of a specified area of a drawing for viewing, or pulling back and viewing the entire scene.

CD (change directory) command, 113
CD-ROM disks, 181
Cell pointers in spreadsheets, 468, 470–71, 579
Cells in spreadsheets, 468, 579
  manipulating, 477–79
  references to, 472–73, 478–79, 490
Cellular networks, 279–80, 579
Censorship, 41
Centered text, 429, 579
Centering in word processors, 413, 579
Central processing units (CPUs), 54–55
  in computer selection, 197
  defined, 579
  instructions for, 63
  properties of, 64–66
  selecting, 67–68
Chain printers, 130, 579
Change directory (CHDIR) command, 113
Channels. See Communication channels
Character enhancement in word processors, 414, 579
Character printers, 126, 579
Character stripping in communications, 325
Charts and graphs, 501–4, 579
  appearance features for, 514–15
  in business, 508–11
  creating, 519–21
  presenting, 522–23
  selecting, 521–22
  spreadsheet functions for, 480
CHDIR (change directory) command, 113
Check boxes in Windows, 156, 158
Checking account banking, 362
China
  market in, 532
  software piracy in, 535
  word processing in, 419
Chips
  defined, 580
  development of, 566, 570, 573
  for microprocessors, 55
  trends in, 541–42
CHKDSK command, 117
Chocolate chip cookies, 338

Christensen, Ward, 288
Civil rights, 383
Classifications of computers. See Categories of computers
Cleaning computers, 202–3
Clicking of mouse, 149
Client/server database architecture, 444–45, 580
Clinton, Bill, 531, 549
Clip art
  defined, 580
  in desktop publishing, 418
  in document design, 429–30
  in graphics, 512
Clocks and clock speeds, 55
  for microprocessors, 64–65
  trends in, 542
Clones, 569
CLS command, 112
Clustered bar graphs, 521
Coaxial cables, 268, 305, 580
COBOL language, 249–50, 567, 580
Codd, Edgar F., 372
Coding programs, 240, 580
Colleges, computer purchases from, 199
Color
  in charts, 520
  in document design, 428
  in graphics, 498, 514
Color Graphics Adapter (CGA), 138
Color printers, 131–32, 580
Columbia River system, fish database for, 377
Columns
  in desktop publishing, 420
  in spreadsheets, 468, 477, 487, 580
COM extension, 108
Command-driven programs, 195, 580
Command-line interfaces, 218–19, 580
Command mode
  in communications, 322
  defined, 580
  in spreadsheets, 469
Command prompt in MS-DOS, 107, 110–11
Commands in MS-DOS, 107, 110–18
Comma spreadsheet format, 476
Commercial on-line services, 291–93, 580

Common carriers, 273–76, 580
Communication channels, 267–69, 580
  bandwidth of, 277
  common carriers, 273–76
  configuration for, 269–71
  sharing, 271–73
  transmission modes in, 276–77
  transmission rates in, 277–78
Communications, 24, 582
  bulletin board systems, 288–89
  for businesses, 293–95
  channels in. See Communication channels
  commercial on-line services, 291–93
  configuration for, 320–21
  connections for, 321–23
  data capture in, 323
  data transmission forms in, 264
  distributed data processing, 280–83
  effects of, 263–64
  electronic mail, 288–90
  facsimile, 290
  file protection in, 325
  file transfer in, 323–25
  international, 529–30
  macros for, 324–25
  modems for, 265–67
  networks in, 278–80
  operating systems for, 214
  parameters for, 320, 580
  servers for, 304–5, 580
  software for, 227, 319–20, 580
  teleconferencing, 291
  trends in, 548–49
  voice messaging systems, 290–91
Compact disc-interactive (CD-I) players, 456
Compact Disc-Read Only Memory (CD-ROM) technology, 457
Compaq computers, 569
Compatibility factors
  in CPU selection, 68
  in DDP, 282
  in secondary storage, 186
Compilers, 246, 580
Compiling programs, 240
Completeness of information, 13, 87, 580
Complex-instruction-set computers (CISC), 65

Massively parallel processing (MPP), 542–43
Mass merchants, buying computers from, 199
Materials, lifting and handling, 361
Mathematical functions
  in spreadsheets, 473
  in SQL, 397
  in word processors, 417
Mauchly, John, 563–65
Maximizing windows, 150
MaxiTrack system, 281
MB (megabytes), 52
Mechanical mouse, 91, 591
Megabytes, 52
MEM command, 118
MEMMAKER command, 118
Memory, 23
  amount of, 60–62
  cache, 59, 579
  conventional, 61, 581
  expanded, 61–62
  extended, 61
  flash, 541, 585
  main, 23, 25, 57, 60–62
  optimizing, 118
  read-only, 57–58, 597
  and speed, 66
  uses of, 59–60
  virtual, 217, 602
Menabrea, Luigi Frederico, 496
Menu bars in Windows, 154–55, 591
Menus
  defined, 591
  for interfaces, 218–19, 591
  for programs, 195, 591
Message characters in transmissions, 278, 591
Message-only BBS systems, 288
Messages
  in object-oriented languages, 248, 591
  sending, 289
Microchips, 55, 591
Microcomputers, 26–29, 591. See also Computers
  care for, 200–3
  communications using, 319–25
  development of, 567
  operating systems for, 218–23
  preparing to buy, 194
  printing devices for, 128–30
  selecting, 195–98
  vendors for, 198–200

Microprocessors, 50, 55–56
  and clock speed, 64–65
  defined, 591
  development of, 567–68
Microsoft Antivirus (MSAV) command, 118
Microsoft Backup (MSBACKUP) command, 118
Microsoft Diagnostic (MSD) command, 118
Microsoft Disk Operating System. See MS-DOS
Microsoft Windows. See Windows program
Microwave signals, 268, 305, 591
Middle-level managers, 332–33
Milbanke, Annabella, 496
Millions of instructions per second (MIPS), 65
Minicomputers, 31–32, 567, 591
Minimizing windows, 151
Minsky, Marvin, 124
Mirror feature in graphics, 513–14, 592
Misuse of information, 41
Mitchell, Artie, 512
Mixed cell references in spreadsheets, 478, 490, 592
MKDIR (make directory) command, 112–13
Mnemonics in assembly language, 245, 592
Modems, 198, 265–67, 568, 577, 592
Modes
  in communications, 321–22
  in databases, 440, 579
  data entry, 85
  in spreadsheets, 469
  transmission, 276–77, 321
  in word processors, 408
Modulation, 265, 592
Modules
  database, 372
  program, 242, 592
Money, electronic movement of, 293
Monitoring
  database performance, 384
  LANs, 312
  medical patients, 367
  programs for, 213
  in SDLCs, 339
Monitors, 134–37
  cleaning, 203
  defined, 592

Monitors, *continued*
  monochrome, 137–38
  for multimedia, 457
  selecting, 197
Monochrome Display Adapter (MDA), 138
Monochrome monitors, 137–38
Monroe, James, 419
MORE command, 115
Motherboards, 56
Mouse, 91
  defined, 592
  development of, 82, 567
  drivers for, 143, 592
  ports for, 142, 592
  using, 149
Mouse pointer, 149, 592
MOVE command, 114
Movies, computers in, 11
Moving
  windows, 153
  worksheet cells, 478
Mrs. Fields Cookies, 338
MSAV command, 118
MSBACKUP command, 118
MSD command, 118
MS-DOS, 107, 221–22
  command prompt in, 107, 110–11, 592
  commands in, 107, 110–18
  CONFIG.SYS file in, 111–12
  date and time in, 111
  defined, 591
  directories in, 108–10, 112–13
  disk management in, 115–18
  file management in, 113–15
  filenames and filename extensions in, 108
  help for, 112
  paths in, 108–10
  starting, 107–8
Multidimensional spreadsheets, 465, 592
Multimedia, 452
  applications of, 457–58
  audio in, 455–56
  defined, 592
  software for, 457
  storage for, 457
  video in, 456–57
Multinational corporations, 530
Multiple block spreadsheet design, 488–91, 592

Multiple instruction multiple data (MIMD) computers, 543
Multiplexers and multiplexing, 271–72, 592
Multipoint channel configurations, 270, 592
Multiprocessing operating systems, 217, 592
Multiscanning and multisync monitors, 136, 592
Multitasking operating systems, 216, 592
Multithreading, 216, 592
Multiuser information systems, 18, 592
Multiuser operating systems, 215, 592
Music, computers in, 9–10
Musical Instrument Digital Interface (MIDI), 455
MYCIN expert system, 337

NAFTA agreement, 532
Names
  for files, 108, 113
  for spreadsheet ranges, 474, 490
Napier, John, 560
Narrow-band channels, 277, 592
NASA, databases for, 446
National Crime Information Center (NCIC), 383
National Information Infrastructure (NII), 549
Natural languages, 247, 437, 592
Near-letter-quality (NLQ) print, 127, 592
Needs factors in computer selection, 197
Negotiating for microcomputers, 196
Nelson, Ted, 452
Netherlands, computing in, 533
Network interface cards, 306, 592
Network operating systems, 306–7, 592
Networks, computer, 24, 278
  architecture in, 592
  cellular, 279–80, 579
  database models for, 379, 592
  defined, 581
  ethics for, 41
  local area. See Local-area networks (LANs)
  security on, 446
  wide-area, 279, 603

Neural networks, 547, 593
Neurosurgery, computers in, 9
Neurosurgical Operating Arm System (NOAS), 9
Newsnet on-line service, 293
Nexis on-line service, 293
NeXT computers, 569
Nodes
  defined, 593
  LAN, 279, 302
Nonbootable data diskettes, 116
None parity in communications, 320
Nonimpact printers, 126, 593
Noninterlaced monitor screens, 136, 593
Nonprocedural programming languages, 247–48, 593
Norton, Peter, 210, 569
Norton Utilities, 210
Notebook computers, 27, 30, 541, 593
Noyce, Robert, 565
Numbers in spreadsheets, 476
Number systems
  binary, 73–75
  decimal, 73
  hexadecimal, 75–78
  octal, 75
Numeric keypads, 90

Object code, 246, 593
Object linking and embedding (OLE), 217
Object-oriented database management system (OODBMS), 381, 593
Object-oriented database models, 380–81, 593
Object-oriented graphics, 497
Object-oriented operating systems (OOP), 544–45
Object-oriented programming languages (OOPLs), 248, 593
Objects, 248
  for databases, 374–75
  defined, 593
Observation as information source, 14
Octal system, 75, 77–78, 593
Odd parity in communications, 320
Office information systems (OIS), 337–39, 593
Off-line modes, 85, 593

Olsen, Ken, 565, 567
On-line help
  in MS-DOS, 112
  in Windows, 161–62
On-line input, 85, 593
On-line modes, 85, 593
On-line real-time processing, 85, 593
On-line reservations systems, 294
On-line services, 291–93
On-screen computer presentations, 522–23
Operating environments, 220, 593
Operating systems (OS), 59, 212–13
  in computer selection, 194–95
  defined, 593
  development of, 573
  differences between, 215–18
  major functions of, 213–14
  for microcomputers, 218–23
  parts of, 213
  trends in, 544–45
  uses for, 214–15, 218
Operational information systems, 334, 593
Operational managers, 333, 593
Optical-bar recognition (OBR), 99, 593
Optical cards, 182, 593
Optical-character recognition (OCR), 100, 593
Optical computers, 541–42, 593
Optical laser disks, 181, 593
Optical-mark recognition (OMR), 99, 594
Optical mouse, 91, 594
Optical recognition, 98–101, 594
Optical scanners, 100–1, 594
Optical storage, 180–83
Optical tape, 183, 594
Optical technology, 594
Option buttons, 156, 158
Order of spreadsheet calculations, 475
Organizational charts, 510–11, 594
Organization of data, 167–69
Orientation of typefaces, 428, 594
Orphan lines, 431, 594
OS/2 operating system, 222
Osborne, Adam, 569
Outline fonts, 429, 594
Output, 22, 25, 125, 594
  computer output microform for, 133

Print servers, 304, 596
Privacy, 40
   in databases, 386
   and government, 46
   legislation for, 42
Problem definition in SDLCs, 341, 596
Procedural programming languages, 247–48, 596
Procedures
   data entry, 83
   defined, 596
   in information systems, 17
Process control, 362, 596
Processing, 22, 542–43, 596
Processing speed, 25
Process in information systems, 18
Prodigy on-line service, 292
Production/operations information systems, 357, 596
Productivity, LANs for, 301
Professional ethics, 40
Program editors, 240, 596
Programmable controllers, 361–62, 596
Programmable file management systems, 374, 596
Programmable read-only memory (PROM), 58
Program Manager, 149–58
Programmers, 236
   defined, 596
   jobs as, 553
   maintenance, 345, 591
   in SDLCs, 339
Programming
   benefits in, 236
   controls in, 85–87
   defined, 581
   languages for. See Languages, programming
   structured, 242–45
Programs. See also Software
   algorithms for, 238
   chart, 501–4
   coding, 240, 580
   compiling, testing, and debugging, 240–41
   control, 213, 581
   design, 498–501, 583
   determining user needs, 237
   development process, 237–42, 596

Programs, continued
   distributing, 241–42
   documenting, 237, 488
   flowcharts for, 238–39, 596
   specifications, 237–38
   well-designed, 236–37
Project justification in SDLCs, 341, 596
Project management in SDLCs, 339–40, 596
Prolog programming language, 251, 596
PROMPT command, 110
Proportional typefaces, 428
Prostheses, designing, 367
Protecting software and data, 203, 325
Protocols
   file-transfer, 324, 585, 596
   in LANs, 306
   in transmissions, 278
Prototype information systems, 345, 596
Prototyping in SDLCs, 345–47
Pseudocode, 238, 596
Publications as information sources, 14
Publishing. See Desktop publishing
Pucks, 92–93, 596
Punched-card machine, 561

Qualitative information, 12
Quantitative information, 12
Quartz crystals, replacements for, 542
Queries, database, 247, 378, 443
   defined, 596
   in relational databases, 380
   with SQL, 393–98
Query by example method, 380, 596
Queues, print server, 304, 597
Quitting Windows, 163

RAM (random-access memory), 57–60, 197. See also Memory
RAM cards, 60
Random-access file processing, 169–70
Range checking in databases, 445
Ranges in spreadsheets
   defined, 597
   names for, 474, 490

Raster graphics, 497, 597
Ratliff, C. Wayne, 436
RD (remove directory) command, 113
Readability
   defined, 597
   in page design, 430–31
Read-only memory (ROM), 57–58, 597
Ready/entry mode for spreadsheets, 469, 597
Real-time banking, 362
Real-time processing, 217, 597
Recalculating spreadsheets, 465, 476, 578
Record-oriented databases, 394, 597
Records, 168, 378, 597
Recovery, data, 46, 187–88
Recycling, 553
Reduced-instruction-set computers (RISC), 65
Redundancy
   in DDP, 282
   in file servers, 313
Reel-to-reel tapes, 173, 175, 597
Referential integrity in SQL, 398, 597
Refresh rates, monitors, 136, 597
Registers, 59, 597
Relational database management systems (RDBMS), 379–80, 597
Relational database models, 372, 379–80, 597
Relative cell references in spreadsheets, 478, 490, 597
Relevance of information, 13
Reliability
   of information, 13, 15
   of programs, 237
   of servers, 303
Removable secondary storage media, 178–79, 457, 597
Remove directory (RMDIR) command, 113
RENAME command, 113
Repair facilities, 195
Repetition control structures, 243, 597
Repetition in document design, 427
Replicating databases, 386
Reports, 125–26
   from databases, 377–78, 443–44
   defined, 597

Software, 17, 21–22, 599. *See also*
    Programs
    acquiring, 228–29
    application. *See* Application soft-
        ware
    commonly used, 224–27
    for data communication, 319–20
    date problems in, 546
    defined, 581
    evaluating and selecting, 194–95
    graphics. *See* Graphics software
    integrated, 227–28, 589
    job-hunting, 555
    language problems in, 534
    for multimedia, 457
    operating systems. *See* Operating
        systems (OS)
    page composition, 417, 420, 594
    piracy of, 44, 535–36, 599
    power-management, 552
    protecting, 203
    sources of, 200
    starting, 229–30
    trends in, 544–47
    types of, 211–12
    user-supported, 300
    workability of, 43
Sonography, 366
Sorting
    databases, 441–42
    defined, 599
    spreadsheet data, 479
Sound boards, 455
Sound in multimedia, 455–56
Sounds of English program, 458
Source code, 246, 599
Source data entry, 84–85, 599
Source documents, 84, 599
Sources of information, 14–15
Soviet Union, software piracy in,
    535
Spaghetti code, 243
Speakers for audio, 455
Special effects, computers in, 11
Specialized application software,
    223, 599
Specialized common carriers, 273–
    75, 599
Special-purpose input devices,
    95–98
Specifications, program, 237–38
Speech coding, 139, 599
Speech recognition, 94–95, 599
Speech synthesizers, 140

Speech-to-speech computerized
    translation systems, 96
Speed
    of computers, 25, 65
    of memory, 66
    of microprocessors, 64–65
    of programming languages, 254
    in secondary storage, 184,
        188–89
    trends in, 542
    of word processors, 406
Spelling checkers, 415, 599
Spinoff Technology Application Re-
    trieval System (STARS) database,
    446
Spinrite program, 188
Spool buffers, 304, 599
Sports, computers in, 9
Spot color, 428
Spreadsheets and worksheets, 225–
    26, 463–65, 568
    benefits of, 465–66
    block design approach for,
        486–91
    built-in functions in, 473, 579
    copying and moving data in,
        477–78
    creating, 468–75
    database functions in, 480–81
    defined, 599, 603
    desktop publishing functions in,
        481
    editing, 475–76
    formatting, 469, 476–77, 489
    graphing functions of, 480
    inserting and deleting rows and
        columns in, 477
    limitations of, 491–92
    moving around in, 471
    planning, 486–87
    printing, 479–80
    saving, 475
    uses of, 466–68
    well-designed, 486
SQL (structured query language),
    380
    basics of, 393
    data integrity in, 398
    defined, 599
    embedded, 393
    history of, 392
    interactive, 393
    mathematical functions in, 397
    queries with, 393–98

SQL, (structured query language),
    continued
    standards for, 392–93
    updating with, 396–97
ST506 interface, 186
Stacked bar graphs, 522
Stacked-line graphs, 508–9, 599
Stacks in hypertext, 453–54
Standard-quality print, 127, 599
Standards
    for databases, 384
    de facto, 221
    defined, 569
    for international computing, 535
    for SQL, 392–93
Star networks, 308, 599
Static electricity, 202
Static RAM (SRAM), 58
Statistical spreadsheet functions,
    473
Status, disk, 117
Status bars in Windows, 158
Status lines
    defined, 599
    in spreadsheets, 469
    in word processors, 407
Stealing data, 45
Stibitz, George, 562
Stock markets, 363
Stop bits in communications, 321,
    599
Storage, 23, 25
    defined, 599
    secondary. *See* Secondary storage
    trends in, 543–44
Strategic managers, 332, 599
String spreadsheet functions, 473
Structured block spreadsheet design,
    486–91, 599
Structured problems, 335
Structured programming, 242–45,
    599
Structured query language. *See* SQL
    (structured query language)
Structures, database, 439
Style checkers, 416
Style sheets, 426, 600
Stylus-based computers, 92
Styluses, 92, 600
Subdirectories, 108–10, 600
Subschema, 382–83, 600
Suess, Randy, 288
Supercomputers, 33, 567, 600
Superconductors, 542, 600

Superimposition of graphic objects, 513, 600
Superstores
    buying computers from, 198–99
    buying software from, 200
    defined, 600
Supervisor programs, 213, 600
Support
    for DDP, 282
    technical, 195, 198, 404–5
Support chips, 66
Surge protectors, 188, 197, 600
Synchronous transmissions, 278, 600
Syntax and syntax errors, 240, 600
SYS extension, 108
System analysis in SDLCs, 340–42, 600
System analysts, 382
    defined, 600
    jobs as, 553
    in SDLCs, 339
System boards, 56
System clocks, 55
    defined, 600
    for microprocessors, 64–65
    trends in, 542
System designers in SDLCs, 339, 600
System design in SDLCs, 342–43, 600
System development life cycles (SDLCs), 339–40, 600
    analysis in, 340–42
    design in, 342–43
    implementation in, 343–45
    maintenance in, 345
    and prototyping, 345–47
System implementation in SDLCs, 343–45, 600
System maintenance in SDLCs, 345, 600
System operators (sysops), 288, 600
System performance in DBMS, 378
System software, 21, 211–12, 600
System studies in SDLCs, 342, 600
System units, 20, 22
    cleaning, 202
    defined, 600

Table properties in SQL, 393–94
Tables for databases, 374, 379
Table spreadsheet functions, 473
Tab settings, 411–12, 600

Tactical managers, 332–33, 601
Taiwan, computing in, 530
Tape
    for backups, 173, 187
    drives for, 141, 172, 601
    optical, 183, 594
    for storage, 172–74
Task List in Windows, 153
Tasks in operating systems, 215
Task Switcher in Windows, 154
Technical support, 204–5
    for microcomputers, 198
    for software, 195
Technological evolution, 570–74
Technophobia, 551
Telecommunication, 263, 601. *See also* Communications
Telecommuting, 295, 320, 601
Teleconferencing, 291, 548, 584
Telephones, cellular, 279
Temperature for computers, 202
Templates
    defined, 601
    for graphics, 514
    for spreadsheets, 466
Terminal emulation, 321
Terminals, 139–41, 601
Terminology, 51
Terrorists, images of, 135
Testing
    computer graphics for, 505
    defined, 601
    programs, 240
    in SDLCs, 343
Text. *See also* Word processors and word processing programs
    in databases, 446
    with graphics, 514
    in graphs, 520
Text Boxes in Windows, 155
Texture in graphs, 520
Thermal printers, 131–32
Thesauruses, 416, 601
Third-generation computers, 570, 573–74, 601
35mm slides, 522
Three-dimensional graphics, 515, 601
386SX microprocessors, 197
Tick marks in graphics, 515
Time bombs, 44–45, 601
TIME command, 111
Timeliness of information, 13, 15
Time on-line status in communications, 325

Time sharing, 215, 601
Time-slice multitasking, 216, 601
Tinker, Miles, 430
Title bars in Windows, 149, 601
Titles
    defined, 601
    in spreadsheets, 477, 488
Token Ring networks, 310–11
Tokens in LANs, 311, 601
Tools, robot operation of, 361
Top-down program design, 242, 601
Top-level managers, 332
Topologies in LANs, 307–9, 601
Touch screens, 94, 601
Trackballs, 91–92, 601
Tracking packages, 281, 294
Tracks in secondary storage, 183, 601
Trade, international, 532
TradeNet network, 530
Training
    computer graphics for, 506–7
    for DDP, 282
    defined, 601
    for jobs, 458
    in SDLCs, 344–45
Transaction processing systems (TPS), 334, 601
Transactions, 12, 85, 334, 601
Transcription errors, 84, 601
Transcriptive data entry, 84, 602
Transferring files, 288, 323–25, 585
Transistor technology, 570, 602
Translating languages, 96, 245, 534, 589
Transmissions
    file, 288, 323–25
    modes of, 276–77, 321
    rates of, 277–78, 320
Transposition errors, 84, 602
Trends
    in communications, 548–49
    concerns in, 551
    in hardware, 540–44
    in information systems, 539–40
    in software, 544–47
    in user interfaces, 549–51
Trojan horses, 44–45, 602
Tukey, John, 565
Turing, Alan, 528, 563
Twisted-pair cable, 268, 305, 602
TYPE command, 115
Typefaces, 428–29, 602